MS-DOS Commands

and Where You'll Find Them in This Book

Y0-BZL-202

New in Version 6

MS-DOS® 6
Companion

MS-DOS® 6
Companion

The Comprehensive Reference That

Fully Explores the Power and

Features of MS-DOS 6

JoAnne Woodcock

PUBLISHED BY
Microsoft Press
A Division of Microsoft Corporation
One Microsoft Way
Redmond, Washington 98052-6399

Copyright © 1993 by Microsoft Press, a division of Microsoft Corporation

Library of Congress Cataloging-in-Publication Data
Woodcock, JoAnne.
    MS-DOS 6 companion / JoAnne Woodcock.
        p.   cm.
    Includes index.
    ISBN 1-55615-550-6
    1. MS-DOS (Computer file)   I. Title.
QA76.76.O63W6618   1993
005.4'469--dc20   93-13266
                                                        CIP

Printed and bound in the United States of America.

1 2 3 4 5 6 7 8 9 AGAG 8 7 6 5 4 3

Distributed to the book trade in Canada by Macmillan of Canada, a division of Canada Publishing Corporation.

Distributed to the book trade outside the United States and Canada by Penguin Books Ltd.

Penguin Books Ltd., Harmondsworth, Middlesex, England
Penguin Books Australia Ltd., Ringwood, Victoria, Australia
Penguin Books N.Z. Ltd., 182-190 Wairau Road, Auckland 10, New Zealand

British Cataloging-in-Publication Data available.

PostScript is a registered trademark of Adobe Systems, Inc. Apple and Macintosh are registered trademarks of Apple Computer, Inc. COMPAQ is a registered trademark of Compaq Computer Corporation. CP/M and Digital Research are registered trademarks of Digital Research, Inc. Deskjet, Hewlett-Packard, LaserJet, PaintJet, Quietjet, Ruggedwriter, and ThinkJet are registered trademarks of Hewlett-Packard Company. Intel is a registered trademark of Intel Corporation. AT, IBM, OS/2, Proprinter, PS/2, and Quietwriter are registered trademarks and PC/XT is a trademark of International Business Machines Corporation. Lotus is a registered trademark of Lotus Development Corporation. Microsoft and MS-DOS are registered trademarks and QBasic, Windows, and Windows NT are trademarks of Microsoft Corporation. UNIX is a registered trademark of UNIX Systems Laboratories. Zenith is a registered trademark of Zenith Electronics Corporation.

The ''Satisfaction Guaranteed'' seal assures the utmost in quality and reliability. If for any reason you are not satisfied with this book, return it within 60 days of date of purchase with your dated sales receipt to the place of purchase. If the place of purchase does not accept returns, you may return the book directly to Microsoft Press for a refund of the lesser of either the purchase price or the suggested retail price. Refunds limited to one per customer.

Acquisitions Editor: Dean Holmes
Project Editor: Ron Lamb
Technical Editor: Seth McEvoy

For Mark and Kate, as always

Contents

SECTION FOUR
MS-DOS UTILITIES AND CUSTOMIZATION

SECTION FIVE
APPENDIXES

Acknowledgments

A great many people contribute to the making of a computer book, not least the brainy and dedicated programmers who spend enormous amounts of time developing the software. Thanks, therefore, go first to the developers at Microsoft who have kept MS-DOS not only evolving but responsive to its users over the years.

At Microsoft Press, thanks go to the following people, in order of their appearance on this project. First were Jim Brown and Dean Holmes of Acquisitions, whose "baby" this book really is, idea-wise. Hard on their heels was Eric Stroo, who read quantities of unedited copy as developmental editor, pointing out flaws in coverage, logic, and presentation. At the heart of the process were Ron Lamb and Seth McEvoy, editor and technical editor, who provided patience and expertise, and who labored diligently to remove embarrassments. Thanks also to Kathy Atkins and the proof crew, who made the words presentable; Lisa Sandburg, who turned scribbles into art; and the editorial and production staff, who turned words on disk into the pages you hold now. Sins of commission and omission belong to none of the above.

Introduction

Long ago (or so it seems), Dean Holmes, Acquisitions Manager of Microsoft Press, set this book in motion by describing it as a portmanteau—an MS-DOS grab-bag of sorts. Well, as heft alone will tell you, the result certainly "portes" its share of "manteaux." But the intent is certainly not to deceive, either by impressing you with the density of MS-DOS or—and this point is important—by intimidating you with detail piled upon detail.

This book is meant to serve you as a reference and a browsable resource when you feel like whiling away a few idle minutes. You don't have to read it all to use MS-DOS well. You don't, in fact, even have to read most of it. Why bother, then? Because an informed computer user is someone who can control, rather than be controlled by, new or unexpected situations. That is the goal of this book: to give you, to the extent you want to take advantage of it, enough background knowledge to enable you to take control of MS-DOS. Along the way, you'll also take a nonprogrammer's look at the personality of MS-DOS, and at the end, you might very well find that what you learn or come to understand a little better here will pop up in surprising ways to make your work with other software more inventive or more intuitive. Understanding MS-DOS, for instance, will make migration to Microsoft Windows and Windows applications more instinctive than labored.

The contents

An operating system is a complex piece of software to which you entrust the most basic, yet necessary and critical tasks you require of your computer: disk management, file management, memory management, device management. To help you see MS-DOS both in whole and in part, the book is divided into five main sections:

- Section One is an overview of MS-DOS, the operating system—what it is, what it means to you, and how it works with your computer. Here, too, you'll find background material on computer hardware and some explanation of the bits, bytes, and binary you might have wondered about at some time.

- Section Two is a survey of the MS-DOS Shell, a graphical environment that can make MS-DOS more intuitive to use than the sometimes terse commands you probably associate with this operating system.

- Section Three comprises a lengthy group of seven chapters describing MS-DOS commands in detail. This section is your reference to MS-DOS. To help you see MS-DOS as form related to function, the commands are grouped by task. For ease of reference, the commands are listed alphabetically and by chapter in tables at the end of Chapter 6, where you'll also find a description of the typographical conventions used throughout the rest of the book.

- Section Four is a collection of chapters that showcase what you can do with MS-DOS. This is where you can find out how you use the new version 6 utilities, such as DoubleSpace and MemMaker. This is also where, at the end of the book, you'll leave the command line and enter the world of macros, of batch files, and (a little bit) of QBasic programming.

- Section Five contains three appendixes, providing the details about esoteric topics such as extended character sets and code pages.

To help you sort the wheat from the chaff, color is used to highlight headings, list items, and other design elements. The same color also appears in examples to show you exactly what you would enter for a particular command, batch file, or macro. For additional details on MS-DOS commands and how they are presented in this book, be sure to check Chapter 6, which begins the command-intensive reference section.

Assumptions about you

You are assumed to be intelligent, as well as reasonably motivated and willing to put a little effort into understanding what goes on inside the magic box. That's it. Enjoy the trip.

OVERVIEW OF MS-DOS

1

MS-DOS

What You'll Find Here: This chapter is about MS-DOS, the operating system—its origins, development, and anatomy, as well as its relationship to Microsoft Windows and other operating systems. Although much of this is background information, you'll find that if you understand what MS-DOS is and (roughly) how it works, you will eventually be able to use its commands comfortably instead of struggling to remember the when, the why, and, especially, the how of using MS-DOS.

*T*he first version of MS-DOS appeared late in the summer of 1981, at the same time the original IBM PC was released. The timing was not coincidental. Microsoft designed MS-DOS version 1 expressly for IBM's first venture into the growing, but then still new, business microcomputer marketplace.

One of three operating systems originally chosen for the PC by IBM, MS-DOS was developed in a small, hot, stuffy, supposed-to-be-locked-at-all-times room in a bank building in downtown Bellevue, Washington. Its competitors were a relatively little-known operating system, SofTech Microsystem's p-System, and a heavyweight contender from Digital Research known as CP/M (Control Program/ Monitor). CP/M was well known and was the dominant 8-bit operating system of the time. Although it had to be revised and updated for the PC's new 8/16-bit 8088/8086 microprocessor, CP/M—or rather CP/M-86, as the new version would be named—was widely believed by industry sages to have the greatest likelihood of becoming the standard operating system on 80x86-based microcomputers. History or the Fates, however, had different plans. CP/M-86 was delayed in development, appeared six months after MS-DOS, and even when available never really caught on. MS-DOS, on the other hand, although it began as an untried, unknown, and untested newcomer, quickly defeated CP/M-86 and in little more than a year became IBM's operating system of choice. Within a decade of its appearance, MS-DOS had become the operating system driving tens of millions of computers in countries throughout the world.

Keeping current

MS-DOS version 1 was serious, albeit baby-sized, software. Four thousand lines of assembly language code that ran in 8 kilobytes of memory, version 1 was smaller than many of today's utilities. Although its basic job description—file management, device management, and information storage and retrieval—was no different from that of MS-DOS version 6, version 1 of MS-DOS managed to be both small and powerful enough to run a business-oriented computer because the machine it ran on was, by modern standards, pretty simple. A standard 1981 IBM PC shipped with 16 K to 64 K of memory and one optional floppy disk drive capable of handling single-sided, 160-K diskettes. As such, the machine was a far cry from modern microcomputers, with their megabytes of memory, multitudes of add-on devices, and hard disks that are now well on their way to gigabytes of storage capacity.

The original IBM PC was so limited that even new computer users of today would consider its capabilities either laughable or pathetic. Still, cynics would do well to remember that just as the first PC was quickly outdated by newer, flashier, more powerful hardware, so too will the powerhouse of today become the dinosaur of tomorrow. Developments pile upon developments in both hardware and software, and they do so at a frenetic pace that makes the computer industry seem to run at a higher clock speed than does the rest of the world.

This constant, rapid change in hardware and user requirements is the primary reason for the numerous updates MS-DOS has undergone since 1981. MS-DOS has grown to match the needs of evolving hardware. In fact, improvements in hardware, more than any other factor, have influenced the timing and capabilities of new releases of MS-DOS—more so in the past than in the present, but hardware is still a significant factor even today.

As it has evolved to work with more devices, larger disk sizes, more memory, and increasingly powerful computers, however, MS-DOS has also remained compatible with earlier versions. This emphasis on backward compatibility ensures that, even though you upgrade to newer hardware and newer versions of MS-DOS, your applications, files, disks, and directories remain usable, and both your files and your knowledge of MS-DOS commands remain portable from one machine to the next. Although each new version of MS-DOS offers more capability than its predecessor, you never have to recopy files as you move from one version to another, nor do you have to replace existing applications or "unlearn" MS-DOS. You simply spend a few minutes upgrading, learn the new MS-DOS commands you need to know, and go on from there.

Such compatibility has its pluses and minuses. Backward compatibility, combined with the large number of existing MS-DOS applications, means that you never have to twiddle your thumbs waiting for programmers to develop applications that can run with your operating system. It is also, however, one of the reasons that MS-DOS, unlike Microsoft Windows or IBM's OS/2 version 2, has not broken away from certain restrictions, such as the 640-K memory barrier or the eight-character filename limit. To remain compatible with low-end computers, existing software, and earlier versions of itself, MS-DOS must continue to recognize and deal with any significant limitations that affect the ways it can work. It cannot go where no MS-DOS has gone before. If it did, it would no longer be MS-DOS as you know it.

Versions of MS-DOS

In its decade-long lifespan, numerous new versions of MS-DOS have been released. Each new version has signaled a more capable MS-DOS, and each has been assigned a number: version 1.1, version 1.25, version 2.1, and so on, through the current version, 6. Whenever MS-DOS undergoes a significant change, the major version number to the left of the decimal point increases. When MS-DOS undergoes a less significant change, the major version number remains the same, but the decimal portion increases. For example, version 1 became version 2

primarily to accommodate the IBM PC/XT. Why was this development so important? Because the XT was the first IBM personal computer to incorporate a hard
disk, and to support the hard disk, MS-DOS in version 2 acquired the ability to
use a hierarchical file system—the directories and subdirectories, trees and paths
without which managing a hard disk would be impossible. In contrast, MS-DOS
version 3.2 differed little from version 3.1, gaining little more than the ability to
recognize and work with 3.5-inch floppy disks: important, but relatively low on
the operating-system Richter scale.

To give some perspective to the various releases of MS-DOS, the following
list identifies the most significant versions and the notable features of each:

- Version 1 was the original MS-DOS, released in August 1981. Shipped on
  a single floppy disk, version 1 included Edlin (the MS-DOS line editor),
  Debug (a program debugger), a file-comparison utility named Filcom,
  the MS-DOS batch interpreter, and the following commands: Directory
  (Dir), Rename (Ren), Erase/Delete (Del), Copy, Type, Pause, Check Disk
  (Chkdsk), Date, Format, System (Sys), and Time.

- Version 1.1, released in May 1982 as an upgrade developed for IBM,
  added support for double-sided, 320-K floppy disks. Essentially the same
  version was released to other computer manufacturers, including COM-
  PAQ and Zenith, as version 1.25.

- Version 2, released in March 1983, was MS-DOS for the IBM PC/XT. One
  of the most significant versions of MS-DOS, version 2 added numerous
  commands, many related to the new hierarchical file system and support
  for hard disks. Also included in version 2 were background printing (the
  Print command) and support for installable device drivers (non-MS-DOS
  programs needed for controlling third-party add-on devices, such as
  video cards, printers, and joysticks).

- Version 2.1, released in October 1983, was essentially version 2 with support for the ill-fated IBM PCjr.

- Version 3, released in August 1984, was MS-DOS for the IBM PC/AT.
  Version 3 added support for 1.2-MB floppy disks and hard disks larger
  than the XT's 5-MB to 10-MB drives.

- Version 3.1, released in March 1985, was version 3 with the addition of
  network support and file sharing.

- Version 3.2, released in January 1986, added support for 3.5-inch floppy
  disks.

- Version 3.3, released in April 1987, appeared at the same time as the IBM
  PS/2 series and added a number of capabilities, including support for
  PS/2 computers; some new commands (Call, Fastopen, Compare (Comp),

Select); some enhanced commands (Fixed Disk (Fdisk), Append, Attribute (Attrib), Backup, and others); and national language support, or code-page switching.

- Version 4, released in February 1988, was an upgrade that did not gain particularly wide acceptance. Version 4 added support for hard disks larger than 32 MB, eliminating the need to create primary and secondary MS-DOS partitions on large hard disks. It also introduced the Memory Display (Mem) command and the MS-DOS Shell.

- Version 5, when released in mid-1991, was widely praised as the most significant update since version 2 or version 3 (depending on the reviewer's opinion). Version 5 added support for memory management. It also gave MS-DOS the ability to conserve conventional memory by loading programs, device drivers, and even part of itself into previously inaccessible portions of memory beyond 640 K. Additional features included online help, an expanded Dir command, several new disk-management utilities (including Undelete and Unformat), and task swapping through an improved MS-DOS Shell.

- Version 6, released in spring 1993, is the latest MS-DOS. Building on the strongest features of version 5, version 6 offers such capabilities as automated memory management, multiple-choice booting, multiple configuration options, extensive online help, and even better disk-management utilities, including antivirus scanning, defragmentation, and disk compression. Version 6 also supports computer-to-computer linkups for file transfers. Most of this book is about version 6.

Kinds of operating systems

MS-DOS is one microcomputer operating system, but it is not the only one. The Apple Macintosh has the Macintosh System, with its familiar program and desktop manager, the Finder. For computers based on the 80x86 microprocessor developed by the Intel Corporation, there are several MS-DOS alternatives, among them Windows, UNIX, and IBM's OS/2 version 2.

Windows

Microsoft Windows can increase the speed and power of a computer with an 80386 or 80486 microprocessor. Currently, Windows exists in two complementary forms: Windows for MS-DOS, which runs on machines such as laptops and typical desktop systems, and Windows NT, which is geared for network servers and very high-end desktop systems. Both forms of Windows push far beyond MS-DOS and its capabilities, most visibly in their ability to use more than the 640 MB of memory to which MS-DOS applications are limited and in their ability to multitask—to run more than one program at the same time.

In a sense, Windows is system software in transition. Originally developed as an operating environment that ran on top of MS-DOS, Windows' primary role was to make using a computer easier and more intuitive by offering a mouse-based, graphical user interface (GUI) based on icons and menu choices and by allowing the user to open and work with more than one application at a time. As hardware became more powerful and GUIs became more popular, succeeding versions of Windows blurred the distinction between environment and operating system by taking over from MS-DOS more and more tasks related to managing system memory and resources.

In its current form, Windows version 3.1 for MS-DOS is an operating system in its own right. It is a unique one, however, in the sense that it complements rather than replaces MS-DOS. Windows for MS-DOS cannot be installed unless MS-DOS is already on the computer, so in this respect, Windows for MS-DOS still functions somewhat like a shell or an operating environment that enhances MS-DOS. Unlike typical shells, however, Windows relies very little, and in some instances not at all, on MS-DOS services for managing memory, attached devices, and even file input and output operations, so from this point of view, Windows is, indeed, a real operating system. Windows NT, which is something of a "big brother" version of Windows for MS-DOS, is even more independent because you do not need MS-DOS at all. Like Windows version 3.1, Windows NT is, however, completely compatible with MS-DOS.

Both Windows for MS-DOS and Windows NT have the ability to run traditional MS-DOS–based applications, confining each MS-DOS–based program to its own on-screen window. Because both forms of Windows are unbound by any of the traditional restrictions affecting MS-DOS, however, they can and do go beyond the capabilities of MS-DOS alone. As already mentioned, Windows in either form easily breaks through the 640-K memory barrier that has plagued MS-DOS applications for years. Windows can also allow Windows-based applications and MS-DOS–based applications to remain active at the same time, and Windows can provide and maintain *virtual memory,* a disk-based temporary storage area that can make a computer work faster and more efficiently.

OS/2 version 2

OS/2 version 2, like Windows NT and unlike Windows 3.1, runs as a totally independent operating system. Comparable in size and scope to Windows NT, OS/2 version 2 is a true 32-bit, multitasking, high-performance operating system. Like

Windows NT, OS/2 version 2 requires much more disk storage space and memory than MS-DOS does, and so it runs especially well on high-performance workstations (as opposed to standard desktop machines with 30-MB to 60-MB hard disks and 2 MB to 4 MB of random access memory, or RAM).

OS/2 version 2 does not require MS-DOS, although it can coexist with MS-DOS on the same hard disk and can, if desired, be set up as a dual boot system—one on which the user can choose to start either operating system. Like Windows, OS/2 version 2 can easily run MS-DOS–based applications as well as applications especially designed for OS/2. When running an MS-DOS–based application, OS/2, like Windows, assigns the application its own memory space and processor time, effectively running the application on its own virtual MS-DOS–based computer within the OS/2 environment.

UNIX

The UNIX operating system has, in one form or another, been in existence longer than MS-DOS and considerably longer than either Windows or OS/2. Originally created for use on minicomputers, UNIX is a powerful multitasking operating system that, in its traditional form, responds to typed commands similar to but often even more abbreviated than those in MS-DOS. On computers running UNIX, MS-DOS can be installed as an alternative operating system. You cannot run both MS-DOS and the UNIX operating system simultaneously, but with versions of UNIX such as the Santa Cruz Operation's Open Desktop system, you can take advantage of MS-DOS commands and the myriad off-the-shelf MS-DOS–based applications with the help of a graphical interface within which you run MS-DOS and an MS-DOS–based application in its own workspace within an open window.

MS-DOS in comparison

MS-DOS is, in many ways, the least powerful of these alternative operating systems for 80x86-based computers. All the others provide multitasking services; the others can work with far more memory than the base 640 K that MS-DOS–based applications can access without additional help; the others offer GUIs. But MS-DOS offers one singular advantage that the others, at least at present, cannot: quantity. Through MS-DOS, you have access to thousands of applications that collectively serve almost every need you can think of. Through MS-DOS, you also have access to large numbers of online databases and bulletin boards, networks large and small, and—importantly—numerous compatible computers to which you can transfer files with ease. Until the world turns to one or another rising star in system software, using a computer with an 80x86 microprocessor essentially means that you need MS-DOS for flexibility as well as productivity.

Compatibility and what it means

MS-DOS–based and Macintosh computers are generally incompatible with one another. A program designed to run on one will not run on the other, although the same basic program can be released in different versions—one for MS-DOS and another for the Mac. This is one very obvious type of incompatibility between these two (and other) microcomputers. There are, of course, other ways in which two such machines can differ even though, in the long run, they both produce the same type of work and can even produce files that are transferable from one to the other.

A computer operating system is designed to make the best possible use of the architecture of the machine on which it runs. This does not mean, however, that there is only one way, or even one best way, to design an operating system. Approaches differ (as do opinions) and, therefore, so do operating systems. The Macintosh, for example, is application based and takes an extremely modular, graphical approach. Graphics are handled by one module; the keyboard, the mouse, and file storage are handled by others. Each of these modules exists to provide resources—data, memory, printing, file management, and so on—to an active application.

MS-DOS, on the other hand, is what you might consider system based. On an MS-DOS–based computer, hardware and software are layered, with hardware at the core, MS-DOS in the middle, and increasingly sophisticated kinds of software running on top of this basic hardware/software partnership. MS-DOS thus manages internal goings-on to create an environment in which applications can run. This is why, when no application is running, MS-DOS displays the system prompt, telling you that the operating system is currently managing the system. MS-DOS is ready to hand temporary, supervised control to an application, but MS-DOS, not the application, runs the show.

Despite these kinds of differences, operating systems can be made to communicate, at least to some extent, although not freely or easily. You can transfer files between an MS-DOS/Windows–based computer or network and its Macintosh equivalent if you have the help of software especially designed to mediate between the two. You can save files in ASCII format and send them via a communications link to another, incompatible computer. You can even transfer formatted files between computers if your application software is designed to read and convert formats from one machine into their equivalents on the other. To actually enable two incompatible operating systems to work together directly, however, you must use software or a software/hardware combination that provides a common link that enables the hardware in one to work with the hardware in the other.

MS-DOS itself

Although MS-DOS is invariably referred to as a single unit, a quick look at your DOS directory is enough to show you that MS-DOS is actually a large number of program and system files. The remainder of this chapter tells about those files and what they do.

The organization of MS-DOS

Of the scores of files supplied with MS-DOS, three are essential: IO.SYS, MSDOS.SYS, and COMMAND.COM. Of these three, IO.SYS and MSDOS.SYS contain so much of the heart of MS-DOS that they are given the hidden, system, and read-only attributes for protection in the root directory of the system boot disk. There, they remain invisible to a normal directory listing, although you can list their names with the *dir /ah* command.

These three files are important because there can be no startup without them. Whenever you start or restart the computer, the bootstrap portion of MS-DOS must be able to find IO.SYS and MSDOS.SYS in the root directory, and it must be able to find COMMAND.COM either in the root directory or in a directory listed in the MS-DOS path.

NOTE: If you have version 6 of MS-DOS and you enable disk compression with DoubleSpace, you add another player to your starting lineup—DBLSPACE.BIN. This file, which sits in about 40 K of memory, gives MS-DOS the ability to work with compressed disks. Unlike the other system startup files, DBLSPACE.BIN has a relatively narrow job description. It is covered later in this book, specifically in Chapters 8 and 14.

IO.SYS

IO.SYS, containing slightly more than 40,000 bytes, is a program with two vital jobs to perform. It initializes the system at startup and provides MS-DOS with a set of default device drivers. *Device drivers* are programs that control the basic input/output devices of the computer, such as the keyboard and display. These drivers in effect give eyes, ears, and hands to the body of MS-DOS. Standard devices include disk drives, the system clock (CLOCK$), and several other devices familiar to anyone who has spent time with the Mode command:

- CON, which is short for console and refers to the keyboard (for input) and monitor (for output).
- PRN, which is short for printer and refers to the first parallel port. PRN usually defaults to (is the same as) LPT1.
- AUX, which is short for auxiliary and refers to the first serial port. AUX usually defaults to COM1.

The startup portion of IO.SYS, called SYSINIT, is the true "bootstrap" part of MS-DOS. SYSINIT loads into memory early in the game and paves the way for MS-DOS to settle in and become active.

MSDOS.SYS

MSDOS.SYS is the portion of MS-DOS commonly known as the *kernel*. Like kernels of corn, nuts, or wisdom, MSDOS.SYS is the "seed" that holds all of the operating system's basic capabilities. The workhorse portion of MS-DOS, MSDOS.SYS contains all the essential disk-management and file-management capabilities of the operating system. MSDOS.SYS also gives MS-DOS the ability to manage memory, supervise application programs, and configure the system for different languages, keyboards, and country conventions.

COMMAND.COM

The most visible portion of MS-DOS when you work from the system prompt, COMMAND.COM is known as the command interpreter and does exactly what you would expect it to. COMMAND.COM is the part of MS-DOS that accepts and carries out your commands, including those that run application programs and batch files as well as traditional MS-DOS commands such as Copy and Directory (Dir).

Internal vs. external commands

MS-DOS includes both internal and external commands. Internal commands are those built into COMMAND.COM; external commands are those that reside on disk until they are needed, at which time they are read into memory and carried out like any other command.

Internal commands include such long-lived, often-used workhorses as Clear Screen (Cls), Copy, and Dir. Most internal commands have been part of MS-DOS since its first release. Some, such as Change Directory (Chdir or Cd), became part of MS-DOS version 2 when the MS-DOS hierarchical directory structure was first implemented. A few others, such as Change Codepage (Chcp) and Load High (Loadhigh or Lh), appeared as internal commands in version 3 and in later versions because they are or might be needed at startup.

External commands are those parts of MS-DOS with filenames such as DISKCOPY.COM, XCOPY.EXE, and CHKDSK.EXE. Some external commands, such as Chkdsk and Format, appeared with version 1 of MS-DOS, but have always led external lives. Most other external commands, however, have been added to MS-DOS since about version 2 and remain as separate files on disk either because they are not often used (File Compare, for example) or because making them internal would cause COMMAND.COM to become too large and require too much of the memory needed by application programs.

In all other respects, however, external commands are no different from internal commands. You request them just as you do any other commands. On a computer with a hard disk, where all these external commands should be in the DOS directory, there's little to distinguish an external command from an internal command other than some slight drive activity as MS-DOS goes out to the disk to fetch the command file.

On a computer without a hard disk, the difference between internal and external commands can be much more noticeable, however, because MS-DOS will look on the current MS-DOS disk for the command file. If MS-DOS fails to find the command on that disk, it responds *Bad command or file name*. To carry out the command, you must find and insert the appropriate MS-DOS disk and give the command again.

NOTE: If you are using MS-DOS from floppy disks, the first and best recommendation is, obviously, to invest in a hard disk. If this is not possible, print the contents of the MS-DOS file named PACKING.LST, which is on Disk 1. This file lists both the files on the distribution disks (filenames ending with an underline, as in format.co_*) and the filenames (with normal extensions) that MS-DOS creates. The easiest way to print the file is to place Disk 1 in drive A and type the command* copy a:packing.lst > prn.

MS-DOS commands, utilities, and tools

MS-DOS has grown enormously from its first release. Along the way, MS-DOS has gained a great deal of capability, thanks to added commands, utilities, and tools designed to help you fine-tune the ways you can manage your computer, your disks, your files, your time, and (in versions 5 and 6) even the way you assign memory to various programs and device drivers. Some of these capabilities are available through the MS-DOS Shell; all can be accessed through the MS-DOS command line, at the system prompt.

Given the large number of external command files now available with MS-DOS, it can be somewhat difficult to keep them straight in your mind. One way to impose order is to differentiate commands from utilities, and both commands and utilities from tools. Such a distinction is artificial in a sense because all commands, utilities, and tools are invoked in the same way—by typing their names at the system prompt—but thinking of them in groups can help you make sense of them all and, by extension, help you see how to use their various capabilities to work with MS-DOS more effectively.

Commands

A command is an instruction you give to MS-DOS that causes it to perform a certain, very specific action. For example, this command

```
C:\>dir
```

causes MS-DOS to list the files in the current directory (here, the root directory of drive C). Although most MS-DOS commands do far more than the simple mnemonic shown above, all commands enable you to control some very specific aspect of the behavior of MS-DOS.

To gain more flexibility, you can qualify most commands with optional parameters and switches. *Parameters,* which most often are drive identifiers and directory names in MS-DOS, focus a command on a particular objective. *Switches,* which are always preceded by a forward slash (/), customize the command or its output.

Thus, you can modify the Dir command with a parameter like this:

```
C:\>dir c:\dos
```

to specify a particular directory you want to view.

You can also modify the command with one or more switches—for example:

```
C:\>dir /o /w
```

tells MS-DOS to run the Dir command and display the result in wide format (*/w*) with subdirectories listed first (*/o*).

And, of course, you can usually include both options, as in this example:

```
C:\>dir d:\ /ah
```

which tells MS-DOS to list all hidden files (*/ah*) in the root directory of drive D.

Commands and their options are described in detail in Section Three.

MS-DOS utilities

Commands let you work with system resources, including data files. Utilities are programs that you start from the command line, like application programs, but that focus on helping you maintain and organize system resources to keep the entire system in good repair and working efficiently. Because data is the most important and least easily replaced of all the information you entrust to a computer, most MS-DOS utilities are involved in protecting, recovering, and optimizing disk-based storage.

Some utilities are old standbys from versions of MS-DOS prior to version 5. Among them are such familiar names as Fdisk, which helps you organize the space on a hard disk, even to the point of dividing the storage area so that you can treat each section as if it were a separate disk drive, and Restore, which returns all or selected files from a backup disk to the disk and directory they originally occupied.

Version 5 of MS-DOS added several new utilities, the most important being

- Mirror, which creates and maintains a record of information about a disk so that you can, if necessary, recover files erased by an ill-advised Delete or Format command.

- Unformat, which reverses (or attempts to reverse) a Format command.
- Undelete, which recovers (or attempts to recover) inadvertently deleted files.

Version 6 of MS-DOS extends the reach of utilities even further with a new, improved Backup utility and a number of new aids for ensuring disk safety and efficient storage. Among these are

- An improved replacement for the version 5 Undelete utility.
- A disk-compression facility called DoubleSpace (Dblspace) that can effectively double disk capacity by storing information more efficiently.
- A disk defragmentation utility, Microsoft Defragmenter (Defrag), that neatens storage and improves disk performance by recombining pieces of files that have been scattered to physically separate regions of a disk as MS-DOS has repeatedly used and reused storage space that has been occupied and then vacated by saved and deleted files.
- Microsoft Anti-Virus aids that find and eliminate computer viruses.

MS-DOS utilities can be invaluable aids in maintaining the integrity of your system and, more importantly, your data. The commands that start MS-DOS utilities are described in Section Three. Use of the utilities themselves is covered in Section Four.

MS-DOS tools

Into the category of tools falls a group of MS-DOS programs that, unlike commands and utilities, helps you turn the computer to tasks that fall outside of normal MS-DOS command use and system maintenance. Like the collected equipment in a carpenter's or a plumber's toolbox, the MS-DOS tools have vastly different jobs to do. The MS-DOS Editor, for example, is a tool that appeared in version 5 to replace the venerable, but admittedly antique, Edlin line editor. A full-screen, menu-based text editor, the MS-DOS Editor functions like a simple word processor, and you can use it with little trouble for creating and editing quick, relatively short text files.

Another valuable tool, again available from version 5 onward, is the Doskey command recorder. With Doskey, you can review, replay, and edit prior commands. If you find you use certain commands frequently, Doskey can also help you assign those commands to macros that you can save and run with a few keystrokes whenever you want.

If you're interested in programming or if you find that you must create an application that you cannot find elsewhere, MS-DOS offers the QBasic interpreter, which enables you to write and run programs written in QBasic—a newer, more powerful dialect of the Basic language that has been part of MS-DOS since version 1. For a quick look at QBasic, see Chapter 20.

Your MS-DOS toolbox also includes a well-known tool called the batch inter-preter, a part of COMMAND.COM that carries out the quasi-programs you put together as sets of commands and conditions in batch files.

Finally, MS-DOS offers both Debug and ANSI.SYS. Debug is primarily a pro-grammer's tool for examining, running, and modifying program files. ANSI.SYS is a screen-and-keyboard device driver you can use instead of the less adaptable MS-DOS default driver. With ANSI.SYS, you can control color, cursor position, and other display features.

The user-oriented MS-DOS tools are covered in Section Four.

2

MS-DOS and the Computer

What You'll Find Here: The "DOS" in MS-DOS tells you that MS-DOS is a Disk Operating System. Much, if not most, of its job deals with storing and retrieving disk-based information, moving programs and data to and from the computer's memory for processing. Although disk management is critical, MS-DOS manages other parts of the computer too. This chapter provides background information about the relationships between MS-DOS and hardware and software, as well as about computers in general. This kind of information provides needed perspective if you want to optimize your system and helps explain the output of the version 6 Microsoft Diagnostics (MSD) command, as well as the output of other system-related commands, such as Mode, Memory Display (Mem), Check Disk (Chkdsk), and DoubleSpace (Dblspace).

When you turn on a computer, electricity washes through the system, making its way to and through the chips and circuit boards that make up the hardware inside the machine. Once inside the computer, this power eventually forms the raw material out of which you construct and save words, numbers, charts, drawings, and even messages to be sent through the telephone system, via modem, from one computer to another.

The flow of electricity inside a computer is as controlled as water within the banks of a river, but without some external intelligence, this power represents nothing more than the potential to do work. The controlling intelligence is, of course, you. But at the levels closest to the hardware, you are represented by the computer's operating system, the software that transfers instructions to the many components, which respond blindly, but at amazing speed, to actions as small as the press of a single key.

Hardware and software, working together, are required to make any computer tick. Hardware, as even new users understand intuitively, comprises the physical parts of a computer. Hardware is touchable, and it is relatively unchanging. Unless modified in some way, the "box," together with its microprocessor, disk drives, and other components, remains the same system throughout its life.

In all the work you do with a computer, however, you don't directly influence much of the hardware. In fact, you don't even see the most important parts of it. You can pound on the keyboard, adjust the color on the screen, insert disks, move and click the mouse, and so on, but you cannot physically move a letter from the keyboard to the screen, retrieve or store a file on a disk, make data available to the microprocessor, draw a circle, calculate a formula, or otherwise control the functioning of the hardware. You can't, but your software can and does.

In name and performance, software is the opposite of hardware. Although not soft to the touch, software is "soft" in two other respects: It is extremely flexible in what it can do, and it is to some degree not truly physical. Software is logic represented by magnetic particles on disk and by changes in voltage in the computer's memory. For all that, however, software is potent logic that turns physics to the manipulation of instructions, ideas, and data.

Types of software

An MS-DOS computer runs at least two, and possibly three, kinds of software, each of which has its own type of work to do. As shown in Figure 2-1, these different types of software run in layers on top of the hardware:

- The MS-DOS operating system. Making up the bottom layer, working most closely with the hardware and forming a base for the other types of software, is MS-DOS. In working with the hardware, MS-DOS acts as an intermediary between higher-level programs and the hardware. In addition, MS-DOS functions as a system superintendent, taking care of such tasks as fetching characters from the keyboard, managing memory, and moving information to and from the disk drives.

- Above MS-DOS is an optional shell or operating environment that overlies the operating system and takes over the task of interacting with you. The MS-DOS Shell is one such environment, but there are others. A shell usually adds to or enhances the basic file-management and disk-management features of MS-DOS. Microsoft Windows, although it occupies this position above MS-DOS in the software hierarchy is, as explained in Chapter 1, a separate operating system rather than a shell— an operating system that, on a typical desktop computer, complements but does not replace MS-DOS.

- At the top of the pyramid are application programs, which do the productive work that makes computers so valuable. Sophisticated as they may be in the work they do, application programs designed for MS-DOS rely on the operating system for file, disk, and memory management, as well as other housekeeping services.

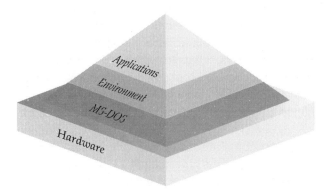

FIGURE 2-1.
Layers of software in a computer.

In some ways, MS-DOS and application software are the equivalents of the conscious and unconscious mind. Because it forms the base layer of software, MS-DOS is the unconscious mind that handles functions comparable to walking, breathing, and blinking.

Application software, in contrast, has "thinking" to do: calculating, formatting, paginating, sorting, and otherwise manipulating data. To free these programs from the need to be both cleanup crew and CEO, MS-DOS takes over the custodial role by providing basic services that the applications can call on for keyboard input, disk storage, video support, and so on. Whenever necessary, an application can simply call on MS-DOS for this kind of assistance and leave the details to the operating system.

So, for example, when a word processor needs to retrieve a file stored on disk, it doesn't have to go to the disk, locate the areas in which the file is stored, and read the file into the computer's memory. It can simply hand the job over to MS-DOS. When the file is no longer needed, the word processor can tell MS-DOS to put the file away, trusting the operating system to find disk space, save the file, and record all storage locations for future reference.

Inside the computer

As you work, MS-DOS picks up what you type, carries it to the microprocessor, hauls it to the monitor, and eventually packs it off to a disk file. To move your work efficiently and in a form the hardware can use, MS-DOS distributes all information—program instructions as well as data—in the *binary digits*, or *bits*, that computer people sometimes assume everyone learns about through osmosis.

Bits and binary arithmetic

In the film "Alien," there's a scene in which Sigourney Weaver sits and stares at a computer monitor, attempting to decipher the message encoded in flickering screenfuls of 1s and 0s. She is, of course, looking at binary digits, the building blocks of bytes. Binary is great for computers, but much less so for humans.

The reason computers take to binary so well is that the two binary digits, 1 and 0, are easily represented both electrically and magnetically inside the machine. In memory or on the high-speed data freeway called the *bus*, binary digits can be represented by simple changes in voltage. So, for example, a high voltage (relatively speaking—not electrocution dosage) can be equivalent to the binary digit 1, and a low voltage can be equivalent to the binary digit 0. On disk, which is the other primary site for computer-based information, binary digits can be represented by differences in the orientation of clusters of magnetic particles. A group, or *domain*, of magnetic particles oriented north-south can represent a binary 1, whereas a domain oriented south-north can represent a binary 0, or vice versa. A bit in a computer is therefore an electrical or magnetic signal that symbolizes a binary 1 or 0.

So far, so good. But binary is not a very intuitive system for humans raised on a decimal diet. Because binary uses only two digits, the representation of a binary number can quickly grow disproportionate to its actual value. For example, 10000 is the binary equivalent of decimal 16. Binary math is even worse. When you add 100 decimal to 100 decimal, the addition looks like this:

01100100

<u>01100100</u>

11001000

Swell.

There is, however, a way to make binary numbers more useful to humans while still maintaining their utility as computer fodder. The trick lies in using groups of bits to represent (slightly) more readable information. On microcomputers, the representation most often used is known as *hexadecimal*, which is numbering to the base 16. Hexadecimal uses groups of 4 bits which, in various combinations, can represent 16 unique digits, as shown below:

Decimal	Binary	Hexadecimal
0	0000	0
1	0001	1
2	0010	2
3	0011	3
4	0100	4
5	0101	5
6	0110	6
7	0111	7
8	1000	8
9	1001	9
10	1010	A
11	1011	B
12	1100	C
13	1101	D
14	1110	E
15	1111	F

Notice that some hexadecimal digits are peculiar. That's because the decimal system runs out of digits when it reaches 9. Hexadecimal, being based on a system with 16 unique digits, must come up with "new" digits to represent 10 through 15. Instead of inventing some new characters, hexadecimal (hex, as it's usually known) resorts to the first five letters of the Roman alphabet. Thus, in hex, the digit corresponding to decimal 10 is A, 11 is B, 12 is C, and so on through F for 15. In hex, then, you can create a number such as FEED or ACED and actually have it represent a numeric value. (FEED is 65,261 decimal and ACED is 44,269 decimal). Figure 2-2 on the following page summarizes this numeric circus by showing conversions from decimal to binary to hexadecimal, and back to decimal.

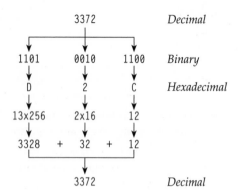

FIGURE 2-2.
Conversion from decimal to binary to hexadecimal to decimal.

Hex to decimal and back again

Although Figure 2-2 shows conversions to and from hexadecimal, you seldom have to go through the contortions when you use MS-DOS. Knowing the conversion procedure can come in handy, though, especially if you want to understand something about computer memory or the output of some MS-DOS commands, such as File Compare (Fc), or if you don't have version 6 and want to use the Mem command to check on memory usage and to figure out the size, location, and availability of upper memory blocks. Upper memory blocks, or *UMBs*, are portions of memory that sit between 640 K and 1 MB on most systems. As described in Chapter 11, they can be put to work holding memory-resident programs and device drivers that would otherwise clog the conventional memory you need for application programs.

To convert hexadecimal to decimal, you multiply the decimal equivalent of each digit by successive powers of 16 as you move to the left, and then add the products, like this:

```
FEED
│││↓
││↓D        = 13         =      13
│↓E  x 16^1 = 14 x 16    =     224
↓E  x 16^2  = 14 x 256   =    3584
F x 16^3    = 15 x 4096  =   61440
                             65261
```

To convert from decimal to hexadecimal, you practice long division instead, as follows:

```
65261/4096 = 65261/16^3 = 15 remainder 3821
 3821/256  = 3821/16^2  = 14 remainder 237
  237/16   =  237/16^1  = 14 remainder 13
   13      =   13        = 13
```

Here, of course, the decimal values 15 14 14 13, when converted to hexadecimal, become FEED.

In addition to the Mem command, hexadecimal makes a token appearance in some other MS-DOS commands, such as Directory (Dir) and Format. The Dir command, for example, displays the volume serial number of a disk (an identification number MS-DOS assigns during formatting) in its second line of output. The volume serial number is always in hexadecimal, like this: 18DE-6BEA. Elsewhere in MS-DOS, when you use the MS-DOS Shell, you can choose to display a file in either hexadecimal or ASCII (plain text) format by selecting a filename and choosing View File Contents from the File menu. Where hexadecimal appears most, however, is in the MS-DOS tool Debug, which programmers use to display the contents of memory and write short programs in assembly language. You'll find more on MS-DOS commands in Section Three.

From bits to bytes

By itself, a bit can convey no meaning outside of a simple two-state situation. Because a bit can represent only 1 or 0, it can be applied only to either/or conditions: ON vs. OFF, YES vs. NO, or TRUE vs. FALSE. But language, mathematics, and art demand far more than duets of logic, and for those purposes, computers (and MS-DOS) rely on larger groups of bits.

As you've already seen, hexadecimal notation groups bits in sets of 4. Groups of 4 bits are often called *nibbles*, or *nybbles*, and as you've seen, a nibble can represent any of 16 unique combinations of 1s and 0s. Sixteen combinations are better than two, but they're still not enough to represent each letter in the Roman alphabet, much less the more complex characters of other languages. Use even more bits, however, and suddenly your horizons expand dramatically. Enter the *byte*, a group of 8 bits. A single byte can make up 256 unique combinations of 1s and 0s, and each of these combinations can be used to represent a letter, numeral, punctuation mark, or other special symbol.

And from bytes to ASCII

Once you know why computers munch on bits and bit combinations with ease, it's an easy step to go from playing with bits to assigning specific meanings to various combinations. This is what *ASCII* (American Standard Code for Information Interchange) is all about. The 256 possible combinations of bits in a byte are used to create a standardized "alphabet"—one in which combination number 65 (decimal) always represents a capital A, 66 always represents a capital B, and so on. ASCII, also referred to as *plain text*, crops up periodically, especially as a file-saving or file-transferring option in communications programs, word processors, and similar applications in which the ability to send, save, or receive readable text, without application-specific formatting or special characters, is important. Within MS-DOS, you have the ability to specify an ASCII option in commands such as File Compare and Copy, which deal with the characters stored in files. ASCII is also the coding scheme used when you create a text file with MS-DOS—for example, with the MS-DOS Editor or by copying from the keyboard to a disk file (*copy con a:myfile*). Appendix A lists ASCII characters, with their decimal and hexadecimal values.

To see the relationship between numbers and readable characters, create a simple text file by copying it from the keyboard to a file. Type the following:

```
C:\>copy con test.doc [Enter]
In Xanadu did Kubla Khan
```

End the file and save it to disk by pressing either F6 or Ctrl-Z.

Now start the MS-DOS Shell, select the file, and use the View File Contents command on the File menu. When you view the contents of a file, the Shell allows you to switch between hexadecimal and ASCII displays. So, for example, TEST.DOC looks like this in hexadecimal:

```
┌──────────────────────── MS-DOS Shell - TEST.DOC ────────────────────────┐
│ Display  View  Help                                                      │
│ ┌ To view file's content use PgUp or PgDn or ↑ or ↓.                   ┐ │
│ │                                                                       │ │
│   000000   496E2058   616E6164   75206469   64204B75   │ In Xanadu did Ku │
│   000010   626C6120   4B68616E                         │ bla Khan         │
│                                                                          │
└──────────────────────────────────────────────────────────────────────────┘
```

but looks like its much more readable self when you press the F9 key to switch to an ASCII display:

```
┌──────────────────────── MS-DOS Shell - TEST.DOC ────────────────────────┐
│ Display  View  Help                                                      │
│ ┌ To view file's content use PgUp or PgDn or ↑ or ↓.                   ┐ │
│ In Xanadu did Kubla Khan                                                 │
│                                                                          │
└──────────────────────────────────────────────────────────────────────────┘
```

When you finish, press Esc to return to the main Shell display. Press F3 to exit the Shell, and then clean up your disk by typing:

```
C:\>del test.doc
```

Full circle to some funny numbers

On the grand scale where you work most of the time, bits and bytes don't have a tremendous amount of meaning, but understanding what they represent goes a long way toward understanding your computer and explaining some rather unlikely units of measure that you encounter every day. Why, for example, does a kilobyte, that basic measure of memory and disk storage, contain 1024 bytes, rather than 1000 as you might expect? Because 1024 is a power of 2, the magic number in computing, whereas 1000 is a power of 10, the magic number in decimal math. Similarly, a megabyte, although often described as one million bytes for the sake of convenience, is actually 1024 x 1024, or 1,048,576 bytes.

As you might expect, the magical 2 also appears in programming languages, such as QBasic. For example, an integer (whole number) value can be either 16 bits or 32 bits long. A 16-bit integer value can be any whole number from –32,768 through +32,767. A 32-bit integer value, known as a long integer, can be any whole number from –2,147,483,648 through +2,147,483,647. Strange choices of upper and lower limits? Not when you understand bits and binary. A group of 16 bits equals 2 to the 16th power, which works out to 65,536 possible bit combinations. Divide that number by 2 to allow for positive and negative numbers, and you come up with 32,768 negative and 32,767 positive numbers (0 accounts for the difference of 1 between negative and positive). Similarly, 32 bits equal 2 to the 32nd power, or 4,294,967,296. Divide by 2, and you have 2,147,483,648 possible negatives, 2,147,483,647 possible positive numbers, and 0.

Whenever you encounter a peculiar number in computing, don't let it throw you. Remember the power of 2. You'll be pretty safe in assuming that the machine is marching to the beat of a binary drum.

From bytes to hardware

So much for computer information, the way it travels, and how you sometimes see it represented. Now it's time to take a brief look at computer hardware and how it works.

A typical computer system consists of a box housing the microprocessor, associated chips and circuitry, one or more disk drives or other forms of mass storage, and a set of plugs and connectors for attaching various external devices to the system. On a desktop model, the screen, or monitor, is usually separate; on a portable computer, the monitor is built in. Depending on the type and size of the computer, the keyboard can be either attached via a long cable or built into the main unit. Some additional devices, including mice and printers, are plugged into connectors and tethered to the machine. Other devices, such as modems and disk drives, can be either internal or external. Some, such as sound boards and video adapters, are internal.

If you could somehow get inside the computer while it was working, you would find rush hour in Silicon City. Bits lumped together into bytes and multiple-byte units speed along a data freeway called the bus, traveling from memory to the microprocessor and from the microprocessor to the various other chips, storage sites, and devices on the system. Depending on the capabilities of the microprocessor, the bus within an MS-DOS computer can range from a mere 8 "lanes" (bits) in width to a megafreeway on which 32 bits can travel abreast.

This electronic infrastructure, complex as it might seem, supports a world in which basically only three things happen: Information arrives, it is changed in some way, and it leaves. This process constitutes the traditional definition of computing: input, processing, output. Processing—manipulating program instructions and data—is primarily the concern of the microprocessor and your application software. Input and output, however, lie mostly in the MS-DOS domain.

The system itself

A computer capable of running MS-DOS is, first and foremost, based on a microprocessor in the 80x86 series of chips pioneered by Intel Corporation. Ranging from the original PC's 8088 relative of the 8086 chip to the current generation of 80486 microprocessors in high-end desktop and portable computers, the 80x86 chips showcase the speed at which computing power has increased in just a few years. The following list describes the main members of the 80x86 series, their dates of introduction, and their basic capabilities.

- The 8086 and 8088: Introduced in 1978, the 8086 and 8088 are almost identical microprocessors. Both have the ability to handle data 16 bits at a time, but the 8088 sends and receives data over an 8-bit bus, whereas the 8086 transfers data 16 bits at a time. The 8088 lay at the heart of the IBM PC, PC/XT, and compatible machines; the 8086 inhabited low-end IBM PS/2 models. Although these chips have been superseded by much more powerful descendants, their influence lives on. Both the 8088 and the 8086 used 20 bits to refer to locations in memory. Two to the 20th power is 1,048,576, or 1 MB. From these chips, then, comes a 1 MB memory address limitation out of which MS-DOS applications can use 640 K. (The remaining 384 K is reserved for system overhead.)

- The 80286: Introduced in 1982, the 80286 powered the IBM PC/AT and compatibles released in 1984. Like the 8088/8086 chips, the 80286 works with 16 bits at a time but can operate in either of two modes, real mode and protected mode. In real mode, it essentially pretends to be an 8086 chip and operates within 8086 limits. In protected mode, the 80286 can refer to as much as 16 MB of memory. It can also keep more than one program active in memory and can protect the memory "owned" by each program from intrusions by other programs.

■ The 80386: Also called the 80386DX, this chip was introduced in 1985. A full 32-bit microprocessor, the 80386 handles and transfers data in 32-bit chunks. It is like the 80286 in being able to operate in either real mode or protected mode, but it differs in two important respects. First, the 80386 can refer to as much as 4 GB (gigabytes—approximately 4 billion bytes) of memory. Second, the 80386 can operate in what is called virtual 8086 mode, a state in which it acts as though it were a number of 8086-based computers, each capable of running a different program.

The 80386SX chip found in some less-expensive 80386-based computers is comparable to the 80386DX, but it transfers data 16 bits, rather than 32 bits, at a time, making it slower than the 80386DX. In addition, the 80386SX can address only 16 MB of memory, but it is otherwise comparable.

■ The 80486: The current top-of-the-line microprocessor in generally available MS-DOS computers, the Intel 80486 is another full 32-bit chip capable of processing and transferring data 32 bits at a time. Like the 80386, the 80486 can refer to as much as 4 GB of memory. Internally, the 80486 improves on the capabilities of the 80386 in several respects, all related to increasing the speed of the chip. For improved performance on numeric calculations (important not only in spreadsheets but also in video graphics), the 80486 relies on a built-in complementary chip called a math coprocessor. Where information access is concerned, the 80486 makes use of caching—a means of storing previously accessed memory locations—to cut down on the time required to fetch information from memory. And to improve speed of execution, the 80486 makes use of a procedure called pipelining, in which instructions literally queue up while waiting for processor time. This pipelining replaces the fetch-an-instruction/carry-it-out/fetch-the-next-one approach to working that was used by earlier microprocessors.

Attached devices

Much, if not most, of the work done by MS-DOS deals with the transfer of information to and from the microprocessor. It is MS-DOS that gets input and moves it into memory, and it is MS-DOS that shifts processed information from memory to permanent storage on disk or to an output device such as the printer. In carrying out these tasks, MS-DOS categorizes devices into those that provide input and those that receive output. The most essential of these input/output devices—keyboard, screen, disk drives, ports, and memory—have their own names and are described in the remainder of this chapter.

Devices and device drivers

Although MS-DOS seems to work intelligently as it moves data here and there throughout the computer, it is, of course, totally brainless. In order to work with a disk drive, a keyboard, or a display monitor, it relies on special programs known as *device drivers*. These device drivers have three purposes: to control the devices for which they are written, to define those devices to MS-DOS, and to shield MS-DOS from having to deal with the unique characteristics of the devices themselves.

You might wonder why, if MS-DOS controls the system, it must use device drivers instead of somehow relying on its own capabilities to "know" about the devices directly. Although device drivers appear to add a layer of complexity to a computer system, in actuality they both simplify operations and add to the reliability of the hardware.

Bear in mind that a computer can have more attached devices than the basic keyboard, screen, and printer supported by MS-DOS. Furthermore, every device attached to a computer system has its own special features and, often, its own special quirks. Printers, mice, video cards, modems, tape drives, and any other kind of hardware you might want to attach to a basic computer system all have their own ways of working. If, as happened early in MS-DOS history, each device manufacturer patched into MS-DOS to enable the operating system to work with new devices, the result would be conflicts among devices and chaos in the computer.

The answer to this potential anarchy comes in the ability of MS-DOS to recognize and work with two different categories of device driver: default and installable. A *default*, or *resident*, device driver is one that is built into MS-DOS and is therefore automatically read into memory and activated whenever you start or restart your computer. Default device drivers control the keyboard, screen, and communications and printer ports as described in the remainder of this chapter.

Because MS-DOS recognizes only a few basic devices on its own, it relies on *installable* device drivers to tell it about all the other devices you might install. Thanks to installable device drivers, MS-DOS can remain stable and yet be "taught" to recognize new devices. Furthermore, these new devices can do whatever the hardware manufacturers want, as long as the manufacturers also create drivers that enable MS-DOS to use their equipment. The result is that both you and your software can make use of the special features of any device with few or no problems. Installable device drivers are, in effect, the means by which a manufacturer can identify its hardware protégé to MS-DOS and, at the same time, enable the device to interact with the operating system and application software. Installable device drivers, which are programs in their own right and must be identified to MS-DOS through Device or Devicehigh commands in CONFIG.SYS, are described in Chapter 10.

Two halves of a whole: the keyboard and the display

The keyboard and the screen, or monitor, are without doubt the most familiar-looking parts of a computer. They don't seem to have much in common, either in appearance or in the ways they are used, but the keyboard and the screen are, nonetheless, related in a very basic way: The keyboard is the primary input device for MS-DOS, and the screen is the primary output device. Because the keyboard and the screen are so closely tied, they are known to MS-DOS by the same name, CON (for console). Together, without any other system components except memory and the microprocessor, the keyboard and screen can fulfill the first and last functions of computing: input and output.

The keyboard

A standard keyboard for a desktop model of an MS-DOS computer has either 101 or 102 keys on it. Because of size restrictions, a laptop or notebook computer generally has fewer and sometimes smaller keys. The layout often differs somewhat from the layout of a full-size keyboard, and some keys can be pressed into dual service—for example, either by being a character key or, when pressed in combination with another key, by functioning as a cursor-movement key or a function key. Regardless of whether it's attached to a full-size or a portable computer, however, a keyboard has the decided advantage of appearing nonthreatening, even to a new user. Figure 2-3 shows a typical desktop keyboard.

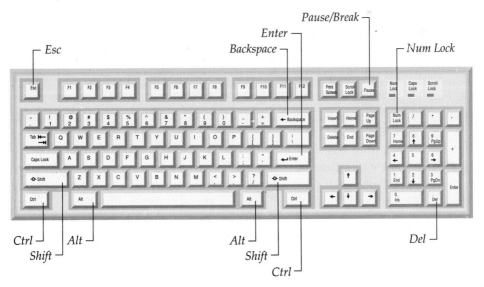

FIGURE 2-3.
A standard keyboard for a full-size desktop computer.

Unlike applications, which generally assign program-specific, predefined tasks to function keys and many key combinations, MS-DOS tends to use the keyboard "as is." It does, however, use a number of noncharacter keys for system control purposes. In addition, because MS-DOS saves the last (and only the last) command you typed in a temporary storage area called the *template*, you can use a number of keys for editing the previous command. Doskey, however, is simpler and more effective.

Keys and key combinations with special meanings to MS-DOS are described in the following list.

Enter. Ends a command you've typed and tells MS-DOS to carry it out. Enter is your means of returning control of the system to MS-DOS so that it can do the work you specified in your command. (Some keyboards call this Return.)

Esc. Cancels a command you've typed, if pressed before you press Enter. Esc moves the cursor to a new line but does not redisplay the system prompt. MS-DOS is, however, waiting for you to type a new command.

Shift. Shifts the alphabetic keys to uppercase and the number keys to special characters. MS-DOS is generally case insensitive (oblivious to differences between uppercase and lowercase), but certain commands, such as Find and File Compare (Fc), make such distinctions and must be specifically told to ignore case.

Ctrl. "Shifts" certain keys to give them a different meaning. Ctrl is generally used to send a program-control command or signal to MS-DOS or another program. The two most common uses of Ctrl with MS-DOS are in the key combinations Ctrl-Break and Ctrl-Alt-Delete:

- Ctrl-Break. Stops and cancels the currently executing command. Unlike Esc, which cancels a command before you press Enter, Ctrl-Break stops a command after MS-DOS has begun carrying it out.

- Ctrl-Alt-Delete. The ultimate escape, Ctrl-Alt-Delete forces the computer to restart and perform the abbreviated startup routine known as a *warm boot*. Ctrl-Alt-Delete, difficult to press accidentally, is the means by which you break out of a bad situation—for example, an application program with a previously undiscovered bug that causes the program— and the computer—to stop responding.

Pause. Stops scrolling in its tracks so that you can read part of a long display (such as a listing of the DOS directory) before it rolls off the top of the screen. Pressing any key restarts scrolling. On high-performance computers, scrolling can be so rapid that stopping the display at a desired point becomes almost impossible. In such situations, the MS-DOS More command or a switch, such as /p (for pause) in the Dir command, offers much more control.

Backspace. Moves the cursor one space to the left, at the same time erasing any character in that position. (This key is often identified by a long arrow pointing left.)

Num Lock. Toggles the numeric keypad between cursor control and numeric entry. This key, unfortunately, usually remains on at startup and is an easy key to forget about...until you press the 4 key repeatedly to move the cursor left and instead produce a string of numerals on the screen. In version 6 of MS-DOS, however, the Number Lock (Numlock) configuration command (described in Chapter 12) can help you out.

Print Screen. When pressed in combination with the Shift key, copies the contents of the screen to a non-PostScript printer. Under MS-DOS, Shift-Print Screen prints the contents of a character-based, alphanumeric display. To print the contents of a CGA, EGA, or VGA screen, you must first use the Graphics command described in Chapter 10.

F3. Displays the contents of the MS-DOS template—the last command you typed. You can use Backspace (and other keys) to edit the command, or press Enter to carry it out again. Chapter 18 describes editing keys in more detail.

F6 or Ctrl-Z. Adds an end-of-file character to a text file. As you saw earlier, you can press F6 or Ctrl-Z when you have finished copying from the keyboard and want the lines you've typed saved as a file on disk.

NOTE: The keys in the preceding list work at the MS-DOS command line identified by the system prompt. Keys with special meanings to other parts of MS-DOS are described elsewhere, as follows: the Doskey command recorder in Chapter 18, the MS-DOS Editor in Chapter 15, and the MS-DOS Shell in Chapters 4 and 5.

The display

A computer display, also called a monitor, looks and (internally) operates much like a standard television. The other half of the MS-DOS CON device, the display is a classic example of "user friendliness"—simple to turn on and adjust, yet the subject of a complex arm of electronics technology. MS-DOS is less active in handling and refining screen displays than it is in other areas, and it is often even programmed out of the picture completely by applications developers who bypass MS-DOS video services in favor of other, more hardware-specific, procedures.

From a user's point of view, MS-DOS and the display also have relatively little to do with one another. Through MS-DOS, you can, however, do the following:

- Use Shift-Print Screen, as described earlier, to send the screen contents to the printer.

- Use the Mode command, as described in Chapter 10, to control the number of characters per line and the number of lines per screen, and to enable code-page switching to display character sets from different languages.

- Use ANSI.SYS, as described in Chapter 10 and Appendix B, to control colors, cursor positions, and other aspects of the on-screen display.

- Use the Displays and Colors commands on the Options menu in the MS-DOS Shell (described in Chapters 4 and 5) to customize the screen while you're working with the Shell.

- Use the Display command on the Options menu of the MS-DOS Editor (described in Chapter 15) to adjust screen colors, tab stops, and the display of on-screen scroll bars that you use with a mouse.

As you work with MS-DOS, display-related terms such as CGA and VGA crop up periodically. Some of these terms might be new to you or, as many people can attest, they might simply be moderately to very confusing and difficult to keep straight. If you need help getting your bearings, the remainder of this section provides a brief introduction to the wonderful world of video.

Types of displays and the differences between them

The display attached to a typical desktop computer is very much like a television in that it is based on *CRT* (*cathode ray tube*) technology. Such a display is also known as a *raster-scan device*. Raster, from the Latin for "rake," refers to the pattern made by an electron beam inside the unit. This beam rapidly sweeps back and forth across and down a phosphor-coated screen and illuminates myriads of small dots, or *pixels*, laid out in rows and columns in the screen coating, as shown in Figure 2-4. Images are created by the pattern of lit and unlit pixels. On a color screen, pixels are are laid down as dots or lines in groups of three—red, green, and blue—and are illuminated in various combinations to create color.

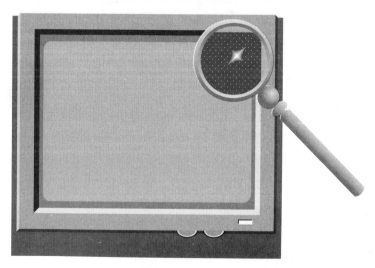

FIGURE 2-4.
The pattern of pixels on a monitor.

Laptop and notebook computers also rely on patterns of lighted pixels to create images, but the background technology differs. Most portable computers create images on flat *LCD* (*liquid crystal display*) screens, in which patterns of light and dark are created by polarized light in combination with electrodes that can block or transmit the light, depending on whether they are turned on or off. Other portable computers use similar flat-panel screens, but images are created by neon gas (*gas plasma displays*) or phosphor (*electroluminescent displays*).

Color screens on portable computers are either *passive matrix* or *active matrix*. In a passive matrix screen, three layers of color—red, blue, and green—are bonded to the screen, and pixels are lighted in varying combinations on a row-and-column basis to create an image. In active matrix, or TFT (*thin-film transistor*), screens, each on-screen pixel is controlled by three tightly aligned transistors bonded to the screen. To create an image, the computer's video circuitry turns the transistors in each pixel on or off, one by one.

Display modes

Just as bits are the basic units from which all internal information is built, pixels are the building blocks of all on-screen (and printed) images, as shown in Figure 2-5. Unless you are a programmer, you don't deal with pixels themselves when you work with MS-DOS. You do, however, encounter the term frequently in relation to screen resolution—the fineness of the image—and in relation to different video display adapters—the circuit boards that drive the display. The differences among various adapter types are outlined in the following list; screen resolutions and the number of colors each can produce are given in Table 2-1 on the following page.

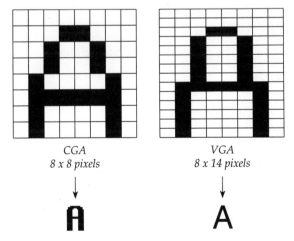

CGA
8 x 8 pixels

VGA
8 x 14 pixels

FIGURE 2-5.
An "A" created by pixels, at different resolutions.

MDA, short for Monochrome Display Adapter. Refers to the circuit board originally required to produce monochrome (background plus one color) displays on the IBM Monochrome Display, which was one of two choices for the original IBM PC. MDA operates in text mode only, meaning that it can reproduce text characters and some line-drawing and box-drawing characters by lighting certain predefined patterns of pixels, but it cannot draw pictures or different character sets, such as italic or script, because those must be created on a dot-by-dot basis. MDA produces 80 characters per line and 25 lines per screen. You cannot specify any other display mode.

CGA, short for Color/Graphics Adapter. The second of the two options provided for the IBM PC. CGA can display either text or graphics (dot-by-dot) mode in up to 16 colors. Widely considered less clear than an MDA display, CGA displays are seldom seen today, at least on new computers.

EGA, short for Enhanced Graphics Adapter. Displays both text and graphics modes, in both monochrome and color, and produces a noticeably clearer display than the CGA does. Although EGA can still produce only 16 colors, it can do so at higher resolutions than the CGA can.

VGA, short for Video Graphics Array. Standard on new computers based on the 80386 microprocessor. VGA displays produce both text and graphics modes and are much clearer than either CGA or EGA. Because VGA display circuitry can produce an analog signal—a variable signal that compares to the signals produced by earlier adapters in the same way a dimmer compares to an on/off switch—VGA displays can produce up to 256 colors at a time, taking them from a pool of 262,144 possibilities. SVGA (Super VGA), which is the current top of the line, is like VGA but capable of even greater resolution.

Display	Mode	Resolution	Colors
MDA	Text	80 characters per line, 25 lines per screen	Monochrome
CGA	Text	40 or 80 characters per line, 25 lines per screen	
	Graphics	320 pixels across, 200 pixels down	16
		640 pixels across, 200 pixels down	4
			2
EGA	Text	Same as MDA and CGA	
	Graphics	Same as CGA, plus	
		320 pixels across, 200 pixels down	16
		640 pixels across, 200 pixels down	16
		640 pixels across, 350 pixels down	Monochrome or 16

TABLE 2-1.
Display types and their features.

(continued)

TABLE 2-1. *continued*

Display	Mode	Resolution	Colors
VGA	Text	Same as MDA, CGA, EGA	
	Graphics	Same as EGA, plus	
		640 pixels across, 480 pixels down	16
		320 pixels across, 200 pixels down	256
SVGA	Text	Same as MDA, CGA, EGA, VGA	
	Graphics	Same as VGA, plus	
		640 pixels across, 480 pixels down	256
		1024 pixels across, 768 pixels down	256

Disk drives

A great many MS-DOS commands and most MS-DOS utilities deal with disks and disk drives. There are two obvious reasons why this is. First, disks and drives are the repositories of all the information you feed into the computer and retrieve from it. Second, MS-DOS needs more help from you in handling disks and drives than it does for any other part of the system. You must tell MS-DOS which disk-based application to run, you must tell it where to find that application, and you must be the librarian in charge of all the programs and data your work requires. Where disks and drives are concerned, you provide the brains, and MS-DOS provides the muscle.

By default, MS-DOS recognizes one more than the last disk drive on your system, identifying them sequentially by letter. A typical system includes one or two floppy drives known to MS-DOS as drives A and B, and one hard disk, always identified as C.

NOTE: Not all drives identified by letter are necessarily physical. A drive can also be logical—a "drive" that MS-DOS uses as if it were a physical component of the system, even though it doesn't actually exist as such. The concept of a logical drive sounds like science fiction, but it does happen to be computer fact. A RAM disk, which you define in memory, is just such a logical drive. So is a network drive that might be physically far distant from the system, but which MS-DOS can treat as an attached drive, thanks to a network connection. Another type of logical drive comes into being when you partition (divide) a large hard disk into sections. You can treat each section, or partition, *as if it were a separate disk drive by assigning a unique drive letter to it. If you use version 6 of MS-DOS and you use DoubleSpace to compress data and gain additional storage, you also divide your physical hard disk into two separate logical drives—usually drive C, which is the "compression" drive on which MS-DOS stores your files, and another drive, which contains your system startup files.*

The anatomy of disks and drives

Physical floppy drives and hard drives differ internally, but both are based on the same kind of mechanism. Each works with the help of an adapter called a *disk controller*, which is usually a separate circuit board inside the system unit and which manages the details involved in ensuring the smooth flow of bits to and from the surface of the disk. Aside from the disk controller, floppy and hard drives both rely on a motor that spins the disk itself; a central axis, or *spindle*, that holds the mounted disk; and *read/write heads* mounted on an arm that moves the heads between the edge and the center of the disk. The structure of a typical hard disk, minus the controller card, is shown in Figure 2-6.

A floppy drive is open, accessible, and of course, vacant until you insert a disk into it. A hard drive, in contrast, is airtight and contains from one to several physically inaccessible disks, or *platters*, already mounted on the spindle. Much more finely machined than a floppy drive, a hard drive must be sealed away from air currents, dust, and pollutants because data is packed tightly onto the surface of each platter and because the read/write heads float at far less than a hair's breadth above the platter when the disk is active.

The disk in a floppy drive rotates about 300 times per minute—fast, but not in comparison to a hard disk, in which the platters spin at about 3600 rotations per minute. This speed and the close tolerances within a hard disk are the reasons why you are cautioned never to jar the computer when MS-DOS is reading from

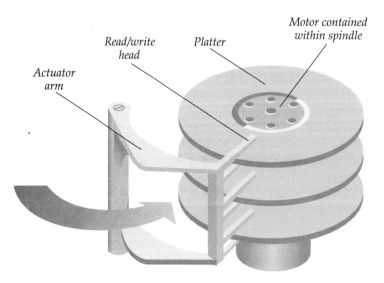

FIGURE 2-6.
The structure of a typical hard disk.

or writing to the disk. Protecting the mechanism also means that, whenever possible, you should avoid turning the system off until the drive is inactive. Although they are far from temperamental, hard disks can be damaged by rough treatment, and such treatment (as well as disk failure, of course) can lead to the dreaded, if rare, *head crash* in which a read/write head strikes the rapidly spinning platter, plowing through and destroying data and quite possibly the disk surface itself.

The physical disk layout

To MS-DOS, a disk is a disk. The primary difference between a floppy disk and a hard disk is that the former is removable and the latter is not. In other respects, the two types of disk are similar, even though they can hold vastly different amounts of information. Regardless of type, all MS-DOS disks are organized into the units you know of as *sides*, *tracks*, and *sectors*.

If you look at the visible portion of the recording surface of a 5.25-inch floppy disk, you see a thin sheet of grayish or reddish brown mylar. This color comes from a thin coating of iron oxide (the "rust" alluded to by some computer writers). It is this coating that stores information in the form of very small magnetic particles handled in small groups called *domains*. This "rust" is not the only coating you find, however. In many hard disks, the platters are often treated with a thin metallic covering that, although still magnetic in nature, uses more closely packed domains and hence enables disk manufacturers to increase storage capacity considerably.

As you no doubt remember from childhood, magnets of any type have two poles, north and south. When MS-DOS, via the drive controller, sends information to disk, a coil in the read/write head transfers electrical impulses to the disk, affecting the polarity of the domains on the surface, making some domains north-south, others south-north. There's a lot more to it than this, of course, because timing enters the picture, but basically, these changes in polarity, known as *flux changes*, can be considered to represent binary 1s and 0s. Flux changes, then, represent all the characters, graphics, and program instructions you store on disk. During a read operation, the read/write head reverses operation, sensing and transmitting back to MS-DOS changes in the polarity of the domains on the portions of the disk surface MS-DOS instructs it to read.

When MS-DOS stores information on disk, it does so in a very orderly, organized manner to ensure that the information is not only saved but can quickly be found and read back into memory. The organization used by MS-DOS relies on a system of disk sides (top or bottom), tracks, and sectors, which are labeled in Figure 2-7 on the following page.

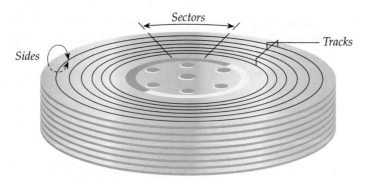

FIGURE 2-7.
The layout of a disk.

The tracks on a disk are often compared to the grooves on a record. (Remember records?) That's not quite accurate, because tracks are generally complete rings, whereas record grooves spiral in toward the center. However, the comparison is otherwise appropriate. Tracks represent the consecutive positions that can be occupied by the read/write heads as they move across the disk surface, between the outside edge and the center.

Whereas the tracks on a disk are a series of concentric rings, sectors are pie-shaped wedges running from the edge to the center. Sectors are the basic storage units of a disk, and each can hold a predetermined number of bytes. As you can see from the description of RAMDRIVE.SYS, which creates a virtual (practically real) disk in your computer's memory, sector size can vary but is always a multiple of 2. RAMDRIVE.SYS accepts sector sizes of 128, 256, 512, and (in some versions of MS-DOS) 1024 bytes, but on physical disks, a typical sector holds 512 bytes. (For details on RAMDRIVE.SYS, check Chapter 11 of this book or the list of parameters for RAMDRIVE.SYS in MS-DOS online Help.)

Tracks and sectors organize the surface of a disk. By means of this arrangement, MS-DOS can pinpoint any location on either side of a disk. Hard disks add another dimension: depth. Remember that hard disks consist of from two to several platters. Each of these platters has a top and a bottom, of course, but the platters themselves are also stacked like pancakes. A *cylinder* is basically a stack of tracks, one above the other, all occupying the same relative location on one side of a platter. You encounter references to cylinders when you investigate the disk drives on your system with the version 6 Microsoft Diagnostics (MSD) command. Otherwise, you probably won't see a reference to cylinders except in the version 4 Format command and the version 3.3 Fixed Disk (Fdisk) command.

Finally, in addition to tracks and sectors, you'll sometimes see references to disk storage in *clusters* (as in the MS-DOS Defragmenter and in the output of the Chkdsk command). Although the term is reminiscent of chocolate, grapes, or pearls, an MS-DOS cluster less delectably represents the smallest unit of storage, in sectors, that MS-DOS uses when saving—and fragmenting—files as it attempts to make the most effective use of available storage on a disk. Cluster size varies with the type of disk you use: two sectors on 360-K and 720-K floppies, only one sector on 1.2-MB and 1.44-MB floppies, and usually either four or eight sectors on a hard disk.

Disk capacities

Disk storage, like memory, is measured in kilobytes, megabytes, and (very occasionally) gigabytes. Actual storage capacity is determined by the number of tracks and sectors on a disk. Normally, the only time you deal with tracks and sectors is when MS-DOS "draws" them onto a disk during formatting; and because you seldom, if ever, need to format a hard disk, the number of tracks and sectors per disk is relevant more to floppy disks than to hard disks. Table 2-2 lists the numbers of tracks and sectors used by MS-DOS in formatting floppy disks of various capacities.

Disk size (inches)	Capacity	Tracks per side	Sectors per track
5.25	360 K	40	9
5.25	1.2 MB	80	15
3.5	720 K	80	9
3.5	1.44 MB	80	18
3.5	2.88 MB	80	36

TABLE 2-2.
Tracks and sectors on floppy disks.

When you buy a hard disk, the statistic that interests you most is the disk's size, or *capacity*. Size varies widely, but on a typical desktop computer hard disk capacity ranges from about 30 MB for a relatively small hard disk to 120 MB for a relatively large one. Even allowing for the doubling of disk capacity provided by the version 6 Dblspace command, however, a 60-MB hard disk should be the minimum size for a non-entertainment-oriented system. A full MS-DOS installation alone requires about 4 MB of disk storage, and programs such as Windows, word processors, and other application software can easily lay claim to an additional 5 MB to 15 MB apiece. Besides, if there's one thing that proves true about any hard disk, it's this: The bigger it is, the more you find to put on it.

Ports

Computer ports, like ports of call, are where shipments arrive from and depart for distant places. Not quite as exotic as distant harbors in tropical waters, computer ports look like drab little plugs, but they have as large—and probably as complex—a job to do as any bustling seaport. Ports are the means by which a computer transfers information in and out of the main console. If you want to send data to the printer, you need a port. If you want to receive a file transmitted via modem, you need a port. If you want your mouse to send clicks to an application, you often need a port. And if you want to connect to a network, or if you want to transfer files with the Interlnk file-transfer utility, you need a port.

Usually located on the back of the system unit, ports are the only visible portions of some complex circuitry that connects an input/output device to the system bus and, hence, to the other active portions of the computer, such as the microprocessor, memory, and disk drives. Some ports, such as the "plugs" for the keyboard and display, are generally built into a computer. Others can either be built in or added later as circuit boards that connect to the bus through one of the computer's internal expansion slots.

To avoid conflict and to ensure that data never goes astray, each port is identified by an address (in hexadecimal) and is assigned its own "call number," called an *interrupt request*, or *IRQ*. If you have version 6 of MS-DOS, you can see both the addresses of your ports and their IRQ numbers by starting the Microsoft Diagnostics utility. If you press Q to display IRQ status, you see a listing like this:

```
 File  Utilities  Help
━━━━━━━━━━━━━━━━━━━━━━━━━━━━━ IRQ Status ━━━━━━━━━━━━━━━━━━━━
 IRQ  Address     Description       Detected              Handled By
 ───  ────────    ───────────       ───────────────       ──────────────
   0  229A:0076   Timer Click       Yes                   Block Device
   1  229A:00CB   Keyboard          Yes                   Block Device
   2  1C94:0057   Second 8259A      Yes                   Default Handlers
   3  1C94:006F   COM2: COM4:       COM2:                 Default Handlers
   4  1E48:02CD   COM1: COM3:       COM1: Serial Mouse    MOUSE
   5  1C94:009F   LPT2:             Yes                   Default Handlers
   6  1C94:00B7   Floppy Disk       Yes                   Default Handlers
   7  0070:06F4   LPT1:             Yes                   System Area
   8  1C94:0052   Real-Time Clock   Yes                   Default Handlers
   9  F000:EECA   Redirected IRQ2   Yes                   BIOS
  10  1C94:00CF   (Reserved)                              Default Handlers
  11  1C94:00E7   (Reserved)                              Default Handlers
  12  1C94:00FF   (Reserved)                              Default Handlers
  13  F000:EED3   Math Coprocessor  No                    BIOS
  14  1C94:0117   Fixed Disk        Yes                   Default Handlers
  15  F000:FF53   (Reserved)                              BIOS

                            ┃    OK    ┃

 IRQ Status: Displays current usage of hardware interrupts.
```

MS-DOS recognizes both major types of ports associated with computers: *serial* and *parallel*. Serial ports transfer information 1 bit at a time; parallel ports transfer information 1 byte at a time, sending the 8 bits in a byte simultaneously over a set of parallel wires. Some devices, particularly communications devices, are serial only and so must be connected to a serial port. Other devices, such as printers, can be either serial or parallel. You can have up to four serial ports on your system. They are known to MS-DOS by the device names COM1, COM2, COM3, and COM4. Parallel ports, of which you can have up to three, are known as LPT1, LPT2, and LPT3.

NOTE: Just to confuse matters, MS-DOS also recognizes a serial device named AUX (for auxiliary) and a parallel device named PRN (for printer). AUX usually defaults to COM1, and PRN defaults to LPT1, so on most computers, you can consider AUX equivalent to COM1 and PRN (which makes a brief appearance the first time you type a Print command) equivalent to LPT1.

By the way, if you look at the preceding illustration, you see that four COM devices share two IRQ lines: COM1 and COM3 use number 4, and COM2 and COM4 use number 3. Although this sharing doesn't always cause problems, certain devices—mice and internal modems, for example—do occasionally conflict if they share the same IRQ and request attention at the same time. If this occurs on your system, you can try to correct the problem by switching one device to a different COM port (so that, for example, the mouse is on COM1 and the modem is on COM2 instead of COM3) or by changing settings on the device so that it uses a different interrupt. (The manual should offer help on this.)

The clock and the bit bucket

In addition to CON, COM, and LPT, MS-DOS recognizes two additional device names: CLOCK$, which refers to the system clock, and NUL, a funny device that goes nowhere.

The CLOCK$ device is the means by which programs and MS-DOS get and set the date and time, which is kept internally as a set of three 16-bit values representing the number of milliseconds that have passed since the "beginning" of time—for MS-DOS, that's January 1, 1980. You never directly manipulate CLOCK$ itself, but whenever you use the Date or the Time command, MS-DOS uses CLOCK$ to find or reset the time for you.

The NUL device, often known as a *bit bucket*, is an odd duck that accepts whatever output you care to send it and makes that output disappear—become nothing, or null. On the surface, NUL would seem to have little use for anything, but its single characteristic can become a strength when you create batch files: To avoid cluttering the screen with command output, you can use the MS-DOS redirection symbol > to send that output to NUL. The command in the batch file will still be carried out, but the screen will remain clear. The use of NUL in batch files is shown in Chapter 19. If you want to experiment with it now, however, three simple commands will do. First create a file named DIR.TXT containing a listing of your DOS directory:

```
C:\>dir c:\dos > dir.txt
```

Now display the file with the Type command:

```
C:\>type dir.txt
```

A long listing will scroll by. Finally, send the output of the Type command to NUL:

```
C:\>type dir.txt > nul
```

MS-DOS pauses for a moment and redisplays the system prompt. Although nothing seems to have happened, MS-DOS carried out the Type command but instead of sending the output to the screen, it sent the output to NUL, where the listing literally disappeared.

Memory

When the IBM PC was released, computer memory was a simple concept. The computer had two kinds of memory: *RAM*, or *random access memory*, and *ROM*, or *read-only memory*. RAM was the memory MS-DOS used for itself, for application programs, and for data. ROM was the memory you didn't have to bother about because it was built into the computer and contained only startup information and some basic instructions that had nothing to do—from a user's point of view—with putting MS-DOS applications to work. Although MS-DOS itself is built into ROM on some machines (laptops), ROM as a type of memory continues to be of little importance to you as a user of MS-DOS. RAM, on the other hand, has given rise to some significant developments having to do with the 640 K of memory MS-DOS applications use.

Addressing memory

When MS-DOS moves information in and out of RAM, it doesn't hurl instructions and data just anywhere. To access the exact information you need processed, at the time it is needed, MS-DOS and the microprocessor together use RAM as if it consisted of an exceedingly large number of pigeonholes, all neatly organized and each able to be referenced, like the boxes in a post office, by a unique numeric address. To access a particular memory location, the microprocessor sends the address over a special bus called the *address bus*. None of this matters unless you are a programmer, but the way in which the microprocessor addresses memory has a great deal to do with the 640-K limit on memory that MS-DOS applications can use directly.

The original IBM PC, remember, was based on the 8088 microprocessor. When accessing memory, the 8088 sent signals over a 20-bit address bus. That meant the microprocessor and, therefore, its operating system, could address however many memory locations as could be described by a unique combination of 20 bits. Twenty bits works out to 1,048,576, or 1 MB, worth of unique addresses and, hence, a maximum of 1 MB of usable memory.

In theory, then, MS-DOS should be able to use a full megabyte of RAM. In practice, however, it cannot because RAM is needed not only by programs but also by hardware, such as the video adapter, which must store an image in memory before sending it to the screen. To serve these needs, the PC's designers set aside the first 640 K as conventional memory for the use of MS-DOS and application software and dedicated the remaining 384 K as reserved, or upper, memory for hardware-related uses.

Conventional memory and the upper memory area

Conventional memory, available in all MS-DOS computers, is the portion people generally mean when they refer to RAM. Also known as *low memory*, this part of memory holds some or all of MS-DOS, as well as application programs, device drivers, and data. *Reserved memory*, although it is set aside for specific uses, commonly contains unoccupied gaps after startup. If you have an 80386-based computer or better, MS-DOS versions 5 and 6—especially version 6 with its auto-mated MemMaker utility—can manage these unoccupied areas as *upper memory blocks*, or *UMBs*, and fill them with appropriately sized device drivers, such as ANSI.SYS and RAMDRIVE.SYS, or memory-resident programs, such as Doskey. Making use of available UMBs in this way can help you increase the amount of con-ventional memory available for use by applications such as word processors and spreadsheets, most of which need as much memory as you can provide.

Beyond 1 MB

In 1981, 640 K of RAM seemed sufficient for the foreseeable future. But then came the revolution. Microprocessors became more powerful, applications grew larger, and people demanded both faster processing and more features. RAM, once thought to be vast at 640 K, began to seem to shrink the way parents do as their children grow. But even though more memory could be added to computer systems, the 640-K sticking point remained. Having extra memory that MS-DOS could not find and use was just like having no extra memory at all.

In the search for ways to move past the 640-K limit without, at the same time, making existing software obsolete, two divergent paths developed. One led to more powerful operating systems, such as Microsoft Windows, that could reach well beyond the 640-K limit yet retain MS-DOS compatibility by creating, in memory, virtual MS-DOS machines to run existing MS-DOS applications. The other path, the one that more directly affects your use of MS-DOS, led to the es-tablishment of two new forms of memory, *expanded* and *extended*. Figure 2-8 on the following page shows these two types of memory in relation to the 1 MB MS-DOS normally uses.

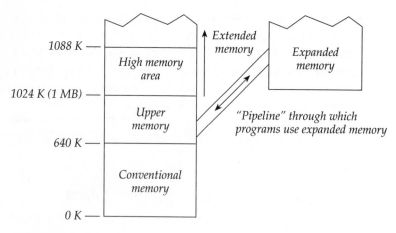

FIGURE 2-8.
MS-DOS manages a variety of memory types.

Expanded memory, or EMS, forms what you can consider a pool of additional memory outside of, and separate from, the 1 MB that MS-DOS can normally use. Expanded memory follows a set of guidelines called the *LIM EMS* (*Lotus-Intel-Microsoft Expanded Memory Specification*). Completely separate from a computer's normal system RAM, expanded memory is made available to MS-DOS by a controlling program known as an *expanded memory manager*, or *EMM*.

The EMM essentially tricks MS-DOS into using memory outside its normal range by setting aside a block of memory somewhere in the 384 K of reserved memory, where MS-DOS can use it. To make portions of expanded memory available, the EMM swaps it, in pieces known as *pages*, into and out of this reserved block. Basically, because MS-DOS can't come to the mountain of expanded memory, the mountain comes to MS-DOS.

Extended memory, in contrast, is growing in acceptance and is much simpler than expanded memory to envision. Extended memory conforms to a standard called the *Extended Memory Specification*, or *XMS*, and simply starts at the 1 MB limit where conventional memory leaves off and keeps going up from there. Adding extended memory to a computer system is essentially like building a second story onto a house.

One portion of extended memory is particularly important to you as a user of MS-DOS. This portion, the first 64 K of extended memory, is called the *High Memory Area*, or *HMA*, and it is the part of memory into which MS-DOS loads part of itself when you add the DOS=HIGH command to CONFIG.SYS.

Although most MS-DOS applications don't make direct use of extended memory, you can use this type of additional memory with MS-DOS to increase the speed of your system with the SMARTDRV.SYS and RAMDRIVE.SYS device drivers. SMARTDRV.SYS creates a *disk cache* in memory, and RAMDRIVE.SYS creates a *RAM disk*, or *virtual disk*, in memory. A disk cache speeds up the system by reducing the number of times that MS-DOS must perform time-consuming disk reads; a RAM disk simulates a disk drive in memory, where MS-DOS, again, can access information more quickly than it can by accessing a real disk drive.

NOTE: If your computer has 1 MB of RAM, it would seem on the surface that you have 640 K of conventional memory, plus 384 K of reserved memory. Not necessarily. On most systems with an 80286 microprocessor or better, you can discount the 384 K of reserved memory and assume that 1 MB of RAM means that your system actually has 640 K of conventional memory, plus 384 K of extended memory.

MS-DOS commands and memory

Altogether, then, a computer can have up to five different kinds of memory:

- Conventional memory: the memory between 0 K and 640 K.
- Upper memory area: the reserved memory between 640 K and 1 MB.
- High Memory Area, or HMA: the first 64 K of extended memory.
- Extended memory: added system memory that begins at 1 MB.
- Expanded memory: a separate bank of system memory made accessible to MS-DOS by an expanded memory manager.

Because conventional memory is limited to a maximum of 640 K but can be used without bother by any MS-DOS program, versions 5 and 6 of MS-DOS include several commands, and two special device drivers, that can help conserve this valuable resource. Most of these commands require an 80386-based computer, but some will work on an 80286-based computer. Your computer must also have a minimum of 1 MB of memory, not counting 384 K of reserved memory. Luckily, this is a standard amount of RAM on current systems. These memory-related features, described in detail in Chapters 11 and 15, are the following:

MemMaker. A version 6 utility, MemMaker can optimize the use of memory on an 80386 or better system with extended memory. MemMaker works by checking for available upper memory blocks and then determining how that memory can best be used for holding programs and device drivers. If you have version 6, run MemMaker. It takes care of all the details, including any necessary changes to CONFIG.SYS and AUTOEXEC.BAT.

HIMEM.SYS and EMM386.EXE. These are device drivers that give MS-DOS the tools it needs to reach beyond the 640-K boundary. HIMEM.SYS, which can be used on a system with an 80286 or better microprocessor, provides access to extended memory. EMM386.EXE, which requires a system with an 80386 or better microprocessor, enables MS-DOS to use some of a system's extended memory to simulate expanded memory for programs that require it. EMM386.EXE also enables MS-DOS to use portions of reserved memory for holding programs and device drivers that would otherwise be loaded into conventional memory.

DOS=HIGH, UMB. This command works with HIMEM.SYS. The HIGH portion of the command instructs MS-DOS to load itself into the high memory area—the first 64 K of extended memory above 1 MB. The UMB portion provides MS-DOS with access to UMBs.

Devicehigh and Loadhigh. These commands, both of which require HIMEM.SYS, EMM386.EXE, and the UMB switch of the DOS command, enable you to move device drivers and memory-resident programs out of conventional memory and into unoccupied UMBs.

3

*Installing and
Starting MS-DOS*

What You'll Find Here: This chapter is about getting MS-DOS up and running. It begins with a description of the Setup program that installs MS-DOS, and then goes on to describe the sequence of events that occur when you start the computer and MS-DOS moves from disk into memory. At the end, you'll find an introduction to AUTOEXEC.BAT and CONFIG.SYS, the two key system files that help you customize MS-DOS for your system and your way of working.

When you first began using a computer, *boot* was probably one of the first "technical" terms you learned. Although you might have been told to *start* the machine or to *turn it on*, before long you found out that starting the computer meant booting the system. Soon after, you found that a *cold boot* meant starting from the On/Off switch, and that a *warm boot* meant restarting the system with the Ctrl-Alt-Del key combination. And you probably figured out for yourself that the term *boot* was a reference to the folklore that advises self-sufficient individuals to pull themselves up by their own bootstraps.

Before any of this booting up can take place, however, MS-DOS must be installed on the system.

Installing MS-DOS

Many, if not most, new computers arrive in your hands or on your desktop with MS-DOS and possibly other software preinstalled. When this is the case, all you have to do is plug the hardware together, turn on the system, and perhaps run Directory (Dir), Check Disk (Chkdsk), or another show-me program such as the MS-DOS Shell or the Windows File Manager to see what's on the hard disk and where. Installing MS-DOS is not difficult, however. If you find that you want or need to set up a new machine or you want to upgrade from an older version of MS-DOS, installation is little more complex than typing one word, *setup*.

Through version 3.3, installing or upgrading MS-DOS involved copying files from the original MS-DOS disks either to a set of floppies or to your hard disk. Beginning with version 4, MS-DOS began to rely instead on its own installation program. Version 4 installation used the MS-DOS Select command. Select was easy enough to use, but in versions 5 and 6, installation can be almost effortless, thanks to a program named Setup. Setup handles a number of tasks, including the following:

File expansion. Unlike earlier versions of MS-DOS, versions 5 and 6 are shipped on disk in a compressed format. Compression, of course, makes the files small enough to fit on fewer floppy disks, but it also makes the files unusable until they are expanded. You can perform this expansion manually with the Expand command, described in Chapter 7, but during installation Setup can do the job more efficiently.

Hardware and memory checks. Before Setup installs MS-DOS, it checks your hardware to determine the kind of computer and display you have, as well as the number and location of COM and LPT ports and the type and amount of memory. It also checks for available space on your hard disk and halts the installation if there's not enough room for MS-DOS. Because Setup performs all these checks, you can, barring hardware compatibility problems, assume that installation will end with MS-DOS configured, though not optimized, for your system. You don't even have to tinker with AUTOEXEC.BAT or CONFIG.SYS because Setup makes the basic changes for you.

Uninstall option. If you are upgrading to a new version of MS-DOS, Setup automatically creates an Uninstall disk and an OLD_DOS.1 directory that you can use if some important hardware or software proves incompatible and you must return to your prior version of MS-DOS. (To "deinstall" MS-DOS, place the Uninstall disk in drive A, reboot, and follow the instructions.)

Customized setup in version 5. With version 5 of MS-DOS, you can make certain choices, such as the language and country conventions you use and whether or not you want to install the MS-DOS Shell.

Customized setup in version 6. In version 6, Setup lets you choose how to install three utilities: Backup, Undelete, and Microsoft Anti-Virus. This version of MS-DOS even manages to reach out to Microsoft Windows. If Setup detects Windows on your system and you choose to install the Windows versions of the Backup, Undelete, and Anti-Virus features, Setup automatically creates a Microsoft Tools group within the Windows Program Manager. You can then run these utilities directly from Windows, rather than having to return to the MS-DOS prompt.

MS-DOS packages

Through version 4, MS-DOS was distributed and supported by computer manu-facturers, or OEMs (original equipment manufacturers). Microsoft, although it was the developer of MS-DOS, sold the operating system primarily through OEMs who, in turn, sometimes modified MS-DOS to suit their own purposes and always provided after-sales support to their customers. Beginning with version 5, however, distribution of MS-DOS changed to reflect the two basic needs of MS-DOS users. An OEM version of MS-DOS was provided for first-time installa-tions on new computers. A second version, the MS-DOS Upgrade package, was released directly by Microsoft for people who already had MS-DOS on their computers but wanted to upgrade to a newer version. Later, a third package emerged, also distributed by Microsoft, that offered both MS-DOS and Windows 3.1 in the same package. If you want or need to install MS-DOS yourself, be sure to get the correct package for the the kind of installation you need to perform.

- The OEM version, supplied or installed by computer manufacturers, is for systems on which MS-DOS does not reside at all.

- The Upgrade package includes a Setup program that must be able to find an earlier version of MS-DOS on your hard disk. Use this to up-grade from any previous version of MS-DOS, from version 2.11 onward.

- The combined MS-DOS and Windows package gives you the ability to upgrade MS-DOS and install Windows or to install Windows only.

The following sections describe, briefly, the basic procedures for installing MS-DOS. Detailed, step-by-step instructions are unnecessary because all versions of Setup prompt you through the entire process and offer on-screen help whenever you press the F1 key.

New installations

NOTE: *The following section assumes you are installing MS-DOS on a hard disk. To install MS-DOS on floppy disks, refer to the section titled, "Installing MS-DOS on floppy disks" later in this chapter.*

A new MS-DOS installation is simple to carry out, and there is only one precaution to bear in mind: If you have floppy disk drives of different sizes (3.5 inches and 5.25 inches), be sure your original MS-DOS disks are the size that fits into drive A.

You can run Setup with either a new or a previously prepared hard disk. If the disk has not yet been prepared for MS-DOS in any way, Setup displays a message telling you so and automatically calls Fixed Disk (Fdisk) and Format, both described in Chapter 8. Fdisk defines the hard disk as one or more logical units called *partitions,* one of which becomes your *primary DOS partition,* the one from which you start MS-DOS. Format, which must always be used after you partition a disk, creates the root directory and verifies the tracks and sectors needed for MS-DOS to use the disk.

To start installation, do the following:

- If the computer is not running, insert Disk 1 in drive A and start the machine.

- If the computer is running, insert Disk 1 in drive A and press Ctrl-Alt-Del to restart the machine.

When the computer starts or restarts, you see an opening screen announcing that the Setup program is active and ready to install MS-DOS. From this point on, follow the instructions that appear on the screen, making whatever choices are appropriate for the way you intend to use the computer. If you are uncertain about anything, press F1 for help or simply choose the default option that Setup highlights in bright letters.

Upgrades

Before release, MS-DOS is tested on a wide variety of hardware and software setups, but not on every conceivable program or piece of equipment you can put in or on your computer. Solutions to problems found during testing are either incorporated in the operating system or provided in the documentation or in special TXT files shipped with the software (which you can read by using the Type command or the MS-DOS Editor). Compatibility issues that have not been found are, of course, neither documented nor fixed. If you have problems upgrading MS-DOS, Setup should give you some idea of what to do next. If you cannot upgrade at all, refer to your documentation or contact Microsoft or your software dealer for help.

Normally, however, upgrading MS-DOS is as simple as installing it for the first time, and in most instances, Setup will run smoothly, especially if your computer is not equipped with numerous add-on devices or memory-management features. Because your hard disk has been in use, however, you might have some extra work to do.

Setup will not run if you don't have enough room for even a minimal MS-DOS installation. You won't damage any software if the upgrade installation fails for lack of room, but if you know your hard disk is full, consider running Chkdsk before starting the installation. MS-DOS version 5 requires at least 2.8 MB of free storage; version 6, with all its added features and utilities, requires about 5.5 MB if you don't install the Windows-based utilities and a little more than 6 MB if you do. It's less frustrating to make room for MS-DOS ahead of time than it is to start Setup, only to have to back out, clean up the hard disk, and start again.

In addition, if your hard disk has been partitioned by non-MS-DOS software, the Setup program might not be able to work with your hard disk as is. If Setup cannot install MS-DOS on your hard disk, it will tell you so, and at that point you might have to quit Setup and then repartition and reformat the disk—probably with the software originally used to prepare the hard disk. To avoid surprises, especially on a well-used, fine-tuned computer, familiarize yourself with potential stumbling blocks by reading the file named README.TXT, which is shipped with MS-DOS. This file gives information on installing MS-DOS with specific kinds of hardware that Setup might not be able to work with. If you use a network, also read the file named NETWORKS.TXT for information on upgrading your network files. You might also want to read the file named OS2.TXT for information about installing MS-DOS on an OS/2 system.

NOTE: README.TXT, NETWORKS.TXT, and OS2.TXT are on Disk 1. To display any of these files, use the Type and More commands: type [filename] ¦ more. *To print the files, use either* copy [filename] prn *or* print [filename]. *(Replace [filename] in each case with the name of the file you want to display or print.)*

Finally, before starting the installation, open your AUTOEXEC.BAT file and disable any existing commands that start disk-caching (other than SMARTDRV) and any delete-protection or anti-virus programs. You can edit AUTOEXEC.BAT with the MS-DOS Editor or with any word processor that saves unformatted text files. To use the MS-DOS Editor, type the following (specifying the root directory ensures that the command opens the file from any current directory on drive C):

```
C:\>edit c:\autoexec.bat
```

To disable a command without deleting it, precede the command with the abbreviation *rem* plus a space, like this:

```
rem c:\utils\bug-off
rem c:\cache-it
```

If you're using the MS-DOS Editor, save the file and quit: Press Alt, F, and X for the Exit command, and press Enter when the Editor displays a *Loaded file is not saved* message.

Restart the computer so that the modified AUTOEXEC.BAT file is carried out, and then run Setup:

1. Place Disk 1 in floppy drive A or B.

2. Make the floppy drive the current drive.

3. Type *setup*.

As for a new installation, follow the instructions that appear on screen. If you need help, press F1 or accept the default.

NOTE: When upgrading an earlier version of MS-DOS, Setup creates a "backup directory" of your earlier version and names it OLD_DOS.1 (or 2 or 3, depending on how many times you run Setup). When you're satisfied that the upgrade is working correctly, you can reclaim the disk space occupied by OLD_DOS with the Delete Old DOS (Deloldos) command. Simply type deloldos *at the system prompt, and MS-DOS will take care of the rest.*

Installing MS-DOS on floppy disks

Although running MS-DOS from floppies seems archaic, you might want to keep a backup in case your hard disk fails. (In version 5, certain upgrade situations also require you to create a set of floppies to install MS-DOS without repartitioning the hard disk.)

You can install either version 5 or version 6 of MS-DOS on floppy disk. Although the process is similar in both versions, the results differ:

■ In version 5, you produce a set of four 720-K disks or seven 360-K disks that, together, represent a complete MS-DOS installation.

■ In version 6, you produce a single floppy disk that provides you with an alternative startup disk containing a minimal, rather than complete, MS-DOS installation.

To create a startup disk with version 6 of MS-DOS, begin with a blank floppy disk that matches your drive A. (Drive B won't do.) Insert the disk and, if possible, place your MS-DOS Setup Disk 1 in drive B to eliminate disk swapping and speed up the process. At the system prompt, type the following (assuming your MS-DOS Setup Disk is in drive A):

```
C:\>a:setup /f
```

Use *b:* instead of *a:* if the the MS-DOS disk is in drive B. From here on, follow the instructions on screen.

To install version 5 of MS-DOS on floppy disks, start with the following:

- Seven 5.25-inch, 360-K disks labeled Startup, Support, Shell, Help, Basic/ Edit, Utility, and Supplemental

or

- Four 3.5-inch, 720-K disks labeled Startup/Support, Shell/Help, Basic/ Edit/Utility, and Supplemental

For the installation, you take either of two approaches, depending on the original disks you have:

- If you have the OEM package, insert Disk 1 in drive A and press Ctrl-Alt-Del to restart the computer. When Setup appears and displays a list of default settings, find the entry labeled *Install To:* and use the direction keys and the Enter key to change the default from *Hard disk* to *Floppy disks.* Follow the remaining Setup instructions as they appear.

- If you have the Upgrade package, insert Disk 1 in drive A or B and type *a:setup /f* or *b:setup /f* as appropriate and press Enter. Follow the remaining Setup instructions.

MS-DOS/Windows installation

Upgrading MS-DOS from the combined MS-DOS/Windows package is the same as upgrading MS-DOS and then moving on to install Windows. Before starting, however, read at least the files named README.1ST, README.TXT, and SETUP.TXT for warnings and for special information about installing MS-DOS and Windows with particular types of hardware and software. Beyond this, upgrade MS-DOS as described earlier. For Windows installation, refer to your documentation.

Culling your MS-DOS directory

With a full MS-DOS installation, you're likely to find at some point that your MS-DOS directory contains a lot of command files that you use seldom, if at all. There's no law stating that all those files must remain on your hard disk simply because Setup put them there. You're free to delete any that you know you don't want or won't use. Although you're the best judge of what to remove, the following list can offer some guidelines:

- MS-DOS files from earlier versions. Among these are such notables as EDLIN.EXE (the Edlin line editor), GWBASIC.EXE (the old Basic shipped with MS-DOS), XMAEM.SYS and XMA2EMS.SYS (two version 4 expanded-memory device drivers), and LINK.EXE and EXE2BIN.EXE (both programmer's tools).

- MS-DOS files that don't apply to your system. Among these are the files related to memory and memory management that require an 80386 or higher microprocessor, or those that need (or work best with) extended or expanded memory. Some examples are EMM386.EXE and SMART-DRV.SYS, and possibly even such useful files as HIMEM.SYS, MEM-MAKER.EXE, CHKSTATE.SYS, and SIZER.EXE, if your system has only 640 K of memory. If you have version 6 and your computer is not a laptop, POWER.EXE is also expendable.

- MS-DOS files you simply don't need. This is where you'll probably find the largest number of disposable files. If you have version 6, for example, and never transfer files through a null modem cable (as described in later chapters), you can eliminate INTERLNK.EXE and INTERSVR.EXE. Other candidates, in versions 5, 6, and some earlier versions, include RAMDRIVE.SYS if you never use a RAM disk; GRAPHICS.COM and GRAPHICS.PRO if you never print screen contents; files with the extension HLP if you're a whiz with MS-DOS and never need on-screen help; and the numerous files related to code-page switching and international language support (NLSFUNC.EXE, KEYB.COM, DISPLAY.SYS, KEYBOARD.SYS, GRAFTABL.COM, 4201.CPI, 4208.CPI, 5202.CPI, LCD.CPI, EGA.CPI, and PRINTER.SYS) if you never use any language or character set other than the one native to your computer.

Do not delete any of the system files—IO.SYS, MSDOS.SYS, and COMMAND.COM and possibly DBLSPACE files—in your root directory. MS-DOS needs these at startup, so if you delete them, your only means of starting MS-DOS will be from a floppy disk (previously prepared) to which you've copied these files either with the System (Sys) command or with the /S switch of the Format command.

If you develop hives at the thought of programming, you might want to remove the files related to the QBasic programming language. You can delete any sample programs you find (those with the extension BAS) and the QBasic help file (QBASIC.HLP), but unless you're certain that you'll never need the MS-DOS Editor, do not delete QBASIC.EXE. The MS-DOS Editor cannot run without access to QBASIC.EXE. Also, in version 6, Help needs QBASIC.EXE to display help files.

Adding or replacing MS-DOS files

Times change and so do people. After installing and using MS-DOS for awhile, you might find options that you considered expendable at installation have become desirable or even necessary. The same is true of command files you delete from your MS-DOS directory. Fortunately, "once gone" does not mean "forever lost." You don't have to reinstall MS-DOS to get the missing files, nor do you have to run Setup. You can use your original MS-DOS disks and the Expand command mentioned earlier.

Described in detail in Chapter 7, the Expand command lets you uncompress individual MS-DOS files. The quickest and least memory-intensive (on your part) method is simply to type *expand*. When you do, MS-DOS prompts for the name of the compressed file:

```
Type the location and name of the
compressed file you want to expand.
(Example: A:\EGA.SY_)


Compressed file:
```

Notice that the example shows an extension ending in an underscore (_). If you list a directory for any of your original MS-DOS disks, you see that all compressed files have such an extension.

Type the name of the compressed file as it appears in the directory for the MS-DOS disk. When you press Enter, MS-DOS prompts for the destination and name of the uncompressed file:

```
Type the location and/or name you
want to give the expanded file.
(Example: C:\DOS\EGA.SYS)


Expanded file:
```

MS-DOS doesn't recognize extensions ending in an underscore when it carries out commands, so the expanded version you place in your MS-DOS directory must have a "normal" extension—COM, EXE, SYS, and so on, as shown. Remember to specify your MS-DOS directory as the destination. Press Enter again, and in a few seconds Expand plumps up the file and places it where you specified.

Although, as you can see in Chapter 7, Expand allows you to specify multiple compressed files in a single command, you'll probably find that expanding files as shown above is easier and just as efficient. If you try to expand several compressed files, you can specify only a disk or directory—no filename—as the destination. Because of this, the expanded files will have the same extension (XX_) that they do in compressed form, and to make the files usable you'll have to use the Rename command to change all extensions.

Booting the system

After you install MS-DOS, you are, as the saying goes, ready to rock and roll. In all versions of MS-DOS, you can perform either a cold boot by turning on the power or a warm boot by pressing Ctrl-Alt-Del.

Startup

When you flip or press the On switch, a computer doesn't shake and stretch like a sleeping dog and then leap to attention. The bootstrap process begins with a series of hardware checks and culminates in the orderly flow of MS-DOS, device drivers, and program files from disk into memory. In a way, startup involves a kind of fast-forward evolution as the computer progresses, without external help, from inert to fully powered and ready for interactive work. Even if you don't care about technology and how a computer works, the process is intriguing, especially because a computer after startup seems to take on an intelligence of its own.

Hardware checks and bootstraps

Versions of MS-DOS, especially version 6, differ in the exact steps they go through at startup, but the general procedure is always the same. First, before MS-DOS even enters the picture, the computer reads in a startup program permanently stored in ROM. This program provides the instructions needed to literally get the computer going in the process known as initialization. This part of the startup process precedes the real bootstrapping that moves MS-DOS from disk into memory.

At the beginning of the initialization process, the computer goes through a series of hardware and memory checks called the POST (Power-On Self Test). The POST ensures that all hardware parts are present and functioning properly. You see part of this testing—during a cold boot only—when your computer displays the results of its memory checking on screen. When you perform a warm boot, the computer skips these checks. After the POST, a secondary part of the initialization procedure runs a program that checks for the keyboard, disk drives, and other devices attached to the computer and readies them for use. You notice this happening when the keyboard lights flash, the disk drives briefly become active, and the system beeps.

When the hardware checks are complete, you usually notice a momentary stillness, and then the startup program begins searching for an operating system. Specifically, it searches drive A and then drive C for a system-formatted disk that contains a small set of bootstrapping instructions in the first, or *boot*, sector of the disk. The contents of this sector are what distinguish a bootable disk from a nonbootable one, and if the startup program does not find a bootable disk, it tells you so with a *Non-System disk or disk error* message.

Assuming that the startup program finds a boot sector with the information it needs, however, bootstrapping begins in earnest. Control of the computer now passes to the bootstrap instructions, and they in turn begin loading MS-DOS into memory. The loading process itself takes place in stages, as MS-DOS moves into memory a piece at a time. During this loading process, each piece of MS-DOS provides the software bootstraps that its successor needs to bring the system closer to full readiness.

During a typical startup, the first stage occurs when the bootstrap instructions search for, and read into temporary memory locations, the system files that form the core of MS-DOS. One of these files is IO.SYS, which, as mentioned in Chapter 1, consists of two parts—a set of device drivers called the BIOS (Basic Input/Output System) and the initialization module called SYSINIT. The BIOS activates the device drivers—CON, COM, and so on—native to MS-DOS. (This BIOS, by the way, is not the same as a very low-level set of non-MS-DOS, ROM-based input/output routines you might have heard of by the name of ROM-BIOS.)

SYSINIT then takes over much of the job of loading the remainder of MS-DOS. In all versions of MS-DOS, SYSINIT first moves itself to an out-of-the-way location in memory, and then moves the MS-DOS kernel, MSDOS.SYS, from the holding area where it was first loaded to the memory area it will occupy for the remainder of the session. Very little time passes while all this is happening, and you actually see very little evidence of all this bootstrapping. The next stage, however, becomes highly visible to you. At this point, MS-DOS is capable of handling basic system functions, so SYSINIT then turns to and processes CONFIG.SYS, loading it into memory and carrying out each line of the file to set up installable device drivers, buffers, and other features that configure MS-DOS to work with the equipment on your system. If you don't have version 6 of MS-DOS, this processing appears as a series of Device and other messages on your screen. If you have version 6, however, fewer messages appear. If you specify either a *clean boot* or an *interactive boot* as described in the next few sections, SYSINIT either skips CONFIG.SYS or stops at each line, waiting for you to indicate whether you want the command carried out.

Finally, SYSINIT loads COMMAND.COM and fades out of the picture, leaving you with a fully functioning computer. At this point, COMMAND.COM takes over, carries out AUTOEXEC.BAT, and ends the bootstrap process by displaying its familiar prompt:

```
C:\>
```

Your computer is ready to go to work.

NOTE: In versions 5 and 6 of MS-DOS, the basic startup described here is expanded in two ways. If your computer has an 80386 or better microprocessor and 350 K or more of extended memory, you enable use of extended memory with HIMEM.SYS and EMM386.EXE, and you include a DOS=HIGH line in CONFIG.SYS, startup ends with part of MS-DOS ensconced in the high memory area. In addition, if you have version 6 and you have set up DoubleSpace to run on your computer, startup involves loading the system file DBLSPACE.BIN into memory so that you will have access to compressed disks, including your primary hard disk. If your CONFIG.SYS includes a Device command naming the device driver DBLSPACE.SYS, a further step involves moving DBLSPACE.BIN to its final location, either at the bottom of conventional memory or, if enough upper memory is available, to UMBs. For more information about loading MS-DOS into the HMA and loading and using DoubleSpace, refer to Chapters 8, 11, and 14.

Startup alternatives

Beginning with version 6, you can specify either a clean boot or an interactive boot by pressing F5 (clean boot) or F8 (interactive boot) after startup but before MS-DOS begins processing CONFIG.SYS. (The clean boot and the interactive boot are described in the following sections.) MS-DOS displays a message telling you *Starting MS-DOS...* before processing begins. When this message appears, a menu of choices appears if you or someone else has set up a multi-configuration CONFIG.SYS as described in Chapter 16. If you don't have a multi-configuration setup, however, and you want to request either a clean or an interactive boot, you have about 5 seconds to press F5 or F8. Five seconds is plenty of leeway, but if you're busy or you don't want to babysit the machine, you can relax and still catch the system at the right time:

1. Make the "mistake" that both inexperienced and experienced users often do: Start or restart the system with a nonsystem disk, such as a document disk, in drive A. Just before MS-DOS starts processing CONFIG.SYS, it will encounter the "bad" disk, pause, and display the message:

    ```
    Non-System disk or disk error
    Replace and strike any key when ready
    ```

2. Now open drive A, press any key to continue, and press F5 for a clean boot or F8 for an interactive boot.

MS-DOS will proceed directly into the type of boot you requested.

Clean boot

When you press F5 after starting or restarting the computer, you signal for a clean boot—one in which MS-DOS performs a minimal startup, ignoring CONFIG.SYS and AUTOEXEC.BAT and loading only the system files it needs to function. A clean boot is quick, and it even skips the time and date prompts MS-DOS normally displays when it does not process an AUTOEXEC.BAT file. The boot process ends with a message, a display of copyright information, and a standard system prompt, like this:

```
MS-DOS is bypassing your CONFIG.SYS and AUTOEXEC.BAT files.

Microsoft(R) MS-DOS(R) Version 6
        (C)Copyright Microsoft Corp 1981-1993
C:\>
```

Long needed, a clean boot can be especially valuable when you experiment with CONFIG.SYS. Sometimes, changes you make to this file can cause the system to "hang," meaning that MS-DOS cannot finish processing CONFIG.SYS. When this happens, MS-DOS cannot start from your hard disk, and you cannot use the computer. Period. The alternative in previous versions of MS-DOS was to start from a system-formatted floppy—assuming, of course, that you had the foresight to create one before tinkering with CONFIG.SYS. If such a floppy disk did not exist and you could not borrow one, well…you could always reinstall MS-DOS.

Interactive boot

When you press F8 after starting or restarting the system, you signal for an interactive boot—one in which MS-DOS stops at each line in CONFIG.SYS, prompting you for a yes or no response to indicate whether you want the line processed. During an interactive boot, such a prompt looks like this:

```
DOS=HIGH [Y,N]?
```

If you press Y, MS-DOS processes the line as it would during a normal boot and then goes on to prompt for the next line in the file. If you press N, MS-DOS skips the instruction and moves on to the next command. When it reaches the end of CONFIG.SYS, MS-DOS asks,

```
Process AUTOEXEC.BAT [Y,N]?
```

Press Y to carry out all the commands in AUTOEXEC.BAT; press N to skip processing and go directly to the copyright information and system prompt shown earlier for a clean boot. (If you want to make your AUTOEXEC.BAT file interactive as well, version 6 of MS-DOS provides the Choice command, which stops and waits for keyboard input, as described in Chapters 12 and 19.)

As you can see, an interactive boot allows you to make decisions about your computer setup whenever you start. It's a useful tool when you're experimenting with device drivers, and it's an alternative you can choose instead of using the version 6 multi-configuration option that customizes startup by turning CONFIG.SYS into a multiple-choice initialization file.

With an interactive boot, therefore, you can decide not only whether you want to activate a network driver, but you can choose the one you want if you have access to two or more. In other circumstances, you might want to control whether MS-DOS creates a RAM disk or whether it configures extra memory in your system as extended, expanded, or both. Prior to the version 6 interactive boot and multi-configuration options, customizing your system configuration meant creating multiple CONFIG.SYS files. To run the one you wanted, you would either have to start the computer, rename the files, and restart the system or (less confusingly) create alternative floppy disks for startup, each with a different CONFIG.SYS and, probably, AUTOEXEC.BAT.

Customizing your system with CONFIG.SYS and AUTOEXEC.BAT

This chapter includes many references to CONFIG.SYS and AUTOEXEC.BAT. If you haven't installed new devices on your system or tried changing your startup, these two filenames might be familiar, but without much meaning beyond "Don't delete these files." Since version 4, MS-DOS has, after all, either created or modified these files for you during installation. Besides, many new computers are shipped with MS-DOS and possibly other software preinstalled, so CONFIG.SYS and AUTOEXEC.BAT are already created for you. And if you're satisfied with the way things work, you have little reason to change your basic startup routine.

These two files, however, are your means of controlling the way MS-DOS uses your computer, and they can contribute significantly both to your knowledge of MS-DOS and to the efficiency of your system. This section describes CONFIG.SYS and AUTOEXEC.BAT: what they do, how they differ, and why you need them.

Unlike MS-DOS command files, which contain program instructions in a machine-language form that you cannot read, both CONFIG.SYS and AUTOEXEC.BAT are readable text files that contain MS-DOS commands. CONFIG.SYS holds the commands that customize MS-DOS to work with the equipment and software on your particular system. AUTOEXEC.BAT, that most useful of batch files, contains commands that customize MS-DOS to work with you. Whenever you start or restart the computer, MS-DOS is programmed to check for and carry out the commands in both of these files—CONFIG.SYS first, followed by AUTOEXEC.BAT. Both files must be located in the root directory of the disk from which you start MS-DOS. If MS-DOS does not find an AUTOEXEC.BAT file, startup ends with prompts for the correct date and time.

Of the two files, CONFIG.SYS is by far the more hardware oriented because it contains the commands that define your system to MS-DOS. Often, a CONFIG.SYS file contains numerous Device or Devicehigh commands that identify various installable device drivers that enable MS-DOS to use equipment such as mice, sound-producing boards, and additional disk drives. In versions 5 and 6, Device and Devicehigh commands serve the added, and very important, role of enabling MS-DOS not only to use, but to configure, memory beyond the 640 K of conventional RAM. Thus, if you have a computer with 2, 4, or 8 MB of RAM, you use Device or Devicehigh commands in CONFIG.SYS to tell MS-DOS how much memory you have, what kind it is, and how you want it set up for use—for example, as extended memory, as expanded memory, or as a RAM disk (with the RAMDRIVE.SYS device driver). Device and Devicehigh commands differ only in that Device loads device drivers into conventional memory, whereas Devicehigh loads (or attempts to load) them into upper memory blocks.

Beyond this, your CONFIG.SYS file is the place where you specify details such as the highest drive letter you want to allow for on your system, how many files can be open at one time, and how many *buffers* (temporary storage areas) you want available. Some of these commands are fairly arbitrary. The Lastdrive command, for example, lets you specify up to 26 possible drive letters on the system. Settings for other commands, such as Files and Buffers, are often specified in the manuals for application programs and other software, and can even be changed for you by installation software.

AUTOEXEC.BAT, on the other hand, is a user's file. More a time-saver than a necessity, AUTOEXEC.BAT contains all the commands you don't want to type each time you start your computer. Like any batch file, it is a repository of MS-DOS commands, parameters, and switches. AUTOEXEC.BAT differs from other batch files, however, in that it is run automatically at startup. Because it is always carried out, AUTOEXEC.BAT is where the MS-DOS Setup program inserts or modifies a Path command that enables MS-DOS to search a directory tree for executable program files. Here, too, is where Setup, in versions prior to 6, includes a Prompt command that defines the traditional MS-DOS C:\> prompt. (Version 6 sets the prompt automatically.)

You can include any valid MS-DOS command in AUTOEXEC.BAT, including those that load *terminate-and-stay-resident* (TSR) programs such as Doskey and Print. You can make the file as short as a few lines or as long as several screenfuls. You can include nothing but a few simple MS-DOS commands, or you can turn AUTOEXEC.BAT into a customized bag of tricks that let you choose which commands you want MS-DOS to carry out.

Beginning with version 6, the key to customizing AUTOEXEC.BAT (and other batch files) is a new command called Choice. In versions prior to 6, the MS-DOS batch interpreter did not have the ability to request and respond to user input during the processing of a batch file. As a result, you could do little to control the sequence of commands carried out in AUTOEXEC.BAT or any other batch file. The Choice command, however, enables you to get keyboard input from within a batch file in much the same way you see MS-DOS wait for, and act on, keystrokes during processing of CONFIG.SYS in an interactive boot. And that means you can make batch files, including AUTOEXEC.BAT, interactive and responsive to different situations.

With Choice, you can set up AUTOEXEC.BAT so that it pauses when you want it to, waits for a keystroke you've defined, and then carries out the option indicated by the key you press. You can even choose to make your AUTOEXEC.BAT file little more than a set of comments and choices that let you determine which options you want to activate for a given session on your computer. You can choose whether to enable file transfer from your laptop computer, jump directly into your spreadsheet program, start a backup procedure, load a set of

Doskey macros, and even to redefine keys on your keyboard. All you need are AUTOEXEC.BAT, a few keystrokes, and a set of special-purpose batch files.

Both CONFIG.SYS and AUTOEXEC.BAT can vary as much as people and the computers they use. There is no "ideal" form for either file, although there are standard ways of putting them together and, sometimes, mandatory sequences in which commands must appear if they are to be carried out correctly. In CON-FIG.SYS, for example, you cannot load device drivers into upper memory blocks until you have enabled use of that memory. Chapter 12 describes the commands you can use in CONFIG.SYS. Chapter 16 tells you how to create customized startup procedures, including a multiconfiguration CONFIG.SYS file. Chapters 18 and 19 describe batch files and the ways you can control the commands they carry out.

GRAPHICAL MS-DOS

4

The MS-DOS Shell: File Management

What You'll Find Here: This chapter and the next one tour the MS-DOS Shell as it appears in versions 5 and 6 of MS-DOS. A particularly useful aid for scanning disks, files, and directories and for viewing file contents, the Shell is a visual interface you can use with mouse or keyboard. This chapter describes the Shell and the ways you can use it in working with files and directories. Chapter 5 covers utilities, programs, customization, and the Task Swapper, a means of switching among several active programs from within the MS-DOS Shell.

*T*he MS-DOS Shell, like any shell, serves a dual purpose: It makes the services of the operating system available to you, and it shields the kernel of the operating system from the chores of checking for and responding to your commands. From a user's point of view, a shell can be as plain as an oyster or as elegant as a nautilus. For example, although you probably never thought of it as one, COMMAND.COM, the command interpreter that brings you the famous MS-DOS prompt, is a shell. COMMAND.COM provides what is called a command-line interface—one in which you type commands at the cursor. COMMAND.COM is usually faster and more efficient than other MS-DOS shells because it is character (text) based and nongraphical, and because it responds to short, sometimes cryptic mnemonics (such as *dir /ad /s /p*). It is also less easy to use than other shells, most of which, including the MS-DOS Shell, have been developed at least in part to help users compensate for COMMAND.COM's taciturn nature.

About the MS-DOS Shell

The MS-DOS Shell (shortened to the Shell from here on) is a visual interface that replaces the system prompt and the command line with an interactive, menu-based and picture-based tool that you can use either from the keyboard or with a mouse. Designed to make using a computer more intuitive, the Shell changes your approach to working with MS-DOS and, to some extent, with application programs. Instead of a system prompt followed by an uncommunicative, blinking cursor, the Shell displays a full screen of information and visual cues that help you locate and manage files as well as carry out common commands easily and without the need to rack your memory for syntax and switches. In a sense, the Shell is the MS-DOS teleprompter.

Although highly visual and clearly related to the Windows File Manager, the Shell is not as truly graphical as Windows and some other non-MS-DOS shells, nor is it as flexible as most. On the other hand, the Shell is less expensive (as in free), and if you don't need real multitasking capability, it offers a good second best—the Task Swapper, which enables you to activate multiple programs and switch among them with a few keystrokes. Not all releases of MS-DOS include the Shell, however. Some OEM releases omit this MS-DOS feature, often because it is not needed with, and actually cannot work at the same time as, Microsoft Windows.

If you have the Shell, you'll find that you can do more from outside the Shell and can generally work more quickly from the system prompt if you know MS-DOS commands fairly well. But if you or those for whom you set up MS-DOS are not accustomed to the command line, the Shell is far friendlier than the MS-DOS prompt in appearance.

Starting the Shell

During setup, version 5 of MS-DOS lets you choose whether you want to run the Shell automatically at startup. If you do, Setup ends your AUTOEXEC.BAT file with the command (*dosshell*) that starts the Shell. In either version 5 or 6, if the Shell does not appear whenever you boot or reboot, you can start it manually by typing a simple command at the system prompt:

```
C:\>dosshell
```

Adding the Shell to AUTOEXEC.BAT

If you run the Shell and find that you want to start it at the beginning of every session, add the *dosshell* command to your AUTOEXEC.BAT, as follows:

1. Start the MS-DOS Editor and open AUTOEXEC.BAT by typing *edit c:\autoexec.bat*.

2. Press Ctrl-End to move the cursor to the line below the last line in the file.

3. Type *dosshell*.

4. Close and save the file by pressing Alt-F-X and then Enter when the *Loaded file is not saved* message appears. The next time you start the system, the Shell will start, too.

NOTE: If your AUTOEXEC.BAT file ends with the command to start an application or other program, adding dosshell *below this command means that the program will start first and the batch interpreter will not carry out the* dosshell *command until you quit the program. Rather than clutter up AUTOEXEC.BAT, start the Shell manually at the appropriate time or use the version 6 Choice command (described in Chapter 19) to give yourself the option of starting either the program or the Shell. In either case, don't leave AUTOEXEC.BAT hanging around waiting for you like a lone sock on the clothesline.*

The Shell screen

When you start the Shell, it begins by displaying its opening screen, overlaid by a constantly changing box in the middle. This box, labeled *Reading disk information*, tells you the Shell is reading the contents of the current drive—probably your hard disk—into memory. On a relatively slow computer (in the 80286 class or lower) with a relatively full hard disk, this startup can take a while. If you plan to work with files on your hard disk, you'll simply have to wait it out, but if you plan to use the Shell to work with files on a floppy disk, you can save some time by making the floppy drive the active drive (by typing *a:* or *b:*, depending on the drive you want) at the system prompt, before you start the Shell. The Shell will read the floppy disk instead, and that will probably be a much faster process.

When the disk contents are in memory and the display settles down, you see
a divided window like the one in Figure 4-1.

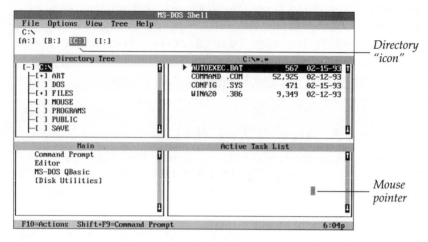

FIGURE 4-1.
The main window of the MS-DOS Shell (text mode).

By default, the Shell starts in nongraphics text mode, as shown. In text mode,
the mouse pointer (if you have a mouse) appears as a bright rectangle, and on-
screen graphics, such as those to the left of directory names in the illustration, are
lines and square brackets. If your video equipment is able to produce graphics,
however, you can use the Display command, described in Chapter 5, to change to
graphics mode you'll see used for Shell illustrations from this point on.

The Shell window

The first time you start the Shell, the main portion of your on-screen real estate is
divided into three smaller windows:

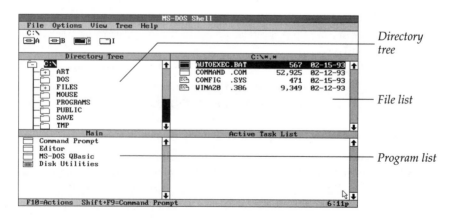

- The Directory Tree graphically outlines the directories and subdirectories on the disk in the current drive.

- The File List displays the names of all files matching the file specification (*.* by default) of the drive and directory shown at the top of the File List window.

- The Program List displays the names of programs and groups of programs, including MS-DOS utilities, that you can run from within the Shell. As described in Chapter 5, you can customize this list by adding or deleting entries to match the way you work.

When you activate the Task Swapper (also described in Chapter 5), a fourth window, titled Active Task List, appears in the lower right quadrant.

Because the Shell is highly interactive and responsive to the mouse as well as the keyboard, its window contains numerous other elements, most of which are more functional than decorative. If you're familiar with a graphical user interface, such as Microsoft Windows—and especially its File Manager—much of the screen makes immediate sense. If your work to date has been primarily with character-based, nongraphical programs and you're unfamiliar with the terminology used in full-screen user interfaces, refer to Figure 4-2 on the next page, which labels other parts of the Shell window.

- Title bar: Identifies the window as belonging to the MS-DOS Shell.

- Menu bar: Displays the menus (lists of commands and other options) you use in working with the Shell.

- Window title: Identifies the smaller "panes" within the main Shell window.

- Selection cursor: Identifies the currently selected item—the one to be affected by your next command. Although the main window can be divided into three or four smaller windows, only one window at a time can contain the selection cursor. In text mode, a dark, right-pointing triangle appears to the left of a filename highlighted by the selection cursor; in graphics mode, both the filename and the small graphic (icon) to the left are highlighted.

- Scroll bar: With the mouse, enables scrolling up and down within the small window to the left of the scroll bar.

- Scroll arrow: Scrolls window contents up or down one line at a time. The scroll arrow responds only to the mouse.

- Scroll box: Indicates, by its position in the scroll bar, your position within the list displayed in a window. You can drag the scroll box (mouse only) to move to the same relative location in the displayed list (beginning, middle, end, and so on).

- Mouse pointer: Self-explanatory; shows the on-screen position of the mouse. The mouse pointer is an arrowhead in graphics mode and a tall, bright rectangle in text mode (compare Figure 4-1 and Figure 4-2).

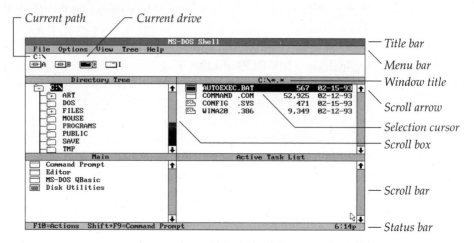

FIGURE 4-2.
The main window of the MS-DOS Shell (graphics mode).

- Status bar: Displays the current time and an on-screen reminder of two commonly used keystrokes: F10, which activates the menu bar, and Shift-F9, which temporarily exits to the MS-DOS prompt. Also displays messages from the Shell to you.

- Current path: Displays the drive and path of the directories and files shown in the Directory Tree and the File List windows.

- Current drive: Displays the current drive.

- Icon: Appearing only in graphics mode, adds visual interest as well as identifies the item to its right. Icons for disk drives appear at the top of the screen. Four other types of icon appear within the Shell windows:

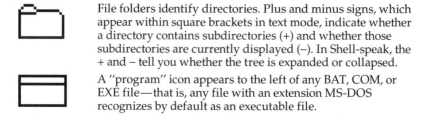

File folders identify directories. Plus and minus signs, which appear within square brackets in text mode, indicate whether a directory contains subdirectories (+) and whether those subdirectories are currently displayed (–). In Shell-speak, the + and – tell you whether the tree is expanded or collapsed.

A "program" icon appears to the left of any BAT, COM, or EXE file—that is, any file with an extension MS-DOS recognizes by default as an executable file.

A "document" icon appears to the left of all other files. Because these "document" icons identify both text and nontext files (such as those with the extensions SYS, DLL, and HLP), they are not a particularly good means of distinguishing true program files from real documents.

 Group icons appear in the lower left window titled Main at startup. Like a folder with a plus sign, a group icon indicates that the item to its right contains other entries.

Using the Shell

The design of the Shell is based on ease of use. Typed commands form the core of your work with MS-DOS at the system prompt; mouse movements and special keystrokes form the core of your work with the Shell.

The mouse

A mouse is simple to use. Push, and the pointer moves toward the top of the screen; pull, and the pointer moves downward. Beyond this, all you need to know are three terms associated with common mouse actions:

- Click, meaning press and release a button quickly. Clicking is usually the means by which you select something, such as a command or a list item.

- Double-click, meaning press and release a button twice in quick succession. Double-clicking is usually a shortcut that both selects and executes an action. For example, if, as described later, you associate a particular extension with a program, double-clicking on a file with that extension starts the program and opens the file.

- Drag, meaning hold down a button while moving the mouse, and then release. Dragging in the Shell is a means of moving files from one disk or directory to another.

The keyboard

Although the Shell is far easier to use with a mouse, you can use the keyboard. In fact, even if you have a mouse you'll probably end up using it for some activities and the keyboard for others. A touch typist, in particular, might find that the benefits of staying in contact with the keyboard outweigh the drawbacks of remembering and carrying out multiple keystrokes.

The Shell includes numerous special keystrokes and key combinations. For reference, the most common keys are listed and defined in Table 4-1 on the following pages.

Additional keys related to specific activities also appear in appropriate sections of this and the next chapter. If you need further information, or if you simply want to browse, consult the Keyboard section of the Shell's online Help facility, which is described in a later section of this chapter.

Navigation keys:

Tab	Moves the selection cursor forward (left to right, top to bottom) within the main Shell window or within a dialog box.
Shift-Tab	Moves the selection cursor in the opposite direction.
Direction keys	Move the selection cursor up or down in a list, one item at a time. Also move the selection cursor left or right within menu names and disk-drive icons.
PgUp, PgDn	Move the selection cursor to the top or bottom of a window, at the same time scrolling up or down one windowful in a long list. In a dialog box, move the cursor to the top or bottom of a group of options.

Control keys:

Enter	Carries out a command or an action.
Esc	Cancels a command or an action; closes a dialog box without carrying out the command.

Function keys:

F1	Requests online Help. To see context-sensitive Help, press F1 after highlighting a menu choice (with the direction keys) or a window area, or while a dialog box requesting additional information is displayed on screen.
F3 or Alt-F4	Quits the Shell and returns to the system prompt.
F5	Causes the Shell to reread the contents of the current drive and redraw the screen. Use this key to update directory and file displays if the screen does not show recent moves, copies, or deletions.
Shift-F5	Redraws the screen but does not update the directory and file lists.
F7	Moves one or more selected files in the File List.
F8	Copies one or more selected files in the File List.
F9	Displays the contents of a selected file; also shifts between ASCII and hexadecimal displays.
Shift-F9	Temporarily exits the Shell and displays the system prompt. Return to the Shell by typing *exit* at the system prompt.

TABLE 4-1.   *(continued)*
Common Shell keystrokes and key combinations.

TABLE 4-1. *continued*

Selection keys:	
Shift-F8	Turns on add mode (indicated by *ADD* in the lower right corner of the status bar) for selecting multiple files.
Shift-Spacebar	When add mode is turned on, selects all files between a previously selected file and the currently highlighted file.
Spacebar	When add mode is turned on, adds the currently high-lighted file to the selection. Use add mode and the Spacebar when you want to select discontinuous files to move, copy, delete, rename, and so on.
Shift-[direction key]	Extends the selection to include multiple files. Add mode can be on or off.
Shift-click	Selects the range of files between the previously selected file and the file the mouse pointer is on. Obviously a mouse-only option.
Ctrl-click	Selects individual files; equivalent to using add mode and the Spacebar. Again, mouse only.

Menus and dialog boxes

Menu choices are the Shell equivalent of typing MS-DOS commands. Dialog boxes are the Shell's means of asking you for command parameters and switches, when appropriate. Together, menus and dialog boxes represent your primary means of getting work done within the Shell.

Although you don't notice at first, the Shell alters the menu bar as you move the selection cursor to different parts of the window. The change is subtle and, the first time you notice, can make you wonder if your eyes need checking: Did you, or did you not, recently see a menu named Tree? Maybe yes, maybe no:

- When the selection cursor is in the File List area in the top half of the window, you see five menus: File, Option, View, Tree, and Help.

- When the selection cursor is in the Program List area in the bottom half of the window, you see only four menus: File, Option, View, and Help. Tree disappears because it is irrelevant in working with programs.

(The Shell also modifies menu choices, but you don't notice the changes until you open the same menu with the selection cursor in different areas of the screen.)

Reading a menu

To open a menu and view the choices it offers, do one of the following:

- Click on the menu name with the mouse.

■ Press either the Alt or the F10 key. When you do, one character in the
menu name is either highlighted (text mode) or underlined (graphics
mode). Press the key representing the highlighted or underlined character. For example, you would press Alt-F (or F10-F) to open the File menu.

When a menu opens, it looks like the one in the following illustration:

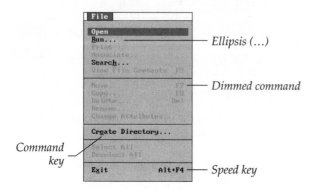

This is the File menu as it appears when the selection cursor is in the File List
area. To see how the menu options are affected by the location of the cursor,

1. Move the selection cursor, if necessary, to the window labeled Directory
   Tree. Open the File menu.

2. Move the selection cursor to the Program List area—for example, to the
   window labeled Main. Open the File menu again.

When you're working in the Program List area, the File menu is much shorter
than the one illustrated above because the Shell modifies the menu to display
commands relevant to working with programs and omits or modifies those related to working with files and directories.

Although a menu is simply a list of choices, the Shell conveys information immediately with the help of the four visual aids labeled in the preceding illustration:

■ An ellipsis tells you that choosing the command will produce a *dialog
box*, in which the Shell will request more information.

■ A dimmed, or grayed out, command is unavailable. The Shell dims and
undims commands depending on what you are doing. Dimmed commands are always those that the Shell determines are inappropriate for
the work you're currently doing.

■ A speed key, when one is displayed to the right of a command, gives you
a keyboard shortcut you can use instead of opening a menu and choosing from it.

■ A command key is the highlighted or underlined character in a menu
item. Pressing the command key chooses the command.

Holding meaningful dialogs

Most MS-DOS commands accept drive letters, paths, filenames, and optional switches, and all MS-DOS commands provide output of some kind, so it comes as no surprise that many commands on the Shell menus produce dialog boxes that the Shell can use as a means of communicating with you. A typical dialog box contains one or more options and, possibly, prompts for information such as a drive, path, or file specification. At the bottom are three or more *command buttons* that you "press" to indicate you have finished with the dialog box. To move from place to place in a dialog box, either click with the mouse or press the Tab key to cycle through the options and command buttons.

Overall, the Shell uses dialog boxes for four purposes. In one instance only— Show Information on the Options menu—a dialog box provides output, like this:

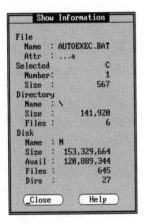

As you can see, the dialog box provides a summary of information related to the currently selected directory and file(s) on the active disk. This is an expanded version of the output of the Chkdsk command.

A second type of dialog box prompts for confirmation before carrying out a potentially destructive command. You can modify the Shell to turn off confirmation, but in at least the situation illustrated below, you're well advised to be conservative:

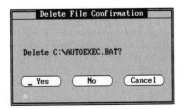

Basically, this is the Shell's equivalent of built-in MS-DOS warnings, such as

```
All files in directory will be deleted!
Are you sure (Y/N)?
```

and switches, such as the Delete command's /P (prompt) switch, which causes MS-DOS to prompt for confirmation before deleting a file.

A third type of dialog box lets you know when a command cannot be carried out, like this:

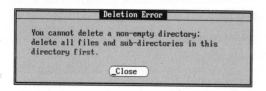

This is obviously the Shell version of a message like this, produced when you try to remove a non-empty directory:

```
Invalid path, not directory,
or directory not empty
```

The fourth, and far and away the most common kind of dialog box, however, is one that requests (or allows you to provide) additional information to make a command more specific. With this kind of dialog box, you provide the equivalents of parameters and switches you would include with comparable MS-DOS commands at the system prompt. One good example of such a dialog box is the one produced by the File Display Options command on the Options menu:

As the labels in this illustration indicate, you provide information in dialog boxes in different ways. Another choice, known as a list box, appears when you choose either the Display command or the Colors command on the Options menu:

- A text box, in which the Shell often displays a default value, such as *.* for a filename, is where you type in variable information, such as a drive, path, or file specification.

- A check box represents an option you can turn on or off at will, either by clicking anywhere on the option line or by tabbing to the option and pressing the Spacebar to turn it on or off. When a check box is turned on, it contains a large X. Options accompanied by check boxes are not either/or propositions, so if a dialog box offers a series of check boxes, you can turn on or off as many as you want.

- Option buttons also represent options you can turn on or off, either by clicking or by using the Tab key and the direction keys. When an option button is turned on, it contains a large, squarish dot in graphics mode, a small dot centered in parentheses in text mode. Option buttons are mutually exclusive. If you choose one from a set, you cannot choose any others.

- A list box shows possible choices, from which you can choose one, either by clicking or by using the direction keys.

Finally, the command buttons at the bottom of every dialog box offer you at least the equivalent of Yes or OK to carry out the command and No or Cancel to close the dialog box without carrying out the command. (You can also cancel by pressing Esc.) Some commands also include a Help button, which you can use to display help related to the command. Because they affect the way the Shell looks on screen, the Display and Colors commands on the Options menu also include a Preview button so that you can see the effect of a change before you make it.

Online Help

The Shell's Help facility provides both general and task-specific information related to using the Shell. Help becomes accessible only after you've started the Shell, but from that point on all you do is press the magic key, F1, or use the Help menu, the rightmost menu on the menu bar:

 or

Like the Help features for MS-DOS commands, the MS-DOS Editor, QBasic, and (in version 6) such utilities as Microsoft Backup, DoubleSpace, and Microsoft Defrag, the Shell's Help facility depends on a special program called a help engine that opens a Help window on screen and, equally important, provides the means by which you can jump froglike in any direction from one topical lily pad to another. You can go forward or backward, or you can follow a trail of cross-references to related topics until you get bored or until you run out of Help, whichever comes first (probably the former).

NOTE: You must have QBASIC.EXE in your path to use the Shell's Help.

The Help menu

Using the Help menu is a good way to get to know the ins and outs of the Shell because you can choose from a number of general topics, including help on using Help (although after two minutes in Help, you're unlikely to get *that* lost). When you use the Help menu, stick to the topics above the horizontal line at the bottom of the menu. The About Shell command, promising as it sounds, merely displays copyright information.

Home base in Help, so to speak, is the Index command on the Help menu. Choosing Index produces this window:

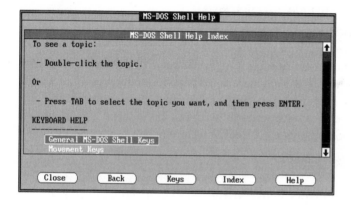

The buttons at the bottom bear quick mention:

- Close closes the Help window and returns you to the Shell proper. Press Esc if you prefer.

- Back takes you back to the previous topic. If there is no previous topic, choosing Back produces a second window that tells you *There is no previous help to go back to.* Press Esc to get rid of the "error" message.

- Keys takes you to keyboard help.

- Index takes you back to the Help index.

- Help gets you help on using Help.

From here on, use the scroll bar or the PgUp and PgDn keys to see more if (as here) the topic covers more than one windowful. References to additional Help topics are displayed in bright characters, so to move to a different topic,

- With the mouse, double-click on any topic reference, such as *General MS-DOS Shell Keys*, in the preceding illustration.

- With the keyboard, press Tab to move the selection cursor to the topic reference you want, and then press Enter.

Context-sensitive help

If you're stuck in a dialog box, don't know what a command does, or are otherwise interested in specific Help information, you don't want to bother searching through Help topics, nor do you have to. When you need quick information relevant to what you're doing,

- Press F1 after highlighting a menu command (use the direction keys) or a list item, or when the selection cursor is in the part of the main Shell window you want help with.

- "Press" the Help button when a dialog box is on display.

In these instances, you go directly to what is called context-sensitive help. The Shell checks what's on the screen and what you've highlighted, and it produces the Help topic related to that particular situation.

If you want to see how this works, try the following example:

1. Place the selection cursor in the Directory Tree window.

2. Press Alt to activate the menu bar, and then press F to open the File menu.

3. Using the direction keys, not the mouse (which would choose a command instead of simply highlighting it), move the dark highlight to Print. Notice that you can request Help on any menu command, not only those that are currently active.

4. Press F1 to see a screenful of information on the Print command.

5. Press Esc to close the Help window.

That's it. Cruise Help as much or as little as you want. You'll find all the information you need for all your Shell activities. Now let's go back to the Shell.

Changing the view

The Shell's default three-window display is one of several available options, all listed on the View menu:

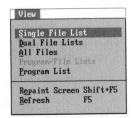

- Single File List divides the screen into two file-related windows, a Directory Tree on the left and a matching File List on the right.

- Dual File Lists is handy when you want to view files on more than one disk or in more than one directory at a time. This option divides the screen into upper and lower halves, each containing drive icons, a Directory Tree, and a File List for one drive or directory. The displays are identical if only one drive or directory is selected.

- All Files displays disk and directory information on the left side of the screen and a File List of all files on the current drive in a large window on the right.

- Program/File Lists is the default Shell window: Directory Tree and File List above, Program List and (if in effect) an Active Task List below.

- Program List divides the screen into a Program List window on the left and, if appropriate, an Active Task List on the right.

When you quit the Shell, the current View status, like other settings, is saved in a file named DOSSHELL.INI in your DOS directory. (The INI extension is short for *initialization*, meaning "what the Shell looks for to find out what it should look like.") DOSSHELL.INI is a text file, so you can easily look at its contents by selecting the filename in the File List and pressing F9 to choose the View File Contents command from the File menu. Shell options are listed at the beginning of the file, under the heading *[savestate]*. The view-related entries are *startup* and *filemanagermode*, which can have the settings listed in Table 4-2.

startup = startprograms	You quit with either Program/File Lists or Program List in effect.
startup = filemanager	You quit with one of the following in effect: Single File List, Dual File Lists, All Files, or Program/File Lists.
filemanagermode = singletree	You quit after choosing Single File List. This has no meaning if DOSSHELL.INI includes *startup = startprograms*.
filemanagermode = twotree	You quit after choosing Dual File Lists. This, too, has no meaning if DOSSHELL.INI includes *startup = startprograms*.
filemanagermode = systemtree	You quit after choosing All Files. Again, this has no meaning if DOSSHELL.INI includes *startup = startprograms*.
filemanagermode = shared	You quit after choosing Program/File Lists.

TABLE 4-2.
Possible startup *and* filemanagermode *settings.*

For more about DOSSHELL.INI, refer to the section titled "More on DOSSHELL.INI" in Chapter 5.

Directories and files

The default Shell window is divided horizontally—roughly across the middle—into two portions, an upper Directory Tree and File List, and a lower Program List. Together, these divisions encompass the two necessary ingredients in any computer's processing diet: data and programs. This chapter covers the data portion; Chapter 5 deals with the programs.

The Directory Tree

Most experienced MS-DOS users can relate stories of known but hopefully unnamed individuals who don't understand directories and thus manage over a relatively short period—weeks or months—to stuff a root directory or a default program directory with masses of data files. While not dangerous (except in the root directory, which cannot hold an unlimited number of files and can, therefore, refuse to accept that one last file), the practice of letting the files fall where they may is not only messy but can make life difficult when it comes to locating specific files or backing up data. Enter subdirectories and, by extension, the directory tree.

As explained in Chapter 9, MS-DOS creates a root directory on every disk you format, and within that root, you can create subdirectories—special-purpose files containing filenames—for different types of files, such as client files, word processing files, spreadsheets, games, utility programs, and so on. Furthermore, within the limits of a 63-character pathname, you can create within any subdirectory as many sub-subdirectories and levels of sub-subdirectories as you need—for example, company A, company B, and company C within a CLIENTS directory. Eventually, as you organize files in more specific directories, the entire structure begins to look like (surprise) the branches of a tree.

Directory-related commands

The command line accepts numerous MS-DOS commands related to manipulating directories. Options in the Shell are less extensive; for example, there are no equivalents of the Xcopy /A, /M, /D: date, /S, and /E switches that selectively copy all or parts of a directory and its subdirectories. The Shell does, however, carry out most common directory-related actions and in some instances gives you flexibility that you cannot match at the system prompt. Within the Shell, for example, you can select files in two different directories for copying, moving, deleting, or renaming. You can also rename a directory—not possible from the command line.

When a directory is selected, a number of commands, primarily on the File menu, are available for use. Not all, however, are related to manipulating directories. Some are simply more "legal" than "illegal" when a directory is selected.

For example, the Display and Colors commands on the Options menu are available, even though the display and screen colors have little or nothing to do with managing directories.

Deleting a directory. To remove a directory, choose Delete from the File menu. Using this command is equivalent to using the MS-DOS Remove Directory (Rmdir) command. You cannot delete a directory that contains files. If you try, the Shell displays the message *You cannot delete a non-empty directory; delete all files and sub-directories in this directory first*. Bear in mind that this message appears if a directory contains files with the hidden or system attributes. If the File List window displays the message *No files match file specifier*, but you cannot remove a selected directory, do the following:

1. Choose File Display Options from the Options menu.

2. Turn on the check box labeled *Display hidden/system files* and press Enter. The previously hidden files will appear.

3. Select the files and choose the Change Attributes command from the File menu.

4. When a dialog box appears, choose the option *Change all selected files at the same time* and press Enter.

5. Select the Hidden attribute and press the Spacebar. Do the same for the System attributes. This removes either or both attributes, so it works even if you don't know which attribute was causing the files to be hidden. Press Enter.

6. Select the files, search your memory to verify that they are not hidden to keep your system from blowing up (as IO.SYS and MSDOS.SYS are in the root directory—which you cannot delete anyway), and then delete them with the Delete command on the File menu.

7. Choose the Delete command again, this time to remove the directory.

NOTE: Because the Shell allows you to select across directories, be careful when you use the Delete command to eliminate files. You could delete some you didn't mean to. For more details, refer to the later section on deleting files.

Renaming a directory. Renaming a directory is simple, as long as you remember that no two directories can have the same name in the same path on the same disk. You cannot, for example, rename C:\BOGUS to C:\FAKE if C:\FAKE already exists.

To rename a directory, select the directory and choose Rename from the File menu; type the new directory name in the dialog box that appears. This command, unfortunately, is not a quick and easy way to alter the structure of a directory tree. You cannot specify a path in an attempt to move a directory from one branch of the tree to another. If the Shell displays a dialog box telling you *Access denied*, check the directory tree; another directory already exists with the name you specified.

Creating a new directory. To create a directory, you use the Create Directory command on the File menu. When you choose this command, you see a simple dialog box that shows the path (*Parent name*) of the new directory and a text box in which you name the directory. Verify that the path is correct before carrying out the command.

You cannot include a path with the new directory name, so bear in mind that the Shell creates the new directory as a *subdirectory* of the current (selected) directory. To ensure that the new directory appears where you want it in your directory tree, select the soon-to-be parent directory before choosing Create Directory.

Showing disk and directory information. The MS-DOS Chkdsk command provides a nice summary of directories, files, and file storage on a disk. The Shell's Show Information command, on the Options menu, provides more, and in a more accessible format. When you choose Show Information, you see information about the currently selected file, directory, and disk. A typical report looks like the following:

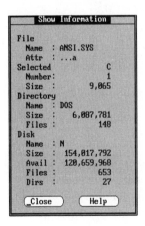

- *File* shows the name of the selected file (the last one highlighted if you select more than one) and its attributes: *r* for read only, *h* for hidden, *s* for system, and *a* for archive, meaning that the file has been changed since it was last saved. A file with none of these attributes shows a series of four dots in the Attr field.

- *Selected* displays the letter of the current drive, the number of files selected, and their combined sizes, in bytes. If directories or files on two or more drives are selected, this section of the report shows the number of files selected on each of two drives but gives the combined sizes of all selected files on all drives.

- *Directory* gives the name of the current directory, its size in bytes, and the number of files it contains. The size of a directory can be very useful when you're wondering whether you can copy an entire directory to a floppy disk. Here you see information only on the most recently selected disk or directory.

- *Disk* gives the volume label (name) of the current or most recently selected disk, its size and available space, and the number of files and directories it contains.

Expanding and collapsing a directory tree

When you work with numerous files, the ability to see directories and their relationships becomes extremely useful, not only as a means of showing yourself how well organized you are but, more practically, as a means of locating and determining where to store or find particular files. Thus, the Directory Tree window gives you a Shell equivalent of the output of the MS-DOS Tree command.

By default, the Shell's directory tree shows the root and the first directory level of the disk in the current drive, like this:

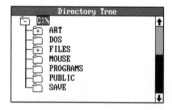

Notice that some folders (square brackets in text mode) to the left of each directory name are blank, whereas others contain either a plus sign or a minus sign. A blank folder (or empty brackets) indicates that the directory to the right does not contain any subdirectories. The plus and minus signs tell you whether another directory level exists immediately below the one shown:

- A plus sign indicates that subdirectories do exist but are not currently displayed.

- A minus sign indicates that subdirectories exist and that those in the level immediately below are displayed.

Directories in succeeding levels have their own icons, each of which can also contain a plus or a minus sign.

Obviously, if the directory tree shows that more levels exist, you want to be able to see them. Equally obviously, there will be times when you will want to see the tree structure only to a certain level, or when you will want to open one particularly twiggy branch of the tree. To open (expand) or collapse (close) all or part of the directory tree, you can use the mouse or the keyboard. You can also use the Tree menu, but the menu really gives you only menu equivalents of the keystrokes listed below:

- With the mouse, click on the icon to the left of the directory. This works both to expand and collapse a (previously expanded) branch.

- With the keyboard, move the selection cursor to the appropriate directory and use one of the following keys:

  □ Plus (+) to expand the branch one level.

  □ Minus (–) to collapse the branch one level.

  □ Asterisk (*) to expand the branch completely to show all levels.

  □ Ctrl-Asterisk (Ctrl-*) to expand the entire directory tree. (You can do this with any directory selected.)

If you practice selecting, expanding, and collapsing directories in the directory tree, you'll notice that the list of files in the File List window changes to match the directory you are working with.

The File List

More useful in many ways than the Directory Tree or the Program List, the File List not only shows the names, sizes, and dates of creation of the files in the currently selected directory, it also provides an easy means of copying, deleting, and—especially—moving files from one disk or directory to another. Most file-related operations are listed on the File menu. This menu is, however, something of a grab bag of commands, two of which—Open and Run—apply as much to programs as they do to files, and one of which, Exit, quits the Shell. Additional commands related to managing and viewing files are on the Options menu and, to some extent, on the View menu.

Selecting files

Within the Shell, you can select one file or many, from one or more disks or directories. In fact, the Shell not only can save time, it can also eliminate scowls if you never use it for much other than selecting files in multiple directories and for moving files from one disk or directory to another.

Selecting a single file is, as already described, a simple matter of pointing and clicking with the mouse or tabbing to the File List and using the direction keys to highlight the file you want. Selecting multiple files is no more difficult. With the mouse, you can do the following:

- Click on the first file you want.

- To select a group of sequential files, click on the first file you want, point to the last file you want to select, hold down the Shift key, and click.

■ To select a discontinuous group of files (files from here and there in the list), hold down the Ctrl key as you point to each file and click.

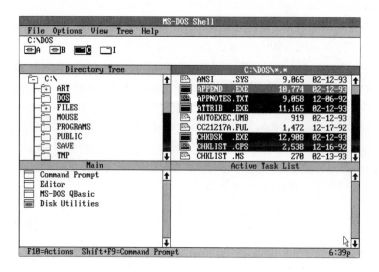

■ To deselect a group of files, click on any file.

With the keyboard, press Shift-F8 to turn Add mode on, and then

■ Press Shift plus a direction key to add files above or below the current file to the selection.

■ Move the highlight with the direction keys and press Shift-Spacebar to select all files between the previous selection and the currently highlighted file.

■ Move the highlight with the direction keys and press the Spacebar to add discontinuous files to the selection.

Press Shift-F8 again when you're ready to turn off Add mode.

You can also choose the Select All and Deselect All commands on the File menu to extend and collapse a selection. Alternatively, press Ctrl-/ (forward slash) to select all files in the current directory, and press Ctrl-\ (backslash) to deselect.

To select files on more than one disk or in more than one directory, do the following:

1. Choose Select Across Directories from the Options menu to enable cross-directory selections. This option is turned on when a small dot appears to the left of the command.

2. Choose Dual File Lists from the View menu to display two separate directory trees and file lists. (You can select from more than two disks or directories, but you can view only two at any one time.)

3. Select files with either the mouse or the keyboard as described earlier.

NOTE: It's easy to forget that you've enabled selection across directories, so be sure to check the list of files to be affected when you use a command such as Copy, Move, or Delete. If the "wrong" files are included, press Esc to cancel the command and turn off Select Across Directories before trying the command again.

After you've selected files, you want to affect them in some way. The following summaries describe (in the order they appear on menus) the remaining file-related commands and how to use them.

Printing one or more files. To print files, you simply select the one(s) you want and choose Print from the File menu. Be sure, however, that the file or files don't contain program-specific formatting codes such as those used by most application programs. The results will not be pleasing. Note that printing from the Shell, like printing from the MS-DOS command line, produces very plain text and can produce either unexpected line breaks or lines that run off the right edge of the page.

Associating file extensions with programs. The Associate command on the File menu enables you to create a link between a filename extension and a program that you run from the Shell. When you associate an extension with a program, selecting a file with that extension both starts the program and opens the file you selected. To associate an extension with a program

1. Select a file (in any directory) with the extension you want to associate with the program, and choose the Associate command.

2. When the Associate File dialog box appears, type the full pathname of the program—for example, *c:\dosword\word.exe*.

To run the program with a selected file, either double-click on the name of the file you want to work with, or select the file with the mouse or the keyboard and choose the Open command from the File menu.

Finding one or more files. No matter how well organized you are, there eventually comes a day and time—usually rushed—when you either can't remember the exact name or spelling of a file you need, or you simply don't know where you saved it. On a hard disk with many directories, trying to find such a needle can make you want to disassemble the haystack.

The Search command on the File menu, like the Directory (Dir) command with the /S switch, finds files that match a file specification you type. The dialog box produced by this command also includes a check box (turned on by default) that tells the Shell to search the entire disk, so a single command can winnow through all the files on a hard disk, from the root to the smallest subdirectory. This command does not accept pathnames, so if you know which directory you want to search, select the directory before choosing the command. Otherwise, put an X in the Search Entire Disk check box to look in all directories. If you use wildcards in the file specification, the effect of the command is to tell the Shell to look everywhere for all files that match.

Viewing files. The View File Contents command on the File menu enables you to look at the contents of a file in either ASCII or hexadecimal format. To view a file, select it and take the easy way: press F9. To switch between ASCII and hexadecimal, press F9 while you're in the View File window. Press PgUp or PgDn to scroll through a long file, and press Esc when you're finished and want to return to the Shell window.

Moving files. Sometimes you'll want to move a file from one directory to another. The version 5 and 6 Shells make the move process effortless, especially if you have a mouse:

1. Select one or more files you want to move. You cannot move files selected from different directories in a single operation; do it one disk or directory at a time.

2. Point to any one of the files and do one of the following:

    □ To move the file to a *different directory* on the *same disk*, drag it to the new directory. If the directory you want is not visible in the Directory Tree window, you can scroll to it: Keeping the mouse button down as you do, either point to the up or down scroll arrow in the Directory Tree window or press the PgUp or PgDn key.

    □ To move the file to the *root directory of a different disk*, hold down the Alt key and drag to the drive icon you want. (If you don't hold down Alt, you copy the file, not move it.)

    □ To move the file to a *different directory on a different disk*, display the directory in a Dual File Lists window, hold down the Alt key, and drag to the appropriate directory. (Here, too, be sure to hold down Alt to perform a move, not a copy.)

NOTE: Depending on which settings are turned on with the Confirmation command on the Options menu, you might or might not see a dialog box asking you to confirm a move when you use the mouse. By default, the Shell requests confirmation when you delete or replace files, and when you perform significant mouse operations, such as moving or copying files. The settings are simple check boxes you can turn off or on with ease. Unless the requests for confirmation annoy you, however, you should consider leaving at least the Confirm On Delete setting turned on. Undoing inadvertent deletions is never fun, even when successful.

To move files with the keyboard (a definite option if you don't want to remember which keys to hold down as you drag):

1. Select the files you want to move.

2. Press F7 or choose Move from the File menu. A Move File dialog box will appear, listing the selected files in a From text box and highlighting the current disk and directory in a To box below it. Type the drive and path of the directory you want to move the files to.

Copying files. To copy files with the mouse you can, as described in the previous section, select and drag. In this case, however,

- Hold down Ctrl as you drag if you're copying files to another directory on the same drive.

- Simply drag if you're copying files to another disk or to a directory on a different disk.

To copy files with the keyboard,

1. Select the file or files to copy. If you've enabled Select Across Directories on the Options menu, the files can be in the same or different directories, on the same or different disks.

2. Press F8 (or take the long way around and choose Copy from the File menu).

3. When the Copy File dialog box appears, type the destination drive and path in the To text box. Press Enter.

Whether you use the mouse or the keyboard, the Shell displays a request for confirmation if you've enabled confirm on replace with the Confirmation command on the Options menu and if a file you are copying already exists on the destination disk or directory.

Deleting files. You can delete one or more files with a single command. If Select Across Directories is enabled, the files can be on the same or different disks and directories. Deleting files is simple: Select one or more files and press Del (or choose Delete from the File menu).

- If you're deleting a single file and Confirm On Delete has been enabled with the Confirmation command on the Options menu, a Delete File Confirmation dialog box appears asking you to confirm the deletion. Press Enter to delete, Esc to cancel.

- If you're deleting multiple files, you see a Delete File box listing the selected files.

- If you can't see all the filenames at the same time, you can check on them by selecting the list box and scrolling with the Home, End, and left and right direction keys.

- Press Enter to delete the first file. If Confirm On Delete is enabled, the Shell prompts for confirmation for each file, as described previously.

You can go merrily on your way deleting here and there, trusting to the Undelete command to save you from momentary bad judgment. Most of the time, Undelete will help you out. But even though deleting is quick and painless, bear in mind that Undelete is a corrective measure, not a license to party.

Renaming files. Where files are concerned, the Rename command on the File menu changes all or part of a filename and extension. To rename a file, select it, choose Rename, and type the new name, extension, or both. However, keep the following in mind:

- You can't specify a different directory. As when you use the Rename command at the MS-DOS prompt, the file you rename must remain on the same disk and in the same directory. (No sneaky way to move files.)

- You can't use wildcards. If you do, an error message appears telling you you've supplied an invalid path and giving you two options: Skip this file and continue or go back and try again. Choose whichever is appropriate.

- You can't assign a filename and extension that already exist in the same directory. Again, if you do, you see an error message. This one tells you *Access denied* and offers the same two choices described above.

NOTE: The Rename command also renames directories. For details, refer to the earlier section "Renaming a directory."

You can select one or more files to rename. If you do, the Shell displays the number of files selected and displays the Rename File dialog box for each one.

If you have a group of files to rename and wildcards will make the job faster, use the Rename command from the system prompt instead of from the Shell. It's faster. For example, if you deleted and now want to restore all the MS-DOS HLP files, exit the Shell, use the Expand command (described in Chapter 8) to uncompress those with the extension HL_, and then use the Rename command at the system prompt to change HL_ to HLP.

Changing file attributes. The Change Attributes command on the File menu is the Shell equivalent of the Attrib command at the system prompt. Unlike the Attrib command, however, Change Attributes applies to files only, not to directories. You can use the Change Attributes command both to change and to view file attributes.

Like the rest of MS-DOS, the command recognizes four attributes:

- Hidden, which hides a file from normal view, as in a directory display.

- System, which indicates a hardware-related program such as a device driver or the IO.SYS file used by MS-DOS. This attribute is used by programmers.

- Archive, which shows whether a file has been changed since it was last saved (backed up). This attribute is used by certain MS-DOS commands, such as Msbackup and Xcopy, to determine whether a file should be copied.

- Read only, which marks a file as readable but not changeable.

You can change attributes for a group of files or on a file-by-file basis, depending on the choice you make in the Change Attributes dialog box. At the bottom of this box is a list of the attributes described above. To turn an attribute on or off, either click on it with the mouse or highlight it with a direction key and press the Spacebar to change the setting. You can set multiple attributes for a single file.

Prompting for confirmation. Because deleting and replacing, with the keyboard or with the mouse, are potentially destructive to data, the Confirmation command on the Options menu allows you to determine whether you want the Shell to prompt for confirmation whenever one of the following is about to occur:

- File deletion

- Replacement of an existing file with another file

- Mouse operation that will move, copy, or delete a file

To set or remove any of these options, choose the Confirmation command and either click on the option or highlight the option with the direction keys and press the Spacebar to turn it on or off. All options are turned on by default. You can set or remove all or any combination you choose, but for your own peace of mind, consider leaving them all turned on.

Changing file-display options. The File List in the Shell looks very much like the output of the MS-DOS Dir command, except that the list usually does not include the time of creation or last modification for each file. As an improvement on the Dir command, the Shell by default lists files in alphabetic order. Often, however, listing files by some other criterion is helpful—for example, when you want to see all the TXT or BAT files on a disk grouped together. To alter the display in the File List, you use the File Display Options command on the Options menu.

When you choose the command, the following dialog box appears:

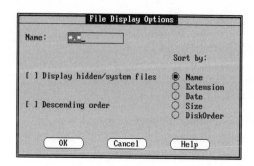

- Fill in the Name text box to limit the file list to a particular set of files—for example, type *.bat* to display batch files only, suppressing the display of all other files in the selected directory.

- Use the check boxes to display hidden and system files and to change to descending (Z to A) sort order in the file list.

- Choose the way in which you want the displayed files sorted: by name, extension, date, size, or the order in which they appear on disk (the order used by the Dir command). You can choose only one option. All but disk order are influenced by your choice of display order in the Descending Order check box.

To return to the default display, specify *.* in the Name box, turn off the check boxes for hidden/system files and descending order, and choose Name as the sort order.

In and out the window

Although the Shell offers many useful commands, it does not always take the place of the much larger and more sophisticated body of commands available from the system prompt. When you want to leave the Shell, you can do so either for good or only temporarily.

To leave the Shell permanently, essentially removing it from the computer's memory, do the following:

1. If you have started the Task Swapper (as described in Chapter 5), switch to and close any open programs. The Shell will not allow you to quit when any Shell-based applications are still running.

2. Press F3 or choose Exit from the File menu.

To leave the Shell temporarily, leaving it in the computer's memory and waiting for your return, do either of the following:

- Press Shift-F9.

- Choose Command Prompt from the Program List, either by double-clicking on the item or by tabbing to it and pressing Enter. If Command Prompt is not displayed, you have moved out of the Main program group. Choose Main from the list, and then choose Command Prompt.

When you leave the Shell temporarily, what actually happens is that the Shell hands control of the computer over to MS-DOS by telling the operating system to start a new version of its primary shell, COMMAND.COM. Essentially, this new version (or instance) of COMMAND.COM runs as the Shell's temporary offspring. But, in a line of succession worthy of royalty, this COMMAND.COM also inherits the ability, in turn, to start other programs, such as external commands and applications. To keep the peace in the system and return to your original Shell, you must go back up the line of succession:

1. If you started an application, quit it. This also applies to MS-DOS "applications" such as the MS-DOS Editor and QBasic but not to typical MS-DOS commands, such as Dir and Chkdsk, which run and neatly end themselves.

2. When the system prompt reappears, type *exit* and press Enter. This is your signal to COMMAND.COM the second that its reign is over, and within a few seconds, it abdicates and returns control to the Shell, which then appears on screen, as you left it.

A little fun

In practice, there's no difference between using Shift-F9 and Command Prompt to exit the Shell temporarily. In truth, there's a small but interesting difference that helps show a little bit about how the Shell actually works. When you run Command Prompt (or any item in the Program List), the Shell, unknown to you, creates a small batch file that contains the command that actually starts the program. This batch file pops into the temporary directory identified by the SET TEMP= line in your AUTOEXEC.BAT file, and you can see it very easily.

First, a little background. A temporary directory is one that MS-DOS and many application programs use as a warehouse for temporary files they create and delete internally as they carry out the tasks you set for them. A word processor, for example, will use a temporary directory for saving records of changes to a document until such time as you save the file on disk.

A temporary directory, if you have one, is always identified by a SET command which, as described in Chapter 12, tells MS-DOS to set a variable named TEMP or TMP (MS-DOS recognizes both) to a particular value—the path to a directory that can be used to store temporary files. This directory can be anything you want, including a RAM disk, but unless you specify otherwise, MS-DOS sets the temporary directory to the DOS directory on your system disk.

To find out the name of your temporary directory, you can type *set* at the system prompt, but this example assumes you're in the Shell anyway, so use the time to get in some practice:

1. In the Directory Tree window, select the root directory of your system disk (C:\ in this example).

2. In the File List window, select your AUTOEXEC.BAT file.

3. Press F9, which is the shortcut key that calls up the View File Contents command on the File menu.

4. Scan your AUTOEXEC.BAT file for a line beginning *SET TEMP=* and note the directory name that follows—for example, *C:\DOS* in the line *SET TEMP=C:\DOS*.

5. Press Esc to quit the View File Contents command.

6. Run Command Prompt from the Program List as described earlier.

Although you haven't seen anything happen, except the appearance of the system prompt, the Shell has created a temporary batch file in your temporary directory and has given it an odd-looking name like 8E97DOSC.BAT. You can't use the Shell to find this file, nor can you use the View File Contents tactic to look at it, because as soon as you return to the Shell, the file will disappear. Instead,

1. Use the Dir command to list all batch files in your temporary directory. Include the path to your temporary directory in the command if necessary. For example, if your temporary directory is C:\DOS, type the command *dir c:\dos*.bat*.

2. If you see more than one batch file, find the one with the latest date and time and with a name ending in DOSC.BAT.

3. Use the Type command to view the file. For example, enter the command *type c:\dos\8931dosc.bat*.

You'll see a simple, one-line batch file:

```
@COMMAND
```

That was a lot of work for a piddling file, but now you've seen how the Shell starts and keeps track of programs you run under its control, and you're a little more the master of your own system. If you return to the Shell and try to view the batch file you just saw, you'll also find that it's disappeared, courtesy of the Shell's handling of your temporary directory.

5

The MS-DOS Shell: Program Management

What You'll Find Here: This chapter moves from the file and directory areas of the Shell window to the Program and Active Task List regions. The Program List is where you list and run MS-DOS utilities, application programs, and even batch files of your own. The Active Task List is where you switch from one open program to another, jumping from task to task without the need to quit one application in order to work with another. In this chapter, you'll find information on running programs and on customizing the Shell window with applications you often use. At the end of this chapter, you'll see how to change the Shell's on-screen display, and you'll take a look at the DOSSHELL.INI file, which stores all the startup information the Shell needs and can help you understand the multiple-configuration option in version 6 of MS-DOS.

*T*he Shell offers numerous, sometimes redundant, ways to manage directories and files. Data, however, forms only half of your creative resources. You also need programs to manipulate the data. Apart from relative ease of use, there are two good reasons for running programs from within the Shell: the Shell's task-swapping capability and its ability to help you organize programs in logical or functional groups.

As you would expect, the Shell offers several ways to run programs. Only one of these ways involves using the Program List area of the window, so this chapter starts off with a summary of methods for starting and stopping programs from within the Shell.

Using programs in the Shell

At the system prompt, you can start a program either by typing its name or by running a batch file that includes the program's startup command. So, for example, to start MYPROG.EXE, you either type *myprog* at the system prompt or include *myprog* in a batch file.

Within the Shell, you can start a program in any of the following ways:

- By typing the program's start command, along with any parameters or switches you need, in the dialog box that appears when you choose the Run command on the File menu. For example, typing *edit myfile.bat* in the Run dialog box starts the MS-DOS Editor and opens a file named MYFILE.BAT.

- By double-clicking on the name of an executable (usually a COM or an EXE) program file, or by highlighting it with the selection cursor and pressing Enter. For example, double-clicking on the name CHKDSK.EXE in the file list for your DOS directory runs the external MS-DOS Check Disk (Chkdsk) command. (When the command program finishes running its course, MS-DOS will prompt you to press a key to return to the Shell.)

- By associating a filename extension with a program, as described in Chapter 4, and then starting the program by selecting an appropriate filename. For example, double-clicking on the name README.TXT in your DOS directory starts the MS-DOS Editor and opens the README.TXT file because the TXT extension is associated with the MS-DOS Editor by default.

- By double-clicking on a program item in the Program List portion of the screen (or by selecting it with the keyboard and pressing Enter). For example, double-clicking on the name Editor in the Program List first produces a dialog box asking for the name of a file (if any) to edit and then starts the MS-DOS Editor.

- By running a second instance of COMMAND.COM and starting the program from the system prompt that appears. You can use this approach if you want to use the Load High (Loadhigh or Lh) command to load a program into free upper memory blocks. If you do this, however, the second instance of COMMAND.COM requires 3 K of memory, and you'll have to remember that your program runs under this alternative command interpreter. When you quit the program, type *exit* to end the second instance of COMMAND.COM and return to the Shell.

When you run a program from the Shell, the Shell hands temporary control of the computer over to the program. During this time, you and the program are in your own little world, and you can pretend the Shell doesn't even exist. When the interlude is over, you return to the Shell in either of two ways:

- If the program runs its course and quits, as is the case with Chkdsk, either the Shell reappears on its own or you see a mostly blank screen with the prompt *Press any key to return to MS-DOS Shell.* You return to the Shell in this manner not only when you run Chkdsk and other external MS-DOS commands such as Format and Memory (Mem) but also when you run a batch file or any other program that does a particular job, retires, and returns control of the machine to MS-DOS.

- If the program does whatever you tell it to, but it doesn't return you to the Shell, you have three options:

  - □ If you're returning to the Shell from the system prompt, type the command interpreter's quit command, *exit.*

  - □ If you're quitting a program, use its quit command. Press a key if the *Press any key* message appears.

  - □ If you want to leave a program temporarily, but you want to have it remain active, press Alt-Tab. If more than one program is active, hold down Alt and press Tab repeatedly until the title *MS-DOS Shell* appears on screen. Release the Alt key. (Note: This option is available only if you enable the Task Swapper before starting the program; for details, refer to the section later in this chapter titled "The Task Swapper.")

The Program List

It's obvious from its name that the Program List is a list of programs you can run from the Shell. At first glance, the Program List is simple and, at least in the default Shell window, mostly vacant.

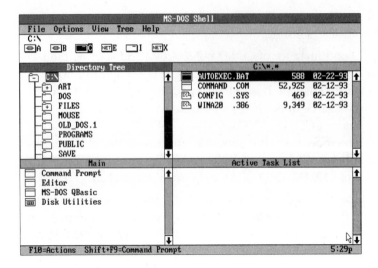

Notice that the window is titled Main, not Program List. If there's a Main, it stands to reason that there are also non-Mains, so where are they? Look at the icon (in graphics mode—in text mode, Disk Utilities is enclosed by brackets) to the left of Disk Utilities. Unlike the other icons in the Main window, Disk Utilities is filled, meaning there's more here than meets the eye. If you double-click on Disk Utilities (or, with the keyboard, highlight the item and press Enter), you'll notice that Main suddenly retreats into an icon of its own, the window title changes to Disk Utilities, and the list in the window changes to display a set of familiar disk-based MS-DOS activities, among them formatting, backup, and disk copying.

Program groups and program items

By example, Disk Utilities provides the key to understanding and, more important, customizing the Shell. The Program List contains two different types of entries called *program groups* and *program items.* A program group, such as Disk Utilities, is a category that includes a collection of programs; a program item, such as Format, is an executable program within a program group. Thus, a program group gives you a means of organizing entries in the Program List; a program item represents a program that actually does some type of work.

Conceptually, program groups and their contents are similar to the directories and subdirectories you create and maintain on a disk. Program groups, however, provide a means of organizing activities rather than files:

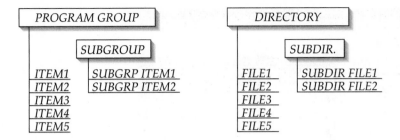

Like branches in the Directory Tree window, a program group can be opened and closed. Opened, a program group displays the items it contains. Closed, a program group looks just like any other entry in the Program List window, except that it has an icon to its left. Because only one program group at a time can be open, opening one program group closes any others in the Program List.

Navigating among program groups and running program items is simple:

- To switch from one program group to another—for example, from Main to Disk Utilities—double-click on the group you want or highlight the group name and press Enter.

- To run a program item in any group, double-click on the item name or—again—highlight the name and press Enter.

Default program groups

Initially, the Program List contains two program groups, Main and Disk Utilities. Main includes the three major "programs" within MS-DOS itself: the Command Prompt, the MS-DOS Editor, and the QBasic interpreter. Disk Utilities in version 5 includes entries that run the Diskcopy, Backup, Restore, Quick Format (Format /q), Format, and Undelete commands.

Disk Utilities in version 6 replaces Backup and Restore with Microsoft Anti-Virus and Microsoft Backup. If you upgrade to version 6, however, you won't see the new utilities unless you expand EGA.INI and rename the file to DOSSHELL.INI. Replacing your old DOSSHELL.INI does eliminate any customizing you've done to the Program List, so you might prefer to expand EGA.INI and edit DOSSHELL.INI as described later in this chapter.

Program-related menus

When you move the selection cursor to a program in the Shell, the commands on the File menu differ substantially from those you see on the same menu when you select a directory or a file.

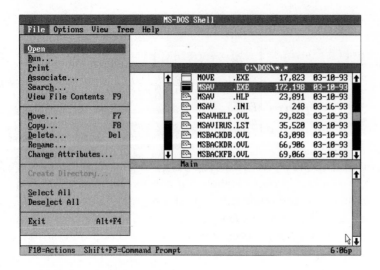

Here all available commands (other than Exit) affect program groups and program items. Commands such as Print, Associate, and View File Contents disappear and are replaced by two program-only commands, Properties and Reorder. The following list briefly describes the function of each command. Later sections of this chapter cover the most important ones in more detail:

- New creates a new program group or program item.

- Open performs one of two functions. If a program group is selected, Open displays the program items within the group. If a program item is selected, Open starts the program.

- Copy duplicates a program item in another group. To use this command, select the program item to copy, open the group to which you want to copy it, and press F2. Note that this command duplicates, rather than moves, a program item. To perform the equivalent of a move, copy the program item and then delete the original.

- Delete eliminates a program item or a program group. As is true of directories, you cannot delete a program group if it contains any program items.

- Properties, described in detail later, is the "big" command. You use it to define a program group or a program item—including help text, defaults, prompts in dialog boxes, memory requirements, and even passwords.

- Reorder changes the order of entries in the Program List. Select the item you want to move, choose the command, highlight the item just above the position you want the item to occupy, and press Enter.

■ Run starts a program. This command produces a dialog box in which
you type the command that starts the program. You can include the
drive and path of a file you want to open, as well as any startup switches
appropriate for the program.

Adding a program group

You can customize the Shell's Program List to match the way you work by adding
your own program groups and, if you wish, groups within groups. The groups
you create, like the ones that appear by default, help you organize program items
by task, sequence, or any other scheme that suits your needs. You might, for example, organize programs related to words, numbers, and fun along the following lines:

Word processing group	Accounting group	Games group
Mighty Write	Ledger Online	Chess Wizards
MS-DOS Editor	Check & CrossCheck	Mutant Goblins
CompuPoet	TaxMANager	Dino Breathers of Worg

Because you can create and delete groups and program items, you don't have
to worry about casting any decisions in concrete. You can redesign the Program
List area whenever you want, to match the needs of the moment.

To create a program group, do the following:

1. Choose the New command from the File menu.

2. When the New Program Object dialog box appears, select Program
Group. Press Enter.

3. A second dialog box, titled Add Group, appears:

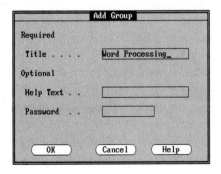

4. A title is mandatory, so type a title for the new group in the Title box
    (*Word Processing,* for example, in the preceding illustration). As you
    create program groups and program items, use a consistent approach to
    capitalization; what you type is what you see in the Program List. Op-
    tionally, you can also include help text and a password. Any help text
    you specify is displayed whenever the group is selected and the user
    presses the F1 key. A password causes the Shell to prompt for the
    password before opening the group. When you finish with the dialog
    box, press Enter. The new program group appears at the bottom of the
    Program List.

Adding a program item

You can add a program item to any existing group, including Main and Disk
Utilities. Unlike most Shell procedures, adding a program item can take you
through a succession of dialog boxes, each of which refines the way the Shell executes the program you specify. Because there is no single path to "walk" as you
move through these dialog boxes, the following sections describe each separately.
By way of example, the illustrations show the addition of a program item that
starts a hypothetical word processor and opens the last file worked on (with the
command-line switch /lastone).

To add a program item, do the following:

1. Open the group.

2. Choose New from the File menu, verify that Program Item (the default)
    is selected, and press Enter.

3. A dialog box titled Add Program appears:

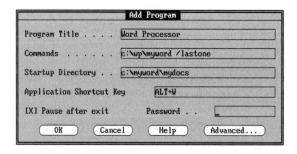

If you're in doubt about any part of this dialog box, move the cursor to
the item in question and press F1 for help information. The following list
briefly identifies how to complete each item:

☐   Type a title for the program item in the Program Title box.

□ Type the command that starts the program in the Commands box. You can include program switches, as shown above, and you can use replaceable parameters (%1, %2, %3, and so on) to prompt the user for variable information, such as drive, path, and file specifications. (For more on this topic, refer to the sections "Replaceable parameters" and "Copy by Date" later in this chapter and to Chapter 18.)

□ Type a drive and path if you want the program to use a particular directory at startup.

□ Type a shortcut key combination if you want to use one to switch to the program while the Task Swapper is activated. A shortcut key combination does not start the program. (A number of Ctrl and Shift key combinations are unavailable for use; to see a list, press F1 when the cursor is in the text box for this entry.)

□ Turn off Pause after exit if you want to return directly to the Shell after quitting the program. If you leave this option turned on, the *Press any key* prompt appears when you quit the program.

□ Type a password if you want the Shell to request a password before it starts the program. A password can be up to 20 characters, including spaces. If you assign a password, be sure it's one you can remember. You can use the Properties command on the File menu to check on all entries in program-item dialog boxes except the password. If you forget the password, you'll have to delete the program item and add it again.

4. Choose OK to add the item, Cancel to quit without adding it, or Advanced (described later) to further refine the program item.

Replaceable parameters

The Shell is one of three parts of MS-DOS that "understand" replaceable parameters. (The others are the batch interpreter and Doskey, as described in Chapter 18.) Essentially, a replaceable parameter is a placeholder that you insert in a command. When MS-DOS—the Shell, the batch interpreter, or Doskey—encounters such a placeholder, it replaces the placeholder with specific information, such as a drive, path, and filename, that you specify at some point before executing the command. Replaceable parameters, like jackets on seats at the movies, let everyone know that something "real" will take their place. Within the Shell, as in batch files, replaceable parameters always take the form of a percent sign followed by a numeral from 1 through 9—that is, %1, %2, %3, and so on through %9.

(Although this is strictly tangential information, you might be interested to note that this %1, %2, %3... form indicates a connection between the Shell and MS-DOS. As noted in Chapter 4, program items are run from small, temporary batch files invisibly created and placed in your temporary directory. Thus, the chain of command goes from the Shell, which creates the batch file, to MS-DOS and its batch interpreter. The batch interpreter, in turn, is designed to recognize a percent sign followed by a single digit as a replaceable parameter, and so it has no difficulty swapping variables in and replaceable parameters out before executing the command that runs a program item from the Shell.)

As mentioned earlier, you include replaceable parameters as part of the command you type in the Commands text box of the Add Program dialog box. If a command includes one or more replaceable parameters, a second dialog box, again titled Add Program, appears when you press the Enter key after defining the program item. Assume you're creating a program item that enables you to view multiple text files, one after the other, with a batch file such as the following:

```
@Echo off
dir %1
echo If these are the files you want to see,
echo press Enter. To quit, press Ctrl-Break.
echo.
pause
copy %1 temp.txt > nul
type temp.txt ¦ more
del temp.txt
```

When you press Enter after creating a program item like the following,

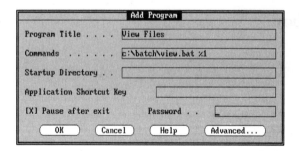

the Shell displays an Add Program dialog box asking you to define the %1 parameter. This is what the box would look like when filled in for the preceding example:

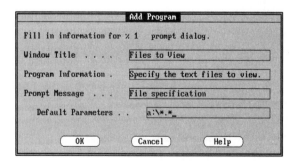

The Shell displays a similar dialog box for each replaceable parameter you include in a program-item command line. In each case, this second dialog box is
where you define what the replaceable parameter stands for:

- Window Title is where you type the title of the dialog-box-to-be.

- Program Information is where you can, if you want, type some explanatory text that will appear at the top of the dialog box. The text can run to
  105 characters, including spaces.

- Prompt Message is where you type a word or two that prompts for the
  variable information that will replace the replaceable parameter.

- Default Parameters is where you can include the parameter the program
  item will default to if the user does not specify any other. Where drive,
  path, and file specifications are involved, leaving the Default Parameters
  box empty causes the program item to default to the current drive and
  directory.

In keeping with the Shell's graphical nature, the information you enter in this
second Add Program dialog box becomes the text of a new, customized dialog
box that appears whenever the program item is run. This new dialog box will, in
turn, prompt the user for the information that the batch interpreter will substitute
for the replaceable parameter.

The Advanced dialog box

The Advanced dialog box offers a number of options you might need in getting a
program to run correctly from the Shell. The dialog box looks like this:

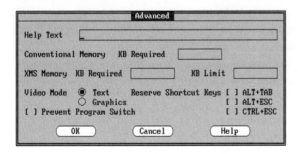

- Help Text lets you enter up to 255 characters, including spaces, of help
  information that the user can access by pressing the F1 (Help) key.
  Although the text box doesn't allow for much formatting, you can insert
  line breaks where you want by entering ^m at appropriate places. To
  insert blank space between lines of text, enter ^m^m. Remember not to
  type spaces before or after ^m unless you want those spaces to appear
  on screen.

- Conventional Memory lets you specify, in kilobytes, the minimum amount of conventional (below 640 K) memory the program needs to run. You'll need to specify this if you get an error message when attempting to run an application while task swapping is in effect. The application's documentation should include minimum memory requirements. The default value is 128 K.

- XMS Memory lets you specify, again in kilobytes, the minimum (KB Required) and maximum (KB Limit) amounts of *extended memory* required by the program. The default minimum is 0 K. The default maximum is 384 K or the amount of XMS memory available, whichever is smaller.

- Video Mode lets you specify whether to run the program in text or in graphics mode. You can probably ignore this option because you need to specify Graphics only if you have a CGA video adapter.

- Reserve Shortcut Keys lets you turn off any or all of the reserved key combinations listed: Alt-Tab, which switches between two active programs; Alt-Esc, which switches to the next active program; and Ctrl-Esc, which switches from an active program back to the Shell.

- Finally, Prevent Program Switch turns off task swapping while you're using the program. Choose this option to disable task swapping while a particular program is in use, essentially giving full, extended control of the machine to the active program.

Program-item properties

The various switches, settings, and replaceable parameters with which you customize the action of a program item are collectively known as its properties. You can view or change the properties of any program item—those you've set with the New command and those that come with the Shell in the Main and Disk Utilities group—whenever you want. The key to doing all this is the Properties command on the File menu. To view the properties of any program item, do the following:

1. Highlight (don't run) the program item.

2. Choose Properties from the File menu.

The Properties command initially displays a dialog box showing the entries that you made in the initial Add Program dialog box: program title, startup command, and so on.

```
┌─────────────────── Program Item Properties ────────────────────┐
│                                                                 │
│  Program Title . . . .  ┌Format─────────────────────────────┐   │
│                         └───────────────────────────────────┘   │
│  Commands  . . . . . .  ┌format %1───────────────────────────┐  │
│                         └───────────────────────────────────┘   │
│  Startup Directory . .  ┌───────────────────────────────────┐   │
│                         └───────────────────────────────────┘   │
│  Application Shortcut Key  ┌────────────────────────────────┐   │
│                           └────────────────────────────────┘    │
│  [X] Pause after exit       Password . .  ┌──────────────┐      │
│                                           └──────────────┘      │
│       ( OK )   ( Cancel )   ( Help )   ( Advanced... )          │
└─────────────────────────────────────────────────────────────────┘
```

To view Advanced settings, if any, choose the Advanced button at the bottom of the dialog box. To view the definitions of replaceable parameters, choose OK. Unlike OK in most other dialog boxes, OK in the Program Item Properties dialog box doesn't execute a command. It simply displays the next dialog box in the series produced by the New (program-item) command.

Examples of adding program items

A preceding example outlined the process of adding a program item titled View Files. The following examples show, in more detail, the addition of three types of program items: The first, Copy by Date, carries out an MS-DOS command; the second, Print Tree, carries out a batch file; the third, Screen Saver, runs a QBasic program that flashes the word *timeout* on the screen until you press a key.

Copy by Date

This sample program item carries out the following MS-DOS Xcopy command:

```
xcopy %1 %2 /d:%3 /s /p
```

Replaceable parameters let the user specify both the source and the destination, as well as limit the copy to files created or modified on or after a specified date. The /s switch allows copying files from both a directory and all its non-empty subdirectories, and the /p switch prompts for confirmation before copying. Viewed with the 20/20 hindsight of the Properties command, the Add Program dialog box looks like this:

```
┌────────────────────────── Add Program ──────────────────────────┐
│                                                                  │
│  Program Title . . . .  ┌Copy by Date────────────────────────┐   │
│                         └────────────────────────────────────┘   │
│  Commands  . . . . . .  ┌xcopy %1 %2 /d:%3 /s /p──────────────┐  │
│                         └────────────────────────────────────┘   │
│  Startup Directory . .  ┌────────────────────────────────────┐   │
│                         └────────────────────────────────────┘   │
│  Application Shortcut Key  ┌─────────────────────────────────┐   │
│                           └─────────────────────────────────┘    │
│  [X] Pause after exit       Password . .  ┌──────────────┐       │
│                                           └──────────────┘       │
│       ( OK )   ( Cancel )   ( Help )   ( Advanced... )           │
└──────────────────────────────────────────────────────────────────┘
```

The following lists show the contents of the series of dialog boxes defining each of the three replaceable parameters. Below the definition of each replaceable parameter is the dialog box that results.

For %1:

Window Title	Files to Copy
Program Information	Specify the files to copy.
Prompt Message	Copy from:
Default Parameters	c:*.*

```
┌─────────────────────█ Add Program █─────────────────────┐
│ Fill in information for % 1   prompt dialog.            │
│                                                         │
│ Window Title  . . . .  │Files to Copy              │    │
│                                                         │
│ Program Information .  │Specify the files to copy. │    │
│                                                         │
│ Prompt Message  . . .  │Copy from:                 │    │
│                                                         │
│   Default Parameters . .  │c:\*.*_                 │    │
│                                                         │
│         ( OK )        ( Cancel )       ( Help )         │
└─────────────────────────────────────────────────────────┘
```

For %2:

Window Title	Destination
Program Information	Specify the file destination.
Prompt Message	Copy to:
Default Parameters	a:

```
┌─────────────────────█ Add Program █─────────────────────┐
│ Fill in information for % 2   prompt dialog.            │
│                                                         │
│ Window Title  . . . .  │Destination                │    │
│                                                         │
│ Program Information .  │Specify the file destination.│  │
│                                                         │
│ Prompt Message  . . .  │Copy to:                   │    │
│                                                         │
│   Default Parameters . .  │a:_                     │    │
│                                                         │
│         ( OK )        ( Cancel )       ( Help )         │
└─────────────────────────────────────────────────────────┘
```

For %3:

Window Title	Date Information
Program Information	Copy files on or after date.
Prompt Message	Date (MM-DD-YY):
Default Parameters	None

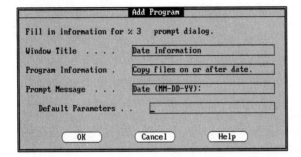

Print Tree

This program item prints a directory tree—a useful means of recording the structure of document directories and files you archive on floppy disks. Although it could be run as a simple Tree command, the program item runs as a batch file instead, to allow the user to choose whether or not to include filenames in the output. The batch file, named TREEPIX.BAT, is assumed to be in a directory listed in the path defined in AUTOEXEC.BAT.

The batch file is as follows (you must have version 6 to run it):

```
@Echo off
REM
REM THIS BATCH FILE PRINTS A DIRECTORY TREE, WITH OR
REM WITHOUT FILENAMES, ON A GRAPHICS PRINTER.
REM ADD THE /A SWITCH TO EACH TREE COMMAND IF USING A
REM NON-GRAPHICS PRINTER.
REM
echo Press Y to include filenames, N for directory
echo tree only. Press Ctrl-Break to cancel.
echo.
choice /c:yn Include filenames
if errorlevel 2 goto nofiles
if errorlevel 1 goto files
:nofiles
tree %1 > prn
goto exit
:files
tree %1 /f > prn
:exit
```

These entries in the Add Program dialog boxes create the program item:

Program title	Print Tree
Commands	treepix %1
For %1:	
Window Title	Drive and Directory
Program Information	Sets the drive and directory for which you'll print a tree.
Prompt Message	Drive and path:
Default Parameters	a:\

Screen Saver

Fascinated as you can become with the Shell, there will be times when you will want to leave it. The mavens of the monitor, however, tell you not to leave the same image on screen for extended periods because you can burn the image into the phosphor lining of the screen. This is true and thoughtful advice, and so the next example provides a crude but effective QBasic program you can run as a screen saver from within the Shell. The basic idea behind a screen saver is to continually change the display so that images don't remain long enough to damage the screen. This program meets the minimum requirements (no fancy graphics or color) by displaying the word *timeout* over and over, at regular intervals, until you press a key.

To create the program, run the MS-DOS QBasic program item. When a dialog box appears asking for the name of a QBasic file, type *savescrn*. Enter these lines (uppercase or lowercase) and save the file:

```
CLS
SCREEN 1
DO WHILE INKEY$ = ""
   LOCATE 12, 17
   PRINT "TIMEOUT"
   SLEEP 1
   CLS
   SLEEP 1
LOOP
SYSTEM
```

Assuming the file is saved in a directory named MYPROGS, the following entries create the program item:

Program title	Screen Saver
Commands	qbasic /run c:\myprogs\savescrn

NOTE: *You can also create a pseudo screen saver with nothing but MS-DOS commands if you're comfortable with batch files. Use two batch files to make the job of turning your "screen saver" off and on really easy. This file protects the screen by changing the prompt to display only a flashing cursor:*

```
@Echo off
prompt $x
cls
```

This one returns the prompt to its normal form:

```
@Echo off
prompt $p$g
cls
```

Don't use this approach for extended periods, though.

The Task Swapper

Whenever you run programs from the Shell, you can either run them one by one, quitting each before starting the next, or activate the Task Swapper and leave each program semidormant in memory so that you can switch from one to another with a few keystrokes. Task swapping, unlike the multitasking that is characteristic of more muscular operating systems such as Windows, does not give programs the ability to continue working when they are off screen. A spreadsheet, therefore, cannot continue to recalculate when you swap it out to work with another program, nor can a word processor paginate or check spelling until you activate it once again. Basically, multitasking is comparable to joining in on a conference call. Task swapping is more like being put on hold. You're there, but as a nonparticipant.

To activate the Task Swapper, do the following:

- Choose Enable Task Swapper from the Options menu.

NOTE: *The Shell Help facility warns you not to run 3270 emulator programs with the Task Swapper; doing so may cause you to be disconnected from the mainframe, with loss of data. This warning also applies to other telecommunications programs.*

Running programs with the Task Swapper

When the Task Swapper is enabled, a new window, titled Active Task List, opens on screen. If you're using the default Shell window, the Active Task List appears to the right of the Program List. Until you start programs, this Active Task List remains blank. To start a program, you can

- Use the Run command on the File menu.
- Double-click on the name of an executable program file or on a filename with an extension associated with a program.

- Run a program item.

Any of these options takes you out of the Shell and into the program. You can also, if you prefer, simply start a program but remain in the Shell. Doing this keeps the program available for later use and is a good, quick means of activating a group of programs you intend to use at some time during your session in the Shell. To start programs without leaving the Shell:

- Press and hold the Shift key while double-clicking on the program name or the name of an associated file.

- Select the program name, either in the File List or in the Program List, or select the name of an associated file and press Shift-Enter.

Switching among active programs

No matter how you start a program, you move among those that are active by doing as follows:

- To go to a program from the Shell, double-click on its name in the Active Task List or select its name and press Enter.

- To go directly to an active program, use the shortcut key combination you assigned when creating the program item in the Add Program dialog box. If there is no such shortcut and you decide you need one, use the Properties command on the File menu to make the change.

- To leave a program and return directly to the Shell, press Ctrl-Esc.

- To choose an active program, hold down Alt and press Tab repeatedly until the name of the program you want appears on screen, and then release the Alt key. To cycle backward, press Shift-Alt-Tab. (This backward movement works only if you start from within a program; if you try from the Shell, you cycle through the on-screen windows.)

- To go from one program to the next, press Alt-Esc; to go to the previous program in the Active Task List, press Shift-Alt-Esc. Note that both these key combinations work only from within a program, not from the Shell.

Quitting after activating programs

Because the Shell is the overseer of the programs you run from the Active Task List, you can temporarily return to the system prompt with the Command Prompt program item or the Shift-F9 key combination, but you cannot quit the Shell completely until you have neatly closed all active programs. When you want to finish up with the Shell, first go to each program in the Active Task List and use whatever quit command it requires. When you quit each program, the Shell closes down the temporary batch file from which the program was started and removes the program name from the Active Task List. When the list is empty, you can use the Exit command on the File menu or (much faster) the F3 key to shut down the Shell.

Display options

And now for the most entertaining portion of the Shell: its display. You can control two related aspects of the Shell's display: its use of text or graphics mode, and (on color screens) the set of colors the Shell uses for various parts of the window.

Text vs. graphics

Most of the illustrations in this chapter and the preceding one have shown the Shell display in 25-line graphics mode. Visually, this mode is the most attractive and readable the Shell offers on computers capable of displaying graphics, but you can choose from other display modes with the Display command on the Options menu. When you choose this command, you see a multiple-choice dialog box like the following:

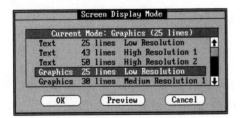

If you want to see what the screen will look like in a certain display mode, select the mode and choose the Preview button. To leave the screen as it was before you began tinkering, choose Cancel.

The choices shown in the preceding illustration represent the display options available on a computer with VGA or better display equipment. If your setup differs, the Shell will alter the list to present only those options that your system can manage.

The first option in the preceding list, 25-line text, is the least demanding display mode and is available on computers with all types of display equipment, from monochrome text-only through super-VGA. Others that are widely available include 43-line text mode and 43-line graphics mode. The remainder, such as 34-line graphics and—at the very highest resolution—60-line graphics, are available only on medium-resolution to high-resolution displays such as VGA.

Whether or not your choices are limited, however, for most work you'll probably find 25-line text or graphics mode the easiest to work with. Higher-resolution display modes can offer large quantities of information in a single window, as shown in Figure 5-1 on the following page.

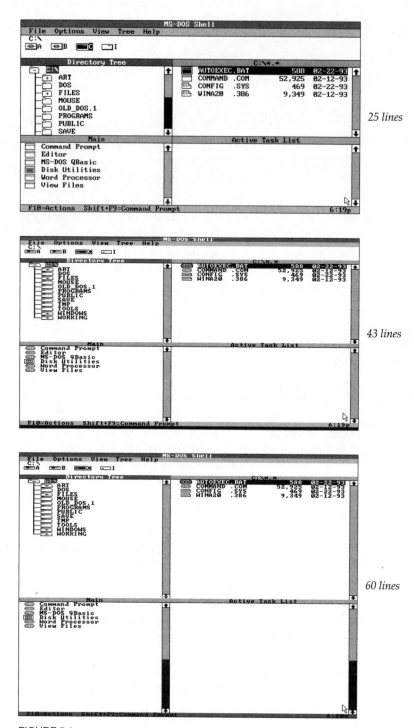

FIGURE 5-1.
The MS-DOS Shell screen in 25-line, 43-line, and 60-line display modes.

But most people would find very small characters visually tiring over extended work sessions.

Colors

The color controls in the Shell are found in the Colors command on the Options menu and, as you'll see a little later, in a screen-definition section of the DOSSHELL.INI initialization file. First, the Colors command.

Choosing Colors from the Options menu produces a dialog box like the following on a computer with a color display:

This illustration doesn't show all possibilities. You need to scroll down to see the remainder of the list.

By default, the Shell uses the color scheme named Ocean, a quiet combination of blue, gray, blue-green, and white. You can, of course, choose any of the others. Some are fun. Reverse, for example, makes you feel as though you're looking at a photographic negative. Others, such as Hot Pink and Emerald City, stand a good chance of blowing your optical fuses if you're a visually sedate being. To preview any color scheme, select it and choose the Preview button. To keep the color scheme you already had, choose Cancel.

Refreshing the screen

One of the most confusing things the Shell can do to you is refuse to display an accurate Directory Tree or File List. This happens not because the Shell is contrary but because it bases these lists on the information it reads into memory, and that information is normally accessed only at the beginning of each session or when you change to a different drive. Combine this remembrance of things past with the ease with which you can slip in and out of the Shell, to and from the system prompt, and you wind up with a potential conflict: the Shell's static memory of your kinetic directory-and-file-related activities.

The logical solution is to use only the Shell's commands to manipulate files and directories because all Shell-based changes to files and directories are immediately reflected on screen. But sometimes you want to use a command from the system prompt—either because it's faster or because its equivalent does not exist in the Shell. When you create, delete, or copy directories or files with MS-DOS commands at the MS-DOS prompt, however, you alter the disk directory—which thus remains accurate at all times—but you do not update the Shell's "memory" of that same directory. The solution for this mismatch is the Refresh command on the Options menu (or the shortcut key, F5).

Refresh causes the Shell to reread the directory of the current drive, updating the Directory and File Lists both in memory and on screen. Use Refresh in the following situations:

- When you exit the Shell and change the contents of the disk directory from the system prompt.

- When you change disks in a floppy drive.

- When you use Undelete, either from the Shell or from the system prompt.

- Most important, when the Directory or File List does not match what you know should be displayed.

One small note: The Refresh command, like many commands on the File menu, comes and goes like the Tooth Fairy. It's there when the selection cursor is in the Directory or File List, but it's gone when the selection cursor is in the program areas of the screen.

Refresh vs. Repaint

The Repaint command appears directly above the Refresh command on the Options menu. Although Repaint would seem to indicate a fresh display, it doesn't exactly. Repaint redraws the screen, but it does not cause the Shell to reread the directory structure of the current drive. Use Repaint if, for some reason, you need to redraw the screen. This might occur because a terminate-and-stay-resident (TSR) program remains on display even after you quit, or because some odd combination of circumstances causes a dialog box to remain partially or incorrectly displayed after you try to close it.

More on DOSSHELL.INI

DOSSHELL.INI is a file that stores all the information the Shell needs to start up already customized to settings you've selected. Although DOSSHELL.INI contains default choices, you modify this file whenever you quit the Shell after changing options such as the display mode and after adding program groups or program items. None of this modification requires human intervention, however, because the Shell itself updates the file when you quit.

You can view DOSSHELL.INI either with the View File Contents command on the File menu or, if you want more flexibility, with a word processor or a text editor such as the MS-DOS Editor. You can also edit DOSSHELL.INI, but if you do, be sure to read the warning at the top of the file:

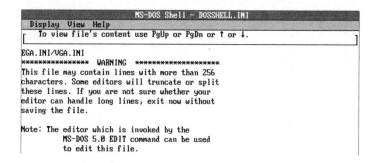

In addition, make a backup copy of the original DOSSHELL.INI so that you can restore the file if your editing goes wrong:

- If the Shell doesn't start by default whenever you boot or reboot the system, just use the Copy command to duplicate the file under another name, such as DOSSHELL.OLD. Be careful, however, not to use any of the extensions MS-DOS uses for other DOSSHELL files: COM, EXE, GRB, HLP, and VID.

- If the Shell starts from your AUTOEXEC.BAT file, the safest way to ensure recovery is to copy DOSSHELL.INI to a bootable floppy. If necessary, you can then replace the edited INI file with the one from the floppy disk without starting the Shell.

If you have version 5 of MS-DOS, DOSSHELL.INI is best suited for browsing, as a means of getting to understand the Shell a little better. If you have version 6 of MS-DOS, however, DOSSHELL.INI can serve another, potentially valuable, purpose by introducing you to the form and format of initialization files similar to one you can create with the version 6 multi-configuration option described in Chapter 16.

Whichever version of MS-DOS you use, DOSSHELL.INI has the same basic form. The file is divided into four major sections: the Shell state, descriptions of program groups and program items, lists of colors assigned to each part of the Shell screen in the color schemes displayed by the Colors command, and associations between filename extensions and programs.

The Shell state

At the top of the file, under the heading [savestate], is a list of status settings that record the status of the screen and various options, such as whether the Task Swapper was enabled when you quit and whether you changed the sort order of files in the File List from the default Name to Extension, Size, or another alternative.

This is the part of DOSSHELL.INI that enables the Shell to "remember" how it was set up when you last used it and to return to the same state at the next startup, whether that happens a minute or a year later. The beginning of this section looks like the following:

```
[savestate]
screenmode = graphics
resolution = low
startup = filemanager
filemanagermode = shared
sortkey = name
pause = disabled
```

As you can see, each of these settings defines some aspect of the Shell's appearance or behavior.

Program groups and program items

Below the startup settings, you see a set of descriptions that are variously indented and enclosed in left and right curly brackets. There is a description for each program group and program item defined in the Shell. If you trace through matched sets of brackets, you can see at least two hierarchies in which descriptions of program items are nested within descriptions of program groups, as shown and labeled in Figure 5-2.

(If you have upgraded to version 6 and want to display the Microsoft Anti-Virus and Microsoft Backup utilities, but you don't want to alter any program groups or program items you've customized, you can do so by editing this portion of your old DOSSHELL.INI file. The trick is to decompress EGA.INI from your original MS-DOS disks and "patch" copies of the relevant descriptions of MSAV and Msbackup from EGA.INI into your existing DOSSHELL.INI file. To do this, use the MS-DOS Editor and the Copy and Paste commands, described later. Be sure to match opening and closing brackets. If you're a little hesitant about doing this, practice on a backup copy of DOSSHELL.INI and try editing a color section first, as described later in this chapter.)

Now, back to DOSSHELL.INI. The first line, *group* =, identifies all of the indented text between it and the next *group* = line (not shown) as the starting point of a program group—in this case, as the next line of text indicates, the Disk Utilities. The part of the description labeled *Program group* defines the title of the group and the help text displayed if you select Disk Utilities and press F1.

Below this, the single line *program* = indicates that the next section of the file describes a program item within the Disk Utilities group. Notice that the brackets and indent levels help both to differentiate one segment of the file from another and to indicate which descriptions are subordinate to others. The remainder of the lines, labeled *Program item* in Figure 5-2, define the Disk Copy program item. Within this description, the first part, labeled *Add Program 1*, lists the contents of

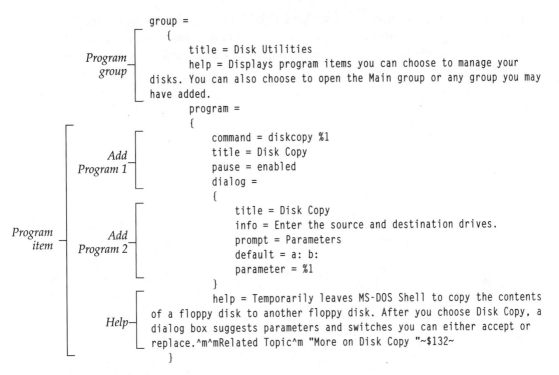

```
                      group =
                         {
                              title = Disk Utilities
           Program               help = Displays program items you can choose to manage your
             group          disks. You can also choose to open the Main group or any group you may
                         have added.
                              program =
                                 {
                                      command = diskcopy %1
              Add                    title = Disk Copy
          Program 1                  pause = enabled
                                     dialog =
                                     {
                                          title = Disk Copy
                                          info = Enter the source and destination drives.
  Program          Add                    prompt = Parameters
    item         Program 2                default = a: b:
                                          parameter = %1
                                     }
                                      help = Temporarily leaves MS-DOS Shell to copy the contents
                                 of a floppy disk to another floppy disk. After you choose Disk Copy, a
              Help            dialog box suggests parameters and switches you can either accept or
                             replace.^m^mRelated Topic^m "More on Disk Copy "~$132~
                                 }
```

FIGURE 5-2.
The anatomy of a program group.

the Add Program dialog box used to define the program item. You can see all this by selecting the Disk Copy program item and choosing Properties from the File menu.

The second part, labeled *Add Program 2*, lists the contents of the Add Program dialog box used to specify the %1 replaceable parameter recognized by the Disk Copy command.

The final portion of the sample, labeled *Help*, shows the help text that appears if F1 is pressed when Disk Copy is selected. Notice the *^m* and *^mm* characters, which produce line breaks as described earlier in the section on adding your own program items. The odd-looking line *Related Topic^m " More on Disk Copy "~$132~* appears at the end of the Disk Copy help text and is a reference to another help topic. The characters *~$132~* represent an internal "flag" that sends the help engine to the correct help text.

Colors

The third portion of DOSSHELL.INI is, like the descriptions of program groups and program items, a list made up of a series of separate, indented descriptions that assign colors to each window element for each color scheme supported by

the Shell. If you're inclined to try editing DOSSHELL.INI, this is a good place to
experiment, especially because you can define your own color scheme and have it
appear in the list displayed by the Colors command. One complete segment of the
color section looks like this:

```
selection =
{
    title = Basic Blue
    foreground =
    {
        base = black
        highlight = brightwhite
        selection = brightwhite
        alert = brightred
        menubar = black
        menu = black
        disabled = white
        accelerator = cyan
        dialog = black
        button = black
        elevator = white
        titlebar = black
        scrollbar = brightwhite
        borders = black
        drivebox = black
        driveicon = black
        cursor = black
    }
    background =
    {
        base = brightwhite
        highlight = blue
        selection = black
        alert = brightwhite
        menubar = white
        menu = brightwhite
        disabled = brightwhite
        accelerator = brightwhite
        dialog = brightwhite
        button = white
        elevator = white
        titlebar = white
        scrollbar = black
        borders = brightwhite
        drivebox = brightwhite
        driveicon = brightwhite
        cursor = brightblack
    }
}
```

To create your own color scheme, you can take either of two approaches:

- If you're hesitant about changing the file, make a backup copy of DOSSHELL.INI and then open the file with the MS-DOS Editor.

- If you're comfortable with editing files, enable task swapping, start the MS-DOS Editor, and open DOSSHELL.INI.

Next, to avoid altering existing color schemes, select an entire color-scheme description, including curly brackets, and copy it with the Copy command on the Edit menu. Move the cursor to another location (the end of the color section is a good spot) and use the Paste command to insert the lines you copied. Name the color scheme in the Title line at the top, and then assign whatever color you want to each window element. To ensure that all colors you specify are those your computer can produce, use color names that already exist in DOSSHELL.INI:

black	brightblack
white	brightwhite
cyan	brightcyan
blue	brightblue
green	brightgreen
magenta	brightmagenta
	brightred

You can also try yellow, brown, and red (which looks like brightred, but does show up in combinations such as red foreground on brightred background). If you specify a color that doesn't exist, you won't break anything, but the color you do see will be unexpected. For example, specifying white on orange produces gray on brightmagenta. In addition, some combinations produce odd results because the color you see on the screen comes from a blending of foreground and background colors.

When you finish, check that each opening bracket—from the beginning of the color section—has a corresponding closing bracket. If you inserted your new color scheme at the end of the descriptions, you'll probably have to add an extra line so that the colors section ends in three closing brackets:

```
        }
    }
}
```

Save the file.

To see the new color scheme:

- Restart the Shell if you quit it to edit DOSSHELL.INI.

- Press Ctrl-Esc if you started the Editor from the Shell.

Choose the Colors command and scroll through the list. Your new color scheme should appear. Choose it. If you don't like the result, edit the same section of DOSSHELL.INI again. Have fun.

Associations

The final, usually short, portion of DOSSHELL.INI lists the filename extensions associated with various programs you run from the Shell. By default, you should see at least the two associations built into the Shell: TXT with the MS-DOS Editor and BAS with the QBasic interpreter:

```
associations =
{
    association =
    {
        program = EDIT
        extension = TXT
    }
    association =
    {
        program = QBASIC /run
        extension = BAS
    }
}
```

SECTION THREE

MS-DOS
COMMANDS

6

About MS-DOS Commands

What You'll Find Here: This chapter begins a section of this book intended as a reference to the numerous commands and device drivers that are a part of MS-DOS. In the following section, you'll find some background on commands and device drivers in general, but more important, you'll find a guide to the contents of the seven chapters that follow. Each of those chapters groups commands, device drivers, or both by the type of work they do: manage files, format and check disks, organize directories, and so on. To help you find what you need, the two tables at the end of this chapter give you two ways of finding information: Table 6-1 shows how commands are grouped within chapters; Table 6-2 lists MS-DOS commands and device drivers alphabetically, with references to the chapters in which they are discussed.

*C*ommands are the tools that enable you to control MS-DOS and, by extension, your computer. Without MS-DOS commands, you could not list a directory, format a disk, create a batch file, or configure your system. At the system prompt, you use commands as the means of transforming your computer from inert hardware to interactive machine.

MS-DOS responds to scores of different commands. Some, such as those that display the time, date, and MS-DOS version number, are quite simple. Others, such as those you use to copy or back up selected files, load programs into high (or extended) memory, automatically optimize memory, monitor file deletions, or even recover inadvertently erased programs and data, are far more complex either in what they do or in the ways you use them. Simple or demanding, however, all this capability lies in the files that MS-DOS Setup copies onto your hard disk at installation.

Although you can make routine procedures semiautomatic by saving MS-DOS commands in a batch file or in a macro, you typically interact more immediately, and more directly, with MS-DOS. More precisely, you interact with its command interpreter, COMMAND.COM, the part of MS-DOS that reads from the keyboard and carries out the commands you type.

The command interpreter

Although knowing how a command is actually carried out matters not at all to you as a user of MS-DOS, this book assumes that you want to know a little more about MS-DOS than "Type X to do Y." In the spirit of adventure, then, this portion of the chapter takes you on a brief walk through the process that COMMAND.COM goes through in interpreting and executing a command. If you're not interested, you won't miss anything by skipping ahead.

From an MS-DOS user's point of view, the cleverest thing about COMMAND.COM is its ability to tell a valid command from an invalid one. Suppose, for example, you type

```
C:\>oh, shut up!
```

and press Enter on one of those days when nothing goes right and MS-DOS has responded *File not found* once too often. Your comment, like all your typing at the system prompt, is processed by COMMAND.COM. Being totally unsympathetic, COMMAND.COM responds as follows:

```
Bad command or file name
```

and redisplays the system prompt so you can try again.

On the other hand, suppose you type

```
C:\>format me a disk, oh mighty one
```

and press Enter. The answer might surprise you. Instead of the *Bad command* message, you see

```
Parameter format not correct - me
```

Why did COMMAND.COM call the first example a bad command but merely balk at the *me* in the second, equally "bad," command? Because COMMAND.COM responded only to the first example; Format responded to the second. Here's what happened.

Whenever you type an MS-DOS command, you use the same general format (options are enclosed in square brackets):

[drive:][path]command [parameter1]...[parameterN] [/switch1]...[/switchN]

The most important part of this line is *command*. If necessary, you can precede the command name with a drive and path, and if you want you can follow the command name with command-specific parameters (usually file specifications), switches, or both.

When COMMAND.COM evaluates and carries out a command, it needs only this part of the command line:

[drive:][path]command

The rest can be ignored briefly until COMMAND.COM can find out whether [drive:][path]command represents a real command. Chapter 1 described how COMMAND.COM checks for commands. Here's a brief recap:

1. First it attempts to match what you typed against the internal commands, such as Dir, that are built into its own program code. If COMMAND.COM does not find an internal match, it attempts to match your command to an executable file.

2. As a first step, it searches all program files in the first directory in the path for a matching file with the extension COM.

3. If no such COM file exists, COMMAND.COM searches the same directory for a file with the extension EXE.

4. If COMMAND.COM again has no success, it finally searches the directory for a file with the extension BAT.

5. If the command you typed is not one that COMMAND.COM can match by the time it has searched each directory in the path, you see the familiar *Bad command or file name* message and are bounced back to the system prompt. This is what happens in the earlier *oh, shut up* example.

Now suppose part of what you type corresponds to a legitimate command name, as in the earlier *format me a disk* example. Here the search for a command file is successful when COMMAND.COM finds FORMAT.COM in your DOS directory. Now the following (greatly simplified) sequence of events occurs:

1. COMMAND.COM sets aside enough memory for the program to run.

2. It transfers into part of this memory a string of bytes known as the command tail. In this command tail are the parameters and switches you typed at the system prompt.

3. It loads the program into memory.

4. It gives temporary control of the computer to the new program (Format in this example).

After all this has occurred (practically in no time from your point of view) the new program is ready to go to work. One of its first actions is to check the command tail to determine whether you typed any parameters and switches that will control its actions:

- If you type a recognizable string of parameters, switches, or both, the program can act on this information, so it carries out the command, quits, and returns control of the computer to COMMAND.COM. This is what happens when, for example, you type *format a: /q*.

- If you type unrecognizable parameters and switches, the program cannot carry out your command. Different programs react in different ways, but they generally go through an "I can't do this" routine and then quit and return you to COMMAND.COM. In the earlier *format me a disk* example, for instance, Format responds to the gibberish it finds in the command tail by displaying the *parameter format not correct* message before exiting and returning control to COMMAND.COM, which displays a new system prompt.

Groups of commands

MS-DOS commands are generally divided into the internal and external categories described above, but in actuality there are four groups of commands: internal, external, configuration, and (in version 6) network.

Whether a command is internal or external hasn't been an issue since hard disks became more or less standard, even on low-end computers. If MS-DOS is on your hard disk, COMMAND.COM can find the files it needs, as long as your DOS directory is in the path defined by the Path command in AUTOEXEC.BAT. (This is guaranteed in versions 5 and 6, because unless you specify otherwise, MS-DOS Setup creates or modifies the Path command for you.) So the only time you might need to worry about internal or external commands is if you're running MS-DOS from floppy disks, a practice definitely not recommended.

Even though distinguishing internal from external commands is of little practical purpose, you might be interested to see what kinds of commands are internal:

■ Commands that are frequently called upon and have been part of MS-DOS since (or nearly since) it was released in version 1. This category includes such time-honored and well-known commands as Directory (Dir), Copy, Type, Time, and Date.

■ Batch commands. This category includes If, For, Goto, and the other batch-control commands recognized and carried out by the batch interpreter (itself a part of COMMAND.COM).

■ Commands that must be in memory because they affect MS-DOS or system setup and commonly appear in AUTOEXEC.BAT files. Included in this category are such commands as Path, which tells MS-DOS where to find command files; Set, which sets environment variables (and can be used to define variables in batch files); and Loadhigh, a recent addition to MS-DOS that loads TSR programs into upper memory blocks.

Batch and internal commands are listed in the following table:

Batch commands

Call	Goto
Choice	If
Echo	Pause
For	Shift

Internal commands

Break	Dir	Ren
Chcp	Erase	Rmdir (Rd)
Chdir (Cd)	Exit	Set
Cls	Loadhigh (Lh)	Time
Copy	Mkdir (Md)	Type
Ctty	Path	Ver
Date	Prompt	Verify
Del	Rem	Vol

For external, configuration, and network commands, it's good to remember the following points:

■ External commands are any for which you can find a COM or EXE file in your MS-DOS directory—for example, CHKDSK.EXE for the Check Disk (Chkdsk) command and MODE.COM for everybody's favorite, the Mode command in all its dazzling variety.

■ Configuration commands are those you use to customize MS-DOS to work with your system. Most, such as the Device, Buffers, and Dos commands, are usable only from CONFIG.SYS. Exceptions are the Break command, which you can use to turn Ctrl-Break checking on or off from the system prompt, and the Rem command, which you can use in batch files to disable commands without deleting them permanently. If you have version 6 of MS-DOS, you also have a group of "initialization" commands you can use in CONFIG.SYS to define menus and to help in creating a set of different *configuration blocks* that can customize startup more than in any other version of MS-DOS. These commands—in particular, Menu Color and Menu Item—are interesting to experiment with.

All of these commands are described in the following chapters. To find specific commands, see Tables 6-1 and 6-2 at the end of this chapter.

Commands, utilities, and programs

Throughout this book, you'll find references along the lines of "the Format command," "the Backup utility," and "your word processing program." All these collections of computer-readable instructions are executed from the system prompt, and many allow optional parameters and switches. So what's the difference between a command and a utility or a program? In one sense, none because all are program files. In another sense, though, the difference is great, and it has to do with the type and amount of work carried out:

■ An MS-DOS command, internal or external, is a set of instructions that carries out one task or closely related variations of a single basic task. The Format command, for example, simply formats a disk. You can customize the command to format the disk in drive A, B, or C; you can specify different disk capacities; or you can request a quick format; but in all cases you still do one thing: format a disk.

■ A utility, whether built into MS-DOS or purchased separately, is a program—small in comparison to an application—that carries out a set of tasks related to some aspect of maintaining or managing your computer. The version 6 backup utility in both the MS-DOS and Windows versions, for example, not only backs up files, it also performs tasks related to backups: It can format the target disk, it can save backup settings and file selections, it can compare backups with the originals to verify accuracy, it can compress backups so that they require less storage space, and it can restore backed-up files.

■ A program, as defined here, is a full-fledged set of instructions that is stored in one or more executable files and that offers more flexibility than either a command or a utility. Generally, a program is something, such as a word processor, that you can turn to creative purposes. MS-DOS is a program, too, however—the one you use creatively to control the computer.

In a sense, the difference between a command, a utility, and a program is a matter of degree: A word processor does more work than a utility such as DoubleSpace, but a utility does more work than a command. Although the boundaries are vague (is the MS-DOS Editor a utility or a program?), you should find it helpful to know that these words do imply comparative differences within the generic group *program* or *executable file* and are not considered equivalent in this book.

Device drivers

As mentioned in Chapter 2, device drivers are programs that enable MS-DOS to work with specific pieces of hardware, such as disk drives and display monitors. Device drivers shield MS-DOS from having to deal with the actual operating characteristics of the devices, so they are, in effect, translators that take over when MS-DOS sends information to, or requests information from, the devices they control.

MS-DOS includes a number of default device drivers (CON, LPT, COM, and so on), which it affords special treatment: It opens and closes them, and it reads from and writes to them as if each were a type of "file" in your system. In working with MS-DOS, you never have to configure these devices with special device drivers, nor do you have to remember anything about them other than their names. In certain commands, particularly the Mode command, you need to know what MS-DOS means by COM1, LPT1, PRN, AUX, and so on. (All this is explained in Chapter 10, "Devices.")

Other device drivers, however, are stored in external files and fall into the installable category. These are device drivers that you must identify to MS-DOS through your CONFIG.SYS file if you want to use them. Some of these, such as HIMEM.SYS and EMM386.EXE, are invaluable aids in optimizing memory use on your system. Because each device driver has its own purpose and its own set of parameters and switches, you'll find them described separately in the following chapters, even though each must be identified to MS-DOS with a Device or Devicehigh command in CONFIG.SYS.

Help with MS-DOS

Online Help with MS-DOS commands is available in both versions 5 and 6. Help in version 5 provides on-screen information about command syntax, including optional parameters and switches. Version 6 help is far more detailed, so the two are described separately here.

In version 5, as in version 6, you can request either a "table of contents" or help on a specific command. In version 5,

- To see a list of commands, with a brief description of each one, type *help* by itself. The list pauses after each screenful; to continue, press any key.

- To see help for a particular command, type the request in either of the following forms, where *[command]* represents the name of the command for which you want help:

    ```
    help [command]
    ```

    ```
    [command] /?
    ```

Of the two, *[command] /?* is slightly faster, but really only because it's easy to remember and saves a few keystrokes. (If you want to see how thorough help is, type *help /?*. You'll see help on getting help.)

In version 6 of MS-DOS, help is customized to a much greater extent and can be accessed through either of two commands, Fast Help (Fasthelp) or Help:

- Fasthelp provides the type of coverage you see in version 5 Help on specific commands—syntax, parameters, and switches—and you access it in much the same way, using either of the following forms:

    ```
    fasthelp [command]
    ```

    ```
    [command] /?.
    ```

- In contrast, the Help command, typed either as *help* or as *help* followed by the name of a command, invokes a more elaborate help system called MS-DOS Help:

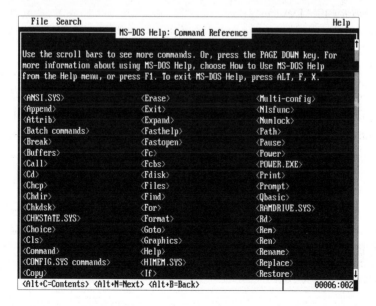

This help appears in a scrollable text-based window with menus (File, Search, and Help) at the top and references to help topics. MS-DOS Help is responsive to both the mouse and the keyboard, so to see help on a particular command (or on any topic displayed between highlighted < and > symbols) simply double-click on the topic or select it with the keyboard and press Enter. MS-DOS Help is very easy to use, and you'll no doubt be clicking your way through commands in no time. If you want more information, however, detailed descriptions of both Fasthelp and Help are in Chapter 13.

The next seven chapters

Each of the next seven chapters begins with an introduction to the subject at hand: files, disks, directories, and so on. In these introductory sections, you'll find the terminology and background information you need to understand how the commands work, what they do, and how they are used. For example, Chapter 7, on files, explains MS-DOS file-naming conventions and wildcards, both of which you must understand to name, save, find, and copy files efficiently. Similarly, the same chapter describes file storage, including the much-mentioned but sometimes little-understood File Allocation Table, or FAT, that indexes all disk storage under MS-DOS. Once you know that the FAT exists, you have a basis for understanding how MS-DOS deletes files and, more important, why delete protection can be essential in recovering deleted files.

After this introductory information, the command descriptions appear alphabetically within each chapter. Each description follows the same format:

- An overview of the command, including syntax and suggestions on when and how to use the command.

- A set of examples in table form, like the following:

Type:	To:
format a: /q	Format a used disk

To help you determine what characters you must type and what information, such as drive letter, you must provide when entering a command, the syntax sections of the command descriptions use the conventions outlined below and illustrated in the following (abbreviated) syntax line:

format *drive*: /q /f:*size* /v[:*label*] /s

- The command name is shown in lowercase, exactly as it must be typed. You can choose to type in uppercase if you wish—that is, either *format* or *FORMAT* in the preceding example.

- Information you provide, such as *drive*, above, is shown in italics. For example, in a real Format command, you might replace *drive* with the letter (followed by a colon) of drive A, like this: *format a:*.

- Optional parameters, such as *[:label]* above, are shown in square brackets. Note that in this example, the parameter not only is optional but also represents information you provide. This particular part of the Format command lets you specify a volume label if you wish, as part of the command line. If you were to make use of this feature, your command might look something like this: *format a: /v:q3 report*.

- Switches that control the way a command works are shown as you should type them. The /s switch is one such example, above. Note that even though switches are optional parts of the command line, they are not enclosed in square brackets as are optional parameters. This convention is used merely to simplify the look of the command syntax, which can become complex and confusing.

If you run into problems deciphering command syntax, the examples that follow the syntax section will clarify matters for you.

Guide to commands

Table 6-1 lists the next seven chapters in this book, along with the commands covered in each.

Chapter 7, "Files"	Attribute (Attrib); Backup; Compare (Comp); Copy; Delete (Del); Expand; Fastopen; File Compare (Fc); Interlnk; INTERLNK.EXE; Intersvr; Move; Microsoft Backup (Msbackup); Rename (Ren); Replace; Restore; Type; Undelete; Verify; Extended Copy (Xcopy)
Chapter 8, "Disks"	Assign; Check Disk (Chkdsk); Defragmenter (Defrag); Disk Compare (Diskcomp); Diskcopy; DBLSPACE.SYS; DoubleSpace (Dblspace); Fixed Disk (Fdisk); Format; Join; Label; Microsoft Anti-Virus (Msav); Mirror; Recover; Substitute (Subst); System (Sys); Unformat; Volume (Vol); VSafe
Chapter 9, "Directories"	Append; Change Directory (Chdir or Cd); Delete Tree (Deltree); Directory (Dir); Make Directory (Mkdir or Md); Path; Remove Directory (Rmdir or Rd); Tree

TABLE 6-1.   *(continued)*
MS-DOS commands and device drivers, grouped by chapter.

TABLE 6-1. *continued*

Chapter 10, "Devices"	ANSI.SYS; Change Codepage (Chcp); Clear Screen (Cls); Country; Ctty; DISPLAY.SYS; DRIVER.SYS; EGA.SYS; Graphics; Graphics Table (Graftabl); Keyboard (Keyb); Mode; National Language Support Function (Nlsfunc); Power; POWER.EXE; Print; PRINTER.SYS
Chapter 11, "Memory"	CHKSTATE.SYS; Devicehigh; DOS (Dos); EMM386; EMM386.EXE; HIMEM.SYS; Load Fix (Loadfix); Load High (Loadhigh or Lh); Memory Display (Mem); Mem-Maker (Memmaker); RAMDRV.SYS; SMARTDRV.EXE
Chapter 12, "System Configuration and Control"	Microsoft Diagnostics (MSD) Configuration: Buffers; Device; Drive Parameters (Drivparm); File Control Blocks (Fcbs); Files; Include; Install; Lastdrive; Menu Color (Menucolor); Menu Default (Menudefault); Menu Item (Menuitem); Number Lock (Numlock); Set Version (Setver); SETVER.EXE; Shell; Stacks; Submenu; Switches
	Batch: Call; Choice; Echo; For; Goto; If; Pause; Remark (Rem); Set; Shift
	Macros: Doskey
	Input/Output Redirection: Find, More, Sort
Chapter 13, "Miscellaneous Commands"	Break; Command; Date; Debug; Dosshell; Edit; Edlin; Exit; Fast Help (Fasthelp); Help; MSCDEX; Prompt; Qbasic; Share; Time; Version (Ver)

Table 6-2 lists the MS-DOS commands and device drivers alphabetically, with references to the chapter in which each is described.

ANSI.SYS	10
Append	9
Assign	8
Attribute (Attrib)	7
Backup	7
Break	13
Buffers	12
Call	12
Change Codepage (Chcp)	10
Change Directory (Chdir or Cd)	9
Check Disk (Chkdsk)	8
CHKSTATE.EXE	11
Choice	12

TABLE 6-2.   *(continued)*
Alphabetic reference to commands and device drivers.

TABLE 6-2. *continued*

Clear Screen (Cls)	10
Command	13
Compare (Comp)	7
Copy	7
Country	10
Ctty	10
Date	13
DBLSPACE.SYS	8
Defragmenter (Defrag)	8
Delete (Del)	7
Delete Tree (Deltree)	9
Device	12
Devicehigh	11
Directory (Dir)	9
Disk Compare (Diskcomp)	8
Diskcopy	8
DISPLAY.SYS	10
DOS (Dos)	11
Doskey	12
Dosshell	13
DoubleSpace (Dblspace)	8
Drive Parameters (Drivparm)	12
DRIVER.SYS	10
Echo	12
Edit	13
Edlin	13
EGA.SYS	10
EMM386	11
EMM386.EXE	11
Exit	13
Expand	7
Fast Help (Fasthelp)	13
Fastopen	7
File Compare (Fc)	7
File Control Blocks (Fcbs)	12
Fixed Disk (Fdisk)	8
Files	12
Find	12

(continued)

TABLE 6-2. *continued*

For	12
Format	8
Goto	12
Graphics	10
Graphics Table (Graftabl)	10
Help	13
HIMEM.SYS	11
If	12
Include	12
Install	12
Interlnk	7
INTERLNK.EXE	7
Intersvr	7
Join	8
Keyboard (Keyb)	10
Label	8
Lastdrive	12
Load Fix (Loadfix)	11
Load High (Loadhigh or Lh)	11
Make Directory (Mkdir or Md)	9
MemMaker (Memmaker)	11
Memory Display (Mem)	11
Menu Color (Menucolor)	12
Menu Default (Menudefault)	12
Menu Item (Menuitem)	12
Microsoft Anti-Virus (Msav)	8
Microsoft Backup (Msbackup)	7
Microsoft Diagnostics (MSD)	12
Mirror	8
Mode	10
More	12
Move	7
MSCDEX	13
National Language Support Function (Nlsfunc)	10
Number Lock (Numlock)	12
Path	9
Pause	12
Power	10

(continued)

TABLE 6-2. *continued*

POWER.EXE	10
Print	10
PRINTER.SYS	10
Prompt	13
Qbasic	13
RAMDRIVE.SYS	11
Recover	8
Remark (Rem)	12
Remove Directory (Rmdir or Rd)	9
Rename (Ren)	7
Replace	7
Restore	7
Set	12
SETVER.EXE	12
Set Version (Setver)	12
Share	13
Shell	12
Shift	12
SMARTDRV.EXE	11
Sort	12
Stacks	12
Submenu	12
Substitute (Subst)	8
Switches	12
System (Sys)	8
Time	13
Tree	9
Type	7
Undelete	7
Unformat	8
Version (Ver)	13
Verify	7
Volume (Vol)	8
VSafe	8
Extended Copy (Xcopy)	7

7

Files

What You'll Find Here: Attribute (Attrib); Backup; Compare (Comp); Copy; Delete (Del); Expand; Fastopen; File Compare (Fc); Interlnk; INTERLNK.EXE; Intersvr; Move; Microsoft Backup (Msbackup); Rename (Ren); Replace; Restore; Type; Undelete; Verify; Extended Copy (Xcopy)

You've doubtless seen TV programs in which a joke depends on an overstuffed closet. Someone opens the door, and a disorganized mess falls out, or someone closes the door only by leaning against it and pushing hard. The joke, such as it is, is old and predictable, but there's a point to mentioning it here: What if MS-DOS, like the fictional owner of the closet, simply shoved data onto disk and kept no record of what went where, or when? Assuming that MS-DOS could retrieve the information at all, you might find the complaining letter you wrote to Microsoft stuffed between Chapters 37 and 38 of your great novel. To its credit, MS-DOS is never as disorganized as a TV jokester, and especially not where your files are concerned. The reason is, of course, that MS-DOS is your only link to stored data once that data has been turned into patterns of magnetic particles on the surface of a disk.

Because MS-DOS logs and tracks all information stored on disk, the only way it allows you to save or access disk contents is through the use of files. Only when you name a file will MS-DOS save it. Only when you provide a filename will MS-DOS run a program or retrieve stored data. To MS-DOS, a file can be as short as one character, or it can be long enough to fill a disk (assuming you could even work with that much data at one time). A file can be a picture of your dog, a speech, or a plan for achieving world peace. The content and size don't matter. To MS-DOS a file is simply a collection of characters you save or retrieve as a unit.

Filenames and extensions

When you save a file, you give it a name of up to eight characters, optionally followed by a period (.) and a three-character extension that further identifies the file. This is the same pattern followed by MS-DOS since its introduction as version 1. In all cases—program files, data files, filenames, or filename extensions—the following rules apply:

- Blank spaces are not allowed, so you can't use names such as MY FILE and THISFILE. OK.

- You can use any combination of alphabetic and numeric characters, as well as certain punctuation marks and special symbols, but the following are not allowed:

  " * + , . / : ; < = > ? [\ ] ¦

Where extensions are concerned, follow the same rules as for filenames, but also keep the following in mind:

- Avoid extensions that have special meaning to programs. Among these are not only such extensions as COM, EXE, and BAT, but "second-tier" extensions such as HLP, BAS, SYS, INI, and DAT.

■ Where possible, allow application programs to assign extensions to data files. Applications usually associate certain extensions with data files, so finding and opening data files is much simpler if you accept the default extension. A word processor, for example, might automatically search for and display the names of all files in the current directory with the DOC extension. If you named a file MYFILE.YES, you would have to specify both the filename and the extension in your file find or file open command.

■ By convention, ASCII files are given the extension TXT, for text. Where such conventions exist, follow them to apply consistency to your files.

Some examples of invalid filenames and valid alternatives follow:

Invalid	Valid	Reason
OH BOY.DOC	OH-BOY.DOC or OH_BOY.DOC	Spaces not allowed; hyphens and underscores are.
TAXES.1992	TAXES.92, 92TAXES.XLS, or 1992.TAX	Extensions must be no more than three characters. (XLS in this example is the extension assigned by the Microsoft Excel spreadsheet application.)
????.NOT	WHY.NOT	Question marks not allowed.
A+.RPT	A-PLUS.RPT	Plus signs can cause error messages or, with the Copy command, unexpected results.
MYCLIENT_10-24-93.LTR	Create a MYCLIENT directory, save file as 10-24-93.LTR	Filename much too long, but the same amount of information can be conveyed, in a more organized fashion through use of directories. See the explanation at the end of this section.

If you want, you can assign some really bizarre filenames, extensions, or both by holding down the Alt key as you type the extended ASCII code for each character on the numeric keypad—for example, Alt-228 for the Greek sigma. Not all characters are valid, however, and as a means of assigning filenames, the exercise is more entertaining than it is useful—especially because you must remember and retype the ASCII codes in order to delete, copy, or otherwise work with the file. If you want to while away some idle moments, however, try creating and saving some files—preferably on a floppy disk—with the Copy command and various combinations of the extended ASCII codes in Appendix A.

MS-DOS is sometimes criticized for limiting users to a maximum of 11 characters, not counting the period, but this complaint is not entirely warranted. Although 8 to 11 characters can sometimes stretch your creativity, consider too that you can create directories within directories to organize your files logically. Assuming that you define and use a directory structure on at least your hard disk, the path to a particular file can be up to 63 characters long. And if half a hundred characters, give or take a few, is not enough to describe a file adequately, perhaps you should look to your own verbosity rather than cast a jaundiced eye on MS-DOS. For instance:

```
C:\ANIMAL\MAMMAL\CETACEA\DOLPHINS\FLIPPER.DOC
```

ought to be enough to help you locate your essay about everyone's favorite sea creature.

Wildcards

When you work with files, especially large collections of files with similar names or extensions, wildcards are a way of life. Available not only at the MS-DOS command line, but within the Shell, Windows, and many application programs, wildcards come in two flavors: ? and *. The question mark can be used to represent any single character in a filename or an extension; the asterisk can be used to represent any number of characters in a filename or an extension. Of the two, the asterisk (*) is no doubt used far more often than the question mark because of its flexibility. Before the version 5 days of Undelete, it also caused numerous loud groans when thoughtlessly used, as in

```
C:\>del *.doc
```

Even now, with Mirror (version 5) and Undelete (versions 5 and 6) to help you out, bear in mind that a Delete (Del) command, coupled with the * wildcard, can cut a wide swath through your files. The only time MS-DOS questions your wisdom in these matters is when you type *del *.** to indicate that you want to delete every file in a directory. At that point, MS-DOS warns

```
All files in directory will be deleted!
Are you sure (Y/N)?
```

Be sure.

Wildcards can be used in numerous ways to specify just about any combination of files you can think of. The following table lists uses for both the question mark and the asterisk and describes the effect in each case:

File specification	Meaning	Valid matches
?OO?.DOC	Any four-character filename with OO as the middle two characters and the extension DOC.	BOOK.DOC, COOK.DOC, POOL.DOC
LETTER.??T	Any file named LETTER with a three-character extension ending in T.	LETTER.TXT, LET-TER.LST, LETTER.BAT
B????ALL.DO?	Any eight-character filename starting with B and ending with ALL, and with a three-character extension starting with DO.	BASEBALL.DOC, BEERHALL.DOT, BENDSALL.DOR
DO*	With the Directory command only: any filename starting with DO, regardless of length or extension.	DOSBOOK.DOC, DOOR.BIG, DOVER, DOUBLE.DIP
	With other commands, such as Copy and Delete: any filename starting with DO, regardless of length, but with no extension.	DO-IT, DONUTS, DOR-MOUSE, and DOVER, but not DOSBOOK.DOC, DOOR.BIG, or DOUBLE.DIP
*DO.DOC	Any filename with the extension DOC. The asterisk at the beginning nullifies the DO ending the file specification.	UNDO.DOC, TODO.DOC, BILLETDO.DOC, but also RHINO.DOC, CLOUD.DOC, SCIFI.DOC
BIG*.	Any filename or directory, of any length, starting with BIG but with no extension. (Note the period in the file specification.)	BIGBUG, BIGMOUTH, BIGBITE, BIG, BIGGER, BIGGEST
*.DOC	Any filename, of any length, with the extension DOC.	ME.DOC, YOU.DOC, THEM.DOC, HARLEY.DOC
README.*	Any file named README, with any extension.	README.DOC, README.TXT, README.WRI
.	Any filename, of any length, with any extension; all files.	Every file in the current directory or the specified path

Types of files

As you work with a computer, you use two basic types of files: program files and data files. Each type complements the other: Program files contain instructions that manipulate data, and data files contain information that give programs something to work with.

For the most part, program files are the untouchables on disk. You don't move them, rename them, or delete them unless you know exactly what you're doing.

This is especially true of Windows and Windows applications, which can install themselves in multiple directories, rather than in a single, easily identified location.

At one time, program files were easy to identify from their extensions: COM, EXE, BAS, and so on. These days, although the COM and EXE extensions still abound, programs often include many other different, and necessary, file types, among them both program files with extensions such as SYS and DLL and readable (but still critical) information files such as WIN.INI and DOSSHELL.INI. As a rule of thumb, you should consider all but INI files off limits. And even with INI files, you should know what you're doing before you dive in with a text editor and modify them to run programs according to your preferences.

Executable, program files—COM, EXE, and others—are stored on disk in a format that makes them unintelligible when displayed, but you can take a look at them with the MS-DOS Type command, with the View File Contents command on the MS-DOS Shell File menu, or—carefully—with the Debug program debugger.

If you want to see what a program looks like, try the following experiments.

1. To see the output of the Type command when you display a program file, type *type c:\dos\doskey.com* at the system prompt. You get beeps and a scattering of strange symbols. That's Doskey, as the Type command encounters it.

2. To see a little more detail, start the Shell, select DOSKEY.COM in your DOS directory, and press F9. At first, there's little to see other than a lot of zeros, but if you press the PgDn key once, your screen should look like this:

```
╔══════════════════════ MS-DOS Shell - DOSKEY.COM ══════════════════════╗
  Display  View  Help
 ┌─── To view file's content use PgUp or PgDn or ↑ or ↓. ─────────────────┐
 │                                                                        │
 │   000130    00000000   0E000000   00000000   00000000   ...............│
 │   000140    00000000   0D0A2D2D   204D6F72   65202D2D   ......-- More --│
 │   000150    004C696E   65206E75   6D626572   3A200000   .Line number: ..│
 │   000160    00000003   00000000   00000000   00000000   ...............│
 │   000170    00750200   00030100   00410100   00000000   .u.......A......│
 │   000180    00000000   003D0516   740F3D05   4B740A80   .....=..t.=.Kt.Ç│
 │   000190    FC48741B   2EFF2E5F   029C2EFF   1E5F022E   ⁿHt.._.£. ._.│
 │   0001A0    891E6502   2E8C0667   020E07BB   6302CF3C   ë.e..î.g...┬c.┴<│
 │   0001B0    10751087   DA803F80   87DA75D8   FBE80D00   .u.ç┌Ç?Çç┌u┘▌ð..│
 │   0001C0    33C0CF0A   C075CD0E   07B802AA   CF505351   3└┴.└u=..┐.¬┴PSQ│
 │   0001D0    52565755   1E06FC2E   89160301   2E8C1E05   RVWU.ⁿ.ë....î..│
 │   0001E0    010E1F0E   07F6062C   0204755F   E85D05BE   .....÷.,..u_ð].┘│
 │   0001F0    27018B0E   28020BC9   7403E8CA   028B3628   '.Ï.(..┌t.ð╨.Ÿ6(│
 │   000200    02C68427   010DC706   18012701   E88301C2   .ä'.∥...'.ðâ.╥│
 │   000210    288B3E18   018B0E28   02B014E3   04F2AE74   (Ï>..Ï.(∥.π.2«t│
 │   000220    18C43E03   01BE2701   8B0E2002   4726880D   .->..┘'.Ï.(.G&ê.│
 │   000230    47F3A4B0   0DAAE94F   01800E2C   0204C43E   GÇⁿñ∥.¬0O.Ç.,..->│
 │   000240    030126C7   4501000D   E93D01C4   3E830147   ..&∥E...O=.->..G│
 │   000250    47B90000   49F6062C   02087503   E9EE008B   G╫Ç.I÷.,..u.ðé.ï│
 │   000260    361A01AC   0AC07433   3C147428   3C247515   6..¼.Lt3<.t(<§u.│
 └◄─┘=PageDown  Esc=Cancel  F9=Hex/ASCII ──────────────────────── 12:32p ─┘
╚════════════════════════════════════════════════════════════════════════╝
```

Here you see a hexadecimal representation of DOSKEY.COM. The left column, which you'll use in a moment, shows the position, or offset, of the first character in the line of digits in the center column, in relation to the beginning of the file. For example, in the preceding illustration, position 000151 (hex) is occupied by character 4C (also hex) which, as you can see in the right column, is the letter L.

3. Press the PgDn key a number of times. Watch the right column, and stop when you see some text beginning with ../REINSTALL. Check the left column. The offset where this text begins to appear should be at line D10H (H indicates hexadecimal):

```
                    MS-DOS Shell - DOSKEY.COM
 Display  View  Help
    To view file's content use PgUp or PgDn or ↑ or ↓.

   000D10    00002F52   45494E53   54414C4C   002F4255    ../REINSTALL./BU
   000D20    4653495A   45002F48   4953544F   5259002F    FSIZE./HISTORY./
   000D30    48002F4D   4143524F   53002F4D   002F3F00    H./MACROS./M./?.
   000D40    2F494E53   45525400   2F4F5645   52535452    /INSERT./OVERSTR
   000D50    494B4500   00020E1F   0E07B430   CD213D06    IKE........|ê=!=.
   000D60    007406BA   E117E9C4   01BE8100   E89903BF    .t.‖ρ.ê─.ⁱü.Ø̃ö.┐
   000D70    3D0EE89E   037474BF   400EE896   03745CBF    =.Ø̃R.tt┐ê.Ø̃û.t\┐
   000D80    480EE88E   03745CBF   120EE886   037444BF    H.Ø̃Â.t\┐..Ø̃â.tD┐
   000D90    260EE87E   03746DBF   2F0EE876   037465BF    &.Ø̃~.tm┐/.Ø̃v.te┐
   000DA0    320EE86E   037466BF   3A0EE866   03745EBF    2.Ø̃n.tf┐:.Ø̃f.t^┐
   000DB0    1D0EE85E   03755FE8   4E033C3D   7403E969    ..Ø̃^.u_Ø̃N.<=t.Θi
   000DC0    01E84303   E85E8389   1E540E2E   800EB00F    .Ø̃C.Ø̃^.ë.T..Ç.▒
   000DD0    02EB992E   800EB00F   01EB912E   800EB00F    .Ø̃ö.Ç.▒..Ø̃æ.Ç.▒
   000DE0    20EB892E   800EB00F   40EB81BB   05138A07     Ø̃ë.Ç.▒θÖⁱⁿ..ë.
   000DF0    430AC074   0A538AD0   B402CD21   5BEBEFB0    C.Lt.Sèⁿⁱⁿ=!Γ∂ⁿ▒
   000E00    00E92E01   2E800EB0   0F08E95F   FF2E800E    .Θ...Ç.▒..Θ_ .Ç.
   000E10    B00F10E9   56FF2EF6   06B00F01   750DB800    ▒..θV .÷.▒..u.┐.
   000E20    48CD2F3D   00487403   E9860056   A1540E3D    H=/=.Ht.θâ.VⁱT.=
   000E30    01017303   B80101B9   FFFF81E9   100E3BC1    ..s.┐..⌐  üθ..;┴
   000E40    76028BC1   508E062C   00B449CD   21B8100E    v.ïⁿPÂ.,.⌐I=!┐..
  <┘=PageDown  Esc=Cancel  F9=Hex/ASCII                              12:40p
```

You're through with the Shell, so press Esc to return to the main window, and then press F3 to quit the Shell.

Now, you'll use the offset you noted in the Shell to help you see DOSKEY.COM through the "eyes" of Debug. Follow the instructions carefully. Debug not only displays, it modifies and saves programs, so don't get adventurous here.

1. To start Debug and load DOSKEY.COM into memory so that you can see its contents, type

```
C:\>debug c:\dos\doskey.com
```

When Debug starts, it displays an unobtrusive prompt, a single hyphen:

```
-
```

2. Just for fun, start by taking a look at a command tail—here, the drive and path you specified for Debug. When Debug loads a COM or an EXE program into memory, the program is preceded by a 256-byte "table" of program-related information. Toward the end of this table, at offset

80H, is the command tail. You can display it on screen with the Debug Dump command, which displays (dumps) the contents of memory. To view the command tail, type

```
-d80
```

You should see something like this:

```
C:\>debug c:\dos\doskey.com
-d80
28F9:0080  00 0D 63 3A 5C 64 6F 73-5C 64 6F 73 6B 65 79 2E   ..c:\dos\doskey.
28F9:0090  63 6F 6D 0D 62 01 52 50-9A 9E 14 87 13 83 3E 64   com.b.RP......>d
28F9:00A0  00 00 74 50 9A 52 04 A7-13 8E 46 08 26 89 84 78   ..tP.R....F.&..x
28F9:00B0  01 0B C0 74 3F C7 46 FC-28 00 8E 46 08 26 FF B4   ...t?.F.(..F.&..
28F9:00C0  78 01 8D 46 FA 16 50 8D-46 C0 16 50 8D 46 FC 16   x..F..P.F..P.F..
28F9:00D0  50 6A 00 6A 00 8E 06 BA-0B 26 FF 1E 4A 01 8D 46   Pj.j.....&..J..F
28F9:00E0  C0 16 50 8B C6 8B 56 08-05 82 01 52 50 9A 98 01   ..P...V....RP...
28F9:00F0  87 13 EB 56 C7 06 64 00-01 00 8D 46 F6 16 50 8B   ...V..d....F..P.
-
```

3. Now take a look at the same part of DOSKEY.COM you just saw in the Shell. Remember that, in the Shell, readable text started appearing at offset D10H. In Debug, however, you have to account for the 256 (100H) bytes of memory containing the command tail and other information, so to see the same part of DOSKEY.COM, you have to add 100H to the offset (D10H) you noted in the Shell. Remember, though, that hexadecimal digits go from 0 through F, not 0 through 9. Thus, when you add 100H to D10H, you get E10H.

To dump this portion of memory, then, you type

```
-de10
```

And you should see something like this:

```
C:\>debug c:\dos\doskey.com
-d80
28F9:0080  00 0D 63 3A 5C 64 6F 73-5C 64 6F 73 6B 65 79 2E   ..c:\dos\doskey.
28F9:0090  63 6F 6D 0D 62 01 52 50-9A 9E 14 87 13 83 3E 64   com.b.RP......>d
28F9:00A0  00 00 74 50 9A 52 04 A7-13 8E 46 08 26 89 84 78   ..tP.R....F.&..x
28F9:00B0  01 0B C0 74 3F C7 46 FC-28 00 8E 46 08 26 FF B4   ...t?.F.(..F.&..
28F9:00C0  78 01 8D 46 FA 16 50 8D-46 C0 16 50 8D 46 FC 16   x..F..P.F..P.F..
28F9:00D0  50 6A 00 6A 00 8E 06 BA-0B 26 FF 1E 4A 01 8D 46   Pj.j.....&..J..F
28F9:00E0  C0 16 50 8B C6 8B 56 08-05 82 01 52 50 9A 98 01   ..P...V....RP...
28F9:00F0  87 13 EB 56 C7 06 64 00-01 00 8D 46 F6 16 50 8B   ...V..d....F..P.
-de10
28F9:0E10  00 00 2F 52 45 49 4E 53-54 41 4C 4C 00 2F 42 55   ../REINSTALL./BU
28F9:0E20  46 53 49 5A 45 00 2F 48-49 53 54 4F 52 59 00 2F   FSIZE./HISTORY./
28F9:0E30  48 00 2F 4D 41 43 52 4F-53 00 2F 4D 00 2F 3F 00   H./MACROS./M./?.
28F9:0E40  2F 49 4E 53 45 52 54 00-2F 4F 56 45 52 53 54 52   /INSERT./OVERSTR
28F9:0E50  49 4B 45 00 00 02 0E 1F-0E 07 B4 30 CD 21 3D 05   IKE........0.!=.
28F9:0E60  00 74 06 BA E1 17 E9 C4-01 BE 81 00 E8 99 03 BF   .t..............
28F9:0E70  3D 0E E8 9E 03 74 74 BF-40 0E E8 96 03 74 5C BF   =....tt.@....t\.
28F9:0E80  48 0E E8 8E 03 74 5C BF-12 0E E8 86 03 74 44 BF   H....t\......tD.
-
```

4. To quit Debug, type *q* and press Enter.

As for data files, they're often simple and highly readable in comparison to program files. This is especially true of plain-text ASCII files, which, as described in Chapter 2, contain nothing but readable characters. Such files are created and stored in the universally recognized ASCII "alphabet" so that they can be easily displayed or transported. One example of such a file is README.TXT, which ships with MS-DOS. Because ASCII files are so readable, viewing one is like reading typed output. The following, for example, is the beginning of the README.TXT file that ships with version 6 of MS-DOS:

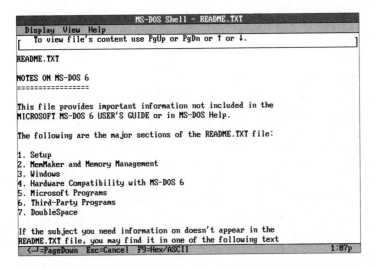

Not all data files are quite so amenable, however. Graphics, charts, spreadsheets, and other data files can be as incomprehensible as program files because they are compressed, specially coded, or contain formatting commands that can be interpreted only by the application that created them. You can see some of this if you have Windows, an application program such as a word processor, or both:

- Use the Type command to display a document you have formatted and saved with an application program. Substitute your own document directory, name, and extension for the path, filename, and extension shown in the following command:

  ```
  C:\>type c:[\path\][filename][.extension]
  ```

  The document formatting will appear as beeps and odd characters intermixed with whatever readable text the Type command can display.

- Use the Type command to display a Windows BMP file. BMP files are bit maps—graphic images—that produce on-screen pictures, such as those on your Windows desktop. For example, to display the HONEY.BMP file, type

  ```
  C:\>type c:\windows\honey.bmp
  ```

File storage

When MS-DOS formats a disk, it divides the disk surface into tracks and sectors, as described in Chapter 8. Sectors are the basic unit of disk storage, just as inches are the basic unit of linear measurement in the United States. When MS-DOS stores a file, however, it does so by filling units called *clusters*. Consisting of one or more sectors, clusters vary in size from one disk to another, but they are always the same size on any particular disk. Depending on disk type and capacity, a single cluster can be as small as one sector (usually 512 bytes) or as large as 32 sequential sectors (16,384 bytes). On floppy disks, a cluster consists of one or two sectors. On a hard disk, a cluster typically covers either 4 sectors (2048 bytes) or 8 sectors (4096 bytes).

Clusters are thus the "bins" into which MS-DOS pours your files when it saves them on disk. Obviously, however, you don't create files by the cluster. Although each file takes up at least one cluster, some files, such as your AUTOEXEC.BAT, can easily be smaller than a single sector. Others, such as a lengthy report, can require dozens of clusters for complete storage. Because neither you nor MS-DOS can predict the final size of a file, MS-DOS allocates clusters to files on an as-needed basis. If a file requires more than one cluster, MS-DOS breaks, or *fragments,* the file into cluster-sized units. (File fragmentation can eventually slow disk-drive performance, but you can deal with this problem easily by running a program such as the version 6 Defrag command; details about this are in Chapter 8.)

Saving files

On a brand-new disk, MS-DOS is able to save files neatly, filling one cluster after the other in an orderly fashion. At this point in the life of a disk, it's easy to think of MS-DOS as comparable to a bottling machine pouring a predetermined amount of, say, milk into an evenly spaced series of same-sized containers.

As the disk becomes used, however, and you begin deleting some files, holes develop where sections of deleted files used to be stored. As these holes develop and you begin saving other files, MS-DOS uses the previously occupied clusters for saving new data. At this point, the situation more closely resembles Donald Duck running back and forth along a conveyor belt, refilling bottles emptied more or less at random by some cartoon nemesis. As a result of all this backing and filling, files become fragmented. Because MS-DOS uses whatever clusters are available, the files can also be widely scattered on the disk surface. Over time, the result is a disk on which more and more files are broken into fragments and stored in nonsequential clusters.

For the most part, file fragmentation doesn't bother you. At most, you might notice that disk accesses take longer. This fragmentation, however, is the reason you're often counseled to use the MS-DOS Copy command to restore order to a much-used floppy disk. The Copy command tracks down the pieces of each copied file, no matter where those pieces are physically located on the disk, and copies them sequentially to the new disk. Diskcopy, in contrast, creates a mirror image of the copied disk, fragmentation and all.

The FAT

As MS-DOS saves and deletes files, it records all its activities in a *File Allocation Table,* or *FAT.* An internal list of disk storage locations and their contents, the FAT is the one part of a disk that belongs wholly to MS-DOS. The FAT is so important that MS-DOS usually keeps a backup copy on the same disk, because it is the only means by which MS-DOS and, therefore, you and your programs, can find and retrieve stored information.

You can think of the FAT as being similar to a numbered list. Except for two lines of "heading" information, the numbered entries in the FAT correspond to clusters on the disk. On a newly formatted disk, each of these cluster-related entries contains a numeric value indicating one of two things: that the cluster is free or that the cluster is bad and should not be used for storage. Essentially, the FAT looks something like this:

FAT entry	Contents	Meaning
0	"Heading"	Disk type
1	"Heading"	Reserved
2	OK	Available
3	OK	Available
4	NO	Damaged
5	OK	Available
6	OK	Available
§		
47	NO	Damaged
48	OK	Available
§		

Now you can envision the way MS-DOS uses the FAT by thinking of how you would follow the clues in a treasure hunt. In this case, however, the "clues" are cluster numbers containing parts of a file, and the "treasure" is a hexadecimal number that tells MS-DOS when it has reached the last cluster containing part of that file.

The starting point in this hunt is the directory entry of the file, where MS-DOS records, in addition to other information, the number of the cluster holding the beginning of the file. This initial clue sends MS-DOS to the entry in the FAT that corresponds to the number of the starting cluster. In that FAT entry, MS-DOS finds another cluster number, which points it to the next entry in the chain listing the file's storage locations on disk. Inspecting one FAT entry at a time, MS-DOS hunts down the cluster numbers containing the file. When it reaches the last cluster, it finds the hexadecimal number (equivalent to END) that marks the end of the chain. Graphically, the process can be illustrated like this:

Directory entry   Starting cluster number

MYFILE.DOC   2

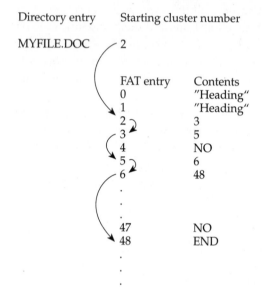

FAT entry   Contents
0   "Heading"
1   "Heading"
2   3
3   5
4   NO
5   6
6   48
.
.
.
47   NO
48   END
.
.
.

As already mentioned, you never deal with the FAT, but understanding how it works can help you understand how MS-DOS deletes files and—more important—why you can undelete some but not others.

When MS-DOS deletes a file, it doesn't go out to the disk and clear out all the clusters in which that file is stored. Rather, it marks the file's directory entry with a special character that makes the file unrecognizable and frees the entry for use in storing information about another file. MS-DOS then goes to the FAT, follows the chain of cluster entries, and frees each of the file's clusters, marking them as again available for use. Until MS-DOS needs the space on the disk, however, the files are still there.

This behavior is what enables Undelete and other file-recovery utilities to track down and restore clusters belonging to "deleted files," that is, if you use the recovery utility before creating or saving too many other files. Once MS-DOS reuses either a file's directory entry or some of the clusters belonging to a deleted file, the deleted information becomes unrecoverable, unless you've had the foresight to run the MS-DOS version 5 Mirror or the version 6 Undelete utility that starts the Delete Sentry or Delete Tracker. (Or, of course, you've started a similar utility that saves deleted files or information about their storage in a protected part of the disk.)

When you work with MS-DOS, you seldom run across references to clusters, but some references can be significant, as you can see from this message, displayed by the MS-DOS Undelete command:

```
** ?ELETED  DOC    12345 8-14-93  2:20a  ...A
Starting cluster is unavailable. This file cannot be recovered
with the UNDELETE command. Press any key to continue.
```

The commands described in the remainder of this chapter all refer to some aspect of file handling with MS-DOS.

Attribute (Attrib)

Any MS-DOS file has certain characteristics, such as size and date and time of creation, that you would consider attributes of the file. MS-DOS also recognizes a set of additional attributes—read-only, archive, system, and hidden—that control access to a file, either by people or by a program such as Microsoft Backup. These attributes can be turned on or off and are stored as part of a file's directory entry. When turned on, they do the following:

- Read-only protects a file or directory from change or deletion by MS-DOS commands.

- Archive indicates, to programs that check for it, that a file has changed since the last backup. Within MS-DOS, you can use the archive attribute with the following programs to control backups and file copies: Ms-backup (available in version 6 only), Restore, and Xcopy.

- System, like the hidden attribute, hides a file from Directory (Dir) and other commands. Whereas the hidden attribute can be applied to any file or directory, system is normally assigned only to special program files that deal with hardware-related operations. Because you can apply it to any type of file, however, the system attribute can be slightly more effective than the more commonly used hidden attribute in keeping files out of sight. Applying the system attribute to a directory does not hide the directory.

- Hidden makes a file or directory invisible to certain MS-DOS commands, such as Dir, Copy, and Del. The hidden attribute offers a simple way to protect information from casual view, but in no way provides real security—especially from people who know how to use MS-DOS.

Command syntax

The syntax for the Attrib command is as follows:

attrib [+ or –*attribute*][*drive*:][*filespec*]/s

+ turns an attribute on, – turns it off.

attribute is one of the following: R for read-only, A for archive, S for system, H for hidden.

drive and *filespec* specify the drive and files for which you want to turn the attribute on or off.

/s extends the Attrib command to include all matching files in all subdirectories of the current or specified directory.

NOTE: To hide and protect its most important files, MS-DOS assigns three attributes— hidden, system, and read-only—to IO.SYS and MSDOS.SYS. The version 6 Xcopy command does not copy files with the hidden and system attributes, so you might remove these attributes temporarily to copy the two MS-DOS files. A more advisable tactic, however, is to use the Sys command or the /S switch of the Format command to transfer these files. Both Sys and Format copy these files without altering their attributes.

Examples

Type:	To:
`C:\SAMPLES>attrib`	Display attributes of all files in the current (SAMPLES) directory.
`C:\FINANCE>attrib +r *.xls`	Apply the read-only attribute to all files with the XLS extension in the current (FINANCE) directory. Opening any of these protected files in Microsoft Excel would produce a message telling the user that the file is read only.
`C:\FINANCE>attrib -r *.xls`	Remove the read-only attribute from all files with the XLS extension in the current (FINANCE) directory. Removing the read-only attribute makes the files available for editing or deletion.
`C:\FINANCE>attrib +a *.xls`	Apply the archive attribute to all files with the XLS extension in the current (FINANCE) directory. This is a useful way of ensuring that the archive attribute is set for a specified group of files you want to copy with: Msbackup (version 6), Xcopy, or Backup (version 5 and earlier).
`C:\PERSONAL>attrib +h c:\personal`	Apply the hidden attribute to the current (PERSONAL) directory. Note that you must specify drive and path to hide a directory; compare the following example.

(continued)

Type:	To:
`C:\PERSONAL>attrib +h /s`	Apply the hidden attribute to all files in the current (PERSONAL) directory and all its subdirectories. This command does not, at the same time, apply the hidden attribute to the current directory or any of its subdirectories.
`C:\PERSONAL>attrib -h *.doc`	Remove the hidden attribute from all files with the DOC extension in the current (PERSONAL) directory. If any or all files have both the hidden and system attributes, attempts to remove either attribute result in an error message such as the following: *Not resetting system file [drive:\path\filename]* or *Not resetting hidden file [drive:\path\filename].* Both attributes must be removed in the same command.

Backup—through version 5 only

Backup, replaced by Msbackup and the Windows Mwbackup utility in version 6 of MS-DOS, is the command you use with earlier versions to archive files. Backup was part of MS-DOS from version 2 through version 5. Although the backup function remained the same, the means used by Backup to accomplish its ends evolved over the years. As a result, before version 5, the wisest approach to the twin procedures of backing up and restoring files was to use the Backup and Restore commands from the same version of MS-DOS.

If you use Backup, bear the following in mind:

- If you back up files to more than one disk, Backup prompts for new disks as required. It also numbers these disks sequentially, so be sure to mark the disks correctly. Restore asks for these disks by number.

- Because Backup has always archived files in a special format, the only way to restore files copied with Backup is the Restore command. You cannot back up with Backup and then restore with Copy or Xcopy.

Backup archives files in special files with the names BACKUP.*nnn* (where *nnn* is a number). It also creates files named CONTROL.*nnn* in which it stores the pathnames of the backed up files. Both Backup files are needed to restore files.

Backup, like other commands, returns an exit code when it terminates. If you run the Backup command from a batch file, you can check for these codes with the errorlevel parameter of the If command and use the code you find to control the outcome of the batch file.

Code	Meaning
0	Success.
1	No files found to back up.
2	File-sharing conflicts prevented backup of some files.
3	Backup was terminated because Ctrl-C was pressed.
4	Backup was terminated because of an error.

Command syntax

The command syntax, parameters, and switches described below are for version 5 of MS-DOS:

backup *source destination* /s /m /a /f[*:size*] /d:*date* /t:*time* /l[*:logfile*]

source is the drive, path, and file specification of the file or files to be backed up. You must specify *source*, but you can specify it as a drive only or as a drive and path. If you include a file specification, you can use wildcards to back up a group of files with one command.

destination is the drive, and only the drive, to which the files are to be backed up. You must specify *destination*.

/s applies the backup to all subdirectories of the specified directory.

/m backs up only changed files and turns off the archive attribute.

/a adds backup files to a backup disk. Normally, Backup deletes all files on the destination disk.

/f[*:size*] formats unformatted backup disks to the capacity specified by *size*. You can enter *size* as one of the following. Be sure to omit spaces if you include *k*, *kb*, and so on:

Disk capacity	Enter as
360 K	*360, 360k, or 360kb*
720 K	*720, 720k, or 720kb*
1.2 MB	*1200, 1200k, 1200kb, 1.2, 1.2m, or 1.2mb*
1.44 MB	*1400, 1400k, 1400kb, 1.44, 1.44m, or 1.44mb*
2.88 MB	*2880, 2880k, 2880kb, 2.88, 2.88m, or 2.88mb*

NOTE: Backup must be able to access the FORMAT.COM file in order to format disks during the backup process.

/d:*date* backs up files modified on or after the date specified by *date*. Use the date format that is normal for your computer or the one that is set by a Country command in CONFIG.SYS. To check the date format, use the Date command at the system prompt.

/t:*time* backs up files modified on or after the time specified by *time*. Use the time format that is normal for your computer or the one that is set by a Country command in CONFIG.SYS. To check the time format, use the Time command at the system prompt.

/l[:*logfile*] creates a log file listing the path and filename of each file in the backup set. If you don't specify *logfile*, Backup assigns the name BACKUP.LOG. The log file is always stored in the root directory of the source drive. New information is added to this file each time you perform a backup.

Examples

Type:	To:
`C:\>backup oldfiles\*.doc a: /s`	Back up all DOC files from the OLDFILES directory and all its subdirectories on drive C to the disk in drive A.
`C:\PLANTS>backup *.* a: /m /a`	Back up all files that have changed from the PLANTS directory on drive C, adding them to the disk in drive A.
`C:\PASTA>backup *.doc` `/d:8-14-93 /s /a`	Back up all DOC files that have changed since 8-14-93 from the PASTA directory and all its subdirectories on drive C, adding them to the disk in drive A.

Compare (Comp)—through version 5 only

The Compare command, originally part of IBM's releases 1.0 and later, appeared in MS-DOS in version 3.3 and disappears once again in version 6. In versions 3.3 through 5, Comp offers a file-comparison alternative to the File Compare (Fc) command, described later. The output of Comp is simpler than that of Fc, but the command itself is less adaptable. Like Fc, however, Comp is best suited to plain-text ASCII files or to binary files, such as executable programs.

Comp matches one file against the other on a byte-by-byte basis and reports on the outcome in one of four ways:

- If the files are the same, both in length and in content, Comp reports

      ```
      Comparing B:FILE1 and B:FILE2...
      Files compare OK

      Compare more files (Y/N) ?
      ```

- If the files are the same length, but the content differs by less than 10 characters, Comp lists where the differing characters appear, showing their positions as offsets (number of characters) from the beginning of the file. Unless you specify ASCII output, Comp gives the hexadecimal values of the characters that differ. The following two side-by-side comparisons show both hexadecimal and ASCII reports for two sample files. The one on the left contains the text *One and two and three and four*; the one on the right reads *One and two and three and five*:

Hexadecimal	ASCII
Comparing B:FOUR and B:FIVE...	Comparing B:FOUR and B:FIVE...
Compare error at OFFSET 1B	Compare error at OFFSET 1B
file1 = 6F	file1 = o
file2 = 69	file2 = i
Compare error at OFFSET 1C	Compare error at OFFSET 1C
file1 = 75	file1 = u
file2 = 76	file2 = v
Compare error at OFFSET 1D	Compare error at OFFSET 1D
file1 = 72	file1 = r
file2 = 65	file2 = e
Compare more files (Y/N) ?	Compare more files (Y/N) ?

- If the files contain 10 or more differing characters, Comp displays the first 10 mismatches with an error report such as the preceding one, but it then ends the comparison like this:

```
§
Compare error at OFFSET 12
file1 = 65
file2 = 73

10 Mismatches - ending compare

Compare more files (Y/N) ?
```

- Finally, if the files are of different sizes, Comp refuses to match them at all and displays the following message:

```
Comparing B:FILE3 and B:FILE4...
Files are different sizes

Compare more files (Y/N) ?
```

Command syntax

The Compare command is always abbreviated Comp. The syntax of the command is as follows:

comp [*file1*] [*file2*] /d /a /l /n=*number* /c

file1 and *file2* are the names of the files to be compared. If the files are not on the current drive or in the current directory, you must include a drive, a path, or both for each file, even if the path to both files is the same. You can use wildcards to compare sets of files. When you do this, Comp pairs the files in set 1 with the files in set 2—that is, it does not compare the first file in set 1 with all files in set 2, and then move on to the next matching file in set 1.

/d displays differences in decimal, rather than the default hexadecimal form.

/a displays differences as ASCII characters, rather than numbers.

/l includes line numbers of differing characters in the output.

/n=*number* compares only the number of lines you specify as *number*.

/c causes the command to ignore differences between uppercase and lowercase in the comparison.

Examples

Type:	To:
`C:\>comp file1 file2`	Compare FILE1 and FILE2, both of which are in the current directory.
`C:\>comp a:is-it.doc b:is-it.doc /d`	Compare the files named IS-IT.DOC on the disks in drives A and B, specifying the output in decimal values.
`C:\>comp maybe.txt a:maybe.txt /a /c`	Compare the file MAYBE.TXT in the current directory with the file of the same name on the disk in drive A, ignoring differences in case and specifying the result in ASCII characters.
`C:\>comp file?.txt b:file?.txt /l`	Compare all TXT files in the current directory that have five-character names beginning with FILE with matching files on the disk in drive B, including line numbers in the output.

Copy

Essentially a means of duplicating information, the Copy command copies files in a number of ways, not only from one disk or directory to another, but to and from devices on your system. For example, MS-DOS users soon learn to copy from the keyboard to a filename to create simple text files. Although it's rarely used in such ways, Copy can also turn your computer into an expensive typewriter by "copying" characters from the keyboard to the printer, and it can combine a set of source files by appending them, one after the other, to a target document.

The Copy command, including all parameters and switches, and its various uses is covered in the following three sections:

- Duplicating files
- Copying to or from a device
- Combining files

NOTE: Except when you combine files, you cannot use the Copy command to copy from multiple subdirectories. For copy procedures that involve different subdirectories or duplicate a directory tree, use the Xcopy command described at the end of this chapter. To move files, use the version 6 Move command, also described later in this chapter.

Duplicating files

Rivaling the Dir command in usefulness, Copy has been an MS-DOS standard since version 1. Copy is more dangerous than Dir, however, both because it actively works with files and because it does not have a built-in safeguard that prevents it from overwriting existing files. To avoid unintentional overwrites with the Copy command, especially when copying from one directory to another, use the Dir command before you copy files. This type of checking can avoid many a misstep if you often use wildcards and you also work with document directories like the following:

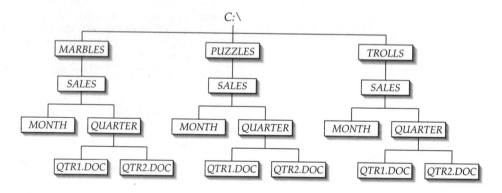

Using the same name for similar files in different directories on the same disk means that the potential for inadvertently overwriting one file with another increases, especially when you're in a hurry. Using the Dir command to check the target directory for matching files puts a check on your impulse to get it over with quickly and protects files with names identical to the ones you plan to copy.

Because copying to a newly formatted disk means that the copied files are stored in consecutive clusters, the Copy command is often recommended as a means of consolidating fragmented files. Consolidating files in this way, however, does not alter the state of affairs on the original disk—nowadays, most likely a hard disk of considerable holding capacity. A much better and far more current method of speeding up access to fragmented files is the version 6 Defrag command (or a defragging utility), either of which will clean up fragmentation on the original disk.

Command syntax

For duplicating files, the form of the Copy command is as follows:

copy [/A or /B] *source* [/A or /B][*destination*][/A or /B] /V

source is the name of the file or files to be copied. You can include a drive, path, or both, and you can use wildcards to specify a set of files.

destination is the disk or directory to which you want to copy the files named as *source*. You can include a drive, path, filename, or some combination of the three. You can also use wildcards to change the names of the copied files. For example, you could change all extensions from DOC to TXT at the destination disk or directory.

To copy to the current drive or directory, omit *destination*, but be sure to specify *source* as a different disk or directory. MS-DOS does not allow you to copy a file to itself. If you attempt this by omitting *destination* or by specifying *source* and *destination* as the same file, MS-DOS refuses to make the copy and displays the following message:

```
File cannot be copied onto itself
        0 file(s) copied
```

/V verifies that the file or files are copied correctly.

/A and /B are switches that indicate file format: /A for ASCII and /B for binary (program code). The /A switch causes Copy to stop reading when it reaches an end-of-file character; /B causes Copy to read the number of bytes specified in the file's directory entry. If you use /B when sending a file to a device, control characters, such as ^Z are treated as data, rather than as device-control signals. If you don't include one of these switches, Copy assumes /A when combining files and copying to a device, /B otherwise. You can't use the /A and /B switches together in the same position.

The /A and /B switches are enormously confusing, because you can put them almost anywhere in the command line, and their position affects what they do. Basically, however, they work as shown in the table on the next page.

Switch precedes filename	Switch follows filename
/A copies up to, but does not include, the first end-of-file character (^Z).	/A adds an end-of-file character to the copied file.
/B copies up to and includes the end-of-file character.	/B does not add an end-of-file character.
/A applies to all files until /B; /B then applies to the preceding file and all following filenames until /A is encountered.	/A applies to the preceding file and all following filenames until /B; /B then applies to the preceding file and all following filenames until /A.
/B is as above, but with /B where /A appears and vice versa.	/B is as above, but with /B where /A appears and vice versa.

If you are now thoroughly confused about the /A and /B switches, a rough rule of thumb to follow is this: If in doubt, leave it out—except when you are working with files containing ^Z and other control characters. To include control characters as data, use the /B switch.

Examples

Type:	To:
`C:\>copy a:readme.txt`	Copy README.TXT from the disk in drive A to the current directory. No destination is necessary because MS-DOS copies to the current directory by default.
`C:\>copy readme.txt a:`	Copy README.TXT from the current directory on drive C to the disk in drive A. Note the colon in *a:*. If you omit the colon, MS-DOS copies the file to a new file named A in the current directory.
`C:\NEWDIR>copy a:*.*`	Copy all files from the disk in drive A to the current (NEWDIR) directory.
`C:\FINANCE>copy qtr?.xls reports`	Copy all XLS files with four-character names beginning with QTR from the current (FINANCE) directory to the FINANCE\REPORTS subdirectory.
`C:\FINANCE>copy qtr?.xls \reports`	Copy all XLS files as in the preceding example, but to the REPORTS directory of the root directory on drive C. Note the \, which indicates that REPORTS is not in the current directory.
`C:\HOTDOGS>copy a:deli?.doc *.txt`	Copy all DOC files on drive A with four-character filenames beginning with DELI to the current directory (HOTDOGS) on drive C, changing all extensions to TXT in the process.

Copying to or from a device

MS-DOS can copy files to and from various input and output devices on the system. The primary input device is the keyboard, CON, and the primary output device is the screen, also CON. Other devices you can use are the printer (PRN or LPT1) and the system bit bucket (NUL). Auxiliary input/output (AUX or COM1), which is usually a modem, is also a possibility, but it is best left alone. Modems need to be set up properly, and communications programs are much more adept and accurate than a simple Copy command could be.

NOTE: You might recall that MS-DOS recognizes one other default device, CLOCK$. Leave it alone. Copying from the clock is useless; copying to it will cause errors and throw system timekeeping out the window.

Command syntax

For copying files to a device, the command form is as follows:

copy *filespec device*

For copying from a device to a file, the command form is as follows:

copy *device filespec*

In both instances:

filespec is the name of the file to copy from or to. You must include at least a filename; drive and path are optional. Note that copying to a file that already exists overwrites the original file.

device is the name of the device to copy from or to—for example, con or prn. The most common forms of copying to or from devices are as follows:

- From the keyboard to a file on disk. This is fast, simple, and often used for creating short text files. You are not using a text editor, however, so the only corrections allowed are backspacing and retyping. You cannot change any line after you end it by pressing Enter. To end a file created in this way, press the F6 key or Ctrl-Z. Either adds an end-of-file character (^Z) to the file and signals MS-DOS that text entry is complete.

- From the keyboard to the printer. This puts your computer in typewriter mode until you press F6 or Ctrl-Z to end the copy process. You could presumably use this procedure to print short notes, but as with copying from the keyboard to a file, no editing beyond backspacing and retyping is possible. Also, if you use a printer such as the HP LaserJet, you'll probably find that the printer does not automatically eject the page when you finish. To produce the hard copy, you can either take the printer off line and press the formfeed button, or you can press the ASCII control code, Ctrl-L, to insert the command for a formfeed wherever you want a new page in the file.

■ From a file to the printer. This use of the Copy command sends the contents of a disk file directly to the printer. Essentially a workaround that omits the MS-DOS Print command, copying from a file to the printer can produce unexpected results if you try to print anything other than a plain ASCII document. Even a short file created and saved as a formatted (non-ASCII) file will contain application-specific formatting and other internal coding that produces odd characters and strange line breaks or page breaks. Lines can also run off the right edge. Windows TrueType fonts emerge as complete gobbledygook on the printed page.

Examples

Type:	To:
`C:\>copy con testfile` *Type something interesting here*^Z [Enter]	Copy the italicized text from the keyboard to a file named TESTFILE in the current (root) directory of the current drive. The ^Z shown here is what you see when you press F6 or Ctrl-Z to end the file.
`C:\>copy con prn` *Here we go a-typing, a-typing. Here we go a-typing to see what we shall see.* ^L^Z [Enter]	Copy the italicized text from the keyboard to the printer. The ^L represents pressing Ctrl-L to eject the page. The ^Z is as described previously.
`C:\>copy testfile prn`	Copy TESTFILE to the printer.
`C:\>copy testfile nul`	To send the contents of TESTFILE to the NUL device. Nothing visible happens, but the file is, indeed, sent to NUL. Not a particularly earthshaking event.

Combining files

When you use the Copy command to combine files, you set in motion the process known as concatenation—literally, the joining of separate items by appending one to the other. Combining files, more than other uses of Copy, can produce unintended results and consequent destruction of an existing file if you don't think the command through before pressing Enter. As described and illustrated below, the way in which you use the command, and the order in which you list the files, determines whether the combined files will be appended to or will overwrite an existing file.

Command syntax

To use wildcards to combine several files into a single destination file, use the following command format:

copy [/A or /B] *sources* [/A or /B] *destination*

sources is the file specification, using wildcards, of the files to combine. You can include a drive and path, if appropriate.

destination is the name of the file in which to combine the files. You can include a drive, path, or both, but you must specify a filename. If the destination file does not exist, MS-DOS creates it. If the file does exist, MS-DOS overwrites its contents with those of the combined files. To ensure no loss of data with this form of the command, use the Dir command to check for the destination filename before using the Copy command.

/A and /B are as described earlier under "Duplicating files."

To combine files with different filenames or to combine files from different drives, directories, or both, use the following command format:

copy [/A or /B] *source1* [/A or /B] + *source2* [/A or /B] +...*sourceN* [/A or /B]
   [*destination*] /V

source1, source2...sourceN are the files to be combined. You can include a different drive and path for each. If you want to add files to an existing file, list that file as *source1* and omit *destination*. This is important because the order of the files causes the copy to proceed in this order:

copy A + B + C + D

destination is the file into which you want to combine the source files. If the file does not exist, MS-DOS creates it. If the file does exist, MS-DOS overwrites its contents.

/A and /B are as described earlier under "Duplicating files."

Examples

Type:	To:
C:\COMBOS>copy a:dinner?.doc menu	Combine all DOC files on the disk in drive A with seven-character filenames beginning with DINNER into the file MENU in the current directory (COMBOS) on drive C.
C:\>copy a:taco+a:burrito+a:tamale c:\combos\menu	Combine the files TACO, BURRITO, and TAMALE on the disk in drive A in the file MENU in the COMBOS subdirectory on drive C.
C:\ALLOFIT>copy c:\moon\luna.doc+ c:\space\stars.doc+c:\planets\ earth.doc stellar.doc	Combine the files LUNA.DOC, STARS.DOC, and EARTH.DOC from three different directories into the file STELLAR.DOC in the ALLOFIT directory on drive C.

(continued)

Type:	To:
`C:\>copy trio+one+two+three`	Add the files ONE, TWO, and THREE, in that order, to the file TRIO.

`C:\PROGS>copy /b module1.prg+`
`    module2.prg+module3.prg`
`    program.prg`
	Combine modules 1, 2, and 3 into the file named PROGRAM.PRG, treating each as binary files.

Delete (Del)

Part of MS-DOS since version 1, the Delete command, also known as Erase, has chugged along with only one real change over the years—the addition of a /p switch in version 4 that causes MS-DOS to prompt for confirmation before deleting files. Although it is much less dangerous now than in the days before Undelete, the Del command is still a tool to be used with care, especially with wildcards, primarily because file recovery cannot always be guaranteed. The Delete Sentry feature in version 6 makes recovery almost foolproof by copying deleted files to a hidden directory, but if you rely on delete-tracking or, especially, on the records kept by MS-DOS in directory entries and the FAT, you could find that a recently deleted file has become unrecoverable, sometimes merely because you saved a small file in the time between deletion and your attempted undelete.

Although long practice with MS-DOS makes for few mistakes, every user of MS-DOS eventually presses Enter a little too soon after typing a Del command with a file specification including wildcards. At such times, it's very easy to overlook the one or two files you need in a directory full of files you want to eliminate, but you can guard against such losses easily. Before you delete the files, use the Dir command with the file specification you intend to use. If Dir doesn't list any surprises, go ahead with your Del command. If you go through the Dir/Del process often enough (in version 6), you might want to automate the procedure with a small batch file like the following:

```
@echo off
dir %1 /on /w /p
choice /c:yn OK to delete<space>
if errorlevel==2 goto quit
if errorlevel==1 goto delete
:delete
del %1
echo Done
:quit
```

In addition to straightforward deletions, the Del command has served long and well as the second half of a "move" command, which was missing from MS-DOS until version 6.

Command syntax

The form of the Del command is simple:

del *filespec* /p

filespec is the name of the file or files to delete. You can include a drive and path, and you can use wildcards. Unless you include the /p switch, MS-DOS carries out the Del command immediately. The only exception to this occurs if you type the wildcard specification *.* for *filespec*, meaning all files. In this one instance, MS-DOS prompts for confirmation before carrying out the deletion:

```
All files in directory will be deleted!
Are you sure (Y/N)?
```

If you're sure you want to delete all the files in a directory, and all files have the same extension, such as DOC, you can type *del *.doc* instead of *del *.* * and MS-DOS will skip the *Are you sure* message. The situation might not happen very often. Then again, if you create and use a lot of document directories, you might find that this approach shaves a second or two off the deletion process. Be sure, of course, that you know what you're deleting.

/p tells MS-DOS to prompt before deleting each file by displaying a message like this:

```
C:\BOGUS\TEST,    Delete (Y/N)?
```

Type Y to delete the file, N to skip and go on to the next file (if any) that matches the file specification you typed.

Examples

Type:	To:

`C:\OLDSTUFF>del *.*`
or
`C:\OLDSTUFF>erase *.*`
	Delete all files in the OLDSTUFF directory.

`C:\NEWSTUFF>del *.bak`
or
`C:\NEWSTUFF>erase *.bak`
	Delete all backup (BAK) files in the NEWSTUFF directory.

`C:\MIXED-UP>del *.doc /p`
or
`C:\MIXED-UP>erase *.doc /p`
	Delete files with the DOC extension, prompting for confirmation, from the MIXED-UP directory.

`C:\>del a:\candy\fudge.old`
or
`C:\>erase a:\candy\fudge.old`
	Delete the FUDGE.OLD file from the CANDY directory on the disk in drive A.

Expand

The Expand command is used for decompressing MS-DOS files when you need to transfer them from the original MS-DOS disks to the disk from which you run MS-DOS. Expand "expands" MS-DOS files from the space-saving compressed form in which they are shipped to the machine-usable form in which they must reside in your DOS directory. Use Expand in the following circumstances:

- You accidentally delete or damage an MS-DOS file.

- You deleted or chose not to install some MS-DOS files, such as Backup for Windows or RAMDRIVE.SYS, because you did not expect to use them and needed space on your hard disk.

Although MS-DOS is shipped on several floppy disks, you don't have to scan them all to find the compressed form of the file you want to expand. Insert Setup disk 1 in your floppy-disk drive and display the text file named PACKING.LST with the following command:

```
C:\>type a:packing.lst ¦ more
```

The file lists the contents of each disk.

As you can see by scanning PACKING.LST, the compressed files on your MS-DOS disks all have extensions ending with an underscore, like this: COM-MAND.CO_. During expansion, files are not only "fattened up" and moved to the disk and directory you specify, the underscore is replaced by the character that turns the compressed version into a normal filename extension. MS-DOS does not have a way of determining what the real extension ought to be, so you must provide the third character of the extension—a simple matter when you're changing CO_ to COM or EX_ to EXE, but not quite so easy to recall when you need to turn CP_ into CPI or VI_ into VID. Here again, rely on the information in PACKING.LST.

Command syntax

When you expand files, you can take the easy way out and let MS-DOS prompt you through the procedure. When you do this, the syntax of the Expand command is simply as follows:

```
expand
```

After you press Enter, MS-DOS first prompts you for the name of the file to expand, like this:

```
Type the location and name of the
compressed file you want to expand.
(Example: A:\EGA.SY_)

Compressed file: _
```

and then prompts for the destination, like this:

```
Type the location and/or name you
want to give the expanded file.
(Example: C:\DOS\EGA.SYS)

Expanded file: _
```

Respond to each prompt as appropriate, and within a few seconds, the uncompressed version of the file will reside in (presumably) your DOS directory.

If you prefer, or if you have several files to expand at the same time, you can make the process faster by using the following syntax:

expand *filespec1 filespec2...filespecN destination*

filespec1 filespec2...filespecN are the drive and file specifications of one or more files to decompress. Expand does not allow the use of wildcards in filenames.

destination is the name of the decompressed file. This should be identical to the name of the compressed file, but with the extension (such as EX_) changed to the recognizable MS-DOS extension (such as EXE). You can specify destination only if you specify a single compressed file.

Examples

Type:	To:
`C:\>expand`	Have MS-DOS prompt you through the expansion of a single file.
`C:\>expand a:help.ex_ c:\dos\help.exe`	Expand the help file in drive A and place it in the DOS directory on drive C.
`C:\DOS>expand a:ramdrive.sy_` `    a:smartdrv.sy_`	Expand the RAMDRIVE and SMARTDRV device drivers in drive A, placing them in the current (DOS) directory as RAMDRIVE.SY_ and SMARTDRV.SY_.
`C:\DOS>ren *.sy_ *.sys`	Rename the expanded files to RAMDRIVE.SYS and SMARTDRV.SYS.

Fastopen

The Fastopen command installs a small, memory-resident program that can speed up disk access by recording the storage locations of recently opened files in a set-aside portion of memory known as the *name cache*. When Fastopen is running, MS-DOS checks the name cache whenever you open a file. If the file was opened earlier in the session, the name cache will contain a record of its storage location on disk, and MS-DOS can go directly to the appropriate disk location to begin reading the file into memory once again. Fastopen does not store actual file contents in memory, as do SMARTDRV and other disk-caching programs, but by storing file locations in fast-access memory, it can speed up applications, such as databases, that frequently open and close the same files.

One of the MS-DOS tools you can use to optimize a computer, Fastopen is a try-it-and-see type of program, as are commands such as Loadhigh and Devicehigh. There are no hard-and-fast rules about what to do and when, so experimenting with Fastopen on your own system will tell you more about its usefulness than any set of instructions can. If you are considering Fastopen, bear the following in mind:

- Fastopen works only with hard disks, but you can use it to track files on up to 24 disk partitions (a lot).

- Fastopen cannot be used on a network.

- Fastopen is really most useful with applications that access the same files repeatedly. In other situations, increasing the number of buffers specified in CONFIG.SYS or loading SMARTDRV might prove much more effective. Also of note: You're unlikely to need both Fastopen and SMARTDRV.

- Fastopen cannot be used with the MS-DOS Shell. If you try this, your system can lock up and require rebooting.

- Fastopen does require memory—about 3 K for itself, plus an additional 48 bytes for each file specified by the n parameter, described below. If you can, maximize available conventional memory by loading Fastopen into upper memory (with the Loadhigh command) or expanded memory (with the /x switch, also described below).

Command syntax

Fastopen can be loaded in one of three ways. Use one form only; you cannot, and should not, load multiple copies of Fastopen. (Descriptions of parameters and switches follow the three formats shown below.)

From the command line (or AUTOEXEC.BAT), use the following form:

fastopen *drive:*[=*n*] [*drive:*][=*n*]... /x

You can also use the following form on an 80386 or better system with available upper memory blocks. (If you have version 6 of MS-DOS, use the Mem command to check on upper memory.) From either the command line or AUTOEXEC.BAT, use the following form:

lh fastopen *drive:*[=*n*] [*drive:*][=*n*]... /x

To save a small amount of memory, use the following form in CONFIG.SYS:

install=[*dosdrive:*][*/dospath/*]fastopen.exe *drive:*[=*n*] [*drive:*][=*n*]...*/x*

drive: is the drive letter, plus a colon, of the hard disk on which you want to track files. You must include at least one drive, but can optionally include others in the same command.

n is the number of files you want to track. Allowable values are from 10 through 999. Bear in mind that each file requires 48 bytes of memory. A large number can require a significant amount of memory—24,000 bytes, for example, if you specify 500 files.

dosdrive: and *dospath*, used only from CONFIG.SYS, are the drive and path of the disk and directory in which FASTOPEN.EXE is stored.

/x specifies that the name cache is to be created in expanded memory. Using expanded memory reduces conventional memory usage to approximately 1 K.

Examples

Type:	To:
`C:\>fastopen c:=20 d:=20`	Install Fastopen in conventional memory, tracking 20 files each on hard drives C and D.

Include in AUTOEXEC.BAT:	To:
`lh fastopen c:=20 d:=20 /x`	Load Fastopen into upper memory blocks, tracking 20 files each on hard drives C and D and creating the name cache in expanded memory.

Include in CONFIG.SYS:	To:
`install=c:\dos\fastopen.exe` `    c:=20 d:=20`	Load Fastopen as above, but from CONFIG.SYS. (Substitute the drive and path of your own DOS directory, if necessary.)

File Compare (Fc)

The File Compare command, typed in the abbreviated form *fc*, compares the contents of two files to determine whether they are the same or different. You can compare either ASCII or binary files. During a comparison, MS-DOS sets aside a buffer large enough to hold 100 lines of the file. If you are comparing ASCII files, MS-DOS searches for a match within those first 100 lines. If enough matches are found to continue the comparison, MS-DOS reads the remainder of the file into memory. If no match is found, the comparison ends with the message

`Resynch failed. Files are too different.`

If you are comparing binary files, MS-DOS compares both files completely, reading additional portions into memory as necessary.

Both the comparison itself and the output of the command can vary, depending on the type of files compared (ASCII or binary) and the switches used. The output of a simple ASCII comparison without switches, however, can give you pause if the files differ substantially, but not enough to end the comparison. The reason for this is the way MS-DOS displays differences in the files (here called FILE1 and FILE2):

- At the start of the comparison, you see a series of asterisks and the name of FILE1, like this: ***** FILE1.
- Below this, you see the last line that matched in both files.
- Below this, you see the lines from FILE1 that (1) follow the last matching line, but (2) differ from the lines that follow the last matching line in FILE2.
- At the end of this, you see the first line in FILE1 that once again matches a line in FILE2.

So far, so good, although these lines are not identified, so you must remember that the first line you see represents the last match and the last line you see represents the first of a new match. Now, however, the situation becomes complicated, because MS-DOS repeats the process for FILE2, displaying, in this order:

- A series of asterisks and the name of FILE2.
- The last line in FILE2 that matched a line in FILE1.
- All the lines in FILE2 that follow the last matching line but differ from lines in FILE1.
- The first line in FILE2 that once again matched a line in FILE1.

If more of the files remain, MS-DOS then repeats the process as many times as necessary. Now if you're confused, here's a way to help it all make sense. If the files are long and you know that they will differ only slightly, stop the output after each screenful with the More command, like this:

`C:\>fc file1 file2 ¦ more`

If the files are long and you don't know what you'll find, send the output to the printer and compare the printed output with a command like this:

`C:\>fc file1 file2 > prn`

In contrast to all this, the output of a binary comparison is simple and easy to read. Suppose, for example, you have the following small batch files:

```
@echo off          @echo off
mode con lines=43  mode con lines=25
cls                cls
```

The only difference is in line 2, in the twenty-sixth and twenty-seventh characters from the beginning. If you perform a binary comparison of the two, the output looks like this:

```
Comparing files FILE1.BAT and FILE2.BAT
0000001A: 34 32
0000001B: 33 35
```

If you have a hexadecimal table and an ASCII table handy, you can interpret this in a breeze:

- 1A is hexadecimal for decimal 26, meaning that the first difference occurs at the twenty-sixth position from the start of the two files. The numbers 34 and 32 give you the hexadecimal values for the characters that differ in the two files: 34 corresponding to the ASCII value of the numeral 4 in FILE1, and 32 for the ASCII value of the numeral 2 in FILE2.

- 1B shows the same type of information for the twenty-seventh character from the beginning: The ASCII character equivalent to hexadecimal 33 is the numeral 3; the ASCII character equivalent to hexadecimal 35 is 5.

Command syntax

To compare ASCII files, use the following format:

fc /a /c /l /lbN /n /t /w /nnnn [drive:][path]file1 [drive:][path]file2

/a, for abbreviate, shortens the output of the command by displaying only the first and last matching lines in each set of differences.

/c, for case, signals MS-DOS to ignore differences between uppercase and lowercase, essentially treating B and b as the same character.

/l, for line (or line-by-line) compares the two files one line at a time and seeks what is called a resynchronization—a set of matching lines—after each mismatch. This is the default setting for an ASCII comparison and produces the output described above.

/lbN, for line buffer, lets you set the number of lines, N, to be read into the buffer. The default is 100 lines.

/n, for number, displays line numbers.

/t, for tabs, leaves tab characters rather than replacing them with spaces. By default, MS-DOS assumes eight spaces per tab stop.

/w, for white space, compresses tabs and multiple consecutive spaces within lines into single spaces. White space at the beginning and end of a line are ignored.

/nnnn is a number you specify to set to number of lines that must match for the files to be considered resynchronized. The default is 2 lines.

drive: and *path* are optional and represent the drive and path for each file to be compared. If the files are not in the current directory, you must specify the drive and path for each.

file1 and *file2*, the only required parameters, are the names of the files to be compared. You can use wildcards as part of the filenames. If you use the asterisk wildcard as part of *file1*, MS-DOS compares each matching file to *file2*; if you use the asterisk as part of *file2*, MS-DOS compares *file1* to each match it finds for *file2*.

For a binary comparison, use the following form:

fc /b [*drive:*][*path*] *file1* [*drive:*][*path*] *file2*

/b signals a binary comparison.

drive:, *path*, *file1*, and *file2* are the same as described for the previous form.

Examples

Type:	To:
`C:\RHYMES>fc cat.doc mat.doc`	Compare the files CAT.DOC and MAT.DOC, both in the current directory of the current drive.
`C:\>fc /c a:*.lst c:\pals\phone.lst`	Compare all LST files on the disk in drive A with PHONE.LST in the PALS directory on drive C, ignoring differences in case.
`C:\VERBOSE>fc /a` `    /n longdoc.one longdoc.two`	Compare LONGDOC.ONE and LONGDOC.TWO in the VERBOSE directory on drive C, abbreviating the output to show only first and last matching lines and including line numbers in the output.
`C:\PICKY>fc /4 a:*.doc same.doc`	Compare all DOC files on the disk in drive A with SAME.DOC in the PICKY directory, stipulating that four consecutive lines must match before the files can be considered resynchronized.
`C:\>fc /b c:\dos\format.com` `    a:format.com`	Make a binary comparison of FORMAT.COM on the disk in drive A with the same file in the DOS directory on drive C.

Interlnk—version 6 only

The Interlnk command is one of three interlocking pieces of MS-DOS version 6—known collectively as Interlnk—that enable you to set up a small but functional mininetwork between two computers. With Interlnk, you can transfer files from one computer to the other and, if you wish, you can use one computer to run a program installed on the other. The Interlnk command, along with its related IN-TERLNK.EXE device driver and the Intersvr file server (both described in this chapter), give you an electronic alternative to what is sometimes called sneakernet—file transfer via floppy disk. More than such basic convenience, however, Interlnk and company serve admirably as a means of passing information between computers with incompatible floppy drive sizes, and they allow you to link one computer, such as your desktop machine, with another, such as a laptop model, to streamline your own work and make it more efficient.

Interlnk, the feature, is easy to use after you set it up on both computers, but because it relies on hardware, three software components, and some networking terminology, it is not necessarily easy to set up the first time around. This rather extended command description covers what you need, how the pieces are related, what the terms refer to, and—perhaps most important—what the basic procedures are.

Before you start, you need to make sure you have a free serial or parallel port on each computer. To connect the ports, you need a cable—either a null modem (basically a serial cable, but with the sending and receiving wires crossed so that information can travel in two directions) or a bidirectional parallel cable. A null modem cable, which was used for testing Interlnk for this book, is quite inexpensive. You'll probably have to call around to computer hardware outlets, and you might have to invest in additional connectors to match the cable to your serial ports, but you should be able to locate a null modem cable for less than $10.

After you cable your computers together, you can install and run Interlnk, as follows:

1. You set up the computer that is to supply programs and files (the server) by running the server program, Intersvr, with the following command:

   ```
   C:\>intersvr
   ```

   If the server is equipped with version 6 of MS-DOS, no preparation is needed before you enter the command. If the server is running an earlier version of MS-DOS, however, you must transfer the Interlnk files to it. For this, you can use a floppy disk with the files on it or, if the computers are already cabled together and you've set up the sending computer, as described later, you can use the /rcopy switch of the Intersvr command. (For more details, refer to the description of Intersvr later in this chapter.)

2. Set up the computer that is to receive files (the client). The first time you use Interlnk, this setup involves modifying CONFIG.SYS and rebooting the computer to install the INTERLNK.EXE device driver. The basic CONFIG.SYS command you need is a line like the following:

   ```
   DEVICE=C:\DOS\INTERLNK.EXE
   ```

Interlnk makes file transfer possible by matching drive letters on the client computer to drives on the server. Thus, if you want to use three drives (say, A, B, and C) on the server, the client computer must have at least three drive letters available in addition to those used for installed drives, RAM drives, network drives, and so on. Be sure the CONFIG.SYS file on the client contains a Lastdrive command that specifies a drive letter high enough to accommodate all the drive letters you need. (For more details on the INTERLNK.EXE device driver, refer to the description of INTERLNK.EXE later in this chapter.)

3. After INTERLNK.EXE is installed, you set up the client computer by running the Interlnk command. The basic command is as follows:

    `C:\>interlnk`

    The Interlnk command makes it possible for the client computer to access files, programs, and printer ports on the server.

After you've set up the computers to share resources, what then? Once setup is complete, sharing resources involves a simple three-step procedure very similar to the setup already described.

1. Run Intersvr on the server. This enables the server to provide files and other resources. When you type *intersvr* to start the server program, the following screen appears:

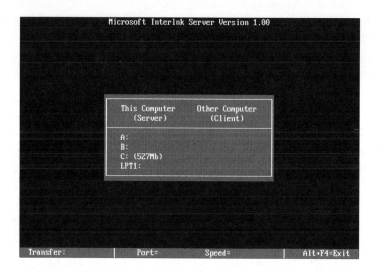

This display means that the server is out of commission—as an independent computer—until you finish using Intersvr. While the server program is running, however, you can use the client computer to access any of the drives or printer ports shown in the Intersvr report.

2. Run Interlnk on the client. This enables the client to use the files, programs, and ports provided by Intersvr. When you start Interlnk on the
client, you see a display very similar to the one shown above:

```
Port=COM1

This Computer          Other Computer
  (Client)               (Server)
- - - - - - - - - - - -   - - - - - - - - - - - - - - - - - - - - - - - -
  K:     equals   A:
  L:     equals   B:
  M:     equals   C: (527MB) CAPPYS PC
  LPT2: equals    LPT1:
```

This report is telling you that drive K on the client computer is redirected (roughly, linked) to drive A on the server, that drive L on the
client is redirected to drive B on the server, that drive M on the client is
redirected to drive C on the server, and that port LPT2 on the client is
redirected to LPT1 on the server. (The text *CAPPYS PC* in the sample
message represents the volume label assigned to the 527 MB drive C on
the server.)

3. Change the current drive on the client to the letter corresponding to the
drive on the server that you want to use. This enables the client computer to use files and other resources on the server. From this point on,
you can use the server drive as if it were on the client. Thus, in the example, if you were to change the current drive to M, the command

```
M:\>dir
```

would produce a directory listing of all the files and directories in drive
C on the server because drive C would be the server equivalent of client
drive M.

*NOTE: If Intersvr is not running on your server at the time you boot the client or run
Interlnk, you'll see the message* Connection NOT established. *Don't worry about this.
The message simply means that Interlnk could not find its partner, Intersvr. When you
start Intersvr on the server, run Interlnk again. The connection will be neatly established.*

Do not use Interlnk with the following commands: Chkdsk, Defrag,
Diskcomp, Diskcopy, Fdisk, Format, Mirror, Sys, Undelete, and Unformat.

Command syntax

The syntax of the Interlnk command takes two forms. To specify the drives you
want to affect, the syntax is as follows:

interlnk *client:=server:*

To see the status of resource sharing, the syntax is simple:

interlnk

client: is the letter of the client drive that you want to redirect to a drive on the server. The drive must be one that appears on the Interlnk and Intersvr reports. Include this parameter when you want to link a specific drive letter with a particular server drive. To cancel redirection of a client drive, include *client:* and an equal sign.

server: is the letter of the server drive that you want linked to the client drive. Again, the drive must be one that appears on the Interlnk and Intersvr reports.

As mentioned earlier, the Interlnk command, typed without parameters, starts Interlnk if it is not already started and produces a report on redirected drives and printer ports.

Examples

Type:	To:
`C:\>intersvr`	Start resource sharing on the server computer.
`C:\>interlnk`	Start resource sharing on the client computer.
`C:\>interlnk q:=c:`	Start Interlnk and redirect drive letter Q to server drive C.
`C:\>interlnk q:=`	Cancel redirection of drive letter Q to the server.

INTERLNK.EXE—version 6 only

INTERLNK.EXE is the device driver that enables a client computer to share resources on a server running the Intersvr program. Because INTERLNK.EXE is a device driver, you must install it with a Device command in CONFIG.SYS before you can make use of resource sharing.

By default, INTERLNK.EXE loads into upper memory, if use of UMBs has been enabled and there is enough room for this rather large (8 K to 9 K) program. This hefty amount of memory is required because INTERLNK.EXE scans all available ports by default and so must load all of itself into memory. To save some memory, narrow the scope of the driver's activities with the following switches (described in more detail later):

- Include the /com switch to eliminate support for parallel ports.

- Include the /lpt switch to eliminate support for serial ports.

- Include the /noprinter switch to eliminate support for printer redirection.

When including a device command for INTERLNK.EXE in CONFIG.SYS, follow two rules: First, be sure CONFIG.SYS includes a Lastdrive command that specifies a last drive letter high enough to accommodate all drives on the system, including RAM drives and network drives. Second, load INTERLNK.EXE *after* other commands, such as one creating a RAM drive, that assign drive letters. MS-DOS assigns drive letters in the order in which these commands appear in CON-FIG.SYS. To ensure that drive redirection does not alter your normal activities and possibly invalidate batch files and macros, load INTERLNK.EXE at or near the end of CONFIG.SYS.

NOTE: The online Help notes for INTERLNK.EXE cover several special circumstances you might want or need to check into. Refer to online Help if you are using Windows or a Microsoft mouse, or if the server is running a version of MS-DOS earlier than 6.

Command syntax

The syntax of the Device command that loads INTERLNK.EXE is as follows:

> device=[*drive:*][*path*]INTERLNK.EXE /drives:*number* /noprinter /com[:*number*
> or *address*] /lpt[:*number* or *address*] /auto /noscan /low /baud:*rate* /v

drive: and *path* are the drive and path to the directory containing INTER-LNK.EXE, most probably the DOS directory on your startup drive.

/drives:*number* specifies the number of drives on the client that you want re-directed to the server. By default, three drives are redirected (typically, A, B, and C). Use this switch if you want to specify a different number. Specify *number* as 0 if you want to redirect printers only.

/noprinter eliminates redirection of printer ports. By default, all printer ports are redirected.

/com:*number* or *address* specifies the COM (serial) port used for connecting the client to the server. Specify *number* as 1, 2, 3, or 4 as appropriate for your com-puter. If you specify *address* instead, specify the four-digit hexadecimal number (such as 03F8H) representing the address of the COM port you want to use. You can see the number and addresses of your COM ports by running the Microsoft Diagnostics utility (type *msd*) and choosing COM Ports from the list of options displayed. If you use the /com switch without specifying a number or an address, Interlnk will scan all COM ports until it finds the one connecting the client to the server. By default, Interlnk scans all COM and LPT ports. By including the /com switch and omitting the /lpt switch, you limit the scan to COM ports only. The colon between /com and *number* or *address* is optional.

/lpt:*number* or *address* is similar to the /com switch, except that it applies to LPT (parallel) ports only. Specify *number* as the number of the LPT port connect-ing the client to the server; valid values are 1, 2, and 3. Specify *address* as the hexa-decimal value representing the address of the LPT port you want to use. Limit the Interlnk scan to LPT ports only by including the /lpt switch and omitting the /com switch. The colon between /lpt and *number* or *address* is optional.

/auto installs INTERLNK.EXE in memory only if the client can connect to the server at startup—that is, only if the server is running Intersvr at the time the client is booted. Use the /auto switch if you want to save memory by loading INTERLNK.EXE only when the server is running. By default, INTERLNK.EXE loads into memory at startup whether or not it can establish a connection to the server. The /auto switch, like the /noscan switch, can add a little extra control to a multi-configuration CONFIG.SYS file.

/noscan installs INTERLNK.EXE in memory without attempting to establish a connection at the time of installation. Like /auto, the /noscan switch will avoid the *Connection NOT established* message if you start the client when Intersvr is not running on the server. Unlike /auto, the /noscan switch would not save memory. Its advantage over /auto, however, is that you would not have to reboot the client in order to install INTERLNK.EXE.

/low loads INTERLNK.EXE into low (conventional) memory, rather than in available UMBs, as happens by default.

/baud:*rate* sets the maximum rate of transmission between the client and the server. The default, as you can see on the bottom of the report screen produced by Intersvr, is 115200. Other valid values for *rate* are 9600, 19200, 38400, and 57600.

/v prevents conflicts with the timer (not the date/time clock) built into each system. Use this switch if the client or server stops running when Interlnk accesses a drive or port.

Examples

Include in CONFIG.SYS:	To:
`DEVICE=C:\DOS\INTERLNK.EXE`	Install INTERLNK.EXE with all defaults—in the upper memory area if possible, with the ability to scan all serial and parallel ports for a connection to the server, and with the ability to redirect printer ports.
`DEVICE=C:\DOS\INTERLNK.EXE /COM:1` `/NOPRINTER`	Install INTERLNK.EXE for COM:1 only, avoiding redirection of printer ports.
`DEVICE=C:\DOS\INTERLNK.EXE /COM:1` `/NOSCAN`	Install INTERLNK.EXE for COM:1 only, suppressing an attempt to connect at the time CONFIG.SYS is processed.
`DEVICE=C:\DOS\INTERLNK.EXE /LOW`	Install INTERLNK.EXE in low memory.

Intersvr—version 6 only

Intersvr is the part of Interlnk that runs on the server, the computer that provides files and programs to the client. If Intersvr is not running, the client cannot connect to the server, nor can it access any drives or printers on the server.

Although the entire three-part entity that enables one computer to use resources on another is, somewhat confusingly, called Interlnk, you should have it clear in your mind that Interlnk (the command) and INTERLNK.EXE (the device driver) are the parts that run on the client, the machine accessing resources. The similarly named Intersvr is the part that runs on the server, the machine that provides resources to the client.

When you run Intersvr, the server computer becomes a temporary slave of the client and remains unusable while the following screen is displayed:

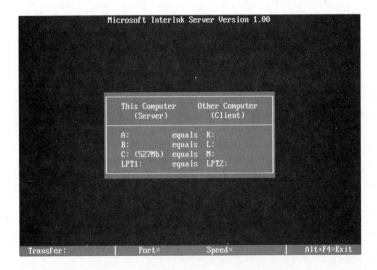

If you start Intersvr while using a multitasking or task-switching environment, such as Windows, the following message appears:

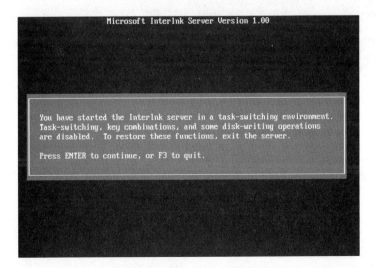

This message tells you that task switching and control keys will be temporarily disabled while you run Intersvr. All will return to normal, however, when you press Alt-F4 to quit Intersvr.

Do not use Intersvr with the following commands: Chkdsk, Defrag, Diskcomp, Diskcopy, Fdisk, Format, Mirror, Sys, Undelete, and Unformat.

In addition to enabling resource sharing on the server, Intersvr has one additional, special use: It enables you to copy the Interlnk files INTERLNK.EXE and INTERSVR.EXE from a computer running version 6 of MS-DOS to another computer (the intended client or server) that is running an earlier version (3.0 through 5) of MS-DOS. You can copy the Interlnk files via floppy disk, or you can let the /rcopy (remote copy) switch of the Intersvr command take care of the procedure for you. To use /rcopy, set up Interlnk on your version 6 computer, cable the computers together, and type the following command:

```
C:\>intersvr /rcopy
```

A remote-copy display like the following appears on the version 6 computer:

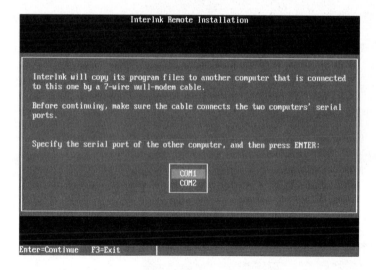

From this point on, follow the instructions that appear, and Intersvr will transfer the two required files for you.

Command syntax

For copying Interlnk files to another computer, the syntax of the Intersvr command is as follows:

```
intersvr /rcopy
```

For enabling the server to provide resources to the client, the syntax of the Intersvr command is as follows:

intersvr [*drive:*] /x=[*drive:*] /lpt[:*number* or *address*] /com[:*number* or *address*]
/baud:*rate* /b /v

drive: specifies a drive on the server that you want to make accessible to the client. By default, all drives are made available. You can include more than one drive in a single command. Separate multiple drives with spaces.

/x=[*drive:*] specifies a drive on the server that you do not want to make accessible to the client. You can include more than one drive in a single command. Separate multiple drives with spaces.

/lpt:*number* or *address* specifies the parallel port connecting the server to the client. If you give the port number, you can specify 1, 2, or 3. If you give the address, specify the four-digit hexadecimal value that represents the port address. If you don't know these values, start the Microsoft Diagnostics utility by typing *msd* and choose LPT Ports from the list that appears. If you include the /lpt switch without a number or an address, Intersvr uses the first parallel port it finds that is connected to the client. The colon between /lpt and the *number* or *address* value is optional.

/com:*number* or *address* works like the /lpt switch, except that it specifies the serial port connecting the server to the client. Valid values for *number* are 1, 2, 3, and 4. The address of a COM port is, again, a four-digit hexadecimal value you can find by starting the Microsoft Diagnostics utility. If you include the /com switch without a number or an address, Intersvr uses the first serial port it finds that is connected to the client. The colon between /com and *number* or *address* is optional.

/baud:*rate* specifies the maximum serial rate of transmission to use. The default is 115200; you can specify 9600, 19200, 38400, or 57600.

/b displays the server screen in black and white and should be used if you have trouble reading a monochrome monitor.

/v prevents conflicts with the timer (not the date/time clock) built into each system. Use this switch if the client or server stops running when Interlnk accesses a drive or port.

Examples

Type:	To:
C:\>intersvr	Start the server and make drives and printers accessible to the client.
C:\>intersvr c: /com1	Start the server, make drive C accessible to the client, and specify COM1 as the port connecting the server to the client.
C:\>intersvr /x=b: /x=d:	Start the server, making all drives except B and D available to the client.

Move—version 6 only

The Move command moves files from one directory to another or from one disk to another. As an added attraction, Move also renames directories, although it does not, unfortunately, have the ability to transfer them from one branch of the directory tree to another. For everyday use, Move is the long-awaited version 6 command that will allow you to retire the trusty old batch file that looks something like this:

```
dir %1 /w /p
copy %1 %2
del %1
```

You can use Move to relocate single files or groups of files, specifying the files individually or with the help of the ? and * wildcards. The basic syntax of the Move command includes one or more source filenames and, optionally, a single destination filename or directory. Using this syntax in various ways, you can

- Move a single file from one disk or directory to another.
- Move a set of unrelated files from one or more disks or directories to a single target disk or directory.
- Move a group of files specified with wildcards to a single target disk or directory.
- Move files to a directory that doesn't exist by specifying the name of the new directory as the target.
- Rename a directory by specifying its old name as the source and the new name as the target. This works as long as you do not change the path to the directory. So, for example, you can change C:\DOGS to C:\CANINES, but you cannot change C:\DOGS to C:\PETS\CANINES.

The Move command is simple to use and displays the source and target pathnames as it moves each specified file, like this:

```
c:\smart\moves.doc => c:\notsmart\oldmoves.doc
```

When you use Move bear the following in mind. First, you cannot combine files by "moving" them to a single filename. If, for example, you try to move files A, B, and C to a single file named D, Move responds as follows:

```
Cannot move multiple files to a single file
```

Second, remember that Move, like Copy, overwrites existing files, without warning you that it will do so. Be sure you want to replace the old file with the one you move.

NOTE: To prune your directory tree, use the version 6 Delete Tree (Deltree) command, described in Chapter 8. To turn the tree into your vision of a bonsai, shape it with Move and clip it back with Deltree.

Command syntax

The syntax of the Move command is as follows:

move /y *filespec1*[,*filespec2*]...[,*filespecN*] *target*

/y (for yes) causes Move to create a new directory you specify as *target* without first prompting for confirmation. If you specify the name of a new directory, but you omit the /y switch, Move displays the message *Make directory "[pathname]"? [yn]*. This switch works only if you specify more than one file.

filespec1, filespec2,...filespecN are the drive, path, and filename of the one or more files you want to move. If you include two or more file specifications, be sure to separate them with commas. You can specify a different drive and path for each file. You can also use wildcards to move a set of similarly named files.

target is the location to which you want to move the file or files. You can include a drive and path as part of *target*. If you are moving a single file, you can also specify a filename. Doing so both moves and renames the file. If you are moving multiple files and specify *target* as the name of a new directory, Move will create the directory for you. Specifying a new directory name does not work, however, if you specify a single source file. Move assumes that the name represents a new filename, rather than the name of a new directory. Also, bear in mind that Move assumes that a directory specified in *target* is a subdirectory of the current or source directory. If you want to move files to a directory in a different branch of the directory tree, include the full path.

Examples

Type:	To:
`C:\CURRENT>move newfile.doc` `c:\archive`	Move the file named NEWFILE.DOC from the CURRENT directory to the ARCHIVE directory.
`C:\CURRENT>move newfile.doc` `c:\archive\oldfile.doc`	Do the same as in the previous example, but rename the file to OLDFILE.DOC.
`C:\>move current\newfile.doc a:`	Move NEWFILE.DOC from the CURRENT directory on drive C to the disk in drive A.
`C:\>move made-it\stock?.xls` `\lost-it`	Move all XLS files with 6-character filenames starting with STOCK from the MADE-IT directory in the root directory to the LOST-IT directory, also in the root. Note the backslash that indicates LOST-IT is in the root. If the backslash were omitted, Move would assume that LOST-IT is a subdirectory of MADE-IT.
`C:\>move \max \min`	Rename the MAX directory to the MIN directory.

Microsoft Backup (Msbackup)—version 6 only

The command listed in online Help as Msbackup is a new and far more efficient Backup utility that considerably outpaces the Backup command found in versions of MS-DOS through 5. Originally a product of Symantec Corporation, Msbackup is included in version 6 of MS-DOS in both Windows and command-line versions. Although the Windows format is more highly graphical than the one you see after starting Msbackup from the system prompt, both forms of the backup utility are similar in the ways they work and the ways you use them—to the point that you can back up from Windows and restore from MS-DOS, or vice versa. Whether you use it from Windows or MS-DOS, however, Msbackup not only can back up files to archive disks, it can also compare the results, restore files when you need them, and maintain special setup files that can establish consistency within backup procedures for different groups of documents.

These setup files actually lie at the heart of the Msbackup command. As you use Msbackup, you can rely on a default setup file named DEFAULT.SET, or you can create whole sets of your own setup files, each customized to a particular backup procedure. The setup file is where Msbackup saves not only all the necessary information related to a particular backup procedure—for example, the weekly backup of all changed files in your REPORTS directory—it also includes the settings you choose for various program options, such as Verify Backup Data, Compress Backup Data, Quit After Backup, and Audible Prompts (Beep). By saving all this information in the setup file, Msbackup ensures that settings remain consistent from one backup to the next, and that you have to do minimal thinking and remembering when you want to back up a set of documents more than once.

When you start Msbackup, it opens (like Microsoft Anti-Virus and Microsoft Undelete) in its own menu-based window, like this:

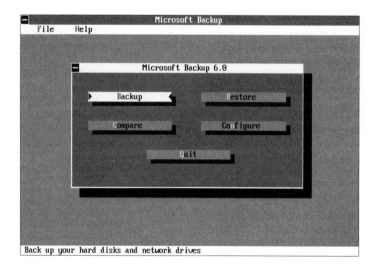

Like the Anti-Virus and Undelete features of version 6, Msbackup is a program in its own right, with capabilities and options too numerous to outline here. This chapter describes the various options available for starting Msbackup from the system prompt. Chapter 15, in Section Four, describes how to use the backup program.

Command syntax

The format of the Msbackup command—that is, the parameters and switches you can use to start the program—is as follows:

msbackup [*setup file*] /bw /lcd /mda

setup file is the name of the Msbackup-maintained setup file. All setup files have the extension SET. Precede the name of the setup file with a drive and path if the setup file is not in the current drive or directory. To start Msbackup and create a new setup file, omit a drive and path and name a setup file that Msbackup cannot find; it will ask whether you want to create the setup file. If you don't specify a setup file, Msbackup assumes the default, DEFAULT.SET.

/bw runs Msbackup in black-and-white, rather than color, on a color monitor.

/lcd runs Msbackup with the video setup for LCD displays, such as those on laptops and notebook computers.

/mda runs Msbackup with the video setup for an IBM Monochrome Display Adapter.

Examples

Type:	To:
C:\>msbackup dosbook	Start Msbackup using the DOSBOOK.SET setup file.
C:\>msbackup /bw	Run Msbackup in black and white. Omitting the name of a setup file causes the program to load DEFAULT.SET.

Rename (Ren)

The Rename (Ren) command has been a part of MS-DOS since version 1. You can use it to change the name, extension, or both name and extension of an existing file. Although the Ren command would seem to be ideal for "moving" a file by renaming its path, you cannot do so. Ren cannot change directory names, so the command is effective only so long as the file you rename remains on the same drive and in the same directory. Unlike the Copy command, Ren contains a built-in safeguard that prevents it from renaming a file with a name that already exists in the same directory. If you attempt to use an existing name, MS-DOS displays the message:

```
Duplicate file name or file not found
```

and returns to the system prompt.

Command syntax

One of the simpler MS-DOS commands, Ren has the following format:

ren *name1 name2*

name1 is the filename you want to change. You can include a drive and path if the file is not in the current directory, and you can use wildcards for any part of the filename or extension. If you use wildcards, the characters represented by the wildcards are identical in both the original and new filenames.

name2 is the name you want to assign the file. Do not include a drive or path. If you do, MS-DOS will display the message *Invalid parameter* and return you to the system prompt.

Examples

Type:	To:
`C:\CHANGE>ren old-dog.doc newtrick.doc`	Change the name of OLD-DOG.DOC in the CHANGE directory to NEWTRICK.DOC in the same directory.
`C:\>ren c:\change\old-dog.doc newtrick.doc`	Rename the same file as above, but from the root directory of drive C.
`C:\>ren a:*.txt *.old`	Rename all TXT files on drive A, keeping the same filenames but changing all extensions to OLD.
`C:\ROMANS>ren caligula.* boots.*`	Rename all files named CALIGULA in the ROMANS directory to BOOTS, keeping all original extensions.

Replace

The Replace command, a part of MS-DOS since version 3.2, was once used as a means of updating MS-DOS files during an upgrade from one version to another (the IBM release of MS-DOS version 3.3). That's of historical interest only, however, especially because the command has changed somewhat in the years since. Currently, the Replace command, despite its name, is included in MS-DOS to help you either replace or *add to* files already on a disk. Whether the command overwrites existing files or adds new ones depends on whether you use the /a switch described below.

The most obvious uses of the Replace command are in

- Upgrading existing files to ensure that they contain the latest version of a program or document.

- Sifting through a group of files when you want to copy only those that are not included in a target directory.

In either case, the Replace command can accomplish in one operation the equivalent of the following:

- Printing a directory listing of the source and target directory or directories.

- Comparing files in the source to those in the target(s). To replace target files, you would have to note those in the source and target that had different sizes, dates, or times. To add files to the target, you would have to note those in the source that did not exist in the target.

- Copying the files you had noted, either singly or in groups with wildcards.

Replace is one of a few MS-DOS commands that records an exit code indicating the outcome of the replace or add procedure. The exit codes are as follows:

Code	Meaning
0	Success.
1	An incompatible version of MS-DOS is installed on the computer.
2	Source files were not found.
3	Source or destination path was not found.
5	Access denied.
8	Not enough memory to complete the command.
11	Error in the command line.

If you run the Replace command from a batch file, you can check for these codes with the errorlevel parameter of the If command and use the code you find to control the outcome of the batch file.

Command syntax

The format of the Replace command bears close scrutiny, simply because it can either replace or add files, depending on how you use it:

replace *source* [*destination*] /a /p /r /s /w /u

source is the file specification of the files you want to copy. You can include a drive and path if necessary. You must specify *source*, regardless of whether you want to replace or add files.

destination is the drive and path to which you want to copy the source files. Because the files retain their original names, you cannot specify a filename. If you omit *destination*, Replace copies files to the current drive and directory.

/a specifies that the source files are to be added to the destination drive or directory. Although it would be nice to combine /a with the /s switch to add files to multiple directories, you cannot do so. You can use /a or /s, but not both in the same command. You also cannot use /u with /a.

/p causes the Replace command to prompt for confirmation before replacing or adding a file.

/r either replaces or adds read-only files, depending on the type of copy you specify. If you attempt to replace a read-only file without using the /r switch, MS-DOS displays the message *Access denied - FILESPEC*; even though it might have already replaced some files, it ends the process at that point.

NOTE: If you replace *a read-only file, MS-DOS assigns the new version the read-only attribute. If you* add *a source file that is read-only, however, the destination copy is not automatically assigned the read-only attribute.*

/s applies a replace procedure to all subdirectories of the destination directory. Unfortunately, the /s switch does not work with the /a switch to add files throughout a branch of the directory tree.

/w causes MS-DOS to display the message *Press any key to continue...* and to wait until you press a key before it starts replacing or adding files. You don't need this switch unless you are working with floppy disks and must swap an MS-DOS disk for the source disk before continuing.

/u, for update, replaces files in the destination directory only if they are older than the source files. The /u switch thus refines a replacement by copying only the source files that are newer than their equivalents on the destination disk and directory. You cannot use the /a switch with /u.

Examples

Type:	To:
C:\RECORDS>replace a:*.*	Replace all files in the RECORDS directory with files from the disk in drive A that have the same name and extension.
C:\RECORDS>replace a:supply.lst /s	Replace all files named SUPPLY.LST in the RECORDS directory and all its sub-directories with matching files from the disk in drive A.
C:\>replace a:*.lst records /a	Add all LST files from the disk in drive A that don't exist in the RECORDS directory.
C:\>replace a:*.lst records /a /r /p	Add all LST files, including read-only files, from the disk in drive A to the RECORDS directory, prompting for confirmation each time.

Restore

The Restore command, the complement of the Backup command in versions of MS-DOS prior to 6, restores files from a backup disk to the directory from which they were archived. If you have version 6 of MS-DOS, back up and restore files with either Msbackup or its Windows version. The Restore command in version 6 is really only for use in restoring files backed up with earlier versions.

Although Backup and Restore in versions of MS-DOS prior to version 5 could be picky about working harmoniously with any other version of MS-DOS, the Restore command in versions 5 and 6 can handle files backed up by any version of MS-DOS back to version 2. When you use Restore, you can restore files to

- The original drive from which they were backed up—for example, to replace files that were unintentionally damaged or deleted.

- To a different drive—for example, to duplicate a set of files on another computer or another disk drive. This use of Backup and Restore is handy when you want to move a group of files that won't fit onto a single floppy disk. "Back up" the files with the Backup command, and then "restore" them to a different drive.

Regardless of the drive to which you restore files, however, Restore is somewhat unforgiving about directories: Although Restore will create the directory for you, the first directory in the path to which you restore files must always have the same name as the directory from which the files were backed up. Beyond this, however, you do have some leeway because subdirectories beyond this first level need not match those recorded on the backup disk. In fact, if a subdirectory does not exist in the main destination directory, Restore, like Xcopy, will create it and populate it with the appropriate files. Thus, for example, you can back up all DOC files from C:\REPORTS and all its subdirectories and then restore the entire set to D:\REPORTS, even though the destination directory does not contain the subdirectories backed up from drive C.

Restore, like Backup, Replace, and certain other MS-DOS commands, returns one of several exit codes on completion. The codes are as follows:

Code	Meaning
0	Success.
1	No matching files were found on the backup disk.
3	Procedure was canceled because Ctrl-C was pressed.
4	Procedure stopped due to error.

If you run the Restore command from a batch file, you can check for these codes with the errorlevel parameter of the If command and use the code you find to control the outcome of the batch file.

Command syntax

The Restore command in versions 5 and 6 of MS-DOS has the following format:

restore *source destination* /s /p /b:*date* /a:*date* /e:*time* /l:*time* /m /n /d

source is the drive containing the backup disk from which you want to restore files.

destination is the drive, path and file specification of the file or files to restore. You can use wildcards to specify a set of files. Remember that the path must begin with the same directory from which the files were backed up.

/s restores files from a directory and its subdirectories.

/p causes Restore to prompt before restoring a read-only file or one with the archive attribute set (meaning that the file has changed since the last backup).

/b:*date* restores files backed up on or before *date*. Use the date format built into your system or the one specified by a Country setting in CONFIG.SYS. To check on the date format quickly, use the Date command at the system prompt.

/a:*date* is similar to /b:*date*, but restores files backed up on or after *date*.

/e:*time* restores files modified at or before *time*. Use the time format built into your system or the one specified by a Country setting in CONFIG.SYS. To check on the date format quickly, use the Time command at the system prompt.

/l:*time* is similar to /e:*time*, but restores files modified at or later than *time*.

/m restores only the files modified since the last backup.

/n restores only the files that don't exist in the destination directory—that is, have been deleted since they were backed up.

/d displays a list of the files on the backup disk that match the file specification you type as part of *destination*. Although the /d switch does not actually restore files, it is useful for checking files on a backup disk—if you know what you're looking for. Otherwise, /d causes Restore to respond—infuriatingly—*WARNING! No files were found to restore*, until you hit upon a file specification that matches one on the backup disk.

Examples

Type:	To:
`C:\>restore a: reports\*.doc /s`	Restore all DOC files from the backup disk in drive A to the REPORTS directory and all its subdirectories, even if those subdirectories have not yet been created.
`C:\RENEW>restore a: *.* /a:12-11-92`	Restore all files modified on or after 12-11-92 from the backup disk in drive A to the current (RENEW) directory.
`C:\>restore a: medics\*.doc /s /d`	Display a list of all DOC files on the disk in drive A that can be restored to the MEDICS directory and its subdirectories.

Type

One of the commands that many MS-DOS users turn to without thinking, the Type command displays the contents of a file on screen. The Type command works best with plain ASCII files. Program files, except for perhaps a copyright notice or the occasional string of text, are uncompromisingly unintelligible. Formatted files saved by a word processor are mostly readable, however, although they, too, can contain unreadable characters—those representing codes recognizable to the application but not to people. Other formatted files, however, such as drawings, spreadsheets, and bit maps, might as well be in hieroglyphs for all the good the Type command does you.

Given those limitations, however, the Type command is not only one of the easiest MS-DOS commands to use, it also proves its utility whenever you want to take a quick look at a readable file. Type is the fastest way to inspect your CONFIG.SYS and AUTOEXEC.BAT files, and it can quickly display any ASCII document, such as the README.TXT and PACKING.LST files shipped with MS-DOS. Type is, to some extent, the Directory command of ASCII files, particularly in combination with the More command, which pauses after each screenful and waits for you to press a key before continuing.

Command syntax

The format of the Type command is simple:

> type *filespec*

filespec is the drive, path, filename, and extension of the file you want to view. You cannot use wildcard characters—for example, you cannot use *type a:*.txt* to view a set of files.

Examples

Type:	To:
`C:\>type a:lilbit.txt`	Display a short file named LILBIT.TXT from the disk in drive A.
`C:\>type c:\dos\readme.txt ¦ more`	Display the file named README.TXT in the DOS directory.

Undelete—version 6 only

Undelete has one mission: to protect you from losing files you've unwisely deleted. In version 6 of MS-DOS, however, Undelete differs from its version 5 complement both in the way it works and in the way you use it. Because of these differences, version 6 Undelete is covered here, version 5 Undelete is covered in the following entry. Version 6 Undelete, which is available in both MS-DOS and Windows versions, is also described in more detail in Chapter 14.

When you delete a file, recall that MS-DOS does not actually remove the data from disk. Rather, it recycles the file's directory entry and marks the clusters occupied by the file as available for reuse. Because the directory entry remains more or less intact and because the information remains on disk until it is overwritten by part or all of another file, utilities like Undelete are able to recover deleted files.

A memory-resident program, Undelete keeps track of the files you delete. (Obviously, if Undelete is never loaded, it can do little in the way of undeleting; even under those circumstances, however, it can try.) When you try to undelete one or more files, Undelete can approach the problem in one of three ways, depending both on the command format you use and on the switches you used when loading it into memory. These three methods are

- MS-DOS. This method relies on the directory and file-storage information recorded by MS-DOS and is the least reliable means of attempting to recover a file. The reason is simple and inarguable: In the time between the deletion and the time you attempt recovery, MS-DOS can very well have overwritten either the file's directory entry, or some or all of the clusters assigned to the file. In either of these situations, partial recovery is the best you can hope for.

- Delete-tracking. This method, more reliable than MS-DOS alone but less reliable than Delete Sentry, is based on a special file called PCTRACKR.DEL. This file contains directory and file-storage information related to each deleted file. Although the directory entry and assigned clusters can, again, be overwritten after the file is deleted, delete-tracking offers Undelete an additional resource to use in attempting to find and recover the file. In some respects, you can think of the delete-tracking file as a secondary copy of the directory and FAT.

- Delete Sentry. The most reliable of the three methods, and the one used by Undelete by default, Delete Sentry sets up a hidden directory named SENTRY in which Undelete saves the actual contents of all deleted files. Because these files are safely tucked away, it doesn't matter whether the originals are overwritten. Undelete can restore what you need directly from its hidden directory. Over time, this directory (typically confined to 7 percent of your hard disk) can become quite full, however, so even Delete Sentry is not completely foolproof: After a certain amount of time elapses (7 days by default), Undelete purges the contents of the directory. Once purged, files are forever gone.

As the preceding items illustrate, there is one good rule to follow in undeleting files: Do it quickly. The longer you wait, the less likely recovery becomes.

When you load Undelete into memory, it refers to an initialization file named UNDELETE.INI, which is stored, after the first time you use the program, in the DOS directory of your hard disk. This file sets a number of options, such as the number of days before files are purged and the percentage of the disk set aside for the SENTRY directory. You can view and change these settings either from the Windows version of the Undelete utility or by editing the UNDELETE.INI file with a text editor, such as the MS-DOS Editor.

NOTE: Unless you use the Windows version, Undelete cannot help you recover deleted directories or the files they contain. If you don't have Windows and you need to recover an entire directory and its files, you might be able to recover the information by re-creating the directory and then using Undelete. This method is effective, however, only if you've protected the drive by using Delete Sentry.

Command syntax

The Undelete command—utility, rather—comes accompanied by a substantial array of parameters and switches. Because Undelete both enables monitoring of deleted files and attempts to recover such files, the command is used in either of two forms.

First, to control Undelete, use the following form:

undelete /load /unload /sdrive/tdrive-entries/status

/load loads Undelete into memory and starts the program with the settings stored in UNDELETE.INI. By default, Undelete enables Delete Sentry when you use the /load switch.

/unload removes Undelete from memory and, obviously, turns off delete protection from that point until you restart Undelete.

/s works just like the /load switch, but it enables Delete Sentry protection for the drive specified by *drive*.

/*tdrive*[-*entries*] loads Undelete into memory and starts delete-tracking for the drive specified by *drive*. Although you're unlikely to need or want to, you can use the *entries* parameter to specify the maximum number of files Undelete tracks in the delete-tracking (PCTRACKR.DEL) file. If you don't specify *entries*, Undelete uses the following values:

Disk capacity	Number of entries	Size of file on disk
360 K	25	5 K
720 K	50	9 K
1.2 MB and 1.44 MB	75	14 K
20 MB	101	18 K
30 MB	202	36 K
32 MB and more	303	55 K

Do not use delete-tracking for drives that have been "unnaturally" united with the Join or Substitute (Subst) command. If you plan to use Assign, do so before starting delete-tracking.

/status displays the type of protection enabled for each drive monitored by Undelete.

Once Undelete is loaded, use the following format to undelete files and to check on or purge deleted files:

undelete *filespec* /ds /dt /dos /all /list /purge[*drive*]

filespec is the drive, path, and file specification of one or more files to un-delete; wildcards are permissible. If you omit *filespec*, Undelete assumes all files (*.*) in the current directory. To avoid a *No entries found* message when you know you deleted an important file, be sure either to change to the appropriate directory or to include the path in *filespec*.

/ds undeletes files stored by Delete Sentry in the SENTRY directory, prompting for confirmation before recovering each file.

/dt undeletes files listed by the Delete Tracker in PCTRACKR.DEL, prompting for confirmation before undeleting a file.

/dos undeletes files on the basis of the directory and file-storage information maintained by MS-DOS, again prompting for confirmation before recovering each file. When you use the /dos switch to recover files, Undelete displays a question mark in place of the first character in the name of each deleted file. If you choose to undelete the file, you'll be asked to type a character to replace the question mark.

/all undeletes all deleted files in the current or specified directory without prompting for confirmation. When you use the /all switch, Undelete tries first to find a Delete Sentry directory. If that fails, it searches for a delete-tracking file. If that, too, fails, Undelete uses the information recorded by MS-DOS. In this last instance, it replaces the question mark representing the first character of each filename with a # sign. If using this symbol would produce a duplicate filename, it then tries the following characters, in order: %, &, the digits 0 through 9, and then the letters A through Z.

/list produces a list of deleted files, but does not actually undelete them. The list you see depends on the type of delete protection you've enabled and on the file specification you provide.

/purge[*drive*] purges the SENTRY directory for the drive specified by *drive*. If you don't specify a drive, Undelete searches for the SENTRY directory on the current drive.

Examples

Type:	To:
C:\>undelete /load	Start delete protection with the settings in UNDELETE.INI, initiating Delete Sentry by default.
C:\>undelete /sd	Start delete protection as above, initiating Delete Sentry only for drive D.
C:\>undelete /status	Check on the status of delete protection for all protected drives on the system.
C:\>undelete c:\oldfiles	Undelete all files in the C:\OLDFILES directory.

(continued)

Type:	To:
`C:\>undelete c:\oldfiles /dos`	Undelete all recoverable files in the C:\OLDFILES directory, using the MS-DOS directory and file-storage information. (You might need to use this method to recover files that Windows Undelete has classified as "poor.")
`C:\>undelete c:\oldfiles /list`	List the names of all deleted files in C:\OLDFILES, without actually undeleting them. This command produces a list based on whatever type of delete protection is in effect for the specified drive.

Undelete—version 5 only

The version 5 Undelete command is similar to the version 6 form, but relies on a delete-tracking (PCTRACKR.DEL) file initiated with the Mirror command, described in Chapter 8. Undelete in version 5 thus does not include a Delete Sentry option and is not as much of a standalone utility as it is in version 6, especially because it is not accompanied by a graphical Windows version.

If you use version 5 of MS-DOS and have not already run the Mirror command, Undelete must rely on the MS-DOS directory and file-storage information. Because of this, you might want either to include Mirror in your AUTOEXEC.BAT file or to include it in a batch file of commands that customize your computer for a particular type of work you do periodically, such as cleaning out old files on your hard disk.

In other respects, the parameters and switches of the version 5 Undelete are similar to those in version 6 of MS-DOS.

Command syntax

The parameters and switches in version 5 Undelete are as follows:

> undelete *filespec* /list /all /dos /dt

filespec is the drive, path, and file specification of the file or files to undelete. You can use wildcards to undelete a set of files. If you omit a file specification, Undelete assumes you mean all files (*.*) in the current directory.

/list produces a list of deleted files without actually undeleting them. This list is based on the MS-DOS directory and file-storage information unless you have enabled delete-tracking with the /t switch of the Mirror command (comparable to the /t switch in the version 6 Undelete command).

/all undeletes all recoverable files. This switch works as described for the version 6 /all switch, except that it does not have the ability to search for a Delete Sentry directory.

/dos bases the file list (with the /list switch) or file recovery on the directory and file-storage information kept by MS-DOS.

/dt bases the file list (with the /list switch) or file recovery on the information logged in the delete-tracking file, PCTRACKR.DEL.

Examples

Type:	To:
`C:\>mirror /ta /tc`	Enable delete-tracking for drives A and C.
`C:\>undelete a:*.doc /list`	List deleted files on the disk in drive A.
`C:\>undelete \oldfiles\*.doc`	Undelete all deleted DOC files in the OLDFILES directory on drive C. This command would use the delete-tracking file if possible, the MS-DOS information otherwise.

Verify

The Verify command, included with MS-DOS since version 2, verifies that data is correctly written to disk. The Verify command can slow down disk writes, but you're unlikely to need it anyway. Both the Copy and Xcopy commands include verify switches of their own, which you can use in cases where accuracy is critical. Other types of disk writes, such as file saves, are most likely going to be under the control of application software, and these programs must assume their own responsibility for accuracy and verification.

Command syntax

The form of the Verify command is simple:

verify on off

on turns verification on, and off turns verification off. If you omit both switches and type only the command name, MS-DOS displays a message indicating whether verify is on or off, like this:

VERIFY is off

Examples

Type:	To:
C:\>verify	Check the status of verification.
C:\>verify on	Turn verify on.
C:\>verify off	Turn verify off.

Extended copy (Xcopy)

The Xcopy command made its appearance as a part of MS-DOS in version 3.2. One of the most useful of MS-DOS commands, Xcopy should come to mind more quickly than the Copy command if you regularly rely on, and copy from, directories and subdirectories.

Whereas the Copy command is highly useful for duplicating single files or sets of files that reside in the same directory, Xcopy can push far into a directory tree, copying all or selected files from a specified directory and all its subdirectories. You can use Xcopy to duplicate an entire branch of the directory tree, or you can use Xcopy to pick and choose among files, copying only those that have the archive attribute set or only those created or modified on or after a certain date.

The only drawback to using Xcopy, especially when you try to duplicate large directories and subdirectories, is the possibility of running out of space on the destination disk. To guard against this, use the Dir command to check the sizes of the directories you want to copy. Be sure to use the /s switch to check subdirectories as well, if you are going to include them in the copy. If you find that the directory or directories are too large to fit on the destination disk,

- Use the version 6 DoubleSpace (Dblspace) command to compress the files on the destination disk.
- Use Msbackup or Backup to make the copy.

If, despite your precautions, you use Xcopy and it runs out of room, you see the message *Insufficient disk space* and Xcopy terminates the copy process. It does not, however, leave you in the lurch with a partial file; it terminates before starting to copy that final file. Because Xcopy displays the names of files as it copies them, you can tell where the copy process stopped: The last filename displayed before the *Insufficient disk space* message is the file that was not copied.

If Xcopy can't tell whether the destination is a filename or directory, it will ask you before beginning the copy.

Xcopy is one of the MS-DOS commands that returns an exit code when it terminates. If you run the Xcopy command from a batch file, you can check for these codes with the errorlevel parameter of the If command and use the code you find to control the outcome of the batch file.

Code	Meaning
0	Success
1	No files found to copy
2	Copy terminated because Ctrl-C was pressed
4	Copy error: not enough memory or disk space, invalid command, or invalid drive specified in the command
5	Error writing to disk

NOTE: Xcopy in version 6, unlike Xcopy in earlier versions of MS-DOS, does not copy hidden and system files. To copy these files with version 6 of MS-DOS, either remove the hidden or system attribute with the Attrib command before using Xcopy, or use the Diskcopy command instead.

Command syntax

The format of the Xcopy command is as follows:

xcopy *source* [*destination*] /a /m /d:*date* /p /s /e /v /w

source is the drive, path, and file specification of the file or files to copy. You can omit the path and filename, but you must specify at least a drive.

destination is the drive, path, and file specification to which you want to copy the source files. You can omit *destination* to copy to the current directory. If you want to duplicate a directory structure exactly, type the name of the top-level directory you are copying as the destination, and end it with a backslash, as shown in the first example in the following "Examples" section.

/a copies specified files only if their archive attributes are set, indicating that they have changed. This switch leaves the archive attribute set on the original file.

/m copies specified files only if their archive attributes are set, but also turns off the archive attribute on the original file.

/d:*date* copies files created or modified on or after the date you specify as *date*. Use the date format normal for your computer or the one set by a Country command in CONFIG.SYS. To check the date format, use the Date command at the system prompt.

/p prompts for confirmation before each file is copied.

/s applies the Xcopy command to all non-empty subdirectories of the directory specified in *source*.

/e, used in combination with /s, applies the Xcopy command to all subdirectories, including empty ones, of the directory specified in *source*. This is the switch combination you need to duplicate a directory structure exactly, if some of the subdirectories do not contain files.

/v verifies each copied file to ensure that the copy was accurate.

/w causes Xcopy to wait until you press a key before starting to copy files.

Examples

Type:	To:
`C:\>xcopy \movies a:\movies\ /s /e`	Copy the MOVIES directory, all files, and all subdirectories even if empty, duplicating the directory structure exactly on drive A. If the MOVIES directory does not exist in the root directory of the disk in drive A, Xcopy will create it. (Note: If you omit the backslash after MOVIES in the destination path, Xcopy will display a message asking whether the destination is a file or a directory.)
`C:\>xcopy movies a: /s /e`	Copy all files and subdirectories of the MOVIES directory, as above, but into the root directory of the disk in drive A rather than into a directory named MOVIES.
`C:\DUCKS>xcopy *.qwk a: /s`	Copy all QWK files in the DUCKS directory and its nonempty subdirectories to the root directory of the disk in drive A.
`C:\POPCORN>xcopy a:\*.doc /d:8-14-93`	Copy to the current directory (POPCORN) all DOC files in the root directory of the disk in drive A that were created or modified on or after 8/14/93.
`C:\BEES>xcopy *.hny a: /m /s`	Copy all changed HNY files in the BEES directory and its subdirectories to the root directory of the disk in drive A, turning off the archive attribute in the copied files—essentially, the equivalent of an incremental backup.

8

Disks

What You'll Find Here: Assign; Check Disk (Chkdsk); Defragmenter (Defrag); Disk Compare (Diskcomp); Diskcopy; DBLSPACE.SYS; DoubleSpace (Dblspace); Fixed Disk (Fdisk); Format; Join; Label; Microsoft Anti-Virus (Msav); Mirror; Recover; Substitute (Subst); System (Sys); Unformat; Volume (Vol); Vsafe.

*F*ast as they are, computers have attention spans measured in microseconds. Furthermore, data in RAM disappears as soon as you turn off or reboot the machine. If it weren't for the disks, which represent a more or less permanent record of your work, you would face a constant either/or choice in working with a computer: Either continually dump data to the printer, or accept that some data will be as ephemeral as snowflakes in July.

Disks and disk layout

Magnetic disks first became the storage devices of preference on desktop computers in the early and mid-1980s. Like floppy disks today, they were plastic pancakes enclosed in stiff, although bendable, vinyl. Then, as now, floppy disks came in different sizes: the familiar 5.25-inch variety (although with far less holding capacity) and a giant-sized version 8 inches across—the Starship Enterprise of floppy disks.

Floppy disks differ considerably from hard disks in certain ways. They are highly portable and can, when locked up, be more secure than hard disks. On a less positive note, they also hold much less information and are more subject to damage from rough handling, sharp objects, and magnetism (which, if inadvertently applied to a disk, can reduce your data to zero and you to tears). Whether you're dealing with floppy disks or hard disks, however, two significant features are the same in both: the physical layout of tracks and sectors on the disk, and the division of the disk, during formatting, into record keeping and storage areas.

Physical layout

As described in Chapter 2, storage on an MS-DOS disk is based on concentric, ringlike tracks and on track segments called sectors. In illustrations, tracks look like clean, evenly spaced ripples on a pond. Although MS-DOS could presumably have been designed to write to and read from a disk in track-sized units, it does not. This is where sectors come in. Sectors are equal-sized segments of tracks, typically holding 512 bytes of information. Groups of sectors form clusters, and these are the units that MS-DOS actually uses as it reads from or writes to a disk.

Together, tracks, sectors, and clusters divide a disk into storage compartments that are uniquely identified by a combination of numbers: the side of the disk they are on (the two sides are labeled 0 and 1 rather than the 1 and 2 you might expect), plus the numbers of the track, sector, and cluster they represent.

Disks vary in the number of tracks and sectors they have on each side. Floppy disks that hold 360 K of information have 40 tracks per side; higher-capacity floppies have 80 tracks per side. Hard disks, with their closer tolerances and much higher capacities, can have upward of 700 tracks per side on each of the two or more platters they contain. The number of sectors per track also varies according to disk capacity: 9 on 360-K and 720-K floppies, 15 on 1.2-MB floppies, 18 on 1.44-MB floppies, and 36 on 2.88-MB floppies (these are supported only in versions 5 and 6 of MS-DOS). On hard disks, the number of sectors per track varies, but typically falls in the 40-to-50 range for 120-MB to 240-MB drives.

Hard disks in particular

Hard disks add two dimensions, depth and great size, to the side/track/sector system of identifying storage locations. These two dimensions give rise to two additional terms that are applied only to hard disks: cylinder and partition.

Cylinders

A hard disk typically contains a number of platters stacked one above the other on a central spindle. These multiple platters mean not only that a hard disk can hold vast quantities of information but that a track on one side of one platter has a corresponding track that occupies the same location on each side of every other platter in the drive. A cylinder represents what you would have if you stacked all the tracks occupying the same relative location on each platter in the hard disk, like this:

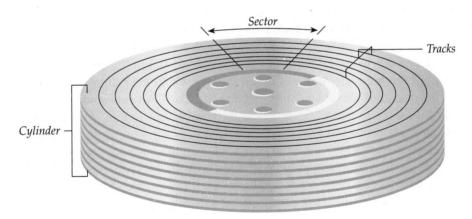

If you were to look down on a cylinder from above, you would see something resembling a Slinky toy—a pile of rings forming a tube. The only real difference would be that the rings of the toy are connected, whereas the tracks in a cylinder are not.

You don't encounter the term *cylinder* in your ordinary work with MS-DOS, but it does show up occasionally—for example, in the disk drive report produced by the Microsoft Diagnostics utility shipped with version 6 and in some versions of the Fdisk program, which creates, modifies, and deletes the second of these hard disk entities, *partitions.*

Partitions

A partition, in contrast to a cylinder, is a section of a hard disk that MS-DOS can physically "wall off" from other sections as a ring-shaped portion of storage space, like this:

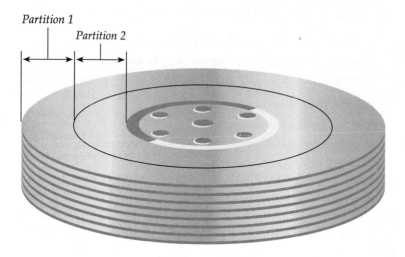

Under MS-DOS, you can have two kinds of partition on a hard disk: a primary DOS partition and an extended DOS partition. Both types of partition can be used for storing programs and data, and both kinds can usually be created, modified, and deleted with the MS-DOS Fdisk command. In practical terms, the only real difference that you see between the two is that the primary DOS partition is the one from which you start and run MS-DOS. An extended DOS partition, if you choose to create one, serves as the home of one or more logical drives, or volumes within the physical hard disk, each of which you format separately, assign its own drive letter, and treat as if it were a physically separate unit.

Partitions, like cylinders, seldom intrude on your everyday work with MS-DOS commands. This does not mean, however, that partitions are unimportant. Both your system's bootstrap program and MS-DOS need information about partitions in order to use the disk without error, and both rely on a tiny, invisible "database" called the partition table to provide that information. The partition table is stored on the disk and is normally off limits to both you and your application programs.

Although you don't normally worry about the partition table, it can, under unusual circumstances (either hardware-based or software-based) become damaged, or corrupted. When that happens, your system refuses to start from the hard disk.

If you have MS-DOS version 5 or you've upgraded from version 5 to 6, and you've used the Mirror command to save your partition table, you can restore that table with the version 5 Unformat /partn command. You must also have a bootable floppy disk.

This floppy disk is your alternative means of getting MS-DOS started, and the copy of the partition table provides you with an uncorrupted version you can use to patch up the damaged table on the hard disk. At a minimum, you can create a bootable disk (before problems occur with your hard disk) with the following command:

```
C:\>format a: /s
```

To ensure that MS-DOS can use your system and its devices, however, you should also copy to this disk basic versions of your CONFIG.SYS and AUTOEXEC.BAT files—*basic,* meaning the essentials, such as device drivers and necessary MS-DOS commands in these files, but not the finely-tuned details.

Once you've created this emergency toolkit, put it away safely and hope you never have to use it. If worst comes to worst, however, you can use the Unformat command as described later in this chapter to rebuild the damaged partition table and make the hard disk bootable once again.

NOTE: A damaged partition table is not the only reason you can have problems accessing your hard disk. If the problem is intermittent, a likely source is the CMOS battery for the system clock. This battery not only drives the clock, it also powers a small portion of RAM that stores, among other things, the type of drive to which your hard disk belongs. If the CMOS battery is the problem, you'll have to replace it and, probably, refresh its "memory" of your startup drive. If you have version 6 of MS-DOS, you should use the MSD utility to check on—and record—this information before the battery runs low.

Parts of a disk

It's easy—and for the most part accurate—to think of a formatted disk as a vast, smooth expanse as unmarked as farmland beneath new snow. In actuality, of course, the farmland consists of cornfields, hayfields, and pastures, each of which will be used for a particular purpose when spring arrives. A formatted disk, too, is divided into different areas—four to be exact—each filling a specific MS-DOS requirement. These parts of the disk—the *boot sector,* one or more FATs, the root directory, and a large, open files area—are always laid out in the same order, as shown on the following page.

Boot sector is in here

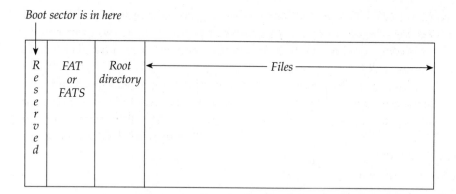

They appear on any formatted floppy disk, primary DOS partition, or logical drive within an extended DOS partition.

The boot sector is always the first sector on a floppy disk or a logical disk (the primary DOS partition or any of the named "drives" in the extended DOS partition) and is a part of the disk you need to care about only to the extent that it does or does not contain the information needed for startup. The boot sector appears on every formatted disk, whether or not it is actually used to start MS-DOS. Think of it as a reserved sector that sometimes serves a special purpose.

After the boot sector comes the disk's FAT, which is usually followed by an extra copy that MS-DOS updates and maintains as insurance in the event the primary FAT is damaged or destroyed. The FAT is described in Chapter 7 and needs no more attention here other than mentioning that the Check Disk (Chkdsk) command sometimes finds problems in the FAT. Details are provided under the heading "Check Disk (Chkdsk)" later in this chapter.

After the two FATs comes an area of considerable interest—the root directory of the disk. The root directory is essentially a table of 32-byte entries, each of which can hold information about one file. The 32 bytes of each directory entry are parceled out among eight fields, as follows:

- Filename: 8 bytes
- Extension: 3 bytes
- File attributes: 1 byte
- Reserved field: 10 bytes
- Time of creation or last modification: 2 bytes
- Date of creation or last modification: 2 bytes
- Number of first cluster used for storing file: 2 bytes
- Size of file: 4 bytes

Notice the sizes of the filename and extension. Here you can see why MS-DOS limits you to filenames no longer than 8 characters and extensions no longer than 3 characters: It doesn't have room for any more.

The file attributes byte, interestingly, uses individual bits in the byte to indicate which file attributes are set. A 1 in bit position 1, for example, indicates that the file is hidden, a 1 in position 6 means the archive attribute is turned on. Here's a table that shows how it works (recall that a byte consists of 8 bits, shown as 0s and 1s below):

Bit settings	Attribute
00000001	Read-only file
00000010	Hidden file
00000100	System file
00001000	Directory entry is disk volume label
00010000	Subdirectory
00100000	Archive attribute set
01000000	No assigned meaning
10000000	No assigned meaning

The size of the root directory varies with the type of disk but is always set at the time the disk is formatted and cannot be changed later on. The holding capacity of the root directory varies with the capacity of the disk: 112 entries on a 360-K or a 720-K floppy, 224 entries on a 1.2-MB or a 1.44-MB floppy, and 512 entries on a hard disk.

When you leave the root directory, you come to the files area, by far the largest on the disk because this is where your files are actually saved—in clusters logged into the FAT. There's really not much to say about the files area, other than it holds files and some of the sectors in it might be "out of service" because the disk surface is damaged. This is, however, the portion of the disk that you normally think of as formatted and available for use. This is also the region in which utilities such as Undelete maintain the hidden directories and files they use to help you out of a jam, and it is the area used by DoubleSpace in version 6 to hold the *compressed volume file* (CVF), which represents a compressed drive.

Formatting

Anyone who has used MS-DOS for a while knows that a disk cannot be used for storage unless it is first formatted. Through version 4 of MS-DOS, formatting was simply formatting: The disk was prepared, and existing storage was marked as empty on each track. A new disk was initialized with a FAT and a root directory, and an old disk was reborn with a new FAT and a new root directory. Versions 5 and 6 of MS-DOS, however, can format a disk in any of three ways: safely, quickly, or unconditionally.

Safe formatting and quick formatting

Beginning with version 5, MS-DOS reduces the risk involved in formatting—especially formatting a hard disk—by performing a *safe format* by default. During a safe format, MS-DOS saves the disk's FAT and root directory in a hidden file on the disk and wipes out the original FAT and root directory, essentially creating a "clean slate" that can be used as if the disk were brand new. MS-DOS does not, however, delete the actual information stored on the disk, so you can, if necessary, use the Unformat command to rebuild the disk.

Quick formatting, which can be performed only on a previously formatted disk and cannot be used to change disk capacity (for example, from 1.44 MB to 720 K), is a fast-forward version of a safe format. A *quick format* starts by saving unformatting information, but from that point is over almost as fast as it starts because the remainder of the format involves nothing more than clearing the very small parts of the disk occupied by the FAT and the root directory. MS-DOS omits the time-consuming process of sector verification and checking for bad sectors. Essentially, a quick format assumes that any bad sectors recorded during the previous format remain unchanged.

Unconditional formatting

In everyday MS-DOS operations, an *unconditional format* occurs when you format a never-formatted floppy disk for the first time, when you reformat a backup disk, or when you specify an unconditional format on either a floppy or a hard disk. During an unconditional format,

- MS-DOS writes sectors onto the disk if it is a floppy disk. (This is why you need an unconditional format if you decide to format a floppy disk to a different capacity.) If the disk is a hard disk, MS-DOS verifies, but does not actually redefine, disk sectors—a process that can still take a significant amount of time.

- MS-DOS checks the disk for unusable (bad) sectors and marks those sectors as unavailable for storage.

- MS-DOS creates the FAT, sets aside the boot sector, and creates the root directory of the disk. If you format the disk as a system disk, MS-DOS also records the initial, short bootstrap program in the boot sector. It makes IO.SYS, MSDOS.SYS, COMMAND.COM, and, if you use version 6, DBLSPACE.BIN the first entries in the root directory, and it copies those files into the files area immediately following the end of the root directory.

Because of its thoroughness, an unconditional format is recommended if you have trouble formatting a floppy disk for the first time, if you want to make the contents of a disk unrecoverable, or if MS-DOS has some difficulty reading from or writing to a disk. Bear in mind, however, that an unconditional format cannot be undone.

The commands described in the remainder of this chapter all cover some aspect of disks or disk management with MS-DOS.

Assign—through version 5 only

The Assign command reassigns a disk drive so that read and write operations directed to it are received by a different drive. Originally included in MS-DOS to allow users to work with programs that expected to find their data files on either drive A or drive B, Assign is dangerous and should be avoided except with programs (if any still exist) that cannot recognize a hard disk. If drives must be redirected, the Substitute (Subst) command, available in versions 3.1 through 6, is preferable to Assign. However, do not run Subst (or Assign) while Microsoft Windows is running. Windows does not recognize the substitution. Use Subst before starting up Windows.

When you use Assign, the letter of the drive you redirect becomes unusable, as do programs and data files on it. In effect, the original drive no longer exists, and you cannot even undo the assignment unless you've copied ASSIGN.COM to the new drive. Because of this, avoid assigning your startup hard disk to another drive. You can use Assign to redirect disk operations from a network drive to a local drive.

NOTE: Some programs need detailed information about drive size and format to work correctly. Assign covers up this information, so it can be dangerous when used with such programs. Within MS-DOS, Assign should never be used with Backup, Restore, Label, Join, Subst, or Print. The Format, Diskcomp, and Diskcopy commands refuse to work with assigned drives. Don't use Copy with Assign; doing so could mean you inadvertently copy a file to a disk containing another file with the same name, destroying the original file.

Command syntax

The syntax of the Assign command is as follows:

> assign = *drive1*[:] *drive2*[:] /sta

drive1 is the drive you want to assign to another drive. You can omit the colon.

drive2 is the drive to which you want disk read and write operations redirected. You can omit the colon.

/sta causes Assign to display the current status of assigned drives. You can abbreviate this switch as /s.

To assign more than one drive in a single command, separate each pair of drives with a space. Each time you type an Assign command, the new drive assignment replaces the old. Typing *assign* by itself, without any parameters or switches, undoes all drive assignments.

Examples

Type:	To:
C:\>assign a = c b = c	Redirect read and write requests from drives A and B to drive C.
C:\>assign /sta	See the current status of assigned drives.
C:\>assign	Undo all drive assignments.

Check Disk (Chkdsk)

Chkdsk is often used as a quick and easy way of finding out about memory use and disk storage. A typical Chkdsk report (shown here for a very new system) looks like the following:

```
Volume MS-DOS_6    created 10-09-1992 11:33a
Volume Serial Number is 1949-5778
120147968 bytes total disk space
    79872 bytes in 2 hidden files
    10240 bytes in 3 directories
  6148096 bytes in 185 user files
113909760 bytes available on disk

     2048 bytes in each allocation unit
    58666 total allocation units on disk
    55620 available allocation units on disk

   655360 total bytes memory
   633792 bytes free
```

(Allocation units are the same as clusters.)

NOTE: If you've compressed the disk by using DoubleSpace, you'll see DoubleSpace chime in with two messages to Chkdsk reports, one telling you that DoubleSpace is checking your drive and one telling you what DoubleSpace finds.

There's more to Chkdsk than you see here on the surface, however. Before producing this report, Chkdsk examines the directory and FAT of the disk or files you specify to determine whether there are any recorded discrepancies that indicate errors in the way files have been allocated and stored on disk. Chkdsk can find a number of different kinds of errors, including damaged directories (about which you can do little) and physical bad sectors on the disk. The two most common uses of Chkdsk, however, involve checking for file fragmentation and attempting to recover digital waifs known as *lost* (or *orphaned*) *clusters.*

File fragmentation occurs as you save and delete files on a disk. Normally, it doesn't cause any problems, but fragmentation can slow disk access by causing

MS-DOS to jump from place to place to find all the clusters belonging to a file. You can check for fragmentation by specifying a file or a set of files when you run the Chkdsk command. If any files are fragmented, Chkdsk reports on them with a message. For example, if you type

```
C:\DONNER>chkdsk thunder.doc
```

you'll see the following at the end of the normal report:

```
C:\DONNER\THUNDER.DOC Contains 2 non-contiguous blocks
```

(Again, DoubleSpace runs its own check if you've compressed the disk.)

Although you can use the wildcard specification *.* to check an entire directory, you cannot check an entire disk unless all files on it are in the same (root) directory. To fix fragmentation, use the Defrag command, which is described later in this chapter.

Lost clusters are caused by a program that misbehaves to the extent that you must shut down or reboot the computer, a thoughtless or uncontrolled urge to press Ctrl-Alt-Del, or a sudden power outage. In all instances, the problem results because the program (and MS-DOS) are not given the opportunity to neatly close the file and update its record on disk. Although marked in the FAT as being in use, lost clusters do not belong to the chain of clusters for any file for which MS-DOS can find a directory entry. They are, in essence, file fragments that have been separated from the remainder of the file. Chkdsk automatically checks for lost clusters, whether you tell it to or not. If if finds any lost clusters, it reports on them with a message similar to this:

```
Errors found, F parameter not specified
Corrections will not be written to disk
    4 lost allocation units found in 1 chains.
    8192 bytes disk space would be freed
```

As you can see, Chkdsk does not attempt to do anything with lost clusters (allocation units) unless you specify the /f switch before running the command. If you use /f, Chkdsk recovers all lost clusters into a file in the root directory and gives it the name FILE0000.CHK. If the file already exists, Chkdsk uses the next number in sequence: FILE0001.CHK, FILE0002.CHK, and so on. Once the lost clusters are recovered in a file, use the MS-DOS Editor or a word processor to view the contents and determine whether you want to save any of the information you find. Usually, lost clusters contain gibberish, so you'll probably want to delete the file to make the space available for more important data.

NOTE: If Chkdsk finds a damaged directory, it might display the message Unrecoverable error in directory. Convert directory to file (Y/N)? *If you press Y, Chkdsk will create a file similar to the one it uses for lost clusters. This file does not, however, contain the contents of any files; those are lost to you. This option is primarily a means of getting rid of a badly damaged directory.*

Chkdsk can also report on another type of storage problem, this one called *cross-linking*. Cross-linked clusters are clusters with too many parents. They come about when the FAT references the same cluster in the chain for two different files—say, files A and B. Both file A and file B thus apparently "own" the cross-linked cluster, even though the data stored in the cluster can obviously belong to only one or the other. Whereas lost clusters can mean that part of a file has been cut off, cross-linked clusters can mean that a change to one of the linked files irreversibly and unexpectedly changes the contents of the other.

Although Chkdsk can find both lost and cross-linked clusters and can report on both, it can help you recover only lost clusters. Cross-linking gives no indication of which file actually owns the linked cluster, so any attempt to salvage cross-linked files is up to you. Such files might be fixable, at least in part, if you can load both linked files, cut them apart at the portion causing the problem, save them both, and then match orphaned clusters to the file that was truncated at the problem point. In some cases, however, cross-linking can turn on itself. If the problem occurs in a program file, for example, the file itself might not be either loadable or fixable.

Command syntax

The syntax of the Chkdsk command is as follows:

chkdsk [*drive:*][*filespec*] /v /f

drive is the letter of the drive on which you want to check file storage.

filespec is, optionally, the path and file specification of one or more files you want to check for fragmentation. You can use wildcards. As already noted, the file specification *.* extends the check to all files in the current or specified directory, rather than the entire disk, unless all files are in the root directory of the disk you specify.

/v lists the names of all files on the disk as Chkdsk runs. This list is in addition to—and more extensive than—the list of files, if any, specified by *filespec*. That is, specifying *chkdsk c:\dos*.* /v* displays the names of all files in all directories on the disk but checks only the files in the DOS directory for fragmentation.

/f fixes storage errors if any are found, including references to lost clusters, which can optionally be collected into the file FILEnnnn.CHK described previously. If /f is used, the contents of lost clusters are not preserved on disk. Because /f can result in changes to the directory and FAT, do not use this switch when open, unsaved files are in memory. Also, do not run Chkdsk from Windows or when you are using the Task Swapper from within the MS-DOS Shell. Do not use the /f switch if you redirect the output of Chkdsk to a file.

Examples

Type:	To:
C:\>chkdsk	Check the status of the current drive (C).
C:\>chkdsk /f	Fix file-storage errors on the current drive (C).
C:\>chkdsk a:*.doc	Check the status of the disk in drive A and check all DOC files for fragmentation.
C:\CASTLE>chkdsk *.*	Check the status of the current drive and check all files in the CASTLE directory for fragmentation.
C:\CASTLE>chkdsk *.* > b:castle.txt	Check the CASTLE directory, as above, but send the output of the command to a file named CASTLE.TXT on the disk in drive B.
C:\>chkdsk /v	Check the status of the current drive (C) and display a list of all files on the disk. (The display scrolls by rapidly on a fast computer.)

Defragmenter (Defrag)—version 6 only

Defrag, new with version 6 of MS-DOS, is based on a utility originally developed for the Norton Utilities (Symantec Corporation). The complement of Chkdsk, Defrag optimizes the physical storage of files and directories on disk by eliminating fragmentation. As mentioned under "Check Disk," file fragmentation is more a nuisance than a serious threat to data integrity and occurs naturally as you add and delete files on a disk. Over time, however, fragmentation can slow disk access by forcing MS-DOS to jump all over the disk to save and retrieve files. Defrag solves this problem and improves disk performance in either of two ways—one quick, the other slower but more effective:

- The quick method recouples fragmented files, but it does not otherwise alter storage on the disk.

- The slower, more effective method performs a full optimization that moves all directories to the beginning of the disk and eliminates gaps in storage space by both defragmenting files and moving all directories and files to one continuous section starting at the beginning of the disk. With this method, Defrag essentially "moves" all empty clusters to the end of the disk rather than leaving them between files.

NOTE: *Do not run Defrag when you are running Windows, and do not run it from the Dosshell Task List.*

Defrag, like most of the utilities that are new in version 6 of MS-DOS, displays a character-based window of its own, like this:

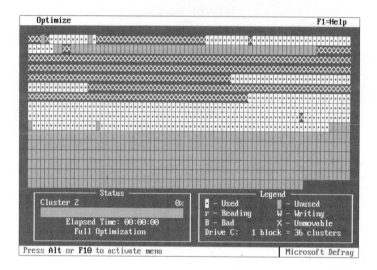

As you can see, the majority of the screen is occupied by a map of the disk you are optimizing. As the defragmentation process goes on—especially if you choose a full optimization—you see the small blocks representing disk clusters being moved from place to place.

When you run Defrag, it returns the following exit codes, which you can check by using the errorlevel option of the If command to control processing in a batch file. For further information, see Chapter 19.

Code	Meaning
0	Success
1	Internal error
2	No free clusters on the disk; at least one is needed for Defrag to function
3	Defragmentation stopped because Ctrl-C was pressed
4	General error
5	Error encountered while a cluster was being read
6	Error encountered while a cluster was being written
7	Allocation error; needs fixing with Chkdsk /f before disk can be defragmented
8	Memory error
9	Insufficient memory

This chapter describes the various options available for starting Defrag from the system prompt. Chapter 14 describes how to use the defragger.

NOTE: Do not use Defrag with drives compressed with DoubleSpace. Use the /defrag switch with the Dblspace command instead.

Command syntax

To start the Defrag utility, you use the following syntax from the MS-DOS command line. The drive parameter and switches described here are optional. You can use them to put Defrag immediately to work, or you can skip them and make the same choices from within the Defrag utility. The syntax is as follows:

defrag [*drive:*] /f /s[:*sortorder*] /u /b /skiphigh /lcd /bw /g0 /h

drive: is the drive containing the disk to defragment. You can specify either a hard disk or a floppy disk, but you cannot attempt to defragment a network drive or one controlled by Interlnk.

/f specifies a full optimization, as described previously. The /f switch cannot be used with /u because the two represent either/or choices.

/s[:*sortorder*] specifies the way in which you want directory entries sorted. The colon is optional. This parameter does not affect the physical layout of files on disk. It is more like using the DIRCMD variable in your AUTOEXEC.BAT file to control the default directory listings produced by the Directory command. Valid entries for *sortorder* are as follows:

- N for alphabetic order (A through Z) by name; -N for reverse alphabetic order (Z through A) by name.

- E for alphabetic order by extension; -E for reverse alphabetic order by extension.

- D for date and time, oldest first; -D for date and time, latest first. (Here -D will probably seem more "natural.")

- S for size, smallest first; -S for size, largest first.

/u specifies an "unfragment-only" optimization—the quick defragmentation described earlier.

/b causes the computer to restart after the disk has been optimized.

/skiphigh loads Defrag into conventional memory, rather than upper memory, where it is loaded by default. If your computer doesn't have upper memory, Defrag automatically goes into conventional memory.

/lcd uses an LCD color scheme, useful for laptops.

/bw uses a black-and-white color scheme.

/g0 disables the graphic mouse cursor and graphical character set.

/h moves hidden files.

Examples

Type:	To:
C:\>defrag	Start the defragmenter. Doing this causes Defrag to start up and then prompt for drive, optimization type, and other choices.
C:\>defrag c: /f	Perform a full defragmentation of drive C. Before beginning the defragmentation, Defrag checks the drive you specify. If no defragmentation is needed, the utility stops and lets you exit by pressing Enter, followed by X.
C:\>defrag b: /f /sn	Perform a full defragmentation of the disk in drive B and specify that directory entries be sorted alphabetically by name.
C:\>defrag a: /u /skiphigh	Peform a partial defragmentation of the disk in drive A, loading Defrag into conventional rather than high memory.

Disk Compare (Diskcomp)

Diskcomp compares two floppy disks on a track-by-track basis to determine whether they are identical. The command has been a part of IBM releases of MS-DOS since version 1.0, and a part of MS-DOS since version 3.2. Diskcomp is simple to use and provides a means of checking whether, and where, the contents of two floppy disks differ. The command is useful if disks are often duplicated and then used for editing, but the process can be tedious on a system with one floppy drive or two floppy drives of different capacities. You'll probably have to swap disks at least once, and possibly several times, even if the computer has a considerable amount of memory and not much to think about.

In comparing disks, bear in mind that Diskcomp performs a track-by-track comparison. It does not check directories, the FAT, or file contents, so it finds two disks identical only if files are stored in exactly the same physical locations on both disks. The Diskcopy command produces this type of duplication; Copy and Xcopy do not. Thus, even though two disks can contain exactly the same files, if the files were transferred with Copy or Xcopy, using Diskcomp will most likely show that the disks are different. Diskcomp also uses the number of tracks and sectors on the first disk as the basis for comparing the second disk, so you cannot compare disks of different sizes or capacities.

Because Diskcomp works only with floppy-disk drives, the drive parameters that you use depend on the current drive and on the number of floppy drives you have:

- If a floppy drive is the current drive, you can simply type the Diskcomp command with no parameters and MS-DOS will use the same drive to compare both floppy disks.

- If you type a single drive parameter, MS-DOS will use the current floppy drive for the second (destination) disk.

- If the current drive is your hard disk, you must specify a drive for both the first and second disks to be compared, even if you specify the same drive for both. If you specify only one drive, such as B, MS-DOS will assume you are comparing your hard disk to a floppy and will refuse to continue.

Regardless of the way you type the Diskcomp command, MS-DOS prompts you through the entire procedure. For example, on a system with one 3.5-inch drive (drive B), you see the following:

```
Insert FIRST diskette in drive B:
Press any key to continue...
```

Insert one of the floppy disks to compare and press a key. MS-DOS then displays

```
Comparing 80 tracks
18 sectors per track, 2 side(s)
```

and then prompts for the second floppy disk:

```
Insert SECOND diskette in drive B:
Press any key to continue...
```

Keep track of which disk is which. It is at this point that you might find yourself being prompted to swap disks several times. (If you get sick of it all, press Ctrl-Break to quit.) When the comparison is complete, MS-DOS displays the result. If the disks are different, you see one or more messages like this:

```
Compare error on
side 0, track 11
```

If the disks are the same, meaning identical information in equivalent sectors on equivalent tracks, MS-DOS displays

```
Compare OK
Compare another diskette (Y/N) ?
```

Diskcomp does not work with network drives or with those reassigned by the Join or Subst command. The command returns the exit codes shown on the next page, which you can check for within a batch file to control the processing of other commands.

Code	Meaning
0	Disks are identical
1	Disks are different
2	Compare ended because Ctrl-C was pressed
3	Critical error, such as a bad sector
4	Initialization error, such as an invalid drive specification

Command syntax

The Diskcomp command has the following syntax:

diskcomp [*drive1:*] [*drive2:*] /1 /8

drive1 and *drive2* are the drives containing the disks to be compared. You can omit both parameters if the current drive is the floppy drive you will use for the comparison. However, specify both if the current drive is a hard disk, such as C. Furthermore, if you have two floppy drives of different sizes or capacities, specify the same drive as both *drive1* and *drive2*.

/1 and /8 are both leftovers from earlier days. /1 compares only one side, even if the disks are double-sided; /8 compares eight sectors per track. Both switches hark back to 5.25-inch floppies with capacities of 160 K, 180 K, and 320 K. (You're not likely to use these.)

Examples

Type:	To:
C:\>diskcomp a: a:	Compare two disks from the current drive (C), using only one floppy disk drive—for example, a 5.25-inch drive. Use this format if the current drive is your hard disk and you have one floppy drive or two floppy drives of different capacities.
A:\>diskcomp	Compare two disks in drive A, as above, but when the floppy drive is also the current drive.
A:\>diskcomp b:	Compare the disk in drive B to the disk in the current drive (A), assuming both drives are the same size and capacity.
C:\>diskcomp a: b:	Compare floppy disks in drives A and B, both of which are the same capacity. Again, the current drive is the hard disk.

Diskcopy

Outwardly, the Diskcopy command is similar to Diskcomp except, of course, that it copies rather than compares floppy disks. Diskcopy has been part of IBM releases of MS-DOS since version 1 and part of MS-DOS since version 2. When you use Diskcopy, MS-DOS duplicates a disk on a sector-by-sector basis, creating a mirror image of the original, including hidden and system files, so you can use this command to duplicate startup disks if necessary.

Because Diskcopy makes such a faithful reproduction, Copy and Xcopy have traditionally been recommended over Diskcopy for duplicating badly fragmented disks. With MS-DOS version 6, you can now use Defrag to optimize disk storage. However, Copy and Xcopy are probably still faster for floppy disks.

When you use the Diskcopy command, the procedure is basically the same as using Diskcomp:

- If the current drive is a hard disk, be sure to specify floppy disk drives for both source and destination. Otherwise, Diskcopy assumes you are attempting to duplicate a hard disk on a floppy, refuses, displays an *Invalid drive specification* message, and quits.

- If the current drive is a floppy drive, you can type the Diskcopy command without drive parameters. Diskcopy will prompt you to swap disks back and forth until the copying is completed.

- If you have two floppy drives of the same capacity and the current drive is a floppy drive, you can type a single drive parameter and Diskcopy will use the current drive as the destination.

When you use Diskcopy, the destination disk can be either formatted or unformatted. If the disk is unformatted, Diskcopy will format the destination disk to the number of tracks and sectors on the source disk. Like Diskcomp, Diskcopy prompts you through the process. Once again, if you are copying from and to the same drive, you will probably have to swap several times. Yawn.

If the source disk has a volume serial number, the destination will be given a new volume serial number.

Diskcopy returns the following exit codes:

Code	Meaning
0	Success
1	Nonfatal error in reading from or writing to disk (significant, but not enough to stop the process)
2	Copy ended because Ctrl-C was pressed
3	Fatal error, such as an unreadable source disk
4	Initialization error, such as an invalid drive specification

Command syntax

The syntax of the Diskcopy command is as follows:

diskcopy [*drive1:*] [*drive2:*] /1 /v

drive1 and *drive2* are the drives containing the disks to be copied from and to. You can omit both parameters if the current drive is the floppy drive you will use for the copy. However, specify both if the current drive is a hard disk. If the two drives are not the same size, Diskcopy will tell you the drives are incompatible and will refuse to make the copy. It will, however, ask you if you want to try again.

/1 copies only one side of the source disk, even if it is double-sided. Like the /1 switch in the Diskcomp command, this switch is a leftover from earlier days.

/v verifies the copy. Use this switch if you must be sure a disk is copied correctly. /v does, however, slow the process and is usually unnecessary.

Examples

Type:	To:
C:\>diskcopy a: a:	Copy two disks from the current drive (C), using only one floppy disk drive—for example, a 5.25-inch drive. Use this form of the command if the current drive is your hard disk and you have one floppy drive or two floppy drives of different capacities.
A:\>diskcopy	Copy two disks in drive A, as above, but when the floppy drive is also the current drive.
A:\>diskcopy b:	Copy the disk in drive B to the disk in the current drive (A), assuming both drives are the same size and capacity.
C:\>diskcopy a: b:	Copy the floppy disk in drive A to the disk in drive B. Both disks should be of the same capacity. Again, the current drive is the hard disk.

DBLSPACE.SYS

You might think that DBLSPACE.SYS, the device driver, controls the actions of DoubleSpace, the program, but it does not. DBLSPACE.SYS has one function in life: to determine the final location of a file named DBLSPACE.BIN in memory. DBLSPACE.BIN is actually the file that enables you to use compressed drives. An important system file, DBLSPACE.BIN is loaded early in the boot process, before CONFIG.SYS and AUTOEXEC.BAT are processed. Because it is loaded even before MS-DOS has access to upper memory or extended memory, DBLSPACE.BIN is necessarily loaded into conventional memory—specifically, at the top of conventional memory. This is where DBLSPACE.SYS comes into play.

When you run DoubleSpace for the first time, you start a Setup program that compresses your startup hard disk. Although you don't see it happen, Setup also adds a Device command to your CONFIG.SYS file. This Device command loads DBLSPACE.SYS, and DBLSPACE.SYS, in turn, becomes the MS-DOS sheepdog that herds DBLSPACE.BIN into its final memory location. Initially, the Device command for DBLSPACE.SYS moves DBLSPACE.BIN to the bottom of conventional memory, out of the way of programs that require access to the file's initial location at the top of conventional memory. You can, however, change the Device command to Devicehigh and cause DBLSPACE.SYS to trot DBLSPACE.BIN all the way to the upper memory area, if enough UMBs are available. Doing this adds about 43 K of conventional memory to the amount your programs and data can use.

Command syntax

The syntax of the Device (or Devicehigh) command, which loads DBLSPACE.SYS from your CONFIG.SYS file, is simple. To load DBLSPACE.SYS and enable it to move DBLSPACE.BIN to the bottom of conventional memory, you use the following command:

device=[*drive:*][*path*]dblspace.sys /move

To load DBLSPACE.SYS and enable it to move DBLSPACE.BIN to the upper memory area, you use the following command:

devicehigh=[*drive:*][*path*]dblspace.sys /move

drive: and *path* are the drive and directory (probably DOS) containing the DBLSPACE.SYS file.

/move moves DBLSPACE.BIN to its final location in memory.

If you use a Devicehigh command, you can include any of the switches and parameters described for Devicehigh in Chapter 12. Better yet, let MemMaker (described in Chapter 11) do the work for you. If you use Devicehigh and your system does not have enough available upper memory, DBLSPACE.SYS will load DBLSPACE.BIN at the bottom of conventional memory instead.

Examples

Include in CONFIG.SYS:	To:
`DEVICE=C:\DOS\DBLSPACE.SYS /MOVE`	Load DBLSPACE.SYS from the DOS directory on drive C and enable DBLSPACE.SYS to move DBLSPACE.BIN to the bottom of conventional memory.
`DEVICEHIGH=C:\DOS\DBLSPACE.SYS /MOVE`	Do the same as in the preceding example, but enable DBLSPACE.SYS to move DBLSPACE.BIN to the upper memory area if available.

DoubleSpace (Dblspace)—version 6 only

DoubleSpace is the version 6 feature that can turn 30 MB of hard disk into 50 MB or more, 120 MB of hard disk into almost 200 MB. It is the new disk-compression utility that increases the amount you can store on a disk without increasing the physical size of the medium (an obvious impossibility). How DoubleSpace manages to stuff more into less space is covered in Chapter 14. Briefly, however, file compression is the key.

When you compress a disk—floppy or hard—DoubleSpace divides the disk into two parts, a small uncompressed portion known as the *host* and a special file known as the *compressed volume file,* or *CVF.* The uncompressed portion, which is assigned its own drive letter, is the part of the disk in which DoubleSpace stores files such as IO.SYS and MSDOS.SYS that cannot be compressed and still remain usable. The CVF, although it is actually a file, becomes the "disk" on which DoubleSpace stores files after it compresses them. Each disk you compress has its own CVF, which is assigned the hidden, system, and read-only attributes and is usually named DBLSPACE.000. (If you have more than one compressed hard disk or if you have both a compressed hard disk and a compressed RAM disk on your system, DoubleSpace distinguishes among them by using 000 for the first drive, 001 for the second, and so on.) Regardless of the extension number, *do not delete or tinker with a DBLSPACE.00N file.* If you delete the file, you can probably recover it by using the Undelete command, but if you destroy the file, you destroy your compressed data. Leave well enough alone, and forget that DBLSPACE.00N even exists.

Disk compression under DoubleSpace is totally transparent. Even though files must be compressed when you store them and uncompressed when you request them, all the work happens on the fly, without your intervention or supervision. You can run compressed programs, view and print compressed documents, and use most MS-DOS commands. The only time you must specifically defer to DoubleSpace is when you want to perform certain disk-related activities, all of which are listed in the syntax section later in this command description and in Chapter 14.

When you choose to compress a disk, you should be aware of the two ways DoubleSpace can work: by compressing and by creating. These terms don't explain themselves particularly well, but here's what they mean:

- Compressing a disk means applying DoubleSpace to the entire disk and everything on it, other than files that must remain uncompressed. The uncompressed portion of the disk is assigned a new drive letter, such as G, but you access the newly compressed drive by its original letter designation, such as C.

■ Creating a new compressed drive means applying DoubleSpace only to the available free space on an uncompressed disk. You can use this option on your startup hard disk or any other hard disk, but you cannot create a compressed drive on a floppy disk. Creating a compressed drive also reverses the drive designations used in compressing a drive: A new drive letter is assigned to the *compressed* portion of the disk, and the original drive letter refers to the uncompressed portion.

When you use DoubleSpace, you can work either from the command line, as described later, or in a menu-based window like this:

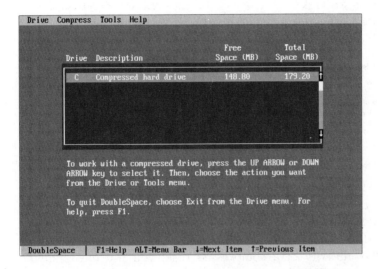

This illustration shows the DoubleSpace window as it appears after you've compressed your hard disk—a requirement if you want full access to the remaining DoubleSpace capabilities. The menus and their commands, as well as a description of DoubleSpace and how it works, are in Chapter 14. The remainder of this description covers using DoubleSpace from the MS-DOS command line.

Command syntax

Unlike most MS-DOS commands, DoubleSpace takes a variety of forms, each of which controls one aspect of using compressed disks. These different command forms represent an amalgam of disk-related tasks. Some are unique to disk compression; others, in the uncompressed world, are handled by MS-DOS commands such as Chkdsk, Format, and Defrag. The foundation of all these DoubleSpace command forms is simply this:

    dblspace

Use this form of the command to open the menu-based DoubleSpace window described earlier. To manage compressed disks, you use one of the command forms listed in the following table.

To:	Use:
Check a compressed disk.	Dblspace /chkdsk
Compress a disk. (This compresses the entire disk and everything on it.)	Dblspace /compress
Create a compressed drive (a CVF) without compressing the entire disk.	Dblspace /create
Defragment a compressed disk.	Dblspace /defragment
Delete a compressed drive. (This is possible only if you've used the /create option to create a compressed drive.)	Dblspace /delete
Format a compressed disk.	Dblspace /format
Find out about a compressed disk.	Dblspace /info
List all the drives on your system, with information about compressed drives.	Dblspace /list
Use a compressed floppy disk.	Dblspace /mount
Stop using a compressed floppy disk.	Dblspace /unmount
Adjust the estimated compression ratio on a disk.	Dblspace /ratio
Change the size of a compressed drive.	Dblspace /size

The following describes each of these commands, and their parameters and switches, in more detail.

To check on the integrity of a compressed disk, you use the following DoubleSpace equivalent of Chkdsk:

dblspace /chkdsk /f [*drive:*]

/chkdsk specifies the task you want done. You can abbreviate this as /chk. /f fixes errors on the compressed disk.

drive, which is optional, specifies the drive to check. If you omit this parameter, DoubleSpace checks the current drive.

For example, type

```
C:\>dblspace /chkdsk /f
```

to check the integrity of the compressed drive C, fixing any errors that are encountered.

To compress a disk, the syntax is as follows:

dblspace /compress *drive1:* [/newdrive=*drive2:*] [/reserve=*size*]

/compress tells DoubleSpace to compress a disk. Remember that compressing a disk means compressing the entire disk and all files on it. To carry out this command on your startup hard disk, DoubleSpace requires a minimum of 1.2 MB of free space. To compress other disks, hard or floppy, DoubleSpace requires a minimum of 0.65 MB of free space. This minimum means that DoubleSpace cannot compress 360-K floppies. You can abbreviate this switch as /com.

drive1: is the letter of the drive containing the disk you want to compress. The disk can be a hard disk, a floppy disk (other than a 360-K floppy), another removable drive, or a RAM drive. You must specify *drive1:*.

/newdrive=*drive2:* is an optional switch that allows you to specify the letter DoubleSpace assigns to the uncompressed host of the compressed drive. If you omit this switch, DoubleSpace assigns the next available drive letter. You can abbreviate /newdrive as /n or /new. To find out which drive letters are available for you to assign, use the Dblspace /list command described later.

/reserve=*size* is another optional switch that allows you to leave a specified amount of disk space, in megabytes, uncompressed. Use this switch to provide enough disk space for files, such as a Windows swap file, that must remain uncompressed.

For example, type

```
C:\>dblspace /compress d: /new=g /res=2
```

to compress hard disk D, assigning the uncompressed portion the drive letter G and reserving 2 MB for the uncompressed drive.

To create a new compressed drive, the syntax is as follows:

dblspace /create *drive1:* [newdrive=*drive2:*] [/size=*compressed-size*]
    [/reserve=*uncompressed-size*]

/create tells DoubleSpace to create a new compressed drive. Remember, you can do this with any hard disk, but not with floppies. You can abbreviate the switch as /cr.

drive1: is the letter of the drive containing the disk to compress. You must specify *drive1:*.

/newdrive=*drive2:* is an optional switch that allows you to specify the letter DoubleSpace assigns to the new compressed drive. If you omit this switch, DoubleSpace assigns the next available drive letter. You can abbreviate /newdrive as /n. To find out which drive letters you can assign, use the Dblspace /list command described later.

/size=*compressed-size*, another optional switch, allows you to specify the amount of space, in megabytes, to assign to the CVF—that is, you can specify how large the compressed drive is to be. If you specify /size, do not specify /reserve. You can abbreviate /size as /si.

/reserve=*uncompressed-size*, also optional, allows you to specify the amount of space, in megabytes, to reserve for the uncompressed drive. To make the compressed drive as large as possible, specify *uncompressed-size* as 0. If you omit both /size and /reserve, DoubleSpace reserves 1 MB of uncompressed space. If you specify /reserve, do not specify /size. You can abbreviate /reserve as /re.

For example, type

```
C:\>dblspace /create d: /n=h /re=0
```

to create a new compressed drive on drive D, assigning the compressed portion the drive letter H and making the compressed drive as large as possible.

To defragment a compressed drive, the syntax is as follows:

dblspace /defragment [*drive:*]

/defragment tells DoubleSpace to defragment the compressed volume file. Unlike the Defrag command you run from the MS-DOS prompt, the DoubleSpace /defragment command simply consolidates empty space at the end of the CVF. This command exists more to help you reduce the size of a compressed drive than to help you speed up system performance (which it probably won't do). You can abbreviate this switch as /def.

drive: is the letter of the drive to defragment. If you omit a drive letter, the command defragments the current drive.

For example, type

```
C:\>dblspace /def d:
```

to consolidate empty space at the end of the CVF of drive D.

To delete a compressed drive, the syntax is as follows:

dblspace /delete *drive:*

/delete tells DoubleSpace to delete the compressed drive. This command can be applied to drives you've compressed with either /compress or /create. You cannot, however, use /delete on your startup hard disk if you've used the /compress switch. The Dblspace /delete command actually deletes the CVF for the drive, essentially deleting every file contained in the CVF. Although you can recover the file with the Undelete command, think before using this command. You can abbreviate /delete as /del.

drive: is the letter of the compressed drive to delete. You must include this parameter.

For example, type

```
C:\>dblspace /del a:
```

to delete the CVF on the floppy disk in drive A. (Before doing this, you would have to mount the floppy disk with the Dblspace /mount command described later in this chapter.)

To format a compressed drive, the syntax is as follows:

dblspace /format *drive:*

/format tells DoubleSpace to format the disk. You must use this command rather than the MS-DOS Format command to reformat a compressed disk. You can abbreviate /format as /fo (or /for or /form...).

drive: is the drive containing the disk to format. If you are formatting a floppy disk, you'll have to use the Dblspace /mount command before issuing the command to format the disk.

For example, type

```
C:\>dblspace /mount a:
```

followed by

```
C:\>dblspace /for a:
```

to mount and then format the compressed floppy disk in drive A.

To find out about a compressed drive, the syntax is as follows:

dblspace /info *drive:*

/info tells DoubleSpace you want to find out about the disk. You can omit this switch as long as you specify a drive letter.

drive: is the letter of the drive for which you want information. You can omit the drive letter if you include the /info switch. If you omit both *drive:* and the /info switch, the command will open the menu-based DoubleSpace window.

For example, type

```
C:\>dblspace /info
```

or

```
C:\>dblspace c:
```

to find out about the compressed drive C. The report produced looks like this:

```
Compressed drive C is stored on uncompressed drive H in the file
H:\DBLSPACE.000.

        Space used:             30.37 MB
        Compression ratio:      1.7 to 1

        Space free:             147.87 MB
        Est. compression ratio: 2.0 to 1

        Total space:            179.23 MB
```

The compression ratio tells you how tightly files are compressed; the estimated compression ratio tells you how DoubleSpace calculates the space available for storing new files. The amount of free space must be estimated because, of course, DoubleSpace cannot determine ahead of time how compactly it can store unknown, unsaved files.

To find out about all local (non-network) drives and available drive letters on your system, the syntax is as follows:

dblspace /list

/list directs DoubleSpace to produce a report like the one on the next page.

Drive	Type	Total Free	Total Size	CVF Filename
A	Compressed floppy disk	2.64 MB	2.64 MB	M:\DBLSPACE.000
B	Floppy drive	0.96 MB	1.16 MB	
C	Compressed hard drive	148.87 MB	179.23 MB	H:\DBLSPACE.000
D	Local RAMDrive	0.63 MB	3.99 MB	
E	Available for DoubleSpace			
F	Available for DoubleSpace			
G	Available for DoubleSpace			
H	Local hard drive	22.41 MB	115.37 MB	
I	Available for DoubleSpace			
J	Available for DoubleSpace			
K	Available for DoubleSpace			
L	Compressed hard drive	6.52 MB	6.52 MB	D:\DBLSPACE.001
M	Floppy drive	0.00 MB	1.39 MB	
N	Available for DoubleSpace			

This report, by the way, shows a 4-MB RAM disk (D) on which a compressed drive (L) has been created. The drive letters shown as available can be specified as new drive letters if you compress or create a new compressed drive with the /compress or /create switch.

To make the CVF on a compressed floppy disk (or on a previously unmounted hard disk) available for use, the syntax is as follows:

dblspace /mount[=*nnn*] *drive1:* [newdrive=*drive2:*]

/mount tells DoubleSpace that you want access to the CVF on the disk in the drive you specify. By default, DoubleSpace searches for the DBLSPACE.000 file. Specify *nnn* if the CVF has a different extension, such as 001 or 002. Remember that you can use the Dblspace /list command to check on compressed volume files. You can abbreviate /mount as /mo.

drive1: is the letter of the drive containing the disk with the CVF you want to mount. You must specify a drive.

/newdrive=*drive2:* lets you specify the drive letter to be assigned to the newly mounted compressed drive. This switch is optional. If you omit it, DoubleSpace uses the next available drive letter. You can abbreviate /newdrive as /new.

For example, to mount the floppy disk in drive A, assuming a CVF named DBLSPACE.000, type

```
C:\>dblspace /mount a:
```

To unmount a compressed drive, making it temporarily unavailable, the syntax is as follows:

dblspace /unmount [*drive:*]

/unmount tells DoubleSpace to take the drive's CVF "off line" for the time being. If you unmount a compressed disk, you cannot use it. You can abbreviate /unmount as /u.

drive: is an optional parameter, but probably one you'll use often. It specifies the drive containing the disk to unmount. If you omit a drive letter, DoubleSpace unmounts the current drive. You cannot, however, unmount drive C.

For example, type

```
C:\>dblspace /unmount b:
```

to unmount the CVF for the floppy disk in drive B. Although MS-DOS can usually detect the difference between a compressed and an uncompressed floppy disk, consider habitually using Dblspace /unmount when replacing a compressed floppy disk with an uncompressed one.

To change the compression ratio DoubleSpace uses in estimating the remaining free space on a compressed disk, the syntax is as follows:

dblspace /ratio[=*n.n*] *drive:* or /all

/ratio tells DoubleSpace to change the compression ratio. Bear in mind that changing the ratio does not change the amount of free space on the compressed disk; it simply changes the way DoubleSpace calculates how much space remains for storing more files, assuming that the files are compressed in proportion to the ratio given. That is, changing a 2 to 1 compression ratio to 3 to 1 will cause DoubleSpace to estimate a larger amount of free space, but doing so will not change the actual compression used, nor will it change the size of the CVF. To see how tightly files are actually compressed, use the /c switch of the Dir command.

You can specify *n.n* as the compression ratio to be used. Any values between 1.0 (1 to 1) and 16.0 (16 to 1) are valid. If you don't specify a compression ratio, DoubleSpace uses the average actual compression ratio for all files on the drive. You can abbreviate /ratio as /ra.

drive: is the letter of the drive for which you want to change the compression ratio. If you include a drive letter, do not use the /all switch. Omit both the drive letter and the /all switch to change the compression ratio of the current drive.

/all, which you can use only if you do not specify *drive:*, applies the change in compression ratio to all currently mounted compressed drives.

For example, type

```
C:\>dblspace /ratio=8.0 b:
```

to set the compression ratio on the floppy disk in drive B to 8 to 1. Doing this would give you a realistic estimate of space remaining if you were using the disk in drive B to store a large number of files such as bitmaps, which are generally compressed at a ratio of about 8 to 1.

To change the size of a compressed drive, which you might do if you needed more or less space for the uncompressed host, the syntax is as follows:

dblspace /size[=compressed-size] or /reserve[=uncompressed-size] *drive:*

/size and /reserve are mutually exclusive switches. Use /size to specify a new size, in megabytes, for the compressed portion of the drive. Use /reserve to specify a new size, again in megabytes, for the uncompressed (host) portion of the drive. If you include /size but omit a new size, and you omit the /reserve switch completely, DoubleSpace makes the drive as small as possible. If you include /size and specify /reserve as 0, DoubleSpace makes the drive as large as possible. You can abbreviate /size as /si and /reserve as /res.

drive: is the letter of the compressed drive for which you want to change the size. You must specify a drive.

For example, type

```
C:\>dblspace /size=120 c:
```

to change the size of compressed drive C to 120 MB (assuming that drive letter C refers to the compressed portion of the disk, and another letter, say M, refers to the host.)

Type

```
C:\>dblspace /size /reserve=0 c:
```

to make compressed drive C as large as possible.

Or type

```
C:\>dblspace /size c:
```

to make compressed drive C as small as possible. (If you're reducing the size of a compressed drive, consider using the Dblspace /defragment command first, to collect all empty space at the end of the CVF.)

Fixed Disk (Fdisk)

Fdisk is a disk-partitioning utility included with IBM releases of MS-DOS since version 2 and with Microsoft releases of MS-DOS since version 3.2. Originally designed to enable the user to create and delete a DOS partition, Fdisk in version 3.3 gained the ability to create either a primary or an extended DOS partition. This capability was included to allow MS-DOS users access to hard disks larger than the 32-MB limit recognized by MS-DOS. Since version 4, however, an extended DOS partition is optional.

Both useful and scary to use (because access to all files on the disk is lost in the process of creating or deleting a partition), Fdisk is a rather spartan, menu-based utility that looks like this:

```
                    MS-DOS Version 6
                 Fixed Disk Setup Program
             (C)Copyright Microsoft Corp. 1983 - 1993

                        FDISK Options

Current fixed disk drive: 1

Choose one of the following:

1. Create DOS partition or Logical DOS Drive
2. Set active partition
3. Delete partition or Logical DOS Drive
4. Display partition information




Enter choice: [1]




Press Esc to exit FDISK
```

The four choices enable you to do the following:

- Create a DOS partition from which you can start and run MS-DOS or create a logical DOS drive within an extended partition if you have created one. You cannot use an extended partition until you define at least one logical drive in it.

- Set the active partition—that is, tell MS-DOS which of the partitions on the disk is the primary (bootable) DOS partition.

- Delete a partition or logical drive. This option leads to four additional choices, one of which (Delete Primary DOS Partition) is dangerous because it eliminates all access to existing files and makes the hard disk unusable until you repartition it. The other options delete an extended partition, a logical drive, and a non-MS-DOS partition (one created and used by another operating system). Although less critical than the first choice, all of these options also make existing files inaccessible.

- Display information about the partitions on the disk. The least risky of the four choices on the main menu, this option tells you how your hard disk is partitioned, and into what sizes. If you choose this option, you'll see information telling you the system uses either a FAT16 or a FAT12. These numbers refer to the number of bits used for FAT entries. The difference is immaterial.

You use Fdisk to either partition or repartition a hard disk. If, however, the hard disk was originally partitioned with another program, be sure to use the original partitioning software. Some such programs work around MS-DOS, and you can make the hard disk unusable if you try to go it alone. If you are in doubt, refer to your MS-DOS documentation or contact the manufacturer or the person who partitioned your hard disk.

NOTE: Fdisk does not work on a drive formed by the Subst command. If you have installed DoubleSpace, Fdisk will not display compressed drive sizes correctly and will not report on all drives represented by compressed volume files.

Command syntax

The command that starts Fdisk is this simple:

fdisk /status

/status displays partition information without starting the Fdisk program.

Examples

Type:	To:
C:\>fdisk	Start Fdisk.
C:\>fdisk /status	Display information about your computer's hard disk(s).

Format

Although it is needed less and less often as floppy disk manufacturers turn to shipping preformatted disks, Format remains one of the most necessary commands in the MS-DOS repertoire. Without Format, you can neither prepare a new, unformatted disk for use nor recycle an old one by reformatting it. If you use Fdisk to partition or repartition a disk, you must always follow up by formatting the new partition. If you create an extended DOS partition and divide it into more than one logical drive, you must format each drive separately.

Earlier in its life, Format was widely considered the most dangerous of MS-DOS commands because formatting was irreversible and the Format command made no distinction between floppy and hard disks. Not a few users of MS-DOS through version 3.1 were dismayed and horrified to find that pressing the Enter key after typing *format* wiped out their hard disks. Because of the potential destruction involved, Format became more sensitive to human fallibility in version 3.2. In all versions from 3.2 onward, Format has both required you to type a drive letter and has consistently displayed the following message if you attempt to format a hard disk:

```
WARNING, ALL DATA ON NON-REMOVABLE DISK
DRIVE X: WILL BE LOST!
Proceed with Format (Y/N)?
```

Since version 5, Format is even less dangerous because it performs a safe format by default and can be reversed by the Unformat command. Even so, however, bear in mind that Unformat is a cure, not a way of life. If you do accidentally format a needed disk, use Unformat immediately.

As mentioned earlier in this chapter, MS-DOS versions 5 and 6 perform any of three types of format: safe, quick, and unconditional. The process is straightforward and accompanied by a number of messages. These messages differ according to the type of format you perform and whether the disk has been previously formatted. Essentially, however, the process always begins with a message. For a hard disk, the message shown above always appears. For a floppy disk, MS-DOS begins by prompting for the disk:

```
Insert new diskette for drive x:
and press ENTER when ready...
```

If the format is to be either a safe or a quick format, you see the following after you press Enter:

```
Saving UNFORMAT information.
```

If the disk is new, you then see messages like this:

```
Formatting 1.44M
 xx percent completed.
```

If the disk was previously formatted, you then see messages like this:

```
Verifying 1.44M
 xx percent completed.
```

If the disk was previously formatted, but to a capacity other than the standard capacity of the disk drive, Format becomes a little more talkative:

```
Checking existing disk format.
Existing format differs from that specified.
This disk cannot be unformatted.
Proceed with Format (Y/N)?
```

This message appears because Format always attempts to format a floppy disk to the capacity of the drive in which you place the disk. That is, if you place a 360-K disk in a 1.2-MB drive, MS-DOS will assume that you want to format the disk to 1.2 MB. If the disk has already been formatted, Format proposes an unconditional format because it must change the number of sectors on the disk. Because formatting a low-capacity disk to a higher capacity than it is designed to accommodate generally results in a drawn-out formatting procedure and large numbers of bad sectors on the formatted disk, the best approach is to cancel the format and retype the command, specifying the correct disk capacity as described in the command syntax below.

Regardless of the type of format you specify, the process ends with the following message:

```
Format complete.
Volume label (11 characters, ENTER for none)?
```

A volume label is somewhat like a filename, but it is a name that you give to the entire disk. Although you don't have to assign a volume label, the name can help you quickly distinguish one disk from another—very useful if you create and save sets of disks. As the message states, you can use up to 11 characters, including spaces. (The label is limited to 11 characters because it is stored in the root directory, in the filename and extension fields of a directory entry.)

After you type a volume label or press Enter to skip labeling the disk, formatting ends with a report on disk storage, a line telling you the MS-DOS–assigned Volume Serial Number (in hexadecimal), and the following message:

```
Format another (Y/N)?
```

If you press Y to indicate that you want to format more disks, bear in mind that the same command applies to them as well, so Format will attempt to give them the same capacity as the disk you just formatted.

The Format command returns the following exit codes:

Code	Meaning
0	Success
3	Format stopped because Ctrl-C or Ctrl-Break was pressed
4	Fatal error; any error other than 3 or 5
5	Format stopped because N was pressed in response to the *Proceed with Format* prompt

Command syntax

NOTE: If you want to format a disk compressed by DoubleSpace, use Dblspace with the /format switch.

Because Format has been part of MS-DOS since version 1, it has gathered a formidable collection of switches, a number of them now archaic.

format *drive:* /q /u /f:*size* /t:*tracks* /n:*sectors* /v[:*label*] /s /b /1 /4 /8

drive is the letter of the drive containing the disk to be formatted.

/q performs a quick format. As in the default safe format, /q causes MS-DOS to save the FAT and the root directory for use if necessary in unformatting the disk. Use this if a floppy disk has no bad sectors (as reported by Chkdsk) and has not caused any read/write errors when used by MS-DOS.

/u performs an unconditional format. You might need this switch in formatting a new disk for the first time. Normally, an unconditional format takes longer than a safe or a quick format. However, even though the combination seems improbable, you can combine the /u and /q switches to specify a "quick unconditional" (unconditionally quick?) format. The /u portion cancels saving the FAT and root directory and the /q portion limits the format to clearing these elements.

/f:*size* specifies the capacity of a floppy disk. Use this parameter if you are formatting a disk to a capacity other than the capacity of the drive. Acceptable values are as follows:

Type:	For:
160, 160k, 160kb	160-K 5.25-inch disk—an antique that is seldom (if ever) needed
180, 180k, 180kb	180-K 5.25-inch disk— almost as old as the above
320, 320k, 320kb	320-K 5.25-inch disk—another "oldie"
360, 360k, 360kb	360-K 5.25-inch disk—aging, but still used
720, 720k, 720kb	720-K 3.5-inch disk—now you're in the modern age (for the moment)
1200, 1200k, 1200kb, 1.2, 1.2m, 1.2mb	1.2-MB 5.25-inch disk
1440, 1440k, 1440kb, 1.44, 1.44m, 1.44mb	1.44-MB 3.5-inch disk
2880, 2880k, 2880kb, 2.88, 2.88m, 2.88mb	2.88-MB 3.5-inch disk—new since version 5, still uncommon

/t:*tracks* and /n:*sectors* are the version 3.2 through 4.1 methods of specifying floppy disk capacities. If you specify one, you must specify both, as follows:

Tracks	Sectors	Disk size
40	9	360-K 5.25-inch disk
80	9	720-K 3.5-inch disk
80	15	1.2-MB 5.25-inch disk
80	18	1.44-MB 3.5-inch disk
80	36	2.88-MB 3.5-inch disk

The /t and /n switches exist primarily for compatibility with earlier versions of MS-DOS; use the /f switch instead.

/v[:*label*] assigns a volume label to the disk, omitting the prompt for a volume label at the end of the format procedure. Use this if you are formatting a single disk or if you want to assign the same volume label to a set of disks.

/s formats a system disk. The format proceeds as usual but ends by copying IO.SYS, MSDOS.SYS, COMMAND.COM, and, in version 6, DBLSPACE.BIN to the new disk so that it can be used for starting the system.

/b allocates space for system files but doesn't copy them.

/1 formats only one side of a floppy disk.

/4 formats a 360-K 5.25-inch floppy disk in a 1.2-MB 5.25-inch drive. Not always reliable—depends on the drive.

/8 formats with 8 sectors per track. Only for antique disks.

Examples

Type:	To:
C:\>format a:	Format a disk in drive A to match the capacity of the drive.
C:\>format b: /f:720	Format a low-capacity 720-K disk in the high-capacity 1.44-MB drive B.
C:\>format a: /q	Quick format a previously formatted disk in drive A. Note that this does not change the capacity of the disk and assumes that the disk capacity is the same as that of the drive.
C:\>format b: /s /v:startup	Format the disk in drive B, copy the system files to it, and assign to the disk the volume label STARTUP.
C:\>format a: /u	Format the disk in drive A unconditionally.

Join—through version 5 only

The Join command was added to MS-DOS in version 3 and enables you to treat directories on one disk as if they belonged to a subdirectory on another disk. When you use Join, MS-DOS temporarily grafts the directory structure of the "provider" disk into an empty subdirectory of the "receiver" disk. Join can be useful if you want to work with a program on one drive and data files on another without having to change drives or type drive letters. The command is confusing, however, and serves no real purpose with current applications, which more or less universally use alternate drives and subdirectories as a matter of course. Join cannot be used with a network drive or on those modified by a Subst or an Assign command, nor should you use it if you plan to use Backup, Restore, Format, Diskcopy, Chkdsk, Fdisk, Label, Mirror, Recover, Sys, Msbackup, Dblspace, Undelete, Unformat, or Diskcomp.

Command syntax

The syntax of the Join command is as follows:

join [*drive1:*] [*drive2:path*] /d

drive1 is the drive containing the directory that is to be connected to another drive. When the drive is joined, the entire directory structure, beginning with the root, is treated as if it were a subdirectory on the second drive.

drive2:path are the drive and path to which the directory on *drive1* will be connected. *path* must be empty. If it does not exist, Join creates it.

/d deletes a join.

If you type the Join command without parameters or switches, it displays the current status of joined drives, like this:

B: => C:\BOGUS

Examples

Type:	To:
C:\>join b: c:\bogus	Treat the root directory and all subdirectories and files on drive B as if they were part of the BOGUS directory on drive C.
C:\>join	View the current status of joined drives.
C:\>join b: /d	Delete the join in the first example.

Label

The Label command displays, changes, or deletes the volume label assigned to either a hard disk or a floppy disk. Label is not one of the more difficult or significant of MS-DOS commands, but it is useful. For example, if your hard disk bears a volume label such as MS-DOS 5, you can use the Label command to change the name to MS-DOS 6 when you upgrade.

The Label command is primarily designed for changing or deleting volume labels. If all you want to do is see or verify a volume label, use the Volume command instead. You'll save a little bit of time.

Command syntax

The syntax of the Label command is both simple and straightforward:

label [*drive:*][*label*]

drive is the letter of the drive containing the disk with the label you want to view, change, or delete.

label is the volume label you want to assign to the disk. You can type in either uppercase or lowercase (MS-DOS will convert alphabetic characters to uppercase). You can include spaces but cannot use the following characters:

" ( ) * + , . / : ; < = > ? [\ ] ^ ¦

If you omit both a drive letter and a label, Label displays a message like the following (the volume serial number does not appear in versions of MS-DOS prior to version 4):

```
Volume in drive C is MS-DOS 6
Volume Serial Number is 1949-5778
Volume label (11 characters, ENTER for none)?
```

At the prompt, type a label and press Enter, or press Ctrl-Break to cancel the command without affecting the existing volume label. If you press Enter and the disk has a label, MS-DOS assumes you want to delete the label and prompts for confirmation:

```
Delete current volume label (Y/N)?
```

Press Y or N as appropriate.

Examples

Type:	To:
`C:\>label ms-dos 6`	Assign (or change) the volume label of drive C to read MS-DOS 6.
`C:\>label`	See the current volume label of drive C (if one exists) and be prompted to change or delete the label.
`C:\>label b:`	See the volume label of the disk in drive B. Press Ctrl-Break to leave the label unchanged. Note that the Volume command would be preferable in this example.

Microsoft Anti-Virus (Msav)—version 6 only

The Microsoft Anti-Virus program, which you start by typing *msav*, is a utility from Central Point Software, Inc. Like the companion Vsafe utility described at the end of this chapter, Msav can help protect your computer from virus invasion. Although both Msav and Vsafe detect viruses, you can think of Msav as an "antibiotic" that you use to clean out any current viral infection, whereas Vsafe is more of a "vaccine" you use to guard against future infection by monitoring your computer and looking for any signs that indicate a possible infection (such as an unexplained attempt to format your hard disk).

Version 6 of MS-DOS includes two versions of the same anti-virus utility: the one described here, which you start at the MS-DOS prompt, and a Windows-based version, which you start and run from within Windows. The appearance of the MS-DOS version is visually not as highly graphical as its Windows counter-part, but both versions of the utility are quite similar in what they do and how they are used.

When you start Microsoft Anti-Virus at the system prompt, you first see the following message:

```
Microsoft Anti-Virus
Copyright (c) 1991-1992 Central Point Software, Inc.
```

Shortly after, the screen clears and is replaced by a character-based window with a menu of commands and options, like this:

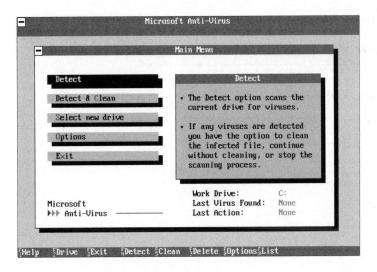

As the illustration shows, numerous commands and options are available from within the anti-virus utility. The following descriptions cover the startup command and its parameters and switches. Chapter 14, in Section Four, tells you about working with the utility itself.

You can run Msav from the MS-DOS prompt, but if you check for viruses on a regular basis, consider putting the command in AUTOEXEC.BAT. The Choice command, described in Section Four, lets you build your AUTOEXEC.BAT file in a way that lets you choose whether to run Msav or skip the check at startup.

Command syntax

To start Msav from the MS-DOS prompt, you use the following command syntax:

msav [*drive1:*][*filespec*] [*drive2:*]...[*driveN:*] /s /c /a /l /r /n /p /f /[video]

drive1, drive2...driveN represent the drive or drives you want to scan for viruses. If you omit a drive, Msav scans the current drive.

filespec is an optional parameter that lets you limit the scan to a particular directory and, optionally, a specific file. If you include a filename, limit the scan to a single drive and directory.

/s, the default, scans the drive or drives you specify but does not remove viruses if it finds any.

/c scans the drive or drives you specify and also removes any viruses it finds. This switch and /s are mutually exclusive. You can use one, but not both.

/a scans all drives other than drives A and B.

/l scans all non-network drives except drives A and B.

/r causes Msav to create a text file named MSAV.RPT that contains a report on the boot sector, number of files checked, number of viruses found, and number of viruses removed. A sample report might look like this:

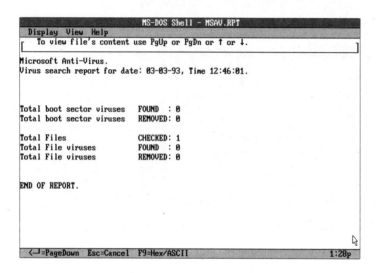

/MSAV.RPT is saved in the root directory of the disk you check. You can use the /r switch with the /n and /p switches as described in the following paragraphs.

The following two switches cause Msav to scan memory and specified drives and directories but without opening the full-screen window shown previously. Use these switches when you want to scan for viruses without leaving the MS-DOS prompt.

/n produces the scan you request but with two refinements: First, it allows you to replace the default message,

```
Microsoft Anti-Virus
Copyright (c) 1991-1993 Central Point Software, Inc.
Working...
```

with a message of your own, which you create and save as MSAV.TXT in the directory containing the MSAV.EXE program file (probably your DOS directory). Second, /n returns an exit code of 86 instead of a warning message if it finds a virus. The /n switch can be useful in batch files where you don't want to display any window from the Msav application.

/p produces a more detailed report of the scan, although still without leaving the system prompt. When you use the /p switch, Msav displays a report like the one shown for the /r switch. MSAV does not, however, save the report unless you also specify /r.

/f turns off the drive, directory, and filename display when you use either the /n or the /p switch. If you don't use /f, the names of drives, directories, and files flash quickly onto the screen as they are scanned.

/[video] stands for a number of video-related switches, enumerated below, that you can use to control the Msav display. Type the switch as /*video* to see the list of choices.

To control the size of characters on the screen, use one of the following:

- /25 for a 25-line display, the default.

- /28 for a 28-line display; VGA only.

- /43 for a 43-line display; primarily EGA, but can be used with VGA adapters capable of simulating EGA mode.

- /50 for a 50-line display; VGA only.

- /60 for a 60-line display; Video 7 display adapters only.

To control color and other display qualities, use the following:

- /bf to have Msav use the BIOS to produce on-screen characters, rather than display them directly. Use this option if characters are incorrectly displayed.

- /bw to run Msav in black and white.

- /ff to turn off snow (screen flickering) control on a CGA screen. Normally, snow control produces a clearer image; turning this feature off can make screen updates faster.

- /in to have Msav run in color even if it doesn't detect a color monitor.

- /lcd to set color on a computer, such as a notebook or laptop, with an LCD display.

- /mono to run Msav in monochrome. Use this with an IBM monochrome monitor if the /bw switch does not produce a clear display.

- /nf to eliminate the use of alternate fonts.

To control mouse operations, use the following:

- /bt to allow the use of a graphics mouse in Windows or graphics fonts with Desqview or UltraVision.

- /le to swap left and right mouse buttons.

- /ngm to use the character-based mouse pointer, a rectangular block, rather than the graphics-based arrow. Using this switch might speed up the mouse a bit.

- /ps2 resets the mouse pointer if it freezes or disappears.

Examples

Type:	To:
C:\>msav	Check all files on the current drive. This form of the command produces the menu-based Msav window.
C:\>msav a: /43 /le	Check all files on the disk in drive A, display the window in 43-line mode, and swap the left and right mouse buttons.
C:\>msav a: /n	Check the disk in drive A without leaving the MS-DOS prompt and display a report on the results of the scan.
C:\>msav c:\newfiles /p /f	Check all files in the NEWFILES directory on drive C without opening the Msav window. Omit the drive, path, and filename display and end by displaying a report on the scan.
C:\>msav /lcd	Check all files on drive C of a laptop or notebook computer, setting a color display customized for an LCD screen.

Mirror—version 5 only

NOTE FOR MS-DOS VERSION 6 USERS: The Mirror command does not exist in version 6, but most of the data protection features it provides are available through the enhanced version 6 Undelete and Unformat commands.

The Mirror command is a utility from Central Point Software, Inc., that serves three purposes which, in combination, protect both your disks and the information stored on them. For both hard and floppy disks, Mirror provides a memory-resident delete-tracking utility that records storage information about deleted files so that you can recover from accidental deletions or formats. Mirror can also save information in the system area of a hard or floppy disk, for use in rebuilding the disk if it is accidentally formatted. For hard disks only, Mirror is able to save a copy of the partition table—a safety measure that enables you to rebuild the table if it is damaged and the disk thus becomes unusable.

Mirror works in partnership with the version 5 Undelete and Unformat commands, which use three special files created by Mirror:

- PCTRACKR.DEL. This file contains storage records for deleted files. PCTRACKR.DEL is the product of Mirror's delete-tracking utility. Because the information it contains can be crucial in restoring deleted files, Mirror protects PCTRACKR.DEL with the system attribute. When you use Mirror to start delete tracking, it displays the following message:

  ```
  Creates an image of the system area.

  Drive C being processed.

  The MIRROR process was successful.

  Deletion-tracking software being installed.

  The following drives are supported:
  Drive C - Default files saved.

  Installation complete.
  ```

  If Mirror finds that delete tracking is already in effect, it does not attempt to install the delete-tracking program again. Instead, the preceding message ends with this:

  ```
  Cannot install. Already resident, or unknown status.
  ```

- MIRROR.FIL. This Mirror file contains a copy of the disk's FAT and root directory for use in rebuilding the disk if it is accidentally formatted or damaged. Mirror assigns this file the read-only attribute to protect it from change. When you use Mirror to create this file, you see the following message:

  ```
  Creates an image of the system area.

  Drive X being processed.

  The MIRROR process was successful.
  ```

- PARTNSAV.FIL. This Mirror file contains a copy of the hard disk's partition table. When you use this part of Mirror, you see the following:

  ```
  Disk Partition Table saver.

  The partition information from your hard drive(s) has been read.

  Next, the file PARTNSAV.FIL will be written to a floppy disk. Please
  insert a formatted diskette and type the name of the diskette drive.

  What drive? A
  ```

Mirror proposes the A drive by default, but you can specify another, such as B. If the table is saved without problem, Mirror responds as follows:

```
Successful.
```

Mirror stores both PCTRACKR.DEL and MIRROR.FIL in the root directory of the disk they protect. It stores PARTNSAV.FIL on a floppy disk because the file is needed only in an emergency in which the hard disk cannot be accessed. You need not continually update PARTNSAV.FIL, but because storage on a disk can change constantly, both PCTRCKR.DEL and MIRROR.FIL are important enough that a Mirror command that creates and updates them should be part of your AUTOEXEC.BAT file.

Command syntax

The Mirror command includes a number of switches that enable the different functions already described. The parameters and switches are described separately in this section.

For unformatting

To create MIRROR.FIL and save information for use in rebuilding a disk, the command syntax is as follows:

mirror *drive1:* [*drive2:*]...[*driveN:*] /1

drive1, drive2...driveN are the letters of the drives for which you want to save FAT and root directory information. You can include multiple drive letters in the same command.

/1 tells Mirror to save only one copy of MIRROR.FIL. If you do not use this switch, Mirror saves the previous copy, if any, as a hidden backup file named MIRROR.BAK.

To save information about the current disk, you can omit a drive letter—that is, simply type *mirror.*

For delete tracking

To work with delete tracking and create or update PCTRACKR.DEL for use in undeleting files, the command syntax is as follows:

mirror /t*drive1*[*-entries*] [/t*drive2*[*-entries*]...[/t*driveN*[*-entries*] /u

/t starts the delete-tracking program.

drive1, drive2...driveN are the letters of the drives for which you want to start delete tracking. You can include multiple drives in a single command. Each drive letter, however, must be preceded by the /t switch. Note that there is no space between /t and the drive letter, nor is there a colon or other separator.

entries is an optional parameter you can include for each drive to specify the maximum number of files to be tracked in PCTRACKR.DEL. You can specify 1 through 999, but you probably won't need to bother with this parameter. The default number of files tracked varies with disk capacity, as shown below. Changing the number of files does not change the size of the delete-tracking file. Use a hyphen before the entry. The following table shows the number of entries and the size of the delete-tracking file for different disk capacities:

Disk capacity	Number of entries	Size of PCTRACKR.DEL
360 K	25	5 K
720 K	50	9 K
1.2 MB and 1.44 MB	75	14 K
20-MB hard disk	101	18 K
32-MB hard disk	202	36 K
Hard disk larger than 32 MB	303	55 K

/u unloads the delete-tracking program from memory.

For saving the partition table of a hard disk

To create PARTNSAV.FIL and save a copy of a hard disk's partition table, the command syntax is as follows:

mirror [*drive:*] /partn

drive is the letter of the drive for which you want to save the partition table. You can omit *drive* if you want to save the table for the current drive, such as C.

/partn starts the part of Mirror that saves the partition table.

Examples

Type:	To:
C:\>mirror	Save FAT and root directory information about the current drive (C).
C:\>mirror c: /tc /ta /tb	Save FAT and root directory information about the current drive (C) and start delete tracking for drives A, B, and C.
C:\>mirror /partn	Save a copy of the partition table for the current drive (C).
C:\>mirror /u	Unload the delete-tracking program from memory.
C:\>mirror /tc - 200	Save FAT and root directory information about the current drive (C) and start delete tracking a maximum of 200 files for drive C.

Recover—through version 5 only

Recover is, or was, the one MS-DOS command most likely to produce a grimace followed by the word "Yuk." Odd that a command with such a salutary name would have such a sinister reputation, but the reason isn't hard to find: data loss. This is a command designed for use only when you have no other way to get a file off a disk, and it is recommended only for those times when a needed disk becomes unreadable because of damaged (not merely bad) sectors or an unreadable root directory.

When you use Recover, MS-DOS examines the disk cluster by cluster, salvaging the contents of readable sectors and discarding the contents of damaged sectors—those that MS-DOS once used for storing information but can no longer read. Damaged sectors are thus not the same as bad sectors, which are relatively common and are routinely reported by the Check Disk (Chkdsk) command. MS-DOS puts bad sectors off limits when the disk is formatted and never uses them for holding information, so you never have to worry about recovering their contents.

You can use Recover to salvage one file or an entire disk. Of the two operations, reclaiming individual files is far less risky than applying the Recover command to an entire disk. When you recover an entire disk, the command wipes out the original root directory and thus destroys whatever directory structure you had built on it. Recover attempts to salvage all subdirectories and the files they contain, to the extent that they are physically undamaged, but the original relationships between and among subdirectories and files will be gone. Furthermore, the root directory of any disk is limited in size, so applying Recover to an entire disk means that the maximum number of files you can recover depends on the maximum number of entries the root directory can hold.

As Recover works, it follows the FAT and places the salvaged information for a file in a new file, which it assigns the name FILE0001.REC. If FILE0001.REC already exists, or if you use Recover to reclaim an entire disk, the command creates a FILEnnnn.REC for each recovered file, assigning the files sequential numbers: FILE0002.REC, FILE0003.REC, and so on.

You cannot use Recover on a network drive.

Command syntax

The syntax of the Recover command is as follows:

  recover [*drive:*][*filespec*]

drive is the letter of the drive containing the disk on which you want to recover one or more files. If you include only a drive specification in the command, Recover attempts to salvage the entire disk.

filespec is the path, if appropriate, and filename of the file or files to be recovered. You cannot use wildcards.

Examples

Type:	To:
`C:\>recover a:hurtfile.txt`	Recover readable sectors of the file named HURTFILE.TXT on the disk in drive A.
`C:\>recover b:\crucial\need-it.doc`	Recover readable sectors of the file named NEED-IT.DOC in the CRUCIAL subdirectory on the disk in drive B.
`C:\>recover a:`	Recover the entire contents of the disk in drive A. Note the warnings in the preceding text regarding potential loss of both the directory tree and data with this form of the command.

Substitute (Subst)

The Subst command assigns a drive letter to a directory so that you can refer to the directory as if it were a disk drive. Essentially, Subst "breaks off" a directory you specify and turns it into a virtual disk drive. Originally designed to enable MS-DOS users to use subdirectories with programs that did not recognize directory structures, Subst now often serves as a convenient time-saver by allowing you to equate a long pathname with a drive letter and thus replace the pathname with the much shorter drive letter in commands.

Because you create a virtual disk drive with the Subst command, you must use a drive letter that falls within the range specified by the Lastdrive command in your CONFIG.SYS. (The Lastdrive command is described in Chapter 12.) Do not use Subst while you are running Windows. Also, avoid the following disk-related MS-DOS commands: Assign, Backup, Chkdsk, Unformat, Undelete with the /s switch, Defrag, Dblspace, Diskcomp, Diskcopy, Fdisk, Format, Label, Mirror, Restore, Recover (avoid this one in any case), and Sys.

Command syntax

The syntax of the Subst command is as follows:

subst [*drive1:*] [*drive2:\path*] /d

drive1: is the letter of the virtual drive you want to "create"—that is, equate with a particular drive and path.

drive2:\path is the drive and directory you want to assign to a virtual drive. You must include a path, but you can specify the root directory (\) to assign an entire disk to a virtual drive.

You can omit both *drive1:* and *drive2:\path* to check on substitutions currently in effect. If you do this, Subst responds with a message like the following:

```
X: => C:\ART\PICASSO\BLUE
```

Here the simple drive letter X is substituted for the much longer and far more cumbersome path to the BLUE subdirectory of the PICASSO subdirectory of the ART directory in the root directory of drive C. It assumes that X is à legitimate drive letter specified by the Lastdrive configuration command.

Examples

Type:	To:
C:\>subst x: c:\art\picasso\blue	Substitute the drive letter X for the path C:\ART\PICASSO\BLUE as in the preceding example.
C:\>subst a: b:\	Substitute the root directory of the disk in drive B for the disk in drive A, in effect reassigning drive B to drive A.
C:\>subst a: /d	Delete the substitution in the preceding example.
C:\>subst	Check on substitutions currently in effect.

System (Sys)

The Sys command has been part of MS-DOS since version 1. You use this command to copy the two hidden files IO.SYS and MSDOS.SYS from one disk to another. In versions 5 and 6 of MS-DOS, the Sys command also copies the command interpreter, COMMAND.COM; earlier versions require you to copy this file separately. In version 6 only, Sys also copies DBLSPACE.BIN to the new disk.

The Sys command does what the /s switch of the Format command does, but without requiring the destination disk to be formatted or reformatted first. Use Format with the /s switch to create a clean, bootable disk; use Sys to upgrade an existing disk without losing any files on it. You cannot use the Sys command with a network drive or with a drive controlled by the Interlnk file-transfer utility in version 6. You also cannot use this command with drives affected by an Assign, Join, or Subst command.

Command syntax

The syntax of the Sys command is as follows:

sys [*source*] *target*

source is the drive and path of the disk containing the system files and COM-MAND.COM. You can omit *source* if the current drive is your startup drive and the files are in the root directory, as all three should be.

target is the drive containing the disk to which you want to transfer the system files. You must specify *target*. You cannot specify a subdirectory.

Example

Type:	To:
C:\>sys a:	Transfer the system files and command interpreter from the current drive, an MS-DOS startup disk, to the disk in drive A.

Unformat

The Unformat command, available in both versions 5 and 6 of MS-DOS, rebuilds (or attempts to rebuild) an accidentally formatted disk or one on which you want to undo an ill-advised Recover command. If you have the version 5 Mirror command, Unformat can also help you rebuild a damaged partition table on your hard disk. A utility developed by Central Point Software, Inc., Unformat adds to MS-DOS a long-needed cure for user shortsightedness. It cannot, however, rebuild a floppy disk you formatted with the /u switch of the Format command, nor can it guarantee full recovery of fragmented files, so you would do well to consider Unformat a rescuer, not a crutch. Unformat can be used with local drives only; you cannot use it on network drives.

To work its magic, Unformat can use the FAT and root directory entries maintained by MS-DOS, but it is much more effective when it can rely on a recent copy of a file named MIRROR.FIL, which is created whenever you use the Format command without the /u switch and is updated when you use the Mirror [*drive:*] form of the version 5 Mirror command.

NOTE: If you upgraded to version 6 from version 5, your old Mirror command still works. If your version 6 of MS-DOS is a new installation, you can order Mirror on the Supplemental Disk from Microsoft if you want, although for the most part you should be able to rely on Format to save the necessary information for you.

Whether you use Format or Mirror to save FAT and root directory information, Unformat works pretty much the same in both versions 5 and 6 of MS-DOS.
When you use the Unformat command, the unformatting process always begins
with the following message:

```
Insert disk to rebuild in drive X:
and press ENTER when ready.
```

As long as you have used either Mirror or Format (the latter is a safe bet if you're
unformatting a disk) the following message appears when you press Enter:

```
Restores the system area of your disk by using the image file created
by the MIRROR command.

    WARNING!!           WARNING!!

This command should be used only to recover from the inadvertent use of
the FORMAT command or the RECOVER command.  Any other use of the UNFORMAT
command may cause you to lose data!  Files modified since the MIRROR image
file was created may be lost.

Searching disk for MIRROR image.

The last time the MIRROR or FORMAT command was used was at hh:mm on mm-dd-
yy.

The MIRROR image file has been validated.

Are you sure you want to update the system area of your drive X (Y/N)?
```

At this point, pressing Y means that Unformat will attempt to rebuild the
disk. Although your other options are limited to one—total loss of all files on the
disk—be sure you want to proceed. Before committing yourself, especially if a
hard disk is involved, you might want to take the time to run a "test" unformat as
described under the command syntax.

If you choose to go ahead and the unformatting process is successful, the procedure ends with:

```
The system area of drive X has been rebuilt.
You may need to restart the system.
```

You can ignore restarting if you've rebuilt a floppy disk.

*NOTE: If you unformat a disk using MS-DOS FAT and directory information, you
might be asked whether to truncate a fragmented file. Unformat cannot reconnect such
fragments, so you have to decide if some is better than none. If a data file is truncated or a
program does not load or work properly, you'll have to copy the complete file to the unformatted disk (if you have a backup copy) or reinstall the program.*

If caution is your motto, you can use the /test switch, described under the command syntax, to see how a disk will be unformatted without actually going ahead and doing the deed. If you use this switch, Unformat assumes there is no record of the original FAT and root directory, and the operation will be a little on the nerve-wracking side—justifiably so if the disk you're unformatting is your hard disk, although the alternative is even more extreme:

```
CAUTION !!
This attempts to recover all the files lost after a
format, assuming you've not been using the MIRROR command.
This method cannot guarantee complete recovery of your files.

The search-phase is safe: nothing is altered on the disk.
You will be prompted again before changes are written to the disk.

Using drive X:

Are you sure you want to do this?
If so, press Y; anything else cancels.
?N
```

If you go ahead, be prepared for a long wait. Unformat reads the disk directly, and this process can take five minutes or more, even on a floppy disk.

Command syntax

The syntax of the Unformat command is much simpler in version 6 than it is in version 5, so the two versions are treated separately below, even though some switches work identically in both.

Version 6 Unformat

In version 6, the Unformat command has the following syntax:

unformat *drive:* /l /test /p

drive is the letter of the drive containing the disk to be unformatted.

/l (lowercase L) causes Unformat to search the disk directly and, when the search is complete, list all the files and directories it finds. When you use the /test switch, unformatting proceeds in two stages, a safe stage during which Unformat checks the disk to determine which files and directories can be recovered, followed by the recovery itself. Because Unformat uses the FAT and root directory information recorded by MS-DOS, fragmented files are only partially recoverable. If you use this switch and the list of files and directories scrolls off the screen, stop scrolling by pressing Ctrl-S and resume scrolling by pressing any key. If you do not include the /l switch, Unformat uses the disk information saved by Format.

/test, like /l, causes Unformat to show how the disk would be unformatted, but it does not actually rebuild the disk. This switch also assumes there is no record of the disk's FAT and root directory other than the information saved by MS-DOS.

/p sends the output of the Unformat command to the printer connected to LPT1. Use this switch with the /l switch to produce a copy of the files and directories that are or would be recovered.

Version 5 Unformat

In version 5, the Unformat command has the following syntax:

unformat *drive:* /j /u /l /test /p /partn

drive, as in version 6, is the drive containing the disk to be unformatted.

/j checks the MIRROR.FIL file saved by Mirror against the FAT and root directory information recorded by MS-DOS. This switch verifies the contents of the Mirror file, but it does not rebuild the disk.

/u causes Unformat to ignore the MIRROR.FIL file, even if it exists. Use this switch only if a disk is corrupted or the Mirror file is so old you do not want to rely on it.

/l is the same as the /l switch in version 6 if you do not also include the /partn switch. If you include both /l and /partn in the same command, /l causes Unformat to display a hard disk's partition table without actually rebuilding it.

/test and /p are the same as the comparable switches in version 6.

/partn, if used with /l, displays the partition table of a hard disk. If used alone, it causes Unformat to display the following message, prompting for the floppy disk (previously made with the Mirror /partn command) that contains a copy of the partition table:

```
Hard Disk Partition Table restoration.

Insert the disk containing the file PARTNSAV.FIL
and type the letter of that disk drive.
What drive? A
```

Insert the disk and type the drive letter if it is not the proposed drive A. Unformat will then use the information on the floppy disk to rebuild the partition table.

Examples

Type:	To:
For version 6	
`C:\>unformat b:`	Unformat the disk in drive B, using the information saved by Format.

(continued)

Type:	To:
`B:\>unformat c: /test`	See how Unformat would rebuild drive C. Note the current drive (B). Also note that the Unformat command would be inaccessible in this situation, so you would need a bootable system disk and a decompressed copy of UNFOR-MAT.COM to carry out the command.
`C:\>unformat a: /l /p`	Send the output of the Unformat /l command to the printer on LPT1.

For version 5 (all of the above, plus the following)

`C:\>unformat b: /u`	Unformat the disk in drive B, using the information recorded by MS-DOS, whether or not a Mirror file exists. When you use this option, subdirectories of the root directory are recovered as SUBDIR.1, SUBDIR.2, and so on. Use the MS-DOS Shell to rename the directories.
`C:\>unformat /l /partn`	See the partition table of the current hard disk (drive C).
`A:\>unformat /partn`	Rebuild the partition table of drive C from the previously created floppy disk in drive A.

Volume (Vol)

The Vol command displays the volume label of a disk—nothing more and nothing less. Use it, instead of the Label command, to check on volume labels without being prompted for a new label. When you use the Vol command, MS-DOS displays a message like the following:

```
Volume in drive C is MS-DOS 6
Volume Serial Number is 1949-5778
```

(The volume serial number appears only in versions 4 and later.)

Command syntax

The syntax of the Vol command is as follows:

vol [*drive:*]

drive is the letter of the drive containing the disk whose volume label you want to check. Omit a drive letter to see the volume label of the current disk.

Examples

Type:	To:
`C:\>vol`	See the volume label of the current drive (C).
`C:\>vol a:`	See the volume label of the disk in drive A.

Vsafe—version 6 only

The Vsafe command, a relative of the Microsoft Anti-Virus command, is a utility from Central Point Software, Inc., that monitors your computer system for signs of virus activity. Unlike Microsoft Anti-Virus, which checks for and removes viruses that have taken up residence on disk or in memory, Vsafe is a memory-resident utility that watches for unauthorized activity, such as attempts to write to the boot sector of a disk, or unexplained activity, such as a change in the size, date, or time recorded in the directory entry of an executable file. If Vsafe detects such warning signals, it warns you with a "ringing" sound and a message asking what you want to do. When you run Vsafe, it gives you the same options Msav gives for combating viruses: You can choose to ignore the warning and continue what you're doing; stop before running a program if Vsafe is indicating that the program is suspect; or update the internal record, which includes file sizes and checksums—a data-verification method the utility uses to detemine whether executable files have changed since they were last used. Vsafe checks against checksums for evidence of changes to executable programs.

When you run Vsafe, you can specify up to eight levels of protection, either from the command line when you start the utility or in a special pop-up window you open by pressing the VSafe hot key—either Alt-V or another Alt-key or Ctrl-key combination that you define. These levels of protection are as follows:

1. Warning of attempts to perform a low-level format (write sectors) on the hard disk.

2. Warning of attempts by programs to remain in memory.

3. Preventing a program from writing to disk.

4. Checking of executable files when you run them.

5. Checking of all disks for viruses hidden in the boot sector.

6. Warning of attempts to write to the boot sector or the partition table of a hard disk.

7. Warning of attempts to write to the boot sector of a floppy disk.

8. Warning of attempts to modify executable files.

The switches you use and the utility's defaults are listed in the command syntax section for this command.

When you start the utility, you see a notice reminding you what the hot key is and a few lines of text telling you how much memory VSafe is using, like this:

```
┌─────────────────────────────────────┐
│          VSafe (tm)                  │
│                                      │
│     Copyright (c) 1991-1993          │
│   Central Point Software, Inc.       │
│      Hotkey:    <Alt><V>             │
└─────────────────────────────────────┘

VSafe successfully installed.
VSafe is using 23K of conventional memory,
             23K of XMS memory,
             0K of EMS memory.

[C:\]
```

To set or change monitoring options, press the hot key, and a small, colorful pop-up window opens in which you set or change options by pressing the number of the option you want. An × indicates that the option is turned on.

Although VSafe is easy to use, remember that it is a memory-resident (also called terminate-and-stay-resident, or TSR) utility. If you are a Windows user, VSafe can warn you of potential problems only if you load and run a program named MWAVTSR.EXE. This program, the Vsafe Manager, opens as an icon in Windows and maintains a "link" to VSafe. To ensure that the Vsafe Manager runs automatically, open your WIN.INI file (in the Windows directory), look at the top of the file for a line that begins *load=*, and edit the line so that it reads *load= mwavtsr.exe*. Save the WIN.INI file, and the next time you start Windows, the utility will be able to communicate with you while you are working in the Windows environment. You can also put the Vsafe Manager icon in your StartUp group.

Command syntax

You start VSafe from the MS-DOS command line. At the same time, you can start the utility according to your preferences by using the following switches, or you can control VSafe options after startup through the windowlike popup described in the preceding section. The VSafe syntax is as follows:

vsafe /*option+* /*option-* /ne /nx /ax /cx /n /d /u

/*option+* or /*option-* is the number of a monitoring option you want to turn on or off at startup. You can include more than one option in a command. Options other than the defaults described in the following list must be specified each time you start VSafe; the program does not "remember" your last settings. The options are shown on the next page.

- /1 warns you of attempts to perform a low-level format on the hard disk. This option is on (/1+) by default. Type /1- to turn it off.

- /2 warns you of a program's attempt to remain in memory. This option is off (/2-) by default. Type /2+ to turn it on.

- /3 prevents programs from writing to disk. This option is off (/3-) by default. Type /3+ to turn it on. Note that turning this option on means that all files essentially become read-only, so VSafe will prompt for confirmation—a time-consuming precaution—before allowing a new or changed file to be saved. The prompt allows you to choose from three options: Stop, Continue, or Boot (reboot the computer). If you want to save the file, choose Continue. Choosing Stop causes VSafe to display a *serious disk error* message and wait for you to type *r* (retry) and choose a different option. Because of the extra work involved in saving a file, be sure you want this option before turning it on.

- /4 causes VSafe to check executable files before running them. This option is on (/4+) by default. Type /4- to turn it off.

- /5 checks the boot sector of all disks for viruses. This option is on (/5+) by default. Type /5- to turn it off.

- /6 warns you if a program attempts to write to the boot sector or the partition table of your hard disk. Both are forbidden territory to most programs. This option is on (/6+) by default. Type /6- to turn it off.

- /7 warns you if a program attempts to write to the boot sector of a floppy disk—another no-no, although not as serious as the same attempt on a hard disk. This option is off (/7-) by default. Type /7+ to turn it on.

- /8 warns you if a program attempts to modify an executable file, a common ploy among viruses. This option is off (/8-) by default. Type /8+ to turn it on.

/ne prevents loading any portion of Vsafe into expanded memory.

/nx prevents loading any portion of Vsafe into extended memory.

/a*x* lets you define the hot key combination as Alt plus the character (*x*) that you specify as part of this switch.

/c*x* lets you define the hot key combination as Ctrl plus the character (*x*) that you specify as part of this switch.

/n allows you to monitor network drives for possible viruses.

/d causes VSafe not to calculate checksums. Turning checksums off does not save any substantial amount of time or energy (at least on your part). Leaving them on provides a good measure of extra protection.

/u unloads VSafe from memory. If you want to unload VSafe from the pop-up window illustrated earlier, you can press Alt-U. Be sure, however, to use the hot key combination to open the popup before pressing Alt-U. This key combination does not work from the command line.

Examples

Type:	To:
C:\>vsafe	Start VSafe with the default options.
C:\>vsafe /8+ or press the hot key to open the pop-up window, and then type *8*	Start VSafe and turn on protection of executable files.
C:\>vsafe /ne	Start VSafe but don't load it into expanded memory.
C:\>vsafe /n	Allow VSafe to monitor network drives.
C:\>vsafe /u or press the hot key to open the pop-up window, and then press Alt-U	Unload VSafe from memory and stop virus monitoring.

9

Directories

What You'll Find Here: Append; Change Directory (Chdir or Cd); Delete Tree (Deltree); Directory (Dir); Make Directory (Mkdir or Md); Path; Remove Directory (Rmdir or Rd); Tree.

How to avoid disaster? Let us count one way.
Files can reach the length and breadth and height of root,
till running out of room, DOS balks and to dismay
states flatly—no regrets—"Not one more can I save."

Ah, the innocent, though in a rush, sits staring all aghast.
Crying aloud, hoping to save both self and file alike,
s/he hears instead sad memory whisper, "Safety now is past.
Directories were e'er the answer." Oh, alas, alas.

*O*K, enough insulting Elizabeth Barrett Browning. That was just for fun. The root directory of a disk, however, is for real, and as hinted at in the preceding verse, it can hold only so many files before it fills up. Long before that point arrives, you can and should create subdirectories—not only for holding the overflow, but also, and more important, for organizing the disk files you save and use more than once. If you're an experienced MS-DOS user, you know that subdirectories are simple to use, and you no doubt make full use of them. To put things in perspective, however, back up a moment and take a quick look at the reasons why subdirectories soon become as essential as cabinets in the kitchen.

The root directory on any disk is large. On a double-density (360-K or 720-K) floppy disk, it can hold 112 entries; on a high-density (1.2-MB or 1.44-MB) floppy, it holds double that amount—224 entries. Either size is almost certainly large enough to hold all the files you want to save on these disks, especially on a 360-K floppy. But even on a disk with such limited capacity, consider the logistics of handling 112 files in a single directory—root or otherwise. MS-DOS does not allow duplicate filenames in the same directory, so you'd need considerable creative flair and inventiveness to come up with 112 different filenames, even allowing for differences among extensions. You'd also need an admirable memory to recall what file contents each of those 112 filenames and extensions referred to. And, of course, you'd have to use wildcards or the /p switch of the Directory command reflexively whenever you ordered MS-DOS to reel off a directory listing.

Now turn your attention to your hard disk. Here you have a root directory of 512 possible entries, minus those needed for COMMAND.COM, IO.SYS, MSDOS.SYS, DBLSPACE.BIN, CONFIG.SYS, AUTOEXEC.BAT, and a few other files, including one named WINA20.386, which supports use of the High Memory Area under Windows. Look at this root directory from two directions. Suppose you have a large hard disk of 120 MB. Divide that amount by, oh, 500 potential entries, and you end up with 240 K per file if you want to take full advantage of the disk's storage space. Big files. On the other hand, those 500 potential entries can also represent the sum of all the files you can save with a program such as your word processor. Assuming that your word processor makes automatic backups whenever you create or change files, you're now looking at a directory capable of holding perhaps less than half of what it had before (less than 250 files). Small directory.

The shape of a directory

Subdirectories are a means of imposing order on disk storage. By enabling you to create groups and subgroups within which to store your files, subdirectories allow you to sort and organize files on disk in the same logical way you would sort and stash more touchable items, from lampshades to lightbulbs. Subdirectories by any name are characteristic not only of MS-DOS, but of other operating systems as well. The Macintosh, for instance, uses the concept of folders, within which other folders can reside.

At heart, subdirectories and related structures are all based on the concept of hierarchies. All start with a top level and branch out and down from there, just like the organization chart in your office or business. This branching effect eventually produces a structure known as a tree, like this:

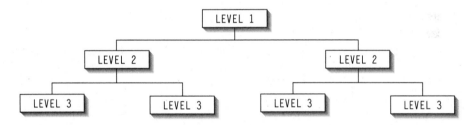

Botanical purists will no doubt note that trees don't usually grow upside down, and so the result of all this branching should more properly be called a root system. Well, language is sometimes imprecise, even in the computer world, where precision in programming is crucial.

Whether tree or root system, the real point illustrated by the preceding diagram is that each succeeding level in a tree is related to the one above, but is neither as important nor as comprehensive as the one above. To describe these relationships, and add mix to the metaphor, you now wander out of the forest and into the family.

In computer terminology, hierarchies of any sort (similar structures are also found in databases) are often referred to in parental terms. So, too, at least to some extent in MS-DOS. Whenever a directory, including the root, gives rise to a subdirectory, the originator is called the parent. For consistency, the offshoot is often called the child, although the term subdirectory probably seems more natural to you. At any rate, just as one individual in a human family can be both parent and child, so too can directories be both parent and child. The diagram on the next page shows the (organizational) parallels between the two.

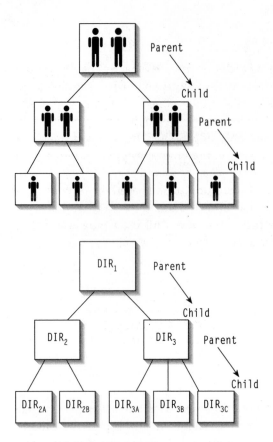

You see a parent directory whenever you run the Directory (Dir) command from any subdirectory: It's that little .. in the second line of the directory listing. Those dots represent the directory immediately above the current directory and appear in any listing that begins below root level, like this:

```
Volume in drive C is MS-DOS 6
Volume Serial Number is 1949-5778
Directory of C:\dos
.            <DIR> 10-06-92   4:02p
..           <DIR> 10-06-92   4:02p
EGA     SYS    4885 03-10-93   6:00a
FORMAT  COM   22717 03-10-93   6:00a
```

The single dot immediately above the symbol for the current directory is a stand-in for the current directory. The later section, "Moving around directories," covers these symbols in more detail.

You might notice, by the way, that . and .. always bear the same date and time stamps, even if the parent was created on a different day and at a different time from the subdirectory. This duplication appears in the subdirectory's listing because the .. entry for the parent directory refers not to the actual parent, but to an entry for the parent within the subdirectory. This entry, like a . entry for the subdirectory itself, always appears as one of the first two entries in a subdirectory. Both the .. and . entries are created at the time MS-DOS creates the subdirectory, and so both have the same date and time. (If such circular references make your head spin, ignore them and just attribute such peccadilloes to the personality of MS-DOS.)

The root vs. subdirectories

Every formatted disk has a root directory. This directory is, in effect, the ancestral directory from which all others spring. Because the root is created when a disk is formatted, MS-DOS gives it a certain size, depending on disk capacity, and that size is divided into 32-byte pigeonholes, one per directory entry. This fixed size and structure means that the root can hold only as many files as the number of directory entries it can contain—512 on a hard disk.

In contrast, a subdirectory—a directory within a directory—can hold as many entries as you want it to because MS-DOS treats all subdirectories as if they were files. Whereas the root directory is more or less engraved on the disk during formatting and cannot be changed (or deleted), MS-DOS handles subdirectories the way it does any other files. As you add to a subdirectory, MS-DOS assigns new disk storage whenever needed, and this is why a subdirectory can grow, for all practical purposes, to any size and can contain as many entries as you care to add to it.

There are, however, two differences between a subdirectory "file" and a normal file, such as a data file. First, the subdirectory's own directory entry includes a setting in the attribute byte that tells MS-DOS that the entry refers to a subdirectory. Second, the subdirectory itself contains a series of directory entries that MS-DOS uses to track down the physical storage locations of the files included in the subdirectory. In effect, using subdirectories is like using indexes within indexes. The diagram on the next page gives you a way to visualize the difference between the root directory and a subdirectory "file."

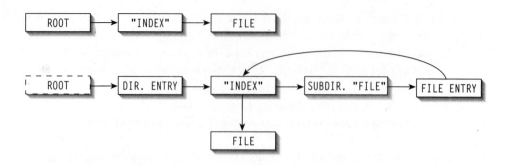

Subdirectory names

Subdirectories, like files, have filenames. Even though subdirectories are files of a special kind, their names follow the same rules that filenames do: up to eight characters, with an optional extension of up to three characters, and no fair using any of the special characters prohibited in normal filenames. Although people become accustomed to seeing subdirectory names without extensions, the judicious use of extensions can help you considerably in naming subdirectories and indicating their relative levels of importance. For example, when you up-grade from version 4 to version 5 of MS-DOS, or from version 5 to version 6, Setup creates a directory named OLD_DOS.1. If, for some reason, you repeat the upgrade without using the Delete Old DOS (Deloldos) command, Setup creates an OLD_DOS.2 subdirectory. In your own work, the same kind of naming can prove equally informative:

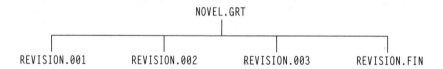

Unless you're the emotional type, and you like subdirectory names that won't be very informative:

NOTE: *MS-DOS limits the length of the search path for executable files (set by the Path command) to 127 characters. Because of this, if you have a choice, opt for short names for program directories. You'll be able to fit more directories into the search path.*

Pathnames

Unless you change the prompt with the Prompt command, MS-DOS sets the system prompt to show the name of the current directory, followed by a greater-than sign:

```
C:\DOS>
```

This prompt shows the current path—the list of subdirectories, starting from the root, that leads to the current directory. When you work with subdirectories and files within subdirectories, you type pathnames to tell MS-DOS the route it must follow, from the current directory, to reach the subdirectory (and file) you want. The full path to a subdirectory starts at the root and proceeds down, level by level, through the subdirectory tree.

When you type a path, you must use backslashes for the following:

- To indicate the root directory (if you are starting from the root)

- To separate directory levels within the pathname

MS-DOS limits the length of the path to a particular subdirectory or file to 63 characters, including backslashes. In practice, however, this limit is usually insignificant. If, as most people do, you habitually use subdirectory names of 8 characters or less, 63 characters provides, at the least, for a formidable seven subdirectory levels—probably far more than you need or want to work your way through, much less type—for example:

```
C:\>cd \dirname1\dirname2\dirname3\dirname4\dirname5\dirname6\dirname7
```

If you use 12-character subdirectory names (as in SDIRNAME.EXT), the 63-character limit still allows four subdirectory levels—again, an adequate number in most circumstances.

The pathname you type with any command depends on what the current directory is. If you're somewhere within the directory tree and you want to go down a level or two, you can omit any subdirectories above the current directory. For example, if you had the following directory structure leading to the file LUAU.DOC,

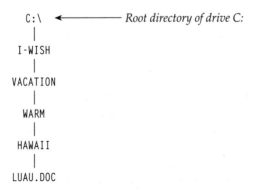

you would type the full path to the file as *c:\i-wish\vacation\warm\hawaii\luau.doc* but if the current directory were WARM, you could type the path to LUAU.DOC as *hawaii\luau.doc*. Notice, by the way, that you don't have to precede the current directory with a backslash unless you are referring to a subdirectory immediately below the root directory.

The search path

By default, MS-DOS looks to the current directory to find all the commands and programs you specify. To avoid typing long pathnames whenever you want to use a different directory, you set a command search path with the Path command. Setup either places this command in AUTOEXEC.BAT or modifies it, if necessary, during installation or upgrade. Unlike a pathname, the search path looks like the following:

```
PATH C:\;C:\DOS;C:\WINDOWS;C:\BATCH
```

Because MS-DOS reads AUTOEXEC.BAT every time your computer starts, a Path command in AUTOEXEC.BAT guarantees that the search path is set whenever you start or restart the computer. You can also modify the path whenever necessary by opening AUTOEXEC.BAT for editing in the MS-DOS Editor or in another program that can edit and save unformatted text files.

After you create a path, MS-DOS searches through it whenever you type the name of an executable file—one with a COM, EXE, or BAT extension. The search proceeds linearly through the subdirectories named in the path, so to save a small amount of time, it's a good idea to position the most often used subdirectories at the beginning of the search path.

NOTE: You can use the Append command to extend the search path or to include document directories in the path MS-DOS searches. Details on both the Path and Append commands appear later in this chapter.

Moving around directories

To MS-DOS, keeping track of the relationship between a parent directory and its subdirectories is paramount for ensuring that your directory structure and, hence, the organization of files on the disk, is maintained correctly. Thus, it doesn't matter whether a parent directory is called DOS or MOSS. What is important is that MS-DOS can tell how these directories are related to the root directory and to others down the line. To track directory relationships, MS-DOS relies on three special symbols:

- A backslash (\) always indicates the root directory of the disk. No matter how far down the directory tree you are, typing a backslash with the Change Directory (Chdir) command always takes you directly to the root. You can also use the backslash as a shorthand reference to the root in other commands, as shown below. You've probably, by the way, noted that the backslash is somewhat ambiguous, because it is also used between directories in a pathname. By itself, however, or immediately following a drive specifier, a backslash always refers to the root directory.

- The single dot (.) always represents the current directory. Because it represents your current location in the directory tree, typing a single dot with the Chdir command doesn't take you anywhere, but you can use this symbol in place of the pathname of the current directory in other MS-DOS commands, such as Xcopy.

- The double dot (..) always represents the parent of the current directory. You can use it with Chdir to move up one level in the directory tree. And you can also use this symbol with other MS-DOS commands, such as Dir, to refer to the parent of the current directory.

Thus, for example, you can move directly to the root from far down the directory tree with a command like this:

```
C:\BOGUS1\BOGUS2\BOGUS3\BOGUS4>cd \
```

Or you can move up one directory level (to BOGUS3) like this:

```
C:\BOGUS1\BOGUS2\BOGUS3\BOGUS4>cd ..
```

Or you can stay in the current directory and request a listing of the directory above with a command like this:

```
C:\BOGUS1\BOGUS2\BOGUS3\BOGUS4>dir ..
```

You can also combine the current-directory symbol with other pathnames to leap like a squirrel from one branch of the directory tree to a separate branch. For example, if your directory tree looks like this,

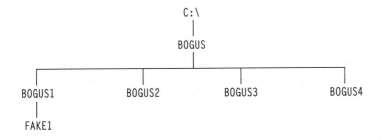

you could jump from BOGUS2 to FAKE1 in BOGUS1 with this command:

```
C:\BOGUS2>cd ..\BOGUS1\FAKE1
```

And, as mentioned earlier, you can save keystrokes by using the backslash, single dot, and double dots in Dir and other commands. The following command, for example, would produce a listing of the root directory:

```
C:\BOGUS\BOGUS2>dir \
```

This command would produce a listing of the files in FAKE1, under the BOGUS1 subdirectory:

```
C:\BOGUS\BOGUS2>dir ..\bogus1\fake1
```

And this would copy BOGUS1, all its files, and all its non-empty subdirectories to the disk in drive A:

```
C:\BOGUS1>xcopy . a: /s
```

The following descriptions cover commands related to managing directories with MS-DOS.

Append

The Append command is one of the more confusing that MS-DOS has to offer, not because it is complicated to use, but because of what it can do. Depending on how you use Append, you can

- Extend the current search path to include document directories as well as the directories listed in the Path command for executable files.

- Extend the current search path to include both document directories and directories containing executable files.

- Control directory searches, depending on whether you include a pathname in the file specification for a data file.

- Assign the list of appended directories to an environment variable which, in turn, can be handed to programs executed by other programs and can be used to control execution of batch files. (The environment is a small portion of memory—256 bytes by default—that contains current MS-DOS settings, such as the prompt and path. Programs use the environment to determine what these settings are. The MS-DOS command interpreter, for example, uses the Path environment variable in locating external command files.)

NOTE: Append in version 4 of MS-DOS differs slightly in capability. If you have version 4, refer to your MS-DOS documentation for details.

When you use Append, MS-DOS searches appended drives and directories *before* it searches the current path. As a result, Append can be useful not only for extending the search path but for cutting the time required to find a file, especially if the file is on a floppy disk and the current drive is your hard disk. Append can also be helpful in eliminating the need to type pathnames. You must always bear in mind, however, that Append can be confusing because it tends to cover up the actual directories in which files are stored. If you use appended directories and then create and save a file, the file is saved not in the appended directory, but in the current directory, unless the program displays or prompts for the directory in which you want to save the file. Even if the program does save to the correct directory, you can inadvertently change or overwrite important data if the new file has the same name as an existing file.

Because most application programs work easily with subdirectories, you should have little need for the Append command. It can be useful, however, under a few somewhat circumscribed sets of conditions:

- If you want to use files on a different drive, such as A, B, or a network drive and directory, without continually changing the current drive. Doing this eliminates some typing, but remember that new files are saved in the current directory, not the appended drive, directory, or both. This approach is useful when you are reviewing, but not altering or creating, data files or, if you are using a network drive, when you want to use a program on the network but save new files in the current directory on your computer.

- If you need a very long path in the Path command but you habitually use different sets of directories for different purposes: programming directories vs. application directories, for example. The Path command limits paths to 127 characters, so to avoid going over this limit, you can shorten the path to the directories you use most often and append the other set of directories when you need them.

- If you receive the *Out of environment space* message at startup, meaning that the environment is too small to hold a lengthy path. You can use Append to extend the search path without enlarging the environment— especially if, as already mentioned, the directories you use depend on the work you are doing. (To change the environment size, you use the /e switch of the Command command, described in Chapter 13.)

- If you want to control the search path from within a batch file. In this situation, you can set and call the Append environment variable to determine or to change the search path for either data files or executable files. If you have version 6 of MS-DOS, you can use the Choice command to give added flexibility to decision making.

Avoid using Append while running Windows, since Windows won't recognize the path created by Append.

Command syntax

The syntax of the Append command includes a number of switches, some of which are mutually exclusive:

append [*drive1:*]*path1*[;][*drive2:*]*path2*[;]...[*driveN:*]*pathN*[;] /x:on /x:off /path:on
/path:off /e

drive1:path1, drive2:path2...driveN:pathN are the drive and path of the directory or directories you want to append. You can specify only a drive letter, only a path, or a combination of the two. If you append more than one drive or directory in a single command, separate the appended paths with semicolons. You can append different lists of drives and directories during a session by reentering the Append command.

/x:on and /x:off determine whether Append searches the list of appended drives and directories for executable programs. The /x:on switch, which you can type as /x, includes the list in the search; /x:off excludes the list. The default is x:off. You can alternate between including and excluding appended drives and directories as often as you want during a session.

/path:on and /path:off determine whether a program, such as the MS-DOS Editor, searches the list of appended drives and directories for data files, if a pathname is included as part of the file specification of the file you want to find. The /path:on switch, which is the default, does cause a program to search the append list, even if you specify a path and filename in a command. The /path:off switch omits the append list if you specify a path and filename. You can turn this switch off and on as often as you want. Using the default /path:on extends the time required to find a file—time you probably don't want to spend if you already know where the file is stored.

/e sets the Append environment variable to the list of appended drives and directories. If you want to do this, *append /e* must be the first Append command you use during a session. If you have already used the Append command, you see the error message *Invalid switch - /e*. You can see the list assigned to Append and other environment variables by typing *set* at the system prompt. The value of the Append variable changes during a session to reflect the current list of appended drives and directories.

If you type the Append command without any parameters, Append displays the current list of appended directories. For example, if drive A and the directory B:\DATA\NEW are appended, typing *append* produces a display like the following:

```
APPEND=A:;B:\DATA\NEW
```

To cancel an Append command, type the command, followed by a semicolon.

Examples

Type:	To:
`C:\>append /e` ***Followed by:***	Prepare Append to assign a list of drives and directories to the Append environment variable. This must be the first Append command of the session.
`C:\>append c:\progs\lib`	Set the Append environment variable to C:\PROGS\LIB. Note that this second Append command actually assigns the variable string to the APPEND variable.
`C:\>append a:;b:`	Append drives A and B to the search path for data files.
`C:\>append a:\batch /x:on`	Append the directory BATCH on drive A and include executable files, as well as data files, in the search path.
`C:\>append /path:off`	Omit appended drives and directories from searches in which you specify a path as part of the name of a data file you want to find.
`C:\>append`	See a list of appended drives and directories.
`C:\>append ;`	Cancel the list of appended drives and directories.

Change Directory (Chdir or Cd)

Chdir is one of the three "true" directory-management commands in MS-DOS, the others being Make Directory (Mkdir) and Remove Directory (Rmdir). These three commands are all that anyone needs to create and manage a directory tree, no matter how large or complex. All three are internal to the MS-DOS command interpreter.

The Chdir command displays or changes the current directory. Period. It's simple to use and operate, yet one of the most valuable tools in your directory kit. Little more need be said about Chdir, other than to note the following:

- When you change directories on a drive, that directory remains current even though you switch to a different drive. (This can cause some momentary confusion if MS-DOS responds *File not found* about a floppy disk because you've forgotten that you changed directories on that drive.)

- You can change directories on a different drive by preceding the path with a drive letter. You do not have to change drives before changing directories.

■ You can use the backslash, dot, and double dot characters to cut down on keystrokes when you change directories.

Command syntax

You can type the Chdir command as either *chdir* or *cd*. The syntax of the command is as simple as its usage:

cd [*drive:*][*path*]

drive: and *path* represent the drive and path to which you want to change. Be sure to type a backslash after *drive:* if you specify both. To display the drive and path of the current directory, type the Chdir command without any parameters.

Examples

Type:	To:
C:\>cd	See the current directory. You shouldn't need this form of the command if the system prompt displays the current directory of the current drive.
C:\>cd b:	See the current directory of the disk in drive B. Note the omission of the backslash between this and the following example.
C:\>cd b:\	Change to the root directory of the disk in drive B.
C:\CATS>cd LIONS\ZOO	Change to the CATS\LIONS\ZOO directory from the CATS directory on drive C.
C:\CATS\LIONS\ZOO>cd ..	Change to the parent directory LIONS of the current directory on drive C.
C:\ZOO>cd ..\pumas	Change to the CATS\LIONS\PUMAS directory from the CATS\LIONS\ZOO directory on drive C.
C:\CATS\LIONS>cd \	Change to the root directory of drive C.

Delete Tree (Deltree)—version 6 only

The Deltree command in version 6 of MS-DOS is incredibly handy. Its job: to lop whole branches, including all contained subdirectories and files, off your directory tree. With Deltree, a single command

deltree [*unwanted directory*]

replaces repetition of the following commands when you want to delete a directory and all its populated subdirectories

```
del *.*
cd ..
rd [unwanted directory]
```

Suppose, for example, you have the following directory tree:

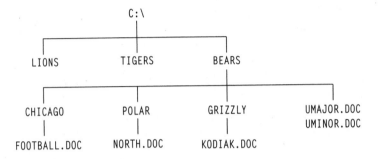

You type this command:

```
C:\>deltree bears
```

and press Enter. What goes? BEARS and everything below it—the directories GRIZZLY, POLAR, and CHICAGO, as well as all files in BEARS and all its subdirectories. If this collection of directories and files were, indeed, what you wanted to eliminate, you can see that Deltree would save a lot of work.

Useful as it can be, however, Deltree can also be dangerous. The reason: Deleted directories are generally not recoverable from the MS-DOS command line. Depending on how a directory tree is structured, Deltree can affect a large number of directories and files, among which it would be easy to overlook the one or two you really needed. If you inadvertently include any needed files or directories in a Deltree command, your only sure means of getting them back is through Windows 3.1 and the Windows form of the version 6 Undelete utility, as follows:

1. Start Windows.

2. Open the Undelete utility.

3. Change to the drive containing the deleted directories.

4. Undelete each directory.

5. Undelete any files you want to recover.

NOTE: If you don't have Windows, and you've been using Undelete with Delete Sentry, you might be able to recover files in a deleted directory with the MS-DOS Undelete command if you use Mkdir to create a new directory with the same path and name as the one you deleted. But you'll have to remember the names of the deleted files and directory.

When you use Deltree, your best approach is to think first and act later. If you have any doubts about what you're going to remove, use the Dir command with the /s and /ahsr switches, to see exactly what Deltree will find. The /ahsr switch is particularly important because Deltree removes files regardless of their attributes. So the hidden, system, and read-only attributes do not offer their usual level of protection for files or directories in the path you specify—even if the path is the root directory containing IO.SYS, MSDOS.SYS, and the other hidden and system files on your startup hard disk. (No, no, no; don't try it.)

Finally, Deltree allows you to use wildcard specifications, but you should be careful with these as well, because Deltree will assume you want to remove every path and file in the current directory that matches the specification you type. If you do use wildcards, be sure *not* to include the /y switch described in the syntax section later. That way, Deltree will prompt for confirmation, like this:

```
Delete directory "a:\lions" and all its subdirectories? [yn]
```

or this:

```
Delete file "c:\io.sys"? [yn]
```

before removing each file and directory that matches your wildcard specification. You'll have a chance to rescue needed subdirectories and files from oblivion.

Command syntax

The syntax of the Deltree command is as follows:

deltree /y [*drive:*]*path*

/y is an optional switch that suppresses the normal Deltree prompt for confirmation before a directory or file is deleted. You should use this switch only if you are certain you know what directories and files will be removed.

drive: represents the letter of the drive containing the disk on which the unwanted directories and files reside. If you omit *drive:*, Deltree assumes you mean the current drive.

path is the path to the directory you want to remove. You must specify a path. You can use wildcards, but as mentioned earlier in the description of Deltree, be sure you know what you're doing.

Examples

Type:	To:
C:\>deltree oldstuff	Delete the OLDSTUFF directory, including all subdirectories and files, on drive C.

(continued)

Type:	To:
`C:\>deltree ???stuff`	Delete every directory, including all subdirectories and files, that begin with three characters and end with STUFF on the disk in drive C. This file specification would, of course, match both OLDSTUFF and NEWSTUFF.
`C:\>deltree /y a:bigtree`	Delete the BIGTREE directory, including all subdirectories and files, on the disk in drive A, without prompting for confirmation. A command for the confident.

Directory (Dir)

The Dir command has been part of MS-DOS since version 1 and is almost certainly the first command any new MS-DOS user learns. In its simplest form, the Dir command tells you what files are located in the current directory of the current drive. Over the years, however, the Dir command has gained far more capability. Currently, it can also help locate files, sort them, display them selectively by attribute, or (in version 6 of MS-DOS) tell you how compactly they are stored by the DoubleSpace (Dblspace) command.

A typical directory listing looks something like the following:

```
Volume in drive C is MS_DOS 6
Volume Serial Number is 1949-5778
Directory of C:\
DOS          <DIR>     10-06-92    4:02p
OLD_DOS  1   <DIR>     08-14-93   10:50a
BATCH        <DIR>     10-09-92   11:04a
COMMAND  COM    52925 03-10-93    6:00a
WINA20   386     9349 03-10-93    6:00a
CONFIG   SYS      234 08-14-93   11:15a
AUTOEXEC.BAT      69 08-14-93   10:42a
WINDOWS      <DIR>     03-20-92    9:37a
        11 file(s)       62577 bytes
                     110121519 bytes free
```

The first line shows the volume label of the current disk and the second shows the MS-DOS–assigned volume serial number. The third line shows the drive and path of the listing that follows. Within the listing itself, <DIR> indicates the name of a directory within the current directory (here, the root). For files and directories alike, the entries, from left to right, identify the filename (such as COMMAND), the file extension (such as COM), the file size (such as 52925), and the date and time of creation or last modification. The second-to-last line of the listing shows the number of files in the listing and the sum of the file sizes shown. (This total does not include the sizes of any hidden or system files in the directory.) The last line shows the number of bytes of available storage remaining on the disk.

So much for the simple side of the Dir command. In actual use, the command is probably the most informative offered by MS-DOS. Working with the information stored in directory entries, the Dir command can go far beyond your simple need to know what's on a disk or in a directory. Using this most basic of MS-DOS commands, you can range from searching an entire disk for a single file to customizing the file lists you see on screen.

At the very least, you can specify which files or kinds of files you want to see by including wildcard characters in the file specification you type with the Dir command. Beyond this, however, the output of the Dir command can be particularly flexible if you also make use of three additional tools, the DIRCMD environment variable, input/output redirection, and piping. (DIRCMD is described in Chapter 12; redirection and piping in Chapter 17.)

Using DIRCMD, for example, you can change the output of the Dir command by setting its "default" with any of the parameters and switches provided for the command itself. Thus, for example, you can decree that Dir always provide a listing sorted alphabetically from A to Z, with directories listed first. (The normal output lists files and directories in the order in which they are saved on disk— that is, the order in which they were added to the root directory or subdirectory in which they are recorded.) If you set such a default with DIRCMD, you can also override it as described in the "Command syntax" section later.

You can't redirect the input to the Dir command because the command must use as its source the directory entries for a disk or directory. You can, however, easily redirect or pipe output at will. Redirecting output means that you send the results of a Dir command to an output device other than the screen—typically, a file or the printer. In contrast, piping means that you take the output of a Dir command and send it, as input, to another command. You can use redirection and piping separately, or you can combine them as shown in the last of the following three examples:

1. If you redirect the output of a Dir command to a device such as your default printer, as shown here,

   ```
   C:\NEWDATA>dir *.xls > prn
   ```

   you can quickly and effectively produce a hardcopy list of selected files—in this example, XLS files in the NEWDATA directory. Using this type of command is an easy way of recording the names of files stored on floppy disks.

2. If you pipe the output of a Dir command, as shown here,

   ```
   C:\NEWDATA>dir *.xls | find "04-15-93"
   ```

you can quickly list all files created or modified on a specific date—in this example, all XLS files created or modified on April 15, 1993. Using piping in this way can help you produce an even more selective list than you can by sorting files by date with the Dir command alone, as described later in this chapter.

3. If you combine piping (¦) and redirection (>), as shown here,

```
C:\NEWDATA>dir *.xls ¦ find "04-15-93" > a:taxes.txt
```

you can produce not only a highly selective list of files, you can also save the output either in a file (as here) or as a printed copy.

Command syntax

The Dir command in versions 5 and 6 of MS-DOS includes a number of useful and easy-to-use switches:

dir [*drive:*][*filespec*] /a[:]*attributes* /o[:]*sortorder* /s /b /l /p /w /c /ch

drive and *filespec* represent the drive, path, and filename of the file or files you want to see listed. If you omit both *drive* and *filespec*, the Dir command lists the contents, except for hidden and system files, of the current directory. You can use the ? and * wildcards to specify a group of files. The question mark can stand for any single character in the file specification, the asterisk for any number of characters.

/a[:]*attributes* displays a list of files with the attribute or attributes you specify. You can specify more than one attribute with a single /a switch, as long as you do not separate the attributes with spaces. The attributes you can specify are as follows:

- H for hidden files; -H for nonhidden files (the default).
- S for system files; -S for nonsystem files (the default).
- D for directories; -D for files other than directories. Both are shown by default.
- A for files with the archive attribute turned on; -A for files with the archive attribute turned off. Both are shown by default.
- R for read-only files; -R for files that are not read-only. Both are shown by default.

Although specifying a "minus" attribute, as for nonhidden files, seems like walking around the block to go next door, the minus sign is useful in overriding an attribute after you've used it to define a specific type of listing with the DIRCMD variable. Note that the colon is optional.

/o:*sortorder* lets you sort the listing alphabetically, numerically, and in any of the other ways described later. You can include more than one sort criterion, as long as you do not separate them with spaces. Note, however, that the order in which you specify sort criteria counts. For example, specifying extension and then name (/oen) sorts a directory first by extension and then by name; specify-ing name and then extension (/one), as might feel more natural, causes the second criterion to kick in only in cases of filename duplication. You can specify the fol-lowing sort orders:

- N to sort alphabetically (A to Z) by filename; -N to sort in reverse alpha-betic order by filename.

- E to sort alphabetically by extension; -E to sort in reverse alphabetic order by extension.

- D to sort in chronological order (both date and time), earliest to latest; -D to sort in reverse chronological order, latest to earliest.

- S to sort by size, smallest first; -S to sort by size, largest first.

- G to sort with all the directories listed ahead of any files; -G to sort with all the files listed ahead of any directories.

- C to sort by compression ratio (as carried out by the Dblspace com-mand), lowest to highest; -C to sort by compression ratio, highest to lowest. This switch is available only in version 6.

/s applies the Dir command to the current directory and all of its subdirecto-ries, listing all occurrences of the filename you specify, preceded by the name of the directory or subdirectory in which each file is stored. On a computer with a reasonably quick hard disk, the Dir command, combined with a wildcard file specification and the /s switch, is a great way to find one or more files when you aren't quite sure where you put them or how you spelled their names.

/b produces a "bare bones" directory listing that shows only path and file-name information—no sizes, dates, or times—for each file that matches the file specification you include in the command. Although the /b switch doesn't seem very useful on the surface, think of it when all you want is a list of the contents of a subdirectory or when you want to redirect a list of filenames to a file or the printer. If you use the /b switch, Dir ignores the /w switch.

/l displays the names of specified files in lowercase—for those times when you really don't want to look at any capital letters.

/p pauses the directory listing after each screenful instead of allowing the list to scroll continuously off the screen. Using /p is similar in effect, if not in opera-tion, to using the pipe symbol (¦) and the More command (described in Chapter 12) as many users often do to halt the display.

/w produces a wide directory listing, displaying directory and filenames only in five columns across the screen:

```
Volume in drive C is MS-DOS 6
Volume Serial Number is 1949-5778
Directory of C:\
[DOS]           [OLD_DOS.1]     [BATCH]         COMMAND.COM      WINA20.386
CONFIG.SYS      AUTOEXEC.BAT    UNDELETE.INI    [WINDOWS]
```

Note that directory names are enclosed in square brackets [ ] to distinguish them from filenames. The /w switch, especially combined with /o:*sortorder* is a handy tool for viewing a lot of directories and files at one time. Also note that the sort order is left to right and then top to bottom.

/c or /ch lists the compression ratios of specified files stored on a disk compressed with the Dblspace command. The compression ratio varies, depending on the type of file you save. The /c switch can be useful in satisfying your curiosity, or in helping you manage DoubleSpace volumes—for example, in determining how to resize one or finding out which types of files (graphics, text, programs, and so on) shrink down most effectively. The /c switch displays the compression ratio based on allocation units (*clusters*) of 8 K. The /ch switch displays the compression ratio based on the cluster size (typically 2 K for a hard disk) of the host—uncompressed—drive..

Examples

Type:	To:
`C:\>dir`	See a listing of the current directory, which happens to be the root of drive C.
`C:\>dir a: /p`	See a list of files on the disk in drive A, pausing after each screenful.
`C:\>dir a:	more`	See the same list as in the preceding example, but using the More command instead of /p.
`C:\BIGDIR>dir *.doc /on /p`	See a list of all DOC files in the BIGDIR directory, sorting them alphabetically by name and pausing after each screenful.
`C:\SECRET>dir /ahr`	See a list of all files in the SECRET directory that have been assigned the hidden and read-only attributes (with the Attrib command).
`C:\>dir /w /ogn`	See a wide listing of directories and files in the root directory of the current drive, grouping directories ahead of files and listing both directories and files alphabetically by name.
`C:\LOST-IT>dir \findme.doc /s`	Search the root and every subdirectory on the current drive for the file FINDME.DOC. Note the use of the \ character to indicate the root from within the current (LOST-IT) subdirectory. You can use the backslash in this way with /s, even though the file you seek is not in the root directory.

(continued)

Type:	To:
`C:\>dir findme.doc /s`	Perform the same search as in the preceding example, but from the root directory. Note that no backslash is included.
`C:\IM-HERE>dir findme.doc /s`	Search the current (IM-HERE) directory and all subdirectories of the current directory for the file FINDME.DOC.
`C:\FLOPPIES>dir a: > jul-rpts.lst`	Redirect a directory listing of the files on the disk in drive A to a "log" file named JUL-RPTS.LST in the FLOPPIES directory on the current drive (C). You could also use >> to append to an existing file.
`C:\FINALS>dir *.xls > prn`	Print a listing of all XLS files in the FINALS directory on the current drive (C).
`C:\>dir /c > a:\compress.txt`	Redirect a listing of the compression ratios of all files on the current compressed drive (C) to a file named COMPRESS.TXT on drive A.
`C:\>dir d:\ /o-c /s /p`	View a list of all files in the root and all its subdirectories on compressed drive D, sorting the files by compression ratio, highest to lowest, pausing after each screenful.

Make Directory (Mkdir or Md)

The Mkdir command creates a new subdirectory. Like its companion directory-management commands, Mkdir needs little explanation, and you don't need a lot of experience in order to use it easily. Note only that the command always creates the new directory in the current directory. To create a directory on a different drive or in a different directory, either change to the other drive or directory, or precede the new directory name with the correct drive and path, as shown in the following examples.

Command syntax

The syntax of the Mkdir command is simple:

md [*drive:*]*path*

drive is the drive on which you want to create the new directory. You can omit this parameter if you are creating a directory on the current drive. (Or you can include it if you're the type of person who likes to be sure.)

path is the path to the new directory. If you are creating the new directory within the current directory, simply type the name of the new directory. If you are creating the new directory in a different branch of your directory tree, precede the new name with the appropriate path. Don't forget to include a backslash for the root, if the path must begin at the very top of the directory tree.

Examples

Type:	To:
`C:\>md new`	Create a directory named NEW in the current (root) directory of the current drive (C).
`C:\NEW>md newer`	Create a directory named NEWER in the current (NEW) directory of the current drive.
`C:\BOGUS>md \new\newer\newest`	Create a directory named NEWEST in the \NEW\NEWER branch of the directory tree on the current drive.
`C:\BOGUS1\FAKE1>md ..\phony`	Create a directory named PHONY in the BOGUS1 directory of the current drive. Note the use of .. to indicate that the new directory is to be created in the directory one level above the current directory.
`C:\>md a:\copies\08-14-93`	Create a directory named 08-14-93 in the COPIES directory within the root directory of the disk in drive A.
`C:\>md a:12-11-93`	Create a directory named 12-11-93 in the current directory of the disk in drive A. Note that this form of the command can cause unexpected results if you forget which is the current directory on a particular drive.

Path

The Path command, which normally appears in AUTOEXEC.BAT, sets the search path that MS-DOS follows in finding executable files. Without a path set by this command, MS-DOS searches for programs only in the current directory—a habit that could cause great wailing and gnashing of teeth if you had to either change directories or type a path before using any program on your hard disk. Lack of a path set by the Path command would be especially irritating these days because programs oriented toward hard-disk use (pretty much all of them) normally propose to install themselves in their own directories. Some, such as Windows, install themselves in multiple directories.

When you set a search path, MS-DOS searches, in order, for programs with the extensions COM, EXE, and BAT. The search always begins in the current directory. If the program is not found, MS-DOS then searches each directory listed in the path. If no executable file is found, MS-DOS displays the message *Bad command or file name* and returns you to the system prompt.

The Path command limits the search path to 127 characters, including the semicolons (as described later) that you use to separate pathnames. To avoid going over this limit, create short directory names for programs if their setup procedures allow you to choose between a default name and your own. You do not generally have to list in the path every subdirectory containing executable files for every application program directory you install. If your path still becomes too long, break it into logical (work-related sections) and attach one section to the search path with the Append command and its /x:on switch.

The Path command is so important that MS-DOS Setup, in versions 5 and 6, automatically sets up an AUTOEXEC.BAT file that includes (among other commands) a path to the DOS directory during a new installation on a hard disk. If you upgrade to a new version of MS-DOS, Setup alters the path—if necessary— to point to your DOS directory. A Path command should appear in any AUTOEXEC.BAT file.

Although the Path command is generally executed from a batch file, especially AUTOEXEC.BAT, you can also set, change, or delete the path from the MS-DOS command line. In everyday use, however, you should have little reason to change the path and practically none to delete it. If you do reset or delete the command path, you can restore it to the one in AUTOEXEC.BAT. If your AUTOEXEC.BAT is very simple, type *autoexec* to rerun AUTOEXEC.BAT from the system prompt. If your AUTOEXEC.BAT is complex, play it safe and restart the system. If you change the path often, you could also create a batch file that has a path statement in it that matches the path in your AUTOEXEC.BAT and call it something like MYPATH.BAT. Then you could run it anytime you want to go back to your original path.

Command syntax

The syntax of the Path command is simple, although you do have to watch your typing carefully to ensure that backslashes appear where needed and that each pathname, if you include more than one, is separated from others by semicolons. Otherwise, the syntax is plain:

path [*drive1:*][*path1*];[*drive2:*][*path2*];...[*driveN:*][*pathN*]

drive1, drive2, driveN and *path1, path2, pathN* are the full drive and path leading to each directory that contains executable files and that you want to include in the search path. Don't forget the backslash for the root directory, if it is needed.

You can include subdirectory names, if necessary. Be sure to type a semicolon between each path and the one following.

If you want, you can type an equal sign between *path* and the first drive and path, like this:

```
path=c:\dos
```

You can type in uppercase or lowercase characters. MS-DOS always converts a path to uppercase for display.

You can check on the current search path by typing *path* at the system prompt, and by typing *path ;* you can delete the current path.

Examples

Include in your AUTOEXEC.BAT file:	To:
PATH C:\DOS;C:\BATCH;C:\WINDOWS	Set the command search path to the DOS, BATCH, and WINDOWS directories whenever you start or restart the system.

Type:	To:
C:\>path	Check on the current search path.
C:\>path ;	Delete the current search path. Note that this command would restrict searches for executable files to the root directory only. MS-DOS would not search any program directories on drive C, including the DOS directory, even for external command files.

Remove Directory (Rmdir or Rd)

The Rmdir command is the third of the three directory-management commands in MS-DOS and, like its companions, is simple to use. Unlike the others, however, Rmdir could also be devastating, especially if you used the command without thinking. Because the consequences of removing an entire directory and all its contents can be considerable, Rmdir does not allow you to remove

- The root directory
- The current directory
- A non-empty directory
- A directory that contains any hidden or system files
- A directory affected by the Substitute or Join command

Once you run this gauntlet, however, and delete a subdirectory, it is gone. If you don't have Windows and the version 6 Windows Undelete, MS-DOS Undelete generally cannot recover the subdirectory or the files it once contained. So think twice before deleting a directory.

On occasion, you might find that attempts to remove a subdirectory continually end in the message

```
Invalid path, not directory,
or directory not empty
```

This message can become infuriating, especially if repeated directory listings show a seemingly empty directory. The solution: Use the Dir command or the Attrib command to check for hidden or system files. If they are the problem, first verify that you do, indeed, want to eliminate them. If so, use the Attrib command to change the hidden or system attributes, delete the files, and then remove the subdirectory. Note that this advice does not apply to the root directory, both because you should never delete the hidden (and system) files IO.SYS, MSDOS.SYS, and (in version 6) DBLSPACE.BIN, and because you cannot delete the root directory of any disk anyway.

If you have version 6 and you want to delete both a subdirectory and the files and subdirectories it contains, use the Deltree command described earlier in this chapter.

Command syntax

The syntax of the Rmdir command is as follows:

rd [*drive:*]*path*

drive is the drive containing the disk on which you want to remove the subdirectory. You can omit this parameter if the subdirectory is on the current drive.

path is the pathname of the directory you want to remove. Unless you specify otherwise by typing a full pathname, MS-DOS assumes that the subdirectory is below the current directory.

Examples

Type:	To:
C:\OLD\OLDER\OLDEST>rd longgone	Remove the LONGGONE directory, which is one level below the current (OLD\OLDER\OLDEST) directory— assuming, of course, that LONGGONE contains no files.

(continued)

Type:	To:
`C:\OLD\OLDER\OLDEST>cd ..` `C:\OLD\OLDER>rd oldest`	Change to the OLDER directory with the Chdir command and then use Rmdir to delete the OLDEST directory. Remember that you cannot delete the current directory.
`C:\OLD\OLDER>rd ..\archaic`	Remove the \OLD\ARCHAIC directory without leaving the current (OLD\OLDER) directory. Note the use of the .. symbol to indicate the directory above the current directory.
`C:\>rd old`	Remove the OLD directory, which is below the current (root) directory.
`C:\>rd a:\cleanup`	Remove the CLEANUP directory on the disk in drive A from the current drive (C).

Tree

Appropriately and rather engagingly named—at least in relation to more powerful but technical-sounding commands such as Chkdsk, Fdisk, and Xcopy—the
Tree command displays a diagram of a disk's directory tree. You can display
subdirectory names only, or you can display both subdirectory names and filenames. You can display part of the tree or all of it. And you can display the output
with graphics characters that produce solid lines that connect branches of the
tree, like this:

```
Directory PATH listing for Volume MS_DOS_6
Volume Serial Number is 1A63-844C
C:.
├──DOS
├──OLD_DOS.1
├──BATCH
└──BOGUS1
     └──BOGUS2
```

Or you can specify ASCII characters that produce universally displayable and
printable lines and "corners," like this:

```
Directory PATH listing for Volume MS-DOS 6
Volume Serial Number is 1A63-844C
C:.
+---DOS
+---OLD_DOS.1
+---BATCH
\---BOGUS1
    \---BOGUS2
```

You can use the > redirection symbol to save the output in a file or to send output to the printer.

Command syntax

The syntax of the Tree command is as follows:

tree [*drive:*][*path*] /f /a

drive and *path* are the drive and pathname of the directory for which you want to display a tree. If you don't include a drive, MS-DOS assumes the current drive. If you don't include a path, MS-DOS assumes the current directory.

/f lists the files in each subdirectory of the tree.

/a causes the command to use ASCII characters rather than the extended (graphics) characters that are the default. The /a switch might be needed if you want to redirect the output to a printer or to a file or if your system is using a national character set (code page) that does not support graphics characters. (Code pages are described in Chapter 10 and Appendix C.)

Examples

Type:	To:
C:\>tree	Display the directory tree of the current drive (C), using graphics characters for the lines connecting the branches of the tree.
C:\>tree /a	Produce the same display as above, but with ASCII characters connecting the branches.
C:\BRANCH\TWIG\LEAF>tree \branch	Display the directory tree of the BRANCH directory, including TWIG, LEAF, and any other subdirectories in BRANCH.
C:\LEAF>tree /f	Display the directory tree of the LEAF directory and any subdirectories, listing the files in each.
C:\>tree a: > prn	Produce a directory tree of the disk in drive A and send the output to a printer that can reproduce graphics characters.
C:\>tree a: /a > prn	Produce a directory tree of the disk in drive A, sending the output to a printer that cannot reproduce graphics characters.

10

Devices

What You'll Find Here: ANSI.SYS; Change Codepage (Chcp); Clear Screen (Cls); Country; Ctty; DISPLAY.SYS; DRIVER.SYS; EGA.SYS; Graphics Table (Graftabl); Graphics; Keyboard (Keyb); Mode; National Language Support Function (Nlsfunc); Power; POWER.EXE; Print; PRINTER.SYS.

*T*his chapter pulls together a set of ruggedly individual MS-DOS commands and device drivers. None affects disks, drives, files, or memory. In all other respects, however, the commands and device drivers covered here have little in common as a group, other than their ability to help you use or control some portion of your hardware. Many are related in some way to the display. Others affect the keyboard, serial ports, and printer. One set manages the multilingual side of MS-DOS by giving your hardware the ability to identify and use the tables of foreign-language characters known as *code pages.*

Devices comprise the varied and complex pieces of hardware that make up the eyes, ears, hands—whatever you want to call them—of a basic computer system. In form and function, devices range from apparently simple (mice) to obviously complex (modems and printers), and from necessary (printers again) to completely optional (joysticks). Taken together, however, devices to a large extent define the computer setup you come to call your own—to the extent that eventually the "feel" of your mouse becomes decidedly different from the feel of someone else's.

No single function or operating characteristic (other than a need for electricity) defines all devices, but that doesn't mean these mechanisms are indefinable. In fact, they have two features in common: They all perform some form of input, output, or both, and they all must be identified to MS-DOS before you can use them.

MS-DOS devices

MS-DOS is designed to recognize two kinds of devices: block and character. *Block devices* are those that transfer information in chunks. The block devices to end all block devices on your system are, of course, the disk drives, which shuttle data to and from memory in the clusters and allocation units that MS-DOS refers to when describing file storage. (In this respect, memory, too, is a block device, but no one ever thinks of it that way.) Under MS-DOS, block devices are pretty much synonymous with disk drives and file storage, and because these topics are covered elsewhere, block devices as a category will now bow politely and depart, leaving the stage to character devices, which form a larger and more diverse lot.

Character devices are pieces of hardware that move information one character (byte) at a time. Into this group fall the keyboard, display, printer, modem, and other non-disk devices you attach to the computer. As described in Chapter 3, the MS-DOS BIOS initializes a basic set of character devices named CON, AUX, and PRN whenever you boot or reboot the computer. These devices are controlled by resident device drivers that are part of the MS-DOS BIOS, much as internal commands are part of COMMAND.COM.

These device names and their associated drivers prepare MS-DOS to use a device named CON as the default for input and output, a device named AUX as the default for serial communications, and a device named PRN as the default for printing. CON sends MS-DOS to the keyboard for input and to the display for output. AUX and PRN are a little stickier, however, and might have confused you somewhat in the past, if you grew up believing, as most people do, that serial communications is the job of a COM port and parallel transmission is the job of an LPT port.

In actuality, AUX and PRN are aliases ("nicknames") that MS-DOS uses internally for *a* serial device and *a* parallel device. However, your computer can have up to four serial ports (COM1 through COM4) and three parallel ports (LPT1 through LPT3), and not a one is named AUX or PRN. Because of this, MS-DOS makes some assumptions about AUX and PRN and, unless you or a program specify otherwise, equates AUX with COM1 and PRN with LPT1. For example, the first time you use the Print command, MS-DOS displays this message:

```
Name of list device [PRN]:
```

MS-DOS is asking you, "Where is the device you want me to treat as the printer (PRN)?" If you press Enter in response, MS-DOS uses its assumption that the PRN device is connected to LPT1, the first parallel port on your system. If the printer you want to use is connected to a different parallel port, you must type the port number (LPT2 or LPT3) to tell MS-DOS to send a file to the correct printer.

Serial communications is essentially the same, but it is complicated by the fact that you must configure a serial port (with the Mode command) before you can use it with MS-DOS. You don't have to think much about AUX, because only a few MS-DOS commands affect serial ports, and of those, most require COM, rather than AUX, as a parameter. You can, however, use AUX in a few cases, such as the following:

```
print /d:aux
```

which identifies a serial printer connected to AUX, the first COM port, as the printer of choice.

Installable device drivers

If you don't customize your system in any way, MS-DOS can work fine with the default devices and device names just described. To expand the basic capabilities of MS-DOS, however, you turn to installable device drivers. These drivers, like applications and external MS-DOS commands, are programs that reside on disk as individual files. Unlike applications and external commands, however, you cannot run installable device drivers from the command line. The only way to activate one is to load it into memory at startup with a Device or a Devicehigh command in CONFIG.SYS, the system configuration file that prepares MS-DOS to work with devices and, often, consists largely of a series of Device or Devicehigh commands.

An installable device driver performs either of two tasks: It enhances MS-DOS capabilities, or it identifies a new device to MS-DOS. The ANSI.SYS device driver, for example, replaces the default CON device driver with enhanced keyboard and screen-handling capabilities. A mouse device driver, on the other hand, adds to MS-DOS by enabling it to take advantage of a device that the basic operating system otherwise cannot recognize and has no ability to use.

Because MS-DOS can work with resident device drivers, installable device drivers, or a combination of the two, it must ensure that the driver you need carries out an action destined for it. To guarantee that devices don't receive scrambled requests (assuming, of course, that they are all properly configured and installed), MS-DOS treats all device drivers in memory as if they formed a chain in which the last device driver to be loaded into memory is the link closest to the "top." When a program requests use of a particular device, MS-DOS searches for the appropriate device by starting at the top of this chain and working "downward" to the end. When it finds a device driver that corresponds to the device specified by the program, MS-DOS stops searching and passes the program's request to the device driver it has found.

The most interesting part of this chaining, however, lies in the way the process works to ensure that any installable device drivers designed to handle the standard MS-DOS CON, AUX, and PRN devices do actually supersede any resident drivers they are meant to replace. Because the resident device drivers are loaded before any installable device drivers, they are always located farther down the chain. Thus, for example, if you load the ANSI.SYS device driver for keyboard control, it is always positioned higher in the chain than the resident keyboard driver. As a result, when MS-DOS carries out a keyboard-related activity, it finds ANSI.SYS before it ever finds the resident driver, and ANSI.SYS always ends up being given control of the keyboard.

Device-related terms and what they mean

Device drivers are important to know about because you need them to load and control devices. But there's a whole other side to understanding devices: the terminology that sometimes makes initiates sound as though they were speaking in tongues. This is especially true of data communications, what with bits per second, parity, data bits, and stop bits swirling through the air like leaves in a windstorm, but other devices have their entertaining moments too. The following sections provide some definitions of the least self-explanatory of these terms.

Scan codes, the keyboard, and extended ASCII

Most of the time, a keyboard is a keyboard. Aside from size and the number of keys on it, a computer keyboard differs little from the typewriter keyboard from which it descended. At times, however, and especially if you are going to enter the world of MS-DOS code-page switching, it helps to understand what scan codes are and how they are related to ASCII and extended ASCII characters.

When you press the A key, the keyboard does not send a little picture of an *A* through the system to the display. It generates a scan code representing a numeric value that identifies the key pressed. That value, alone or in combination with the scan code generated by a key such as Shift or Ctrl, is then converted into a particular ASCII value by special ROM software called the *keyboard handler*, and this ASCII value, in turn, corresponds to a letter, number, punctuation mark, or symbol defined by the ASCII code. When you release the key or keys, the keyboard generates another scan code, this time the equivalent of "All done." So, for example, pressing Shift-A to generate a capital A sends two scan codes that can be converted into the ASCII value representing capital A. Releasing the keys ends that particular keyboard event. And, of course, holding the keys down long enough (a length of time you can control with the Mode command, described later in this chapter) causes the keystroke to be repeated. At any rate, once converted to an ASCII code, the character can then be pushed into a buffer for MS-DOS to retrieve and pass along to a waiting program.

Together, all the character-related keys on your keyboard produce what is known as the standard ASCII character set—the first 128 characters in the ASCII table shown in Appendix A. As you can see from the table, however, ASCII actually allows for 256 possible characters—standard ASCII, plus an additional 128 characters usually known as extended ASCII, which begin with ASCII code 128 decimal (80 hexadecimal). These extended ASCII characters are less rigidly defined than standard ASCII, but they generally include the accented characters and line-drawing and box-drawing symbols known as the IBM extended character set. These are the characters illustrated in the ASCII table in Appendix A.

Although your keyboard does not include any labeled keys for extended ASCII characters, you can produce them, and MS-DOS can interpret them. To do so, you hold down the Alt key and type on the numeric keypad the ASCII value of the character you want. Many people use this method to produce symbols, lines, and boxes on screen from within a batch file. MS-DOS has another use for extended ASCII, however: code pages.

A code page is, briefly, an ASCII table in which the upper 128 ASCII values are assigned to the characters used in one or more related languages. For example, in the English-language code page, ASCII value 155 is the cent symbol (¢), whereas in the Multilingual code page, the same ASCII value represents the character ∅. When you use code pages, you thus enable MS-DOS to interpret a particular ASCII value as whatever character corresponds to that value in the code page in effect at the time.

In the mostly unilingual United States where this book was produced, code pages are not widely used, but if you live or work in a multilingual environment, you can use code pages to display and print characters for languages other than the one supported by your hardware. Even though MS-DOS can use six code pages, the ones generally available to you depend on the default, or hardware, code page built into your keyboard and display. Setting country and language conventions can be somewhat confusing because you use several different commands to enable their use and to switch from one code page to another. See "Change Codepage (Chcp)," later in this chapter, for more information about code pages. If you want to internationalize your system, refer to Appendix C and your documentation for details.

Ports and communications

Most computers are equipped with one or two serial ports and at least one parallel port. Serial ports transfer information bit by bit and are most commonly used for modems and mice. Parallel ports transfer information byte by byte and are generally used for printers. Where MS-DOS is concerned, there's not much you have to know about a parallel port other than the number of the one to which your printer, if it operates in parallel mode, is connected. Serial ports, however, because they are used for communications, are associated with several terms that don't usually turn up in everyday language, especially these: baud, bps, parity, data bit, and stop bit. If you use your computer for communications, you don't necessarily have to know what these words mean, because the computer or service with which you connect will tell you what settings to use. On the other hand, step-by-step, connect-the-dots, and multiple-choice approaches to things really take you only so far.

Communications is a fascinating topic in its own right, and it's replete with far more esoteric terms than baud and parity, but MS-DOS requires you to know only the five terms just mentioned, so that's where this chapter (and book) will start and stop.

First, what is *baud*? This is a term dating back to the days of telegraphy and a French engineer named Jean-Maurice-Emile Baudot. Commonly considered to represent the speed, in bits per second (bps), at which a modem can transmit data, baud is a misleading term. Here's why. Technically, baud is a measure of the number of events, or signal changes, that occur in 1 second of transmission— for example, how many times the signal switches from low to high frequency in a single second. Each of these events encodes data. If a single event encodes 1 bit, baud is an accurate measure of transmission speed because the number of baud really does equal the number of bits per second transmitted. And, in fact, at very low modem speeds, the term is accurate. A 300-baud modem, for example, does actually transmit 300 bits per second. At the higher transmission speeds currently in wide use (2400, 4800, and 9600), however, several bits of data are crammed into a single event, so baud no longer applies as a real measure of transmission speed. A 9600 "baud" modem, for example, encodes 4 bits per event. Thus, it operates at 2400 baud (2400 events per second times 4 bits per event), but its true transmission speed, the rate at which bits are sent, is 9600 bits per second. The upshot is this: Even though you specify "baud" when defining a serial port to MS-DOS (with the Mode command), you should really use the term "bits per second." It's more accurate.

Data bits and stop bits are the number of bits used to encode a single transmitted character. Unlike keyboard-to-display or memory-to-file data-transfer operations, communications relies heavily on both the sending and receiving computers agreeing on certain rules so that each can distinguish one character from the next in the stream of bits arriving at and departing from each computer. These rules are particularly important in asynchronous communications of the type used between modems because transmission does not always occur at a steady rate. For example, if you are on line with a data service, you might type furiously for a minute or so and then sit idly for a time while you read the screen. Neither the sending nor the receiving computer can tell when you're going to start typing, nor how fast, so they must both be prepared to interpret transmitted characters in some other way. That way is to use a specified number of bits for each character and a "marker" that separates the end of one character from the beginning of another.

The bits used to encode each character are known as *data bits,* and they can range from as few as 5 to as many as 8. The most common usage, however, is either 7 or 8 data bits per character. The marker between characters is known as the number of stop bits. Under MS-DOS, this value can be 1, 1.5, or 2, depending on the speed of transmission. Like the term *baud,* however, *stop bits* is somewhat misleading. In actuality, stop bits are timing signals rather than true bit values (0 or 1). It makes sense. How else would you encode 1.5 stop bits? The most common, however, is 1 stop bit.

Parity refers to the form of error checking used to verify that characters are accurately sent and received. Parity is based on the addition of a special parity bit to each transmitted character. Depending on the type of parity used, this bit is set to either 1 or 0 by the sending computer. Parity checking is not performed when 8 bits are used for a character, but it is usually done for 7-bit characters. MS-DOS supports several different forms of parity checking:

- N, for none, meaning no parity bit is used.

- O, for odd, meaning the parity bit is either set or not set to make an odd number of 1s in the transmitted character.

- E, for even, meaning the parity bit is either set or not set to make an even number of 1s in the transmitted character.

- M, for mark, meaning the parity bit is always set to 1. In this form of error checking, an incorrectly set parity bit would indicate an error.

- S, for space, meaning the parity bit is always set to 0. Here, as in mark parity, error checking is limited to the possibility that the parity bit is incorrectly set.

The commands and device drivers described in the remainder of this chapter all cover some aspect of device management—other than disk drives and memory—with MS-DOS. Disks and files are covered in Chapters 7, 8, and 9; memory in Chapter 11.

ANSI.SYS

ANSI.SYS, once—and probably still—beloved by MS-DOS users who like to tinker under the hood, is an installable device driver that has accompanied every version of MS-DOS since 2.0. A tool that greatly expands your ability to control the keyboard and the display, ANSI.SYS replaces the default MS-DOS console device driver (CON) with a set of special commands that you can use for any of the following tasks:

- To position the cursor anywhere on screen.

- To control the color and attributes (such as bold or underlined) of both the text characters and the background on which they appear.

- To redefine the character produced when you press a particular key.

- To assign a sequence of characters, such as a program startup command, to a key or a key combination.

ANSI.SYS is useful and pleasant to experiment with if you're interested in customizing your display in ways such as adding color to your prompt or displaying flashing warnings and notes from within a batch file. In everyday use of MS-DOS, however, you don't actually need ANSI.SYS unless you want to use the Mode command to change the number of lines your screen can display—for example, if you want to be able to switch between a 25-line display and a 43-line display at will and you have an EGA or better monitor.

There are two ways to look at ANSI.SYS: as the device driver you load as an MS-DOS "command" from within CONFIG.SYS and as a tool you use in customizing your keyboard and screen. The following table shows the kinds of things ANSI.SYS can do.

Type:	To:
Cursor control:	
Esc[*lines*A	Move the cursor up the number of lines specified.
Esc[*lines*B	Move the cursor down the number of lines specified.
Esc[*cols*C	Move the cursor right the number of columns specified.
Esc[*cols*D	Move the cursor left the number of columns specified.
Esc[*line;col*H	Move the cursor to the specified line and column.
Esc[*line;col*f	Move the cursor to the specified line and column (same as Esc[*line;col*H).
Esc[s	Save the cursor position (related to the following).
Esc[u	Move the cursor to the position last saved with Esc[s.
Screen control:	
Esc[2J	Clear the screen and move the cursor to the home position (upper left corner).
Esc[K	Erase from the cursor to the end of the line.
Esc[=*screenmode*h	Set the display mode to the mode specified. The meaning of *screenmode* depends on your adapter.
Esc[=*screenmode*l	Reset the display mode as in the previous command.
Esc[=*graphicsfunction;...;* *graphicsfunction*m	Set the graphics mode, including text attributes, foreground and background color.
Keyboard control:	
Esc[*keycode;string;...*p	Redefine a key represented by *keycode* using a *string* for the new definition.

Details on these parameters and their use are in Appendix B. The syntax you use for loading ANSI.SYS is described on the following page.

Command syntax

Like any device driver, ANSI.SYS must be loaded with a Device or a Devicehigh command in CONFIG.SYS. The form of the command is as follows:

DEVICE=[*drive:*][*path*]ANSI.SYS /x /k /r

drive and *path* are the drive and path of the disk on which ANSI.SYS is stored. Unless you've moved the ANSI.SYS device driver, it is in the DOS directory of your startup drive.

/x allows you to reassign certain duplicate keys independently on a 101-key keyboard. These duplicates, known as the *extended keys*, are the two small groups of keys to the left of the numeric keypad, as shown here:

Extended keys

The extended keys perform the same functions as the identically labeled light-colored keys on the numeric keypad, and most software does not distinguish between the two. To treat these duplicates as different keys that can be assigned to different functions, include the /x switch in the Device command that loads ANSI.SYS. The /x switch is especially useful if long practice has made reaching for the numeric keypad almost instinctive. If that's the case, you can reassign the extended keys to often-used macros, batch files, foreign-language characters, or any other keystrokes you wish were a standard part of the keyboard.

/k, in many ways the opposite of /x, causes software to ignore extended keys. This switch exists for the benefit of people with software that cannot correctly interpret extended keystrokes. By including the /k switch, you force ANSI.SYS to ignore extended keys, essentially treating your keyboard as if it were an older, XT-style keyboard. The /k switch is related to the SWITCHES=/K command (described in Chapter 13), which turns off extended keys on a 101-key keyboard. If you include both ANSI.SYS and the SWITCHES=/K command in CONFIG.SYS, add /k to the ANSI.SYS line.

/r, new in version 6, adjusts scrolling when ANSI.SYS is used with screen-reading software for people who have disabilities. This switch helps improve readability.

Examples

Include in CONFIG.SYS:	To:
`DEVICE=C:\DOS\ANSI.SYS`	Load the ANSI.SYS driver from the DOS directory on drive C.
`DEVICEHIGH=C:\DOS\ANSI.SYS`	Load ANSI.SYS into upper memory, if enough upper memory (4 K) is available. If not enough memory is found, ANSI.SYS will be loaded into conventional memory.
`DEVICE=C:\DOS\ANSI.SYS /X`	Load ANSI.SYS and ensure that it can distinguish between extended keys and their duplicates on the numeric keypad.

Change Codepage (Chcp)

The Change Codepage (Chcp) command enables you to make your computer multilingual by switching from one code page—one set of national-language characters—to another as you work. When you use Chcp, the command causes MS-DOS to switch to the code page you specify so that you can type, display, and print characters from a language other than the "native tongue" built into your computer. Before you use Chcp, however, you must lay a fair amount of ground-work by preparing your computer for code-page switching—a process that involves Device, Mode, and National Language Support Function (Nlsfunc) commands, as described in Appendix C. You can see your current code page by typing *chcp* on a line by itself.

Once your computer is set up for code-page switching, changing from one character set to another is a breeze. You simply type the Chcp command and the three-digit number of the code page to which you want to switch. MS-DOS supports the six code pages shown on the following page.

Code page	Character set
437	English language; includes accented characters for most western European languages.
850	Multilingual (Latin I); closely resembles code page 437, but is more truly European. Includes more accent marks and accented characters than code page 437, to cover most languages based on the Latin alphabet.
852	Slavic (Latin II); similar to code page 850, but includes characters for Slavic languages based on the Latin alphabet.
860	Portuguese; includes characters used specifically in the Portuguese language.
863	Canadian-French; similar to code page 437, but includes characters used both in English and in Canadian-French.
865	Nordic; similar to code page 850, but also includes characters for Norwegian and Danish.

The Chcp command changes the code page for all devices on the system (keyboard, display, and printer) that you have set up to use code-page switching. To change code pages for a single device—the console or the printer—use the Mode Codepage Select command described later in this chapter.

Command syntax

The syntax of the Chcp command is as follows:

chcp [*codepage*]

codepage is the number of the code page you want to use: 437, 850, 852, 860, 863, or 865. You cannot change code pages unless you have first prepared the system, prepared the code pages, and started national-language support with the Nlsfunc command. For any given country, MS-DOS allows you to switch between two code pages. You cannot switch among all six code pages at will. If you omit the *codepage* number, Chcp will display the current code page.

Examples

Type:	To:
C:\> chcp	Display the current code page.
C:\> chcp 850	Switch to the Multilingual code page from a compatible code page.
C:\> chcp 865	Switch to the Nordic code page from a compatible code page.

Clear Screen (Cls)

If there is any MS-DOS command you don't have to think about, that command is Cls. All you need to know is that typing three letters—*cls*—wipes the screen and moves the cursor to home base, the upper left corner of the screen. Using Cls is thus like giving yourself a new, blank sheet of paper: an uncluttered space to fill up as you will. Although Cls is useful anytime you are working at the system prompt and feel the need for a fresh start, the command is even more helpful when used from within a batch file or a Doskey macro. Clear the screen both to ensure that output will appear where you want, without having to compete with information already on the screen, and, just as important, to ensure that unexpected or unnecessary scrolling doesn't cause the user to miss needed output, such as the results of a Directory (Dir) or a Memory Display (Mem) command.

Command syntax

The Cls command is always typed as follows:

    cls

There are no parameters or switches.

Example

Type:	To:
`C:\>cls`	Clear the screen.

Include in a batch file:	To:

`@echo off`
`cls`
`dir %1 /w /p`
	Clear the screen and display a wide listing, with pause if needed, of a user-specified directory. (The Echo command suppresses display of the commands in the batch file.)

Include in a Doskey macro:	To:
`wdir=echo off$tcls$tdir` `$1 /w /p$techo on`	Perform the same task as above, but with a memory-resident macro. (The second Echo command here redisplays the system prompt, which is turned off by the first Echo command in the macro.)

Country

Country is a configuration command that enables MS-DOS to support international language conventions. On a visible level, Country sets the formats used on your computer for date, time, currency, and decimal separators—for example, whether the date is shown as 12-25-1993 or 12/25/1993, as it is in the United States, or as 25.12.1993, as it is in Germany. On a less visible level, the country setting also determines the following: correct conversion of lowercase to uppercase characters, correct sort order of characters and strings, and valid characters for use in filenames.

Country settings are stored in the file named COUNTRY.SYS, which Setup installs in your DOS directory. At startup, MS-DOS defaults to a particular country setting (usually the United States). You can change this, however, by pointing the operating system to COUNTRY.SYS and by specifying the country code— equivalent to the international dialing prefix—of the country whose conventions you want to use.

Internationalization commands in MS-DOS are tied to code pages. Where the Country command is concerned, this connection means that choosing a country determines which of the six code pages supported by MS-DOS you can use. For each country supported by the Country command, you have access to two code pages: one the default for the country, the other an alternate, but compatible, character set. Thus, for example, if you use the Country command to indicate that you want to adopt the conventions used in Belgium, you are able to use code pages 850 (Multilingual) and 437 (English language).

If you use the Country command, it must appear in the CONFIG.SYS file. Like other configuration commands, Country cannot be used directly from the system prompt.

Command syntax

The syntax of the Country command is as follows:

COUNTRY=*country*[,][*codepage*][,][*filespec*]

country is the code number of the country you want to specify. You can specify your own country if you want to simplify use of the Nlsfunc command, described later. For valid country code numbers, see Table 10-1.

codepage specifies the country code page. This is an optional parameter, but if you include it, you must separate the country and code page with a comma. (See Table 10-1.)

filespec is the drive, path, and filename of the file containing country-specific information. By default, MS-DOS looks for COUNTRY.SYS in the root directory of the current drive. If you use a different country file, or if (as is probably the case) MS-DOS Setup placed COUNTRY.SYS in your DOS directory, include this parameter. Precede the file specification with a comma—two commas if you omit the *codepage* parameter.

Country	Code	Valid code pages (default listed first)
Australia (International English)	061	437, 850
Belgium	032	850, 437
Brazil	055	850, 437
Canadian-French	002	863, 850
Croatia	038	852, 850
Czech Republic	042	852, 850
Denmark	045	850, 865
Finland	358	850, 437
France	033	850, 437
Germany	049	850, 437
Hungary	036	852, 850
Italy	039	850, 437
Latin America	003	850, 437
Netherlands	031	850, 437
Norway	047	850, 865
Poland	048	852, 850
Portugal	351	850, 860
Serbia (Yugoslavia)	038	852, 850
Slovakia	042	852, 850
Slovenia	038	852, 850
Spain	034	850, 437
Sweden	046	437, 850
Switzerland	041	850, 437
United Kingdom	044	437, 850
United States	001	437, 850

TABLE 10-1.
Country codes and valid code pages supported by MS-DOS. (Country codes and code pages are also supported in localized versions of MS-DOS for the following: Arab countries, Israel, Japan, Korea, People's Republic of China, and Taiwan.)

Examples

Place in CONFIG.SYS:	To:
`COUNTRY=039`	Set country conventions to Italy and omit a code page when COUNTRY.SYS is in the root directory of the startup drive.
`COUNTRY=049,,C:\DOS\COUNTRY.SYS`	Set country conventions to Germany and omit a code page but specify COUNTRY.SYS, in the DOS directory, as the country file.
`COUNTRY=002,863,C:\DOS\COUNTRY.SYS`	Set country conventions to Canadian-French, specify code page 863, and specify COUNTRY.SYS, in the DOS directory, as the country file.

Ctty

Ctty is an MS-DOS command few people need or use. The command name itself, pronounced "see-tee-tee-wye," represents a throwback to days of old when large computers used teletypewriters, or TTY devices, as remote communications terminals designed strictly for input and output. As its name implies, Ctty switches standard input and output from the default keyboard and screen to an alternative device, essentially turning control of your computer over to the other device—a specialized input/output device, for example, or another computer. In all such cases, the alternative device is connected through one of the serial or parallel ports on the computer being controlled. If you use the version 6 Interlnk utility, you'll see Ctty come into play when you transfer Interlnk files from one computer to another with the Intersvr /rcopy command.

Command syntax

The syntax of the Ctty command is as follows:

ctty *device*

device is the name of the device—on your system—that connects the alternative input/output device. You can use the following MS-DOS device names: PRN, LPT1, LPT2, LPT3, AUX, COM1, COM2, COM3, and COM4. To return input and output to your computer's keyboard and screen, specify the default device, CON.

Examples

Type:	To:

`C:\>mode com1 baud=96 parity=n`
`    data=8 stop=1`
 	
followed by:
 	
`C:\>ctty aux`
	Set up the first serial port (COM1) for communications, at 9600 baud, no parity, with 8 data bits and 1 stop bit.
	
	Assign input and output to the device connected to the COM1 port.

`ctty con`	Reestablish the keyboard and display as the input/output devices on the controlled computer. Note that this command must be sent by the device to which control was assigned with the Ctty command. If you're using Intersvr /rcopy, the sending device is in the computer from which you transferred the Interlnk files.

DISPLAY.SYS

Despite its name, DISPLAY.SYS does not control your normal viewing activities. The Berlitz of video, DISPLAY.SYS is an installable device driver that enables an EGA, a VGA, or an LCD display to handle the multilingual chores of code-page switching. You do not have to install DISPLAY.SYS unless you need the ability to display characters from one or more languages other than the one your display is built to support. To enable the same type of support for your printer, you use the companion device driver PRINTER.SYS, described later in this chapter.

Although an EGA, a VGA, or an LCD display comes with a built-in hardware code page for its own "native" language, it is not equipped to reproduce "foreign" characters—those it does not recognize. All three display types can, however, light on-screen pixels in any shape you care to run through video memory, so to reproduce alternate character sets, all you need to do is provide a template for the characters you need and enable the display to use them. The templates are stored in code pages, which you make available through the Nlsfunc, Mode, and Chcp commands. DISPLAY.SYS is the device driver that offers the software support that prepares your display to reproduce the varying character sets in up to six alternative code pages.

The following sections describe the use of DISPLAY.SYS and its several parameters. To enable code-page switching, however, bear in mind that you must
follow a procedure comparable in scope, though not in intent, to the steps you
take in fine-tuning memory use on your system. Appendix C gives you the hows
and whys of setting up a system for code-page switching.

Command syntax

You install DISPLAY.SYS with a Device or a Devicehigh command in CON-
FIG.SYS. The following syntax lines show the Device command. If your system
has 8 K of upper memory available, you can substitute Devicehigh where Device
is shown below:

>   DEVICE=[*drive:*][*path*]DISPLAY.SYS
>   CON[:]=(*displaytype*[,*hwcodepage*][,*codepages*])

or

>   DEVICE=[*drive:*][*path*]DISPLAY.SYS
>   CON[:]=(*displaytype*[,*hwcodepage*][,(*codepages,subfonts*)])

drive: and *path* are the drive and path to the disk and directory in which
DISPLAY.SYS is stored. MS-DOS Setup should have placed the device driver in
your DOS directory.

displaytype is the kind of display you have. You can specify either EGA (which
also covers VGA) or LCD. MS-DOS won't stumble if you specify MONO or CGA,
but you'll just be wasting your time and energy. Monochrome and CGA displays
don't support code-page switching.

hwcodepage is the number of the code page built into your display—the native
language of the "tube." Include this parameter to ensure that you can switch back
to the original code page. The hardware code page can be any of the following:

Code page	Character set
437	English language
850	Multilingual (Latin I)
852	Slavic (Latin II)
860	Portuguese
863	Canadian-French
865	Nordic

codepages is the number of alternate (prepared) code pages you want to display to use. This parameter reserves memory space for the number of code pages
you want to use. If your display is an EGA or a VGA, you can specify a value in
the range 0 (pretty useless, since if you specify *no* memory, you won't be able to
store any characters) through 6; if your display is an LCD, specify 1.

subfonts tells MS-DOS the number of fonts (character bit maps) supported for each code page by your hardware. Usually there's only one font for each code page, but some display systems might allow for more than one font per code page. Special fonts are stored in code-page information (CPI) files named EGA.CPI and LCD.CPI in your DOS directory. If you omit the parameter, MS-DOS will default to 2 possible fonts for EGA and VGA displays, 1 for LCD. Notice that you must separate *codepages* and *subfonts* with a comma and enclose both within a separate set of parentheses.

NOTE: If you use a third-party device driver for your display, install the third-party driver ahead of DISPLAY.SYS in your CONFIG.SYS file to avoid having the other driver invalidate DISPLAY.SYS. Also load ANSI.SYS before DISPLAY.SYS.

Examples

Include in CONFIG.SYS:	To:
`DEVICE=C:\DOS\DISPLAY.SYS` `CON:=(EGA,437,2)`	Enable an English-language EGA or VGA display to display characters in two alternate code pages.
`DEVICEHIGH=C:\DOS\DISPLAY.SYS` `CON:=(EGA,437,2)`	Do the same as the previous example, but load DISPLAY.SYS into 8 K of upper memory.
`DEVICE=C:\DOS\DISPLAY.SYS` `CON:=(LCD,850)`	Enable an LCD display with a Multilingual hardware code page to display one additional code page (the default for LCD displays).

DRIVER.SYS

The DRIVER.SYS device driver performs two tasks: It lets you identify an external floppy drive to MS-DOS and, more fun, it lets you "clone" a floppy drive, turning one into two by assigning two separate drive letters to a single physical drive. DRIVER.SYS exists to provide support for logical—not physical—floppy drives. On your system, remember, MS-DOS distinguishes between physical drives, which are actual, touchable pieces of hardware, and logical drives, which are drives represented by drive letters. You use logical drives when, for instance, you connect to a network server as drive X or when you partition a hard disk and divide it into multiple "drives," each assigned a different drive letter. In the case of DRIVER.SYS, you apply the concept of logical drives to the floppy drives on your computer.

It's easy to see that DRIVER.SYS can be essential if you attach an external floppy drive to the system. In order for you to use the drive, you must be able to tell MS-DOS to assign it a drive letter, and that's what you do with DRIVER.SYS. Less obvious, perhaps, is how or why you would want to use DRIVER.SYS with the existing physical drives on your computer. But suppose you have, as many people do, two internal floppy drives of different capacities: drive A is a 5.25-inch drive and drive B is a 3.5-inch drive. Suppose further that you sometimes need to copy files from and to floppy disks of the same capacity—5.25-inch to 5.25-inch, for instance. You can use Diskcopy, but you cannot use Copy or Xcopy, because the command you need would be something like *copy a:*.doc a:*, and MS-DOS refuses to copy files if the process results in copying a file to itself. The solution: Install DRIVER.SYS so that MS-DOS assigns two drive letters to the same physical drive.

When you install DRIVER.SYS, you create a new logical drive and MS-DOS assigns it the next available drive letter on your system. Thus, if you have floppy drives A and B, plus hard drive C, MS-DOS can assign drive letter D to either drive A or drive B. (DRIVER.SYS does not work with hard disks.) But, you might be wondering, how does MS-DOS know which drive I mean, and how do I find out which drive letter it assigns? The answer to the first question is all in the Device command you use to install DRIVER.SYS. MS-DOS will tell you the new drive letter (D, for example) with the following message:

```
Loaded External Disk Driver for Drive D
```

If the message scrolled by too fast, you can also see the new drive letter by doing one of the following:

- If you have version 6 of MS-DOS, reboot the system and press F8 for an interactive boot when the message *Starting MS-DOS* appears.

- If you have version 6 and you've installed DoubleSpace, type *dblspace /list* and look for the new drive letter.

- If you don't have version 6 of MS-DOS, reboot and press the Pause key to stop scrolling as CONFIG.SYS is processed. (You'll have to be fast.) Otherwise, try changing the current drive to the letter following the letter of the last drive on your system. For example, if you have drives A, B, and C, try changing the current drive to D. If you already have "real" drives A through E (the last drive letter MS-DOS recognizes by default), take a look at CONFIG.SYS with the Type command and note the highest letter specified in the Lastdrive command. Work your way up through the letters until the light flashes on the drive you cloned with DRIVER.SYS. You're there.

Command syntax

You install DRIVER.SYS with a Device or Devicehigh command in CONFIG.SYS. The following syntax lines show the Device command. DRIVER.SYS takes up a minuscule 224 bytes, so if your system has this small amount of upper memory available, you can substitute Devicehigh where Device is shown below:

DEVICE=[*drive:*][*path*]DRIVER.SYS /d:*drivenumber* /c /f:*drivetype* /h:*heads*
/s:*sectors* /t:*tracks*

drive and *path* are the drive and directory where DRIVER.SYS is stored. This should be your DOS directory.

/d:*drivenumber* is the number used internally by MS-DOS for the floppy drive to which you want to assign a new drive letter. MS-DOS accepts any number in the range 0 through 127 and assigns them sequentially. Your first floppy drive (A) is always drive 0, your second floppy drive (B if you have two) is 1, your third floppy drive (must be external) is 2, and so on. If you have one floppy drive, which you can refer to as either A or B, it is drive 0.

/c, for change-line support, tells MS-DOS that the floppy drive in question is able to detect when the drive latch has been opened and closed and, thus, whether the disk has been changed. If the drive does have change-line support, disk access is speeded up because MS-DOS doesn't verify the status of the disk in the drive. You'll have to consult your disk-drive documentation to find out about change-line support.

/f:*drivetype* identifies the type of floppy drive you are specifying. Use one of the following:

Number	Drive type
0	360 K, 5.25 inch (also for 160 K, 180 K, and 320 K)
1	1.2 MB, 5.25 inch
2 (default)	720 K, 3.5 inch
7	1.44 MB, 3.5 inch
9	2.88 MB, 3.5 inch

If you specify a drive type, you can omit the three following switches (/h, /s, and /t), unless the number of heads, tracks, or sectors for your drive differs from the defaults listed below. Conversely, if you use the three following switches, you can omit /f.

/h:*heads* identifies the number of heads in the drive. MS-DOS accepts values from 1 through 99; the default is 2. If you don't know how many heads the drive contains, check your documentation or—if you have version 6—start the Microsoft Diagnostics and press D for drive information. You'll find the number of tracks ("cylinders") and sectors here as well.

/s:*sectors* gives the number of sectors per track on a formatted disk. MS-DOS accepts values from 1 through 99; defaults for drive types listed under the /f switch are shown on the following page.

Drive type	Sectors per track
0	9
1	15
2	9
7	18
9	36

/t:*tracks* gives the number of tracks per side. MS-DOS accepts values from 1 through 999; the default is 40 for drive type 0, 80 for all others.

NOTE: You cannot use DRIVER.SYS to try to change the physical description of a floppy drive—that is, to fool MS-DOS into using a 1.2-MB, 5.25-inch floppy drive as if it were a 1.44-MB, 3.5-inch floppy drive. The drive characteristics you specify must match the physical characteristics of the drive. If you need to define or redefine a physical drive to MS-DOS, use the DRIVPARM command, but don't assume you can monkey with drive characteristics there, either.

Examples

Include in CONFIG.SYS:	To:
`DEVICE=C:\DOS\DRIVER.SYS` `/D:0 /C /F:1`	Have MS-DOS assign a second drive letter to a 1.2-MB, 5.25-inch floppy drive A with change-line support.
`DEVICEHIGH=C:\DOS\DRIVER.SYS` `/D:1 /F:7`	Have MS-DOS assign a second drive letter to a 1.44-MB, 3.5-inch floppy drive B, placing the device driver in upper memory.
`DEVICEHIGH=C:\DOS\DRIVER.SYS` `/D:1 /H:2 /S:18 /T:80`	Do the same as in the preceding example, but define the drive by number of heads, sectors, and tracks instead of by drive type.
`DEVICE=C:\DOS\DRIVER.SYS` `/D:2 /F:7`	Install a device driver for an external, 1.44-MB floppy drive on a system with two internal floppy drives.

EGA.SYS

The EGA.SYS device driver is necessary only if you have an EGA display, you use the MS-DOS Shell, and you activate the Task Swapper. This is the device driver that enables the Shell to save and restore your on-screen display as you switch from one active program to another. If you use a mouse with the Shell, install EGA.SYS ahead of the mouse driver in your CONFIG.SYS file to save some memory.

If you are using version 5 of MS-DOS on a system with an EGA display and you chose to install the Shell during Setup, EGA.SYS is probably already in your CONFIG.SYS file.

Command syntax

You install EGA.SYS with a Device or a Devicehigh command in CONFIG.SYS. The following syntax lines show the Device command. If your system has 3 K or more of upper memory available, you can substitute Devicehigh where Device is shown below:

DEVICE=[*drive:*][*path*]EGA.SYS

drive: and *path* are the drive and path to the directory where EGA.SYS is stored. This should be your DOS directory.

Examples

Include in CONFIG.SYS:	To:
`DEVICE=C:\DOS\EGA.SYS`	Install EGA.SYS and ensure that the Shell can restore your screen when you use the Task Swapper.
`DEVICEHIGH=C:\DOS\EGA.SYS`	Install EGA.SYS, as in the previous example, but load the device driver in upper memory.

Graphics Table (Graftabl)—through version 5 only

Graftabl is a display-related command designed for use only if you use code-page switching on a computer with a CGA display, which might be unable to display the extended characters—those with ASCII codes above 127—used in code pages for language-specific characters and symbols. Higher-resolution displays, such as EGA and VGA, use the DISPLAY.SYS device driver to enable multilingual character displays. They should have no need for the Graftabl command.

Graftabl is a memory-resident program that occupies about 1 K. Once in memory, it remains until you reboot the system. When you load Graftabl, it displays a message such as the following:

```
Previous Code Page: None
Active Code Page: 437
```

Although the distinction isn't very obvious, note that Graftabl simply enables the display to produce characters stored in a particular code page. It does not actually change the code page currently in use on the system. To change from one code page to another, you enable code-page switching with the Nlsfunc, Mode, and Chcp commands, as described in Appendix C.

Graftabl, like certain other MS-DOS commands, produces a number of exit codes that you can check to determine whether and how well a Graftabl command is carried out. If you use batch files, you can use the errorlevel parameter of the If command to check these exit codes and control the outcome of the batch file. The exit codes are

Exit code	Meaning
0	New code page loaded successfully; no previous code page in memory.
1	New code page successfully replaced previous code page.
2	File error.
3	Command error; no action taken.
4	Incorrect MS-DOS version running; version 5 needed.

Command syntax

The syntax of the Graftabl command is simple:

graftabl[*codepage*] /status

codepage is the number of the code page for which Graftabl is to produce characters. You can specify any of the following:

Code page	Character set
437	English language
850	Multilingual (Latin I)
852	Slavic (Latin II)
860	Portuguese
863	Canadian-French
865	Nordic

/status, which you can abbreviate /sta, is an optional switch you can use to display the number of the current code page; for example, typing *graftabl /sta* will produce the following result:

```
Active Code Page: 850
```

Typing *graftabl* alone produces the same result.

Examples

Type:	To:
`C:\>graftabl 850`	Enable MS-DOS to display characters in the Multilingual code page on a CGA display running in graphics mode.

`C:\>graftabl /sta`
or
`C:\>graftabl`
	Display the number of the active code page.

Graphics

The Graphics command loads a small (6 K), memory-resident utility that enables you to use Shift-Print Screen to print the contents of a graphics screen produced by a CGA, an EGA, or a VGA display adapter. MS-DOS has long had the built-in ability to print the contents of a text-based screen of the sort you see when you're working at the system prompt. When you're working with a graphics-based program, however, as you do when running the MS-DOS Shell in graphics mode, using Shift-Print Screen without the Graphics command can produce strange output: odd characters, page breaks you didn't know existed, and indecipherable patterns of light and dark that bear no resemblance to what you see on screen. In order to print such a screen, you use the Graphics command to give MS-DOS the more sophisticated screen-dumping tools it needs to scan and send the screen contents to the printer.

Although the Graphics command can be useful, you should not assume it's the cure-all for every pretty picture you ever wanted to commit to paper. It's not. Despite its name, the Graphics command is not the equal of graphics-printing programs of the kind you'd expect with Windows. Graphics has, in fact, no effect on Windows and Windows–based applications at all, for the simple reason that MS-DOS sits on the sidelines while Windows is running. (MS-DOS does control any active window in which you're running an MS-DOS–based application, and you might be able to print the contents of that window, but don't try it. The experiment can be risky, resulting in serious video errors that lock up your system and force you to reboot.)

The basic rule to follow in dumping screens to your printer is this: If you try to print screen contents while an MS-DOS–based application is running and the outcome does not resemble the screen at all, load the Graphics program and try again. Be sure, however, to specify both the kind of printer you have and the location of the printer profile file named GRAPHICS.PRO. This file includes escape sequences and display instructions that enable Graphics to use your printer correctly. To people, the profile is readable, but not especially informative to those who don't know a lot about printers. You might need to display GRAPHICS.PRO, however, if you use the /printbox switch described later.

When you print screen contents, the Graphics program shades the output in up to four gray shades if the printer you specify is either *color1* or *graphics*, as described later, and the screen resolution is in 320 by 200 (pixel) color graphics mode. The output will be oriented sideways on the page—that is, rotated 90 degrees so that the width of the screen is aligned along the long edge of the paper—if the screen resolution is 640 by 200.

The Graphics program cannot send screen contents to a PostScript printer. If you use a non-PostScript laser printer, remember that you might have to take the printer off line and press the formfeed button or send a new-page escape character to force the printer to eject the page.

Command syntax

The Graphics command includes a number of parameters and switches. The full syntax is as follows:

graphics *printertype filespec* /r /b /lcd /printbox:std /printbox:lcd

printertype identifies the type of printer you are going to use. You can specify any of those in the left column of the following table:

Printer type	Printer name
IBM printers:	
color1	IBM Personal Computer Color Printer, black ribbon
color4	Same as above, with RGB (red, green, blue, and black) ribbon
color8	Same as above, with CMY (cyan, magenta, yellow, and black) ribbon
graphics	IBM Personal Graphics Printer, IBM Proprinter, or IBM Quietwriter
graphicswide	IBM Personal Graphics Printer with 11-inch carriage
thermal	IBM PC-Convertible Thermal Printer
Hewlett-Packard printers:	
hpdefault	Any Hewlett-Packard PCL (Printer Control Language) printer

(continued)

Printer type	Printer name
deskjet	Hewlett-Packard DeskJet
laserjet	Hewlett-Packard LaserJet or LaserJet Plus
laserjetII	Hewlett-Packard LaserJet II
paintjet	Hewlett-Packard PaintJet
quietjet	Hewlett-Packard Quietjet
quietjetplus	Hewlett-Packard Quietjet Plus
ruggedwriter	Hewlett-Packard Ruggedwriter
ruggedwriterwide	Hewlett-Packard Ruggedwriter Wide
thinkjet	Hewlett-Packard ThinkJet

filespec is the drive, path, and filename of the printer profile file. If you are using GRAPHICS.PRO, the file should be in your DOS directory. If you are using a customized profile file, specify the appropriate drive, path, and filename. You can omit the drive and path if the file is in the current directory. If you load one profile file and later attempt to load another with a second Graphics command, the new profile must be smaller than the old one. If the file is larger, you must restart the system first.

/r prints the screen as you see it—that is, light characters on dark background. Use this switch to reverse the image, printing dark on light. You'll probably want to remember this when printing screens such as those you see in the Shell to avoid a very dark printout.

/b prints the screen background in color if the printer you use is either color4 or color8.

/lcd causes Graphics to use the (pixel) height-to-width aspect ratio characteristic of LCD screens instead of the default CGA aspect ratio the program normally uses. Using the /lcd switch is the same as using the /printbox:lcd switch described next.

/printbox:std and /printbox:lcd, which can be abbreviated as /pb:std and /pb:lcd, determine the size of the print box which, in turn, determines the relationship between the printed graphic's height and width. Use /printbox:std for CGA, EGA, and VGA screens, /printbox:lcd for LCD displays. If you are uncertain whether one or the other is supported by your printer, use the MS-DOS Editor to display GRAPHICS.PRO and look for a line like this under the description of your printer:

```
PRINTBOX STD,2,2,ROTATE
```

Examples

Type:	To:
`C:\DOS>graphics`	Load the Graphics program without specifying printer type. This command assumes that GRAPHICS.PRO is in the current directory.
`C:\>graphics laserjetii` `c:\dos\graphics.pro /r`	Load the Graphics program, specify a LaserJet Series II printer, identify the location of the GRAPHICS.PRO profile, and print screens as dark characters on a light background.
`C:\>graphics color4` `c:\dos\graphics.pro /b`	Load the Graphics program, specify an IBM color printer, identify the location of the GRAPHICS.PRO profile, and print background color.

Keyboard (Keyb)

The Keyboard (Keyb) command sets your keyboard to the layout and characters of a language other than United States English. Keyb is one of several commands in your multilingual repertoire and can be used either with or without the code-page switching enabled by Nlsfunc, Mode, and Chcp, described in Appendix C.

When you use Keyb, you are telling MS-DOS to alter its normal layout, such as the one used in the United States, so that you can use the layout and characters associated with the keyboard of a particular country, such as France or Germany. On the French keyboard, for instance, the locations of the Q and A keys are the reverse of their locations in the United States layout. On the German keyboard, the Z and Y keys swap places. Because the Keyb command enables MS-DOS to interpret keys according to these and other country-specific or language-specific layouts, specifying the German keyboard and pressing the keys that spell *keyb* in the United States layout produces *kezb* instead. Similarly, pressing the unshifted 9 in the top row of the United States layout produces *ç* in the French layout.

After you change from one keyboard layout to another, you can switch between the original layout, which is built into ROM, and the alternate layout, which sits in memory, with the following keys:

Press:	To:
Ctrl-Alt-F1	Switch to the default layout.
Ctrl-Alt-F2	Switch to the alternate layout.
Ctrl-Alt-F7	Switch to the "typewriter mode" used in some countries.

Although simple to use, the Keyb command can cause a little head-scratching because it's one of the MS-DOS commands that uses code pages, yet it doesn't always require you to change code pages to use the layout and characters of another country and language. The reason for this seeming inconsistency is that code pages vary, but not extensively. You find many similarities from one code page to another. For example, even though only the Nordic and Multilingual code pages contain the character Ø, the character ç appears in all six code pages supported by MS-DOS. As a result, you can often change the keyboard layout without changing code pages and still type many, if not most, of the characters you need. The English-language code page (437), for instance, can be used successfully to type accented words in French, German, and Italian. To gain access to all of the characters in a given language, however, you do have to change to the code page that supports it best and that change, of course, means preparing for code-page switching.

Whether or not you actually change code pages when you use the Keyboard command, you must match the layout you choose to the code pages—either built in or previously prepared—that are supported by your system and that work with the language. If you do not follow these rules, MS-DOS does the best it can, but you can see error messages such as these:

```
Code page requested (xxx) is not valid for given keyboard code
```

and:

```
One or more CON code pages invalid for given keyboard code
```

The Keyb command, like certain other MS-DOS commands, produces a number of exit codes that you can check to determine whether and how well the command is executed. If you use batch files, you can use the errorlevel parameter of the If command to check on these exit codes—for example, to ensure compatibility between the layout and the active code page—and control the outcome of the batch file. The exit codes are

Exit code	Meaning
0	Success.
1	Invalid keyboard code, code page, or command syntax.
2	Bad or missing keyboard definition file.
4	Error related to CON (keyboard) device.
5	Requested code page has not been prepared for use.

Command syntax

You can use the Keyb command by itself, either from the command line or from a batch file, or you can point MS-DOS to the KEYB.COM file with an Install command in CONFIG.SYS. The following description covers the Keyb command syntax. For the Install command, refer to the example later in this description and to Chapter 12.

The syntax of the Keyboard command is as follows:

keyb *countrycode,[codepage][,filespec] /e /id:NNN*

countrycode is the two-letter code of the country whose keyboard layout you want to use. Valid country codes are listed in Table 10-2.

codepage is the number of the code page you want to use with the keyboard layout. If you don't include this parameter, MS-DOS uses the current code page. Valid code pages for each layout are shown in Table 10-2.

filespec is the drive, path, and filename of the keyboard definition file that contains the keyboard layout information. By default, MS-DOS searches the path for KEYBOARD.SYS, so you need to include the file specification only if the file is not in the current path or you are using a different keyboard definition file.

/e notifies MS-DOS that you are using an enhanced (101-key or 102-key) keyboard with an 8086-based computer. You need this switch only if you are using an XT-class computer.

/id:*NNN* specifies the number (*NNN*) of the keyboard you are using. You need this switch only for countries with more than one keyboard layout (France, Italy, and the United Kingdom). See Table 10-2 for keyboard identification numbers.

Country	Country code	Code pages	Keyboard IDs
Belgium	be	850, 437	
Brazil	br	850, 437	
Canadian-French	cf	850, 863	
Czech Republic	cz	852, 850	
Denmark	dk	850, 865	
Finland	su	850, 437	
France	fr	850, 437	120, 189
Germany	gr	850, 437	
Hungary	hu	852, 850	
Italy	it	850, 437	141, 142
Latin America	la	850, 437	
Netherlands	nl	850, 437	
Norway	no	850, 865	
Poland	pl	852, 850	
Portugal	po	850, 860	
Slovakia	sl	852, 850	

TABLE 10-2.   *(continued)*
Country codes, code pages, and keyboard identification numbers.

TABLE 10-2. *continued*

Country	Country code	Code pages	Keyboard IDs
Spain	sp	850, 437	
Sweden	sv	437, 850	
Switzerland (French)	sf	850,437	
Switzerland (German)	sg	850, 437	
United Kingdom	uk	850, 437	166, 168
United States	us	437, 850	
Yugoslavia	yu	852, 850	

Examples

Type:	To:
`C:\>keyb gr`	Switch to the German layout (assuming either code page 437 or 850 is active).
`C:\>keyb fr,850`	Switch to the French layout and specify code page 850 (assuming code-page switching is enabled).
`C:\>keyb it,850 /id:141`	Switch to the Italian layout, specifying code page 850 and keyboard ID 141.

Include in CONFIG.SYS:	To:
`INSTALL=C:\DOS\KEYB.COM FR`	Set up the French layout at startup with the Install command in CONFIG.SYS. You can use this method of switching keyboards only with countries that have the same default code page as your own. (CONFIG.SYS is processed before MS-DOS reaches any code-page switching commands in AUTOEXEC.BAT.)

Mode

The Mode command is where MS-DOS separates the dilettantes from the true believers. If you're comfortable with Mode, you're comfortable with computers. Through Mode, you configure and control the display, keyboard, printer, and communications ports—all the standard-issue devices (except for disk drives) on the system.

Because Mode works with so many different kinds of devices, dealing with it is a lot like dealing with your dog's new litter of puppies. The best way (perhaps the only way) to keep your sense of humor and see the parts in relation to the whole is to look at Mode as a collection of functions and explore them one at a time. Although there's no overriding reason to do so, the following sections start with the simplest uses of Mode and move on from there. The last two topics cover serial ports and code-page switching, arguably the least friendly parts of this command.

Controlling the keyboard rate

Press a key, and a character appears on screen. Hold down a key, and the character repeats. The speed at which the keyboard repeats a character is called its *typematic rate,* and this rate consists of two parts: the rate of repetition and the amount of time that passes before repetition begins. If you're an average typist, the typematic rate probably doesn't matter very much, but if your fingers are so fast that your keyboard sounds like an unmusical "Flight of the Bumblebee," you can have a little fun with a very simple form of the Mode command. This one controls both the rate of repetition and the pause that precedes it to make the keyboard responsive to your typing abilities. Try this form of the Mode command, especially if your work often requires that you press the same key repeatedly— even such nonprinting keys as the Spacebar and the cursor-movement keys. A word of caution is in order here, though: If you set the typematic rate to the fastest possible repetition, type with a light touch and keep your eyes open. Characters will fly onto the screen, and the cursor-movement keys will move you through a document so quickly you might lose more time than you gain because you consistently overshoot your target.

Command syntax

To control the typematic rate, the form of the Mode command is

mode con[:] rate=r delay=d

con applies the Mode command to the keyboard. You must include this device name. You don't need to type a colon after con, but you can if you want to.

rate=r and delay=d control the rate of repetition and the length of time before a keypress is repeated while a key is held down. For rate, you can specify r as any unit value from 1 through 32. The higher the value, the faster the rate of repetition, ranging from about 2 to 30 characters per second. The default rate is 20 or 21 units, depending on your keyboard. For delay, you can specify d as any value from 1 through 4, where 1 equals 0.25 second, 2 equals 0.5 second, 3 equals 0.75 second, and 4 equals 1 second. The default delay is 2 or about half a second. If you include rate, you must include delay and vice versa. MS-DOS won't adjust one without the other.

You can simply type *mode con* and omit both rate and delay, but doing this gives you a different form of the Mode command: one that displays the status of the display.

Examples

Type:	To:
C:\>mode con rate=32 delay=1	Set the fastest typematic rate, with the highest rate of repetition and the shortest delay.
C:\>mode con rate=1 delay=4	Set the slowest typematic rate. (This makes the cursor act as if it's slogging through a swamp. Sit back and have a cuppa.)
C:\>mode con rate=28 delay=1	Set a fast, but not overfast, typematic rate.

Controlling the display mode

Although MS-DOS often cedes control of the display to application programs with their own preferences and speed requirements, you can set the number of displayed lines and the number of characters (either 40 or the more normal 80) per line. This capability can be very useful if you need large, clear characters on screen, or if you sometimes want to see significant amounts of information on screen at the same time—a long directory listing, perhaps. Using the Mode command to control the display in this way, you can easily switch all the way from an easily readable 40 characters per line and 25 lines per screen to the MS-DOS default of 80 characters and 25 lines per screen or to an even more compact 80 characters and 43 or 50 lines. The ability to select display modes can be made even easier with small, simple batch files or, if you have version 6, with display-related choices in your AUTOEXEC.BAT file that appear automatically at startup. If you do make use of this part of the Mode command, however, you'll have to install the ANSI.SYS device driver in CONFIG.SYS.

A number of other display-control options are available through the Mode command, but for the most part these options are holdovers from the days when display choices were limited to the clear but inflexible 80-column IBM Monochrome Display Adapter (MDA) and the less clear but more colorful 40-column or 80-column capabilities of CGA displays. Contemporary displays, such as EGA and VGA, combine the clarity of the MDA with the visual appeal of the CGA to make choices such as enabling or disabling color unnecessary. Still, in the interest of completeness, the following descriptions outline all options currently available for controlling display characteristics.

Command syntax

The most important and useful of the display-related Mode options is the one that allows you to set the number of lines per screen and the number of characters per line. The syntax takes one of the following three formats. The first is as follows:

mode con[:] cols=*c* lines=*n*

con is the MS-DOS name for the console—here, the display. You must include con; the colon is optional.

cols=*c* is the number of columns (characters) per line. You can specify either 40 or 80. If you specify 40 characters per line, the screen shows 25 lines per screen, regardless of the number of lines you have specified.

lines=*n* is the number of lines per screen. If you have an EGA display, you can specify either 25 or 43. If you have a VGA display, you can specify 25, 43, or 50 (small, but effective for minimizing use of the PgDn key).

The second format is best if you have a good memory:

mode ,*n*

n again specifies the number of lines—25, 43, or 50—per vertical inch. Note that this use of the Mode command can omit the preliminary *lines=* identifier. If you include only *n* in the command, be sure to precede the value with a comma.

Although these forms of the Mode command require you to install ANSI.SYS, they are more effective than comparable choices, such as the co40 and co80 options described next, because the display mode you set, if you retain 80 characters per line, carries over into certain programs, such as the QBasic interpreter and the MS-DOS Editor.

The third format is useful with an MDA or a CGA display:

mode *displaymode* [,*n*] [,*shift*[,t]]

displaymode is any one of the following:

- 40 or 80, which specifies 40 or 80 characters per line.
- bw40 or bw80, which specifies 40 or 80 characters per line on a CGA display with color disabled.
- co40 or co80, which specifies 40 or 80 characters per line on a CGA display with color enabled.
- mono, which specifies a monochrome adapter with 80 characters per line.

shift instructs MS-DOS to shift screen output on a CGA display to the left or right. Type *l* or *r*, the only permitted values.

t instructs MS-DOS to display a test pattern on the screen and to ask you to indicate whether the orientation is correct or should be shifted farther left or right.

NOTE: If you shift screen output in CGA mode and you have specified 80 characters per line, the shift will be two characters to the right or left.

Examples

Type:	To:
(The following examples assume that the line DEVICE=C:\DOS\ANSI.SYS is in CONFIG.SYS.)	

`C:\>mode con lines=43`
or:
`C:\>mode ,43`
	Set the display mode to 43 lines per screen. (The example assumes that the default of 80 characters per line is already in effect.) You must have an EGA or better monitor to display 43 lines. Note the leading comma in the second command.

`C:\>mode con lines=25`	Set the display mode to 25 lines per screen (again, assuming 80 characters per line).
`C:\>mode con cols=40`	Set the display mode to 40 characters per line.
(The following examples don't require ANSI.SYS.)	
`C:\>mode co40`	Set the display mode to 40 characters per line on a CGA display. This command would work on an EGA or better display as well, but co40 and its allies are pretty antiquated and are better replaced by the *col=* and *lines=* parameters.
`C:\>mode co80,1,t`	Set the display mode to 80 characters per line, color enabled, on a CGA screen, at the same time shifting the image to the left two characters and displaying a test pattern.

Include in a batch file:	To:

`@echo off`
`mode con lines=43`
`cls`
	Change to a 43-line display mode from within a batch file. Remember, ANSI.SYS must be installed.

Displaying device status

In addition to configuring devices, the Mode command by itself reports on whether and how you have used it to affect those devices. When you request device status, Mode can report either on all devices on the system or on just the one you request. It all depends on how you type the command, as described in this section. Beyond this, there's little to be said about this use of the Mode command, other than to note that the command can produce some rather lengthy output and that it tells you about code-page status—whether or not you've enabled code-page switching. The following lines show a fairly typical report on device status, with brief explanations of what the different lines mean. Just type *mode*:

```
Status for device LPT1:
------------
LPT1: not rerouted
Retry=NONE
Code page operation not
supported on this device
```

The printer is connected to the first parallel port (LPT1). *not rerouted* means Mode has not been used to send output to a serial port, such as COM1. The printer is set up for no retries on timeouts (printer errors). The last line tells you that code-page switching has not been enabled for this printer.

```
Status for device LPT2:
------------
LPT2: not rerouted
```

LPT2 is the name MS-DOS recognizes for the second parallel port. This system does not actually have an LPT2 port, so the message is somewhat confusing. All it means, however, is that Mode does not detect redirection of LPT2.

```
Status for device LPT3:
------------
LPT3: not rerouted
```

Same as above.

```
Status for device CON:
-----------
Columns=80
Lines=43
No code page has been selected
Hardware code pages:
   code page 437
Prepared code pages:
   code page 850
   code page not prepared
MODE status code page
function completed
```

This, of course, is the display. The report shows that the screen is set to 80 columns and 43 lines. The remainder of the report has to do with code-page switching, which has been enabled for this sample report. The first line, telling you no code page is selected, means that the display is using the default (hardware) code page, 437. The lines describing prepared code pages tell you that this system is set to use up to two prepared code pages, of which one (850) has been described to MS-DOS and is available for use. The last line tells you that Mode has checked code page support for the display.

(continued)

```
Status for device COM1:
------------
Retry=NONE
```

This is the first (and only) serial port on the system. For COM ports, Mode merely tells you the retry status in cases of timeouts where the port cannot send or receive. Even though a COM port might be set up for a particular baud rate and other communications settings, you do not see them in this report. If you have version 6 of MS-DOS, you can find this information by starting the Microsoft Diagnostics and checking the COM ports.

Command syntax

The syntax of the Mode command when used to display device status is as follows:

mode [*device*] /status

device is the name of the device for which you want a status report. If you omit this parameter, you see a complete report like the preceding one, describing all active devices on the system. Valid device names are CON, PRN, LPT1, LPT2, LPT3, COM1, COM2, COM3, and COM4. Although AUX usually defaults to COM1, Mode responds *Invalid parameter - aux* if you try to use this device name. Also, although PRN is usually equivalent to LPT1, reports for the two devices differ—only LPT1 includes rerouting and retry status and thus is the more complete. You can add a colon to the end of any device name (for example, LPT1:).

/status, which you can also abbreviate as /sta, is a switch you need only when you want to check on a parallel port that has been redirected to a serial port. Remember this switch. If you omit /status with a redirected port, the command you type (*mode lptx*) cancels redirection. See "Redirecting a printer to a serial port," later in this chapter.

Examples

Type:	To:
C:\>mode	Check on the status of all devices on the system.
C:\>mode con	Check on the status of the display.
C:\>mode lpt1	Check on the status of the first parallel port if it has not been redirected to a serial port, or cancel redirection of LPT1.
C:\>mode lpt1 /sta	Check on the status of the first parallel port if it *has* been redirected to a serial port.

Configuring a parallel printer

When you attach a parallel printer to your system, you do little more than plug the printer cord into an outlet and run a parallel cable between the printer and a parallel port on your computer. All the other work of running and using the printer is normally handled by your application programs and your printer driver, both of which should work seamlessly together. Under MS-DOS, printer use is confined to the Print command (covered later) and the Copy command, which can copy from the console or a file to the printer. Configuration control covers two areas: setting the number of lines per inch and the number of characters per line and setting the retry method—the MS-DOS response to a timeout error that occurs in transmission.

Setting lines per inch and characters per line is the print equivalent of the *mode con cols=x lines=y* command you use with the display. Although you can control line spacing and character size far more effectively through your applications, the MS-DOS capacity to set printer lines and character size can be useful when you're working at the system prompt and you want a "quick-and-dirty" way to print certain types of documents—for example, a file full of electronic mail messages, an ASCII-formatted file you've downloaded from a bulletin board or a network, or (a real possibility) MS-DOS readme or help information. You can put this capability of the Mode command to work if you have an IBM-compatible or an Epson-compatible printer. Control of character size and line spacing does not affect other printers, such as the Hewlett-Packard LaserJets.

You probably don't really need the ability to specify a particular retry method in response to a timeout error. In fact, if you use a printer on a network, ignore the retry setting completely to avoid tying up network lines unnecessarily. However, if you find that your non-networked printer cannot keep up with your computer or if printouts are incomplete, try either the e or r retry setting. If you don't specify a retry method, MS-DOS defaults to None, meaning it does not make repeated attempts to send data to a printer that does not respond.

Command syntax

The syntax for using the Mode command to configure a parallel printer is as follows:

    mode lpt*n*[:] [cols=*c*] [lines=*l*] [retry=*r*]

or, if you have a good memory:

    mode lpt*n*[:] [*c*][,*l*][,*r*]

lpt*n* is the parallel port to which the printer is connected. You can specify 1, 2, or 3 for *n*. You must include this parameter. (You can add a colon if you want.)

cols=*c*, or just plain *c*, specifies the number of characters per line. You can specify either 80 (the default) or 132.

lines=*l*, or just plain *l*, specifies the number of lines per inch to be printed. You can specify either 6 (the default) or 8. Note that if you use the short form of the command and include both *c* and *l*, you must insert a comma between the two.

retry=*r*, or just plain *r*, specifies the retry action to take when MS-DOS tries to use a busy or an unresponsive port. The default is none, or n. Note that if you use the short form, you must precede this parameter with a comma (two commas if you omit *l*). Other valid choices for *n* are

- e, which reports "error" if the port is busy.

- b, which reports "busy" from a status check of a busy port.

- p, which causes continual retries until the printer responds. (Be careful with this setting. You can break out of repeated retries by pressing Ctrl-Break, but you can also cause serious problems with Windows that force you to shut down all applications and reboot the system.)

- r, which reports "ready" even if the port is busy.

Examples

Type:	To:

`C:\>mode lpt1 lines=8`
or:
`C:\>mode lpt1 ,8`
	Set the printer to 8 lines per vertical inch. (Note the comma indicating that a value for *c* is omitted in the short form of the command.)

`C:\>mode lpt1 cols=132 lines=8`
or:
`C:\>mode lpt1 132,8`
	Set the printer to 132 characters per line and 8 lines per vertical inch. Again, note the comma in the short form of the command.

`C:\>mode lpt1 ,,e`	Report "error" if the printer port is busy. This is the short form, and since no columns or lines were specified, two commas are needed.

Redirecting a printer to a serial port

The syntax description under "Displaying device status" made a point of telling you about redirected parallel ports. This section tells you how to go about redirecting one. The procedure is simple—once you've prepared the serial port, as described in the next section, "Configuring a serial port."

By default, MS-DOS assumes that PRN refers to a parallel printer. Printers come in two varieties, however: parallel and serial. Some printers, in fact, can be switched from one to the other with the help of a few small DIP switches contoured for fingers roughly the shape and size of those on a Barbie doll. But all that's another story. Here, the subject at hand is how to tell MS-DOS to use a serial printer by redirecting output from an LPT port to a COM port, and that's easy. All you have to know in advance is which parallel port you want to redirect and which serial port you want to redirect to. Those facts, unfortunately, are not always known, but there are ways to find out.

Your LPT port is almost certainly going to be LPT1, unless you have more than one printer, and if you have more than one parallel printer, you should already know which is which. If you don't, choose an LPT port with the printer setup commands in one of your application programs, print a short document, and see where it emerges or type *dir > lpt1* to redirect a directory listing to LPT1. Try it again for LPT2, LPT3, and so on. The COM port can be a little more difficult than an LPT port to figure out because it can be connected to a modem, a mouse, or another serial device, but even here you have some steps to take. First, foremost, and easiest of all, check the back of your computer and hope that the ports are labeled for you. If the ports aren't labeled, here's what you do:

- If you have version 6 of MS-DOS, start the Microsoft Diagnostics utility and check the settings listed for COM ports. This will at least tell you how many COM ports are installed. You can check IRQ status to see which COM ports have mice or other known devices attached. But you still might have to experiment.

- If you don't have version 6, check your documentation or ask someone who knows. If you still can't find out, type the Mode command without any parameters to check on device status. If this doesn't work, check your CONFIG.SYS and AUTOEXEC.BAT files to see if you can determine whether a device is using a particular COM port. (You might find a clue in a Device command or a command-line switch.) If all else fails, resort to trial and error, redirecting the default parallel port to each COM port in turn. Start with the highest-numbered COM port and send a short test file to the printer each time until you succeed. You might cause your system to hang and need to reboot, but sooner or later you'll find the COM port you need.

Once you know which ports to use, the rest is simple.

Command syntax

The syntax for redirecting a parallel printer to a serial port is as follows:

    mode lpt*n*[:][=com*n*[:]]

lpt*n* is the name of the parallel port to redirect. You can specify *n* as 1, 2, or 3. You can add a colon to the name of the parallel port if you want to; the same goes for the serial port.

com*n* is the name of the serial port to which you want to redirect printing. You can specify *n* as 1, 2, 3, or 4, depending on how many serial ports are on your system.

To cancel redirection, type *mode lptn*, omitting the name of the COM port.

Examples

Type:	To:
`C:\>mode lpt1=com1`	Redirect printing from the first parallel port to the first serial port on the system.
`C:\>mode lpt1`	Cancel redirection of LPT1 to COM1. Note that you should type *mode lpt1 /status* if you've redirected a parallel port to a serial port and you just want to check its status.

Configuring a serial port

Before you can use a serial port, whether for a modem, a printer, or another serial device, you must configure the serial port so that it operates at an appropriate speed for the device and uses the correct parity setting, data bits, start bits, and stop bits.

If you're using a serial port for a mouse, the mouse installation program should take care of all the details for you. If you're using a modem, your communications program should provide a command or a menu that sets the serial port without your having to use the Mode command. If you are setting up a serial printer, however, you'll probably have to pay your respects to Mode by using it first to configure the serial port and again, in a different form, to redirect printing from the parallel port (LPT) MS-DOS assumes by default to the serial (COM) port you have configured.

When you use Mode to configure a serial port, you should not have to come up with baud, parity, data bits, or any other settings out of thin air. Check the documentation for the device or service you will be communicating with.

Command syntax

When you set up a serial port for communications, whether to a bulletin board or a printer, the syntax is as follows:

mode com*n*[:] [baud=*b*] [parity=*p*] [data=*d*] [stop=*s*] [retry=*r*]

or:

mode com*n*[:] [*b*][,*p*][,*d*][,*s*][,*r*]

NOTE: If you use the short form of this command, note the comma that precedes each parameter. If you omit a parameter, thus accepting the default for it, you must include two commas in its place—one for the parameter you omit and another as a leading character for the next parameter. For example, if you omit a value for d but include b, p, and s, you would type the command as mode comn b,p,,s *(substituting real values for n, b, p, and s, of course).*

com*n* is the serial port you want to configure. *n* can be 1, 2, 3, or 4. You can add a colon to the COM port if you want to (COM1:).

baud=*b*, or just plain *b*, gives the baud rate—really, the speed of transmission in bits per second—to be used. MS-DOS accepts the following:

For transmission speed of:	Type as:
110	110 or 11
150	150 or 15
300	300 or 30
600	600 or 60
1200	1200 or 12
2400	2400 or 24
4800	4800 or 48
9600	9600 or 96
19,200 (not supported on all systems; check your documentation)	19200 or 19

parity=*p*, or just plain *p*, is the type of parity—error checking—to be used. MS-DOS supports the following parity values:

For parity of:	Type as:
None	N
Odd	O
Even (the default)	E
Mark	M
Space	S

data=*d*, or just plain *d*, gives the number of data bits per transmitted character. MS-DOS supports 5, 6, 7 (the default), and 8. Not all computers support 5 and 6 data bits.

stop=*s*, or just plain *s*, gives the number of stop bits, or timing signals, that indicate the end of a transmitted character. MS-DOS supports 1, 1.5, and 2. The default is 2 if the transmission rate is 110; for all other speeds, the default is 1. Not all computers support 1.5 stop bits.

retry=*r*, or just plain *r*, is for use in setting up a serial printer. As in the form of the Mode command used in configuring a parallel printer, the retry setting tells MS-DOS how to respond even if the printer is busy or unable to accept transmission. Specifying this parameter causes MS-DOS to make part of the Mode command memory resident. In general, avoid using the retry parameter unless your printer documentation or an application program recommends a particular setting. Do not specify retries for a network printer so that you don't accidentally tie up a printer. Acceptable values are as follows:

Retry value	Meaning
N (the default)	No retries.
E	Report "error" if the printer is busy.
B	Report "busy" if the printer is busy.
P	Continue trying until successful; break out of this cycle by pressing Ctrl-Break.
R	Report "ready" even if the printer is busy.

Examples

Type:	To:

`C:\>mode com1 baud=9600`
or:
`C:\>mode com1 96`
	Set the first serial port to transmit and receive at 9600 bps, using defaults for all other values (even parity, 7 data bits, and 1 stop bit).

`C:\>mode com2 baud=2400`
`    parity=n data=8`
or:
`C:\>mode com2 24,n,8`
	Set the second serial port to 2400 bps, no parity, and 8 data bits, using the default of 1 stop bit.

`C:\>mode com2 baud=2400 data=7`
or:
`C:\>mode com2 24,,7`
	Set the second serial port to 2400 bps and 7 data bits, using the defaults of even parity and 1 stop bit.

Place in AUTOEXEC.BAT:	To:

`mode com2 baud=96 parity=n data=8`
or:
`mode com2 96,n,8`
followed by:
`mode lpt1=com2`
	Set the second serial port to 9600 bps, no parity, 8 data bits, and the defaults of 1 stop bit and no retries and then redirect the default parallel printer (LPT1) to the newly configured serial port for printing on a serial printer. Placing the commands in AUTOEXEC.BAT ensures that the serial port configuration and printer redirection are carried out each time the computer starts up.

Setting up code pages on devices

It would be nice if MS-DOS made preparing for—and using—code-page switching parts of a single command. Oh, well. Other parts of this book, especially Appendix C, dig into the art of using code pages. This part of the chapter guides you through a look at the four closely related forms of the Mode command shown on the next page.

- Mode Codepage Prepare lets you set up a code page for use with the device you specify—either the display (CON) or a parallel printer (LPT*x*). You must use this form of the Mode command before you can change or select alternate code pages.

- Mode Codepage Select lets you choose the code page you want to use with your display or printer. This command is similar to Change Codepage (Chcp), but selects a code page only for the device you specify. Chcp selects a code page for both the display and printer at the same time, if both devices are already set up for code-page switching.

- Mode Codepage Refresh lets you reinstate a display or printer code page that has been lost due to hardware error. You shouldn't need this command very often.

- Mode Codepage Status lets you check the numbers of the built-in (hardware), active, and prepared code pages for the device you specify. If you omit the /status switch, you'll still get the same status report. This command produces a report much like the one you see when you request a device status report (described earlier) with the Mode command:

```
Active code page for device CON is 850
Hardware code pages:
  code page 437
Prepared code pages:
  code page 850
  code page not prepared
Mode status code page function completed
```

The *code page not prepared* line means that MS-DOS is set up to use a second alternate code page with the display, but only one (850) has actually been prepared.

Before you can use these Mode commands, remember that you must first set up your system for code-page switching. If you haven't satisfied some or all of the MS-DOS requirements for code-page support, using these Mode commands will net you messages such as *Code page not prepared*, *Device error during select*, and *Code page operation not supported on this device*.

Command syntax

The syntax for the four forms of Mode already described is as follows:

mode *device* cp prepare=((*codepage*) *filespec*)

mode *device* cp select=*codepage*

mode *device* cp refresh

mode *device* cp /status

You can spell out cp as codepage if you want, and you can use the following abbreviations: prep for prepare, sel for select, ref for refresh, and sta for status.

device is the name of the device affected by the command. You can specify CON for the display and LPT1, LPT2, or LPT3 for a parallel printer. As with all device names, you can add a colon (for example, LPT1:).

codepage is the number of the code page you want to prepare or select. Valid code pages, as listed elsewhere in this chapter, are 437 (English language), 850 (Multilingual, or Latin I), 852 (Slavic, or Latin II), 860 (Portuguese), 863 (Canadian-French), and 865 (Nordic). You can prepare more than one code page in the same command, but separate each code-page number with a space.

filespec is the drive, path, and filename of the code-page information (CPI) file for the device you specify in the command. MS-DOS uses CPI files to determine how to display or print the character sets stored in alternate code pages.

If you have version 6, you received one CPI file with it—EGA.CPI for an EGA or a VGA display.

If you have version 5 of MS-DOS, you'll also have the following CPI files. (Although version 6 doesn't supply them, you probably don't need them.)

- LCD.CPI for the IBM PC Convertible.
- 4201.CPI for the IBM Proprinter II or III, Model 4201 or 4202, or a compatible printer.
- 4208.CPI for the IBM Proprinter X24E Model 4207, XL24E Model 4208, or a compatible printer.
- 5202.CPI for the IBM Quietwriter III or compatible printer.

Examples

Type:	To:
`C:\>mode con cp` `    prep=((850)c:\dos\ega.cpi)`	Prepare an EGA or a VGA display to use one alternate code page (850). Include a command such as this (with other code-page switching commands) in AUTOEXEC.BAT or in another batch file to automate code-page preparation.
`C:\>mode con cp` `    prep=((850 865)c:\dos\ega.cpi)`	Same as above, but prepares two alternate code pages (850 and 865). Separate the code-page numbers with a space.
`C:\>mode lpt1 cp` `    prep=((850)c:\dos\4201.cpi)`	Prepare an IBM Proprinter II or III, Model 4201 or 4202, or a compatible printer to use one alternate code page (850). As mentioned above, include a command such as this as part of a set of code-page switching commands in AUTOEXEC.BAT or in a batch file if you want.

(continued)

continued

Type:	To:
`C:\>mode con cp sel=850`	Select code page 850 for use with the display.
`C:\>mode lpt1 cp ref`	Reinstate a code page that has been lost or scrambled by a printer problem.
`C:\>mode con cp /sta`	Check on the status of hardware, prepared, and active code pages for the display.
`C:\>mode con cp`	Produce the same status report that the /status switch does.

National Language Support Function (Nlsfunc)

The Nlsfunc command is the "key" that turns on the MS-DOS ability to use alternate code pages. Once you turn on this support, you can use the code-page related forms of the Mode command described previously, and you can use the Change Codepage (Chcp) command to switch among hardware and prepared code pages.

To enable code-page switching, Nlsfunc relies on the file of country-specific information stored in either COUNTRY.SYS or (if you have one) an alternate country file. Although Nlsfunc looks for this file in the root directory of your startup drive, MS-DOS Setup copies COUNTRY.SYS to your DOS directory, rather than to the root directory. Thus, unless you move COUNTRY.SYS to the root directory (not recommended if you like keeping the root directory uncluttered), you might have to point Nlsfunc to COUNTRY.SYS or its equivalent. There are two ways to do this:

- Include a Country command in CONFIG.SYS. Take this approach if you frequently use code-page switching and you also want or need to specify to MS-DOS a country other than the one for which your computer was built. (Recall that the syntax of the Country command is, in part, *country=countrycode,,countryfile*, where *countrycode* is the three-digit international dialing prefix of the country for which you want to set up the system and *countryfile* is the drive, path, and filename of the file containing country-specific information.)

- Include the name of your country file as a parameter when you use the Nlsfunc command. Take this approach if you sometimes use code-page switching or if you do not want to include a Country command in CONFIG.SYS.

If you do not specify a path to COUNTRY.SYS or its equivalent either in CONFIG.SYS or with the Nlsfunc command, MS-DOS doesn't tell you something's missing until you try to switch to a different code page with the Chcp command. At that time, you see the message *Cannot open specified country information file.* From here, it's back to square one. Nlsfunc is memory resident, and you cannot load it twice, so if you see this error, you must restart the system, this time specifying the country file in the Nlsfunc command.

Command syntax

The syntax of the Nlsfunc command is as follows:

nlsfunc [*countryfile*]

countryfile is the drive, path, and filename of COUNTRY.SYS or an equivalent country information file.

You can use Nlsfunc, in the form shown here, from the MS-DOS command line. If you prefer, you can instead save a small (usually quite small) amount of memory by specifying the NSLFUNC.EXE program as part of an Install command in CONFIG.SYS. The Install command is described in Chapter 12.

NOTE: Do not run Nlsfunc if you are running Microsoft Windows. Your computer might stop functioning.

Examples

Type:	To:
`C:\>nlsfunc`	Enable code-page switching, assuming that the path to COUNTRY.SYS or its equivalent has already been identified by a Country command in CONFIG.SYS.
`C:\>nlsfunc c:\dos\country.sys`	Enable code-page switching when CONFIG.SYS does not include a Country command.

Include in CONFIG.SYS:	To:
`INSTALL C:\DOS\NLSFUNC.EXE` `C:\DOS\COUNTRY.SYS`	Start Nlsfunc and identify the country information file with an Install command in CONFIG.SYS.

Power—version 6 only

The Power command works with the related POWER.EXE device driver to reduce energy consumption while applications and devices on your computer are idle. Power is especially appropriate for use on laptop and notebook computers that rely on batteries, but you can run it on a normal desktop system even though such machines, despite their capabilities, generally don't require significant amounts of electricity to begin with.

To use the Power command, you must first install the POWER.EXE device driver with a Device command in CONFIG.SYS. Once the device driver is loaded, you use the Power command itself to regulate the device driver's enthusiasm for conserving energy and to turn off power saving when it is not needed. When you use the Power command, you see a message like the following:

```
Power Management Status
-----------------------
Setting =  ADV: REG
CPU: idle 46% of time.
```

The last line of this display is particularly interesting, if for no other reason than it can show you how much time the system spends twiddling its electronic thumbs. The percentage varies, of course, according to the work going on inside. The preceding message reflects a desktop computer doing nothing but running MS-DOS. If background processing were going on—under Windows, for example—the CPU would be far more active.

Both Power and the POWER.EXE device driver conform to the APM (Advanced Power Management) specification.You can use the Power command whether or not your computer supports this specification, but there will be a difference in the way the STD switch of the command works, as described in the following syntax section. If you use a portable computer, your documentation should be able to tell you whether this specification is supported by your machine.

Command syntax

The syntax of the Power command includes several simple switches:

    power [adv:max][adv:reg][adv:min][std][off]

NOTE: Choose only one of these switches at a time. Typing power *with no switches will give you a report on power usage.*

adv lets you turn the Power "thermostat" up or down to regulate the degree of power conservation. You can specify max, reg (the default), or min efficiency. If you find that an application or device does not respond adequately, turn power conservation down with this switch.

std, on a system that supports the APM specification, tailors Power to use the power-management features of your computer. If the computer does not support the APM specification, you will not harm the machine by inadvertently using this switch. It will merely turn off power conservation, just as the switch described next does.

off turns off power conservation.

NOTE: All of these switches can also be used when you install the POWER.EXE device driver, so you can set the switch or switches you want from CONFIG.SYS and later use the Power command to alter the settings—for example, to set power management to minimum when you want to use a program (such as a spreadsheet) or a device (such as a modem or fax) that can make heavy demands on the CPU and can be slowed down by overly aggressive power management.

Examples

Type:	To:
C:\>power adv:max	Set power management to maximum efficiency.
C:\>power std	Set power management to use the features built into the computer.
C:\>power	Check on current power conservation status.
C:\>power off	Turn off power management.

POWER.EXE—version 6 only

POWER.EXE is the device driver that enables power management on a computer, as described in the preceding section. Before you can use the Power command, you must load POWER.EXE with a Device command in CONFIG.SYS. You do not have to use a Devicehigh command, because POWER.EXE loads into upper memory, if it is available, by default.

Command syntax

For the most part, the parameters and switches that control POWER.EXE are the same as those you use with the Power command. The syntax does, however, require a Device command and a file specification, as follows:

DEVICE=*filespec* [adv:max][adv:reg][adv:min][std][off]/low

filespec is the path to the drive and directory in which POWER.EXE is located. This is probably your DOS directory.

adv sets the degree of power management you require. As with the Power command, you can specify max, reg, or min. The default is reg.

std specifies that POWER.EXE is to use the APM (Advanced Power Management) support built into the computer. Here, as in the Power command, using this switch on a computer that does not support the APM specification turns off power management.

off turns off power management, as it does with the Power command.

/low, which is available only with POWER.EXE, loads the device driver into low (conventional) memory even if upper memory is available. Use this switch if you have other uses for upper memory, or set up your CONFIG.SYS file so that all the device drivers and programs you want to load into upper memory are loaded first.

Examples

Include in CONFIG.SYS:	To:
`DEVICE=C:\DOS\POWER.EXE`	Load POWER.EXE with the default (reg) level of power management.
`DEVICE=C:\DOS\POWER.EXE STD`	Load POWER.EXE with the APM capabilities of the computer.
`DEVICE=C:\DOS\POWER.EXE /LOW`	Load POWER.EXE into low memory, even if upper memory is available.

Print

The Print command, a part of MS-DOS since version 2, obviously prints documents. Less obviously, the Print command gives MS-DOS a limited (very limited) form of multitasking. It does this by loading itself as a memory-resident program called a *print spooler,* which allows printing to take place as a background process, during intervals when the system is otherwise idle. You can use Print for a single document, or you can queue and print a set of documents using a single command. During the printing process, Print sends file contents to the printer until it encounters an end-of-file character, the familiar ^Z (ASCII character 32 decimal or 1A hexadecimal), which you produce by pressing Ctrl-Z or the F6 key when copying from the console to a disk file. Print stops as soon as it reaches ^Z, even if the character occurs within the body of a file, so if you have to print a file containing control codes, use the Copy command with the /b switch instead.

A useful tool for printing certain types of documents, Print can rapidly produce hard copy without your having to start a word processor or even a text editor such as the MS-DOS Editor. Print is not, however, all things to all documents. It is well suited for printing text-only files, but for formatting, Print correctly interprets only ASCII codes, such as linefeeds, tabs, and carriage returns. Thus, it has no ability to understand or interpret the special, usually application-specific, characters that define how documents produce graphics, character formats (such as italics), paragraph alignment, columns, variable line spacing, and other niceties of page layout. Using Print with such documents generally results in wasted paper covered with output that ranges from gibberish to sentences that break in odd places, run off the page, and even print a word or two to a page. From the MS-DOS command line, however, Print is unbeatable for printing plain-text files, including unformatted electronic mail (email) messages, files transmitted or downloaded via modem, and, especially, the MS-DOS TXT and PACKING.LST files.

As already mentioned, you can specify a number of files to print in a single command. When you do this, Print arranges the specified files in a queue and prints them one after the other. While this printing is going on, you can return to other work, but because the print queue is being handled as a background task, you might well find that an application or, especially, your keyboard becomes sluggish. Generally speaking, even though MS-DOS can handle both printing and keyboard input, you'll get the best of all possible worlds by letting Print run its course before starting or returning to an application. (This slowdown is not, by the way, an indictment of Print or MS-DOS. The same type of performance hit affects Windows with Print Manager, as you can easily see by playing Solitaire while you're printing a long document.)

By default, Print assumes that the print device is PRN, which is usually the first parallel port, LPT1. Bear in mind, however, that Print is merely the agent by which you send files to the printer; it is not the manager of the printer port itself, nor does it "know" which printer you mean to use. Thus, if the printer you want is attached to a different port, either parallel or serial, you must identify the port. In addition, if you're sending to a serial port, you must first configure the port with the Mode command. You can identify the printer port either by using the /d:*device* switch described in the following syntax section or by letting Print prompt for the printer, which it does the first time you use the Print command during a session with MS-DOS:

```
Name of list device [PRN]:
```

If the printer is attached to LPT1, pressing Enter will cause the program to use the default PRN device. If you want to use a different printer, you can specify LPT2 or LPT3 for a parallel printer or COM1 through COM4 for a serial printer. When Print is ready to work, it responds with the message:

```
Resident part of PRINT installed
```

This message is followed by *PRINT queue is empty* if you did not include the name of a file or files to print as part of the command. If you did specify one or more files, Print displays the names of all files in the queue, like this:

```
C:\BOGUS\FILE1.TXT is currently being printed
C:\BOGUS\FILE2.TXT is in queue
```

One final note about Print is in order. You might be accustomed to using the Copy command to "copy" short text files to the printer. If you have a LaserJet or similar printer, Print is often a better choice because you don't have to take the printer off line and press the formfeed key or use a command (*echo*[Ctrl-L]>prn) to send a formfeed character to the printer in order to eject the page.

Command syntax

Print includes a number of parameters and switches that fall into two considerably different groups: Some control the way Print operates; the rest let you specify the documents to be printed. Even though these two sets of options can be combined in a single command, they are treated separately in the following descriptions to present a clearer picture of Print (the process), as opposed to Print (the producer of printouts). Examples following both syntax descriptions, however, show how these parameters and switches can be used both separately and in combination.

Defining print characteristics

Print has certain default settings, such as the size to which the queue can grow. You can change these settings, but because Print is memory resident, you can define the way it operates only the first time you use the command during a session. To change operating characteristics a second time, you must reboot the system. To define the way Print works, you use the following form of the command.

print /d:*device* /q:*queuesize* /b:*buffersize* /u:*interval* /m:*maxtime* /s:*timeslice*

/d:*device* is the name of the port connecting the computer to the printer you want to use. Print assumes LPT1 (PRN). You can specify LPT2 or LPT3 for a parallel printer or COM1, COM2, COM3, or COM4 for a serial port. This switch must precede any file specifications (described in the following section) that you include as part of the command. Like all device names, you can add a colon (for example, LPT1:).

/q:*queuesize* specifies the maximum number of files Print will place into its print queue. By default, Print allows 10 files. You can specify from 4 through 32 files.

/b:*buffersize* determines the size of the buffer (temporary memory storage area) that Print uses as a holding area for data waiting to be transmitted to the printer. The default buffer size is 512 bytes—small, but probably adequate if your printer has a buffer of its own. The minimum buffer size is the same as the default; you can specify a maximum buffer of 16,384 bytes.

/u:*interval* specifies the length of time, measured in ticks of the computer's internal timer, that Print is to wait for the printer to become available—that is, how long Print will remain ready to transmit before giving up its share of the computer's time. The default is 1; you can specify from 1 through 255. Note that although you are accustomed to measuring time in seconds, Print (and your computer) measure time in much smaller intervals called *ticks*. The computer's internal timer, which provides the "clock" for all system events, "ticks" at a rate of 18.2 times per second.

/m:*maxtime* specifies the maximum length of time, again measured in timer ticks, that Print can take to print a single character. The default is 2; you can specify from 1 through 255. Increase this value if you consistently receive error messages because printing occurs too slowly.

/s:*timeslice* specifies the amount of time, in timer ticks, that Print has for transmitting to the printer. This time slice is the window that opens periodically so that Print can launch characters outward to the printer port. The default is 8; you can specify from 1 through 255. Note that the larger the time slice given to Print, the smaller the time slice(s) given to other programs.

Specifying files and controlling the queue

Although you can define the print spooler only the first time you use the Print command, you can print files at any time. You can add to the queue while other files are being printed, take files out of the queue before they are printed, or cancel a print job completely by canceling the queue. The syntax for controlling the print queue is as follows:

print *filespec* /t /c /p

filespec is the drive, path, and name of the file or files to be printed. You can type multiple file specifications in a single command by separating them with spaces, and you can use wildcards to specify a group of files with similar names or extensions.

/t cancels the print queue.

/c and /p manage the queue. The /c switch removes a file or files from the queue; /p adds a file or files to the queue. You can use both /c and /p in the same command, but trying to do so might make you feel as though you're (a) taking an IQ test and (b) getting a headache. Strongly reminiscent of the equally exasperating /a and /b switches in the Copy command, /c and /p work as follows:

- The /c switch removes from the queue all files that follow its position in the command line, up to but not including any file that precedes a /p switch. When /c comes after a file specification, it removes from the queue the file that precedes its position on the command line and all following files, up to but not including a file specification that precedes a /p switch.

- The /p switch works like /c, but it adds to the queue instead. Thus, /p adds to the queue all files that follow its position in the command line, up to but not including any file that precedes a /c switch (which is removed from the queue). Similarly, when /p comes after a file specification, it adds that file and all following files to the queue, up to but not including a file that precedes a /c switch.

To clarify matters, the diagram on the next page shows how the /c and /p switches work: + means a file is added to the queue and − means a file is removed.

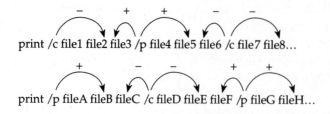

```
print /c file1 file2 file3 /p file4 file5 file6 /c file7 file8...
```

```
print /p fileA fileB fileC /c fileD fileE fileF /p fileG fileH...
```

NOTE: Each print queue entry (drive, directory, subdirectories, and filenames) must be 64 characters or less.

Examples

Type:	To:
`C:\>print /d:lpt2`	Instruct Print to use the printer connected to LPT2.
`C:\>print /d:lpt2 c:\myfile.txt`	Instruct Print to print the file named MYFILE.TXT on the printer connected to LPT2.
`C:\>print /b:1024 /q:5`	Set the buffer size to 1024 bytes and the queue size to 5 files for the default print device, PRN (LPT1).
`C:\>print /d:com1 /u:10 /m:4 /s:16`	Instruct Print to use the serial printer connected to COM1 and allot more than the default amount of time for printing: a wait period of 10 timer ticks (roughly 0.5 second), with 4 ticks for printing a character and 16 ticks of scheduled background print time. Note that these settings would slow other system activities appreciably.
`C:\>print newmail\mail?.txt`	Print all files in the NEWMAIL directory that have the TXT extension and five-character filenames beginning MAIL.
`C:\>print a:bills.txt b:pay.txt` `    c:\tax\taxes.txt`	Print the file BILLS.TXT from the disk in drive A, the file PAY.TXT from the disk in drive B, and the file TAXES.TXT in the directory TAX on the disk in drive C.
`C:\>print /t`	Cancel the print queue.

PRINTER.SYS—through version 5 only

PRINTER.SYS is the code-page equivalent of the DISPLAY.SYS device driver, except that it provides support for code pages on an IBM-compatible printer connected to a parallel printer port. An installable device driver, PRINTER.SYS must be identified to MS-DOS through a Device or Devicehigh command in CONFIG.SYS.

Like your keyboard and display, your printer comes with a built-in hardware code page for its own "native" language. To print "foreign" characters—those it does not recognize—the printer must be given a template, or a code page, that contains regular and extended ASCII codes, along with the characters assigned to them. The templates themselves must be made available to the system through the Nlsfunc, Mode, and Chcp commands. PRINTER.SYS, in contrast, is the install-able device driver that enables the printer to reproduce the character sets you choose to use.

The following sections describe the use of PRINTER.SYS and its several parameters. Appendix C tells you how to set up a system for code-page switching.

Command syntax

The syntax of the command that installs PRINTER.SYS is as follows. The Device command is used here; if your system has enough upper memory available, you can substitute Devicehigh instead:

DEVICE=[*drive:*][*path*]PRINTER.SYS LPT*n*=(*printer,hwcodepage,codepages*)

drive: and *path* are the drive and directory in which PRINTER.SYS is stored. This should be the DOS directory on your startup drive.

lpt*n* is the parallel port to which the printer is connected. You can specify LPT1, LPT2, or LPT3.

printer identifies the type of IBM or compatible printer you use. You can specify one of the following:

Use:	For:
4201	IBM Proprinter II or III (including XL), Model 4201 or 4202
4208	IBM Proprinter X24E Model 4207 or IBM Proprinter XL24E Model 4208
5202	IBM Quietwriter III Model 5202

hwcodepage is the code page built into your printer. You can specify one of the following: 437 (English language); 850 (Multilingual, or Latin I); 852 (Slavic, or Latin II); 860 (Portuguese); 863 (Canadian-French); 865 (Nordic).

codepages is the number of code pages, in addition to the hardware code page, that you want to use with your printer. The code pages you use must be compatible with the hardware code page, so this value should be either 1 or 2.

Examples

Include in CONFIG.SYS:	To:
`DEVICE=C:\DOS\PRINTER.SYS` `LPT1=(4201,850,2)`	Set up an IBM Proprinter II or III Model 4201 or 4202 or a compatible printer for use with two code pages in addition to the built-in Multilingual code page 850.
`DEVICEHIGH=C:\DOS\PRINTER.SYS` `LPT1=(4201,850,2)`	Do the same as above, but load the PRINTER.SYS device driver into available upper memory.

11

Memory

What You'll Find Here: CHKSTATE.SYS; Devicehigh; DOS (Dos); EMM386; EMM386.EXE; HIMEM.SYS; Load Fix (Loadfix); Load High (Loadhigh or Lh); Memory Display (Mem); MemMaker (Memmaker); RAMDRIVE.SYS; SIZER.EXE; SMARTDRV.EXE.

*M*emory is made of this: chips, volatility, and tiny storage cells called capacitors. Memory is also a gaggle of regions named conventional memory, the upper memory area, the high memory area, extended memory, and expanded memory. To MS-DOS and the microprocessor, memory is numbers known as addresses. But to many people, memory is mostly a place of smoke and mirrors where only the clever dare to walk.

In actuality, memory probably is the most confusing topic you encounter in working with MS-DOS, and for several reasons: the design of the 8088/8086 chips and the impact of that design on MS-DOS; hexadecimal numbers, which form the ABCs of memory reference; and memory-related terminology, most of which is achingly nonintuitive. To de-confuse some of these issues, the first part of this chapter takes you on a tour of memory and MS-DOS, starting with the basics.

ROM vs. RAM

ROM and RAM sound like nicknames for the twin founders of Rome, but as you probably already know, these terms are just acronyms for read-only memory and random access memory, the two types of nondisk storage built into your computer. ROM contains permanently inscribed instructions that perform such essential tasks as starting the bootstrap process and providing MS-DOS with the low-level input/output routines known as the ROM BIOS. On some machines, ROM is even the carrier of MS-DOS itself. When you work with a computer, however, you don't deal with ROM. Invariably, you deal with RAM.

To the eye, RAM is a set of small, rectangular chips laid out in rectangular banks inside the computer. Externally, these chips are unprepossessing; internally, they are powerhouse complexes of tiny, battery-like "cells" called *capacitors*, each of which can be electrically charged to hold one bit—a single 1 or 0. Because the microprocessor does not easily access individual bits, these capacitors are managed in groups of eight to store the bytes that make up all computer-based information. And, of course, the sum of these bytes represents all the kilobytes or megabytes of memory in which MS-DOS stores not only the characters you type, but the applications that process your thoughts.

As you learned early on, RAM, unlike ROM, is volatile. As long as you feed it electricity, RAM holds its contents. As soon as you turn off the computer, RAM loses everything stored in it, and woe to the person who forgot to save unsaved files. In actuality, RAM is even more volatile than you might have thought, because the RAM chips in most computers are of the type known as *dynamic RAMs*, or *DRAMs*.

Dynamic RAMs, unlike the more stable *static RAMs* (*SRAMs*) sometimes used for on-chip caches, wax and wane like the beam of a fading flashlight. In order for data to remain stable in dynamic RAM, the capacitors holding that data must be bathed periodically with electricity in a process known as refreshing. This refreshing happens automatically and very rapidly, so its only real effect on you is its impact on the speed at which the microprocessor can access data. That speed, however, is already great enough that you won't spend inordinate amounts of time chewing your nails, even with a slow computer. What affects you far more than either volatility or the electronic pause that refreshes is the amount and types of RAM a computer contains and the way in which this RAM is configured for use by MS-DOS.

Memory types revisited

Chapter 2 described, briefly, the types of RAM you can install in an MS-DOS–based computer. As you might recall, these types of memory are clearly organized and lie within very specific boundaries. Figure 11-1 on the next page shows how you can pull everything together with the help of a takeoff on an old nursery rhyme.

Here's a closer look.

Conventional and upper memory

The "house that DOS built" represents 1 MB of memory divided somewhat lop-sidedly into 640 K of *conventional memory* and 384 K of *upper memory*. Because it is the kind of RAM MS-DOS was designed to use, conventional memory is the prin-cipal holding area for programs, data, device drivers, and—even in versions 5 and 6—at least part of MS-DOS itself. The amount of conventional memory in an MS-DOS–based computer depends on the amount of installed RAM and can, at least in theory, consist of as little as 64 K. No modern application program would be able to run on such a lean machine, however, so a typical MS-DOS–based computer contains a full 640 K of conventional memory.

Above conventional memory, sitting in the space between 640 K and 1 MB, comes the 384-K upper memory area, sometimes abbreviated UMA. The upper memory area is the portion of RAM traditionally reserved for ROM programs and for video and other hardware uses. Beginning with version 5 of MS-DOS, the upper memory area on computers with 80286 and better processors and at least 350 K of extended memory can also be opened up for loading device drivers and certain *terminate-and-stay-resident* (*TSR*), or simply *memory-resident*, programs, thus freeing valuable space these programs would otherwise require in the admittedly cramped 640 K of conventional memory.

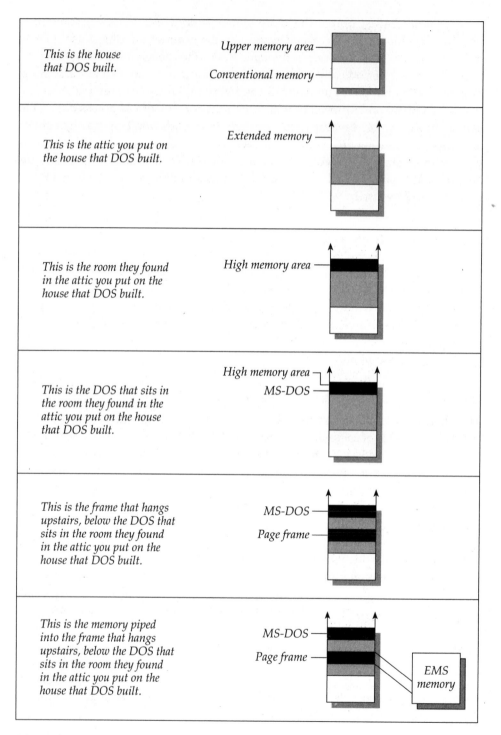

FIGURE 11-1.
How random access memory is organized.

Extended memory

Extended memory begins at 1 MB and goes on up—typically to a maximum of 16 MB. The actual ceiling depends mostly on the depth of your pockets (how many additional MB you buy) and the design of your hardware. Extended memory is often described as *XMS memory* after the set of rules (*Extended Memory Specification*) that governs the way this kind of memory is used by programs. Although extended memory is commonly used as a home for a RAM drive, a SMARTDRV.EXE disk cache, or both, MS-DOS cannot access extended memory on its own. To use extended memory, you must install HIMEM.SYS (or another extended memory manager), which enables programs to use extended memory without conflict.

The HMA

The *high memory area,* or *HMA,* occupies the first 64 K (minus 16 bytes) of extended memory, immediately above the 1-MB boundary. This memory region is really special because MS-DOS should no more be able to "see" it than you can see the top of your head. Yet, MS-DOS not only can find the HMA, it can use this small portion of memory as a home for a large part of itself. By loading into the HMA, MS-DOS neatly moves itself out of conventional memory, where it would otherwise reside, and thus makes even more conventional memory available to satisfy the memory hunger of programs and data.

NOTE: A combination of hardware and software trickery enables MS-DOS to access the HMA directly. The way this is done is described briefly later in this chapter—after you've been introduced to the joys of protected mode and segmented addresses.

Expanded memory

Expanded memory, or *EMS,* sits to the side of all the preceding types of memory. You add expanded memory to your system as a separate hardware module that you use with the help of a special program called an *expanded memory manager,* or *EMM.* Developed as a means of enabling MS-DOS to access more than the 640 K it was designed to use, expanded memory use is based on a procedure called *bank switching,* in which blocks of memory are taken from the expanded memory "pool" and swapped, usually in 64-K blocks, into a reserved portion of the upper memory area—the page frame diagrammed and labeled in Figure 11-1.

Although you, as a computer user, see little if any of the details underlying the use of expanded memory, an extensive set of rules governs the way in which it is handled by the operating system and by application software. Under MS-DOS (and Windows), the standard used for expanded memory management is known as the *Lotus-Intel-Microsoft Expanded Memory Specification,* or *LIM EMS.*

Like MS-DOS, the LIM EMS has been updated several times since its introduction in the mid-1980s. MS-DOS versions 5 and 6 follow the most current version, LIM EMS 4.0. If you have version 6 of MS-DOS and you enable expanded memory, you see the LIM EMS version number displayed by the /d switch of the Memory Display (Mem) command and by the Microsoft Diagnostics utility.

MS-DOS does not directly support expanded memory. However, some programs require expanded memory, so the EMM386.EXE driver enables MS-DOS to use extended memory in a way that simulates expanded memory on computers that have an 80386 or better processor and sufficient extended memory. You can also use the EMM386 *command* to turn access to this simulated expanded memory on or off.

Addressing memory

Descriptions of memory generally use terms such as area, block, region, and portion, all of which convey the impression that memory can be sliced up like a pie, labeled, and served up to waiting software as needed. Although these terms are indeed accurate, they also tend to cover up the concept of *addressable memory*, which is the amount of RAM that a microprocessor can actually access and which represents the way the computer's microprocessor, MS-DOS, and software for MS-DOS actually make use of RAM. Memory addressing, as a tool, is far more important to programmers than it is to MS-DOS users, but even a basic grasp of the topic can help you see why memory is divided into so many different types and understand that the amount of memory the microprocessor can use is not necessarily the same as the amount of physical RAM installed in the computer.

To see how addressable memory works, change your view slightly by thinking of RAM not as a vast open field you can fill with programs and data, but as a collection of 1-bit capacitors, bundled 8 to a byte. Now consider that a microprocessor, when it refers to memory, must be able to pinpoint individual bytes or groups of bytes that contain the instructions or data required to carry out a given task. Without this ability to locate information, the microprocessor could not load and run software correctly, nor could it find and process your data. The location of each byte of memory is called an *address*.

Because all work inside a computer is handled numerically, in binary form, the microprocessor finds specific areas in memory by "broadcasting" addresses over the dedicated set of wires known as the *address bus*. Address buses for different microprocessors come in different sizes, or widths, depending on the number of lines they contain. Each address line carries 1 bit at a time, so the number of lines determines the number of bits that can be used to create a memory address. And, naturally, the more bits the microprocessor can use, the larger the number it can generate.   .

Now you come to the heart of the matter, at least where MS-DOS is concerned. The 8086, the chip for which MS-DOS was designed, uses a 20-bit address bus, so the largest memory address the 8086 can generate can contain 20 bits. To determine how many unique numbers these 20 bits can represent, you would calculate 2 to the 20th power, which is 1,048,576.

To look at it another way that's perhaps a little easier to understand, simply write the largest 20-bit number possible, a string of twenty 1s: 11111111111111111111. To determine what this value represents in more human terms, convert the binary value to decimal. (If you have Windows 3.1, save your brain and use the Calculator accessory.) No matter how you convert binary to decimal, however, the result is 1,048,575. That's 1 less than 1,048,576, but don't forget that a string of twenty 0s is a legitimate address, too. When you count 0 as part of the package, the result is, once again, 1,048,576. Therefore, regardless of how you get there, you can say with assurance that the highest point in memory the 8086 can reach is the 1,048,576th byte, which happens to be the last byte in 1 MB of RAM. In other words, the 8086 has what is known as a 1-MB *address space.*

Not surprisingly, MS-DOS, which was designed for the 8086, and software designed for MS-DOS stay within the same 1-MB boundary—at least most of the time. On computers with 80286 or better microprocessors, however, both MS-DOS (versions 5 and 6) and MS-DOS software can wander farther afield, for reasons you'll see in the next section.

When you diagram the address space of the 8086, you produce a memory map like the following:

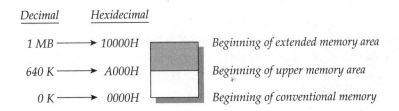

Decimal	*Hexidecimal*		
1 MB ⟶	10000H		*Beginning of extended memory area*
640 K ⟶	A000H		*Beginning of upper memory area*
0 K ⟶	0000H		*Beginning of conventional memory*

Notice here that significant addresses are shown as hexadecimal numbers that appear to be equivalent to values—0 K, 640 K, and 1 MB—you would be more inclined to think of as units of measure. The two sets of values are actually different ways of saying the same thing. You can easily see that 0000H and 0 K can be, and are, equivalent. But how does A000H equal 640 K? Remember, 640 K, even though it refers to kilobytes, is still a decimal number. Written out, 640 K is 640 times 1024 bytes per kilobyte, or 655,360. And 655,360 in hexadecimal is A000H. Similarly, 1 MB is 1024 times 1024, or 1,048,576, which is 10000H.

If you have a computer with an 80286 or better processor and some extended memory and you're using version 6 of MS-DOS, you can see a memory map— the upper memory area for your own computer—by starting the Microsoft

Diagnostics utility and choosing Memory from the opening set of options. The map you see will be much more detailed than the preceding diagram because it labels 16-K segments of memory. The following diagram of the first megabyte of memory, however, should help you get your bearings:

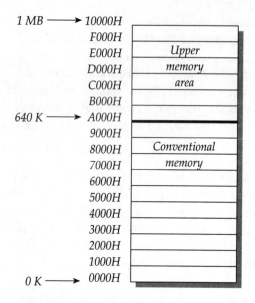

Going beyond 1 MB

The preceding section emphasized the 8086 microprocessor, which has pretty much been replaced by its more powerful 80286, 80386, and 80486 descendants. Why dwell on the past? For the simple reason, often repeated, that MS-DOS was designed for and remains primarily wedded to the 8086 chip. Thus, the design and memory limitations of the 8086 influence, to a great extent, the design and memory limitations of MS-DOS.

These days, however, most computers have more powerful microprocessors, and these microprocessors have capabilities that open the door to more and better memory use. Basically, two related factors in 80286 and better microprocessors enable use of memory beyond or outside of the traditional 1-MB address space of the 8086. They are larger address buses and two new ways of working known as *protected mode* and *virtual 86*, or *V86, mode*.

Bigger buses

As you've seen, the 8086 can address 1 MB of memory because it has a 20-bit bus. How much memory can 80286 and better microprocessors address—at least in theory? The 80286 has a 24-bit address bus, so it can generate 2 to the 24th addresses, which works out to 16 MB of memory. The 80386 and 80486 microprocessors (in their DX incarnations) are far more powerful. Blessed with a 32-bit bus, these microprocessors can generate more than 4 billion addresses to reach a potential maximum of 4 GB of memory. That's a whopping amount of RAM by any current standard, but there's a catch, one that neatly leads into the next topic—modes of operation. To access memory beyond 1 MB, 80286 and better microprocessors must operate at a higher level than the 8086. This is where you encounter the differences among the *real mode* native to the 8086, protected mode, and virtual 86 mode. In many ways, these modes define the differences between the 8086, the 80286, and the 80386 and 80486 microprocessors.

Multitudes of modes

An 8086 chip has only one way of working, real mode, which basically means that the chip uses 1 MB of memory and can run only one program at a time, letting that program take over the computer during its moment in the sun. Real mode doesn't have much meaning where the 8086 chip is concerned because to it, real mode is the only mode there is. Where real mode does become significant is with the 80286 and better microprocessors. These chips, with their greater memory-addressing capabilities and more sophisticated memory-management features, can operate in modes that take them far beyond the 1 MB of memory accessible in real mode. To remain compatible with the 8086 and its software base, however, these chips can also "dumb down" and operate in real mode. Thus the following applies:

- In real mode, an 80286 or better microprocessor throttles back and acts just like an 8086/8088 chip. In this mode, the microprocessor can run MS-DOS and any software designed for MS-DOS.

- In protected mode, the microprocessor becomes responsive to software instructions that unleash its ability to address far more than 1 MB of memory, and—just as important—enable the chip to handle multitasking. Protected mode is exploited by the MS-DOS HIMEM.SYS device driver on 80286 and better computers to enable the microprocessor to access extended memory. On computers based on the 80386 and 80486 microprocessors, protected mode is also used by Microsoft Windows.

- In virtual 8086 mode, which kicks in under protected mode, the 80386 and 80486 chips open the door to the world of virtual computing—a place like Wonderland where nothing is as it seems, where a 1-MB piece of memory can appear to software to comprise a separate, independent, 8086 computer. Both the 80386 and 80486 chips can create such simulated, memory-based 8086 computers, each of which can, under an operating system such as Windows, be used to run a different MS-DOS program. The software key to this virtual 8086 computing is a technique called *virtual addressing,* which enables Windows to "split off" independent, protected blocks of memory from anywhere in RAM and treat each, no matter where it is physically located, as if it were the 1 MB of memory accessible to an 8086 computer. Under MS-DOS, virtual 86 mode is used by EMM386.EXE in simulating expanded memory with extended and in providing upper memory blocks for loading device drivers and TSR programs.

To help you get your bearings, the following table shows how these operating modes are related to 80x86 microprocessors:

Processor	Real mode	Protected mode	Virtual 8086 mode
8086/8088	X		
80286	X	X	
80386	X	X	X
80486	X	X	X

Now, with a basic understanding of the first 1 MB of RAM, plus the alternatives opened up with the help of protected and virtual 86 mode, you can move on to the fine points of the upper memory area, the HMA, and various memory-related terms and workarounds.

Filling the upper memory area

Twenty-bit addresses explain why MS-DOS can refer to only 1 MB worth of RAM, but they still do not explain why MS-DOS works in the 640 K of conventional memory. This is where the human factor enters in. As described in Chapters 1 and 2, MS-DOS was created for a specific machine, the IBM PC. As part of their job, the PC's designers had to wrestle with ways to divide the 1 MB worth of addressable memory MS-DOS would be able to work in. Not only would memory be needed for programs, data, and MS-DOS itself, some memory would have to be reserved for other purposes: video, hardware, the ROM BIOS, and other, anticipated-but-still-undeveloped ROM software.

To provide for these needs, the PC's designers declared the addresses in the top 384 K of RAM off limits, leaving those in the lower 640 K for applications, data, and the MS-DOS program itself. At the time, this decision seemed appropriate, and so MS-DOS was created to respect these limits. As the PC industry evolved, however, this essentially arbitrary division came to be more of a burden than it was a blessing. Applications grew in size and power, as did MS-DOS itself. Within a few years, the lower 640 K of RAM was bulging with bytes, whereas the upper memory area remained sparsely populated, with gaps of 64 K or more separating relatively small islands reserved for, and inhabited by, video images, hardware buffers, and ROM software.

In theory and in practice, these unused memory addresses can be used to help ease the "RAM cram" afflicting the lower 640 K of memory. At this point, however, memory gets a little sticky. When you talk about 1 MB of RAM, you most likely picture some vast carpet of capacitors extending, unbroken, to a line marked 1 MB. Not so. Picture instead a memory map like the following:

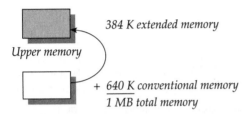

384 K extended memory

Upper memory

+ <u>*640 K conventional memory*</u>
1 MB total memory

Notice that this diagram shows 640 K of conventional memory, a gap where 384 K of upper memory ought to be, followed by an additional 384 K of *extended* memory. Such a layout is typical of 80286 and better systems with 1 MB or more of RAM. Within the upper memory gap, certain addresses are reserved for, and used by, hardware and the ROM BIOS. The remainder of those addresses are unused and therefore available for holding TSRs and device drivers. To use these vacant addresses, however, MS-DOS must find a way to associate them with physical, installed RAM. That way involves the 384 K of extended memory and the EMM386.EXE device driver.

EMM386.EXE, if you'll recall, provides two services: One, it uses extended memory to simulate expanded memory; two, it acts as a memory manager known as a UMB provider. When wearing the latter hat, EMM386.EXE makes upper memory "available" by rerouting programs and device drivers destined for the upper memory area to addresses in equivalent portions of extended memory, in effect "backfilling" the upper memory area with physical RAM from extended memory. The result, in everyday terms, is comparable to your having mail delivered to a post office box rather than to your home. As far as the postal service (MS-DOS) is concerned, you "live" at the post office (UMA), even though your actual residence might be miles away or even in another town (extended memory).

Regions and UMBs

The result of this software hocus-pocus is the creation of upper memory regions and *upper memory blocks,* or *UMBs.* A region, which you find referenced only by version 6 of MS-DOS, refers to any continuous block of space that appears between "inhabited" portions of upper memory, as shown on the next page.

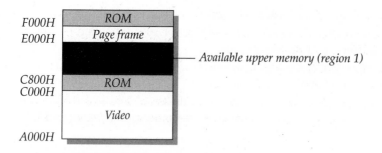

This diagram shows one available upper memory region, region 1, which appears between C800H and E000H. Small as it looks, this block contains more than 90 K of additional space, which could be used to hold device drivers and programs that otherwise would have to be loaded into conventional memory. If the upper memory area on this computer included another free region, say at E400H to E800H, that area would be named region 2. A third region, if it existed, would be region 3, and so the naming would continue, to the top of available upper memory.

A UMB refers to actual, usable memory within a region. A UMB, like a disk sector, is a way of lumping bytes together as a larger group. Unlike a sector, however, a UMB does not have a fixed size. It can be as small as a few hundred bytes or as large as an entire upper memory region. Essentially, you should think of UMBs simply as continuous blocks of memory that MS-DOS uses in parceling out portions of the upper memory area as it processes your CONFIG.SYS and AUTOEXEC.BAT files: X KB to one device driver, Y KB to another, Z KB to a TSR, until it has loaded all the device drivers and programs you specified or it has run out of free UMBs—at which point, any additional software you aimed at the upper memory area is automatically loaded into conventional memory instead.

Shadow RAM and the HMA

Although using extended and expanded memory can be, and usually is, straightforward, you must always remember that MS-DOS has traditionally been confined to a 640-K playpen. In making use of memory beyond 640 K, including the upper memory area, the going can become tortuous and filled with high-tech terminology. When you clear away the excess verbiage, however, the reason all those terms exist becomes simple to understand: Under MS-DOS, the ability to use UMBs, the HMA, extended memory, and expanded memory is based on workarounds of one type or another that somehow "trick" the operating system into working with memory it is not designed to recognize. And those workarounds have a tendency to generate their own exotic language. This book has neither the time nor the space to go into details, but the following brief explanations should help you peer through the glass, however darkly, when you encounter some of the parameters and switches attached to memory-related MS-DOS commands.

Shadow RAM

Many computers include a semi-real form of RAM known as *shadow RAM*. Although the term brings to mind some horned and fleecy comic-book defender of justice, in fact shadow RAM is a portion of upper memory (scavenged from extended memory) that is used on some computers to hold programs, such as the ROM BIOS, that would otherwise have to be read from ROM each time they were accessed. Reading from ROM is slower than reading from RAM, so "shadowing" ROM into RAM improves a computer's operating capabilities.

The software that enables shadow RAM generally comes to life early in the bootstrap process. If you're in a memory crunch, the HIMEM.SYS device driver can help you disable shadow RAM—at the probable expense of a slightly slower machine. You might also be able to turn shadowing on or off through your computer's setup program. For this, you'll need to check your hardware manual.

The HMA

The most interesting part of extended memory is the HMA, the first 64 K directly above the 1-MB boundary. This is the region where, since version 5, MS-DOS has been able to settle in to optimize memory use by leaving as much conventional memory as possible for programs and data to use. The HMA is interesting because of the way in which it was found or, perhaps, created. The HMA is not truly a different region of memory in the same way that extended memory is different from conventional memory.

Earlier in this chapter, you found that MS-DOS is able to use 1 MB of memory because it uses 20-bit addresses. Actually, the process is more complicated than that, because these 20-bit addresses are generated as the sum of a 16-bit portion called the *segment* and a second 16-bit portion called the *offset*. Do you need to care about this? No. But a little background can help fill you with admiration for some devilishly clever trickery that led to the HMA.

To begin with, you need to understand how two 16-bit numbers—at least in the 8086/MS-DOS scheme of things—can add up to one 20-bit address that references a specific memory location. The way it's done is like this:

1. Take the 16-bit segment portion of the number and write it as a hexadecimal value. That gives you a four-digit number between 0000H and FFFFH—that is, 0 through 65,535, which works out to 64 K.

2. Multiply the hexadecimal segment number by 16. This is the equivalent of shifting the number left and tacking a zero on the end: 1234 becomes 12340. (If you find this confusing, think of how you multiply a decimal number: 5 times 10 is 50—you shift the 5 one place to the left and add a zero. Same thing in hexadecimal.)

3. Take the 16-bit offset portion of the address and add it to the shifted
    segment value—for example, 12340 + 5678. The result is 179B8 or, in
    decimal, 96,696. This is known as an *absolute address,* the location of a
    very specific place in memory.

Given this background, think about microprocessors of the 80286 or better
persuasion. These microprocessors contain not 20 address lines, as did the 8086,
but 24 or 32 of them. In addition, the 80286 and above are capable of operating in
protected mode. When running MS-DOS, however, they pretend to be 8086
microprocessors, and as part of real mode, they disable all but 20 of their address
lines, limiting memory access to the standard 1 MB for which MS-DOS remains
notorious.

Now you can turn your attention to a group of programmers working some
time in the late 1980s. These programmers found that it was possible to turn on, or
enable, the 21st address line—known as the A20 line—of an 80286 or better
microprocessor operating in real mode. By itself, the ability to turn on the A20
line would seem to be nothing more than a hardware oddity. Note, however, that
an active A20 line would allow the creation of 21-bit, rather than 20-bit, addresses.
Combine this capability with large segment and offset values, plus a shift of the
address to the left to fill the bit value opened by the new address line, and the
result becomes a way to create addresses ranging from FFFF0H (1,048,560)
through 10FFEFH (1,114,095)—in other words, addresses ranging from just under
1 MB (1,048,576) through 1 MB plus 64 K minus the 16 "overlapping" bytes represented by the values between 1,048,560 and 1,048,576. Voilà. The HMA arrives,
fully accessible to MS-DOS.

The commands described in the remainder of this chapter cover some aspect
of memory or memory-management with MS-DOS.

CHKSTATE.SYS—version 6 only

CHKSTATE.SYS is a device driver that enables MemMaker to keep track of the
memory optimization process. The device driver is mentioned here because it appears in online Help. What should you do with it? Leave it to MemMaker.

Devicehigh

The upper memory equivalent of the Device command (described in Chapter 12),
the Devicehigh configuration command enables you to load individual device
drivers into available UMBs. To use Devicehigh, however, you must

- Have an 80386 or better computer with at least 350 K of extended
  memory.

- Install the HIMEM.SYS extended memory manager.
- Install EMM386.EXE or another UMB provider.
- Create a link to upper memory with the Dos=umb command.

The MS-DOS commands you need, in the order in which they must appear in CONFIG.SYS, are shown in the examples section later in this chapter.

Devicehigh is highly useful for adding a device driver to CONFIG.SYS or for fine-tuning the loading of a device driver into high memory, but if you don't want to bother tinkering, the version 6 MemMaker utility gives you an excellent alternative for optimizing upper memory use. If your CONFIG.SYS file already contains Device or Devicehigh commands for all device drivers you need at startup, the MemMaker utility will automatically adjust those commands to make the best possible use of available UMBs.

If you want to use the Devicehigh command, you must edit your CONFIG.SYS file, either changing an existing Device command to Devicehigh or adding a new Devicehigh command to load a new driver you want to install. Before editing your CONFIG.SYS file, however, run the Memory Display (Mem) command both to see how much space your device drivers currently require when loaded into conventional memory and to see how much upper memory is available. If you have version 5 of MS-DOS, use the Mem /p command (and be prepared for a little hexadecimal arithmetic). If you have version 6 of MS-DOS, use Mem /c to see how much space the drivers require, and then use Mem /f to see how much upper memory is available and in which region. Edit CONFIG.SYS and restart the system to verify that your Devicehigh commands work as you anticipated, and then run the Mem commands again. If MS-DOS was not able to load a device driver into upper memory, even though you specified Devicehigh, you will find the driver in conventional memory.

Command syntax

The basic syntax of the Devicehigh command is simple, but you can customize the command considerably (as MemMaker does) with switches that determine where and into what size UMBs a particular device driver is loaded. The basic syntax is as follows:

devicehigh = *filespec* [*parameters*]

The more elaborate form, for version 6 only, is as follows:

```
devicehigh /L:region1[,minsize1];region2[,minsize2]...;regionN[,minsizeN]
/s=filespec [parameters]
```

filespec is the drive, path, and filename of the device driver to load into upper memory. The equal sign between *devicehigh* and the remainder of the command is optional.

parameters is a list of any parameters needed by the device driver. A Devicehigh command for the DISPLAY.SYS device driver, for example, would look something like this:

```
DEVICEHIGH=C:\DOS\DISPLAY.SYS CON=(EGA,437,2)
```

where *CON=(EGA,437,2)* would be the parameters required by the DISPLAY.SYS device driver.

The following options fine-tune the use of upper memory. These are the switches added by MemMaker. If you want to use them, refer to the description of the Mem command later in this chapter for information about how to check on both memory use and available upper memory regions.

/L:*region* specifies that the device driver is to be loaded into a particular upper memory region (numbered 1, 2, 3, and so on). You can also use this option if you have a device driver that uses more than one memory region and thus needs access to additional UMBs. The Mem /m and Mem /f commands can help you determine the best use of this switch. You can include more than one region number with the /L switch by separating the numbers with semicolons.

The optional *minsize* parameter, which must be preceded by a region number followed by a comma, allows you to specify—in bytes—the minimum size of the UMB into which the device driver is loaded. Include this parameter if the device driver grows after being loaded into memory and thus requires more space than is indicated by its file size. If the driver does not load correctly or the system halts during processing of CONFIG.SYS, this parameter might cure the problem. To determine whether a driver needs more space than anticipated, load it into conventional memory, check on the amount of memory it is using, and then compare that value with the driver's file size (determined with a Dir command). If you specify more than one region with the /L switch, you can include a *minsize* for each.

/s optimizes memory by making a UMB as small as possible while a device driver is being loaded into it. This switch is only effective if used with the /L switch and a UMB for which you've specified a minimum size. You might want to leave this switch to MemMaker to ensure that inadequate UMBs don't cause a device driver to be loaded incorrectly—and don't cause your system to "hang" at startup.

Devicehigh made its appearance in version 5 of MS-DOS, in a similar but less comprehensive form that you use in either of the following two ways:

devicehigh=*filespec* [*parameters*]

where *filespec* and *parameters* are as described for the version 6 command, or

devicehigh size=*minsize filespec parameters*

where size=*minsize* specifies the minimum kilobytes (K) of memory (in hexadecimal) that must be available for Devicehigh to load the driver into upper memory. This parameter performs essentially the same function as *minsize* in version 6, but it is somewhat more difficult to use because it requires you to enter a hexadecimal, rather than decimal, value.

If you use version 5 of MS-DOS, refer to your documentation for more details about this command.

Examples

Include the following in CONFIG.SYS:	To:
DEVICE=C:\DOS\HIMEM.SYS DEVICE=C:\DOS\EMM386.EXE RAM DOS=UMB DEVICEHIGH=C:\DOS\ANSI.SYS	Load the ANSI.SYS device driver into upper memory, after having enabled use of extended memory and the upper memory area with the HIMEM.SYS, EMM386.EXE, and Dos commands.
DEVICE=C:\DOS\HIMEM.SYS DEVICE=C:\DOS\EMM386.EXE RAM DOS=UMB DEVICEHIGH /L:1=C:\DRIVERS\DRIVE-IT.SYS	In version 6, load a driver named DRIVE-IT.SYS into region 1 of the upper memory area. This command could also be typed *DEVICEHIGH= L:1C:DRIVERS\DRIVE-IT.SYS*. You can put a space or an equal sign after the word *devicehigh* or before *filespec*.
DEVICE=C:\DOS\HIMEM.SYS DEVICE=C:\DOS\EMM386.EXE RAM DOS=UMB DEVICEHIGH=L:1,9040 C:\DOS\ANSI.SYS	In version 6, load the ANSI.SYS driver into upper memory, specifying region 1 and a minimum UMB size of 9040 bytes.
DEVICE=C:\DOS\HIMEM.SYS DEVICE=C:\DOS\EMM386.EXE RAM DOS=UMB DEVICEHIGH L:1;2 C:\DRIVERS\DRIVE-IT.SYS	In version 6, load a driver named DRIVE-IT.SYS into upper memory, allowing it to use regions 1 and 2.
DEVICE=C:\DOS\HIMEM.SYS DEVICE=C:\DOS\EMM386.EXE RAM DOS=UMB DEVICEHIGH SIZE=10 C:\DRIVERS\CONTROL.SYS	In version 5, load a driver named CONTROL.SYS into upper memory, specifying that at least 16 K (10 H) of memory must be available before the driver can be loaded.

DOS (Dos)

Next to Clear Screen (Cls), DOS (Dos) is about the simplest MS-DOS command you can use. Despite its simplicity, however, Dos is one of the operating system's big memory winners. Through this command, you accomplish either or both of the following:

- Loading a large part of MS-DOS into the HMA, out of conventional memory where it would occupy valuable real estate needed by other programs.

- Opening a pipeline to the upper memory area, where Devicehigh, Loadhigh, and Memmaker can save even more memory by moving device drivers and programs from conventional to upper memory.

A command you include in your CONFIG.SYS file, Dos works with HIMEM.SYS to load MS-DOS into the HMA on any 80286 or better computer with at least 1 MB of RAM (of which 350 K or more is extended memory). If you want to enable use of UMBs, you must also load a UMB provider. This is an easy task on 80386 and 80486 computers because the EMM386.EXE device driver in versions 5 and 6 does the job handily. On an 80286 machine, however, you must use an alternate non-MS-DOS UMB provider.

Command syntax

The syntax of the Dos command is as follows:

dos=[high or low][,umb or noumb]

high and low specify whether MS-DOS is to be loaded into the HMA (high) or into conventional memory (low). low is the default.

umb and noumb specify whether MS-DOS is to manage (umb) or not manage (noumb) any available upper memory blocks, making them available for device drivers and programs. noumb is the default.

A real mix-and-match command, Dos allows you to specify high/low and umb/noumb in any order you choose, in the same command or in different commands. If you include both options in the same command, be sure to separate them with a comma as shown in the following examples. You can place the Dos command anywhere in CONFIG.SYS.

Examples

Include in CONFIG.SYS:	To:
`DEVICE=C:\DOS\HIMEM.SYS` `DOS=HIGH`	Load MS-DOS into the HMA. Note that these commands would not allow use of UMBs, as shown in the next example.

`DEVICE=C:\DOS\HIMEM.SYS`
`DEVICE=C:\DOS\EMM386.EXE RAM`
`DOS=HIGH,UMB`
	Load MS-DOS into the HMA and open a line to the upper memory area.

`DEVICE=C:\DOS\HIMEM.SYS`
`DEVICE=C:\DOS\EMM386.EXE RAM`
`DOS=UMB,HIGH`
	Do the same as in the previous example. Note that the order of the high and umb options reverses the order shown above.

`DEVICE=C:\DOS\HIMEM.SYS`
`DEVICE=C:\DOS\EMM386.EXE RAM`
`DOS=HIGH`
`DOS=UMB`
	Do the same as in the second example. Here the two options are in separate commands, on separate lines.

`DEVICE=C:\DOS\HIMEM.SYS`
`DEVICE=C:\DOS\EMM386.EXE RAM`
`DOS=HIGH`
`BUFFERS=20`
`FILES=30`
`DEVICEHIGH=C:\DOS\ANSI.SYS`
`DOS=UMB`
	Load MS-DOS into the HMA, open a line to the upper memory area, and load the ANSI.SYS driver into UMBs. Note here that Buffers and Files commands separate the two Dos commands (messy, but workable). Note also that DOS=UMB can appear after the Devicehigh command.

EMM386 and EMM386.EXE

EMM386.EXE is a beast with two faces: It is a device driver, which you load with a Device command in CONFIG.SYS, and it is also a command you can type as *emm386* at the system prompt. Both the device-driver part and the command part of its personality come from the same MS-DOS file, EMM386.EXE.

Command or device driver, EMM386.EXE works only on an 80386 or better computer with extended memory. If installed, EMM386.EXE the device driver performs two functions: It enables MS-DOS to simulate expanded memory by converting some of the computer's extended memory, and it enables the use of UMBs for loading device drivers and programs. Once EMM386.EXE is installed as a device driver, EMM386 the command lets you control program access to (simulated) expanded memory and, if your computer is equipped with a Weitek coprocessor, lets you turn support for the coprocessor on and off.

NOTE: If you use Windows in 386 enhanced mode, you need to use EMM386.EXE to provide expanded memory only if you use non-Windows–based programs that require expanded memory. Windows in 386 enhanced mode can provide expanded memory as necessary.

If you have an 80386 or better computer, you'll want to include EMM386.EXE in CONFIG.SYS, if for no other reason than to gain access to the upper memory area. When you install EMM386.EXE under version 5, you see a report on its status whenever you start your computer. When you install EMM386.EXE under version 6, the driver is more reticent, producing its report only if an error occurs, if the Device command in CONFIG.SYS includes a /v (verbose) switch, or if you press the Alt key while EMM386.EXE is being loaded. At other times, in both versions 5 and 6, you can request a status report at the system prompt by typing *emm386*. If you use EMM386.EXE to provide access to UMBs but you don't use expanded memory, the report looks something like the following in version 6:

```
MICROSOFT Expanded Memory Manager 386   Version 4.45
Copyright Microsoft Corporation 1986, 1993

Expanded memory services unavailable.

    Total upper memory available  . . . . . .    0 KB
    Largest Upper Memory Block available  . .    0 KB
    Upper memory starting address . . . . . .  B000 H

EMM386 Active.
```

If you also use EMM386.EXE to simulate expanded memory, the report includes details on both expanded and upper memory, as in the sample on the following page.

```
MICROSOFT Expanded Memory Manager 386   Version 4.45
Copyright Microsoft Corporation 1986, 1993

   Available expanded memory . . . . . . . .  1024 KB

   LIM/EMS version . . . . . . . . . . . . .   4.0
   Total expanded memory pages . . . . . . .    88
   Available expanded memory pages . . . . .    64
   Total handles . . . . . . . . . . . . . .    64
   Active handles  . . . . . . . . . . . . .     1
   Page frame segment  . . . . . . . . . . . E000 H

   Total upper memory available  . . . . . .     0 KB
   Largest Upper Memory Block available  . .     0 KB
   Upper memory starting address . . . . . . C800 H
```

EMM386 Active.

The following sections describe EMM386 as both a device driver and a command.

EMM386.EXE, the device driver

To simulate expanded memory with EMM386.EXE, you must precede the command that loads EMM386.EXE with a DEVICE=HIMEM.SYS line in CONFIG.SYS. If you want to use the upper memory area as well, you must also include a DOS=UMB line somewhere in CONFIG.SYS. The position of this command doesn't matter, but for neatness and readability, you'll probably want to put it just below EMM386.EXE.

For the most part, you don't have to worry much about specifying parameters with EMM386.EXE, even though the driver does offer a substantial number of moderately to extremely exotic options. If you are planning to use EMM386.EXE as a UMB provider, however, note from the following descriptions that you must include either a ram or a noems switch as part of the Device command that loads this driver into memory. This is important. Forgetting to include one of these switches means that you can end up sitting with furrowed brow wondering why the Emm386 and Mem commands report 0 K upper memory when you're convinced that dozens to hundreds of kilobytes ought to be available.

Two further notes are in order. First, if you use the more advanced switches included with EMM386.EXE, do so carefully. Memory use is critical on a computer, and you must take pains to ensure that you do not try to use addresses in upper memory that are reserved or needed by other device drivers or programs. A serious mistake can cause your computer to hang, so even though you can perform a clean boot (with the F5 key in version 6), you might want to leave memory optimization to MemMaker. If you do experiment with EMM386.EXE, consider doing so either in one section of a CONFIG.SYS file designed for multiple configurations (as described in Chapter 15) or on a bootable floppy containing both your CONFIG.SYS and AUTOEXEC.BAT files. The latter approach ensures that you don't have to change your startup files until you are certain the system is working properly. Also, it is the only way to go if you have version 5.

The second point to remember has to do with the SMARTDRV.EXE device driver. If you have version 6 of MS-DOS and you use SMARTDRV.EXE to create a disk cache in extended memory, you might have to specify a feature called double buffering if one of the following applies to your computer:

- Your system is based on the Micro Channel Architecture (MCA) bus design.

- Your system contains a hard disk or other device with a Small Computer System Interface (SCSI) or an Enhanced Small Device Interface (ESDI) controller.

Most hard disks don't need double-buffering, but if you want to check for yourself, you can run through a series of steps outlined in MS-DOS online Help. To find these steps,

1. Type *help smartdrv.exe* at the system prompt.

2. Press Enter.

3. Read the top of the Notes screen, which appears next, and follow the steps outlined under the heading "Determining whether you need to use double buffering."

Command syntax for EMM386.EXE in version 6

The Device command for loading EMM386.EXE at startup must appear in your CONFIG.SYS file. The complete syntax is shown below. Because this device driver includes so many options, those more likely to be used are shown in boldface type in the complete syntax and are grouped together in the partial syntax shown below it. Note that you do not use Devicehigh with this driver:

device=***filespec*** [on or off or auto] [*memory*] [min=*minimum EMS/VCPI memory*] [w=on or off] [m*n*][frame=*address* or /P*address*] [P*n*=*address*] [x=*address range*] [i=*address range*] [b=*address*] [l=*minimum XMS memory*] [a=*alternate registers*] [h=*handles*] [d=*DMA memory*] [**ram**[=*address range*]] [**noems**] [**novcpi**] [**highscan**] [**verbose**] [win=*address range*] [**nohi**] [rom=*address range*] [**nomovexbda**] [altboot]

device=*filespec* [on/off/auto]
[ram][noems][novcpi][highscan][verbose][nohi][nomovexbda]

filespec, the most important of the EMM386.EXE parameters, gives the drive, path, and filename of the device driver.

on, off, and auto are three switches that control EMM386.EXE activity:

- on, the default, activates EMM386.EXE to enable use of UMBs and provide programs that need it with access to expanded memory.

- off essentially puts EMM386.EXE to sleep. Including this switch in
  CONFIG.SYS shuts off access to expanded memory until you activate
  EMM386.EXE from the command line (with the EMM386 command).
  You can use off only if you do not enable or use UMBs. Use this option
  only if a program cannot run while EMM386.EXE is active.

- auto activates and deactives EMM386.EXE as necessary, depending on
  program requirements.

memory specifies the amount of extended memory, in kilobytes, that you want
EMM386.EXE to provide to requesting software as simulated expanded memory,
or VCPI (Virtual Control Program Interface) memory. The default is the amount
of extended memory, less whatever has been reserved or allocated as extended
memory. Specify *memory* as a multiple of 16, in the range 64 through either 32768
or the amount of available extended memory, whichever is less. If you use a value
that is not a multiple of 16, EMM386.EXE rounds that value down to the nearest
appropriate value.

*NOTE: VCPI is the name of a set of rules related to the EMS specification. VCPI enables
programs controlled by software routines called DOS extenders to run on a system where
access to high memory is handled by a control program—EMM386.EXE—that runs the
system in V86 mode. EMM386.EXE provides VCPI support, if you need it. If you don't
know whether a program uses VCPI memory, check your documentation.*

min=*minimum EMS/VCPI memory* specifies the minimum amount of memory,
in kilobytes, that you want to reserve for EMS/VCPI use. Using this switch reduces the amount of available extended memory by preventing other programs
from using the amount you specify. The default is 256 K; you can specify any
amount from 0 through the amount specified by the *memory* parameter. If you
specify an amount greater than that given by the *memory* parameter, the minimum you specify takes precedence. If you use the noems switch, the value of min
is, obviously, 0 because noems invalidates use of EMS memory.

w=on or off turns the support for a Weitek coprocessor on or off; the default
is off.

m*n* positions the EMS page frame at a specific base address in upper memory.
Specify *n* as a value between 1 and 14, as follows:

Specify:	For page frame starting at:
1	C000H
2	C400H
3	C800H
4	CC00H
5	D000H
6	D400H
7	D800H
8	DC00H
9	E000H
10	8000H
11	8400H
12	8800H
13	8C00H
14	9000H

Use the values between 10 and 14 only if your computer has 512 K of conventional memory.

frame=*address* is comparable to the m parameter but allows you to specify the actual address of the page frame. You can specify addresses from 8000H through 9000H and from C000H through E000H, in 400H (1024-byte) increments. You can also specify frame=none to provide expanded memory but disable the page frame. Doing so, however, can cause problems with some EMS programs.

/P*address* performs the same task as frame=*address*. Specify *address* as a hexadecimal value from 8000H through 9000H or from C000H through E000H, using 400H increments, as described earlier.

P*n*=*address* goes beyond the preceding switches by allowing you to specify the locations of EMS pages (the blocks of bytes that are swapped into and out of the page frame). In this switch, *n* is the number of a page and can be from 0 through 255; *address* is the segment address for the page and can be from 8000H through 9C00H and C000H through EC00H, in 400H increments. Pages 0 through 3 must be contiguous. You cannot specify addresses for pages 0 through 3 if you use the m, frame, or /P switches, all of which allow for four pages within the 64-K page frame they set up.

x=*address range* keeps the range of segment addresses you specify from being used as an EMS page frame or being considered part of available UMBs. You can specify addresses from A000H through FFFFH. EMM386.EXE rounds values down to the nearest 4-K boundary. Separate the beginning and ending addresses with a hyphen (for example, B000-BFFF). The complement of the i switch described next, x takes precedence if you include both switches and their ranges overlap.

i=*address range* uses (includes) the address range you specify as the location for an EMS page frame or UMBs. As with x, you can specify addresses from A000H through FFFFH, which are rounded down, if necessary, to the nearest 4-K boundary. Again, separate the beginning and ending addresses with a hyphen.

b=*address* specifies the lowest segment address—in conventional memory—that can be used for bank-switching (swapping) 16-K EMS pages into memory. You can specify addresses from 1000H through 4000H. The default is 4000H.

l=*minimum XMS memory* specifies the minimum amount of extended memory, in kilobytes, that must be available after EMM386.EXE is loaded. Type this switch as the letter L, not the numeral 1. The default is 0.

a=*alternate registers*, used for multitasking, specifies the number of fast alternate register sets (small segments of memory used for vital program information) that should be allocated to EMM386.EXE. You can specify 0 through 254; the default is 7. Using this switch adds about 200 bytes for each register set to the memory that EMM386.EXE requires.

h=*handles* specifies the number of handles ("aliases" for files and some devices) that EMM386.EXE can use. You can specify 2 through 255; the default is 64, as you can see from the report produced by the EMM386 command.

d=*DMA memory* reserves the amount of memory you specify, in kilobytes, for use as a buffer (temporary storage area) during DMA (direct memory access) transfer operations. DMA bypasses the microprocessor and shuttles information directly between a device and memory. You can use values between 16, the default, and 256 with this switch. If you use this switch, ignore floppy disk DMA and specify the size of the largest transfer that will occur while EMM386.EXE is active—for example, during a tape backup procedure. To determine this value, you must know your hardware and software.

ram=*address range* opens the upper memory area for use in providing UMBs, but does not eliminate use of expanded memory. Specify an address range if you want or need to limit UMB use to a particular region. Omit the range to enable EMM386.EXE to use whatever memory is available for UMBs.

noems shuts off access to expanded memory, but it does open the upper memory area for use as UMBs. Use this or the ram switch to enable EMM386.EXE to act as a UMB provider.

novcpi eliminates support for programs that use VCPI. If you use this switch, you must also use noems. Using both noems and novcpi reduces the amount of extended memory allocated.

highscan controls the behavior of EMM386.EXE at startup. Normally, the driver scans most of the upper memory area; specifying highscan causes EMM386.EXE to be more aggressive. Use highscan if you want to try to get a bit more memory. On some computers, however, it will have no effect or may cause your computer to hang or behave oddly.

verbose causes EMM386.EXE to display status and error information at startup, as is the default in version 5 of MS-DOS. verbose can be abbreviated as /v or just plain v. You can also get the same messages by pressing the Alt key when EMM386.EXE loads.

win=*address range* reserves the range of addresses you specify for use by Windows. You can specify addresses from A000H through FFFFH; if necessary, EMM386.EXE will round the values down to the nearest 4-K boundary. If specified ranges overlap, this switch takes precedence over the ram, rom, and i switches but loses out to the x switch.

nohi loads all of EMM386.EXE into conventional memory rather than loading part (about 5 K) into the upper memory area, as happens by default. Using this switch increases the amount of upper memory available for use as UMBs.

rom=*address range* specifies a range of addresses to be used as shadow RAM. You can specify A000H through FFFFH, separating the starting and ending addresses with a hyphen (for example, F000-FFFF). If necessary, EMM386.EXE rounds down to the nearest 4-K boundary. Before using this switch, check your computer's documentation to see whether shadow RAM is already in effect. If your machine doesn't have shadow RAM, this switch may speed up your programs.

nomovexbda keeps EMM386.EXE from moving some system information called the extended BIOS data from conventional memory to upper memory.

altboot tells EMM386.EXE to use an alternate handler to restart your computer when you press Ctrl-Alt-Del. Use this if pressing Ctrl-Alt-Del doesn't reboot your computer when you have EMM386.EXE loaded.

Command syntax for EMM386.EXE in version 5

EMM386.EXE exists in both versions 5 and 6 of MS-DOS, in somewhat different forms. Basically, the version 6 device driver offers more options. The following syntax shows the version 5 parameters. Where necessary, version differences are identified; as in the version 6 syntax, parameters and switches most likely to be used are shown in boldface type:

device=*filespec* [on or off or auto] [*memory*] [w=on or off] [m*n*][frame=*address* or /P*address*] [P*n*=*address*] [x=*address range*] [i=*address range*] [b=*address*] [l=*minimum XMS memory*] [a=*alternate registers*] [h=*handles*] [d=*DMA memory*] [ram] [noems]

Most of the switches are as described for the version 6 syntax. The ram switch in version 5, however, does not take a range of addresses as it does in version 6.

Examples

Include in CONFIG.SYS:	To:
DEVICE=C:\DOS\HIMEM.SYS DEVICE=C:\DOS\EMM386.EXE NOEMS DOS=UMB	Enable and load EMM386.EXE, specifying no expanded memory and ensuring that MS-DOS can use available UMBs for device drivers and TSR programs.
DEVICE=C:\DOS\HIMEM.SYS DEVICE=C:\DOS\EMM386.EXE RAM DOS=UMB	Enable and load EMM386.EXE, allowing for an EMS page frame, with remaining upper memory to be used for UMBs.
DEVICE=C:\DOS\HIMEM.SYS DEVICE=C:\DOS\EMM386.EXE NOEMS ·NOVCPI DOS=UMB	In version 6 only, enable and load EMM386.EXE, omitting EMS/VCPI support, to leave as much extended memory as possible available for use.
DEVICE=C:\DOS\HIMEM.SYS DEVICE=C:\DOS\EMM386.EXE 1024 DOS=UMB	Enable and load EMM386.EXE, specifying 1024 K of EMS/VCPI memory and ensuring that MS-DOS is able to use extended memory for UMBs and as XMS memory.

EMM386, the command

Although EMM386 is not the most often needed of the commands in your MS-DOS arsenal, it can be helpful—possibly necessary—if you regularly use an application that requires expanded memory and you also use a program, such as Windows, that prefers extended memory. You type this command at the system prompt to control support for expanded memory. The command does not work, however, if you have loaded the EMM386.EXE device driver with the noems switch—that is, you cannot tell the device driver to provide the maximum possible amount of extended memory at startup and then expect to turn expanded memory support off and on from the system prompt. You are also limited by the fact that you cannot turn off expanded memory support if EMM386.EXE is also acting as a UMB provider. The two capabilities, in this case, go hand in hand. Turning expanded memory support off is useful when you want to use a program that does not support (or recognize) EMS/VCPI memory. Windows version 3.0, when running in standard mode, is such a program. Do not, however, use EMM386 while Windows is active.

Command syntax

The syntax of the EMM386 command is as follows:

    emm386 [on or off or auto] [w=on or off]

on, off, and auto allow you to control support for expanded memory use. The switches are as described for the EMM386.EXE device driver. on, the default, activates support for expanded memory; remember, however, that you cannot load EMM386.EXE with no such support and then turn expanded memory support on from the command line. off turns off expanded memory support. auto provides expanded memory support only when programs require it.

w=on or off turns support for the Weitek coprocessor on or off.

Examples

Type:	To:
C:\>emm386	View a report on expanded memory support, including its current status.
C:\>emm386 off	Turn off expanded memory support. This switch does not work if EMM386.EXE is providing UMB support as well as expanded memory support.
C:\>emm386 auto	Provide expanded memory support when and as programs need it.
C:\>emm386 w=off	Turn off support for the Weitek coprocessor.

HIMEM.SYS

HIMEM.SYS is an extended memory manager, a program that enables MS-DOS to use and manage extended memory. Its primary duties are two: To ensure that extended memory is neatly allocated and to prevent conflicts between programs that use extended memory. In addition to managing all of extended memory, HIMEM.SYS also opens up the HMA, the special region to which MS-DOS, in versions 5 and 6, can relocate itself, to vacate as much conventional memory as possible for use by other programs. As the key to memory use beyond 1 MB under MS-DOS, HIMEM.SYS works on any 80286 or better computer with at least some extended memory. If you have such a computer, HIMEM.SYS is a necessary part of using the machine as efficiently as possible.

HIMEM.SYS, like all other MS-DOS device drivers, must be loaded with a Device command in CONFIG.SYS. You cannot use a Devicehigh command, because this driver represents the first of several configuration commands that enable use of the upper memory area for loading other device drivers, as well as TSR programs.

Command syntax

Although HIMEM.SYS can be customized with a number of switches, you can probably ignore most of them. Of all those described in the following paragraphs, the one most likely to be used is the /machine switch, and that is required only with certain computers. The full syntax, however, is as follows:

device=*filespec* /a20control:on or off /cpuclock:on or off /eisa
    /hmamin=*minimum memory* /int15=*amount* /numhandles=*handles*
    /machine:*machine code* /shadowram:on or off /verbose

filespec is the drive, path, and filename of the device driver.

/a20control:on or off determines whether HIMEM.SYS is to take control of
the A20 line, the twenty-first address line, which opens the HMA for use. The
default is on. If you specify /a20control:off, HIMEM.SYS takes over the A20 line
only if it is turned off when HIMEM.SYS is loaded.

cpuclock:on or off lets you control the interaction between HIMEM.SYS and
the computer's clock speed. The default is off. Use this switch if the clock speed of
the computer changes when you load HIMEM.SYS. Turning this on will slow
down the Himem command.

/eisa is needed only on an EISA (Extended Industry Standard Architecture)
system with more than 16 MB of memory. If you have such a computer, /eisa enables HIMEM.SYS to allocate all available extended memory in the computer.

/hmamin=*minimum memory* lets you control use of the HMA by specifying
the minimum amount of memory a program needs in order for it to use the HMA.
This portion of memory can be used by only one program at a time, so you'll
probably want to hand it over to MS-DOS, rather than to an application. To control
use of the HMA, however, you can specify an amount of memory from 0 through 63
(kilobytes). The first program to meet that requirement gains control of the HMA.
The default setting, 0, hands the HMA to the first program that requests it. This
switch has no effect if you are running Windows in enhanced mode.

/int15=*amount* specifies the amount of extended memory, in kilobytes, to be
set aside for programs that use a method based on Interrupt 15 to access extended
memory. For such programs, you might have to set aside a special "pool" of extended memory for their use. The default setting for this switch is 0; specify an
amount from 64 through 65535, or as much memory as your computer has available. To ensure that a program receives as much memory as it needs, set the value
to 64 K more than the program actually needs.

/numhandles=*handles* lets you specify the number of extended memory block
handles that can be used at the same time. The default is 32; you can specify from
1 through 128. Each handle uses up 6 bytes of memory. This switch has no effect if
you are running Windows in enhanced mode.

/machine:*machine code* is a switch that enables HIMEM.SYS to work with the
program that handles the A20 line on certain computers. Use this switch if
HIMEM.SYS does not run correctly or if you cannot get access to the HMA. To
specify a particular computer, use either the machine code (awkward) or the
equivalent number (much easier) shown in the following list. Note that some code
numbers apply to more than one make or model of computer:

Machine code	Code number	Computer
at	1	IBM AT or 100% compatible
ps2	2	IBM PS/2
ptlcascade	3	Phoenix Cascade BIOS
hpvectra	4	HP Vectra (A and A+)
att6300plus	5	AT&T 6300 Plus
acer1100	6	Acer 1100
toshiba	7	Toshiba 1600 and 1200XE
wyse	8	Wyse 12.5 Mhz 286
tulip	9	Tulip SX
zenith	10	Zenith ZBIOS
at1	11	IBM PC/AT (alternative delay)
at2	12	IBM PC/AT (alternative delay)
css	12	CSS Labs
at3	13	IBM PC/AT (alternative delay)
philips	13	Philips
fasthp	14	HP Vectra
ibm7552	15	IBM 7552 Industrial Computer
bullmicral	16	Bull Micral 60
dell	17	Dell XBIOS

/shadowram:on or off turns shadow RAM on or off. This switch is unnecessary unless your computer has less than 2 MB of memory and uses shadow RAM. On such machines, HIMEM.SYS might attempt to disable shadow RAM to free extended memory for use by Windows. If you do not want shadow RAM disabled, use the on option. To turn off shadow RAM, set this switch to off.

/verbose, or /v, displays status and error messages while HIMEM.SYS is loading. Press Alt while HIMEM.SYS is loading to get the same messages.

Examples

Include in CONFIG.SYS:	To:
`DEVICE=C:\DOS\HIMEM.SYS`	Load HIMEM.SYS to enable use of extended memory on an 80286 or better computer.

`DEVICE=C:\DOS\HIMEM.SYS`
`DEVICE=C:\EMM386.EXE RAM`
`DOS=HIGH,UMB`
	Load HIMEM.SYS and enable use of both expanded memory and available UMBs, as well as loading MS-DOS high.

`DEVICE=C:\DOS\HIMEM.SYS` `    /MACHINE=8`	Load HIMEM.SYS and enable use of the HMA on a Wyse 12.5 mHz 286 computer.
`DEVICE=C:\DOS\HIMEM.SYS /V`	Load HIMEM.SYS and display status reports and messages during loading.

Load Fix (Loadfix)

As the name implies, Load Fix (Loadfix) is a "fix it" command. Designed to provide an escape hatch for certain programs that cannot run when loaded into the first 64 K of conventional memory, Loadfix ensures that such programs are loaded above this troubling 64-K boundary. Try this command if you receive the message *Packed file corrupt* when loading a program.

Command syntax

The syntax of the Loadfix command is as follows:

loadfix *filespec* [*parameters*]

filespec is the drive, path, and filename of the program to load.

parameters represents any startup parameters you want to include as part of the startup command.

Examples

Type:	To:
`C:\>loadfix c:\apps\myprog /l`	Load the program named MYPROG above 64 K and start the program with the last (/l) file used.

Or include in AUTOEXEC.BAT or another batch file:	To:
`loadfix c:\apps\myprog /l`	Load the program above 64 K at startup or whenever you run the batch file containing the command.

Load High (Loadhigh or Lh)

The Loadhigh command, which can also be abbreviated Lh, is a companion to the Devicehigh command. Where you use Devicehigh to load device drivers into UMBs, you use Loadhigh to load memory-resident (TSR) programs, such as Doskey, into upper memory regions. Unlike Devicehigh, however, which always appears in CONFIG.SYS, you use Loadhigh either from the system prompt or—more typically—from AUTOEXEC.BAT at startup. Although Loadhigh can be extremely simple to use, it does require a little preparation. If you want to go beyond the basics and use this command to really pack the upper memory area with programs, you'll spend some quality time with the Mem command, as well.

To prepare your system for Loadhigh, you must do the following, in the order shown here:

1. Enable use of extended memory with a DEVICE=C:\DOS\HIMEM.SYS line in CONFIG.SYS.

2. Enable a UMB provider. On an 80386 or better system, you can do this with a DEVICE=C:\DOS\EMM386.EXE line below the HIMEM line in CONFIG.SYS. On an 80286 system, or one on which you use a different UMB provider, the appropriate Device line will, of course, depend on the program you use.

3. Enable use of UMBs with a DOS=UMB line, again in CONFIG.SYS.

Once you've laid the necessary groundwork, MS-DOS will attempt to find enough free upper memory to hold each program you want to load into UMBs. If there is not enough room for a particular program, MS-DOS ignores the Loadhigh command and loads the program into conventional memory automatically.

Although you can tinker with Loadhigh on your own, a good way to go about using upper memory efficiently is to start by clearing unnecessary programs from your AUTOEXEC.BAT file and then running the MemMaker utility. Mem-Maker will add the Loadhigh command to any programs it determines will fit into (and run from) UMBs. If you want to experiment with Loadhigh on your own, perhaps changing the order in which programs appear in AUTOEXEC.BAT and other batch files so that the largest or most necessary ones are loaded first, the /f and /m switches of the Mem command are invaluable in showing you how much upper memory is available (/f) and how much is needed by a particular program (/m). Combine these switches with file sizes you determine with the Dir command, and you should have most of the information you need to begin creating or fine-tuning an upper memory patchwork based on the Loadhigh command. As a rule of thumb,

- Use Mem /f to determine how many upper memory regions you have and how large they are.

- Use Mem /m (followed by the program name) to determine how much memory a program needs when loaded and to determine whether the program uses more than one "piece" of memory (some do).

- Use the file size shown by the Dir command to see roughly how much memory the program needs, at least initially. In some cases, a program grows during the load process, so compare the file size with the amount of memory the program needs when running. If the final program size is larger than the file size, you can specify a required minimum amount of upper memory with the version 6 form of Loadhigh, described later. (If you have version 5 of MS-DOS, you don't, unfortunately, have the same control.)

Command syntax

The syntax of the Loadhigh command includes one plain form that applies to both versions 5 and 6 and one fancy form that applies to version 6 only. The plain syntax is as follows:

loadhigh *program* [*parameters*]

The fancier form, which MemMaker uses and you can, too, to control where programs are loaded in upper memory, is as follows:

loadhigh [/l:*region*[,*minsize*][;*region*[,*minsize*]...[;*region*[,*minsize*]] /s *program*
[*parameters*]

program, in both forms of the command, is the drive, path, and filename of the program you want to load into upper memory.

parameters, again in both forms of the command, represents any parameters you include as part of the program's startup.

/l, an L not a 1, lets you specify one or more upper memory regions the program can occupy or use. The /l switch must be followed by a colon (:) and a region number. If you omit either, Loadhigh displays the error message *LoadHigh: Invalid argument*.

region is the number of the upper memory region you want the program to occupy. If necessary, for programs that require more than one memory location, you can specify two or more regions by separating the region numbers with semicolons, as shown in one of the following examples. To load a program into conventional memory but allow it to use upper memory, specify region 0 (conventional memory) and an upper memory region. If you type the /l switch and its following colon but omit a region number, you see the message *A bad UMB number has been specified*.

minsize specifies the minimum amount of memory the program needs. Loadhigh does not load a program unless the targeted region contains at least as much available memory as the program's file size. If the program grows larger than its file size once it is in memory, however, use the *minsize* parameter to ensure that the program will not be loaded unless the region contains enough memory to accommodate both the program's load size and the minimum you specify. If you're not interested in squeezing out the last possible few bytes of upper memory, consider relying on MemMaker to determine whether this parameter is needed by any of the programs you want to load high.

/s, a tricky switch, optimizes memory use by shrinking a targeted UMB to the minimum size specified with the *minsize* parameter before a program is loaded. This switch works only if you also include /l and *minsize*. Because you can't see into the computer while programs are loaded, consider leaving this switch to MemMaker.

Examples

Type or include in AUTOEXEC.BAT or another batch file:	To:
lh doskey	Load the Doskey command and macro recorder into any suitable region in upper memory.
lh /1:1 doskey	Load Doskey into region 1 (on a computer with a region 1 of suitable size).
lh /1:2 print /d:lpt2	Load the MS-DOS print spooler into region 2, specifying that Print is to use the printer attached to the LPT2 printer port.
lh /1:0;2,42384 /s c:\dos\smartdrv.exe	Load the SMARTDRV.EXE disk-cache program into conventional memory, allow for use of a minimum of 42,384 bytes of upper memory in region 2, and shrink the targeted UMB to the specified minimum size at load time. (This example is taken from an AUTOEXEC.BAT file optimized by MemMaker.)

Memory Display (Mem)

Everyone's favorite—and only—MS-DOS command for peering into the murk of PC memory, the Memory Display (Mem) command appeared in version 5 and has been strengthened considerably in version 6. In both versions of MS-DOS, however, the objective of the command is the same: to let you see how memory is being used on your system. As described under Loadhigh, Mem is useful not only for satisfying your curiosity, but for the much more practical task of helping you make the most efficient possible use of RAM. Use Mem

- To see how much memory, and of what kind, a computer contains.
- To see how much of each type of installed memory is used and how much remains free.
- To see the sizes of the largest continuous blocks of conventional and upper memory you can use for loading programs.
- To see whether MS-DOS is running in the HMA.
- To see where and how programs and device drivers are loaded into conventional and upper memory. (If you have version 6 of MS-DOS and your computer is set up for UMB use, you can spend an interesting few minutes comparing a printed copy of the Mem /d report with the map of upper memory displayed by the Microsoft Diagnostics utility.)

Valuable as it is, Mem needs little explanation beyond this. You should note, however, that the command and its output are not the same in versions 5 and 6. The version 6 reports are easier to read and easier, even for a novice, to understand. Hexadecimal appears (naturally) in the segment addresses that form part of detailed memory listings, but file sizes are all given in bytes and kilobytes. The version 6 output is also more clearly laid out, and it is, overall, more informative.

In both versions 5 and 6 the output of the Mem command varies somewhat, depending on how your system is configured:

- Extended (XMS) memory is reported only if the system includes memory above 1 MB.

- Expanded (EMS) memory is reported if it conforms to the LIM EMS 4.0 specification and you have installed expanded memory or you have enabled EMM386.EXE to simulate expanded memory in the Device command that loads EMM386.EXE from CONFIG.SYS.

- Upper memory is reported only if you have installed a UMB provider, such as EMM386.EXE, and you have enabled upper memory use with the DOS=UMB command in CONFIG.SYS.

- Hardware-based RAM and ROM, such as video and BIOS memory, are displayed as Adapter RAM/ROM (version 6 only).

The most comprehensive report in either version 5 or 6 appears when you use the /d switch. The actual output of the /d switch, however, differs significantly between the two versions of the command. The following excerpt shows part of a version 6 report produced with the /d switch:

```
Conventional Memory Detail:
   Segment          Total         Name          Type
   -------      ---------------   -----------   --------
   00000         1039   (1K)                    Interrupt Vector
   00040          271   (0K)                    ROM Communication Area
   00050          527   (1K)                    DOS Communication Area
   00070         2656   (3K)      IO            System Data
                                  CON           System Device Driver
                                  AUX           System Device Driver
                                  PRN           System Device Driver
                                  CLOCK$        System Device Driver
                                  A: - C:       System Device Driver
                                  COM1          System Device Driver
                                  LPT1          System Device Driver
                                  LPT2          System Device Driver
                                  LPT3          System Device Driver
                                  COM2          System Device Driver
                                  COM3          System Device Driver
```

(continued)

```
                                      COM4        System Device Driver
    00116              5664    (6K)   MSDOS       System Data
    00278             14048   (14K)   IO          System Data
                        768    (1K)      SETVERXX Installed Device=SETVER
                       1136    (1K)      XMSXXXX0 Installed Device=HIMEM
                       4128    (4K)      EMMXXXX0 Installed Device=EMM386
⋮
Upper Memory Detail:
  Segment  Region      Total        Name         Type
  -------  ------   ----------------  -----------  --------

   0B13A     1        4224    (4K)   IO          System Data
                      4192    (4K)      CON       Installed Device=ANSI
   0B242     1        1216    (1K)   IO          System Data
                      1184    (1K)      E:        Installed Device=RAMDRIVE
   0B28E     1        4656    (5K)   IO          System Data
                      4624    (5K)      POWER$    Installed Device=POWER
   0B3B1     1       17616   (17K)   MSDOS       -- Free --
   0C801     2       43472   (42K)   IO          System Data
                     43440   (42K)      DBLSSYS$ Installed Device=DBLSPACE
   0D29E     2       22016   (22K)   MSDOS       -- Free --
   0F001     3       32752   (32K)   MSDOS       -- Free --
Memory Summary:
  Type of Memory           Total      =      Used       +       Free
  ---------------       ----------------    ----------------    ----------------

  Conventional          655360  (640K)     71536   (70K)     583824  (570K)
  Upper                 126016  (123K)     53632   (52K)      72384   (71K)
  Adapter RAM/ROM       131072  (128K)    131072  (128K)          0    (0K)
  Extended (XMS)*      7476160 (7301K)   5739456 (5605K)    1736704 (1696K)
  ----------------      ----------------    ----------------    ----------------

  Total memory         8388608 (8192K)   5995696 (5855K)    2392912 (2337K)

  Total under 1 MB      781376  (763K)    125168  (122K)     656208  (641K)

  Handle    EMS Name      Size
  -------   --------      ------
      0                   060000

Total Expanded (EMS)              7929856  (7744K)
Free Expanded (EMS)*              1966080  (1920K)
```

* EMM386 is using XMS memory to simulate EMS memory as needed.
  Free EMS memory may change as free XMS memory changes.

```
Memory accessible using Int 15h           0    (0K)
Largest executable program size      583632  (570K)
Largest free upper memory block       32752   (32K)
```
MS-DOS is resident in the high memory area.

```
XMS version  3.00; driver version  3.09
EMS version  4.00
```

Command syntax

The syntax of the Mem command, neither complex nor difficult to use, differs in versions 5 and 6, as does the meaning of one switch, /p. Switches can either be abbreviated or typed out, as shown in the following lines. First, the syntax for Mem in version 6 is as follows:

    mem /c /d /f /m program /p

Spelled out, the version 6 command reads as follows:

    mem /classify /debug /free /module program /page

In version 5, the syntax is similar, but less comprehensive, as follows:

    mem /c /d /p

Or, spelled out, it is as follows:

    mem /classify /debug /program

Note that /p stands for *page* in version 6, but *program* in version 5.

/c, or /classify, in both versions lists programs loaded into conventional and upper memory and gives the size of each program. The end of the report—more detailed in version 6—summarizes memory use on the system. If you have version 6, you can use the /p switch to halt scrolling of a multiple-screen display. If you have version 5, use the More command instead, as shown in the following examples section.

/d, or /debug, in both versions produces the most information. Using this switch causes Mem to list all programs, device drivers, and areas of free memory in the conventional and (if it has been activated) the upper memory areas. The report this switch produces, as shown previously, is the most detailed, in either version 5 or 6 of MS-DOS, that you can produce with the Mem command. As mentioned earlier, use the /p switch in version 6 or the More command in version 5 to halt scrolling.

/free, in version 6 only, produces a report showing the amount of free conventional and upper memory available on your computer. The report looks something like the following:

```
Free Conventional Memory:

    Segment       Total
    -------    ----------------
    00690          80    (0K)
    006A6          96    (0K)
    01176         176    (0K)
    01181       88608   (87K)
    02723      495040  (483K)

Total Free: 584000  (570K)
```

(continued)

```
Free Upper Memory:

  Region   Largest Free      Total Free       Total Size
  ------   -------------    -------------    -------------
     1     17616  (17K)     17616  (17K)     27760  (27K)
     2     22016  (22K)     22016  (22K)     65504  (64K)
     3     32752  (32K)     32752  (32K)     32752  (32K)
```

/m *program*, in version 6 only, shows memory use for the program or device driver you specify as program. You can separate the switch and the name of the program or device driver with a space, as shown here, or you can type the switch and its modifier as either /m:*program* or (though it's confusing) m*program*. Regardless, this switch produces a report like the following:

```
SMARTDRV is using the following memory:

  Segment  Region       Total        Type
  -------  ------    -------------    --------
   01ECA               14736  (14K)   Program
                      -------------
  Total Size:          14736  (14K)
```

/p, or /page, in version 6 only, causes the Mem command to "page" through its output, stopping after each screenful and waiting until you press a key. This switch is the Mem command's built-in Pause command and even includes a *Press any key to continue...* prompt at the bottom of each screen.

/p, or /program, in version 5 only, causes the Mem command to produce a report midway between the reports produced by the /c and /d switches. The output lists the names, locations, and sizes of programs and device drivers in memory, but not in quite the detail shown by the /d switch.

Examples

Type:	To:
C:\>mem	See a summary report of memory use (either version 5 or 6).
C:\>mem /d /p	See a detailed listing of device drivers, programs, and free memory, pausing after each screenful. The report includes program locations and sizes, as well as a detailed summary of available and free memory on the system (version 6 only).

(continued)

Type:	To:
`C:\>mem /p ¦ more`	See a report midway between a summary and a complete listing, showing programs, sizes, and memory addresses, pausing after each screenful. This report also includes a summary of available and free memory, although not in the detail provided by version 6 of MS-DOS (version 5 only).
`C:\>mem /f`	See a summary report of free conventional and upper memory (version 6 only).

`C:\>mem /m mydriver`
or
`C:\>mem /m myprog`
	See a report on memory use by the MYDRIVER device driver or the MYPROG program. Note that you do not have to specify a drive and path with the driver or program name (version 6 only).

MemMaker (Memmaker)—version 6 only

MemMaker is clever and fun to use. New in version 6 of MS-DOS, MemMaker is a full-screen utility that prompts you through the process of improving memory use on an 80386 or 80486 computer with extended memory. Actually, MemMaker does most of the work itself; it

- Examines current memory use on your system.

- Restarts the system to find out how programs and device drivers are loaded into memory. (When you think about MemMaker "watching" while your system reboots, these particular restarts come to resemble the MS-DOS version of an out-of-body experience.)

- Uses its findings to "consider" up to several thousand alternative configurations that might improve memory use.

- Changes your CONFIG.SYS, AUTOEXEC.BAT and (if appropriate) Windows SYSTEM.INI files to use conventional and upper memory as efficiently as possible, given the configuration defined in these files.

As a last step, MemMaker double-checks its work by restarting your computer with the new configuration. Before quitting, it also asks you to verify that your system is working properly. If you answer no, MemMaker lets you choose to either undo the changes or keep the changes, exit, and do some troubleshooting on your own, with the help of your MS-DOS 6 User's Guide.

If you're interested in taking a look behind the scenes, use a text editor or the Type command to view the file MEMMAKER.STS in your DOS directory. This file contains before and after information on available memory, as well as details about the programs and device drivers MemMaker found in AUTOEXEC.BAT and CONFIG.SYS.

Because Windows has its own way of working with memory, you should not run MemMaker while Windows is active. Chapter 14 describes the use of Mem-Maker in more detail. The following sections describe the command-line options you can use in starting this program.

Command syntax

The syntax for starting MemMaker is as follows:

memmaker /b /batch /session /swap:*drive* /t /undo /w:*space1,space2*

/b runs MemMaker in black and white. You need this only if you have a monochrome screen and MemMaker is not correctly displayed.

/batch tells MemMaker to run itself—that is, to run in batch mode and assume the default whenever it normally prompts for a choice. If you use this switch, be sure to remove all disks from your floppy drives before running Mem-Maker. If an error occurs, MemMaker restores all original settings. After optimi-zation, you can view the MEMMAKER.STS file mentioned earlier for information about the drivers and programs MemMaker considered.

NOTE: *Batch mode is not fully automatic. If you've set up a menu as part of a multi-configuration CONFIG.SYS file, MemMaker needs you to choose from the menu during the two times it restarts your computer. Running MemMaker with a multi-configuration CONFIG.SYS is not, however, the best approach to optimizing memory use. See Chapter 14 for details.*

/session is a private switch used by MemMaker while it's working. Ignore this switch.

/swap:*drive* tells MemMaker where to find your startup files if the current drive letter is not the same as the startup drive letter. You need this switch only if you use disk-compression software (*not* including DoubleSpace, Stacker, and SuperStor) that swaps logical drives after startup. Specify *drive* as the letter of the original startup drive.

/t disables detection of the IBM Token Ring network. Obviously, you need this switch only if you use such a network and have trouble running MemMaker.

/undo, probably the most likely of the MemMaker switches to be used, reverses all the changes made by MemMaker to your CONFIG.SYS, AUTOEXEC.BAT, and (if appropriate) Windows SYSTEM.INI files. This switch is your safety net, the one to be used if changes made by MemMaker cause error messages or problems running device drivers or memory-resident programs.

/w:*space1,space2* sets aside—or doesn't set aside—spaces in upper memory for Windows to use as temporary storage areas called *translation buffers,* which it needs when running MS-DOS–based (not Windows-based) applications. By default, MemMaker does not set aside any translation buffers.

Examples

Type:	To:
C:\>memmaker	Start the MemMaker utility.
C:\>memmaker /undo	Undo changes made by MemMaker.
C:\>memmaker /batch	Run MemMaker in batch mode and exit when through.

RAMDRIVE.SYS

RAMDRIVE.SYS, one of the two MS-DOS device drivers (the other being SMARTDRV.EXE) that can make good use of extended memory on your computer, sets up a virtual disk drive in memory. Once created, a RAM drive can be used as if it were another, extremely fast, piece of hardware on the system. The great advantage of a RAM drive is, therefore, that it enables MS-DOS to access programs and files at memory speeds, rather than at the considerably slower speeds involved in reading from a physical disk drive. The disadvantage is that the "drive" exists only in memory. You cannot expect a RAM drive to hold its contents after you turn off the computer. If you create and use a RAM drive, always remember to save its contents to a real disk before you shut down or reboot. If you're the forgetful type, use the RAM drive from a batch file that ends only after carrying out a Copy or an Xcopy command.

To create a RAM drive, you add a Device or a Devicehigh command to CONFIG.SYS. If you want, you can create more than one RAM drive by adding a Device or Devicehigh command for each separately. The Ramdrive command will select a drive letter for you, usually the first available. You can create the drive in conventional, expanded, or extended memory. Of these choices, conventional memory is the least desirable because whatever memory the RAM drive uses (64 K by default, more if you say so) becomes memory that other programs cannot use. The best choice, in terms of speed and (memory) affordability, is extended memory, which places the RAM drive out of the way, yet accessible to MS-DOS, as long as you've installed HIMEM.SYS or another extended memory manager that conforms to the XMS rules and regulations. Expanded memory, which also places the RAM drive out of the normal MS-DOS realm, is somewhat slower than extended memory, but it is still a better choice than conventional memory. To place the RAM drive in expanded memory, you must install HIMEM.SYS and EMM386.EXE or use another expanded memory manager.

To create and use RAM drives effectively, you should give some thought to the amount of memory you can afford to spare and the types of files you plan to "install" on the RAM drive. If you create a large RAM drive (several megabytes, for example), think about whether 64 directory entries, the default, is sufficient. If you also use the SMARTDRV.EXE disk cache described later and your system does not have masses of extended or expanded memory, you might also have to think about balancing the amount of memory you devote to each driver. Once created, however, you'll find that a RAM drive is lightning fast and acts just like any other drive. You can run Check Disk (Chkdsk) on a RAM drive, you can list its directory, and you can create, populate, rename, prune, and delete subdirectories on it. Just remember to save everything on it.

Many people, by the way, simplify life and disk storage by creating a small RAM drive and pointing the TEMP and TMP variables to a directory on it. TEMP and TMP (some programs use one, some use the other) tell applications and other software where to store the temporary files they create while active. Under normal operation, the program deletes these temporary files before quitting. Over time, however, you can find that your temporary directory slowly fills with temporary files that are not deleted because of software or hardware problems. Temporary files, however, cannot survive a shut down or a reboot, so using a RAM disk as their temporary home guarantees that they disappear each time you pack up for the day.

Command syntax

RAMDRIVE.SYS (known as VDISK.SYS in IBM releases of MS-DOS) has been part of MS-DOS since version 3.2. The command and its default settings have varied somewhat, depending on the MS-DOS version and, in some cases, on whether you were using RAMDRIVE.SYS or VDISK.SYS. To avoid getting lost in thickets of versionary brambles, the following syntax describes RAMDRIVE.SYS as it exists in versions 5 and 6 of MS-DOS. Note that you can replace Device with Devicehigh if your computer has 1 to 2 MB of available UMBs:

device=*filespec* [*disk-size*] [*sector-size*] [*directory-entries*] /e /a

filespec is the drive, path, and filename of the RAMDRIVE.SYS device driver.

disk-size specifies the size of the RAM drive you want to create. The default is 64 K. You can specify from 4 through 32767 in version 6 or from 16 through 4096 in version 5 (note the difference). This is probably the only parameter you'll really need to include.

sector-size specifies the number of bytes per sector to be used for the RAM drive. The default is 512, as is typical for real disk drives. You can also specify 128 or 256, but the default is probably best. If you specify a sector size, you must also specify a disk size.

directory-entries specifies the number of directory entries for the root directory of the RAM drive. The root directory, remember, must accommodate both files and subdirectories. The default is 64, probably adequate for most needs, but if you create a very large RAM drive that will typically contain a large number of files, be sure the root directory is large enough to hold the maximum number of files and directories you expect the drive to hold. You can specify from 2 (too few) through 1024 (probably too many) directory entries. If necessary, MS-DOS will round the number up to fill a complete sector. If you specify the number of directory entries, you must also specify both the disk size and the sector size. If memory is too limited for MS-DOS to create a RAM disk of the size you specify, it will attempt to create a RAM disk with 16 directory entries. To check on this, use the Chkdsk command to verify the size of the RAM disk.

/e creates the RAM disk in extended memory. Use this switch if your computer has both extended and expanded memory, and you can spare extended memory for the job.

/a creates the RAM disk in expanded memory (or expanded memory simulated by EMM386.EXE). Use this switch if your computer has both extended and expanded memory, but extended memory is in short supply.

NOTE: If you don't use the /e or /a switch, remember that your RAM drive will be in conventional memory and will take space away from your programs.

Examples

Include in CONFIG.SYS:	To:
`DEVICE=C:\DOS\RAMDRIVE.SYS 32`	Create a 32-K RAM drive in conventional memory. Bear in mind that this is not a particularly desirable setup. It can, however, speed up operations on a floppy-only system with a full 640 K of RAM.

`DEVICE=C:\DOS\HIMEM.SYS`
`DEVICE=C:\DOS\EMM386.EXE NOEMS`
`DOS=UMB`
`DEVICEHIGH=C:\DOS\RAMDRIVE.SYS 1024 /E`
	Load the RAMDRIVE.SYS device driver into upper memory and create a 1024-K RAM drive in extended memory. Note that the preceding commands set up the computer to use extended memory and UMBs but no expanded memory.

`DEVICE=C:\DOS\HIMEM.SYS`
`DEVICE=C:\DOS\EMM386.EXE RAM`
`DOS=UMB`
`DEVICEHIGH=C:\DOS\RAMDRIVE.SYS 1024 /A`
	Create the same setup as the preceding example, but with the RAM drive created in expanded memory simulated by the EMM386.EXE device driver.

(continued)

Include in CONFIG.SYS:	To:
DEVICE=C:\DOS\HIMEM.SYS DEVICE=C:\DOS\EMM386.EXE NOEMS DOS=UMB DEVICEHIGH=C:\DOS\RAMDRIVE.SYS 4096 512 256 /E	Create a 4096-K RAM drive with a possible 256 directory entries in extended memory. Note that the sector size (512) is included, even though it is the same as the default because both disk size and sector size must be included if the number of directory entries is specified.
DEVICE=C:\DOS\HIMEM.SYS DEVICE=C:\DOS\EMM386.EXE NOEMS DOS=UMB DEVICEHIGH=C:\DOS\RAMDRIVE.SYS 512 /E DEVICEHIGH=C:\DOS\RAMDRIVE.SYS 1024 /E	Create two separate RAM drives, one of 512 K and one of 1024 K, in extended memory. Note that each RAM drive must have its own Device or Devicehigh line in CONFIG.SYS.

SIZER.EXE—version 6 only

SIZER.EXE is, like CHKSTATE.SYS, the property of the version 6 MemMaker utility. MemMaker uses SIZER.EXE to help optimize memory use by tracking the size of device drivers and TSR programs in memory. Pretend SIZER.EXE does not exist; leave it to its rightful owner.

SMARTDRV.EXE

SMARTDRV.EXE is similar to RAMDRIVE.SYS in enabling a computer to work faster. Unlike RAMDRIVE.SYS, however, which creates a simulated disk drive in memory, SMARTDRV.EXE sets aside a portion of memory for use as a disk cache, a temporary holding area for information recently read from or about to be written to disk. Using a disk cache can speed up file access considerably because it is much faster for MS-DOS to check memory for a file or part of a file than it is for the operating system to go out to disk, find the file, and read it into memory. Although caching a file does not seem particularly effective on the surface, the report on the next page, generated while this chapter was being written, shows just how often references to the cache can be successful—that is, result in "hits." You see this report if you're running either version 6 of MS-DOS or Windows 3.1.

NOTE: If you use Windows with version 6 of MS-DOS, you can see a more graphical report—replete with help, options, and a chart showing the cache hit rate—live and in living color. To produce this report, open the File Manager in Windows and double-click on SMARTMON.EXE in your DOS directory.

To see a typical report on SMARTDRV.EXE, type *smartdrv /s* at the MS-DOS prompt. An example is shown on the next page.

```
Microsoft SMARTDrive Disk Cache version 4.1
Copyright    1991,1993 Microsoft Corp.

Room for    256 elements of 8,192 bytes each
There have been 2,962 cache hits
      and    1,373 cache misses

Cache size: 2,097,152 bytes
Cache size while running Windows: 2,097,152 bytes

             Disk Caching Status
  drive   read cache   write cache   buffering
  ---------------------------------------------
    A:      yes           no            no
    B:      yes           no            no
    C:      yes           yes           no
For help, type "Smartdrv /?".
```

This example is slightly skewed because it represents the results of caching a
single word processing file. MS-DOS would obviously be less successful if you
were using a program that jumped from one file to another. Most computer work
does, however, rely on repeated access to one or more files and for that, a
SMARTDRV.EXE cache makes a lot of sense. You can cache both uncompressed
and compressed DoubleSpace disks.

As you can see from the preceding report, SMARTDRV.EXE distinguishes
between read caching and write caching. Read caching is what you just covered.
Write caching is the temporary storage of information destined for disk. When
you enable write caching, MS-DOS essentially waits for an opportune moment,
as when you're busy thinking, to access the disk. This hiatus can be dangerous if
you turn off the computer or hit the reset button before the information has been
saved. MS-DOS, however, like Asimov's robots, follows certain laws, and chief
among them is this one: MS-DOS will not, through any action or omission of action, allow harm to befall your data. Thus, even if you don't save the file,
MS-DOS automatically writes it to disk at frequent intervals. Furthermore,
SMARTDRV.EXE includes a switch (/c) that allows you to save at any time. And,
write caching is normally disabled for floppy drives (where the disk could conceivably be changed before data is saved) and for remote drives you connect to
in version 6 with Interlnk (because the connection could be broken before the
data is saved).

*NOTE: The Buffering column shown in the preceding report (not shown in version 5)
tells you whether you need to install the version 6 double-buffering capability of
SMARTDRV.EXE. Double buffering is a means of enabling certain hard disk controllers
to use memory provided by EMM386.EXE. To provide double buffering, you must add a
Device line for SMARTDRV.EXE to your CONFIG.SYS file. Version 6 provides detailed*

help information on determining whether you need double buffering. To see this help, follow the steps described earlier in this chapter under the entry for EMM386.EXE.

SMARTDRV.EXE appears in both versions 5 and 6 of MS-DOS. There are differences, however. Version 6, which offers little support for expanded memory, always creates the cache in extended memory. Version 5 can create the cache in either extended or expanded memory. Version 5 does not support double buffering, however, nor does it support as many parameters and switches as does the version 6 program.

Command syntax

You can start SMARTDRV.EXE from the command line, but the logical place to put so valuable a command is your AUTOEXEC.BAT file. Some of the following parameters and switches are of the "setup" variety you would include in AUTOEXEC.BAT; a few others, such as /c and /r, assist you in using and controlling SMARTDRV.EXE once it is loaded. The following syntax describes SMARTDRV.EXE in version 6 of MS-DOS. The section following this one describes SMARTDRV.EXE in version 5.

The syntax to load and control SMARTDRV.EXE is as follows:

[*drive:*][*path*]\SMARTDRV.EXE [*drive1+* or −] [*drive2+* or −]...[*driveN* + or −]
    [/e:*element size*] [*initial cache size*] [*Windows cache size*] /b:*buffer size* /c /r /l
    /q /s /v

The syntax to enable double buffering for SMARTDRV.EXE is as follows:

device=[*drive:*][*path*]\SMARTDRV.EXE /double_buffer

drive and *path* are the drive and path leading to the SMARTDRV.EXE file—probably drive C and your DOS directory.

drive1, drive2,...driveN are the drive or drives for which you want to enable or control caching (with the + and − symbols). You can use these parameters from the command line to control caching of specific drives. By default, SMARTDRV.EXE sets up both read and write caching for your hard disk and read caching for each floppy disk drive and all Interlnk drives. SMARTDRV.EXE does not cache RAM drives, CD-ROM drives, network drives, compressed drives, or Microsoft Flash memory card drives.

+ and −, immediately following a drive letter (no colon) enable and disable caching, as follows:

- + enables both read and write caching. So, for example, *a+* causes SMARTDRV.EXE to cache both reads and writes for floppy drive A.

- − disables all caching for the drive you specify. So, for example, *a−* causes SMARTDRV.EXE to eliminate caching for floppy drive A.

To enable read caching but not write caching, simply specify a drive letter.

/e:*element size* specifies the number of bytes SMARTDRV.EXE transfers at one time. The default is 8192; you can specify 1024, 2048, or 4096 instead. Use this switch in AUTOEXEC.BAT. Specifying a smaller element size slightly decreases the amount of upper memory (conventional memory if the program is loaded low) used by SMARTDRV.EXE.

initial cache size specifies the size of the cache, in kilobytes, that SMARTDRV.EXE sets up when you start it. If you use this parameter, specify *initial cache size* as part of the command in AUTOEXEC.BAT. Obviously, the larger the cache, the more "hits" MS-DOS will make when checking for information in the cache. The default cache size depends on the amount of memory in your computer, as shown in the table following the description of the companion parameter, the *Windows cache size*.

Windows cache size specifies the size, in kilobytes, to which SMARTDRV.EXE will shrink the cache when you run Windows. Again, if you use this parameter, specify it in AUTOEXEC.BAT. Windows has its own methods of dealing with memory, and because MS-DOS and Windows work closely together, this parameter allows you to specify how small an MS-DOS cache you want to maintain while Windows is running your computer. As with the initial cache size, the Windows cache size depends on the amount of extended memory in the computer, as follows:

Amount of extended memory	Initial cache size	Windows cache size
1 MB or less	All of available extended memory	0 K
1 MB to 2 MB	1 MB	256 K
2 MB to 4 MB	1 MB	512 K
4 MB to 6 MB	2 MB	1 MB
More than 6 MB	2 MB	2 MB

/b:*buffer size* specifies the amount of memory set aside for a special cache called a read-ahead buffer. A read-ahead buffer is used to hold information that occurs past the portion of a file copied into memory during a "normal" caching operation. In a sense, the read-ahead buffer is the SMARTDRV.EXE version of going above and beyond the call of duty. Instead of reading X bytes into memory, SMARTDRV.EXE reads X bytes plus the amount specified by *buffer size*, thus increasing the likelihood that needed information will be in memory rather than on disk. By default, the read-ahead buffer holds 16 K; you can specify any multiple of the values—1024, 2048, 4096, or 8192—acceptable for element size. (See the /e switch, above). As with other size parameters, if you use this, specify the size of the read-ahead buffer in your AUTOEXE.BAT file. The smaller the value you specify, the less conventional memory SMARTDRV.EXE requires. Specifying a small element size with the /b switch can save 10 K or more of memory, so if memory is at a premium, you might want to experiment with this switch to determine whether a larger read-ahead buffer or more memory for loading programs enhances your system.

/c is a small but mighty switch, not to be forgotten, because it causes SMARTDRV.EXE to write all cached information to disk. Pressing Ctrl-Alt-Del will not cause loss of unsaved information, but you should definitely use this switch before pressing the reset button on your computer (if it has one). Use this switch from the command line.

/r clears the cache and restarts SMARTDRV.EXE. Use this switch from the command line.

/l loads SMARTDRV.EXE into conventional memory rather than the upper memory area where it loads by default, assuming that upper memory is enabled and contains enough free UMBs (about 28 K by default) for SMARTDRV.EXE. Use this switch, if you need it, from AUTOEXEC.BAT. If you enable double buffering, /l might be able to speed up your system if it is running slowly.

/q tells SMARTDRV.EXE to be quiet—that is, not to display status and error messages. This switch can be useful for a system on which you want to suppress error messages. The /q switch can be used from AUTOEXEC.BAT or the command line. However, SMARTDRV.EXE is normally "quiet" when it loads and only gets "noisy" when you call it later.

/s produces a status report like the one shown earlier in the description of SMARTDRV.EXE. This one is useful from the command line.

/v tells SMARTDRV.EXE to display status and error messages during startup, in case you want to see how it loaded. This is the opposite of /q.

/double_buffer is used only when you need to enable double buffering on your system. Remember that this switch must appear in a Device command in CONFIG.SYS. You do not use it in AUTOEXEC.BAT.

SMARTDRV.EXE in version 5

SMARTDRV.EXE in version 5 of MS-DOS is much simpler than it is in version 6. The syntax for the version 5 command is as follows:

[*drive:*][*path*]\SMARTDRV.EXE [*initial cache size*] [*Windows cache size*] /a

drive and *path* specify the location of the SMARTDRV.EXE file.

initial cache size, as in version 6, sets the size of the disk cache. The default is 256 K; you can specify values from 128 through 8192.

Windows cache size, again as in version 6, specifies the size to which Windows can shrink the cache. Specify a value if you do not want Windows to shrink the cache to 0 while it is running.

/a creates the disk cache in expanded memory, rather than the extended memory SMARTDRV.EXE uses by default. Use this switch if your system has more available expanded memory than extended.

Examples

Use the following command:	To:
In AUTOEXEC.BAT	
SMARTDRV	Start SMARTDRV.EXE with all default settings. Note that this command omits the drive and path and must therefore follow a Path command defining the DOS directory (versions 5 and 6).
In AUTOEXEC.BAT	
SMARTDRV /E:4096 /B:4096	Start SMARTDRV.EXE, specifying 4096 for both the element size and the read-ahead buffer. This command can cut memory use about in half (version 6 only).
In CONFIG.SYS	
DEVICE=C:\DOS\SMARTDRV.EXE /DOUBLE-BUFFER	Enable double buffering from CONFIG.SYS and start SMARTDRV.EXE with default settings from AUTOEXEC.BAT (version 6 only).
In AUTOEXEC.BAT	
SMARTDRV	
In AUTOEXEC.BAT	
C:\>smartdrv /s	Check on the status of the disk cache (version 6 only).
C:\>smartdrv /c	Save all cached information on disk (version 6 only).
In AUTOEXEC.BAT	
SMARTDRV /A	Create the disk cache in expanded memory (version 5 only).

12

System Configuration and Control

What You'll Find Here: For finding out about your computer—Microsoft Diagnostics (MSD); for system configuration—Buffers, Device, Drive Parameters (Drivparm), File Control Blocks (Fcbs), Files, Include, Install, Lastdrive, Menu Color (Menucolor), Menu Default (Menudefault), Menu Item (Menuitem), Number Lock (Numlock), Set Version (Setver), SETVER.EXE, Share, Shell, Stacks, Submenu, and Switches; for controlling batch files—Call, Choice, Echo, For, Goto, If, Pause, Remark (Rem), Set, and Shift; for command recall and macros—Doskey; for input/output redirection—Find, More, and Sort.

*T*he commands in this chapter, more than most others covered in this book, help you leave the realm of comfortable beginner and ascend to the world of confident intermediate user and beyond. These are the commands that help you manage the computer itself, not simply the files, programs, and directories you tell the machine to use on demand. As you can see from the opening paragraph, the commands described here can be grouped into several categories:

- "Everything you ever wanted to know about your computer" offers the version 6 Microsoft Diagnostics utility.

- "Making it work the way you want" covers all the configuration commands not included in the preceding chapters more specifically devoted to devices and memory.

- "Putting MS-DOS on autopilot" describes the batch commands that help you control the actions of the batch interpreter.

- "Making life easier" puts forward another single entrant, the Doskey command.

- "Having fun with MS-DOS and making it more useful too" covers the input/output redirection commands—Find, More, and Sort.

Everything you ever wanted to know about your computer

If you have version 6 of MS-DOS (or Windows version 3.1), typing the letters M, S, and D calls up the handy utility more formally known as Microsoft Diagnostics. This is a menu-driven program that appears in a text-based window and enables you to peer into the hardware maze that makes up the entity you call "My Computer." Through the MSD program, you can take a look at memory use, disk drives, video, device drivers, serial and parallel ports, and so on.

You should avoid starting the utility when Windows is running. Although you won't hurt anything by doing so, the information MSD displays on memory, video, and other hardware might not be accurate. This cautionary note aside, you start the MSD utility simply by typing its initials at the system prompt:

```
C:\>msd
```

When the program first starts, you see a message from Microsoft and a flashing note telling you that *MSD is examining your system....* When the program has gathered all the information it needs, the screen changes to the following:

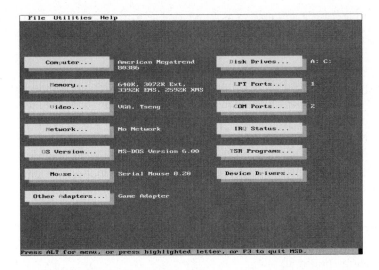

The File and Utilities menus, as you'll see, deal with specialized tasks. Help, however, does nothing more than tell you about the version of MSD you have. Usually your main concern will be the "buttons" in the middle of the screen. Press the highlighted (or colored) letter of the button you want, and MSD will display information about that aspect of your computer. For example, pressing P for Computer produces a display like this:

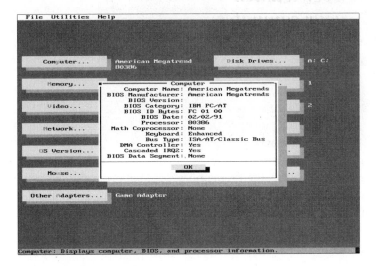

When you finish viewing a screen, press Enter or Esc to return to the main "control panel." To quit MSD, press F3 or, if you like using menus, press Alt-F followed by X.

If you're interested in exploring with MSD, the following steps should get you started. Note, however, that the illustrations show screens in 43-line mode. If you install ANSI.SYS from your CONFIG.SYS file, you might also want to set the screen mode to 43 lines rather than the usual 25 with the *mode con lines=43* command before you start MSD. Using a compact display can be especially helpful if you plan to check on memory use. Unlike some programs, MSD maintains the screen mode you set under MS-DOS, and setting the screen to 43 lines means you can easily see the entire memory map without scrolling.

To take a tour of MSD and see some of its capabilities, do the following:

1. Start by using a menu command. Press Alt-U to open the Utilities menu. Press Enter to choose the Memory Block Display command. A screen like the following should appear:

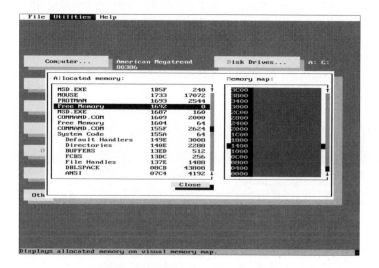

2. Now take a look at exactly where, in memory, various programs and device drivers are residing. Use the direction keys or your mouse to scroll through the list in the box labeled *Allocated memory*. As you highlight different entries, notice that their locations in memory are highlighted in the box on the right, labeled *Memory map*. Press Enter when you've seen enough.

3. For another exercise, press P to view a report on your computer. Note the name of your BIOS manufacturer. Press Enter to remove the report.

4. Press Alt-U to open the Utilities menu again, but this time, press B to choose the Memory Browser command. A box like this appears:

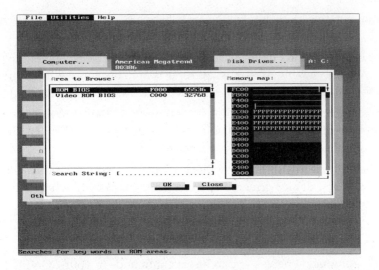

5. Now you're going to search memory for a specific set of characters. This example assumes that the Area To Browse box includes a highlighted entry for ROM BIOS:

   ☐ If you have a mouse, click on the dotted line to the right of the text *Search String*.

   ☐ If you don't have a mouse, press Tab twice to move the cursor to the dotted line.

6. Type (uppercase or lowercase doesn't matter) the name of your ROM BIOS manufacturer. A report like the following should appear:

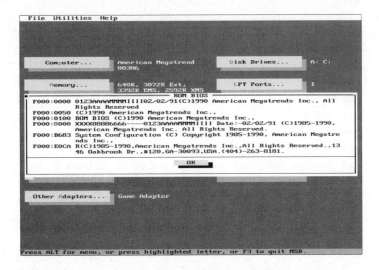

Press Enter when you've seen enough. Press F3 to quit.

To round out this description of MSD, here's a quick look at the menu commands:

- Print Report on the File menu lets you choose to print a copy of the report you are viewing. (Initially, all reports are checkmarked, meaning you'll get a report covering all choices on the MSD Startup screen.)

- Choosing one of the startup files (for example, CONFIG.SYS) listed at the bottom of the File menu displays the contents of the file. The Find File command does the same for other files.

- On the Utilities menu, Memory Block Display, as you've seen, lists the programs and device drivers in memory and shows you where they are located.

- Memory Browser lets you search ROM for a specific string of text or numbers.

- Insert Command enables you to insert commands in your CONFIG.SYS or AUTOEXEC.BAT file. This is not the best way to edit these files, however. The MS-DOS Editor is much faster and better.

- Test Printer lets you choose a printer type and printer port and send a test—a set of ASCII characters—to the printer, to verify that all is working correctly. (This command can be useful if you need a printout of the lower 127 ASCII characters; if you want all 255, success will depend on your printer.)

- Black & White (or the F5 key) displays MSD in black and white.

MSD was originally designed to help Microsoft's technical support staff find out about the computer configurations of people calling for help. As you can see, however, it's also a safe way to satisfy your curiosity and find out numerous details about your computer and the devices attached to it.

Making it work the way you want

The commands grouped in this category are all configuration commands—those that help you define your computer setup to MS-DOS so that programs and devices run correctly. Version 6 of MS-DOS includes two types of configuration commands. There are the traditional ones you've used for years to install devices and provide system settings, such as the number of files and the number of buffers, and there is a new set of six commands (Include, Menucolor, Menudefault, Menuitem, Numlock, and Submenu) that help you create a startup menu and define configuration "blocks," each of which lets you start the computer in a unique way—for example, choose whether to connect to a network or choose whether to enable expanded memory. The best of these new commands, Numlock, performs a service that's been needed for years: turning off the Num

Lock key at startup. (No more pressing a direction key only to see a string of 4s, 2s, 6s, or 8s on the screen!)

All of these configuration commands are described, in alphabetic order, in the later section headed "System configuration commands." Cross-references to configuration commands described in other chapters are also included.

Using configuration commands

Whenever you install or upgrade version 5 or 6 of MS-DOS, the Setup program creates or modifies your CONFIG.SYS and AUTOEXEC.BAT files to reflect the new status of MS-DOS on your system. CONFIG.SYS (and AUTOEXEC.BAT) can, of course, be modified at other times as well. If you use the version 6 Mem-Maker command or if you would like to be able to choose from alternate startup configurations, you will almost certainly edit CONFIG.SYS as part of the optimizing or customizing process.

Any file—CONFIG.SYS, AUTOEXEC.BAT, or another batch file—that you expect MS-DOS to read must, of course, be saved in plain ASCII, or plain-text, format—that is, the file cannot contain any application-specific formatting or editing codes that MS-DOS does not recognize. To edit an MS-DOS file, you can use the MS-DOS Editor, another plain-text editor (such as Edlin, if you're so inclined), or any word processor that permits saving without formatting. For ease of editing, however, the MS-DOS Editor or a similar plain-text editor will work better than your word processor because the Editor provides exactly the type of no-hassle save you need, whereas you'll have to specifically instruct your word processor to save CONFIG.SYS without formatting.

Editing CONFIG.SYS through version 5

Through version 5 of MS-DOS, using configuration commands is a relatively simple matter of including those you need and omitting those you don't. That sounds simple, but sometimes, especially if you're tinkering with loading device drivers and programs into upper memory, you can produce a significant pain in your head if a change you make causes your system to stall during startup. Through version 5, remember, MS-DOS does not support the version 6 safety feature called a clean boot—that is, a boot procedure that, when you press F5, bypasses both CONFIG.SYS and AUTOEXEC.BAT. In versions 5 and earlier, therefore, if your system hangs during startup, you cannot boot from the hard disk. At that point, your only alternatives are to reformat the hard disk and reinstall MS-DOS or to boot from a system-formatted emergency floppy. The latter option, of course, assumes that you had the prescience to create such a disk before making that cursed change to CONFIG.SYS.

If you have version 5 or earlier of MS-DOS, the soundest approach to editing CONFIG.SYS involves the following two precautions:

- If the installation manual for a program or a device tells you how to change CONFIG.SYS, follow the instructions to the letter and double-check your typing before saving the file.

- If you're experimenting on your own, particularly with memory, create a system disk for use in drive A and copy CONFIG.SYS and AUTOEXEC.BAT to it. If the floppy disk is already formatted, transfer the MS-DOS system files to it with the command *sys a:*. If the floppy needs formatting, swat two flies with the same blow with the command *format a: /s*. Now you can experiment all you want on the floppy, knowing that you can always boot from the old version of CONFIG.SYS on your hard disk whenever you want.

Personal experience shows this to be sound advice.

Editing CONFIG.SYS in version 6

Beginning with version 6 of MS-DOS, your creative horizons expand dramatically where CONFIG.SYS is concerned. At the same time, your need for the safety net provided by a bootable floppy decreases to nil (or close to it) thanks to both the clean boot described in the preceding section and an interactive boot feature that allows you (by pressing the F8 key) to walk through CONFIG.SYS line by line, choosing whether you want each command to be carried out. All this and more is described in Chapter 16, "Controlling Startups." For your convenience, however, the following summary describes options that are available only in version 6 of MS-DOS.

Changing your configuration

You can customize loading of CONFIG.SYS at boot time. This feature alone means that you no longer have to wish you could choose configuration commands at startup, nor do you have to create alternate boot disks or rename different configuration files to reboot with a specific system setup. If your alternatives are few—for instance, you simply want to be able to choose whether to enable expanded memory or install network drivers—press F8 to step through CONFIG.SYS. If your alternatives are more demanding—for instance, you want to choose which of several different sets of drivers to install, with memory use optimized for each configuration—create a multiple-configuration CONFIG.SYS file with a separate installation block for each choice. Place any commands that you always want carried out in a block named [common], as shown in the following (simple) example:

```
[MENU]
MENUITEM=STANDARD
MENUITEM=RAM-DRIVE

[COMMON]
DEVICE=C:\DOS\SETVER.EXE
DEVICE=C:\DOS\HIMEM.SYS
DEVICE=C:\DOS\EMM386.EXE NOEMS
DOS=HIGH,UMB
SHELL=C:\DOS\COMMAND.COM C:\DOS\ /P
NUMLOCK=OFF

[STANDARD]
DEVICEHIGH=C:\DOS\ANSI.SYS
FILES=30
BUFFERS=30
LASTDRIVE=E

[RAM-DRIVE]
DEVICEHIGH=C:\DOS\RAMDRIVE.SYS 1024 /E
FILES=40
BUFFERS=20
LASTDRIVE=E
```

Chapter 16 tells you how to construct a CONFIG.SYS file like this one; the commands are described later in this chapter, except for the DOS=HIGH,UMB line (which is described in Chapter 11).

Special characters

Beginning in version 6, MS-DOS also has the ability to interpret two special characters—the semicolon and the question mark—when you include them in CONFIG.SYS.

■ A semicolon (;) at the beginning of a line indicates that the line represents a comment and is not to be processed. The semicolon is an alternative to the REM command usually used to disable a command or insert an explanatory note. Using it will neaten up your CONFIG.SYS file. For example,

```
;DEVICEHIGH=C:\DOS\RAMDRIVE.SYS 1024 /E
```

causes MS-DOS to ignore the command that would otherwise load RAMDRIVE.SYS into upper memory and create a 1024-K RAM drive in extended memory. At the same time, the command remains in CONFIG.SYS, so all you need to do to reactivate it is delete the semicolon. This small character can also prove useful if you want to try out two different forms of a command to see which works better on your system— for instance, whether creating a smaller SMARTDRV.EXE cache has any effect on speed. Insert both commands in CONFIG.SYS. Disable one and test the system, and then disable the other and try again.

■ A question mark (?) inserted immediately *after* the name of a command causes MS-DOS to stop and ask whether you want the command processed. If you don't want to use the F8 key to step through an entire CONFIG.SYS file, a question mark inserted in strategic spots will serve just as well in helping you control whether certain commands are carried out. For example, the command

```
DEVICE?=C:\DOS\EMM386.EXE RAM /HIGHSCAN
```

causes MS-DOS to ask whether you want to install EMM386.EXE and provide access to both extended and expanded memory with the RAM switch and to scan for extra available UMBs. You can use the question mark to control CONFIG.SYS processing of alternate forms of the same command—for example, the following two commands in CONFIG.SYS

```
DEVICE?=C:\DOS\EMM386.EXE RAM
DEVICE?=C:\DOS\EMM386.EXE NOEMS
```

would allow you to load EMM386.EXE as a UMB provider but let you choose whether to enable expanded memory use, as well, at each start-up. However, if you think you will do this more than once or twice, a multiple-configuration CONFIG.SYS would be better.

Putting MS-DOS on autopilot

Autopilot means batch files, of course. A batch file, even one so special as AUTOEXEC.BAT, is simply a collection of commands that MS-DOS interprets and carries out, one after the other. The only time MS-DOS stops during the processing of a batch file is when it comes to a Pause command or (in version 6 only) a Choice command that requests the user to select from a set of options by pressing the key that corresponds to the person's choice.

Batch files can be as short as one line or long enough to fill several pages with text. Regardless of length, however, they must always

■ Be saved in plain-text (ASCII) format.

■ Contain commands that MS-DOS can recognize and carry out.

Beyond this, batch files can be constructed to do anything you want them to do. They are your means of shaping MS-DOS to your own needs and preferences in computer work. The only other part of MS-DOS that offers such customization is the macro-generating feature of the Doskey utility.

Batch files are, to some extent, programs that you write using the language of MS-DOS. They differ from the COM and EXE files that represent executable programs in several respects, however:

- They consist of readable words, parameters, and switches rather than the indecipherable symbols typical of executable program files.

- They always have the BAT extension.

- They are carried out by a special part of COMMAND.COM called the batch interpreter.

- They can contain certain special commands, such as If and Goto, that let you control the order of execution. Some of these commands, such as Echo and Set, can be used from the command line; most, however, can be carried out only by the batch interpreter.

Although each batch file you create runs the same commands each time, you are not limited to the same unchanging output. With the help of replaceable parameters—which you insert in commands as %1, %2, %3, and so on through %9—you can make any batch file accept variable information, such as drive, path, and file specifications. Replaceable parameters are nothing more than placeholders for information you provide when you type the command that runs the batch file. If, for example, you use %1 and %2 as placeholders for two different variables, you run the batch file by typing its name, followed by the actual values you want MS-DOS to substitute for %1 and %2 as it carries out the commands in the file. For example, suppose you include the following command in a batch file:

```
dir %1 %2
```

Thanks to the replaceable parameters %1 and %2, this line is the equivalent of any Dir command you can type that includes two variables—file specifications, switches, or a combination of the two. You can, for example, substitute a drive, path, and file specification for %1 and substitute any valid switch in the Dir command for %2. By way of example, the following commands show just a few ways this line could be interpreted within the batch file:

```
dir c:\myfiles\*.txt /od
dir a: /ah
dir /ah /os
dir findme.doc /s
dir c:\bigdir /p
```

And so on, and so on.

For more information on batch files and how you construct them, refer to Chapter 18, "Batch Files and Macros," and Chapter 19, "Controlling Batch Files."

Making life easier

Making life easier means using Doskey, the command recorder and macro facility, to save keystrokes. If you've ever attempted to remember and retype the syntax of some of the lengthier MS-DOS commands, you'll appreciate knowing that using Doskey can help you keep your blood pressure under control. Can you, for example, remember everything you need to know about editing an EMM386.EXE line in CONFIG.SYS? How do you type the Xcopy command that turns off archive attributes, copies files edited on or after a specific date, and duplicates a branch of the directory tree, empty subdirectories included? And if you have version 5, what's the Backup command that formats unformatted disks, creates a log file, and backs up all files in all subdirectories of the source directory, but only if they've been edited on or after a specified date? With Doskey, you don't have to worry about any of this. You can list and review commands you've typed, select a specific command to rerun, edit a previous command, and even save long commands as macros you run with a few keystrokes. You can, for instance, use the following Doskey command:

```
doskey sos=fasthelp $1
```

to create a macro that produces abbreviated help for version 6 whenever you type *sos* followed by the name of an MS-DOS command.

When you load Doskey, you load a small (4-K) memory-resident program that creates its own private buffer, into which go copies of all the commands you type and execute from that point on. If you use the default buffer size of 512 bytes, Doskey can remember about two or three dozen commands and display them, numbered for your convenience, whenever you press the F7 key. If you want to rerun an earlier command, press F9, type the number of the command you want, and press Enter twice. You can clear the buffer whenever you want, by pressing Alt-F7. This capability, combined with the ability to redirect a list of Doskey commands to a file, provides you with an easy way of creating and "debugging" a batch file. Clear the buffer and execute each command (other than remarks) that you want to include in the batch file. When you know the commands work together to produce the results you want, redirect the command list from the buffer to a file. Edit the file, adding replaceable parameters and remarks, and save it for future use.

Details on Doskey, including special keystrokes and ways to edit a command, are in Chapter 18, "Batch Files and Macros." In that chapter, you'll also find more information on using Doskey to create batch files and macros.

Having fun with MS-DOS and making it more useful too

In this context, having fun with MS-DOS means using input redirection to get input from a source other than the keyboard and using output redirection or piping to send output somewhere other than the screen. Perhaps the process doesn't sound exactly festive, but it beats having fun with Dick and Jane.

Input redirection usually means telling MS-DOS to use a file as input. Redirection of this type isn't often used, but when it is, it is generally associated with the Sort command, which can sort columns (as in a database) either alphabetically or numerically. Output redirection, which is far more common than input redirection, is usually used to send the output of a command to a file. You can also redirect output to the printer if you don't feel like using the Print command. Piping is something of a hybrid between input and output redirection. It sets up a temporary link between commands by turning the output of one into the input of another. The most obvious use of a pipe occurs when you use the More command, which takes the output of another command, such as Dir or Mem, and pauses scrolling after each screenful, waiting until you press a key to resume scrolling.

Redirection and piping make use of three special symbols:

- The < symbol tells MS-DOS to redirect input, as in the following

```
C:\>sort < c:\bigbucks\sales.txt
```

which tells the Sort command to sort the data (assume a column of numbers) it finds in a plain-text file named SALES.TXT in the C:\BIGBUCKS directory.

- The > symbol tells MS-DOS to redirect output, as in the following

```
C:\>dir a:\*.doc > alist.txt
```

which sends the output of a Dir command that lists all DOC files on the disk in drive A to a file named ALIST.TXT in the root directory of drive C. Redirecting the output of the Dir command can be particularly useful when you want a quick means of listing the files on a floppy disk: Type the Dir command you need and redirect the output to the printer with a command like the following:

```
C:\>dir a: > prn
```

- The ¦ symbol is placed between two commands to tell MS-DOS to use the output of the command to the left of the pipe as the input of the command to the right, as in the following

```
C:\>find /i "heroes" \fables\legends.txt ¦ find /i "beowulf"
```

which uses the Find command twice—first, to find every line in \FABLES\LEGENDS.DOC that contains the word *heroes*, and then to sift through each matching line for the word *beowulf*. You can use Find with a formatted file, such as one produced with a word processor, but be prepared to see odd symbols or truncated lines and to hear the occasional beep. Another common use of the pipe symbol is with the Type command, which displays the contents of a file, followed by the More command, as shown on the next page.

```
C:\>type \fables\legends.txt ¦ more
```

This example would stop scrolling of the LEGENDS.TXT file after each screenful. Actual readability of the file would, of course, be affected by any formatting codes embedded in the file by a word processor. You'll also be interested to note that you can scroll through a file with More and the input-redirection symbol, like this:

```
C:\>more < \fables\legends.txt
```

Here you're telling More to take its input from the file. When you use More, use whichever form of the command you prefer.

As you can see from these examples, redirection and piping enable you to bypass the normal keyboard/screen defaults for input and output. For more details on redirection, and on the three filter commands (Find, Sort, and More) often used with redirection symbols, refer to Chapter 17, "Redirection, Pipes, and Filters."

The commands described in the remainder of this chapter all deal with some aspect of system configuration and control. They are grouped in the categories outlined above.

Finding out about your computer

This category has a single entry, the Microsoft Diagnostics utility.

Microsoft Diagnostics (MSD)—version 6 only

As mentioned at the beginning of this chapter, Microsoft Diagnostics, or MSD, is a tool for peering at the configuration and memory use of your computer. The command syntax is a simple *msd*. No switches or parameters are required, as long as the directory containing MSD.EXE is in the current path. For a description of MSD and its uses, refer to the earlier section titled "Everything you ever wanted to know about your computer."

System configuration commands

This category includes the following: Buffers; Country (see Chapter 10); Device; Devicehigh (see Chapter 11); DOS (Dos, see Chapter 11); Drive Parameters (Drivparm); File Control Blocks (Fcbs); Files; Include; Install; Lastdrive; Menu Color (Menucolor); Menu Default (Menudefault); Menu Item (Menuitem); Number Lock (Numlock); Set Version (Setver) and SETVER.EXE; Shell; Stacks; Submenu; Switches. All but Country, Devicehigh, and Dos are described, in alphabetic order, below.

Buffers

The Buffers command sets aside a specified number of storage areas—buffers—for holding information read from or about to be written to disk. A part of MS-DOS since version 2.0, the Buffers command is in many respects a limited precursor of the SMARTDRV.EXE disk cache, which appeared in version 5. Like SMARTDRV.EXE, Buffers can use both a normal cache and a secondary cache, in which it stores "read-ahead" portions of files—information from a file requested by a program, but located beyond the part of the file actually requested. At this point, however, Buffers and SMARTDRV.EXE part company. Buffers creates a number of small holding areas, each of which holds about 530 bytes.

On 8086 and 80286 systems, setting an optimum number of buffers can speed performance by limiting physical disk access. Because each buffer requires a certain amount of memory, however, too many buffers can slow performance by reducing the memory available to programs. This impact is less critical in versions 5 and 6 of MS-DOS, both of which create buffers in the HMA, if space there is available and if you don't specify more than 48 buffers.

Determining the best number of buffers for your system generally requires experimenting to achieve a balance between performance and memory requirements. As a starting point, you can use the following guidelines:

- For programs such as word processors, specify 10 to 20 buffers.
- For programs that use many files or for systems on which you create a lot of directories, specify 20 to 30 buffers.

In some cases, the manual for a program will tell you the optimum setting to use.

Command syntax

Buffers can be used only from CONFIG.SYS. The syntax for the command is as follows:

buffers=*primary buffers*[,*secondary buffers*]

primary buffers sets the number of disk buffers. You can specify 1 through 99. Default settings, which are based on the amount of conventional memory in the system, are as follows:

Conventional memory	Primary buffers	Memory used (bytes)
Less than 128 K on a system with 360-K disk drive(s)	2	N/A
Less than 128 K on a system with drive(s) larger than 360 K	3	N/A
128 K to 255 K	5	2672
256 K to 511 K	10	5328
512 K to 640 K	15	7984

secondary buffers sets the number of "read-ahead" buffers; note that this value, if included, must be preceded by a comma. If you specify secondary buffers, the recommended number is 8. The default is 0. Do not specify secondary buffers if you are using a SMARTDRV.EXE disk cache.

Examples

Include in CONFIG.SYS:	To:
BUFFERS=25	Set the number of primary buffers to 25.
BUFFERS=20,8	Set the number of primary buffers to 20 and the number of secondary buffers to 8.

Country: See Chapter 10, "Devices"

Device

The Device command appears in CONFIG.SYS more often than any other command for the simple reason that you need it or its version 5 and 6 companion, Devicehigh, to identify any non-native device driver to MS-DOS. Without a Device (or Devicehigh) command in CONFIG.SYS, MS-DOS is unable to use any of the add-on devices you attach to your system. More important, perhaps, Device is the version 5 and 6 tool you need to load HIMEM.SYS, which enables use of extended memory, and EMM386.EXE, which acts as your UMB provider and can simulate expanded memory for programs that need it. Device is also required if you need to provide the double-buffering capability for SMARTDRV.EXE that allows SCSI and other disk controllers to use high memory provided by EMM386.EXE. And if you have version 6 of MS-DOS, Device (or Devicehigh) is also related to using DoubleSpace, Interlnk, and Power.

Device supports the following MS-DOS version 6 device drivers (references to the chapters in which they are described are in the column to the right):

Device driver	Chapter
ANSI.SYS	10
DISPLAY.SYS	10
DRIVER.SYS	10
DBLSPACE.SYS	8
EGA.SYS	10
EMM386.EXE	11

(continued)

Device driver	Chapter
HIMEM.SYS	11
INTERLNK.EXE	7
POWER.EXE	10
RAMDRIVE.SYS	11
SETVER.EXE	This chapter
SMARTDRV.EXE	11

These are, of course, in addition to any third-party drivers you install with Device to control a mouse, scanner, joystick, or other add-on hardware.

If you want to push your system beyond the bare essentials, Device is necessary. To understand all your options in terms of loading device drivers and conserving memory, refer to the Devicehigh command, in Chapter 11, as well.

Command syntax

Device can be used only from CONFIG.SYS. The syntax of the command is as follows:

device=[*drive:*][*path*]*filename* [*parameters*]

drive, *path*, and *filename* specify the location of the device driver to load.

parameters represents any required or optional parameters you want to specify for the device driver.

Examples

Include in CONFIG.SYS:	To:

`DEVICE=C:\DOS\HIMEM.SYS`
`DEVICE=C:\DOS\EMM386.EXE NOEMS`
`DOS=HIGH,UMB`
	Enable use of extended memory and the upper memory area on a system with at least 350 K of extended memory. The order of the commands here is critical.

`DEVICE=C:\DOS\ANSI.SYS`	Load the ANSI.SYS expanded keyboard and screen driver into conventional memory.
`DEVICE=C:\DOS\POWER.EXE`	Load the version 6 power-management device driver. Even though you use the Device command, POWER.EXE loads into upper memory by default, if enough memory is available. To specify loading into conventional memory, you would add the /low switch to the command line.

(continued)

Include in CONFIG.SYS:	To:
`DEVICE?=C:\DOS\RAMDRIVE.SYS 1024 /E`	Cause MS-DOS to prompt for confirmation (with the ? symbol) before loading the RAMDRIVE.SYS device driver into conventional memory and creating a 1024-K RAM drive in extended memory. This example is usable only with version 6 and is included to show the use of both the question mark and driver parameters in a Device command.

Devicehigh: See Chapter 11, "Memory"

Dos: See Chapter 11, "Memory"

Drive Parameters (Drivparm)

Drive Parameters (Drivparm), one of the least used commands, can and often does go unnoticed throughout a person's career with MS-DOS. The only time you need it is when you have to define or redefine a block device—a device that handles information in chunks rather than a byte at a time. Where MS-DOS is concerned, you can consider a block device to be synonymous with a disk drive.

When you use Drivparm, you change the values in an internal table that MS-DOS checks for the size, heads, and other characteristics of a disk or tape drive. These values, in turn, help the operating system read from or write to the drive reliably. You do not need Drivparm to define or identify your main floppy and hard drives, however. The command is necessary for drives identified to MS-DOS through a Device command in CONFIG.SYS. Needless to say, Drivparm, if you use it, must follow the Device command, if any, that loads the device's driver. In all cases, the characteristics you define for a block device must be physically supported by the drive. You cannot, for instance, decide to tell MS-DOS that external drive F supports 1.44-MB floppies if the hardware itself would make a liar out of you. As you can see from the switches described later, you might have to consult your hardware manuals for some details.

Command syntax

Drivparm can be used only from CONFIG.SYS. The syntax of the command is as follows:

drivparm=/d:*drivenumber* /c /f:*formfactor* /h:*heads* /i /n /s:*sectors* /t:*tracks*

/d:drivenumber is a value from 0 through 255 that identifies the drive you want to redefine. Drives are numbered as follows: A = 0, B = 1, C = 2, and so on. This switch must always appear first in the Drivparm command.

/c specifies that the drive has the ability to detect whether the door is closed.

/f:formfactor identifies the drive type, as follows:

Value	Drive type
0	160-K, 180-K, 320-K, or 360-K 5.25-inch disk
1	1.2-MB 5.25-inch disk
2	720-K 3.5-inch disk
5	Hard disk
6	Tape drive
7	1.44-MB 3.5-inch disk
8	Read/write optical disk
9	2.88-MB 3.5-inch disk

If you omit this switch, MS-DOS assumes 2. (If you're wondering what happened to values 3 and 4, they're gone; they were once used to refer to 8-inch floppies.)

/h:heads specifies the number of read/write heads. Values for *heads* can be 1 through 99; the default depends on the drive type you specify with the /f switch.

/i identifies an "electronically compatible" 3.5-inch floppy drive that works with the existing drive controller in your system. You need the /i switch if your computer's ROM BIOS does not support 3.5-inch disk drives.

/n indicates that the drive is nonremovable.

/s:sectors specifies the number of sectors per track and can be in the range 1 through 99. The default depends on the drive type you specify with the /f switch.

/t:tracks specifies the number of tracks per side. The default depends on the drive type you specify with the /f switch.

Examples

Include in CONFIG.SYS:	To:
`DRIVPARM=/D:3 /F:7`	Define a 1.44-MB floppy disk drive as drive D, assuming the defaults for heads, sectors, and tracks.
`DRIVPARM=/D:1 /S:9 /T:80`	Redefine drive B with 9 sectors per track and 80 tracks per side. The hardware must be able to support this capacity.

File Control Blocks (Fcbs)

You use the File Control Blocks (Fcbs) command to tell MS-DOS how many files it can open at the same time using internal file-information structures known as *file control blocks,* or *FCBs.* FCBs contain such housekeeping information as the file-name and file size. Important as FCBs sound, the Fcbs command is really necessary only with older programs that rely on FCBs for storing information about open files. Most programs rely on a newer, simpler method that involves managing open files with the use of an ID code called a *handle.* Include an Fcbs command in CONFIG.SYS only if a program specifically requires you to do so. Otherwise, set the number of files that can be open at the same time with the Files command, described in the next entry.

Command syntax

Fcbs can be used only from CONFIG.SYS. The following syntax describes the Fcbs command as it exists in versions 5 and 6 of MS-DOS; in earlier versions of MS-DOS, the syntax differs. If you have version 4 or earlier, refer to your documentation. If you have version 5 or 6, the syntax is as follows:

FCBS=*files*

files is the number of files using file control blocks that can be open at one time. You can specify 1 through 255; the default is 4. If you need this command, be sure to specify a large enough number of files. MS-DOS might close the oldest file if the number of open files exceeds the number specified with the Fcbs command.

Example

Include in CONFIG.SYS:	To:
FCBS=8	Set the number of files that can be open using FCBs to 8.

Files

The modern-day version of Fcbs, the Files command tells MS-DOS how many files controlled by file handles can be open at the same time. File handles are 16-bit codes assigned internally by MS-DOS. When a program needs to use a particular file, it uses the handle to identify the file it needs. The number of files you specify determines how much memory is reserved for an internal table that contains handle-based information about open files. The larger the number of files, obviously, the more memory is reserved.

Your CONFIG.SYS file might well contain a Files command, placed there by the person who set up your computer or, perhaps, by an application that requires more than the 8 files set by default. If you have to insert or change a Files command yourself, program documentation usually tells you what value to use.

Command syntax

Files can be used only from CONFIG.SYS. The syntax of the command is simple:

files=*files*

files specifies the number of files that can be open. You can specify 8 (the default) through 255 (too many). Typical settings are in the 20 to 30 range. If you run Windows, you might need a setting as high as 40.

Example

Include in CONFIG.SYS:	To:
FILES=30	Set the number of files that can be open at the same time to 30.

Include—version 6 only

The Include command is usable only in CONFIG.SYS and only if you've defined multiple configuration blocks, as described in Chapter 16, "Controlling Startups." The purpose of Include is to help you limit the amount of repetition in a CONFIG.SYS file. To use Include, you first define a set of commands as a named block in a multiple configuration file—essentially creating a CONFIG.SYS "subroutine." Once you've defined this subroutine, you can then run the commands it contains from within any other block in CONFIG.SYS by inserting a simple INCLUDE=SUBROUTINE command wherever you want those particular commands to be carried out.

Include is a useful aid in simplifying and modularizing your CONFIG.SYS file. By eliminating the need to type the same commands in several blocks, Include helps you see the unique parts of each configuration block. Include can also be valuable in helping you determine whether various startup configurations do or do not work together. Overall, however, unless your CONFIG.SYS file is long and complex or you really enjoy organizing the commands in CONFIG.SYS, you probably won't find Include as beneficial as some of the other new configuration commands in version 6 of MS-DOS—the Menuitem command, for example, which lets you define and name different startup options, or the soothing Numlock command that turns the Num Lock key off for you.

NOTE: If you want some control over whether certain CONFIG.SYS commands are carried out but you don't have the time or inclination to sort the file into blocks and use the Include command, consider putting the question mark to work. Remember that a question mark after the name of a configuration command causes MS-DOS to prompt for confirmation before carrying out the command.

Command syntax

Include can be used only from CONFIG.SYS. The syntax of the command is as follows:

include=*blockname*

blockname is the name of the configuration block containing the commands you want to carry out from another block.

Example

The following shows a sample CONFIG.SYS file in which a base configuration block is called with the Include command in two different startup options:

```
[menu]
menuitem=no_frills,Basic Startup
menuitem=ramdrive,Start RAM drive,No ANSI

[base_config]
device=c:\dos\himem.sys
dos=high,umb
devicehigh=c:\mouse\mouse.sys
buffers=20
lastdrive=F
numlock=off

[no_frills]
include=base_config
device=c:\dos\emm386.exe ram
devicehigh=c:\dos\ansi.sys

[ramdrive]
include=base_config
device=c:\dos\emm386.exe noems
devicehigh=c:\dos\ramdrive.sys 1024 /e
```

Install

The Install command provides an alternative to loading memory-resident programs from the command line or from AUTOEXEC.BAT. When you load a program with Install, MS-DOS does not create an environment (block of information about system settings, such as the current path and prompt), so you can save some (usually small) amount of memory. Although Install might seem the practical choice, balance its use against the amount of conventional memory you can save by loading the same program into UMBs with the Loadhigh command. Install does not support loading into upper memory, so if you figure that out of sight is as good as out of mind, Loadhigh might provide the better solution, even if it does use some upper memory.

You can use the Install command with the following programs: Keyb, Nlsfunc, Share, and Fastopen. It also works with programs such as Doskey, but you should avoid its use with other programs unless your documentation indicates that you can use Install. To avoid problems, do not use Install with programs that use shortcut keys or environment variables or that rely on COMMAND.COM to handle critical errors (such as "no disk in drive" or "I'm about to blow up").

NOTE: All Install commands are loaded after any Device command and before the command interpreter.

Command Syntax

Install can be used only from CONFIG.SYS. The syntax is as follows:

install=[*drive:*][*path*]*filename* [*parameters*]

drive, path, and *filename* specify the location of the program file. Include the filename extension.

parameters represents any required or optional parameters you specify as part of the program's command line.

Examples

Include in CONFIG.SYS:	To:
`INSTALL=C:\DOS\FASTOPEN.EXE C:`	Start the MS-DOS Fastopen program for drive C. Fastopen keeps track of file locations to help speed up disk access.

`INSTALL=C:\DOS\SHARE.EXE`
 	
And include in AUTOEXEC.BAT:
 	
`LH /L:2 C:\DOS\SHARE`
	Enable file-sharing. Note that the Loadhigh command shown for AUTOEXEC.BAT would do the same job, but position SHARE.EXE in region 2 of the computer's upper memory area.

Lastdrive

The Lastdrive command defines the highest letter that MS-DOS can use in referring to disk drives. By default, MS-DOS recognizes one letter more than the highest drive letter on your system. So, for example, if you have drives A, B, and C, MS-DOS recognizes the letters A through D by default. Although one letter more than the number of physical drives would seem to be adequate, this is very often not the case. Bear in mind that drive letters refer to logical drives. Logical drives are not always the same as physical drives. If you regularly access network drives, for example, each of the drives you connect to requires a drive letter while you are using it. If you create one or more RAM drives, each RAM drive requires its own drive letter. If you use DoubleSpace (in version 6) to compress a drive, you need drive letters for both the compressed and uncompressed portions of the affected drive. And, of course, if you created an extended MS-DOS partition some time in the past, you already know that each logical drive created within that partition needs its own drive letter. Given all these possibilities, it's easy to see that a mere four or five drive letters could be used up quickly. On the other hand, you probably want to bear in mind that each drive letter you allow for requires some small amount of memory. MS-DOS allows for a maximum of 26 possible drive letters (A through Z). If you reserve space for them all, Lastdrive will require about 2 K of conventional memory.

Command syntax

Lastdrive can be used only from CONFIG.SYS. The syntax of the command is simple:

> lastdrive=*letter*

letter is the highest drive letter you want MS-DOS to use. You can specify any letter through Z.

Example

Include in CONFIG.SYS:	To:
LASTDRIVE=M	Set M as the highest drive letter MS-DOS can recognize.

Menu Color (Menucolor)—version 6 only

The Menu Color (Menucolor) command, present only in version 6, lets you set the text and background colors MS-DOS uses when it displays the startup menu choices you define as part of a menu block at the beginning of your CONFIG.SYS file. These choices, as described in Chapter 16, "Controlling Startups," allow you to choose from alternative configurations by pressing the number corresponding to the menu option you want. Menucolor provides the decorative part of this menu building by letting you set the colors used in the menu. The command itself is simple to use and understand. The only restriction on it is that Menucolor can appear only in the menu block portion of your CONFIG.SYS file, as shown in the example later in this chapter.

Command syntax

As already mentioned, Menucolor can be used only from CONFIG.SYS. The syntax of the command is as follows:

> menucolor=*text*[,*background*]

text defines the color used for the menu text; *background* defines the background color on which the text is displayed. The default is white text on a black background. To display a different text color and, optionally, a different background color, specify for each a value corresponding to the following colors:

Color number	Color	Color number	Color
0	Black	8	Gray
1	Blue	9	Bright blue
2	Green	10	Bright green
3	Cyan (blue-green)	11	Bright cyan
4	Red	12	Bright red
5	Magenta (purple)	13	Bright magenta
6	Brown	14	Yellow
7	White	15	Bright white

You cannot omit the *text* parameter and specify only a background color. If you do, MS-DOS uses the background color you specify as the color for *text* and keeps the default background. If you do specify a background color, the color covers the entire screen. Both text and background colors remain in effect until processing of CONFIG.SYS is complete. If you choose a color number from 8 through 15, be prepared for a surprise. On some displays, these colors blink.

Examples

Include in CONFIG.SYS:	To:
[menu] menuitem=no_frills,Basic Startup menuitem=ramdrive,Start RAM Drive menucolor=15,3	Display a menu including two choices, *Basic Startup* and *Start RAM Drive*, in bright white text on a cyan background.
[menu] menuitem=no_frills,Basic Startup menuitem=ramdrive,Start RAM Drive menucolor=2	Display the same menu, but in green characters on a black background (the default).

Menu Default (Menudefault)—version 6 only

The Menu Default (Menudefault) command, also available only in version 6, lets you automate the processing of a multi-configuration CONFIG.SYS. You use Menudefault to set the default menu choice and, if you want, to specify the amount of time MS-DOS is to wait before processing CONFIG.SYS with the startup configuration indicated by the default. To use Menudefault, you have to set up your CONFIG.SYS file with a menu block and with a separate configuration block for each startup option. The command must appear in the menu block of CONFIG.SYS. Menudefault can be helpful if you often start with the same configuration and would prefer not to babysit the computer, waiting to press a key, each time you boot or reboot.

When you use Menudefault, MS-DOS highlights the default choice when it displays the startup menu. If you also specify a timeout period, a countdown appears below and to the right of the menu, like this:

```
MS-DOS 6 Startup Menu
=====================

   1. Basic Startup
   2. Start RAM Drive

Enter a choice: 1      Time remaining: 15
```

When the count reaches 00, the default menu choice is carried out. If you're experimenting with different configuration blocks and your CONFIG.SYS includes a Menudefault line with a specified timeout, you can disable the line temporarily by preceding it with a REM or a semicolon.

Command syntax

The syntax of the Menudefault command is as follows:

menudefault=*blockname*[,*timeout*]

blockname is the name of the configuration block to set as the default. Remember to type the name of the configuration block (the name that appears in square brackets at the beginning of the block). Do not specify any descriptive text that you might have defined with the Menuitem command. (If this sounds confusing to you, refer to the Menuitem command, later in this chapter.)

timeout specifies the amount of time, in seconds, that MS-DOS is to wait before carrying out the default configuration choice. You can specify any value from 0 through 90. If you specify 0, MS-DOS will bypass the menu display completely and swing directly into processing the default configuration. If you don't include a timeout value, MS-DOS will highlight the default choice but will wait until you press Enter before it begins processing.

Examples

Include in CONFIG.SYS:	To:

`[menu]`
`menuitem=no_frills,Basic Startup`
`menuitem=ramdrive,Start RAM Drive`
`menucolor=15,3`
`menudefault=1,15`
	Display a menu including two choices, *Basic Startup* and *Start RAM Drive*, in bright white text on a cyan background. Set *Basic Startup* as the default, which is to be carried out after 15 seconds have elapsed.

`[menu]`
`menuitem=no_frills,Basic Startup`
`menuitem=ramdrive,Start RAM Drive`
`menucolor=2`
`menudefault=2`
	Display the same menu, but in green characters on a black background (the default), and set the default to the block named *ramdrive*. Because no timeout is specified, MS-DOS will highlight the *ramdrive* choice but wait until a key is pressed.

Menu Item (Menuitem)—version 6 only

The Menu Item (Menuitem) command allows you to define a startup option for the menu of a multi-configuration CONFIG.SYS file. When you use Menuitem, you tell MS-DOS, "I want you to offer whatever I define here as a configuration option whenever I start or restart the computer." When you choose a menu item defined with this command, MS-DOS carries out, in this order: any commands that appear without a header or in a block named [common] at the beginning of CONFIG.SYS; all commands in the configuration block specified by the menu item; all commands at the end of CONFIG.SYS that appear in a second, optional, [common] block.

A Menuitem command must always appear in a menu block, as shown in the example later, and it must correspond to the name of a configuration block in CONFIG.SYS. You can use Menuitem parameters both to identify a configuration block and to define the text that MS-DOS displays to represent the option in the startup menu. MS-DOS allows up to nine menu items in a menu block. If you need more than nine startup options (a lot), you can break the menu block into submenus with the Submenu command described later.

Command syntax

As already mentioned, you can use Menuitem only from the menu block in a CONFIG.SYS file. The syntax of the command is as follows:

menuitem=*blockname*[,*menu text*]

blockname is the name of the block that contains the configuration commands you want carried out as part of the startup option indicated by the menu item. The block name can contain up to 70 characters, but it cannot include any spaces or any of the following symbols:

\ / , ; = [ ]

Because a block name simply identifies a configuration block, you'll probably want to keep it short, but descriptive.

menu text defines the text you want MS-DOS to use for the menu item when it displays the startup menu. Like a block name, the menu text can contain up to 70 characters. There are, however, no restrictions on spaces or special characters. If you specify menu text, especially when setting up a computer for an inexperienced user, you'll probably want to make good use of the descriptive potential of 70 characters. MS-DOS reproduces your text exactly, including uppercase and lowercase. If you don't specify any menu text, MS-DOS uses the block name when it displays the menu.

Example

Include in CONFIG.SYS:	To:

```[menu]```
```menuitem=no_frills,Basic Startup```
```menuitem=ramdrive,Start RAM Drive```
	Display a menu including two choices, *Basic Startup* and *Start RAM Drive*.

Number Lock (Numlock)—version 6 only

The Number Lock (Numlock) command controls whether the Num Lock key is turned on or off at startup. If you've been irritated in the past by a Num Lock key that's turned on by default whenever you boot or reboot, use the Numlock command and offer thanks to whoever included it in version 6 of MS-DOS.

Numlock is so simple to use, nothing much really need be said about it. Put it in the menu block if you want Num Lock turned on or off at every startup; put it in a configuration block if you sometimes want Num Lock turned on, other times want it turned off. Numlock can go anywhere in CONFIG.SYS.

If you don't create a multi-configuration CONFIG.SYS, place Numlock wherever you want, or use the question mark, like this:

```
NUMLOCK?=OFF
```

to have MS-DOS ask before turning the Num Lock key off.

Command syntax

The syntax of the Numlock command is as follows:

```
numlock=on or off
```

on tells MS-DOS to turn the Num Lock key on (or leave it on) at startup; off tells MS-DOS to turn the key off (or leave it off).

Example

Include in CONFIG.SYS:	To:

```[menu]```
```menuitem=no_frills,Basic Startup```
```menuitem=ramdrive,Start RAM Drive```
```numlock=off```
	Turn the Num Lock key off each time you start or restart the computer. Notice that the command is in the menu block of the sample CONFIG.SYS file.

```[no_frills]```
```include=base_config```
```device=c:\dos\emm386.exe ram```
```devicehigh=c:\dos\ansi.sys```
```numlock=off```
	Turn the Num Lock key off whenever you use the "no frills" startup configuration. Notice that the command here is in a configuration block of the CONFIG.SYS file. If you put Numlock here, you would leave it out of the menu block.

(continued)

Include in CONFIG.SYS:	To:
| ```
[ramdrive]
include=base_config
device=c:\dos\emm386.exe noems
devicehigh=c:\dos\ramdrive.sys 1024 /e
numlock=on
``` | Turn the Num Lock key on (or ensure that it stays on) whenever you use the "ramdrive" startup configuration. Once again, the Numlock command is in a configuration block, not the menu block. |

Set Version (Setver) and SETVER.EXE

The Set Version (Setver) command, executed by the SETVER.EXE program file, exists to help programs that cannot work with versions 5 and 6 of MS-DOS. Although most programs can run with versions 5 and 6, even if they were designed to run with earlier versions of MS-DOS, some do have difficulties. If the problem is not compatibility (or lack of it), you can use the Setver command to alter a structure called a version table, which then reports to the program that it is running with the version of MS-DOS it needs, instead of the actual MS-DOS version installed on your computer.

Although Setver itself is not a configuration command and can be run from the command line, it is included in this section because it cannot be used at all unless the version table has been loaded into memory, and that is done with a Device command in CONFIG.SYS (*device=c:\dos\setver.exe*). This command is placed in CONFIG.SYS for you by the version 5 and 6 Setup programs. Once the table is in memory, you can display it, add an entry to it, or delete entries from it as required.

Using Setver is not to be done lightly. Changing the MS-DOS version number reported to a program can cause problems with your system. These problems are potentially serious enough that Setver displays a warning message when you change a version number or add a program to the version table. In version 6, the message is as follows (in version 5, the message is quite similar):

```
WARNING - Contact your software vendor for information about whether a
specific program works with MS-DOS 6. It is possible that
Microsoft has not verified whether the program will successfully run if
you use the SETVER command to change the program version number and
version table. If you run the program after changing the version table
in MS-DOS 6, you may lose or corrupt data or introduce system
instabilities. Microsoft is not responsible for any loss or damage, or
for lost or corrupted data.
```

If you proceed, Setver changes the version table, and the change becomes effective the next time you start the system.
```

Command syntax

Assuming that SETVER.EXE is loaded with a Device command in CONFIG.SYS as described earlier, the syntax of the Setver command takes the following forms.

To display the version table, the command is as follows:

setver [*drive:\path*]

To change the version table, the command is as follows:

setver [*drive:\path*]*programname n.nn*

To delete an entry and, optionally, suppress the message accompanying the deletion, the command is as follows:

setver [*drive:\path*]*programname* /delete /quiet

drive and *path* in all instances are the drive and path to the SETVER.EXE file—probably C:\DOS. You should be able to omit this parameter.

programname is the name of the program for which you want to set or delete the MS-DOS version number.

n.nn represents the major and minor version numbers you want MS-DOS to report to the program—for example, 4.01 or 5.00.

/delete, or /d, removes the entry for the specified program from the version table.

/quiet, or /q, suppresses the deletion message that would otherwise be displayed.

Examples

Type:	To:
`C:\>setver`	Display the current version table—assuming that SETVER.EXE has been loaded from CONFIG.SYS.
`C:\>setver c:\dos program.exe /d`	Delete the version-table entry for PROGRAM.EXE.
`A:\>setver program.exe /d /q`	Delete the version-table entry for PROGRAM.EXE, suppressing output of the /d switch.

Shell

The Shell command, usable only from CONFIG.SYS, specifies the name and location of the command interpreter to use. The default, of course, is the MS-DOS COMMAND.COM program, which typically resides (after Setup, a Sys command, or the Format /s command) in the root directory of your boot disk. If COMMAND.COM is your command interpreter and is in the root directory of the boot drive, you need a Shell command in CONFIG.SYS only if you want to specify an environment size or other startup switch for COMMAND.COM. If COMMAND.COM is in your DOS directory and not in the root, you need a Shell command in CONFIG.SYS, even if you want to use COMMAND.COM's default settings. And, of course, you need a Shell command if you want to use an entirely different command interpreter. See Chapter 13 for more information on COMMAND.COM.

Command syntax

The Shell command can be used only from CONFIG.SYS. Its syntax is as follows:

shell=[*drive:*][*path*]*filename* [*parameters*]

drive, path, and *filename* specify the location of the command interpreter to use. You must include at least a filename.

parameters represents any command-line parameters or switches to be carried out when the command interpreter is loaded.

Examples

Include in CONFIG.SYS:	To:
SHELL=C:\DOS\COMMAND.COM C:\DOS\ /P	Tell MS-DOS to use its own COMMAND.COM, which is in the DOS directory, rather than the root, which MS-DOS searches by default. The parameters included here tell MS-DOS to search C:\DOS if it needs to reload part of COMMAND.COM and to make the command interpreter permanent in memory. (See the description of the COMMAND command in Chapter 13 for more information about such switches.)
SHELL=C:\COMMAND.COM /E:512 /P	Tell MS-DOS to use COMMAND.COM, which is in the root directory, but to increase the environment size to 512 bytes and, again, to make the command interpreter permanent.
SHELL=C:\SHELLS\DO-IT.COM	Use the DO-IT.COM command interpreter located in the C:\SHELLS directory.

Stacks

The Stacks command tells MS-DOS how many stacks—small portions of memory used for temporarily saving program information—to set aside for use when hardware interrupts occur. Hardware interrupts are requests for service from devices, such as disk drives, mice, communications ports, or even the micro-processor itself. In a sense, the stacks managed by MS-DOS are like electronic bookmarks or sticky tags. When a hardware interrupt occurs, MS-DOS switches to one of the reserved stacks before giving control of the system to the interrupt handler, the program that services the interrupt request. The interrupt handler, in turn, uses the stack to hold information about the status of the system—essentially marking the computer's place so that it doesn't lose track of what it was doing. When the interrupt has been serviced, the stack is released for use by another interrupt handler. This ongoing process of recycling available stacks is known as *dynamic allocation*. You don't have to worry much about stacks, but if you receive an "Internal Stack Overflow" message, increasing the number of stacks should fix the problem.

Command syntax

The Stacks command can be used only from within CONFIG.SYS. The syntax is as follows:

stacks=*stacks,size*

stacks is the number of stacks to be set aside. You can specify 0 or 8 through 64. Setting aside 0 stacks means that the computer must be able to reserve enough memory for handling hardware interrupts. If you use 0 and your system does not function properly, set a value in the range 8 through 64 (lower is better).

size is the size of each stack in bytes. You can specify 0 (with 0 stacks) or 32 through 512.

MS-DOS uses the following defaults:

Computer	Default stacks
Original IBM PC, PC/XT, or PC-Portable	0
Other computers	9 stacks, each of 128 bytes

Examples

Include in CONFIG.SYS:	To:
STACKS=9,256	Use the default number of stacks (9) but increase the size of each to 256 bytes. Note that the two values are separated by a comma. If your CONFIG.SYS file contains a Stacks command like this, don't mistakenly interpret the command as meaning you have 9,256 stacks.

Submenu—version 6 only

Submenu is one of the half dozen version 6 commands that allow you to create a multi-configuration CONFIG.SYS file. You use Submenu to create a menu item that, instead of being carried out directly, presents the user with a second set of options from which to choose. If you diagram the process, it looks like this:

```
MS-DOS 6 Startup Menu
=====================


   1. Main menu item 1
   2. Main menu item 2
   3. Submenu item        ──────────▶  MS-DOS 6 Startup Menu
                                       =====================


                                         1. Submenu item 1
                                         2. Submenu item 2
```

As you can see from the diagram, Submenu can help you refine startup choices by subordinating some options below other, more important, alternatives. For more details on using Submenu, refer to Chapter 16, "Controlling Startups."

Command syntax

The syntax of the Submenu command, almost identical to the syntax of the Menuitem command, is as follows:

submenu=*blockname*[,*menutext*]

blockname is the name of the configuration block defining the submenu. You can use any name you want, including *submenu* (which can make the logic of your CONFIG.SYS file easier to decipher). The block name can consist of up to 70 characters, but you cannot include spaces or any of these characters:

\ / , ; = [ ]

To carry out its mission, the submenu block must, obviously, contain at least one Menuitem command. If it does not, MS-DOS executes the following: any "universal" commands at the beginning of CONFIG.SYS that apply to all the defined configuration blocks; any commands in a [common] block at the beginning of CONFIG.SYS; any valid configuration commands in the submenu block; any commands in a [common] block at the end of CONFIG.SYS.

menutext defines the text you want MS-DOS to use for the submenu item. Like a block name, the menu text can contain up to 70 characters. There are, however, no restrictions on spaces or special characters. If you specify menu text, especially when setting up a computer for an inexperienced user, you'll probably want to make good use of the descriptive potential of 70 characters. MS-DOS reproduces your text exactly, including uppercase and lowercase. If you don't specify any menu text, MS-DOS uses the block name when it displays the submenu.

Example

The following sample CONFIG.SYS file uses a submenu to allow the user to choose whether to enable expanded memory as part of a basic startup:

```
[menu]
submenu=submenu,Basic Startup
menuitem=ramdrive,Create RAM Drive

[submenu]
menuitem=ems,Yes To Expanded Memory
menuitem=noems,No To Expanded Memory

[common]

device=c:\dos\himem.sys
dos=high,umb
devicehigh=c:\mouse\mouse.sys
buffers=20
lastdrive=M
files=30
numlock=off

[ems]
device=c:\dos\emm386.exe ram

[noems]
device=c:\dos\emm386.exe noems

[ramdrive]
include=noems
device=c:\dos\ramdrive.sys 2048 /e
```

Switches

The Switches command is primarily for use in a few special cases. You need it if you find that certain programs do not work correctly with your enhanced (101-key or 102-key) keyboard or if you use Windows 3.0 *and* move the WINA20.386 file out of the root directory (not a recommended maneuver). If you have version 6 of MS-DOS, you can use the Switches command to disable the F5 and F8 keys that, respectively, cause MS-DOS to perform clean and interactive boots. If you disable these keys, you can also use the Switches command to eliminate the 2-second delay that MS-DOS allows for pressing these keys. The pause occurs after the message *Starting MS-DOS...* appears on screen. If you're tinkering with CONFIG.SYS, you should not disable the F5 and F8 keys.

Command syntax

The Switches command can be used only from CONFIG.SYS. Its syntax is as follows:

switches=/w /k /n /f

/w is needed only if you use Windows version 3.0, you want to run Windows in enhanced mode, and as mentioned above, you move the WINA20.386 file out of the root directory of your startup disk. If all of the preceding are true, you must add a SWITCHES=/W line to CONFIG.SYS. In addition, you must add a Device command naming the new location of WINA20.386 to the [386Enh] section of the Windows file named SYSTEM.INI. (For details on this, refer to your Windows 3.0 documentation.)

/k causes an enhanced keyboard to behave as if it were a conventional (XT-style) keyboard. If you use this switch and you also install ANSI.SYS, you must include a /k switch in the Device line that loads ANSI.SYS. (For information about ANSI.SYS, refer to Chapter 10, "Devices.")

/n, in version 6 only, prevents use of the F5 and F8 keys at startup. You might want to use this switch, and the next, if you are setting up a menu-driven system for someone else and want to avoid the clean and interactive boot options. But you run the risk of locking yourself out. If you do, prepare a system-formatted floppy disk as an alternative startup disk.

/f, in version 6 only, eliminates the 2-second pause that allows the user to press F5 or F8 at startup.

Examples

Include in CONFIG.SYS:	To:
SWITCHES=/K	Force an enhanced keyboard to act like a conventional keyboard.
SWITCHES=/K DEVICE=C:\DOS\ANSI.SYS /K	Do the same as in the previous example, but also load ANSI.SYS into memory.
SWITCHES=/N /F	Disable the F5 and F8 keys and eliminate the 2-second pause at startup.

Batch commands

This category includes the Call, Choice (version 6 only), Echo, For, Goto, If, Pause, Remark (Rem), Set, and Shift commands.

Call

The Call command performs a single important function: It allows you to call and run a batch file from within another batch file and then return to the original file to continue execution. Simple as the process sounds, MS-DOS does not normally return to, and complete, a batch file that contains the name of a second batch file. Instead, it leaves the original batch file at the point at which you name the second and carries on from the beginning of batch file number two, forgetting about any uncompleted commands in the original. The Call command appeared in MS-DOS version 3.3. Prior to that version, you could accomplish the same goal, but less efficiently, with the /c switch of the Command command, described in Chapter 13.

When you use Call, you include as part of the command the name of the batch file you want MS-DOS to carry out. As when you run a batch file from the system prompt, you can also include command-line parameters, switches, replaceable parameters (%1, %2, %3, and so on), and environment variables (for use with the Set command). You should, however, avoid using pipes and redirection symbols.

Command syntax

The syntax of the Call command is as follows:

call [*drive:*][*path*]*filename* [*parameters*]

drive, path, and *filename* specify the location of the batch file you want to call. You can omit the BAT extension, and you need include *drive* and *path* only if they are not part of the search path defined by a Path command or an Append command (with the /x:on switch).

parameters specifies any parameters needed by the batch file you are calling— for example, drive letters, directory names, and replaceable parameters.

Example

Suppose you create two batch files named MICKEY.BAT and DONALD.BAT.
MICKEY.BAT contains the following:

```
@echo off
echo A message from MICKEY before calling DONALD
echo.
call %1
echo A message from MICKEY after carrying out DONALD
```

DONALD.BAT contains this:

```
@echo off
echo.
echo A message from DONALD
```

Typing this command

```
C:\>mickey donald
```

would produce the following:

```
A message from MICKEY before calling DONALD
A message from DONALD
A message from MICKEY after carrying out DONALD
```

The first and third lines of output here are produced by MICKEY.BAT, before and after calling DONALD.BAT. The batch file is kept simple with Echo commands to make the sequence of events obvious. (The *echo.* commands add space by echoing blank lines on the screen.) Except for showing how the Call command works and, perhaps, being marginally entertaining, these batch files are useless. The following, more practical, pair let you use the number of bytes of storage needed by a specified set of files to determine whether to use a file-compression program or simply to use Copy to copy the files to a disk in a specified drive.

The following file does most of the work, calling a second batch file named COMPRESS.BAT if the user presses 1 to indicate that the files specified as %1 should be compressed onto the disk in the drive specified as %2:

```
@echo off
cls
dir %1 | find "file(s)"
if not exist %1 goto end
echo.
echo Use the number of bytes displayed above
echo to decide whether to compress or copy
echo the files you specified.
echo.
echo Type 1 to compress, 2 to copy.
echo.
choice /c:12 /n Compress files onto drive %2
if errorlevel 2 goto copy
if errorlevel 1 call compress.bat %1 %2
goto end

:copy
echo Copying %1 to drive %2
copy %1 %2

:end
```

And this is the COMPRESS.BAT file called by the previous batch file:

```
@echo off
echo.
echo Ready to compress files to drive %2
pause
c:\squeezem\squeeze.sqz %2:packed.sqz %1
```

If you need a more detailed explanation of the commands in these files, refer to Chapter 19. You'll find line-by-line descriptions there.

Choice—version 6 only

The long-needed Choice command *finally*, in version 6 of MS-DOS, enables a batch file to prompt for keyboard input. With Choice, you can display a message asking the user to press a key, you can define the keystrokes that represent acceptable responses, and you can design your batch file to carry out different sets of commands, depending on which choice is made. Beginning with version 6, Pause is no longer your only legal way of asking the user to press a key. Nor do you have to rely on on-screen menus with different options, each of which quietly calls a different batch file. Nor do you have to write or find an assembly language program that gets keyboard input, or purchase a utility that provides enhancements not built into the MS-DOS batch interpreter.

Choice works by storing the user's keystroke as an errorlevel value. Suppose, for example, you design a Choice command that displays this prompt:

```
Ready to format [Y,N,C]? _
```

In response to the prompt, the user can press Y for yes, N for no, or C for cancel. Choice will wait for a key to be pressed and assign it an errorlevel value: 1 for the first key defined (Y), 2 for the second (N), and 3 for the third (C).

To find out which key was pressed, the next part of your batch file must check for each possible key, in descending order, like this:

```
if errorlevel 3 [take action 3]
if errorlevel 2 [take action 2]
if errorlevel 1 [take action 1]
```

It's important to remember this upside-down order because errorlevel is true not only for the value you specify, but for all greater values as well. Thus, you must work from the largest to the smallest values to be sure you control the outcome of the batch file correctly.

NOTE: If, instead of pressing one of the defined keys, the user presses Ctrl-C or Ctrl-Break to end the batch file, Choice returns the errorlevel value 0. If any other key is pressed, Choice makes the computer beep. If an error occurs, Choice returns the errorlevel value 255, which you could use to trap unknown errors.

Command syntax

The Choice command includes a number of switches. The default prompt (using the default choice of YN) looks like this:

```
[Y,N]?_
```

You can specify the characters to be displayed, and you can dress up the basic prompt with text. The command is case insensitive and, in fact, displays keyboard input in uppercase regardless of whether the Shift key was held down. You can, however, use the /s switch, described later, to make the command treat uppercase and lowercase differently. The complete syntax is as follows:

choice /c:*keys* /n /s /t:*default,time* [*prompttext*]

/c:*keys* defines the keys that can be pressed in response to the prompt. The default is YN. If you use the /c switch, the keys you define are displayed as a basic prompt: They are separated by commas, inside square brackets, followed by a question mark. The colon preceding *keys* is optional, but visually useful when you glance at the command—something you'll probably do in polishing a batch file.

/n suppresses the prompt, but it does display any text you define as *prompttext*.

/s makes the command case sensitive so that uppercase and lowercase input are treated differently.

/t:*default,time* lets you set the default character and the amount of time you want Choice to wait before before assuming the default. You must specify *default* as one of the characters you defined or as one of the default YN choices; *time* can be any value from 0 through 99 (seconds). Specifying 0 means that the default is automatically carried out—which means, of course, that there's not much point in offering a choice in the first place.

prompttext specifies any text you want displayed as part of the prompt. Spaces count here, so if you want an extra space between the prompt text and the cursor, be sure to press the Spacebar at the end of the text message. Use quotes if you include a slash (/) so that MS-DOS won't think you're adding another switch.

Examples

Include in a batch file:	To:
choice /c:abc	Define allowable keys as A, B, and C and to display the prompt as *[A,B,C]?*
choice /c:abc /n Please press A, B, or C<space>	Define allowable keys as A, B, and C and to display the prompt as *Please press A, B, or C<space>_*. (Read *<space>* as a press of the Spacebar, not as text.)
choice /t:y,10	Use the default YN characters, specifying Y as the default choice after 10 seconds. This prompt would be displayed as *[Y,N]?*

Echo

The Echo command performs two tasks: It turns command echoing (the display of commands) on or off, and it echoes (displays) messages on screen. Although this command is generally used from within a batch file, it can be typed at the system prompt as well.

Simple to use and understand, Echo incorporates a few special tricks into its repertoire:

- Typing *echo* at the system prompt causes Echo to display the current echoing status, on or off.

- Typing *echo off* at the system prompt causes Echo to suppress the prompt and display only the flashing cursor.

- Including *echo off* in a batch file causes Echo to suppress the display of batch commands until an *echo on* command is encountered. Starting a batch file with *@echo off* suppresses the display of Echo and all subsequent commands until *echo on* appears.

- Including *echo.* (*echo* followed by a period) causes Echo to display a blank line. Note that there is no space between the command and the period.

Command syntax

The syntax for the Echo command takes one of the following two forms:

echo on or off

echo *message*

on and off turn echoing on or off.
message is any text that you want displayed on screen.

Examples

From the system prompt, type:	To:
`C:\>echo`	Display the current echo status.
`C:\>echo off`	Turn echo off and suppress the system prompt, displaying the cursor only.
`C:\>echo on`	Turn echoing on.

Include in a batch file:	To:
`@echo off`	Avoid displaying the commands in the batch file.
`echo.`	Echo a blank line, as in the following multiline message.

`echo Place a formatted disk in`
`echo drive A and`
`echo press a key when ready`
`echo.`
	Display the message *Place a formatted disk in drive A and press a key when ready* on three separate lines and follow the message with a blank line.

For

For is one of several commands that help you control the execution of commands in a batch file. (The others are Call, Choice, Goto, If, and Shift.) A means of saving both work and time, For loops through a group of items, usually files, applying a command you specify to each one. Although the syntax looks somewhat convoluted, the following semiliterate sentence can help you see how For works:

for [each file] in [the set old?.txt] do copy [each file to drive a:]

The variables in this command are shown in square brackets. Translated, the command would be, "For each file that matches the file specification OLD?.TXT, do copy that file to the disk in drive A." As MS-DOS executed this For command, the meaning of the command would change for each file, like this:

for old1.txt in [the set old?.txt] do copy old1.txt to a:

for old2.txt in [the set old?.txt] do copy old2.txt to a:

for old3.txt in [the set old?.txt] do copy old3.txt to a:

and so on.

As you can see, For can help you apply a command to numerous items in a set. You must also remember, though, that when MS-DOS executes a For command, it is somewhat like one of the animated brooms in Disney's version of *The Sorcerer's Apprentice:* It goes back and forth through the same line in the batch file, applying whatever command you specify until it has exhausted all items in the set you define. This single-mindedness can produce frustration at times. For example, if you were to use this For command:

for [each file] in [the set old?.txt] do type [each file]

MS-DOS would use the Type command to display each file that matched the file specification OLD?.TXT. Notice, however, that there is no pause built in here. So executing this command with files that filled more than one screenful would require you to sit with your finger hovering over the Pause key. Otherwise, the files could flash by so quickly you couldn't read them. The For command supports redirection to some extent, but you would find both redirection and piping useless. Neither of the following, for example, would help stop scrolling:

for [each file] in [the set old?.txt] do type [each file] ¦ more

for [each file] in [the set old?.txt] do more < [each file]

MS-DOS would ignore the pipe and the More command in the first instance and report *File not found* in the second. Remember, too, that a /p switch, even if supported by a command such as Dir, will not always stop scrolling. For example,

for [each file] in [the set c:\dos*.exe] do dir [each file] /p will not stop scrolling after each screenful because the /p switch is applied to each instance of the Dir command, not to the set of Dir commands that equal one screenful.

Command syntax

The For command can be used either from the system prompt (a useful means of avoiding repeated typing of the same command) or from within a batch file. The only difference between the two uses is in the number of percent signs you include before the replaceable variable, as described later. From the command line, the syntax is as follows:

for %*variable* in (*set*) do *command* [*parameters*]

From within a batch file, the syntax is as follows:

for %%*variable* in (*set*) do *command* [*parameters*]

In both forms of the command the words *for, in,* and *do* are required.

%*variable* or %%*variable* is a replaceable variable you specify as a single character—for example, %f or %%f. During processing of the For command, the variable you specify is replaced by each filename or other item you specify as belonging to *set*. You can choose any character you like as a replaceable variable, but you must avoid the numerals 0 through 9, which are used as replaceable batch parameters. Note that you must use %% with batch file variables in For statements.

(*set*) represents the group of files or other items you want the For command to process. You must include the parentheses. You can use wildcards, drive letters, and directories, and you can specify more than one item by separating the items with a space or a comma, as in (*.doc* *.txt*). The items you specify here take turns starring as the replaceable variable described previously.

command is the MS-DOS command you want carried out for each item in (*set*).

parameters represents any parameters or switches you want included as part of *command*.

Examples

If using For from the command line, type:	To:
`C:\>for %f in (1 2 3) do echo %f`	Echo each item in the set 1 2 3 to the screen.
`C:\BATCH>for %f in (*.bat) do print %f`	Print each batch file in the current directory (C:\BATCH).

(continued)

If using For from a batch file, include:	To:
`for %%f in (*.bat) do print %%f`	Print each batch file in the current directory. This example is included simply to show the difference between typing a For command at the system prompt and using it from a batch file. Note the two percent signs.
`for %%f in (%1) do move %%f %2`	In version 6 only, move each file in a set specified as the first replaceable parameter (%1) typed with the name of the batch file to the drive or directory specified by the second replaceable parameter (%2). For example, if the batch file were named MOVEM.BAT, the command to move all DOC files from C:\DOCS to A:\OLDDOCS would be *movem c:\docs*.doc a:\olddocs.*

Goto

The Goto command controls the order in which commands are carried out by sending the batch interpreter to a particular location in a batch file. When you use Goto, the "key" is a label you include that heads the section of the batch file you want to jump to. Goto is most often used as part of an If statement that lets you process specific commands based on whether a condition is true or not true. Goto can be used only in batch files, never from the command line.

When you use Goto, the label you choose must appear both in the command and in the line in the batch file that marks the destination of the command. Within the Goto command, you can type the label with or without a preceding colon— for example, *goto start* and *goto :start* would both be acceptable. The label that marks the destination, however, must always be preceded by a colon. Do not include any commands in a label line. They will be ignored.

Command syntax

The syntax of the Goto is simple:

goto *label*

label is an identifier that marks the destination of the Goto command. The label cannot include spaces, semicolons, colons, slashes, backslashes, square brackets, or equal signs. Although you can make a label as long as you want without causing an error, the batch interpreter reads only the first eight characters. Thus, the two labels *threedognight* and *threedogday* would be considered identical. When labels are identical, Goto sends processing to the first label that appears in the batch file, as shown in one of the following examples.

Examples

The following batch file shows a simple use of Goto that sends processing to the beginning of the file unless the user presses N in response to the Choice command:

```
@echo off
:start
echo 1
echo 2
echo 3
choice Continue
if not errorlevel 2 goto start
```

The following example includes the two labels *threedognight* and *threedogday* mentioned earlier under the "Command syntax" heading:

```
@echo off
:threedognight
echo 1
echo 2
choice Continue
if errorlevel 2 goto threedognight
if errorlevel 1 goto threedogday
:threedogday
echo 3
echo 4
```

This batch file would never end and would never echo 3 and 4 to the screen because the batch interpreter would consider both labels identical and skip to the first label (*threedognight*) in the batch file regardless of the key pressed. The only way to get out of this mess would be to press Ctrl-Break, which stops processing and asks whether to terminate the batch file.

If

If is the command you turn to whenever you want a command carried out only in certain circumstances—for example, to copy a file only if it does not exist on the target disk or, in version 6, to jump to a set of commands and carry them out only if the user types a particular character, such as Y or N. Because you use If in conditional situations, this command lets you control which MS-DOS commands are executed as a batch file runs and, therefore, lets you control the outcome of the batch process itself.

You can use If in any of three situations: to determine whether a file exists, to determine whether two strings are identical, and to retrieve an errorlevel value.

Furthermore, you can use If in either of two forms: "If this, then do that" and the complementary "If not this, then do that." All told, then, you can use If in three circumstances, each with two types of evaluation, as follows:

- Checking whether a file exists. This lets you set up a batch file so that a particular command affects only a particular file or set of files. You would use this form of If, for example, when you wanted to move, copy, or delete selected files, and you could set up the command in either of the following forms:

    1. If the file exists, do [command].

    2. If the file does not exist, do [command].

- Checking whether two strings are identical. This is often used to verify that a replaceable parameter contains a certain set of characters. Another, related, use is in comparing a replaceable parameter against nothing—that is, an empty string—so that you can stop a command when the last file in a set has been processed. On a somewhat more exotic level, this type of evaluation is also used with variables you've defined with the Set command. (One example appears below; more details are in Chapter 19, "Controlling Batch Files.") The two forms in which you can check strings with If are as follows:

    1. If string 1 equals string 2, do [command].

    2. If string 1 does not equal string 2, do [command].

- Retrieving errorlevel values. This puts If to work in two very different ways. The first, available in MS-DOS since version 2, checks the error-level value returned by certain MS-DOS commands, such as Format, Backup (prior to version 6), and Xcopy. Because these values indicate whether the command was completed correctly or was halted for some reason, you can use errorlevel values as pointers (with the Goto command) to jump to sections of the batch file related to each type of outcome. The second, and far more interesting use of errorlevel, at least in terms of batch-file personality, exists—in version 6 only—as a means of retrieving the key pressed in response to a Choice command. Choice, in combination with If, at long last gives batch files the ability to act upon keyboard input. The forms of If, when used with errorlevel, are as follows:

    1. If errorlevel value equals X, do [command].

    2. If errorlevel value does not equal X, do [command].

Command syntax

The syntax of the If command is as follows. Separate lines are shown for each of the three possible conditions you can evaluate.

if [not] exist *filename command*

if [not] *string1==string2 command*

if [not] errorlevel *value command*

command is the MS-DOS command plus any acceptable command-line switches or parameters you want carried out if the condition is true.

filename is the name of the file to check for. To check for a set of related files, specify *filename* as a replaceable parameter. You can also use this form of the If command in combination with For, if you want to apply the same If command to each file in one or more sets, as in the following:

```
for %%f in (%1) do if exist %%f [command]
```

Or you can test for the existence of a group of unrelated files by using If in combination with the Shift command, like this:

```
:start
if exist %1 [command]
shift
if {%1}=={}goto end
goto start
:end
```

To test for the existence of a directory, use a replaceable parameter and specify the NUL device as a filename, as in the following:

```
if exist %1\nul [command]
```

string1 and *string2* are the strings you want to compare. To test for a replaceable parameter that might have been omitted when the batch file was started, or to test for an empty string, enclose *string1* in a pair of unique characters that MS-DOS will accept. Specify *string2* as the characters only. Curly brackets are used in the Shift example above to help make the If command more readable. Most people, however, use quotation marks.

value is used only when checking for errorlevel. Specify *value* as the error-level number you want to check for. When checking for errorlevel values, remember that MS-DOS considers If errorlevel to be true for the specified value and all greater values. To eliminate other possible "true" values, use the If not form of the command (for a situation with only two possibilities), or set up a series of If errorlevel commands to test for all possible values, in descending order.

Examples

The following sample batch files show various uses of the If command. They are designed, however, to clarify command syntax rather than to illustrate good uses of the If command. For details, refer to Chapter 19, "Controlling Batch Files."

Include in a batch file:	To:
`if exist a:%1 goto nocopy`	Branch to the label :nocopy if the file specified with the %1 replaceable parameter exists on the disk in drive A.
`for %%f in (%1) do if not exist a:%%f` `    copy %%f a:`	Copy each file in the set specified by the %1 replaceable parameter if the file does not already exist on the disk in drive A.
`if "%1"=="" goto end`	Branch to the label :end if the file specified by the %1 replaceable parameter equals nothing but a set of quotation marks—that is, represents an empty string, meaning MS-DOS can find no other files.
`for %%f in (%1) do if not "%1"==""` `    find /i "%2" %%f`	Search each file in the set corresponding to the file specification %1 for the string specified as %2, stopping when the last matching file has been processed.

`choice /n Press Y or N`
`if errorlevel 2 goto no`
`if errorlevel 1 goto yes`
	Branch to the label no if the user presses N in response to the Choice command; branch to the label yes if the user presses Y in response to the Choice command. Note that the first key defined (Y) returns errorlevel 1, but the If commands are placed in descending order.

`if errorlevel 5 goto end`
`if errorlevel 4 goto error`
`if errorlevel 3 goto halt`
`if errorlevel 0 goto end`
	Branch to the label end if the Format command returns exit code 5; to the label error if the command returns exit code 4; to the label halt if the command returns exit code 3; and to the label end if the command exits successfully with code 0.

Pause

After all the preceding exercise with the If command, you'll be happy to find that Pause is remarkable in its simplicity. This is, in fact, a command whose output you've often seen while using MS-DOS:

```
Press any key to continue . . .
```

When you create batch files, you too can cause MS-DOS to display this message simply by inserting the one-word, no-switches, no-parameters Pause command. Use it, as MS-DOS does, to halt scrolling and give the user time to read the screen, consider options, change disks, or any combination of the three. Especially in versions of MS-DOS prior to version 6 (which offers the more flexible

Choice command), Pause is often used in combination with an Echo command to let the user choose whether to continue or to end batch processing by pressing Ctrl-Break; an example of this usage is shown later. You can use Pause, unlike most other batch commands, at the system prompt. There's little reason to do so, however, unless you feel like making sure the command works as advertised.

Command syntax

The syntax of the Pause command is simple:

```
pause
```

Example

The following batch file uses a Dir command to produce a list of files about to be deleted. The /w switch lists the files in wide format, and the /p switch ensures that the command pauses after each screenful (if a great many files match the %1 replaceable parameter). The second Echo command asks the user to verify that the listing contains no surprises. The remaining Echo and Pause commands instruct the user to press Ctrl-Break to terminate processing or to press any key to delete the files.

```
@echo off
cls
echo The following files will be DELETED.
echo.
dir %1 /w /p
echo.
echo To quit now, press Ctrl-Break.
echo.
echo To delete the files
pause
del %1
```

Remark (Rem)

The Remark command performs two related functions in a batch file or in your CONFIG.SYS file: It allows you to insert explanatory comments, and it allows you to "comment out" commands that you don't want to delete completely but don't want processed either. In both cases, Rem works by instructing MS-DOS to ignore any text or command that follows on the same line. Because of this, Rem must always appear at the beginning of the line.

NOTE: *Beginning in version 6, you can use a semicolon instead of Rem to disable commands in CONFIG.SYS, for greater readability. However, the semicolon does not work in batch files.*

Command syntax

The syntax of the Rem command is as follows:

rem [*comment*]

or, when used in CONFIG.SYS in version 6:

; [*comment*]

comment, in either syntax, is any text you want to include on the line. The line can be up to 127 characters long, but it cannot contain any redirection symbols (< or >) or pipes (¦).

Examples

Include in a batch file:	To:
`rem Batch file created 6/6/92`	Include a remark noting the date on which the file was created.

Include in CONFIG.SYS:	To:
`rem devicehigh=c:\dos\ansi.sys`	Disable a Devicehigh command in CONFIG.SYS that loads ANSI.SYS into UMBs.
`;devicehigh=c:\dos\ansi.sys`	Do the same as in the previous example, but use the semicolon (version 6 only).

Set

The Set command, unlike the other commands described in this section, is not a true batch command. The command is included here, however, because it is used for setting environment variables and can be called from within a batch file when you want to add to or modify part of the environment. The environment is a series of strings in the form *name=value*. The left side of this equation represents a variable name. The right side represents the actual information corresponding to the variable name. The most familiar of all environment variables is this one:

prompt=pg

which defines the system prompt. The prompt and other variables, including the command path, are set by MS-DOS at startup as a set of very basic information about the computer. This information originally belongs to COMMAND.COM, but it can be passed to other programs that need it.

The point of an environment variable, at least in the context of this book, however, is that the name represents specific information you can define and redefine as necessary. And the way you view and define environment variables is with the Set command. Furthermore, once defined, a variable name can be used in batch files as a shorthand reference—something like a replaceable parameter—to the information it represents. Wherever you want to substitute the value of the variable for the variable name in the batch file, you simply enclose the variable name in percent signs, like this: *%prompt%*. One of the following examples shows how this is done.

MS-DOS and most application programs are designed to recognize certain variable names. The most often used are COMSPEC, which identifies the path to COMMAND.COM; PROMPT, which defines the system prompt; PATH, which specifies the current command path; SHELL, which identifies the command interpreter (usually COMMAND.COM); DIRCMD, which lets you define a "default" format, such as wide (/w), for your directory listings; and two special variables named TEMP and TMP, which are generally accepted as "default" names for temporary directories. You can, however, name any type of environment variable you want.

As already mentioned, Set is not a "true" batch command. You can use it from batch files and from CONFIG.SYS, but you can also use it from the system prompt. Also note that you do not use Set to change the prompt or path. Even though Set displays these variables and can be used to control the values associated with them, you normally use the Prompt and Path commands to make any changes you consider necessary.

Command syntax

The syntax of the Set command is as follows:

set[*name*=[*value*]]

name is the name of the variable you want to define or modify.

value is the string you want to assign to the variable name.

If you type the command without any parameters, Set displays the current environment. If you type *name* followed by only an equal sign, MS-DOS clears the variable—that is, associates the variable name with nothing—and omits the variable name from the display.

Examples

Type:	To:
`C:\>set`	Display the current environment settings.
`C:\>set include=c:\include`	Set a variable named *include* to the path C:\INCLUDE. (This variable would be used by programmers.)
`C:\>set user=kate`	Set a variable named *user* to the name *kate*.

Include in a batch file:	To:
| ```
@echo off
echo This batch file is for %user%
echo The current path is %path%
``` | Cause a batch file to display the name of the user for whom it was designed and to display the current command path. If, for example, the *user* variable had been set to *kate*, as shown in the previous example, and the current path were C:\DOS;C:\KATE, this batch file would display *This batch file is for kate.* *The current path is C:\DOS;C:\KATE.* |

Include in AUTOEXEC.BAT:	To:
| ```
set dircmd=/og /w
set temp=d:\temp
set tmp=d:\tmp
``` | Set the "default" directory listing to a wide format with directories listed first, and set directories named TEMP and TMP on drive D for temporary storage. Both *temp* and *tmp* are included here to allow for common variations in spelling. |

Shift

The Shift command is used when you want to create a batch file that uses more replaceable parameters than the 10 you can supply with the %0 through %9 replaceable parameters that MS-DOS recognizes, and also when you want to give a batch file the flexibility to perform the same operation (for example, a copy, delete, or move) as many times as needed but cannot do so with wildcards or global filenames.

Seeing the Shift command in operation is like watching people in a queue. As each item (person) reaches the head of the line, all of those behind move up one place closer to the front. Thus, as Joe is being helped, Jess moves to the head of the line. When it's Jess's turn, Anita takes Jess's spot, while Joe walks off into the sunset. It's the same with replaceable parameters and the Shift command. If, for example, your batch file moves files and you want the user to be able to specify anywhere from 1 or 2 to 10 or more files to be moved, you include a Shift command and construct the batch file so that the person can type the names of as many files as necessary when starting the batch file. As each file is moved, the Shift command takes care of moving the second file into first place, the third into second, and so on.

Command syntax

The syntax of the Shift command is as follows:

    shift

That's it.

Example

The following very simple batch file shows the Shift command at work. The heart of the file is between the *:start* label and the *goto start* line. Type the lines as shown and save the file as TEST.BAT:

```
@echo off
cls
:start
if "%1"=="" goto end
echo %1
shift
goto start
:end
```

To see the file at work, type *test* followed by as many words, numbers, or characters as you want, separating them with spaces. Try this, for example:

```
test I am trying out a batch file that shows how the Shift command works
```

Without Shift, the batch file would repeat endlessly, echoing the first word until you pressed Ctrl-Break.

Command recall and macros

Command recall and macros can save a lot of retyping. Both are accomplished with the help of the Doskey utility included with versions 5 and 6 of MS-DOS. The following description applies to Doskey as a command, with parameters, that you execute from the command line. Chapter 18, ''Batch Files and Macros,'' tells how to put Doskey to work.

Doskey

Doskey stores commands as you enter them, keeping them in a buffer so that you can later review, reuse, and edit them as you work. A memory-resident program, Doskey can be loaded into either conventional memory or UMBs. In either location, it requires about 4 K of memory.

As already mentioned, Doskey functions not only as a command editor but as a program that enables you to save sets of MS-DOS commands as macros. In many respects, macros are comparable to batch files, even to the extent that they can accept replaceable parameters. Unlike batch files, however, macros, once loaded, remain in memory and so are slightly faster to run. They do, however, occupy room in the Doskey buffer, so if you're working with a large number of commands, you might have to increase the buffer size to accommodate both commands and macros.

Command syntax

The syntax of the Doskey command is as follows:

doskey /reinstall /bufsize=*size* /macros /history /insert /overstrike
    macro=commands

/reinstall installs a new copy of Doskey and clears the Doskey buffer. Each time you use this switch, you increase the memory required by about 4 K.

/bufsize=*size* specifies the size, in bytes, of the Doskey buffer. The default is 512 bytes; minimum buffer size is 256 bytes.

/macros, or /m, displays a list of the Doskey macros—both macro names and commands—in memory. You can use this switch with the redirection symbol > to save macros in a batch file. The file must, however, be edited before you can use it to load the macros into memory at another time. For details, refer to Chapter 18.

/history, or /h, displays all of the commands currently in the Doskey buffer. You can redirect this list to a batch file, but you'll probably want to edit the file before running it as a thoroughly "debugged" batch program. An easier way to display commands is to press the F7 key, as described in Chapter 18.

/insert and /overstrike determine whether the text you type while entering and editing commands replaces existing characters (the default) or is inserted between existing characters. You can pick only one of these.

macro=commands is the form in which you create Doskey macros. *macro* represents the name you want to assign the macro; *commands* represents the commands you want the macro to carry out. For details on this, refer to Chapter 18.

Examples

Type:	To:
`C:\>doskey`	Load Doskey into conventional memory.
`C:\>lh doskey`	Load Doskey into the upper memory area.
`C:\>doskey /reinstall`	Load a new copy of Doskey and clear the command buffer.
`C:\>doskey /macros`	List macros currently in the buffer.
`C:\>doskey /macros > macros.txt`	Save the macros in a file named MACROS.TXT.
`C:\>doskey /history`	List previously executed commands.
`C:\>doskey subdirs=dir $1 /ad /w`	Create a macro named SUBDIRS that lists only subdirectories of the directory specified by the Doskey replaceable parameter $1. This macro displays the directories in the wide format.

Redirection, piping, and filter commands

Input/output redirection and piping are closely tied to the three commands—
Find, Sort, and More—known as *filters*. The commands are so named because
they "strain" input or output, altering it in some way to provide you with specific
information. Although input/output redirection doesn't always require the use of
filter commands, the two subjects are closely related and are usually considered
two aspects of one highly useful MS-DOS capability. For details on redirection
and piping, and their uses with both filter and non-filter commands, refer to
Chapter 17, "Redirection, Pipes, and Filters."

Find

The Find command doesn't find specific files in a directory. For that, you have
the /s switch in versions 5 and 6 of MS-DOS. Find dives deeper, to act as the MS-
DOS equivalent of the Search command your word processor and other applications offer. With Find, you can search one or more files for specific strings of text.
The files can be formatted or unformatted, but searching formatted files can
cause beeps, odd scanning, and screenfuls of information interrupted by the occasional carriage return produced by the Enter key.

When you use Find, it displays each line that contains the string you search
for. You can use Find either with files you specify or as a filter, taking its input
from the keyboard or from the redirected or piped output of another command.
Unlike most MS-DOS commands, Find is sensitive to the difference between uppercase and lowercase. Thus, if you tell it to find the string *ms-dos*, it will do so,
but it will skip all occurrences of *MS-DOS*. To overcome this literal-mindedness,
remember to include the /i switch that tells Find to ignore case. If you use Find a
lot, you'll probably end up typing /i almost automatically.

You should also note that Find recognizes carriage returns but does not take
them into account as it works. Two words separated by a carriage return are, to
Find, exactly that: two words with a carriage return in the middle. If those two
separated words are the ones you seek, Find will not declare a match because of
the intervening carriage return. If you search a file in which line breaks are produced by carriage returns, bear this idiosyncrasy in mind. Finally, remember that
Find, like the Type command, does not accept wildcard characters as part of a file
specification. If you want to search a set of files, either list each filename as part of
your Find command or make the Find command part of a For command. You can
do the latter either from the system prompt or in a batch file (preferable if you use
Find fairly often).

Find returns the following errorlevel values on completion. You can use
these codes with the errorlevel parameter of the If command to control actions
within a batch file:

Exit code	Meaning
0	Successful search, with at least one match found.
1	Successful search, but no match found.
2	Unsuccessful search.

Command syntax

The syntax of the Find command is as follows:

find /v /c /n /i *"string"* [*filespec1*] [*filespec2*]...[*filespecN*]

/v tells Find to display all lines that do not contain the specified string.

/c tells Find to display a count of the lines containing the string, but not the lines themselves.

/n tells Find to number the lines, displaying the line number in square brackets at the beginning of each line that contains the string. The /n switch does not work with /c.

/i tells Find to ignore differences between uppercase and lowercase.

"string" is the string you want to search for. You must always enclose the string in quotation marks. Spaces count, so you can use preceding and trailing spaces to ensure that Find searches for whole words (*" liar"*) rather than finding the string wherever it occurs (*"familiar"*). This trick can work against you, however, if you include a trailing space and the word you seek appears just before a carriage return, a period, or other punctuation.

filespec1, filespec2...filespecN are the files to search. Include the drive and path for any file that is not in the current directory.

Examples

Type:	To:
`C:\>find /i "heart " valentne.txt` `    anatomy.txt`	Find the word *heart*, spelled in any combination of uppercase or lowercase, in the files named VALENTNE.TXT and ANATOMY.TXT. Note that the space following the string would eliminate *heartfelt*, *heartily*, and *heart-shaped*.
`C:\>find /c "Microsoft" book.doc`	List the number of lines containing the word *Microsoft* in the file BOOK.DOC.
`C:\>find /n /i " contract" legal.txt`	Display and number each line in the file LEGAL.TXT that contains the word *contract*, spelled in uppercase or lowercase.
`C:\>for %f in (*.txt) do find /i` `    "cake" %f`	Find the word *cake*, without regard to case, in all files in the current directory with the TXT extension.

More

The command-line version of the /p switch included in Dir and a few other MS-DOS commands, the More command has but one function: to display one screenful of information at a time, pausing and waiting for you to press a key before continuing. Present in MS-DOS since version 2.0, More was long the near-indispensable companion of anyone who regularly displayed long directories. It continues to be just as useful in controlling the display of lengthy files.

Command syntax

You can use More in either of the following two forms. The first form relies on the input-redirection symbol (<) to tell More where to find its input. The second uses the pipe to send the output of a command, such as Dir or Type to More for controlled display:

more < *filespec*

command ¦ more

filespec is the drive, path, and filename of a file you want to display one screenful at a time.

command is the MS-DOS command that produces the output you want to pipe to More for display.

Examples

Type:	To:
`C:\>type longdoc.txt ¦ more`	Display the file LONGDOC.TXT one screenful at a time.
`C:\>more < longdoc.txt`	Do the same as in the previous example, using input redirection to specify the filename.

Sort

The Sort command takes input, sorts it by column into ascending or descending order, and either displays the results or sends its output to a file or a device (such as the printer). When counting columns, Sort uses the row/column arrangement you see on your display in character mode—that is, one column equals one character across the screen. Like any sorting program, Sort relies on you to ensure that the characters you want to sort are arranged trooplike in recognizable (and countable) columns. Sort is fast and reliable and can handle files up to 64 K in size. Do not, however, expect it to do the impossible by asking it to sort a formatted spreadsheet or another file in which some data occupies single rows while other data overflows into a second or third row. The result could be havoc, as even your spreadsheet program would agree. Keep Sort for cleanly arranged, plain ASCII files.

When sorting, Sort arranges characters in ASCII order, according to the country and code page defined for the computer. If you are sorting extended characters—those with ASCII values above 127—they are sorted according to the character table defined for your country by the MS-DOS COUNTRY.SYS file or an alternative file you specify in CONFIG.SYS.

For more on the Sort command, including examples of how you would use it, refer to Chapter 17, "Redirection, Pipes, and Filters."

Command syntax

Sort is a protean command that can take many forms, depending on where it gets its input and where it sends its output. The basic syntax of the Sort command, however, takes either of two forms, depending on whether you are sorting a file or sorting the output of another command, such as Dir. The two forms are as follows:

sort /r /+n < *source* > *destination*

command ¦ sort /r /+n > *destination*

/r sorts in reverse order, Z to A or 9 to 0. If the column contains both letters and numerals, the letters are sorted first.

/+n specifies the column to be sorted. The default is column 1.

source specifies the file from which Sort is to get its input, and *destination* specifies the file (if any) to which Sort sends its output. Do not specify the same file for both *source* and *destination*.

command is the MS-DOS command, if you choose to use this form of the Sort command, that is used to pipe its output to Sort as the input source.

Examples

Type:	To:
`C:\>sort < table.txt`	Sort the file TABLE.TXT in ascending order according to the characters in column 1.
`C:\>sort /r < table.txt`	Sort the file TABLE.TXT, as in the previous example, but arrange the output in reverse order.
`C:\>sort /+10 < table.txt`	Sort the file TABLE.TXT according to the characters in column 10.
`C:\>sort < table.txt > newtable.txt`	Sort the file TABLE.TXT with the default settings and redirect the output to the file NEWTABLE.TXT.

(continued)

Type:	To:
`C:\>dir ¦ sort /r /+14`	Sort the current directory on column 14 (where the entry <DIR> appears) in reverse order. This command is the equivalent of the version 5 and 6 *dir /ad* command, although with less elegant output because all lines of the directory, including the header, are sorted.
`C:\>dir ¦ sort /+14 ¦ find "<"`	Sort the current directory, as in the previous example, but clean up the output by piping it to a Find command that lists only lines containing the < character. Once again, this example is more for show than for actual use, as the version 5 and 6 *dir /ad* command does the job as well, and with less bother.

13

Miscellaneous Commands

What You'll Find Here: Break; Command; Date; Debug; Dosshell; Edit; Edlin; Exit; Fast Help (Fasthelp); Help; MSCDEX; Prompt; Qbasic; Share; Time; Version (Ver).

*T*his chapter is a symphony of unrelated commands, some of which you might use frequently (Help and Fast Help), others of which you might never want or need to activate (Edlin, Debug, Qbasic). They are here, however, for completeness, to round out this section on MS-DOS commands. Because there is no coherent theme binding these commands together, the best approach to covering them is to jump right in.

Break

Break is a command you can use from the system prompt or as a command in CONFIG.SYS. Its purpose is to turn Ctrl-C checking on or off. Ctrl-C is, in most cases, identical to Ctrl-Break so we'll use the term Ctrl-C for both. As you probably know by now, both key combinations represent your means of canceling a command, stopping MS-DOS in midstride whenever you want to break out of an executing program. By default, MS-DOS checks for Ctrl-C only when it reads from the keyboard or writes to a character device (screen, printer, or communications port). By turning Break on, you can extend Ctrl-C checking so that MS-DOS checks for Ctrl-C more often, such as when it is reading from or writing to disk. Setting Break to on means that you won't have to wait as long for Ctrl-C to stop a program that is ignoring the keyboard and screen while processing data. At the same time, however, extended Ctrl-C checking also means that your system can slow down somewhat.

Command syntax

The syntax of the Break command is as follows:

> break [=] on or off

> on turns extended Ctrl-C checking on.
> off turns extended Ctrl-C checking off.
> Typing Break without a switch displays the current status:

> BREAK is off

or

> BREAK is on

> The equal sign is optional.

Examples

Type:	To:
C:\>break	Display the current status of Ctrl-C checking.
C:\>break on	Turn on extended Ctrl-C checking.

Include in CONFIG.SYS:	To:
break on or: break=on	Enable extended Ctrl-C checking at startup.
break? on or: break?=on	Have MS-DOS prompt for confirmation before enabling extended Ctrl-C checking at startup (version 6 only).

Command

When you type the name of a file that ends in COM, EXE, or BAT, MS-DOS loads and runs the program represented by that filename. When you start or restart the computer, the bootstrap process ensures that MS-DOS runs the file named COMMAND.COM, which activates the command interpreter, which, in turn, takes on the job of interpreting and carrying out keyboard commands. If, while you're using MS-DOS, you type the Command command, MS-DOS loads and runs a new instance of COMMAND.COM, providing you with a secondary copy of the command interpreter. You can remove each extra copy by using the Exit command.

In a way, the Command command leads you into a funhouse of mirrors. Each time you type the command, a new copy of COMMAND.COM takes over, ready to respond to Directory (Dir), Path, Delete (Del), Date, and other MS-DOS commands. Every time you type *command*, you end up with an identical copy of COMMAND.COM, each one sitting in about 3 K of memory. (If you type it enough times, you'll run out of memory.) The interesting part of all this is that you need the original COMMAND.COM to run the new COMMAND.COM, so each copy of COMMAND.COM you load is a child of the copy that came before. And to back up through the chain of COMMAND.COMs, you must do so one copy at a time, using the Exit command to tell each copy to take a hike and move you one step closer to the original COMMAND.COM.

In and of itself, Command would seem to be fairly irrelevant. Who, after all, needs multiple copies of a command interpreter, especially when the original is perfectly capable of handling all the file and disk operations you're likely to use under MS-DOS? In versions of MS-DOS prior to 3.3, Command (with the /c switch) proved highly useful to creators of batch files because it was the only way in which you could call a batch file from within another batch file, and then return execution to the original. (In normal circumstances, chaining to another batch file invariably terminates execution of the file you chain from.) With the advent of version 3.3, however, the Call batch command made this use of the Command command unnecessary.

Even today, however, Command continues as an unsung and usually unseen companion of certain programs, among them the MS-DOS Shell. Whenever you tell the Shell to suspend itself temporarily and take you to the system prompt, you are using the Command command to "clone" a secondary copy of COMMAND.COM. It is this copy of COMMAND.COM, not the one that was in charge when you started the Shell, that carries out the commands you then type at the system prompt. This passing of the baton from the original command interpreter to its temporary successor is also the reason why, when you want to return to the Shell, you must type *exit* to return control to the originating program and its copy of COMMAND.COM.

In everyday use, you probably won't need the Command command, although you can, in version 6, use its /k switch to advantage in customizing the way you run MS-DOS from within Windows. On a practical level, however, if COMMAND.COM is not in the root directory of your startup disk, Command does play a role in how your system runs. In fact, you're likely to see Command as the "object" of a Shell command in CONFIG.SYS. The reason has to do with the way COMMAND.COM runs in memory. COMMAND.COM loads into memory in two distinct parts: a resident portion that remains inviolate while MS-DOS is running, and a transient portion that can, when necessary, be overwritten (and thus destroyed in memory) by programs that need the memory space. If the transient portion must be reloaded, MS-DOS must be able to find COMMAND.COM on disk. To do this, it refers to the COMSPEC variable in the environment, which is automatically set at startup. COMSPEC, however, is affected by a Shell command in CONFIG.SYS. And Shell, in turn, is the command you need to define the path to COMMAND.COM if the file is not in the root directory of your startup disk. Boxes within boxes, but all related in the end.

As for Command itself, you should know that the secondary copy of COMMAND.COM that you load inherits a copy of the current operating environment. This environment, as mentioned elsewhere, contains a series of variable names that are associated with strings defining such important items as the system prompt, command path, startup configuration (in version 6), and temporary directory or directories. Because the secondary copy of COMMAND.COM inherits a copy of the current environment, it has access to these environment settings. When you load this secondary copy of COMMAND.COM, you can specify a different environment size, either larger or smaller. However, any changes you or a program make to the environment under this new copy of COMMAND.COM are not passed back to the environment owned by the original. You cannot, therefore, change the path or define a variable after using Command and expect that change to remain in effect when you return to the original command interpreter.

You can use the Command command from the system prompt, from a batch file, or, as previously mentioned, as the object of a Shell command pointing MS-DOS to the location of COMMAND.COM.

Command syntax

When used to load a secondary copy of COMMAND.COM, the syntax of the Command command is as follows:

command [*drive:*][*path*] [*device*] /e:*size* /k *filename* /p /msg /c *string*

When used with a Shell command in CONFIG.SYS, the syntax used with Command is as follows:

shell=[*dospath*]command.com [*drive:*][*path*] [*device*] /e:*size* /p /msg

drive: and *path* are the drive and path that tell COMMAND.COM where to look when it needs to reload its transient portion. You can omit them in the first (command) form of the Command command if COMMAND.COM is in the root directory of the startup drive, or if the COMSPEC variable has already been set by a previous loading of COMMAND.COM. You must include these parameters with the Shell command.

dospath, included only with the Shell command, is the drive and path to COMMAND.COM. Although its use seems redundant, it is a useful part of the Shell command. (For more information, refer to the Shell command in Chapter 12.)

device is the name of an alternate device, such as AUX, that the command interpreter is to use for input and output.

/e:*size* specifies the size of the environment, in bytes, the new copy of COMMAND.COM is to have. The default is either 256 or the size of the current environment, whichever is larger. You can specify 160 through 32768. MS-DOS uses this value, rounded up to the next 16 bytes.

/k *filename*, available in version 6 only, runs the program or batch file specified by *filename* before it displays the system prompt. If you use this switch with Windows, add /k to the Optional Parameters box in your DOSPRMPT.PIF file. Open the DOSPRMPT.PIF file with the Windows PIF Editor and type /k in the

Optional Parameters box. Don't use this switch with the Shell command in CON-
FIG.SYS; if you do, programs you install might not be able to change your
AUTOEXEC.BAT. You can use this switch to run alternate startup files for MS-
DOS programs in Windows.

/p makes the copy of COMMAND.COM permanent, meaning that the Exit
command is disabled. This switch should appear only with a Shell command in
CONFIG.SYS. If you use it from the system prompt, you cannot exit the new copy
of COMMAND.COM and return to the original. This switch also causes COM-
MAND.COM to carry out your AUTOEXEC.BAT file.

/msg causes Command to store all error messages in memory, rather than
leaving some on disk, for retrieval if and when they are needed. Use this switch
only if you run MS-DOS from floppy disks and you don't want to go back to your
original boot disk just for a message.

/c *string* causes COMMAND.COM to carry out the command specified by
string and then exit. You can use this switch from the command line to run a batch
file, command, or program and to avoid having to type *exit* to return to the original command interpreter. This is the old way of calling one batch file from another. Use Call instead, if you're in a batch file.

Examples

Type:	To:
`C:\>command /e:512`	Run a new copy of COMMAND.COM with a 528-byte environment (512 plus 16 bytes).
`C:\>exit`	Exit from the secondary copy of COM-MAND.COM and return to the original.
`C:\>command /k altstart.bat`	Start a new copy of COMMAND.COM after running the file ALTSTART.BAT. You could also run this from Windows by including */k c:\altstart.bat* in the Optional Parameters box of the DOSPRMPT.PIF file.

Include in a batch file or type at the system prompt:	To:
`command /c runit.bat`	Start a new copy of COMMAND.COM, run the file named RUNIT.BAT, quit the secondary copy of COMMAND-.COM, and return to the original command interpreter. If included in a batch file, this command would allow execu-tion to continue after RUNIT.BAT had finished.

Include in CONFIG.SYS:	To:
`shell=c:\dos\command.com c:\dos\` `    /e:1024 /p`	Set the COMSPEC variable to C:\DOS\COMMAND.COM, start the command interpreter with a 1040 (1024 plus 16) byte environment, and make the copy of COMMAND.COM permanent.

Date

The Date command allows you to display or change the date kept by the system clock. The date, like the time, is used by MS-DOS in dating files and directories and, in version 6, in keeping track of the number of days till deleted files are to be purged.

If, as is usually the case, your computer has a battery-controlled clock/calendar as part of its built-in CMOS setup, you don't have to worry about setting the date. The system does it automatically. Nor do you have to worry about leap years or months with differing numbers of days. All this is accounted for. If you do have to check or change the date, however, you use the Date command.

When you type the Date command, MS-DOS displays the following:

```
Current date is Thu 12-31-1992
Enter new date (mm-dd-yy): _
```

To change the date, type a new value as described later. To leave the date as displayed, press Enter. To change the date without having MS-DOS prompt for it, type *date* followed by the date you want to set—for example, *date 8-14-93*.

Command syntax

The syntax of the Date command is simple:

date [*mm-dd-yy*]

mm-dd-yy sets the month, day, and year you specify. The format you use here, however, depends on the date format set by the Country setting in your CONFIG.SYS file. In the United States, the default is as shown. In other countries, however, you might enter the date as *dd-mm-yy* or *yy-mm-dd*. Separate the month, day, and year values with hyphens, slashes, or periods. Values accepted by MS-DOS for month, day, and year are as follows:

mm	1 through 12
dd	1 through 31
yy	80 through 99 or 1980 through 2099

Examples

Type:	To:
C:\>date	Display the current date and a prompt for a new date.
C:\>date 12-11-93	Change the system date to December 11, 1993.

Debug

Debug is a tool for viewing and changing files at a very low (assembly language) level as well as running a program under a controlled set of circumstances to find subtle errors. With Debug, you can perform tasks like the following:

- Assemble and unassemble programs, meaning you can convert assembly language statements to executable machine code and vice versa.
- Run programs and find errors (called *debugging* by programmers).
- View the contents of specified memory ranges.
- View the contents of the microprocessor's registers (small, temporary storage areas for holding instructions and data).
- Perform hexadecimal arithmetic.

Although it can be useful in creating advanced batch files and is the delight of technically adept users who enjoy probing the insides of program files, Debug does not make much sense if you are not a programmer. Nor is this utility for casual use. It can, in fact, be dangerous. Unlike most of MS-DOS, Debug assumes you know what you are doing. As such, it provides little, if any, protection from inadvertent presses of the Enter key—to the point that it has been known to scramble crucial data on system disks, making them unusable. All this is not meant to warn you away from Debug completely, but if you want to use Debug seriously, refer to the MS-DOS online Help in version 6 and, more importantly, to a book that covers the subject in detail.

Dosshell

The Dosshell command starts the MS-DOS Shell. Use of the Shell itself is covered early in this book, in Chapters 4 and 5. The following descriptions show how to start the Shell from the command line.

Command syntax

The syntax of the Dosshell command is as follows:

dosshell /t[:*resolution*[*number*]] /g[:*resolution*[*number*]] /b

/t starts the Shell in text mode.
/g starts the Shell in graphics mode.
/b starts the Shell in black-and-white.

resolution, for both text and graphics modes, specifies the resolution category you want. You can specify L (low), M (medium), or H (high). The actual category or categories you can specify, however, depend on the type of video hardware you have. To determine which categories are available, start the Shell with a simple *dosshell* command. Open the Options menu, choose the Display command, and scroll through the list of display options that appears in the resulting dialog box. The list looks like the following, and will include all the categories available for your hardware:

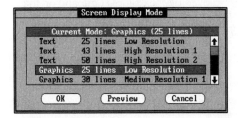

The next time you start the Shell, you can specify any valid category in the Shell's startup command and thus avoid having to set the display after the Shell gets going. You can abbreviate resolution as *res*.

number is necessary only if you want to specify a screen resolution with more than one choice. On some computers, for example, the video hardware supports two high-resolution text displays: one of 43 lines and the other of 50 lines. Once again, you can use the Display command from within the Shell to determine whether *number* is necessary for certain resolutions. If, for example, your hardware supports the two high-resolution text displays, the list box produced by the Display command will show the entries *Text 43 lines High Resolution 1* and *Text 50 lines High Resolution 2*, both of which are visible in the preceding illustration.

Examples

Type:	To:
C:\>dosshell /g	Start the Shell in graphics mode, with the default 25-line, low-resolution screen.
C:\>dosshell /g:h2	Start the Shell in graphics mode, with the 60-line, high-resolution screen (on a system that supports this type of display).
C:\>dosshell /t:h1	Start the Shell in text mode, with the 43-line, high-resolution screen (if available). This is a useful choice, especially when you plan to work with large directories.
C:\>dosshell /b	Start the Shell in black-and-white (monochrome-2 color) mode. This switch overrides the color choices displayed by the Colors command on the Shell's Options menu, so starting the Shell with /b effectively disables color throughout the session.

Edit

The Edit command, in versions 5 and 6, starts the MS-DOS Editor, a full-screen, menu-based text editor for creating, modifying, and saving plain-text (ASCII) files. Beginning in version 5, the Editor replaces the serviceable but geriatric Edlin. The Editor, along with its menus, commands, and keystrokes, is described in detail in Chapter 15. The following descriptions tell how to start the Editor from the MS-DOS command line.

NOTE: *The Editor is less a "word processor" than it is a part of the QBasic interpreter, and it relies on the file QBASIC.EXE to function. Do not delete QBASIC.EXE if you want to use Edit.*

Command syntax

The syntax of the Edit command is as follows:

edit [*filespec*] /b /g /h /nohi

filespec is the drive, path, filename, and extension of a file you want to edit. If the file does not exist—that is, you haven't typed the name of a file you want to create—the Editor creates the file(name) and starts with a blank screen. If you do not include *filespec*, the Editor starts with a blank screen. In this case, you can later save any file you create with the Save As command on the Editor's File menu. Unlike word processors, the Editor does not assign a default extension. To load or save a file with a specific extension (a batch file, for example), be sure to include the extension as part of the file specification.

/b starts the Editor in black and white. You might need this switch if you use a monochrome monitor.

/h displays the most lines possible for your monitor.

/g tells the Editor to provide the fastest possible updating on a CGA monitor. You do not need this switch with EGA, VGA, or other monitors.

/nohi sets the Editor to work with an 8-color monitor. (The Editor is designed to work with 16 colors.)

Examples

Type:	To:
`C:\>edit c:\autoexec.bat`	Start the Editor and open the file AUTOEXEC.BAT for viewing or editing.
`C:\>edit b:\cakes\ale.txt`	Start the Editor and open or create the file named ALE.TXT in the CAKES directory of the disk in drive B.
`C:\>edit newfile /g`	Start the Editor with fast screen updates on a CGA monitor and, at the same time, open or create a file named NEWFILE. Note that omitting the file extension means the Editor would not open or create NEWFILE.DOC, NEWFILE.TXT, or any other NEWFILE plus extension.

Edlin—through version 5 only

Edlin, the command, calls up Edlin, the text editor. Familiar to many long-time MS-DOS users, Edlin is a line-oriented plain-text editor, meaning that you create and edit ASCII files on a line-by-line basis. To create a new file, you can simply type, ending each line by pressing the Enter key. To edit a particular line, however, you call for the line by number. Whichever line you last displayed or worked on becomes what Edlin considers the current line, the line that marks your position in the file. Because Edlin works strictly by line number, you cannot scroll up or down in a file. You must specifically turn Edlin's attention to the line you want.

Although the description of Edlin so far would indicate that it is not the ideal choice for editing text files, there are instances in which Edlin can be much faster than the MS-DOS Editor. If you want to bang out a quick note, make a simple change to a batch file, or even create a small batch file you know will not require much fine-tuning, you'll find that Edlin loads and saves the file much more quickly than the Editor can. The Edlin commands, which are briefly described here, are terse and not easy to remember, but if you stick to the basics—inserting, deleting, and editing within a line—Edlin does, indeed, sometimes have the edge on the Editor.

Edlin is absent in version 6 of MS-DOS, but you can use it if you've upgraded from version 5 or earlier and the file EDLIN.EXE is in the current command path. Version 6 of MS-DOS is not designed to work with Edlin, and requesting help will net you the response *No match found*, but version 6 does still support Edlin, if it exists on your machine.

Edlin is not covered elsewhere in this book, so the following descriptions and examples represent something of a goodbye to an old friend. Surly as it sometimes is, Edlin has, since version 1 of MS-DOS, provided a real alternative to using a word processor for unformatted text files. Besides, it's kind of fun to use.

Command syntax

The syntax of the Edlin command is as follows:

    edlin *filespec* /b

filespec is the drive, path, filename, and extension of a file you want to create or edit. You must include *filespec*, and you must be very specific as to the location and extension of the file. Edlin is very literal.

/b tells Edlin to ignore the end-of-file character (Ctrl-Z) in the file you're loading. If you're working on a file that has Ctrl-Z in the middle, you'll need this.

Commands and examples

The Edlin editing commands are those you can use after starting Edlin. They are briefly described here in alphabetic order after the descriptions of the two "general" commands—Edit Line and Help—which allow you to work on specific lines and call for help. The following applies to Edlin as a whole:

- A line, to Edlin, consists of all the characters you type up to a press of the Enter key. The maximum line length is 253 characters.

- When you edit a line in Edlin, it displays two lines, as follows:

      3:*line 3 of the file
      3:*

  The top line shows the line as it currently exists. This line is called the template. The bottom line is where you type the line as you want it to be. This line is called the new line. The asterisk after the line number indicates that the line is the current line. An asterisk is also the Edlin prompt, as you can see in the first line of the following:

```
*3
  3:*line 3 of the file ──── Template
  3:* ──────────── New line
```

- ■ To edit a line, you can do the following:
    - □ Press F1 or the right direction key to copy one character at a time from the template to the new line.
    - □ Press Backspace or the left direction key (from somewhere within the line), to delete one character at a time from the new line.
    - □ Press F2, followed by a character key, to copy from the template up to, but not including, the character you pressed, to the new line.
    - □ Press F3 to copy the entire template (useful when you want to add to the end of the line) to the new line.
    - □ Press F4, followed by a character key, to delete the template up to the first instance of the character you pressed.

Changes to the template do not take effect until you press Enter. To cancel what you've done, press Ctrl-C.

NOTE: Where a command accepts or requires one or more line numbers, you refer to the line by actual number (as in 14d). If you want to get fancy, you can also use the + and − symbols to refer to the line +x lines below the current line or −y lines above the current line. This can be confusing, though, especially if you delete, copy, or move lines, because Edlin renumbers the lines automatically. If you use + and −, use the List or Page command frequently to be sure you know which line you're referring to. You can also use # (number sign) to stand for the line after the highest line in your file, and . (period) to stand for the current line.

The Edlin commands are as follows. For more details, you can also refer to your version 5 or earlier MS-DOS documentation.

Edit Line

[*line*] displays the specified line. For example,

```
*3
```

displays line 3.

```
*+3
```

displays the line 3 lines below the current line. (Below means a line number that is "higher"—for example, 6 is below 3 and 3 plus 3 equals 6.)

Help

? displays a list of Edlin commands. Note that you type this command at the Edlin prompt. It is not the same as typing *help edlin* or *edlin /?* at the system prompt. For example,

```
*?
```

displays a list of Edlin commands and command syntax, part of which looks like the following:

```
Edit line            line#
Append               [#lines]A
Copy                 [startline],[endline],toline[,times]C
Delete               [startline][,endline]D
End (save file)      E
. . .
```

whereas the following command

```
C:\>edlin /?
```

produces online help about Edlin.

Append

*[lines]*a appends the specified number of lines from disk to the file in memory. Edlin normally reads a file until available memory is about 75 percent full. You use the Append command when a file is too large to fit in memory. Before you use Append, use the Write command to write the beginning (presumably edited) portion of the file back to disk. For example,

```
*50a
```

appends (loads in) 50 lines of the file you're currently editing into memory.

Copy

[firstline],*[lastline]*,*toline[,times]*c copies the lines from *firstline* through *lastline* to the line specified by *toline*, duplicating the copied lines as many times as you specify with the optional *times* parameter. The syntax, like that of Move, is confusing, but the following example should help you see what happens:

```
*5,10,20,2c
```

copies lines 5 through 10, inclusive, to the position just above line 20. The 2 in this command tells Edlin to copy the lines twice. If the current line were 5, you could also type the following:

```
*  ,10,20,2c
```

or

```
*  ,+5,+15,2c
```

Delete

[*firstline*][*,lastline*]d deletes the range of lines from *firstline* through *lastline*. To delete a single line, omit *lastline*. To delete the current line, type *d* without any parameters. For example,

    *3d

deletes line 3 of the current file.

    *3,5d

deletes lines 3 through 5.

End Edit and Quit

e, with no parameters, ends the current editing session and saves the file. Quit, abbreviated q, ends the session without saving the file. If you use the Quit command, Edlin prompts for confirmation with the message *Abort edit (Y/N)?* Press Y to confirm, N to cancel and return to the Edlin prompt. For example,

    *e

ends the session and saves the file, including any changes you have made.

    *q

prompts for confirmation before ending the session. If you press *Y*, all changes you made to the file are lost.

Insert

[*line*]i inserts a new line above the line you specify as *line*. To insert lines at the end of a file, specify *line* either as the next line in the sequence or use the # (number sign) followed by i or—if you are lazy—any line number greater than the number of lines in the file. You must use the Insert command first when starting Edlin with a new file. To insert a number of sequential lines, you need to use the Insert command only for the first new line. Edlin will continue inserting new lines after it each time you press Enter. When you're tired of entering new lines, press Ctrl-C at a blank line. For example,

    *20i

inserts a new line immediately before line 20.

    *100i

when used with a file 20 lines long, inserts new lines at the end of the file (starting at line 21).

List

[*firstline*][*,lastline*]l displays the range of lines from *firstline* through *lastline*. If you omit *firstline* (but include the comma before *lastline*), List displays up to one screenful, beginning 11 lines before the current line and ending at *lastline*. If you omit *lastline*, List displays up to one screenful, beginning with *firstline*. If you omit both first and last lines, List displays up to one screenful, beginning 11 lines above the current line. For example,

```
*1,5l
```

displays lines 1 through 5.

```
*,75l
```

displays up to one screenful, beginning 11 lines above the current line and ending at line 75 (if line 75 is part of that screenful).

```
*l
```

displays up to one screenful, beginning 11 lines above the current line. If the current line is less that 11, it will display the lines starting at line 1.

Move

[*firstline*],[*lastline*],*toline*m moves the range of lines from *firstline* through *lastline* to the position above the line specified as *toline*. For example,

```
*20,30,10m
```

moves lines 20 through 30 to the position above line 10.

Page

[*firstline*],[*lastline*]p displays the lines from *firstline* through *lastline*. Although Page is very similar to List, there are some differences. When you use Page, the line you specify as *lastline* becomes the current line; when you use List, the current line remains unchanged. In other respects, omitting *firstline* (but including the leading comma) displays up to one screenful, ending with *lastline*. If you omit *lastline*, Page displays up to one screenful, beginning with *firstline*. If you omit both the first and last line, Page displays up to one screenful, beginning with the line after the current line. For example,

```
*p
```

displays one screenful of the file, beginning with the line after the current line. Use this form of the command to "scroll" through a file. Remember, however, that the current line changes each time.

```
*,40p
```

displays one screenful of the file, ending at line 40.

```
*40p
```

displays one screenful of the file, beginning with line 40.

NOTE: A default screenful for paging is 23 lines of text. You can change the number of lines displayed, however, with the Mode con lines = *command. Note that the number of lines will be one more than you will be able to display.*

Quit

See the entry for End Edit and Quit.

Replace

[*firstline*][*,lastline*][?]r[*oldstring*][Ctrl-Z*newstring*] searches the range from *firstline* through *lastline*, replacing any occurrence of *oldstring* with *newstring*. This command, one of Edlin's better brain-twisters, obeys the following rules:

- The optional question mark (?) causes Edlin to prompt for confirmation before each replacement.

- Ctrl-Z (or F6), which appears on screen as ^Z, is required to separate the text you specify as *oldstring* from the text you specify as *newstring*.

- Any spaces between parameters following the r in the command are taken literally. You can search and replace any character you can type, *except* Ctrl-Z.

- Replacements are case sensitive, meaning that Replace will match uppercase and lowercase. Thus, if you specify *oldstring* as *Butter* but the file contains only *butter*, Replace will respond *Not found*. Also, remember that Replace does not normally distinguish between whole words and parts of words. Thus, if you specify *butter*, Replace finds not only *butter*, but *butterfly*, *butterfish*, and *butterball*.

- If you omit *firstline*, Replace begins at the line following the current line. If you omit *lastline*, Replace stops at the end of the file. If you omit *oldstring*, Replace uses either the last *oldstring* you specified in a Replace command or the last string you specified in a Search command, whichever is more recent. You must, by the way, press Ctrl-Z even if you omit *oldstring*. On the other hand, if you omit *newstring*, be careful: Replace uses the last *newstring* you specified in a Replace command if possible, but if you haven't used the command in the current session, Replace deletes all occurrences of *oldstring*.

By way of example,

```
*1,40?rbutter^Zoleo
```

replaces all occurrences of *butter* with *oleo* in lines 1 through 40, prompting before each replacement.

```
*?rbutter^Zoleo
```

replaces as in the previous example, but from the line following the current line through the end of the file.

Search

[*firstline*][*,lastline*][?]s*string* searches the range from *firstline* through *lastline* for the string specified as *string*. Including ? in the command causes Search to prompt for confirmation after each match. The Search command is very similar to the Replace command, except that its job is limited to finding text, rather than finding and replacing it. For example,

```
*1,40?sbutter
```

searches for all occurrences of *butter* in lines 1 through 40, prompting with an *O.K?* each time it finds a match. The search continues until you press Y to indicate you've found the correct line.

```
*?sbutter
```

searches as in the previous example, but starts from the line after the current line and continues to the end of the file.

Transfer

[*toline*]t*filespec* transfers (inserts) the file specified by *filespec* into the current file, at the position just above the line specified by *toline*. The file specification can include a drive and path, but must at least include a filename (and an extension, if appropriate). For example,

```
*4tb:\nuts\pecans.txt
```

inserts the file named PECANS.TXT from the NUTS directory on the disk in drive B above line 4 in the current file.

Write

[*lines*]w writes the number of lines specified by *lines* to disk. Use this command only if a file does not fit completely into memory. To save a file, all of which is in memory, use the End Edit command. For example,

```
*150w
```

writes the first 150 lines of a file to disk.

Exit

The Exit command is what you use to quit one copy of COMMAND.COM and return to the program that called the command interpreter. The Exit command is simple, and you need to use it only when exiting a secondary copy of COMMAND.COM. The only time Exit does not work is when you start COMMAND.COM with the /p (permanent) switch. For more details, refer to the earlier description of the Command command.

Command syntax

The syntax of the Exit command is simply as follows:

```
exit
```

Examples

Type:	To:
`C:\>exit`	Return to the program that called the secondary copy of COMMAND.COM. The calling program can be the MS-DOS Shell, Microsoft Windows, or any program that "shells" out to MS-DOS.

Fast Help (Fasthelp)—version 6 only

Fast Help (Fasthelp) is to version 6 of MS-DOS what Help was to version 5: a means of displaying a description of each command supported by MS-DOS, along with the syntax for that command. Fasthelp is, essentially, condensed Help. Instead of a text window with menus and cross-references to topics you can jump to with the mouse or keyboard, a Fasthelp display gives you just the facts you need to use a command or quickly refresh your memory. You can use Fasthelp to view

- A list of MS-DOS commands, displayed one screenful at a time, with brief, one-line descriptions of each.

- Help on a specific command.

Typical Fasthelp output (here for the Date command) looks like this:

```
Displays or sets the date.

DATE [mm-dd-yy]

  mm-dd-yy    Sets the date you specify.

Type DATE without parameters to display the current date setting and
a prompt for a new one.  Press ENTER to keep the same date.
```

Command syntax

You can display the information produced by Fasthelp in either of two ways:

　　fasthelp [*command*]

　　command /?

command is, of course, the name of an MS-DOS command, including Fasthelp.

Examples

Type:	To:
C:\>fasthelp	See a list of MS-DOS commands, one screenful at a time, with a brief description of each.
C:\>fasthelp /?	See Fasthelp on Fasthelp.
C:\>fasthelp format	See Fasthelp on the Format command.
C:\>format /?	See the same as the previous example.

Help

The Help command works differently in versions 5 and 6 of MS-DOS. In both versions, however, the command serves to call up online help on MS-DOS commands. Online help is described in Chapter 6. The following descriptions tell how to access Help.

Command syntax

In version 6 of MS-DOS, the syntax of the Help command is as follows:

help /b /g /h /nohi [*topic*]

/b allows you to use a monochrome display with a color graphics (CGA) video card.

/g provides the fastest possible updating on a CGA monitor. You do not need this switch with EGA, VGA, or other monitors.

/h displays the most lines per screen that your video hardware can accommodate.

/nohi allows use of a monitor that does not support high-intensity character display.

[*topic*] represents the name of a command for which you want to request help. You can specify any topic, including those such as *Batch commands* and *CONFIG.SYS commands*, that you find listed on the opening Help screen (the one you see when you type *help* without a *topic* parameter).

In version 5 of MS-DOS, the syntax of the Help command is simpler:

help [*command*]

command, in this instance, is the name of any legitimate MS-DOS command. Depending on the software installed on your system, *command* might also include the names of commands supported by third-party utilities and other programs. MS-DOS Help has been designed so that developers can add to it if they wish.

Examples

Type:	To:
C:\>help	See help on Help.
C:\>help format	See help on the Format command.
C:\>help /h batch commands	See help on batch commands displayed with the largest number of lines per screen supported by your video hardware (version 6 only). Typing *help/h batch* would have the same result.

MSCDEX—version 6 only

MSCDEX, short for Microsoft CD Extensions, is a new version 6 command that enables MS-DOS to access CD-ROM drives. In a sense, this command is the middle link in a chain: At one end is the CD-ROM drive; at the other is the device driver that defines the drive to MS-DOS. In the middle is MSCDEX, which enables the driver and makes a connection between it and a logical drive letter that you can use to refer to the CD-ROM drive, just as you use A, B, and C to refer to the disk drives on your system.

When you install a CD-ROM drive, part of the installation involves placing a Device or a Devicehigh command for the drive in CONFIG.SYS. This Device or Devicehigh command enables MS-DOS to find and load the driver at startup. You must complete this part of the installation before you can use MSCDEX. The Device or Devicehigh command that you need in CONFIG.SYS takes the following form:

device=[*drive:*][*path*]CDdriver /d:*drivername*

drive and *path* specify the drive and directory containing the CD-ROM driver shown in the syntax line as *CDdriver*. The /d switch is required and must be followed by a unique driver name that generally looks something like MSCD000. Check your CD-ROM drive's documentation and installation instructions for the details you need. If you have more than one CD-ROM drive, you must use a separate Device or Devicehigh command for each drive in CONFIG.SYS. While you're working on your CONFIG.SYS file, check your Lastdrive command to be sure you've specified a high enough last drive letter to cover the CD-ROM drive. (If you need help with this, refer to the Lastdrive command in Chapter 12.)

Once you've made the appropriate change(s) to CONFIG.SYS, you can use the MSCDEX command either from the system prompt or, more likely, from your AUTOEXEC.BAT file.

Command syntax

The syntax of the MSCDEX command is as follows:

mscdex /d:*drivername* /e /k /s /v /l:*driveletter* /m:*number*

drivername is the identifying name of the CD-ROM drive, such as MSCD000. This name must match the driver name you specify with the /d switch in the CONFIG.SYS command that loads the device driver. If you have more than one CD-ROM drive, repeat the /d:*drivername* switch for each drive, separating the switches with a space, as shown in one of the later examples.

/e enables the driver to use expanded memory, if available, to store sector buffers.

/k enables MS-DOS to recognize CD-ROM volumes (discs) encoded in Kanji (Japanese characters). By default, MS-DOS does not recognize Kanji.

/s allows sharing of a CD-ROM drive on an MS-NET or Windows for Workgroups server.

/v causes MSCDEX to display memory information when it starts.

/l:*driveletter* specifies the letter you want to assign to the CD-ROM drive. As already mentioned, be sure the Lastdrive command in your CONFIG.SYS file allows for enough drive letters. If you enable more than one CD-ROM drive with this command, MS-DOS assigns subsequent available drive letters.

/m:*number* specifies the number of sector buffers allocated to the drive.

Examples

The following example shows a Device command in CONFIG.SYS and the matching MSCDEX command you would use for a CD-ROM drive with a device driver named ROMDRIVE.SYS in the C:\CDROM directory. The driver name is assumed to be MSCD000.

The command in CONFIG.SYS would be as follows:

```
DEVICE=C:\CDROM\ROMDRIVE.SYS /D:MSCD000
```

The MSCDEX command to install the CD-ROM drive as drive M in AUTOEXEC.BAT would be as follows:

```
mscdex /d:mscd000 /l:m
```

To do the same, but enable the CD-ROM driver to use expanded memory, the command would be as follows:

```
mscdex /d:mscd000 /e /l:m
```

To enable MS-DOS to use two CD-ROM drives named MSCD000 and MSCD001, the MSCDEX command (assuming that both drives had been identified in CONFIG.SYS) would be as follows:

```
mscdex /d:mscd000 /d:mscd001 /l:m
```

In this case, the first CD-ROM drive would be assigned drive letter M; the second would be assigned the next available drive letter, such as N.

Prompt

The Prompt command sets the system prompt. In versions 4 and later, MS-DOS is set up to show the system prompt as the current drive and directory, followed by a greater-than sign, like this:

```
C:\>
```

if your current drive and directory is the root of drive C. This prompt is so common that many people probably consider it the default always used by MS-DOS. In fact, it was not. The default omits the current directory and looks like this:

```
C>
```

Simple or complex, when you want to customize your system by changing the prompt, you do so with the Prompt command. Because Prompt responds to the dollar sign ($) followed by certain predefined characters, it's easy to display such information as the date, time, and MS-DOS version number. If you're an ANSI.SYS fan, you can use the $e characters supported by the Prompt command to go all out and customize the prompt with color or to control the location at which the prompt is displayed. Regardless of your experience with MS-DOS, Prompt is one command you can experiment with as much as you want without worrying about causing indigestion to either MS-DOS or your computer. If you're going to experiment, the command you can use to return everything to "normal" is as follows:

```
prompt $p$g
```

This command, or one like it, might be in your AUTOEXEC.BAT file. Prompt, by itself, sets the prompt to the equivalent of ng—that is, the current drive and the greater-than sign, but *not* the current path.

NOTE: ANSI.SYS control sequences involving color can backfire on you and refuse to go away, but even such sticky prompts can be taken care of by rebooting.

Command syntax

The syntax of the Prompt command is as follows:

prompt [*text*]

text can be any text or message you want to display. You can use one or more of the following dollar-sign plus character combinations to produce the effects described. You can type the characters in either uppercase or lowercase.

Use:	To:
$Q	Display an equal sign.
$$	Display a dollar sign.
$T	Display the time.
$D	Display the date.
$P	Display the current drive and path.
$V	Display the MS-DOS version number.
$N	Display the current drive.
$G	Display a greater-than (>) sign.
$L	Display a less-than (<) sign.
$B	Display a pipe (¦).
$_	Insert an enter and a linefeed character, which moves the remainder of the prompt to a new line.
$E	Enter an ASCII escape code (ASCII 27). Use this when you enter ANSI.SYS control sequences.
$H	Enter a Backspace character, which deletes the displayed character immediately to the left.

Any other combination of the dollar sign and a character displays nothing but the cursor.

Examples

Type or include in a batch file:	To:
prompt What would you like me to do?	Change the prompt to *What would you like me to do?* _
prompt pg	Return the prompt to *C:\>*_
prompt d_t_pg	Change the prompt to three lines showing the date, time, and current drive and directory, as follows: *Sun 01-03-1993* *3:28:30.25* *C:\>*_
prompt $e[36;40m$p$g	Display the prompt as the current drive and directory, but in cyan characters on black (with the ANSI.SYS control sequence $e[36;40m). Note that ANSI.SYS must be loaded from your CONFIG.SYS file if you want to use ANSI control sequences. In addition, you should note that this prompt displays all MS-DOS output, including command output, in cyan on black.
prompt $e[36;40m$pge[m	Do the same as in the previous example, but display only the prompt in cyan on black.

Qbasic

The Qbasic command starts the QBasic interpreter, a working environment in which you can create and execute programs written in the QBasic language. QBasic, as a programming language, is not within the scope of this book, although Chapter 20 does give you a quick and very superficial look at it. If you use QBasic, however, the following descriptions tell how to use it from the command line.

Command syntax

The syntax of the Qbasic command is as follows:

qbasic /b /editor /g /h /mbf /nohi /run *filespec*

/b displays QBasic in black and white, even if you have a color monitor.

/editor starts the MS-DOS Editor. This switch produces the same result as typing *edit* at the system prompt.

/g provides the fastest possible updating on a CGA monitor. You do not need this switch with EGA, VGA, or other monitors.

/h displays the most lines per screen that your video hardware can accommodate.

/mbf converts the built-in functions MKS$ and MKD$ to, respectively, MKSMBF$ and MKDMBF$, and it converts the built-in functions CVS and CVD to, respectively, CVSMBF and CVDMBF. The MKS$ and MKD$, and the CVS and CVD functions convert numbers to strings, and vice versa. MKSMBF$ and MKDMBF$ convert IEEE-format numbers to Microsoft Binary Format (MBF) numeric strings, and CVSMBF and CVDMBF convert those strings back to IEEE-format numbers.

/nohi allows use of a monitor that does not support high-intensity character display.

/run *filespec* runs the program specified as *filespec*. Typing /run is optional. If you just type a filename after Qbasic, the file will be loaded but not run. If the filename has the BAS extension, you can omit the extension.

Examples

Type:	To:
`C:\>qbasic c:\dos\gorilla`	Start QBasic and load and display the file GORILLA.BAS (a sample QBasic program included with version 5 of MS-DOS).
`C:\>qbasic /run c:\dos\gorilla`	Run the GORILLA.BAS program.
`C:\>qbasic /b`	Start QBasic in black and white.

Share

The Share command, present in MS-DOS since version 3, provides a user-controlled means of supporting file sharing and locking in a networking environment. When you use the Share command, you install a memory-resident program named SHARE.EXE. This program acts as a monitor for all network file sharing, tracking open files and validating read and write requests to ensure that two people do not attempt to modify the file at the same time. When loaded with its default settings, Share occupies about 6 K of memory. You can install Share in either of two ways: by entering the command at the system prompt or from a batch file, or by installing SHARE.EXE with an Install command in CONFIG.SYS. If you choose to use Install, Share takes up slightly less memory.

Command syntax

The syntax for the Share command is as follows:

> share /f:*bufferspace* /l:*locks*

To load SHARE.EXE with the Install command, the syntax is as follows:

> install=[*drive*:][*path*]SHARE.EXE /f:*bufferspace* /l:*locks*

/f:*bufferspace* specifies the amount of room, in bytes, that Share sets aside for holding file-related information—the full pathname, plus a small amount of overhead. The default is 2048 bytes, enough room for about 100 files with average-size (20-byte) paths.

/l:*locks* specifies the number of entries set aside for an internal table that contains file-locking information, which is needed to prevent simultaneous access to the same region of the same file by two people. Each entry in the table corresponds to one lock on one region of an open file. The default, 20, means that Share will support 20 locks at the same time.

drive and *path* are the drive and path to the SHARE.EXE file.

Examples

Type:	To:
`C:\>share /f:4096 /l:50`	Install the file-sharing program, setting aside 4096 bytes for file-related information and enabling 50 locks at the same time.
Include in CONFIG.SYS:	
`install=c:\dos\share.exe` `    /f:4096 /l:50`	Do the same as above, but loading SHARE.EXE from your CONFIG.SYS file.

(continued)

Type:	To:
Include in CONFIG.SYS:	
`install?=c:\dos\share.exe` `/f:4096 /l:50`	Do the same as above, but prompt for confirmation before loading SHARE.EXE from CONFIG.SYS (version 6 only).

Time

The Time command is the complement of the Date command. Time allows you to display or change the time kept by the system clock. The time, like the date, is used by MS-DOS in time-and-date stamping files and directories.

If, as is usually the case these days, your computer has a battery-controlled clock/calendar as part of its built-in CMOS setup, you don't have to worry about setting the time at startup. You do, however, use the Time command to match your system to different time zones and to match changes caused by daylight saving time.

When you type the Time command, MS-DOS displays the following:

```
Current time is  2:05:05.40p
Enter new time: _
```

To change the time, type a new value as described in the "Command Syntax" section. To leave the time as displayed, press Enter. To change the time without having MS-DOS prompt for it, type *time* followed by the time you want to set—for example, *time 9:40a.*

NOTE: The format used by MS-DOS in displaying the time is determined by the country setting in your CONFIG.SYS file (or by the default hardware code page built into your computer). If your country format allows time to be displayed in either 12-hour or 24-hour format, be sure to type an a or a p after the time to specify 12-hour format.

Command syntax

The syntax of the Time command is as follows:

time [*hours:minutes:seconds.hundredths*][a or p]

hours, minutes, seconds, and *hundredths* specify the time you want to set. Separate hours, minutes, and seconds with colons (:). If you care to race the clock, separate seconds from hundredths of seconds with a period (.). Valid values are as follows:

hours	0 through 23
minutes	0 through 59
seconds	0 through 59
hundredths	0 through 99

a and p specify the time according to a 12-hour clock. If you want a 12-hour format, be sure to specify p for times after noon.

Examples

Type:	To:
C:\>time	Display the current time and a prompt for a new time.
C:\>time 6:40p	Change the time to 6:40 at night for a 12-hour clock.
C:\>time 18:40	Do the same as in the previous example for a 24-hour clock.

Version (Ver)

The Version command displays the number of the version of MS-DOS you are using. Enough said.

Command syntax

The syntax of the Version command is as follows:

    ver

Example

Type:	To:
C:\>ver	Display the MS-DOS version number. Include such a command in a batch file if it is important to display or determine the version of MS-DOS that is running on the computer.

MS-DOS UTILITIES AND CUSTOMIZATION

14

Optimizing and Protecting Storage: Disks and Memory

What You'll Find Here: The two parts of your computer you entrust with data are its memory and its disk drives, especially its hard disk. It's difficult to go too far overboard in protecting these vital resources. After all, a computer is a computer, but data is irreplaceable. This chapter is about using MS-DOS tools to make the best possible use of both memory and disk storage. None of the tools described here exists in versions of MS-DOS prior to 5. Most are new with version 6; two in particular—DoubleSpace and MemMaker—will easily convince you that version 6 is worth the price of admission.

*T*his chapter is about optimizers of the computer kind, a set of utilities that help tune your system and keep it running efficiently. These tools are organized and described here as follows:

- For using disk space efficiently:
  - □ DoubleSpace (Dblspace), the version 6 disk doubler
  - □ Defragmenter (Defrag), the version 6 disk compaction utility
- For using memory efficiently:
  - □ MemMaker (Memmaker), the version 6 memory maximizer
- For protecting disks and memory:
  - □ Microsoft Anti-Virus, the version 6 equivalent of your antibody system
  - □ VSafe, the version 6 memory-resident virus monitor
- For managing disk-based information:
  - □ Microsoft Backup (Msbackup), the version 6 librarian and archivist
  - □ Undelete and Unformat, the versions 5 and 6 file and disk recovery twins
  - □ Delete Tree (Deltree), the version 6 pruning tool for (carefully) lopping branches off overgrown directory trees

Using disk space efficiently

There are three aspects to using disks efficiently: organization, maintenance, and physical storage. Organization is a matter of setting up subdirectories that match the way you work and think. Although people can give you guidelines about defining and maintaining a directory tree, the choice is ultimately up to you. You must decide whether you want applications in subdirectories of the root directory (where they usually propose to install themselves) or in subdirectories of an APPS or PROGRAMS directory that clearly separates software from data files. Similarly, you are the final arbiter when it comes to deciding whether documents should be grouped by type (letters, sales reports, mailing lists, graphics), by program (word processor, spreadsheet, database, paint program), by relationship (personal, business, project, client), or some other logical breakdown that makes sense to you.

Disk maintenance boils down to housekeeping. It is to your hard disk what clearing your desk and file drawers is to your office: clutter removal. To help you in this effort, MS-DOS has always offered the Delete and Copy commands. Versions 2 through 5 include Backup and Restore, and versions 3.2 onward provide

Extended Copy (Xcopy) as well. Beginning with version 6 of MS-DOS, you have the more capable Microsoft Backup utility, which offers three-in-one maintenance: file comparison and restoration as well as backup. And for those times when the *All files in directory will be deleted!* message gets on your nerves when you're cleaning out a subdirectory, version 6 provides major surgery in the form of Deltree. All these commands, including their syntax and uses, are described in Chapters 7, 8, and 9. Msbackup and Deltree are also described in a little more detail at the end of this chapter along with the Undelete and Unformat commands, which help you recover from too-fast presses of the Enter key.

In contrast to organization and maintenance, optimizing physical storage means making the best use of available space on your hard disk and, to the extent you choose, on your floppy disks. To do this, you combine the data compression provided by DoubleSpace with the disk compaction provided by Defrag to store your program and data files as neatly and as tightly as possible on disk. Prior to version 6 of MS-DOS, compaction and compression were available only from non-Microsoft providers of MS-DOS utility software. Beginning in version 6, however, both features are available through the DoubleSpace and Microsoft Defragmenter utilities.

DoubleSpace

When you first use DoubleSpace, you can feel as though you've just gotten something for nothing—as, indeed, you have. As you'll see in the sample output later in this section, DoubleSpace can actually "expand" a 120-MB hard disk so that it can hold 180 MB or more. So how does DoubleSpace make this growth happen, and where does the space come from?

Start with a simple problem and an equally simple solution. Suppose you had 10 inflated balloons that you wanted to pack into a shoebox. How would you do it? By letting out the air. DoubleSpace does the same thing—roughly. To make your disk seem larger, it squeezes the "air" out of your files so that they take up less storage space. Depending on how you look at it, you can either say that your disk grows by so many megabytes or that your files shrink by the same proportion. The result is still the same: no change in the physical disk, but more available storage nonetheless.

Whether you're talking about hypothetical balloons or real files, however, there's another aspect to compression. Compressed balloons lack a certain aesthetic appeal. Compressed files *cannot* be used by MS-DOS until they are fattened up again. You've seen this with the compressed files you receive on your original MS-DOS disks. To use them, you must rely on MS-DOS Setup or the MS-DOS Expand command to decompress the files. The same holds true of files compressed by DoubleSpace, with one big difference: DoubleSpace compresses and decompresses your files on the fly, as you use them. The process is rapid and, to you, invisible.

How does it work?

When you think about DoubleSpace and try to envision what it does, it's tempting to picture something like the following happening.

$\boxed{FILE.EXE}$ = 1200 bytes

$\boxed{\text{\scriptsize FILE.EXE}}$ = 532 bytes

Conceptually, this diagram does represent what happens when you use DoubleSpace. Files do, indeed, shrink down so that they occupy less physical space on the disk. In reality, however, DoubleSpace is both less simple and far more intriguing.

When DoubleSpace compresses a disk, it divides the disk into two portions, one uncompressed and the other compressed. The uncompressed part, called the *host* of the compressed drive, is assigned a drive letter of its own. Unless you specifically access this host by drive letter, it never shows up in your normal work with MS-DOS. Even so, it serves two vital purposes. First, the uncompressed drive is where DoubleSpace stores files that cannot be deflated and still remain usable. Among these are the system files (IO.SYS and MSDOS.SYS), and the Windows swap file (if you run Windows version 3.1 in 386 enhanced mode). Second, and far more relevant in terms of disk compression, a large part of this host drive is set aside as a special file known as a *compressed volume file*, or CVF. This file, usually named DBLSPACE.000, becomes, in effect, the compressed drive you see whenever you use the Directory (Dir) and Check Disk (Chkdsk) commands to check on files and available disk space.

To understand how a compressed drive suddenly becomes a file, you have to leave old ways of thinking behind—that is, you must understand that the compressed portion of your drive doesn't really exist or at least not as a physical disk drive. The following diagram, more accurate than the previous one, shows how a CVF is related to a compressed disk drive. (Shaded areas represent files.)

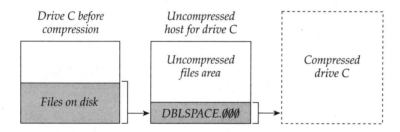

Although the compressed drive works exactly as it always has, the alchemy that is DoubleSpace quietly mediates between what you've got and what you think you've got. Whenever you save a file on a compressed disk, DoubleSpace shrinks the file and stores it in DBLSPACE.000. When you retrieve such a compressed file, DoubleSpace pulls it from DBLSPACE.000, inflates it, and presents it to you in the old familiar form. When you request a directory listing for a compressed file, you see the actual, not compressed, size of the file. In all respects but one—the amount of physical storage required—that file is unchanged as far as you are concerned.

As you can see, DoubleSpace is a sophisticated piece of software. To do its work, it relies on files named DBLSPACE.BIN and DBLSPACE.INI, as well as the DBLSPACE.000 you've already met. All of these files are stored on the uncompressed portion of a disk, and all are assigned the hidden, system, and read-only attributes for maximum protection from prying eyes and inadvertent Delete commands. The relationships among these files and the compressed and uncompressed portions of a disk are close to the point of entanglement, but located at the heart of disk compression is DBLSPACE.BIN.

DBLSPACE.BIN has more in common with IO.SYS, MSDOS.SYS, and COMMAND.COM than it does with other, more familiar MS-DOS files such as FORMAT.COM and CHKDSK.EXE. An add-on to the operating system itself, DBLSPACE.BIN is a system file that gives MS-DOS a brain boost of around 40,000 bytes. These bytes represent the program instructions that enable MS-DOS proper to access and use any hard or floppy disks you compress with the DoubleSpace command. DBLSPACE.BIN—like IO.SYS, MSDOS.SYS, and COMMAND.COM—appears on your startup hard disk and on every floppy system disk you create with version 6 of MS-DOS.

Whenever you boot or reboot the computer, DBLSPACE.BIN is loaded into memory very early in the process. The file doesn't provide any screen output as it moves into memory, but by the time you see the *Starting MS-DOS* message on screen, DBLSPACE.BIN is already resident and ready to go to work. It is thus processed before CONFIG.SYS and AUTOEXEC.BAT.

Because DBLSPACE.BIN is a system file, it loads into conventional memory—actually, the top of conventional memory—at startup. A highly movable beast, however, it doesn't necessarily stay put. When you run the DoubleSpace Setup program, described later, Setup places a Device or a Devicehigh command in CONFIG.SYS that loads the device driver named DBLSPACE.SYS. When loaded by means of a Device command, this driver has one purpose in life: to relocate DBLSPACE.BIN to its final resting place at the bottom of conventional memory. If the driver is loaded with a Devicehigh command and your computer has enough upper memory available, it moves DBLSPACE.BIN clean out of conventional memory and into UMBs.

DBLSPACE.INI and DBLSPACE.000 are both used by DBLSPACE.BIN in managing your compressed disks. DBLSPACE.000, of course, represents the compressed portion of a disk. DBLSPACE.INI contains initialization (startup) commands that define the disk drives on your system—for example, the number of removable drives, the first and last (but not always only) drive letters DoubleSpace considers available for use, and an association between the drive letters that define the compressed and uncompressed drive letters representing your startup hard disk. The most important thing to remember about these or any other DBLSPACE files is this: Leave them alone. If you tamper with them, you risk losing every file on your compressed disk. Need any more be said?

Setting up DoubleSpace

You can use DoubleSpace on both hard disks and floppy disks, and you can even use it to compress RAM drives, as described briefly later in this chapter. When you run DoubleSpace for the first time, the command starts a Setup program, which configures your system for DoubleSpace and compresses a disk you specify—by default, your primary (startup) hard disk. Until you run through this Setup program, you cannot use DoubleSpace as a utility to compress removable disks, such as a floppy. After setup is complete, however, DoubleSpace reverts to utility form and allows you to view and manage any compressed or compressible disks when and as you choose.

Express vs. Custom setup

When you run DoubleSpace the first time, it offers two choices: Express setup or Custom setup. An Express setup, by default, compresses an entire hard disk and all the files on it. A Custom setup lets you choose between compressing the disk and creating a new compressed drive. After you've run DoubleSpace Setup for the first time, you can compress and create new compressed disks either with the Compress menu in the DoubleSpace window or with the Dblspace /compress and Dblspace /create commands you use from the command line.

How does creating a compressed drive differ from compressing an existing drive? When you create a new compressed disk, you tell DoubleSpace to leave existing files on the disk alone and simply compress whatever free space remains on the disk (almost all of it if the disk is newly formatted). When you compress an existing disk, you compress all the files on your disk. The following table compares the two options:

Compress existing disk:	Create new compressed disk:
Preferable if the disk is getting full.	Possibly preferable if the disk contains a large amount of free space.
Time-consuming, because Double-Space both compresses and verifies compression of all existing compressible files.	Faster than compressing an existing disk.

(continued)

Compress existing disk:	Create new compressed disk:
DoubleSpace assigns the current drive letter to the compressed drive and a new (higher) drive letter to the uncompressed drive.	DoubleSpace assigns the current drive letter to the *uncompressed* drive and a new drive letter to the compressed drive. Bear in mind that this reversal means you (and your batch files) will have to refer to the compressed drive by a new drive letter.
Not easily reversible.	Compressed disk can be deleted and space can be recovered.

The following two reports show the results of both options on the same hard disk. When a new drive is created, the result is as follows:

```
DoubleSpace has created drive H by converting free space
from drive C.

      Space used from drive C:      70.6 MB
      Free space on new drive:      141.3 MB
      Compression ratio:            2.0 to 1
      Total time to create:         1 minute

Drive C still contains 2.0 MB of free uncompressed space.
```

Note that drive C is down to 2 MB of uncompressed space. When the same disk is compressed:

```
DoubleSpace has finished compressing drive C.

      Free space before compression:   62.5 MB
      Free space after compression:    131.6 MB
      Compression ratio:               1.6 to 1
      Total time to compress:          12 minutes

DoubleSpace has created a new drive H that contains 2.0 MB
of uncompressed space. This space has been set aside for
files that must remain uncompressed.
```

Although this procedure took 11 minutes longer than the other, note that drive H is now the drive with 2 MB of uncompressed space, while the more familiar drive C contains 131.6 MB of free space. On your own system, choose the option that suits you best.

Even though DoubleSpace Setup is largely automatic, consider the factors on the following page before you run the program.

- Express setup is recommended, but it can take a long time if the disk is large and full of files. If you're going to use Express setup, run DoubleSpace Setup when you have some time to spare or you won't be needing the computer for a while. If you'd like a trial run before committing your hard disk to DoubleSpace, you can try Custom setup and choose to create a new compressed disk. Such a disk can be deleted later; an Express setup cannot easily be undone. (Removing DoubleSpace from your hard disk is possible, but not a chore to be taken lightly. If you must remove DoubleSpace, refer to the README.TXT file in your DOS directory.)

- If you plan to choose an Express setup, audit your hard disk first. Delete or back up old files, remove programs you don't use, and clean out temporary directories. If you've been using MS-DOS for a while and have no problems with it, use the Delete Old DOS (Deloldos) command to remove the backup OLD_DOS directory.

Running DoubleSpace Setup

Once you know what you want to do, start DoubleSpace Setup simply by typing the DoubleSpace command:

```
C:\>dblspace
```

When the Setup program starts, you see the following screen:

```
Welcome to DoubleSpace Setup.

The Setup program for DoubleSpace frees space on your hard
disk by compressing the existing files on the disk. Setup
also loads DBLSPACE.BIN, the portion of MS-DOS that provides
access to DoubleSpace compressed drives. DBLSPACE.BIN
requires about 40K of memory.

If you use a network, then before installing DoubleSpace,
start the network and connect to any drives you normally use.

  o To set up DoubleSpace now, press ENTER.

  o To learn more about DoubleSpace Setup, press F1.

  o To quit Setup without installing DoubleSpace, press F3.
```

Even if you have supreme confidence in your knowledge and Microsoft's competence, don't start by pressing Enter. Instead, press F1 to to request information about DoubleSpace. As mentioned earlier, there's no uninstall or uncompress option if you use Express setup. Once you compress the files on your primary hard disk, you're committed, so you might as well find out about DoubleSpace ahead of time. When you've read enough, press Esc to return to Setup proper.

During Setup, DoubleSpace carries out the following actions:

- It runs Chkdsk on your hard disk.

- It restarts your computer. (If your computer doesn't restart, turn it off and then on; doing so might make you feel as if you're "breaking" something, but it does work.)

- It compresses the disk.

- It defragments the disk.

- It modifies CONFIG.SYS and AUTOEXEC.BAT, as needed.

- It creates the invisible file named DBLSPACE.INI, which defines your disk drives and available drive letters.

When all is complete, you press Enter to return to MS-DOS and your newly compressed disk drive. The following example shows the type of report you can expect when you run Chkdsk on a compressed drive (here, a 120-MB hard disk):

```
Volume MS-DOS_6    created 01-12-1993 8:28p
Volume Serial Number is 1BE4-1B3A

183648256 bytes total disk space
    81920 bytes in 2 hidden files
   294912 bytes in 36 directories
 44433408 bytes in 1068 user files
138838016 bytes available on disk

     8192 bytes in each allocation unit
    23604 total allocation units on disk
    18134 available allocation units on disk

   655360 total bytes memory
   586608 bytes free
```

Notice that Chkdsk reports very large allocation units—much larger than the 2048 typical of a hard disk. Although these allocation units don't affect normal use of the drive, their size is one reason why you cannot use the Format command on a compressed disk. To reformat a compressed disk, you must use the DoubleSpace /format option described later and in Chapter 8.

Once you've compressed your hard disk, you can use DoubleSpace options, either from menus you access by typing *dblspace*, or from the command line, to manage this disk as well as any floppy disks (even RAM disks) you choose to compress.

Using DoubleSpace with floppy disks

To compress a floppy disk, you need at least 0.65 MB of free space on the disk (so this requirement leaves floppies 360 K and smaller out of the running). Once compressed, the floppy is then capable of holding considerably more data than before—an excellent option for backups or the Xcopy command. Once compressed, however, a floppy disk can be used

- Only on a computer running DoubleSpace.
- Only after you've mounted it with the dblspace /mount [*drive:*] command. (The word *mount* comes from the days of tape storage, when reels of tape had to be walked to, and mounted on, the tape drive—your history lesson for the day.)

The following Chkdsk report shows storage on a compressed 1.44-MB disk:

```
Volume Serial Number is 1BFD-035C

2768896 bytes total disk space
2768896 bytes available on disk

   8192 bytes in each allocation unit
    338 total allocation units on disk
    338 available allocation units on disk

 655360 total bytes memory
 586608 bytes free
```

Because floppies are so highly portable, you can easily lose track of whether a compressed disk has been mounted or not. The situation can be frustrating when you're in a hurry and can prove momentarily disorienting if you type the Dir command and don't see the list of files you expect to see. As already mentioned, floppies cannot be read until they are mounted with dblspace /mount [*drive:*]. To avoid confusion with compressed floppies, keep some stick-on dots or labels on hand and use them to code or color code your disks. Also, get in the habit of typing the Dir command. As soon as you see a file named READTHIS.TXT, you know you're dealing with a compressed floppy. If you want to make life easier for yourself, create a batch file like the following for each floppy drive:

```
if exist a:readthis.txt dblspace /mount a:
```

or use the following command and type the batch-file name and the drive letter without a colon:

```
if exist %1:readthis.txt dblspace /mount %1
```

All this takes some getting used to.

NOTE: You can use compressed drives from within Windows. Both the compressed and uncompressed portions of your primary hard disk will appear as drive icons in the Windows File Manager. If you want to use files on a compressed floppy, however, be sure to mount the disk before starting Windows. You cannot mount a disk while running Windows, even if you shell out to the MS-DOS prompt, and if you don't mount the disk, Windows will be able to "see" only the READTHIS.TXT file on the floppy.

Compressing a RAM drive

The DoubleSpace online Help and documentation don't mention compressing RAM drives, but you can do it. You don't have quite as much to gain from compressing a RAM drive as you do from compressing physical disks because the RAM drive remains compressed only until you shut down. Thus, you must either compress the drive each time you start up, or you must create a batch file that does the job for you. On the other hand, DoubleSpace views a compressed RAM drive as a local hard drive, so you don't have to mount the RAM drive. Furthermore, compressing a RAM drive does mean that you can stuff a lot of compressed files into memory, so the time spent on startup might prove worth the trouble, especially if your system is a little short on memory, if you habitually use your RAM drive for data files and programs, and if the speed of a virtual drive is important to you.

If you use the dblspace /compress option on your RAM drive, you can maximize the amount of compressed storage by specifying a reserve of 0.13 MB (the smallest amount possible) in a command like the following:

```
dblspace /compress d: /reserve=.13
```

This command would turn a 4-MB RAM drive into a 7.5-MB RAM drive with 0.1 MB set aside as uncompressed storage. Bear in mind, however, that such a RAM drive allows very little room for files, such as a Windows swap file, that must remain uncompressed. Evaluate your system and be sure you set aside enough reserve storage. If you omit the /reserve switch, DoubleSpace will set aside 2 MB of uncompressed storage. In the case of a 4-MB RAM drive, the result would be an uncompressed 2-MB volume and a compressed volume allowing about 3.8 MB of storage.

A quick look at DoubleSpace commands

Chapter 8 described using DoubleSpace from the command line. The following brief list should help you find your way around DoubleSpace and its menus. If DoubleSpace is a new and confusing utility for you, spend some time roaming through its Help files.

When you type the DoubleSpace command any time after installing DoubleSpace and compressing your hard disk, the utility opens with a screen like the one shown on the following page.

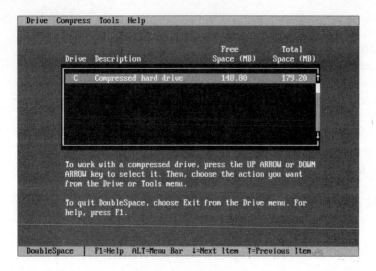

This screen shows all compressed drives and any floppy disks you mounted before typing *dblspace* to open the window.

As the instructions at the bottom of the screen tell you, use the direction keys to highlight the disk you want. To work with the disk, use the following commands:

- Choose Info from the Drive menu to see the following details: the letter of the disk's host drive; the amounts of its total, used, and free space; and its compression ratio (the amount by which files are compressed).

- Choose Change Size from the Drive menu to change the size of the compressed drive. When you choose this command, the following screen appears:

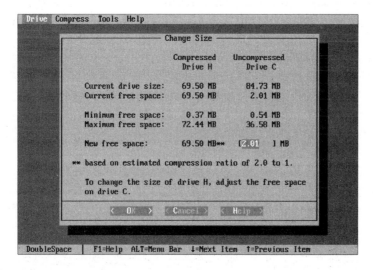

Change the value in the New Free Space line for the uncompressed drive. If that sounds a little backward, remember that the compressed drive is stored on the uncompressed drive.

- Choose Change Ratio to change the estimated compression ratio for the compressed drive. (Remember that you can see the actual compression ratios of your files with the /c switch of the Dir command.) The estimate is the ratio that DoubleSpace uses as a working figure when determining how much free space exists on the compressed drive. (DoubleSpace obviously can't know ahead of time just how tightly it will be able to compress future files.) If you use this command, don't worry overmuch about specifying a too-high compression ratio, such as 5 to 1. If Double-Space cannot compress files to that extent, it won't. Setting the ratio too high does, however, mean that you're causing DoubleSpace to overestimate the actual amount of free space on the disk.

- Choose Mount from the Drive menu to mount a compressed disk. As described earlier, this command is necessary when you're working with floppy disks. DoubleSpace mounts hard disks and RAM drives automatically.

- Choose Unmount from the Drive menu to unmount a disk. Again, this command applies primarily to floppy disks. (Switching to and using an uncompressed floppy also unmounts a compressed disk.)

- Choose Format from the Drive menu to format a compressed disk. DoubleSpace cautions you to be very careful about doing this because formatting of this type is irreversible. Bear in mind that formatting a compressed disk does not return the disk to its former, uncompressed state. Formatting simply clears out the CVF and all the files in the CVF, essentially leaving you (or your disk) holding an empty bag.

- Choose Delete from the Drive menu to delete a compressed drive. Doing this means that you delete the CVF and everything it contains. The space formerly occupied by the CVF once again becomes available for use. Deleting a compressed floppy disk essentially makes it an uncompressed disk again. (You will need to erase the little READTHIS.TXT file.)

- Choose Exit to leave DoubleSpace.

- Choose Existing Drive from the Compress menu to compress a disk. When you press Enter, DoubleSpace will scan all drives (including RAM drives) on your system for compressible disks. Choose the drive letter you want.

- Choose Create New Drive from the Compress menu to create a new compressed drive. When you choose this option, DoubleSpace lists the uncompressed hard disks and RAM drives on your system, as well as uncompressed host disks if they contain available space. This command does not apply to floppies.

- Choose Defragment from the Tools menu to defragment—tighten up storage—on a disk you have selected. Use this command before changing the size of a compressed disk. What this option really does is move all the files in the CVF to the front. It doesn't actually move the files on your drive as the Microsoft Defrag command does. Defragment works with both hard disks and floppies. Use this option when you won't need your computer for a while. Defragging can take a long time.

- Choose Chkdsk from the Tools menu to run the DoubleSpace version of Chkdsk on a compressed disk. Like regular Chkdsk, it lets you choose between simply checking or both checking and trying to fix file-storage errors. (It's really checking the CVF.)

- Choose Options from the Tools menu to set the last drive letter available for DoubleSpace to use and to set the number of removable-media drives (floppies, Bernoulli drives, flash memory cards) on your system.

- Choose the Help menu if you run into trouble or need additional information.

Defrag

The version 6 disk defragmenter, Microsoft Defragmenter, is related to a Norton Utilities program and arrived in MS-DOS via Symantec Corporation. Its purpose: to optimize disk storage by eliminating fragmentation and, if you so choose, by physically rearranging directories and files so that directories are at the beginning of the disk and all gaps—free spaces—are at the end.

Like DoubleSpace, Defrag is a more colorful utility than you'd normally expect of black-and-white MS-DOS. Although text-based, like all MS-DOS utilities (other than the version 6 Windows forms of Anti-Virus, Msbackup, and Undelete), Defrag operates in a full-screen window and interacts with you via menus and dialog boxes. As is typical of such utilities, it also offers fairly extensive online Help.

NOTE: Defrag works only on uncompressed drives. If you try to defragment a compressed disk, Defrag might do some work on it, but will hand the actual defragmenting to DoubleSpace.

When you start Defrag, the opening screen looks like this:

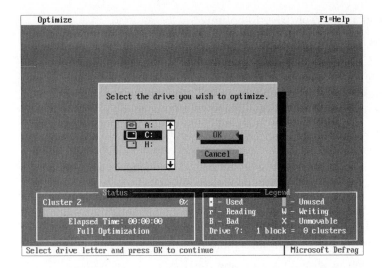

Select the disk you want to optimize, and from this point on, Defrag pretty much takes over and runs itself. First it analyzes the disk you specify to determine how badly fragmented it is. Depending on the results of this check, Defrag makes a recommendation: either full optimization if the disk needs a complete tune-up or unfragment files only if the disk is mildly fragmented. The recommendation looks like this:

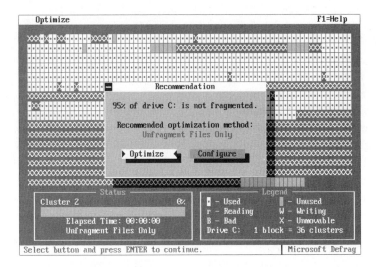

At this point, you can simply press Enter to start the process, or you can choose the Configure button to open the Optimize menu and make some choices of your own:

■ Begin Optimization to start optimizing.

- Drive to select a different drive to optimize.

- Optimization Method to choose between full optimization and unfrag-menting only. A full optimization unfragments files, moves directories to the front, and moves all free space to the end of the disk. Unfragment-ing consolidates fragmented files, but it does not move directories and does leave gaps between files. A full optimization takes longer.

- File Sort to specify the order in which you want files sorted within each directory (unsorted, or by name, extension, data and time, or size, in as-cending or descending order). Note that this doesn't affect the order of the files on the disk, just the way they're displayed.

- Map Legend to see pretty much the same information you see in the Legend box at the bottom of the full-screen window.

- About Defrag to see copyright information.

- Exit to leave Defrag without optimizing the disk.

Other than this, there's little to know ahead of time before running Defrag, other than the fact that full optimization can take a fairly long time, especially on a full hard disk. You won't need this utility often, but if you find that disk access is slowing down, if you want to check on file storage, or if you simply feel like straightening up your hard disk, Defrag is the tool you need. Use it periodically, or after deleting large numbers of files or directories, to keep your hard disk well in hand.

NOTE: *If you start Defrag from Windows, you may lose data.*

Using memory efficiently

Version 5 of MS-DOS gained the capability to load device drivers and memory-resident programs into UMBs, thereby freeing conventional memory for applica-tion programs and data. MS-DOS relied on you, however, to modify CONFIG.SYS and AUTOEXEC.BAT and thereby tell it what programs to load into UMBs and in what order. While this process could be a welcome challenge for people who enjoy tinkering under the hood, going beyond the basics could be more of a headache than a pleasure for many. Determining the best way to rank UMB-destined drivers and programs depended a great deal on experimentation, ex-perience with MS-DOS, and—unfortunately—a better knowledge of computers and hexadecimal numbering than most MS-DOS users could lay claim to.

Version 6 of MS-DOS changes much of that with MemMaker, the memory-optimization utility for the rest of us. Running MemMaker is generally a simple matter of typing its name, sitting back, and waiting for the system to reboot with CONFIG.SYS and AUTOEXEC.BAT optimized to make the best use of available

UMBs. The basics of using MemMaker are covered in the command description in Chapter 11. The following descriptions offer some additional insights; Chapter 16 covers memory optimization with multi-configuration startup files.

To use MemMaker, you must have an 80386 or better system with enough extended memory (about 350 K) to provide UMBs. The MemMaker program itself offers two optimization choices: Express and Custom. If you simply want to make your system more efficient, Express should work fine. In some cases, Custom will be a better choice. In deciding whether and how to use MemMaker, consider the following:

- If MS-DOS is simply the "thing" you boot with before jumping into exclusive use of Windows and Windows applications, you don't need MemMaker.

- If you use both MS-DOS applications and Windows, but you do not run MS-DOS applications from within Windows, you can benefit from using MemMaker to optimize memory for your MS-DOS applications. Run the Custom setup and answer No to the question *Optimize upper memory for use with Windows?* when the Advanced Options screen appears.

- If you use MS-DOS applications only, run MemMaker's Express setup, at least for the first time. As described here, you might find yourself wanting to work with MemMaker a little more later on.

- If you have an EGA or a VGA (not a Super VGA) monitor, run MemMaker's Custom setup and answer Yes to the question *Use monochrome region (B000-B7FF) for running programs?* EGA and VGA displays don't use this portion of upper memory.

The next part of your decision-making involves you. How interested are you in squeezing memory for every last byte you can get out of it? If your system is running truly and well, start it up as usual, including whatever memory-resident software you use. Do not, however, start Windows. Now, run MemMaker as already described and see what happens. Most likely, you'll end up with a few to a few dozen extra K of upper memory.

NOTE: When you run MemMaker, your original CONFIG.SYS and AUTOEXEC.BAT (and Windows SYSTEM.INI if changed) are saved with the UMB extension. If you have problems with your system after running MemMaker, you can use the memmaker /undo command to return the system to its former state.

If you want to tinker under the hood and do a real tune-up, you probably have to do a little more preliminary work. MemMaker is clever, but it does not do your thinking for you. Even though it can add some exotic switches that include and exclude certain addresses in upper memory, MemMaker takes what it finds in your CONFIG.SYS and AUTOEXEC.BAT files and goes from there. If, for example, your CONFIG.SYS is loaded with device drivers tossed in over the years in haphazard order, MemMaker doesn't clean house before it gets to work. Instead, it assumes that the order it finds is the order you want, and it optimizes your CONFIG.SYS and AUTOEXEC.BAT accordingly. It does not, nor should you expect it to, scan these files, determine the optimum order in which drivers and TSRs should be loaded, and then edit the lines accordingly. That job is still yours. You do, however, have a friend in need: a file named MEMMAKER.STS.

When you run MemMaker, it creates the file named MEMMAKER.STS (STS is short for status) and saves the file in your DOS directory. If you want to optimize memory even more effectively, run MemMaker with your system as is. When MemMaker finishes and your system reboots, print MEMMAKER.STS. The section you're interested in is headed *[SizeData]*. This is where MemMaker stores information about the memory requirements of each device driver and TSR loaded from CONFIG.SYS and AUTOEXEC.BAT. A typical entry looks like this:

```
Command=C:\DOS\SETVER.EXE
Line=8
FinalSize=832
MaxSize=12048
FinalUpperSizes=0
MaxUpperSizes=0
ProgramType=DEVICE
```

The figure you want is in the *MaxSize* line. This figure, 12048 in the preceding example, tells you the maximum amount of memory the device driver or program requires when loading into memory. Using MaxSize as a guide, order the lines in CONFIG.SYS and AUTOEXEC.BAT so that the drivers and programs requiring the most memory are loaded first. Run MemMaker again, and this time memory optimization should be even better.

NOTE: The size requirements in MEMMAKER.STS are collected during the optimization process by a MemMaker tool named SIZER.EXE. A command for SIZER.EXE is added to the beginning of each command that loads a device driver or program from CONFIG.SYS and AUTOEXEC.BAT and is removed after optimization, before your system reboots a final time. You can't use this program on your own, without MemMaker. MS-DOS just tells you it found an unrecognized command in line xx of the file.

Finally, bear in mind that MemMaker must deal with a vast pool of device drivers and TSR programs. Even though MemMaker normally runs without problem, not all software is going to fit happily into the MemMaker mold. If you have problems starting your system or running a particular device driver or program, see the file named README.TXT in your DOS directory and the section titled "Troubleshooting While Using MemMaker" in your MS-DOS 6 User's Guide. Both offer specifics you won't find here.

Protecting disks and memory

Version 6 of MS-DOS includes three utilities—Microsoft Anti-Virus, Microsoft Backup, and Undelete—that you can run either from MS-DOS or from Windows. When you run the version 6 Setup program, it gives you a choice of setting up each of these utilities in one of three ways:

- Both MS-DOS and Windows. This option is expensive in terms of disk space, but it means you can run the utilities from either environment. If you have some disk storage to spare, consider this option for the Undelete utility. In a pinch, you can use the MS-DOS version of Undelete to recover at least portions of files that are partially damaged by overwrites and that Windows Undelete refuses to restore. Conversely, you can use Windows Undelete to recover directories you mistakenly deleted.

- Windows only. This is the proposed choice if Setup detects Windows on your system during the software and hardware check it runs before beginning the MS-DOS installation. If you use Windows regularly, this is the choice for all three utilities.

- MS-DOS only. This is obviously the only option if you don't have Windows, but it can also be useful if you do a lot of maintenance and housekeeping from the system prompt, or if you run Windows only now and then—for games, perhaps, although that would be comparable to using a racehorse for rides in the park.

When Setup displays its suggestions for installing these utilities, you can change the proposed installation as follows:

1. Press a direction key to highlight the entry to change.

2. Press Enter to see a list of options.

3. Choose the type of setup you want and press Enter again to make the change.

Whether you run these utilities from MS-DOS or from Windows, for the most part they work the same. Anti-Virus and the backup utility are displayed in text-based windows under MS-DOS and in graphical windows in the Windows environment. Undelete scrolls its output the way a typical MS-DOS command does when used from the command line, but it appears in its own window when invoked from Windows. All utilities are, of course, prettier under Windows.

If you run these utilities from MS-DOS, you can use the command-line syntax described in Chapters 7 and 8. If you run them from Windows, you use the icons in the Microsoft Tools program group, described next.

The Microsoft Tools group

If you choose to run one or all of the Microsoft Anti-Virus, Microsoft Backup, and Undelete utilities from Windows, part of your MS-DOS installation involves a little backstage hocus-pocus in which Setup quietly goes out and creates a Windows program group called Microsoft Tools. This group contains an icon for each utility you chose to install as a Windows application. You don't see the group created during MS-DOS Setup, but the next time you run Windows, a program group like the following appears in the Program Manager:

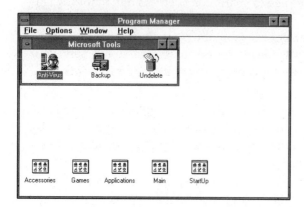

To run a utility, double-click on the program item, as you usually do in Windows. And, if you have Windows for Workgroups, the new tools also appear in the File Manager Toolbar.

The utilities and how you use them

The following descriptions assume that you know your way around text-based MS-DOS windows, graphical Windows windows, or both, so you won't find click-this, press-that, step-by-step instructions. Also, the utilities and their startup parameters (some of which are more extensive from the system prompt) are covered in Chapters 7 and 8, so coverage here provides more of an overview of each utility. If you need specifics to use any of these programs, bear in mind that online Help is always available, both from the utility's Help menu and whenever you press the F1 key.

Microsoft Anti-Virus for Windows

Microsoft Anti-Virus for Windows is a utility licensed from Central Point Software, Inc., the creators of several valuable utilities incorporated in versions 5 and 6 of MS-DOS, among them Mirror and Undelete.

NOTE: The command-line version of Microsoft Anti-Virus is abbreviated MSAV and is controlled by a group of files whose names contain the characters MSAV. Microsoft Anti-Virus for Windows is controlled by a group of files whose names contain the characters MWAV.

When started from the MS-DOS command line, the Anti-Virus window looks like this:

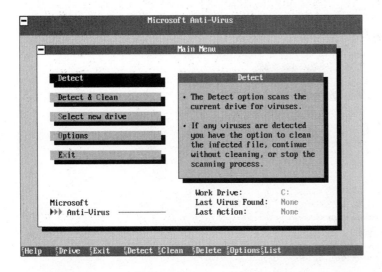

When run from the Microsoft Tools group in Windows, Anti-Virus looks like the following. (The bugs might give you pause....)

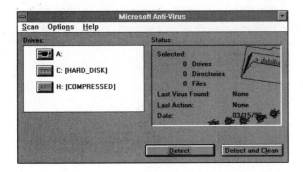

A virus, as you probably know by now, is a stealthy, self-replicating, usually small, and often inimical program that can sneak into a computer over a network connection or a phone line or from a contaminated floppy disk. Depending on the type of "disease" it spreads, a virus can damage program files, data files, or both; it can alter the computer's ability to work; and if it is particularly extreme, it can damage or destroy a disk's boot sector or partition table. Although viruses as a group are somewhat overglamorized by news reports, they are not pleasant. You can develop a feel for their intent (as well as an opinion of their creators' mental ages) very easily:

1. From the MS-DOS prompt, type *msav* to start the Anti-Virus utility. When the Main Menu appears, press F9.

   From Windows, double-click the Anti-Virus icon in the Microsoft Tools group. Open the Scan menu and choose Virus List.

   The virus lists are similar in both environments. This is what the list looks like in the MS-DOS version:

2. Double-click on a virus name that catches your eye to see a description of the virus and what it can do. (If you don't have a mouse, highlight the virus name and press Enter.) When you've seen enough, press Esc twice to return to the main window.

The information you see in this Virus List window comes from a database of several hundred known viruses that Microsoft Anti-Virus for Windows can recognize and protect your system from. For further information on viruses in general:

1. Start Anti-Virus Help. In the MS-DOS window, press F1 and then F4; in Windows, simply open the Help menu.

2. Choose Glossary. When the glossary appears, here's what you do:

   □ In the MS-DOS window, scroll through the list of definitions that appears.

   □ In Windows, click on any word you want to know more about. A definition will appear in a box on screen. To get rid of the definition, press Esc or click anywhere on the screen.

Setting options and eliminating viruses

Interesting as the virus list can be, the reason you run Microsoft Anti-Virus is to protect your system against invasion. As a first step, you should check to see which of a number of optional settings are turned on. The settings most likely to be needed are turned on by default, but you might find that you can do without some and want others. Rather than run a virus scan twice because you forgot or didn't know about a particular setting, check the options:

- From the MS-DOS window, press F8 or choose Options from the Main menu (the window that appears when you start Microsoft Anti-Virus).

- In Windows, choose Set Options from the Options menu.

In the MS-DOS window, the following dialog box appears:

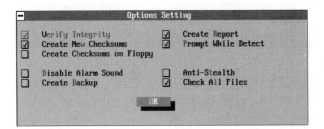

The Windows version is quite similar.

Create New Checksums. Turned on by default, this option appears below the Verify Integrity option in the Set Options dialog box. The two options are covered here in reverse order because Verify Integrity depends on information gathered and stored by Create New Checksums.

Checksums are calculated values based on the actual bytes that make up computer files and are traditionally used to verify data integrity when activities, such as transmission and disk writes, could conceivably alter file contents. To verify that a file has not changed, a checksum calculated before the event is compared with a checksum calculated afterward. If the two checksums match, the chances are great that data integrity has been preserved.

When Create New Checksums is turned on, Microsoft Anti-Virus calculates a checksum, based on file size, for each executable file in each directory on your hard disk. It then saves the checksum along with the file size, date, and file attributes, in a verification file named CHKLIST.MS. There is a separate CHK-LIST.MS file for each directory on the disk, but overall, these files do not take up inordinate amounts of disk space. The CHKLIST.MS file for a DOS directory, for example, is only about 3000 bytes.

NOTE: CHKLIST.MS looks pretty meaningless, but you might enjoy taking a brief look at it with a text editor. Be careful not to make any changes to the file, however.

Verify Integrity. Turned on by default, Verify Integrity uses the information in CHKLIST.MS to determine whether a file—executable, not document—has changed since the last virus scan. Verify Integrity offers protection against viruses that are not listed in the Virus List database. If you turn this option on and some anomaly is found for a given file when the Prompt While Detect option is also on (which it is by default), Microsoft Anti-Virus displays a Verify Error dialog box with the following choices:

- Update. Choose this if the file has legitimately changed—for example, you've overwritten an old program file with a newer version. If you choose Update, Microsoft Anti-Virus assumes that file integrity has not been compromised and updates the file information in CHKLIST.MS.

- Delete. This choice appears if either the file size or the checksum has changed. Choose Delete if you cannot account for the change and you want to delete the file.

- Repair. The companion to Delete, this choice appears if less critical information, the file's date or time, has changed. Choose Repair if you want to return the file's date and time to their original settings.

- Continue. Choose this option to continue the scan without updating, deleting, or repairing the suspect file.

- Stop. Choose this option to end the virus scan.

Create Checksums On Floppies. Turned off by default, this option enables you to extend checksum protection to floppy disks. Create Checksums On Floppies does not work on write-protected disks (such as those on which new software is typically shipped), but it is good protection if you transfer shareware or programs you've developed to other computers via floppy disk.

Disable Alarm Sound. This option is turned off by default. Turn it on if you don't want to hear a warning sound whenever Microsoft Anti-Virus finds a virus or other potential problem.

Create Backup. Turned off by default, this option makes a backup copy of an infected file before cleaning the file. The backup copy is given the extension VIR and should be used only if the cleaned file doesn't run and either the risk outweighs loss of the program or you've turned on the Anti-Stealth option (described later) and suspect that the problem found by Microsoft Anti-Virus does not represent an unknown virus type. To avoid having to make this choice on a system with a formerly virus-free hard disk, run a virus scan on floppy disks containing new programs before you install the programs on your hard disk. If you use Windows, you can do this easily with the drag-and-drop scanning feature, described later in the section "Stopping viruses before they strike." Don't become paranoid, however. Remember that infection is very rare on genuine, paid-for, shrink-wrapped software from reputable software developers.

Create Report (MS-DOS only). When turned on, this option creates a virus-scan report named MSAV.RPT, which is saved as an ASCII (text) file in the root directory of the drive you scan. The report essentially provides "hard copy" of the report displayed after a scan.

Prompt While Detect. This option is turned on by default. Leave it on if your computer contains valuable information or if it is at risk—for example, because you go on line a great deal or because you often copy promiscuous floppy disks that have made the rounds of other computers. When this option is on and you scan for viruses with the Detect command, Microsoft Anti-Virus warns you if it finds either verification errors or actual viruses in the system. Verification errors were described earlier for the Verify Integrity option. If Microsoft Anti-Virus finds a virus, it displays a Virus Found dialog box with these choices:

- Clean. Choose this to eliminate a virus from an infected file without damaging the file itself.

- Stop. Choose this option to stop the virus scan.

- Delete. The default choice, Delete uses MS-DOS to delete the file. When MS-DOS deletes a file, its contents remain on disk until they are over-written by a new file. Thus, deleting leaves the virus on disk but immobilized until it is overwritten.

- Wipe (Windows only). A choice that appears if you've turned on Wipe Deleted Files, this option really cleans house by eliminating every trace of the infected file.

- Continue. Choose this to continue the virus scan.

Anti-Stealth. Turned off by default, the Anti-Stealth option enables you to protect the system from Stealth viruses (ones that can fool normal detection methods but can be found by Stealth-specific techniques). Anti-Stealth adds to the protection against unknown viruses that is provided by the Verify Integrity option, described earlier.

Check All Files. Turned on by default, this causes Microsoft Anti-Virus to check every file in every directory on the disk, not only the executable files. Such an exhaustive check is a relatively lengthy process that can take several minutes on a large, well-used hard disk. After running a complete scan, you might want to turn this off, especially if you also rely on Create New Checksums to warn you of changes in any executable files. Although that level of protection is not as complete, it is probably sufficient if you do not normally use your computer to communicate or to download files and you feed it only legally obtained programs.

Wipe Deleted Files. Turned off by default, this Windows-only option replaces the Delete button in the Virus Found dialog box with a Wipe button you can use to eliminate all traces of an infected file. Wiping makes sure that Undelete can't recover the deleted file—all the clusters of the file are overwritten.

Running Microsoft Anti-Virus

Once all the options are set to your preferences, running Microsoft Anti-Virus is a snap:

1. From the command line, type *msav* (plus switches, if you want, as described in Chapter 8). From Windows, double-click on the utility's icon in the Microsoft Tools program group.

2. If necessary, select the drive you want to check. (In the MS-DOS window, use the Select new drive button.)

Now you can perform either of two types of virus scans: detect or clean.

- Choose Detect to check the disk without automatically eliminating viruses along the way. If a virus is detected, Microsoft Anti-Virus displays the Virus Found and Verify Error Warning dialog boxes described earlier.

- Choose Detect And Clean to both find and remove viruses on the system. If you leave the Verify Integrity option turned on in the Set Options dialog box, Detect And Clean gives you a Verify Error warning if it encounters problems with executable files and the information stored in CHKLIST.MS.

For hassle-free upgrades

If you use Microsoft Anti-Virus, there's one time you might wish it were a little less zealous about protecting your system: when you upgrade software. Remember that the Create New Checksums option is turned on by default. For everyday use, that's fine. When you upgrade to new software, however, many, if not most, of the upgrade program files will have the same names as your existing files, but they will also have different dates, times, and probably sizes. The next time you run Microsoft Anti-Virus on the disk, it will find each and every one of these differences and alert you to the possibility that the change indicates a potential virus. With some software, such as MS-DOS or Windows, Microsoft Anti-Virus is going to make a lot of these "virus" catches. To avoid having to respond to each one, do the following when upgrading software:

1. Run Microsoft Anti-Virus before installation to verify that your system is clean. When the check is complete, press the F7 key to delete the existing checksum files.

2. If your new software is not shrink-wrapped or if you want to be very sure of the upgrade files, scan the floppies before installation.

3. Install the new software.

4. Run Microsoft Anti-Virus again, this time to create new checksums and protect your system for the future.

Stopping viruses before they strike

It sometimes seems as though the words "if only" could be the motto of the human race. You've no doubt indulged in some of this, probably with regret. Remembering your feelings, then, take a look at two ways to guard against viruses: drag-and-drop virus scanning and a memory-resident virus monitor called VSafe. If you use these and your computer still becomes infected, at least you'll be able to say "I did what I could" rather than "If only I had...."

Drag-and-drop scanning (Windows only). Viruses often travel from one computer to another via infected files on floppy disks. Because of this, Microsoft Anti-Virus, in partnership with Windows, lets you do a drag-and-drop virus check, examining a disk for contamination before you load a new program into memory or install it on your hard disk. Drag and drop is simple, especially if you're already comfortable with dragging to move or copy files:

1. Working from the Windows File Manager, display the files on the disk you want to check.

2. Select one or more filenames and drag them to the MWAV.EXE entry in the file list for your DOS directory. For this approach, you have to display two File Manager windows. Choose New Window from the File Manager's Window menu, choose Tile to display both the old and new file-list windows, select your DOS drive and directory in one of them, and scroll until MWAV.EXE appears.

If Confirm On Mouse Action is turned on when you drag a filename to the MWAV.EXE entry in the File Manager's file list, you first see a message asking *Are you sure you want to start MWAV.EXE using [filename] as the initial file?* Odd though the question might appear, click Yes. Microsoft Anti-Virus then appears on screen and swings into its usual memory scan, followed by a Detect scan. At the end, it displays a report like this one if no viruses are found:

If Microsoft Anti-Virus does find a virus, refer to the options described for the Virus Found dialog box in the earlier section, "Prompt While Detect."

Monitoring the system with VSafe

In addition to checking disks for dormant viruses, you can also use the VSafe command from the system prompt to run a memory-resident program that continually watches over the system, checking for virus activity. (The VSafe command and its command-line switches were described in Chapter 8.)

VSafe sits in a few dozen kilobytes of memory and monitors your system for viruses and virus activity. When you press Alt-V, a small pop-up window appears in which you can view and select options specifying the types of protection you want.

Checking for the most significant types of virus activity, the types that can most seriously damage your system, is turned on by default. To turn any options on or off, simply press the number of the option.

Running VSafe in the Windows environment. Even though VSafe is an MS-DOS program that you start from the MS-DOS command line, if you're a Windows user, you'll be interested to note that VSafe can continue working and can notify you of potential problems when you switch to working in the Windows environment. The key to doing this is a program called the VSafe Manager, which is in your DOS directory under the name MWAVTSR.EXE.

To run the VSafe Manager, make the following change:

```
load=mwavtsr.exe
```

to WIN.INI. Or, if you always run VSafe (from AUTOEXEC.BAT, for example) install the VSafe Manager in your Startup program group as follows:

1. Open the Startup program group.

2. Start the File Manager and resize its window so that you can see both it and the Program Manager.

3. In the File Manager, select your DOS directory. Find the file MWAVTSR.EXE and drag it to the Startup program group. The VSafe Manager icon will appear.

4. To save yourself the bother of minimizing the VSafe Manager each time you start Windows, verify that the VSafe Manager icon is selected in the Startup program group window. Choose Properties from the Program Manager's File menu and click the check box to the left of Run Minimized.

Either way you do it, the VSafe Manager will ensure that the version of VSafe you start at the MS-DOS command line will be able to send any warning messages to you while you are working in Windows.

A memory-resident program by definition performs some type of monitoring of system activities. VSafe, for example, checks for virus activity, the Undelete Delete Tracker and (in version 6) the Delete Sentry keep track of file deletions, and an electronic mail program checks for mail messages. Because these types of programs never know when they'll be called on, they remain in memory, but they relinquish control of the computer to other programs until they're needed. At that time, however, they must be able to interrupt an active program to let you know something has happened. In the Windows environment, which is distinct from the MS-DOS environment, these monitors continue to watch the system. The

VSafe Manager, in effect, watches the watcher, providing you with a means of controlling it and providing it with a means of communicating with you.

The following illustration shows the VSafe Manager as you see it after restoring it from an icon to an active window:

To set VSafe options, you click the big button in the middle of the window. When you do, you see a dialog box like this:

These are options you can turn on or off from within Windows, even though you started the program from MS-DOS.

NOTE: You must start VSafe, the program, before starting Windows if you want the VSafe Manager to watch for viruses. You cannot start Windows and then use the MS-DOS Prompt program item to exit to MS-DOS in order to start VSafe because you forgot about it. If you use VSafe, you might want to run Windows from a batch file like the following:

```
@Echo off
vsafe
win
```

to ensure that you never start one without the other.

Managing disk-based information

Managing disk-based information covers a lot of ground. As mentioned earlier in this chapter, one of the most important facets of this management is the creation and maintenance of a directory structure that matches the way you think and work. MS-DOS can't help with this, but it can help significantly when it comes to archiving important files and clearing old, unneeded files from your hard disk. Aside from DoubleSpace and Defrag, both of which make physical storage much more efficient, MS-DOS version 6 provides a new, improved backup utility and a long-needed, if somewhat dangerous, Deltree command.

Microsoft Backup

Beginning with version 6 of MS-DOS, you can perform backups from MS-DOS, from Windows, or (if you install both options) from both. Microsoft Backup in version 6 is completely different from the Backup command in earlier versions of MS-DOS. Chapter 7 described the syntax for the Msbackup command. This section covers use of the utility in more detail. Microsoft Backup runs in a menu-based window and looks remarkably similar in both the MS-DOS and Windows environments.

The first time you run Microsoft Backup, either from the command line or from Windows, the program tells you that it must run a compatibility test for floppy disks before it can guarantee reliable backups. The message you see looks like this:

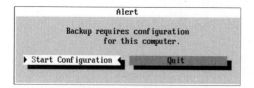

The test itself is somewhat lengthy because it involves backing up a set of files and then comparing the backups to the original to verify accuracy. Most of the test, however, is automated, so basically all you do is select the drive to test and insert floppy disks as requested. Run the compatibility test for each drive and whenever you change the configuration of your system.

The following sections briefly describe the backup, compare, and restore options. Excellent—and much more detailed help—is also available in the Microsoft Backup online Help, which you can access through the Help menu or by pressing F1 whenever you need more information.

The process

Although the *actions* of backing up, comparing, and restoring files are considerably different, with Microsoft Backup, the *process* is similar in all three cases—so similar that once you go through one backup, the chances are good you'll have no problems comparing or restoring backed-up files. What might give you pause, however, are some of the terms Microsoft Backup uses. The best way to define these is to take a walk through the backup process.

Backup. When you make backups, you begin by making certain decisions. At the very least, this involves deciding which files you want to back up and which drive to back up to. But as you'll see later, Microsoft Backup also allows you to make other choices, such as whether you want the utility always to format the backup disks and whether you want it to compress the backups so that they occupy less space on disk. To do all this, you make selections in the Backup window:

- In the MS-DOS Backup window, verify that the Backup button is high-lighted and press Enter.

- In the Windows version, click the large Backup button below the menu bar. The resulting screen looks like the following when you run Microsoft Backup from the command line:

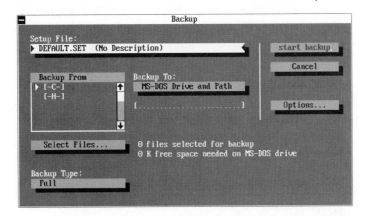

Ignoring the list box titled Setup File for a moment, take a look at the other boxes in the window:

- Backup From lets you select the drive to back up from. This box lists the hard drives, RAM drives, compressed and uncompressed drives, and network drives on your computer.

- Backup To lets you select the drive to back up to. Click to open the box, and you'll see a set of icons listing the floppy drives configured for your system—one for each possible disk capacity—plus an item shown as MS-DOS Drive And Path, like this:

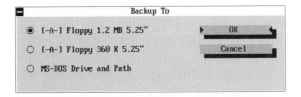

Choose MS-DOS Drive And Path to back up to a different drive or a device other than one of your floppy drives. This is also the option you must use if you want to back up to a floppy disk compressed with DoubleSpace. In this case, however, be sure to mount the disk ahead of time. Also, don't try to cram too much onto the compressed disk. If Microsoft Backup runs out of room, it quits, and you're left with nothing to show for your efforts. As a rule of thumb, you can assume that a compressed 1.44-MB floppy will take about 2 MB of backed-up data.

- Backup Type lets you select the type of backup to perform:
  - ☐ Full backs up all the files you select.
  - ☐ Incremental backs up all new or changed files since the last full or incremental backup.
  - ☐ Differential backs up all new or changed files since the last full backup.

The remaining choices in the Backup window allow you to specify the what, when, and how of backing up:

- Start Backup obviously sets the process in motion.
- Select Files opens a new window that resembles the File list in the MS-DOS Shell and the File Manager in Windows:

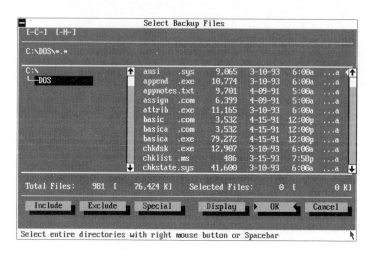

Here you see a directory tree on the left, a list of files in the current directory on the right, and a row of special buttons at the bottom:

- ☐ Include and Exclude open nearly identical windows in which you can specify sets of files for inclusion and exclusion. For example, if a directory contains files with different extensions, you can choose to include all DOC files in the backup. Conversely, use Exclude to eliminate files you don't want to back up—for example, all BMP files in a document directory.

(In the Windows version of Backup, fill in the path and file specification, and click the radio button next to the Include or Exclude label to tell Backup what you want to do. Click the Add button to the right, and a description of your choice will appear in the Include/Exclude list.)

After you've created an Include/Exclude list, you can edit it at any time. In the MS-DOS Backup window, choose Include or Exclude, choose the Edit Include/Exclude List button, and choose Edit from the dialog box that appears. In the Windows version, select the item you want. To delete an entry in either the MS-DOS or Windows version, select the entry and choose the Delete button. Choose OK to record your choices and close the window.

☐ Special opens a dialog box that enables you to back up files with directory entries indicating they were created or changed within a particular time period. This dialog box also lets you exclude from a backup files with read-only, system, and other attributes.

☐ Print (Windows only) lets you print directory and file information, either on a printer or by "printing" to a file on disk. Note that this button prints information about all the directories and files on the current drive or all drives. It does not list just those files you've selected for backup.

☐ Display produces a dialog box in which you can customize the display of directories and files—for example, whether all or just those matching a file specification (file filter) are displayed and whether they are sorted by name, extension, size, and so on.

☐ Legend (Windows only) displays descriptions of the various types of legends—small rectangular icons—that appear to the left of drives, directories, and files selected for backup.

☐ OK and Cancel, as usual, either "set" or cancel your choices.

And now, what of the Setup File list box that you ignored awhile back? By way of example, suppose that after making all your selections, you find that your backup will involve the following:

■ Backup of all spreadsheets and macros in C:\BIGBUCKS.

■ Backup of all word processor documents and macros in C:\NEWDOCS.

■ Exclusion of all hidden and read-only documents in both directories.

Suppose further that you're a lawyer conducting bankruptcy proceedings for a notorious international personality and you want to perform this same backup procedure at the end of every day, to keep your archived copies as current as possible. Does that mean you have to go clicking your way through Microsoft Backup once a day, making all these choices? Obviously not. What you do after making or modifying your choices is save them all as a *setup file*, which is more or less a backup-specific initialization file.

When you first use Microsoft Backup, you see one entry in the Setup File list, DEFAULT.SET followed by the somewhat less than helpful annotation *No Description*. This file contains the default settings built into Microsoft Backup. To save your own settings, you use either the Save Setup or the Save Setup As command on the File menu:

- Use Save Setup to save any new or changed settings in the setup file currently highlighted in the Setup File list box (DEFAULT.SET if you haven't created any other setup files).

- Use Save Setup As to save file specifications and other settings in a new setup file or to save changes to an existing setup file under a new name. Save Setup As opens a dialog box in which you can assign the setup file a name and a description:

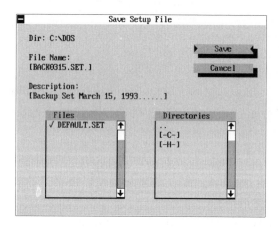

You can also choose a directory in which to save the file by clicking your way through the directories listed in the Directories box. By default, Microsoft Backup proposes to save all setup files in your DOS directory.

NOTE: Setup files are both readable and informative, and you can view their contents easily. To get a feel for one, try starting the MS-DOS Editor or Windows Notepad and viewing DEFAULT.SET in your DOS directory. Be sure not to save any inadvertent changes.

Cycles and catalogs. If you take backups seriously, you perform them periodically, at regular intervals: daily, weekly, monthly, or whatever. Microsoft

Backup doesn't keep track of when you use a particular setup file to back up a group of files, but it does work in backup cycles. To Microsoft Backup, a backup cycle begins with a full backup—the kind you should do when you first back up a set of files—and continues through each succeeding incremental or differential backup performed with the same setup file. A new cycle begins the next time you perform a full backup.

NOTE: To switch from a full backup to an incremental or a differential backup, open the setup file and then choose the backup type you want.

To determine when a new cycle begins, Microsoft Backup must be able to track successive backups for a particular setup file. To do this tracking, the utility uses two special types of file called a *master catalog* and a *backup set catalog*.

A master catalog contains a sequential record of all the backups done for a given setup file. Microsoft Backup creates a master catalog for each setup file you use and stores the catalog on the disk from which you back up files. The master catalog has the same name as the setup file, but with the extension CAT. Catalog files are stored in your DOS directory by default.

As you perform successive backups, Microsoft Backup also creates a series of backup set catalogs, one catalog file for each backup. One copy of this catalog file goes in the catalog file path on the disk from which you back up (source disk). A second copy, stored as part of the backup set, also goes on the last (target) disk that receives the backup. You can use this second copy, if necessary, to recover a catalog you've inadvertently deleted or destroyed on the source disk.

Essentially a log that enables Microsoft Backup to find, compare, and restore files, a catalog file has a coded filename in which each part tells you something about the backup. In the catalog name CC30811A.FUL, for example,

- The first character (C) tells you the first drive that was backed up.
- The second character (also C in this example) tells you the last drive backed up.
- The third character (3) is the last digit of the year of the backup.
- The fourth and fifth characters (08) give the month of the backup.
- The sixth and seventh characters (11) give the day of the backup.
- The eighth character (A) gives the sequence order of the backup. The first backup for any particular setup file is A, the second is B, the third is C, and so on.
- The extension tells you the type of backup: full (FUL), incremental (INC), or differential (DIF).

By this time, your head is probably reeling as you try to picture cycle after cycle and catalogs within catalogs, so the diagram on the next page can help you see how cycles and catalogs are related.

```
Setup file = SAMPLE.SET


Full backup ——→ Master catalog (SAMPLE.CAT)
                      |
                      Catalog file 1 (CC30117A.FUL)┐
Partial backup ———→ Catalog file 2 (CC30128B.INC) ├— Cycle 1
Partial backup ———→ Catalog file 3 (CC30207C.INC)┘


Full backup ——→ Master catalog (SAMPLE.CAT)
                      |
                      Catalog file 1 (CC30214D.FUL)┐
Partial backup ———→ Catalog file 2 (CC30221E.INC) ├— Cycle 2
Partial backup ———→ Catalog file 3 (CC30228F.INC)┘
```

And so on.

You might have noticed from this diagram that Microsoft Backup is capable of producing an endless stream of catalog files as your backup experience progresses. Unless you really need records going back to the dawn of backup history, these old catalog files will eventually be as welcome as that stack of old magazines you've been meaning to recycle. Luckily, eliminating old catalogs is a lot simpler than hauling magazines to the recycling center:

1. Choose Options in the Backup window.

2. Turn off the Keep Old Backup Catalogs setting (turned on by default).

From here on, no matter how many new backup cycles you begin, Microsoft Backup will keep and display only one complete set of catalogs—those for the current backup cycle. Old catalogs will disappear when you begin a new cycle.

Compare and Restore. When you want to verify that files are backed up accurately, click the Compare button in the Microsoft Backup window. The Compare window, which looks much like the backup window, appears:

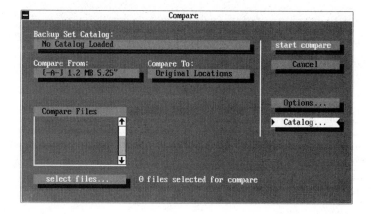

When you need to restore files from your backup disks to their original or alternate locations, click the Restore button. The Restore window is identical to the Compare window, except that the word *Restore* appears in place of *Compare*.

In both windows, the list box titled Backup Set Catalog is where you choose the catalog file containing the set of backup files you want to compare or restore. Initially this list shows the master catalogs and catalog files in the catalog file path. If you want to work with a catalog that is not displayed:

- In the MS-DOS window, choose Catalog from the Compare window. Select the catalog you want and press Enter, or choose Retrieve to load a catalog on the backup disk.

- In the Windows window, choose Load from the Catalog menu. Select the catalog you want and press Enter. If the catalog you want is stored with the backup on a floppy disk, choose Retrieve from the Catalog menu instead.

NOTE: Two other commands also appear on the Catalog menu and are available from the Compare and Restore windows. The Rebuild command helps you recover a catalog that has been damaged or destroyed on the backup drive. The Delete command deletes a catalog you no longer need or want.

Other than the Backup Set Catalog option, the other choices in the Compare and Restore windows are self-explanatory and easy to use:

- Select the drive containing the backup files from the list titled Compare (Restore) From.

- Select the files to compare or restore with the Select Files button.

- Select the location of the files to compare or restore from the Compare (Restore) To list. If you open the list, you'll see that you can choose an alternative drive or directory, as well as the original location.

Microsoft Undelete

The third disk-management utility to consider is Microsoft Undelete, which can truly be a friend in need, especially if you're inclined to use wildcards in deleting files and have a tendency to type first and whack your forehead after the fact. Microsoft Undelete is particularly valuable if you use the Deltree command or if you're a Windows user and use Windows' capability to delete whole, populated directories with a single command. Directories, even more so than files, have in the past been difficult to recover. Here, however, are two points to remember:

- If you don't have Windows and the Windows version of Microsoft Undelete, be very careful when you use Remove Directory or Deltree. You usually cannot use Microsoft Undelete from the command line to recover deleted directories. (If you re-create the original directory name, you might be able to undelete any files in it from the command line, but this tactic works only if you protect deleted files with Delete Sentry.)

■ With Windows and Microsoft Undelete, recovering directories is doable and even simple if you act fast enough, although you'll have to carry out more than one undelete to recover both the directory and its subdirectories and files.

The best protection against needing the heroic measures provided by Microsoft Undelete, of course, is to systematically back up your critical data onto floppies.

Microsoft Undelete ultimately (although not entirely) bases its magic on the disk-based index to file and directory storage known as the File Allocation Table, or (affectionately) the FAT. As described in Chapter 7, "Files," the FAT is maintained by MS-DOS and contains pointers to the actual disk locations in which files are stored. In the FAT, MS-DOS records the number and locations of the disk clusters—multibyte storage units—that hold individual files and directories. Without the FAT, MS-DOS cannot find or store your files.

You never manipulate the FAT directly, but you do need to know that when you delete a file or directory, MS-DOS records, in the FAT, that the clusters occupied are now free and available for storing new information. The file or directory contents don't actually disappear immediately. They can, however, be quickly overwritten by new information—so quickly that saving even a small file after a deletion can mean that part of the deleted information becomes unrecoverable. Forever.

Because data-bearing clusters can be recycled so rapidly by MS-DOS, the riskiest type of undelete a data-recovery program can perform is to go into the FAT, find the clusters in which a deleted file or directory was stored, and mark them as once again unavailable. Such an undelete can usually be accomplished if you try to recover the data immediately, but too much depends on the FAT. The way this index is structured, the information about storage clusters actually forms a chain in which one entry points to the next. As MS-DOS stores new files and uses formerly occupied clusters, it alters the chain of pointers in the FAT. Thus, if one point in the chain—one cluster of many in a file—is used to store another file, the chain is broken and any clusters beyond that point are lost. The effect is literally as if you took a link out of a real chain connecting your car to a tow truck on a steep hill.

Protecting deleted files and directories

Because the risk of data loss is so great if undelete utilities have to rely only on information in the FAT, MS-DOS includes two memory-resident utilities that can help preserve the integrity of deleted files and directories, at least for a while.

These utilities, Delete Tracker and Delete Sentry, are both accessible to Microsoft Undelete, and using either one of them can mean the difference between saving and losing deleted files.

Delete Tracker, the less effective of the two, makes its own record of the FAT information pinpointing the chain of clusters used to store a file. Delete Tracker does not actually save the data. Any or all of the clusters can still be reused by MS-DOS, but by recording the storage locations of a deleted file, Delete Tracker does give you a means of finding out whether any of the data is salvageable.

Delete Sentry, the most reliable method of protecting your data, actually saves the contents of deleted files in a hidden directory named SENTRY. Furthermore, Delete Sentry saves those files even after you turn off the computer, protecting them either until you purge the files or until a user-specified amount of time passes. Because it saves your data, Delete Sentry enables you to recover files in pristine condition—most of the time. The catch, however, is that Delete Sentry requires a certain amount of disk space for saving deleted files, and you must specify that amount. If the space you allot becomes full of deleted files and you do nothing about culling them, Delete Sentry will begin to replace the oldest ones with newer deletions.

Chapter 7 covers using Microsoft Undelete from the command line. The following descriptions apply to using this utility from within Windows.

Enabling delete protection in Windows

Within Windows, you can easily add protection for deleted files and directories:

1. Start Microsoft Undelete by double-clicking on its icon in the Windows Tools group.

2. Choose Configure Delete Protection from the Options menu in the Undelete window that appears. When you choose this command, Microsoft Undelete displays a dialog box like this:

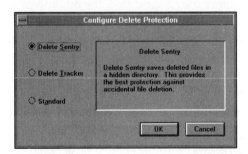

Notice that a description of the selected option appears in the box to the right of the three choices. As you click on different choices, this description changes to tell you about the level of protection offered by each.

3. To choose the type of protection you want, click on it and click OK.

If you choose either Delete Sentry or Delete Tracker, another dialog box appears. For Delete Sentry, you see this:

- Click the Drives button to specify the drives you want to protect.

- Use Only Specified Files to limit saves to files of a particular type. To specify the file type, click in the Include box. You can include a drive and path if you want.

- Click in the Exclude list, press Ctrl-End, and type a minus sign followed by a wildcard file specification for any files you don't want to protect.

- Turn off the check box for archived files if you want to save files you back up and delete. (Saving these is overkill, really.) Remember, though, that programs such as Backup and Xcopy may or may not alter the archive bit. Be sure you know which files are archived.

- The last two options are related. Specify the number of days you want the files kept in \SENTRY before they are purged, the amount of space you want to allot for deleted files, or both. Think about your work habits when making these choices and try to balance time and space requirements. If necessary, because your disk space is limited, you can type the percentage as a fraction, such as *10.5*.

- Click OK. Another dialog box will appear, asking you to reboot the computer so that delete protection will be in effect. Click OK. Once you reboot, Delete Sentry will be ready to go to work.

If you choose Delete Tracker when you configure delete protection, you see a simpler dialog box:

- Click on the drive or drives you want to protect. If you make a mistake, click on the drive again or click the Clear button.

- After you make your choices, click OK. As for Delete Sentry, you'll see a dialog box asking you to reboot. Click OK and reboot the computer to enable Delete Tracker.

Recovering files

Whether you protect deleted files and directories with MS-DOS only, with Delete Tracker, or with Delete Sentry, whenever you start Microsoft Undelete, you see a window like this:

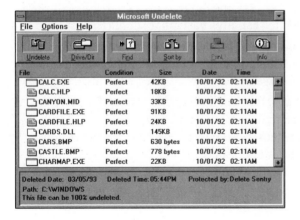

The file list taking up most of the window lists the files and directories you've deleted in the current directory, both with and without any delete protection you've enabled. Files and directories undeleted by MS-DOS are preceded by a question mark—a sure indicator that MS-DOS has marked their disk space as available for new files.

In addition to directories and filenames, you see their condition, size, and date and time of creation or last modification. At the bottom of the window, Microsoft Undelete displays information about the selected file. As for the rest of the window,

- Click the Info button, press Alt-I, or choose File Info from the File menu to see more information about the highlighted file.

- Click the Drive/Dir button, press Alt-D, or choose Change Drive/Directory from the File menu to display the names of deleted files on a different drive or in a different directory.

- Click the Find button, press Alt-N, or choose Find Deleted File from the File menu to search for a particular file. When this dialog box appears:

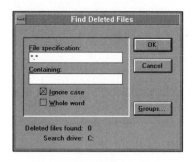

  □ Type a file specification to display a particular set of files.

  □ Type text in the Containing text box to display files containing specific text. Modify the search with the Ignore Case and Whole Word check boxes if necessary.

  □ Click the Groups button and select a Windows program item from the resulting dialog box to search for deleted files associated with a particular program. The Edit button in the Groups dialog box lets you customize the search, if necessary.

- Click the Sort By button, press Alt-S, or choose Sort By from the Options menu to change the sort criteria from name (the default) to other attributes, such as extension, size, or condition.

- Click the Print button or choose Print List from the File menu to print a list of deleted files.

- Choose Select By Name and Unselect By Name from the Options menu to select and deselect files that match a file specification you type. This is a quick way to select a group of files to undelete.

As for undeleting itself, remember that the condition of a deleted file or directory determines whether you can undelete it with Microsoft Undelete. If the file or directory is in excellent condition, you should have no trouble. If its condition is good, the data is recoverable, but some clusters might already have been overwritten by other files. If a file or directory is in poor or destroyed condition, Microsoft Undelete will not even attempt the undeletion from Windows. For critical information in either of these conditions, try using Undelete from the MS-DOS command line as described in Chapter 7.

If Microsoft Undelete can recover a file or directory, the process is simple:

1. Select the file or directory as described previously. If you cannot locate a file, think about whether it might be in a deleted directory. If so, use the procedure described here to undelete the directory. Display the contents of the recovered directory and continue undeleting in layers, through subdirectories, until you reach the file you want.

2. If you simply want to undelete the selected file or directory, click the Undelete button, press Alt-U, or choose Undelete from the File menu. If the file is protected by MS-DOS, you'll first have to provide a letter to replace the question mark produced by MS-DOS.

   If you want to restore the file to a different drive or directory, choose Undelete To from the File menu and either type the new path and filename or select the drive or directory from the Directories list. Note that you cannot use Undelete To if you undelete a directory. Directories can be restored only to their original locations.

15

The MS-DOS Editor

What You'll Find Here: This short chapter is an introduction to the MS-DOS Editor supplied with versions 5 and 6 of MS-DOS. The successor to the late and largely unlamented Edlin line editor, the MS-DOS Editor is a menu-oriented, text-based, full-screen editor you can use for creating and editing plain-text files. If you've found some of the material in preceding chapters a little heavy going, this chapter will provide a welcome breather. The MS-DOS Editor is simple to use and easy to learn.

*T*he MS-DOS Editor is, basically, a plain-vanilla word processor. You can use it to create, edit, save, and print ASCII files, but it lacks the whizbang formatting and page-layout capabilities, the macro language, and the spell-checking, hyphenation, annotation, and other features characteristic of a real word processor. Where MS-DOS is concerned, however, the MS-DOS Editor has one default capability that your word processor must be told to provide: the ability to save text files without the program-specific formatting and other characters that the Type command and the batch interpreter cannot handle. Such text files are, of course, the form in which you create and save CONFIG.SYS, AUTOEXEC.BAT and other batch files, and Doskey macros. Because the following chapters delve into the fine and sometimes fancy world of controlling MS-DOS through plain-text files, this chapter covers the basics of working with the MS-DOS Editor. As previously mentioned, the coverage will be brief and to the point, especially because you can keep Help on screen whenever you want, referring to it as you work.

About the MS-DOS Editor

The most interesting aspect of the MS-DOS Editor, at least from the point of view of understanding how MS-DOS works, is the MS-DOS Editor's relationship to QBasic. It is a component—a "module" if you will—of the QBasic environment. Even though it might seem that a text editor and a programming environment have little in common, bear in mind that you can't write programs without an editor of some type. The MS-DOS Editor provides the paper, pencil, and eraser you need to create and edit programs written in the Basic programming language. Because Basic programs are stored as ASCII files, it's only a small jump to using the QBasic Editor as an editor for other text files as well. After all, a text file is a text file, whether it contains Basic instructions or batch commands.

Although the MS-DOS Editor/QBasic family tree is interesting, you might suppose it is also irrelevant. A search of your DOS directory will quickly show a file named EDIT.COM, and this, you would assume, runs the MS-DOS Editor. A closer look at the file details, however, shows that EDIT.COM is a mere 413 bytes in length, hardly enough to provide file-creation and text-editing capabilities in even the most tightly coded program instructions. In actuality, EDIT.COM, although it might seem more important than QBASIC.EXE, is really just a small program that allows you to tap into the text-editing capabilities of QBasic. To run the MS-DOS Editor, you need QBASIC.EXE. If you delete QBASIC.EXE from your DOS directory, you can't use either QBasic or the MS-DOS Editor. (If you're strapped for space, however, you can delete QBasic Help if you won't be programming in QBasic.)

The moral of the story: If you want to use the MS-DOS Editor, as you probably will if you create even simple batch files, leave QBASIC.EXE alone.

Starting the MS-DOS Editor

Here's a pretty useless party trick you can use to convince your friends you've gone around the bend. Type

```
C:\>qbasic /editor c:\autoexec.bat
```

The MS-DOS Editor will start up with AUTOEXEC.BAT on display. Wow. (But at least it shows that QBasic and the MS-DOS Editor really are relatives.) The better way to start the MS-DOS Editor is, of course, to use the Edit command, described in Chapter 14. The most essential part of the command,

```
edit
```

starts the MS-DOS Editor. Period. When you use this form of the command, you start off with a clean slate. To save time, start the MS-DOS Editor and open an existing file or assign a name to a new file-to-be with an Edit command in the following form:

edit [*path*][*filename*][*.ext*]

When you include a filename, the MS-DOS Editor searches the path you specify for the filename *and* extension you type. Unlike word processors, the MS-DOS Editor neither assigns nor searches for a default extension, such as TXT or DOC, and this can take a little getting used to. For example, if you specify

```
C:\>edit c:\dos\readme
```

the MS-DOS Editor searches for a file with the name README and no extension. To find README.TXT, you would have to include the extension in the command line. This literal-mindedness on the MS-DOS Editor's part might cause temporary frustration if you habitually use batch files. You can become so accustomed to typing the name of the batch file without an extension that you unthinkingly type

```
C:\>edit batfile
```

instead of

```
C:\>edit batfile.bat
```

when you want to work with the file in the MS-DOS Editor.

NOTE: If you have good eyesight and a monitor capable of displaying more than the usual 25 lines, you might find the /h switch useful. This switch starts the MS-DOS Editor with the highest number of lines your monitor can display.

A look at the MS-DOS Editor

When you start the MS-DOS Editor without specifying a filename, it opens with a screen like the following:

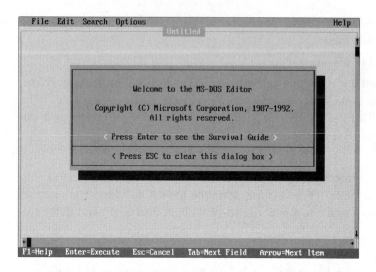

If you press Enter (which you might want to do the first time you use the MS-DOS Editor), the screen divides into an upper Help window and an initially small lower editing window like this:

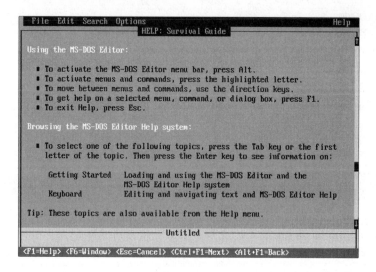

Here's what you can do with these two windows:

- If you have a mouse, move the cursor between windows by clicking in the window you want. To change the sizes of the windows, place the mouse pointer on the horizontal line across the top of the editing window and drag up or down.

- If you use the keyboard, press F6 to move the cursor between windows. To change window sizes, hold down Alt and press the plus key or the minus key. You can use either the top row of the keyboard or the numeric keypad (with Num Lock turned either on or off).

The Help window at the top can be useful when you're becoming accustomed to the MS-DOS Editor, especially if you use the keyboard rather than a mouse. You don't, however, have to start with the Survival Guide to display the Help window. Whenever you're working in the MS-DOS Editor, with or without a file open, you can display the Help window very quickly:

1. Open the Help menu at the top left of the screen.

2. Press Enter to display help on Getting Started; choose Keyboard to display keyboard help.

To view specific topics, move the mouse pointer to any Help topic displayed between left-pointing and right-pointing triangles and click the *right* mouse button. With the keyboard, tab to the item you want and press Enter.

To keep the Help window out of the way while you're working on a file, drag it with the mouse or use Alt-plus or Alt-minus (depending on where the cursor is) to reduce the Help window to a small, horizontal bar across the top of the screen.

Before you leave the startup window, make note of the following:

- The shaded horizontal bar at the bottom is a scroll bar. The MS-DOS Editor allows individual lines of a file to be up to 255 characters long. If you enter very long lines, you can use this scroll bar with the mouse to move quickly to the left or right in the current line.

- The divided horizontal bar below the scroll bar displays two items of interest: status messages at the left and the current row and column location of the cursor at the right (for example, 00001:022, meaning row 1, column 22). Status messages change according to what you are doing. After you start the MS-DOS Editor and press Esc to get rid of the Survival Guide message, for instance, the status portion of the message bar tells you to press F1 for Help or press Alt to activate menus—those being the only actions other than typing that you can do at the time. When you open a menu, the message changes to display a brief description of the currently highlighted menu command.

Editing files

The MS-DOS Editor's Keyboard Help topics list all the different keystrokes you need to move around in a file, as well as those you need to select and edit text. There's no point repeating the same information, so the following simply provides you with ways to accomplish the most common text-entry, navigation, and editing tasks.

To create a file, here's what you do:

- Press Enter at the end of each line.

- Press Tab to indent the line 8 spaces. (This is the default; you can change the number of spaces with the Display command on the Options menu.)

- Press Ctrl-P, followed by a control character to enter a special character. For example, Ctrl-P followed by Ctrl-G inserts the control character that produces a beep; Ctrl-P followed by Esc inserts the Esc character.

- Press Backspace to delete an indent.

- Press Home and Enter to insert a line above the current line.

- Press Del to delete the character above the cursor or, if text is selected, to delete the text.

- Press Ins to toggle between insert mode and overtype mode.

To move around in a file, follow these steps:

- Press the direction keys to move left or right one character or up or down one line.

- Press Ctrl-Left direction key or Ctrl-Right direction key to move left or right one word.

- Press Home to move the cursor to the beginning of the current line (to the first character if the line is indented).

- Press End to move the cursor to the last character of the current line.

To select text, do this:

- Press Shift-Left direction key or Shift-Right direction key to select one character to the left or right.

- Press Shift-Ctrl-Left direction key or Shift-Ctrl-Right direction key to select one word to the left or right.

- Press Shift-Down direction key to select the current line and move the cursor to the line below the selected line.

- Press Shift-Up direction key to select the line above the current line.

To cut, copy, and paste, here's the procedure:

- Press Ctrl-Ins to copy selected text to the Clipboard (a buffer where information is stored temporarily).
- Press Shift-Ins to paste Clipboard contents to the location of the cursor.
- Press Shift-Del to delete selected text to the Clipboard (also known as cutting).

The menus

In addition to keystrokes and mouse actions, you use the commands on five menus to work with files in the MS-DOS Editor. These menus and their commands are described in the following lists.

The File Menu opens, saves, and prints files and closes the MS-DOS Editor.

- New causes the MS-DOS Editor to close the current file and open a new, unnamed file. If the current file contains any unsaved changes, the MS-DOS Editor displays the following dialog box:

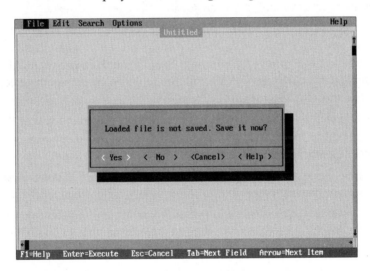

Choose Yes to save the changes, No to discard them, Cancel to change your mind, or Help to request help in figuring out what to do.

- Open causes the MS-DOS Editor to open an existing file. To help you choose, it displays a dialog box listing files in the current directory. (Here, the MS-DOS Editor assumes TXT files by default, but you can type another filename specification to list other files.) If the file you want is in a different directory, you can either type the full path or choose a directory from a list in the dialog box. Once again, if the current file contains unsaved changes, the MS-DOS Editor displays the *Loaded file is not saved* dialog box and refuses to open the new file until you respond.

- Save saves the current file. If the file has not yet been named, the MS-DOS Editor displays a dialog box prompting for a name. Remember to include the extension.

- Save As both names and saves a file. The command produces a dialog box in which you can specify both a filename (and extension) and a directory.

- Print prints a file. Before printing, this command displays a dialog box that lets you specify whether to print the entire document (the default) or only the selected text.

- Exit quits the MS-DOS Editor. Again, you're prompted to save the file if it contains unsaved changes.

The Edit menu lets you cut, copy, paste, and clear selected text.

- Cut removes selected text and places it on the Clipboard. When you cut text, you can reinsert it elsewhere in the file, so you can think of this as something of a "move" command. Bear in mind, however, that text remains on the Clipboard only until it is replaced by other cut or copied text. The shortcut key for Cut is Shift-Del.

- Copy copies selected text to the Clipboard. This command leaves the selected text in place, so it functions as the MS-DOS Editor version of a duplicating machine. The shortcut key for Copy is Ctrl-Ins.

- Paste inserts Clipboard contents at the cursor position. You can paste either cut or copied material. The shortcut key for Paste is Shift-Ins.

- Clear removes selected text and gets rid of it. When you clear text, you do not move it to the Clipboard. Once cleared, the text is gone. The shortcut key for Clear is Del.

The Search menu lets you search for or replace text you specify.

- Find finds the text you specify in the following dialog box:

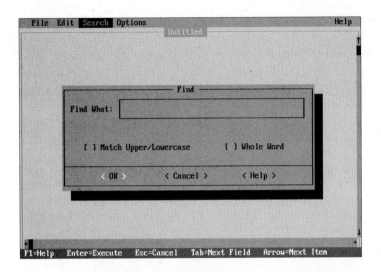

Select Match Upper/Lowercase if you want to find only occurrences that exactly match the text you type in the Find What box. Select Whole Word if you want to limit the search to words, not parts of words, that match the text you specify.

■ Repeat Last Find repeats the last search you specified. The shortcut key for this command is F3.

■ Change is the MS-DOS Editor's replace command, and it produces the following dialog box:

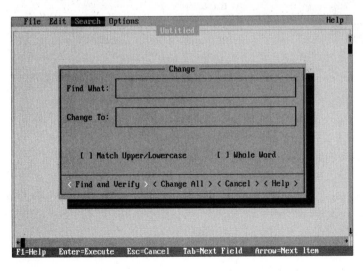

As you can see, it is similar to the Find dialog box, except that you specify the text you want the search text changed to. Choose Find And Verify if you want to approve each change before it is made; choose Change All if you're confident of your search criteria and just want the command carried out. (If you choose Change All, it wouldn't hurt to at least scan the file for possible errors after the search.)

The Options menu lets you control, to some extent, how the MS-DOS Editor works.

- Display is the most fun of the MS-DOS Editor's commands. It produces the following dialog box, in which you can control the foreground and background colors in the editing window of the screen:

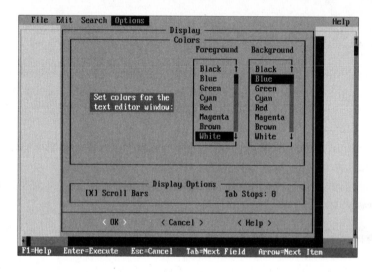

Foreground represents the characters you type; background is the main screen color. The box to the left of the color lists gives you a preview of what your choices will look like. The two choices in the Display Options box at the bottom of the dialog box let you turn scroll bars on and off (X means they are turned on) and set the number of spaces for tab stops (8 by default).

- Help Path, which you probably don't need, displays a dialog box in which you can specify the path to the MS-DOS Editor's Help file. Use this command if, for some reason, you move EDIT.HLP out of your DOS directory, where it's placed during Setup.

The Help menu, as you've already seen, provides online Help.

Now, on to more fun stuff.

16

Controlling Startups

What You'll Find Here: This chapter describes the new, and welcome, ways in which version 6 of MS-DOS can hand the reins of system control over to you at startup. If you've ever wished you could choose whether to load network drivers from CONFIG.SYS, version 6 provides the means. If you've ever wanted the ability to choose between a basic configuration and a more elaborate one that loads ANSI.SYS or creates a RAM drive, your days of wanting are over. Even if your computer is a simple, solitary soul, version 6 can help you optimize your system for different applications—enable EMS memory, for example, for your spreadsheet program, but disable EMS memory and create a RAM drive when you're going to be processing words. This chapter outlines the what, the how, and the why of controlling startup. Of course, nothing in life is perfectly easy. Because every computer and every computer user differs, you still have to figure out the when and the where.

W hereas past versions of MS-DOS ran CONFIG.SYS and AUTOEXEC.BAT automatically and noninteractively, version 6 provides alternatives that allow you to determine how your computer is configured at startup. These alternatives range from a very basic clean boot that bypasses CONFIG.SYS and AUTOEXEC.BAT to a potentially elaborate set of startup configurations you create as blocks of commands that you can group and choose among with multi-configuration commands in CONFIG.SYS. If you decide to control your system from a multi-configuration file, you'll have the ability to customize your computer the way you want for a particular session with MS-DOS, your hardware, and your applications.

CONFIG.SYS then and now

Through version 5 of MS-DOS, you probably held a few computing truths to be painfully self-evident: Don't format your hard disk; don't delete AUTOEXEC.BAT; don't turn off the system when the drive light is on; and don't get too wildly experimental with CONFIG.SYS. This last "don't" was particularly important because CONFIG.SYS was processed automatically during startup, without offering you any interactivity. If you inadvertently made the wrong change to CONFIG.SYS and rebooted the system, there was always the possibility, however slim, that the change would cause your system to hang, with the result that MS-DOS could not complete the boot process. This potential outcome was especially significant in version 5, because changing memory switches or loading the wrong device driver into UMBs could stall CONFIG.SYS and set up an impassable roadblock between you and your hard disk. And, of course, no hard disk, no MS-DOS. No MS-DOS, no computer.

Beginning with version 6, you no longer have to treat CONFIG.SYS as the vulnerable underbelly of MS-DOS, because it no longer is. The reasons are the following:

- The version 6 clean boot allows you to bypass CONFIG.SYS and AUTOEXEC.BAT by pressing F5 when the message *Starting MS-DOS* appears at startup. (MS-DOS gives you about a 5-second grace period during which you can specify either the clean boot described here or the interactive boot described next.) Opting for a clean boot essentially lets you pretend you're booting from a system-formatted, no-frills floppy. No matter how badly you mess up CONFIG.SYS or AUTOEXEC.BAT, you can always access your hard disk by way of a clean boot.

- The version 6 interactive boot allows you to step through CONFIG.SYS one command at a time, choosing whether you want to process each one. To request an interactive boot, you press F8 when the *Starting MS-DOS* message appears. If you think a modification to CONFIG.SYS is causing your system to hang, you can use an interactive boot to skip the questionable command and see whether your system starts properly. If you're optimizing memory use, an interactive boot lets you experiment with different configurations and device drivers.

- The version 6 multi-configuration commands allow you to design a custom setup. In addition to using these commands to give yourself different startup options, you can use multi-configuration commands to try out different CONFIG.SYS options. Make your normal, tried-and-true startup one section of your CONFIG.SYS, and make a second part an experimental one that you can assign a name such as *test*. Place the CONFIG.SYS commands you're trying in this test portion of your multi-configuration file, and see what happens when you reboot. If your computer doesn't start correctly, you always have the option of booting normally with the nontest commands.

- The version 6 question mark (?) allows you to tell MS-DOS to prompt for Y or N before processing a CONFIG.SYS command. You can use the question mark, as described in Chapter 12, to test new or modified lines in CONFIG.SYS. If you don't want to bother with multi-configuration commands, you can also use it as a quick-and-dirty version of a Choice command you run from CONFIG.SYS.

NOTE: Just because version 6 of MS-DOS supports multi-configuration CONFIG.SYS files doesn't mean that you have to use one. You can leave your CONFIG.SYS file exactly as is, and MS-DOS will be perfectly capable of starting the system from it. If you want to specify a clean or an interactive boot, you won't have any problems there, either.

From the top

If you haven't worked much with your CONFIG.SYS file, your first order of business is to become familiar with the way it looks and what it does. The easiest way to explore is to use the MS-DOS Editor described in the preceding chapter. Use the command descriptions in Chapter 12 to decipher your own CONFIG.SYS. Pay special attention to commands using the Device, Devicehigh, and DOS (Dos) configuration commands.

The examples in this chapter show different ways a basic CONFIG.SYS file can evolve into a multi-configuration set of options. The left column of the following table shows a typical version 6 CONFIG.SYS file for an 80386 or better computer with 2 MB or more of extended memory; the right column briefly explains what each command does:

`DEVICE=C:\DOS\HIMEM.SYS`	Loads the driver that manages extended memory.
`DEVICE=C:\DOS\EMM386.EXE NOEMS`	Loads the driver that provides UMBs and could, if NOEMS were changed to RAM, simulate expanded memory.
`DOS=HIGH,UMB`	Loads MS-DOS into the HMA and makes UMBs accessible.
`DEVICEHIGH=C:\DOS\RAMDRIVE.SYS 1024 /E`	Creates a 1024-K RAM drive in extended memory.
`SHELL=C:\DOS\COMMAND.COM C:\DOS\ /P`	Defines COMMAND.COM as the MS-DOS shell.
`DEVICEHIGH=C:\DOS\SETVER.EXE`	Loads the MS-DOS version table into UMBs.
`DEVICEHIGH=C:\DOS\DBLSPACE.SYS /MOVE`	Loads the program that moves DBLSPACE.BIN to UMBs.
`BUFFERS=30`	Sets the number of buffers to 30.
`FILES=30`	Sets the number of files that can be open to 30.
`LASTDRIVE=Z`	Sets the last drive letter MS-DOS recognizes to Z.

When MS-DOS processes a CONFIG.SYS file like this one, it romps through the commands one after the other, setting up your hardware according to the Device, Devicehigh, Shell, Dos, and other commands in the file. The file consists of a single block of commands processed pretty much from beginning to end.

Of blocks and headers

To turn a simple (or not-so-simple) CONFIG.SYS into a multi-configuration file, you make use of three version 6 options: a *startup menu, configuration blocks,* and *block headers*. A startup menu describes the different configuration options and lets you choose the one you want. A configuration block contains the configuration commands you want to process for a particular startup. A block header is a name you assign that acts as a label for a particular configuration block and serves as a link between the menu item and the configuration block itself. The following diagram should help you see how these items are related:

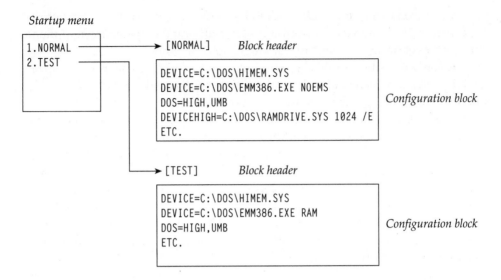

Startup menu

```
1.NORMAL ─────────┐──────► [NORMAL]      Block header
2.TEST   ───────┐ │
                │ │  ┌──────────────────────────────────────┐
                │ │  │ DEVICE=C:\DOS\HIMEM.SYS              │
                │ │  │ DEVICE=C:\DOS\EMM386.EXE NOEMS        │
                │ │  │ DOS=HIGH,UMB                          │   Configuration block
                │ │  │ DEVICEHIGH=C:\DOS\RAMDRIVE.SYS 1024 /E│
                │ │  │ ETC.                                  │
                │ │  └──────────────────────────────────────┘
                │ │
                │ └─► [TEST]          Block header
                │
                │    ┌──────────────────────────────────────┐
                │    │ DEVICE=C:\DOS\HIMEM.SYS              │
                │    │ DEVICE=C:\DOS\EMM386.EXE RAM          │   Configuration block
                │    │ DOS=HIGH,UMB                          │
                │    │ ETC.                                  │
                │    └──────────────────────────────────────┘
```

The next several sections of this chapter describe these elements in more detail. Although a startup menu normally appears at the beginning of a multi-configuration CONFIG.SYS file and, frankly, offers the most entertainment when you experiment, you're going to be stuck with the dour old work-before-play approach to life here: configuration blocks and headers first, and then the fun can begin. For detailed descriptions of the multi-configuration commands themselves, refer to Chapter 12.

A note about order

If you're familiar with editing CONFIG.SYS in version 5 of MS-DOS, you might have wondered why you could place a DOS=HIGH,UMB command anywhere in CONFIG.SYS and have the command carried out correctly, even if it appeared before the Device commands enabling HIMEM.SYS and EMM386.EXE. After all, both drivers are needed before MS-DOS can load into the HMA and can make use of available UMBs. Version 5 has the ability to "read" CONFIG.SYS and "remember" the DOS= command as it goes about loading your device drivers and processing other configuration commands.

Version 6 of MS-DOS shows even more independence of spirit, in that it looks for, and executes, multi-configuration blocks no matter where they appear in CONFIG.SYS. You can, for example, place a startup menu at the end of CONFIG.SYS and still be confident that the menu will appear before any commands in the file are processed. This twist of intelligence on the part of MS-DOS, however, can lead to a poorly designed and confusing CONFIG.SYS file. Even though you can scramble configuration blocks and still come up with a working system, let logic prevail. Build your multi-configuration file block by sensible block. That way, you won't end up with a CONFIG.SYS version of the unstructured "spaghetti code" that once caused wailing and gnashing of teeth among (human) interpreters of Basic programs filled with Goto commands.

The only exception to this rule occurs if you run MemMaker to optimize a CONFIG.SYS in which you've defined multiple configuration blocks. Taking this approach to optimization is not the best or even the recommended way to fine-tune CONFIG.SYS, because MemMaker optimizes the file only for the current configuration. If you do run MemMaker on a multi-configuration file, however, you'll find that it places certain commands at the beginning of your CONFIG.SYS file. Among these commands are the Dos= command and Device commands for SETVER.EXE, HIMEM.SYS, and EMM386.EXE. These commands do not form a configuration block, nor are they preceded by a header. In order for MS-DOS to process your CONFIG.SYS correctly, these MemMaker-positioned commands must always appear before any multi-configuration commands, including those that define your startup menu.

Configuration blocks

The heart of a multi-configuration file consists of typical configuration commands grouped in configuration blocks, each of which sets up the computer in a particular way. Regardless of what it does, each configuration block begins with an identifying header consisting of a *block name* surrounded by square brackets. In the preceding diagram, for example, the configuration block named NORMAL disables EMS memory and creates a 1024-K RAM drive in extended memory. The configuration block named TEST, on the other hand, enables EMS memory and, were it more complete, might also set the last drive to H, load ANSI.SYS in UMBs, and, perhaps, load code-page switching.

If the typical CONFIG.SYS file shown earlier represented the block named NORMAL in a multi-configuration file, the complete header and configuration block would look like this:

```
[NORMAL]

DEVICE=C:\DOS\HIMEM.SYS
DEVICE=C:\DOS\EMM386.EXE NOEMS
DOS=HIGH,UMB
SHELL=C:\DOS\COMMAND.COM C:\DOS\ /P
DEVICEHIGH=C:\DOS\SETVER.EXE
DEVICEHIGH=C:\DOS\DBLSPACE.SYS /MOVE
BUFFERS=30
FILES=30
LASTDRIVE=Z
```

If you've spent any time examing INI (initialization) files such as those created by the MS-DOS Shell, Microsoft Backup (Msbackup), Undelete, and Windows, headers and configuration blocks probably don't look all that strange. The primary difference between a multi-configuration file and a typical INI file is that you create the former, while a program creates and modifies the latter behind the scenes as a tool for "remembering" what it's supposed to look and act like the next time you start it.

Headers

As already mentioned, each block header provides the link between a choice on the startup menu and the commands to be carried out. The block name between the square brackets in a header can be up to 70 characters long, so you can be as descriptive as you want. As you'll see in the later section on menus and menu items, however, the block name does not necessarily have to appear on the startup menu, so you can choose short, simple block names and still associate them with longer, more descriptive choices on the startup menu.

The block name cannot contain spaces or any of the following characters: backslash (\), forward slash (/), comma (,), semicolon (;), equal sign (=), or square brackets ([or]).

Reducing repetition

When you create a multi-configuration CONFIG.SYS file, you can use a *common block*, the Include command, or both to eliminate repetition of certain commands.

Common blocks

A common block always has the header [COMMON] and contains commands that you want processed every time the computer is started. When MS-DOS encounters a common block, it carries out the commands in it regardless of which of your other configuration blocks is chosen. So, for instance, you might choose to include a LASTDRIVE=Z command in a common block so that the last drive MS-DOS recognizes is set to Z no matter which startup configuration is selected. You can include more than one common block in CONFIG.SYS.

The following example shows a short CONFIG.SYS file in which a common block precedes two startup options, one disabling EMS memory and the other providing access to both EMS and XMS memory.

```
[COMMON]
DEVICE=C:\DOS\HIMEM.SYS
DOS=HIGH,UMB
SHELL=C:\DOS\COMMAND.COM C:\DOS\ /P
LASTDRIVE=Z

[NORMAL]
DEVICE=C:\DOS\EMM386.EXE NOEMS
BUFFERS=30
FILES=30

[EMS]
DEVICE=C:\DOS\EMM386.EXE RAM
BUFFERS=25
FILES=25
```

The CONFIG.SYS file in this example is incomplete because it lacks a block defining the startup menu, but in other respects, it is workable. Note that the common block includes the command DEVICE=C:\DOS\HIMEM.SYS, but each configuration block starts EMM386.EXE in a different way. When you're editing CONFIG.SYS, be sure that HIMEM.SYS precedes EMM386.EXE no matter which configuration option is chosen. Bear in mind that EMM386.EXE cannot load if HIMEM.SYS is not already in memory.

In the same vein, if you create a common block, give some thought to where it appears in CONFIG.SYS, as well as what commands you include in other configuration blocks. It's natural to assume that a common block should appear before specific configuration options, but the block's location also depends on what you include in the common block. Although MS-DOS can carry out most configuration commands in a common block without problem, it cannot, for example, carry out Devicehigh commands until you've installed both HIMEM.SYS and EMM386.EXE. Suppose, for example, that you have created the following CONFIG.SYS file:

```
[COMMON]
DOS=HIGH,UMB
SHELL=C:\DOS\COMMAND.COM C:\DOS\ /P
DEVICEHIGH=C:\DOS\SETVER.EXE
DEVICEHIGH=C:\DOS\DBLSPACE.SYS /MOVE
LASTDRIVE=Z

[NORMAL]
DEVICE=C:\DOS\HIMEM.SYS
DEVICE=C:\DOS\EMM386.EXE NOEMS
BUFFERS=30
FILES=30
```

(continued)

```
[EMS]
DEVICE=C:\DOS\HIMEM.SYS
DEVICE=C:\DOS\EMM386.EXE RAM
BUFFERS=25
FILES=25
```

Notice the Devicehigh commands in the common block. MS-DOS would be able to process this CONFIG.SYS file, but you would find that both SETVER.EXE and DBLSPACE.SYS end up loaded in conventional memory. The reason is this: HIMEM.SYS and EMM386.EXE won't be enabled until later, when the commands in either NORMAL or EMS are carried out. And, as you know, if MS-DOS cannot load a device driver into the upper memory area, it loads it into conventional memory instead. To clean up this faulty CONFIG.SYS file, you could place the common block at the end of CONFIG.SYS, or you could include two common blocks. In this case, moving a single common block to the end of the file makes the most sense, at least in terms of length. The choice you make will, of course, depend on your own CONFIG.SYS. A CONFIG.SYS with a single common block at the end would look like this:

```
[NORMAL]
DEVICE=C:\DOS\HIMEM.SYS
DEVICE=C:\DOS\EMM386.EXE NOEMS
BUFFERS=30
FILES=30

[EMS]
DEVICE=C:\DOS\HIMEM.SYS
DEVICE=C:\DOS\EMM386.EXE RAM
BUFFERS=25
FILES=25

[COMMON]
DOS=HIGH,UMB
SHELL=C:\DOS\COMMAND.COM C:\DOS\ /P
DEVICEHIGH=C:\DOS\SETVER.EXE
DEVICEHIGH=C:\DOS\DBLSPACE.SYS /MOVE
LASTDRIVE=Z
```

The same CONFIG.SYS with two common blocks would look like this:

```
[COMMON]
DOS=HIGH,UMB
SHELL=C:\DOS\COMMAND.COM C:\DOS\ /P
LASTDRIVE=Z

[NORMAL]
DEVICE=C:\DOS\HIMEM.SYS
```

(continued)

```
DEVICE=C:\DOS\EMM386.EXE NOEMS
BUFFERS=30
FILES=30

[EMS]
DEVICE=C:\DOS\HIMEM.SYS
DEVICE=C:\DOS\EMM386.EXE RAM
BUFFERS=25
FILES=25

[COMMON]
DEVICEHIGH=C:\DOS\SETVER.EXE
DEVICEHIGH=C:\DOS\DBLSPACE.SYS /MOVE
```

Both approaches use a common block at the end, as recommended in the MS-DOS documentation. Some applications append commands to CONFIG.SYS when they are installed, including a common block, even if it doesn't contain any commands, ensuring that application-added commands will be carried out no matter which startup configuration you choose.

Include

In contrast to a common block, the Include command allows you to name a configuration block that you want processed as part of another configuration block. To use Include, you begin by creating a sub-block, as it were, of commands that you want to use in more than one of your complete configuration blocks. One obvious example would be along these lines:

```
[BASE_SETUP]
DEVICE=C:\DOS\HIMEM.SYS
DEVICE=C:\DOS\EMM386.EXE NOEMS
DOS=HIGH,UMB
LASTDRIVE=M
```

In creating your other configuration blocks, you can then use the Include command to "insert" the BASE_SETUP commands wherever you want them carried out in CONFIG.SYS. For example,

```
[NORMAL]
INCLUDE=BASE_SETUP
DEVICEHIGH=C:\DOS\RAMDRIVE.SYS 1024 /E
BUFFERS=20
FILES=20

[NETSETUP]
INCLUDE=BASE_SETUP
DEVICEHIGH=C:\NET\MYNET.SYS
BUFFERS=30
FILES=30
```

As you can see here, Include helps make a CONFIG.SYS file more readable by eliminating repetition of commands. When you use Include, you and everyone else can immediately see that in each configuration block all commands other than Include are unique.

NOTE: *Although a common block and Include can be valuable tools for organizing the commands in CONFIG.SYS, you should avoid both if you plan to use MemMaker to optimize memory use as described later in this chapter.*

Startup menus and menu items

Now for the fun. A *startup menu* is a special block that always begins with the header [MENU]. Reason dictates that a startup menu should appear at the beginning of CONFIG.SYS, but as mentioned earlier, you can put it somewhere else. A typical startup menu looks like this:

```
MS-DOS 6 Startup Menu
=====================
    1. Basic Startup
    2. Create RAM Drive

Enter a choice: 1
```

Within a startup menu, you include a Menu Item (Menuitem) command for each (automatically numbered) menu choice you want to define. As described in Chapter 12, the Menuitem command takes two parameters, one of them optional:

menuitem=*blockname*[,*menutext*]

where *blockname* is the name of the configuration block you want processed if the menu item is selected, and *menutext* is an optional description of up to 70 characters that is displayed instead of the block name on the menu. Menu items are a lot easier seen than described, so the following simple examples should suffice.

Suppose you create two startup configurations named NORMAL and EMS. If you omit *menutext* when creating the menu items, like this,

```
[MENU]
MENUITEM=NORMAL
MENUITEM=EMS
```

the startup menu shows the names of the configuration blocks:

```
MS-DOS 6 Startup Menu
=====================
    1. NORMAL
    2. EMS

Enter a choice: 1
```

On the other hand, if you include both the block name and some text, like this,

```
[MENU]
MENUITEM=NORMAL,Normal Startup - No Expanded Memory
MENUITEM=EMS,Startup with Expanded Memory
```

the displayed menu is considerably more descriptive:

```
MS-DOS 6 Startup Menu
=====================
    1. Normal Startup - No Expanded Memory
    2. Startup with Expanded Memory


Enter a choice: 1
```

Notice that your use of uppercase and lowercase in the menu text controls capitalization in the displayed menu choices.

Adding color

Normally, MS-DOS is a black-and-white animal unless you use ANSI.SYS, the MS-DOS Shell, the MS-DOS Editor, QBasic, or one of the menu-based version 6 utilities, such as Msbackup. If you define a startup menu, you can add a Kodachrome moment to your otherwise monochrome MS-DOS existence. Once defined, the menu color remains untouched until output scrolls to a new screen or processing of AUTOEXEC.BAT begins. The color then reverts to your usual black-and-white display.

To colorize a startup menu, you use the Menu Color command and place the definition in your menu block. Briefly, the syntax of the command is as follows:

menucolor=*text*,[*background*]

where *text* is the text color and *background*, if included, is the screen color. Specify either or both as numbers corresponding to the following colors:

Color number	Color	Color number	Color
0	Black	8	Gray
1	Blue	9	Bright blue
2	Green	10	Bright green
3	Cyan (blue-green)	11	Bright cyan
4	Red	12	Bright red
5	Magenta	13	Bright magenta
6	Brown	14	Yellow
7	White	15	Bright white

NOTE: If you want bright white text of the type you normally see on screen, specify 15 rather than 7. Also, be prepared for a possible surprise: On some displays, specifying 8 through 15 produces the color you specify, but the text will blink on and off like the normal MS-DOS cursor. The effects of some color combinations haven't been seen since the psychedelic sixties.

Defining and timing a default configuration

If you're like most people and use one startup configuration far more often than others, or if you simply detest babysitting your computer, you'll appreciate the Menu Default (Menudefault) command, which allows you to specify a default configuration and set it running automatically if you don't choose a different configuration within a fixed amount of time. Like the other menu commands, Menudefault is simple:

menudefault=*blockname*[,*timeout*]

where *blockname* is the name of the configuration block you want to define as the default, and the optional *timeout* specifies the number of seconds (0 through 90) until the default configuration is processed.

When you use Menudefault and specify a time, your startup menu gains one added piece of information:

```
MS-DOS 6 Startup Menu
=====================
   1. Normal Startup - No Expanded Memory
   2. Startup with Expanded Memory
Enter a choice: 1      Time remaining: 15
```

When the countdown reaches 0, MS-DOS kicks in and carries out the default configuration. You will, however, still have to press Y or N for either of the following conditions: if you indicate that you want to step through CONFIG.SYS or if you use the question mark in a configuration command to cause MS-DOS to prompt for confirmation before processing the command.

Submenus

Submenus, as described in Chapter 12, allow you to break a menu down into two levels. You might do this if your list of configuration blocks and menu items runs to more than the nine allowed by MS-DOS or if you want to set up the computer with options like the following:

Menu item 1: Normal startup

    Submenu item 1: RAM drive, no EMS

    Submenu item 2: EMS, no RAM drive

Menu item 2: Network Startup

In a situation like this, if the user chose menu item 1, a second, very similar, menu would appear offering the two choices shown for submenu items 1 and 2. The skeleton of a simple CONFIG.SYS file defining these options might look like the following:

```
[MENU]
MENUITEM=NORMAL,Normal Startup
MENUITEM=NETWORK,Network Startup
SUBMENU=OPTIONS,RAM Drive or EMS

[OPTIONS]
MENUITEM=RAM,RAM Drive, No EMS
MENUITEM=EMS,EMS, No RAM Drive

[COMMON]
DEVICE=C:\DOS\HIMEM.SYS
DOS=HIGH,UMB
LASTDRIVE=M

[NORMAL]
DEVICE=C:\DOS\EMM386.EXE NOEMS HIGHSCAN
BUFFERS=20
FILES=20

[RAM]
INCLUDE=NORMAL
DEVICEHIGH=C:\DOS\RAMDRIVE.SYS 1024 /E

[EMS]
DEVICE=C:\DOS\EMM386.EXE RAM

[NETWORK]
DEVICE=C:\DOS\EMM386.EXE NOHI
DEVICEHIGH=C:\NETWORK\NETWORK.SYS
BUFFERS=30
FILES=30

[COMMON]
```

Wheels within wheels, cogs turning...turning.

Number Lock (Numlock)

Whatever you do with CONFIG.SYS, don't forget the Number Lock (Numlock) command. You can put Numlock anywhere you want, in one line of a simple CONFIG.SYS file or in two or more places in a maze of configuration blocks. As described in Chapter 12, Numlock turns the Num Lock key on or off. And as any word-oriented user of computers knows, Num Lock should be turned off at startup. If it is not, the key can make numeric messes when forgetful people attempt to use the direction keys on the keypad.

Using the Numlock command is about as difficult as hitting a wall switch:

```
numlock=on
```

turns the key on.

```
numlock=off
```

turns the key off.

If you sometimes use your computer primarily for numeric entry and at other times use it primarily for processing words, even the simplest of CONFIG.SYS files can ensure that you start up with Num Lock in the correct mode. For example, suppose you use EMS memory with your spreadsheet, but XMS memory and a RAM drive with your word processor. To set up your computer for these uses and ensure that Num Lock is on for your spreadsheet but off for your word processor, you could create a multi-configuration file like this one:

```
[MENU]
MENUITEM=NUMBERS
MENUITEM=WORDS

[BASE_SETUP]
DEVICE=C:\DOS\HIMEM.SYS
DOS=HIGH,UMB
LASTDRIVE=M

[NUMBERS]
DEVICEHIGH=C:\DOS\EMM386.EXE RAM
NUMLOCK=ON

[WORDS]
DEVICEHIGH=C:\DOS\EMM386.EXE NOEMS
DEVICEHIGH=C:\DOS\RAMDRIVE.SYS 1024 /E
NUMLOCK=OFF
```

Question marks and semicolons

Punctuation might be something you learned and forgot most of after Composition 101, but when you're working with CONFIG.SYS, two punctuation marks can make your life simpler:

- The question mark lets you step through portions of CONFIG.SYS by causing MS-DOS to prompt for confirmation before carrying out a specified command. You can use the question mark in either a "normal" or a multi-configuration CONFIG.SYS. The prompt does not appear, however, if the question mark is in a default configuration block that MS-DOS carries out automatically.

- The semicolon lets you eliminate all those REMs your CONFIG.SYS might have collected over the years as you and your installed software disabled configuration commands without deleting them from the file.

The question mark gives you a means of selectively stepping through CONFIG.SYS at startup, choosing whether or not to process certain commands. In that sense, inserting a question mark in a configuration command is much like giving yourself a customizable version of the F8 (interactive boot) key. You can use the question mark with any configuration command other than those that define menus and multiple configurations. Place the question mark before the equal sign in the command for which you want to be prompted, like this:

```
COUNTRY?=033
KEYB?=FR,,C:\DOS\KEYBOARD.SYS
```

In these examples, MS-DOS would prompt for confirmation twice: once before setting the system's country conventions to French and again before adjusting the keyboard layout to match the one used in France.

A semicolon, when it appears as the first character in a line, works much like the REM command you can use in CONFIG.SYS and your batch files: It causes MS-DOS to ignore everything that follows on that line. Use a semicolon to disable a CONFIG.SYS command without actually deleting it (useful both when you're testing configuration commands and when you want to save a complex command for a rainy day) and to begin comment lines that describe your CONFIG.SYS file. For example,

```
;DEVICEHIGH /L:1,44256 =C:\DOS\DBLSPACE.SYS /MOVE
```

would disable, without deleting, the Devicehigh command that enables DBLSPACE.SYS to move DoubleSpace to region 1 of your computer's upper memory area. Likewise, the two lines at the beginning of this example,

```
;THE FOLLOWING BLOCK REPRESENTS A BASE CONFIGURATION
;FOR THIS SYSTEM. DO NOT DELETE.

[BASE_SETUP]
DEVICE=C:\DOS\HIMEM.SYS
DEVICE=C:\DOS\EMM386.EXE NOEMS
DOS=HIGH,UMB
LASTDRIVE=M
```

would tell you and others that the configuration block named BASE_SETUP is an essential part of CONFIG.SYS.

Linking CONFIG.SYS and AUTOEXEC.BAT

If you've tried an interactive boot, you already know that MS-DOS steps through each command in CONFIG.SYS (or the configuration block you specify) and ends with the message:

```
Process AUTOEXEC.BAT [Y,N]?
```

Perhaps you were a little surprised by this, thinking that an interactive boot meant interacting with AUTOEXEC.BAT as well as CONFIG.SYS. Well, obviously interactivity doesn't extend quite that far. But version 6 of MS-DOS does offer you other ways to skin this particular feline. One is the Choice command described in Chapter 12 and, in more detail, in Chapter 19. If you create a multi-configuration CONFIG.SYS, another is a new environment variable named CON-FIG. (If you aren't comfortable with batch files as yet, skip the following descriptions for now. You won't hurt anything by waiting awhile.)

The Choice command, as you probably know by now, allows you to tailor AUTOEXEC.BAT or any batch file to accept keyboard input by displaying a prompt like the *Process AUTOEXEC.BAT [Y,N]?* message shown previously. Using Choice, you can have AUTOEXEC.BAT prompt for instructions or confirmation and thus customize AUTOEXEC.BAT to match the options you select in CON-FIG.SYS. For example, suppose you don't go to the trouble of creating a multi-configuration CONFIG.SYS, but you do use the question mark to cause MS-DOS to prompt before loading some device drivers you use now and then. Such a CONFIG.SYS file might look something like the following (for ease of reading, the two options are grouped at the end):

```
DEVICE=C:\DOS\HIMEM.SYS
DEVICE=C:\DOS\EMM386.EXE NOEMS
DOS=HIGH,UMB
SHELL=C:\DOS\COMMAND.COM C:\DOS\ /P
DEVICEHIGH=C:\DOS\SETVER.EXE
DEVICEHIGH=C:\DOS\DBLSPACE.SYS /MOVE
BUFFERS=30
FILES=30
LASTDRIVE=Z
DEVICEHIGH?=C:\DOS\RAMDRIVE.SYS 1024 /E
DEVICEHIGH?=C:\DOS\ANSI.SYS
```

If you choose to create a RAM drive (drive D, say), you might also want to be able to use it as a home for your temporary directory, which otherwise is C:\TEMP. If you load ANSI.SYS, you might also want to load a batch file (named SCREENS.BAT) that creates memory-resident Doskey macros you can use to switch between 25-line and 43-line display modes. You might also want the

luxury of deciding, while AUTOEXEC.BAT is being processed, whether to load
VSafe to monitor your system for virus activity. With the Choice command, you
can do all three in an AUTOEXEC.BAT like the following:

```
@ECHO OFF
LH C:\DOS\SMARTDRV.EXE 2048
PATH C:\DOS;C:\BATCH;C:\PROGS
CLS
ECHO CHOOSE A TEMPORARY DIRECTORY:
ECHO.
ECHO C:\TEMP
ECHO D:\TEMP
ECHO.
CHOICE /C:CD Press C or D
IF ERRORLEVEL 2 SET TEMP=D:\TEMP
IF ERRORLEVEL 1 SET TEMP=C:\TEMP
CLS
ECHO LOAD SCREENS.BAT?
ECHO.
CHOICE
IF ERRORLEVEL 2 GOTO NEXT
IF ERRORLEVEL 1 CALL C:\BATCH\SCREENS.BAT
:NEXT
CLS
ECHO START VIRUS SCANNING?
ECHO.
CHOICE
IF ERRORLEVEL 2 GOTO END
IF ERRORLEVEL 1 LH C:\DOS\VSAFE
:END
```

If you create a multi-configuration CONFIG.SYS file, linking your choice to
AUTOEXEC.BAT is much easier, thanks to the CONFIG variable. When you
choose a particular configuration block during startup, MS-DOS sets the CON-
FIG variable to the name of the configuration block you choose. For example, if
your CONFIG.SYS includes two blocks named NORMAL and RAMDRIVE and
you choose NORMAL from the startup menu, MS-DOS adds this entry to the
environment:

```
CONFIG=NORMAL
```

You can see this and other environment variables by typing *set* at the command prompt.

As described in Chapters 12 and 19, the name of an environment variable can
be included in a batch file, and the batch interpreter will substitute the actual
name of the variable for the variable itself. To do this, you enclose the variable
name in percent signs, like so:

```
%CONFIG%
```

You're no doubt way ahead of the game by now. The key here is the Goto batch command. Using Goto and the CONFIG variable, you can define blocks of commands in AUTOEXEC.BAT that match the startup option you choose in CONFIG.SYS. For example, suppose you have the following pretty simple CONFIG.SYS file:

```
[MENU]
MENUITEM=NORMAL
MENUITEM=RAMDRIVE

[BASE_SETUP]
DEVICE=C:\DOS\HIMEM.SYS
DEVICEHIGH=C:\DOS\EMM386.EXE NOEMS
DOS=HIGH,UMB
SHELL=C:\DOS\COMMAND.COM C:\DOS\ /P
DEVICEHIGH=C:\DOS\SETVER.EXE
DEVICEHIGH=C:\DOS\DBLSPACE.SYS /MOVE
BUFFERS=30
FILES=30
LASTDRIVE=Z

[NORMAL]
INCLUDE=BASE_SETUP
DEVICEHIGH=C:\DOS\ANSI.SYS
NUMLOCK=OFF

[RAMDRIVE]
INCLUDE=BASE_SETUP
DEVICEHIGH=C:\DOS\RAMDRIVE.SYS 1024 /E
```

Depending on the option you choose, suppose you want to do the following in AUTOEXEC.BAT:

- For all configurations: Set the path, set up a SMARTDRV.EXE cache, start Undelete with the /S (Sentry option), and enable VSafe.

- For the Normal option: Load Doskey into the upper memory area, load your Doskey macros (in MACROS.BAT), and set the temporary directory to C:\TEMP.

- For the Ramdrive option: Set the temporary directory to D:, which is your RAM drive.

Here's how you do it all in AUTOEXEC.BAT, with CONFIG and Goto:

```
@ECHO OFF
PATH=C:\DOS;C:\BATCH;C:\PROGS
C:\DOS\SMARTDRV.EXE 2048
UNDELETE /SC
LH VSAFE
```

(continued)

```
GOTO %CONFIG%
:NORMAL
LH DOSKEY
CALL MACROS.BAT
SET TEMP=C:\TEMP
GOTO END
:RAMDRIVE
SET TEMP=D:
:END
```

As you can see from this example, the batch interpreter compares the value of %CONFIG% to the names of your two startup options. If the value of %CON-FIG% is NORMAL, the Goto command sends execution to the section of AUTOEXEC.BAT beginning with the label :NORMAL. (To avoid having the commands in the RAMDRIVE section carried out, the NORMAL section ends with the command GOTO END.) If the value of %CONFIG% is RAMDRIVE, the GOTO command sends execution to the label :RAMDRIVE, instead, skipping over the commands in NORMAL.

Simple, clean, quick, and customizable. Not that bad for a 10-year-old operating system.

Optimizing a multi-configuration file

Although MemMaker is a handy and easy-to-use aid in optimizing memory use, it requires some help from you when you create a multi-configuration CON-FIG.SYS file. You can run MemMaker on a multi-configuration CONFIG.SYS, but not without some advance preparation. This is because MemMaker analyzes and works with the device drivers and TSR programs that are active at the time you optimize memory. If you create multiple configurations, obviously only one of those startup sets will be active when you run MemMaker. As a result, Mem-Maker will optimize memory use for that configuration, but not for any others. In fact, in optimizing for one configuration, MemMaker might make one or more alternatives less memory-efficient. It's also possible that MemMaker's handiwork could keep your computer from starting properly.

To optimize a multi-configuration CONFIG.SYS, you have to treat each potential startup option as if it were your one and only. That means you must create a separate—and complete—configuration block for each startup option you want, even if doing so requires repetition of some configuration commands in each block. For example, suppose you have the following CONFIG.SYS file, complete with Include commands:

```
[MENU]
MENUITEM=NORMAL
MENUITEM=RAMDRIVE

[BASE_SETUP]
DEVICE=C:\DOS\HIMEM.SYS
DEVICEHIGH=C:\DOS\EMM386.EXE NOEMS
DOS=HIGH,UMB
SHELL=C:\DOS\COMMAND.COM C:\DOS\ /P
DEVICEHIGH=C:\DOS\SETVER.EXE
DEVICEHIGH=C:\DOS\DBLSPACE.SYS /MOVE
BUFFERS=30
FILES=30

[NORMAL]
INCLUDE=BASE_SETUP
DEVICEHIGH=C:\DOS\ANSI.SYS

[RAMDRIVE]
INCLUDE=BASE_SETUP
DEVICEHIGH=C:\DOS\RAMDRIVE.SYS 1024 /E
```

To optimize memory use for this file, you should first save a backup copy of CONFIG.SYS under a name, such as CONFIG.ABC, which doesn't exist in your root directory. Next, using a text editor, you should break CONFIG.SYS into two new files, assigning them temporary names, such as CONFIG.111 and CONFIG.222. Each new CONFIG file would have to contain all the commands necessary for a complete startup, as follows.

For CONFIG.111, type this:

```
DEVICE=C:\DOS\HIMEM.SYS
DEVICEHIGH=C:\DOS\EMM386.EXE NOEMS
DOS=HIGH,UMB
SHELL=C:\DOS\COMMAND.COM C:\DOS\ /P
DEVICEHIGH=C:\DOS\SETVER.EXE
DEVICEHIGH=C:\DOS\DBLSPACE.SYS /MOVE
BUFFERS=30
FILES=30
DEVICEHIGH=C:\DOS\ANSI.SYS
```

For CONFIG.222, type this:

```
DEVICE=C:\DOS\HIMEM.SYS
DEVICEHIGH=C:\DOS\EMM386.EXE NOEMS
DOS=HIGH,UMB
SHELL=C:\DOS\COMMAND.COM C:\DOS\ /P
DEVICEHIGH=C:\DOS\SETVER.EXE
```

(continued)

```
DEVICEHIGH=C:\DOS\DBLSPACE.SYS /MOVE
BUFFERS=30
FILES=30
DEVICEHIGH=C:\DOS\RAMDRIVE.SYS 1024 /E
```

Save each file. To optimize each startup, rename the file to CONFIG.SYS (for example, *ren config.111 config.sys*), restart the computer, and run MemMaker. When the file has been optimized, save it under its old, non-SYS name. Rename the other CONFIG file (for example, *ren config.222 config.sys*), restart the computer, and run MemMaker again. When both files have been optimized, use your text editor to combine the two, adding whatever menu commands are needed at the beginning. Save the file as your new, optimized, CONFIG.SYS.

17

Redirection, Pipes, and Filters

What You'll Find Here: There's a video game called Pipe Dream in which the player attempts to put differently shaped pieces of pipe together to keep water from spilling. This short chapter is about the less intriguing but sometimes fun MS-DOS equivalents of those video-game constructs: the redirection and pipe symbols that help you channel the flow of command input and output, and the closely related Find, Sort, and More commands that join and filter the input and output you direct.

*M*S-DOS is often castigated by the graphically minded for being so unfriendly that it requires you, the user, to type commands. Perhaps it is unfriendly to some people, but in comparison to some non-graphical operating systems, others find MS-DOS positively puppyish. MS-DOS also has a certain pleasant directness about it: Type a command, and get results. (OK, not always the results you intended, but certainly the results you requested.)

This equivalence of keyboard equals input, screen equals output makes MS-DOS both fast and easy to understand. Between you and the results you seek from a Directory (Dir) command or a Make Directory (Mkdir) command, there is only MS-DOS. Sometimes, however, you want more control over what goes in and what comes out. At those times, MS-DOS offers flexibility in the form of re-direction, pipes, and filter commands.

Redirection

As explained in Chapter 12, you can redirect both input and output. Input redirection allows an MS-DOS command to get input from a file rather than from the keyboard; output redirection allows a command to send its results somewhere other than the screen—usually to a file or the printer. Redirection always relies on the following symbols:

- A less-than symbol (<) tells MS-DOS to get command input from the source following the symbol. Input redirection isn't used very often, but when it is, it is usually associated with a filter command. For example, the command *more < c:\dos\readme.txt* would display the README.TXT file one screenful at a time; the command *sort < mylist.txt* would sort the lines in the file MYLIST.TXT.

- A greater-than symbol (>) tells MS-DOS to send command output to the file or device name following the symbol. Output redirection is used much more often than input redirection, commonly as a means of saving the output of a command such as Dir or Check Disk (Chkdsk) in a disk file or sending it to the printer. For example, the command *dir > filelist.txt* would save the output of the Dir command in a file named FILELIST.TXT.

- Two greater-than symbols (>>) tell MS-DOS to append the output of a command to an existing file. You use this form of redirection when you want to add to, rather than replace, the contents of a file. For example, the command *dir >> c:\floppies\dirlists.txt* would append the output of the Dir command to a file named DIRLISTS.TXT in the FLOPPIES directory of drive C.

Some uses for redirection

The following description applies to redirecting output. We'll concentrate on output redirection because input redirection is used less often. Redirected input is, in fact, almost synonymous with use of the filter commands, and so is described later in this chapter. Because filters are involved, you'll find that redirecting input offers more creative channels than redirected output. The latter, however, occupies a valuable, if utilitarian, place in MS-DOS.

The most common use of redirection in the history of MS-DOS has almost certainly been redirection of the output of the Dir command to either a file or the printer as a means of creating a permanent list of the files on a disk or in a directory. Since the arrival of version 5, this use has gained even greater flexibility because the Dir command itself includes numerous ways to sort files and to list those with specified attributes. If you work with a lot of floppy disks or directories, the following simple and often-mentioned use of output redirection can make library duty much simpler by printing a list of files for you:

   dir [*disk* or *directory*] > prn

Insert the letter of the disk drive or the name of the directory, and off you go. Because redirection doesn't interfere with allowable switches, you can customize this command as much as you want. For example,

- *dir a: /b > prn* would print only the names and extensions of the files on drive A, omitting file sizes, dates, and times.

- *dir c:\bmp /c > prn* would, in version 6 only, print an expanded listing of the files in the BMP (bitmap) directory, including compression ratios as well as names, extensions, sizes, dates, and times.

- *dir /ad /on > prn* would print an alphabetized list of directories in the current directory of the current drive.

- *dir bmp /on /s > prn* would print alphabetized lists of all files in the BMP directory and all its subdirectories, including an identifying header for each directory.

With some printers, such as Epson dot-matrix printers, you can redirect command output and receive pages of printed copy in return, so any of the preceding examples would work no matter whether the output were a few lines or a few pages long. With some printers, such as Hewlett-Packard LaserJets, however, you might become frustrated if you redirect output that goes on for more than one page, because the printer does not use a formfeed (Ctrl-L) character to eject the last page. Normally, this conservatism on the part of your printer doesn't matter because your application software ensures that all pages of your document are printed and ejected. When you redirect the output of an MS-DOS command, however, the last page or pages of output can remain in the printer's buffer until you take the printer off line and press the formfeed button. The simplest solution in this case is to redirect the output to a file and then print the file. You can do this quickly with a small batch file like the following:

```
@echo off
dir %1 > dosdir
print dosdir
echo When printing is complete
pause
del dosdir
```

NOTE: Echo and Pause commands following the Print command in the preceding batch file are included to avoid an error message telling you about a sharing violation. If you omit the Pause command, MS-DOS might try to delete the DOSDIR file while it is being printed. The Echo command simply displays a message while Pause gives MS-DOS a short breather. Press any key when printing is complete, or nearly so.

Just because redirection is used so often with Dir doesn't, of course, mean other commands needn't apply. You can, for example,

- Redirect the output of the Chkdsk command to a file or to the printer to receive a report on fragmentation and available space.

- If you're working with CONFIG.SYS and AUTOEXEC.BAT and you want to optimize the order in which device drivers and programs are loaded, redirect the output of *mem /c* or *mem /d* to list the drivers and programs in memory, along with their sizes and the amount of upper memory remaining for use.

- If you've loaded Doskey and you want to keep a list of commands you've entered, either for historical purposes or to serve as the basis of a new batch file, use *doskey /history > [filename]* to redirect the commands in the Doskey buffer to a filename you specify. Similarly, if you've been making your keyboard work faster and easier with a series of Doskey macros, use *doskey /macros > [filename]* to save the macros in a file. With a little bit of editing, as described in the next chapter, you can easily use that output to create a batch file that creates and loads the macros for you whenever you want.

- Finally, if you assign the hidden, system, or read-only attributes to your files, you might want to keep a (discreet) list of such files. For that, redirect the output of either the Attribute command or the Dir command with the /a switch—for example, use *dir [directory] /ah > prn* to print a list of hidden files in the directory you specify.

Piping

Piping, unlike redirection, acts as a conduit between MS-DOS commands by turning the output of one command into the input for another. The simplest and most self-explanatory use of the pipe is in the following command, a standard means of viewing long directories for years, until the /p switch appeared in the Dir command:

```
dir ¦ more
```

Here, the pipe takes the output of the Dir command and turns it into the input of the More command, which then displays the output one screenful at a time. Other common commands used with More include

- The Type command, for scrolling through long text files, like this:

  ```
  type karenina.txt ¦ more
  ```

- The Find command, for viewing more than one screenful of lines containing a specified string, like this:

  ```
  find "DOS" c:\dos\readme.txt ¦ more
  ```

- A combination of commands, which can sometimes become fairly elaborate and usually involves Find, Sort, or both, like this:

  ```
  dir c:\dos ¦ find "EXE" ¦ sort ¦ more
  ```

Regardless of how you use the pipe symbol, however, there's a little more than meets the eye. While piping output from one command to another, MS-DOS actually sends the output through one or more behind-the-scenes temporary files. These temporary files don't usually show up on screen and are seldom seen in directory listings because MS-DOS deletes such files as soon as they are no longer needed. In addition, if you have set the TEMP variable in your environment, MS-DOS places its temporary files in the temporary directory specified by the variable, so you're unlikely ever to see them. If you want a glimpse of these elusive beasts, however, there is a way.

1. First, type *set* to use the Set command to check on your temporary directory. You should see something like the following:

    ```
    CONFIG=Normal
    COMSPEC=C:\COMMAND.COM
    PROMPT=$P$G
    PATH=C:\DOS;C:\BATCH;C:\PROGS
    TEMP=C:\TEMP
    ```

    Note the drive and directory indicated by TEMP. You're going to eliminate the line for a short time.

2. To "unset" your TEMP variable, type the following:

    ```
    C:\>set temp=
    ```

3. Now, change to your DOS directory. This exhibition won't work unless you request a listing of the current directory. Type the following:

    ```
    C:\DOS>dir | more
    ```

    MS-DOS displays the contents of your DOS directory one screenful at a time. Scan the list, and you should see one or two 0-byte files with peculiar filenames that look like random collections of characters—for example, BBAIBOEH and BBAIBOFC. Depending on your version of MS-DOS, you might find one of these filenames at the beginning of the listing and one at the end, or you might find both at the end. Wherever you find them, those are the temporary files created to help MS-DOS pipe the output of Dir to the More command. Note the first three or four characters.

4. At the system prompt, use the Dir command to find the filenames you just saw. They won't be there. As soon as MS-DOS finished carrying out the *dir | more* command, it deleted the temporary files.

5. Reset your TEMP variable by typing the Set command again, this time followed by the drive and name of your temporary directory. For example

    ```
    C:\DOS>set temp=c:\temp
    ```

Examples in the remainder of this chapter show how you can use piping in other ways. If you plan to use this feature, especially with the Find and Sort commands, be sure to set the TEMP variable so that temporary files don't intrude on your command output.

Filters

Although filters sound like they belong on cigarettes or water faucets, they are special—and aptly named—commands in the MS-DOS world. Filters are commands that take input and "strain" it in some way to produce the output you want. MS-DOS includes three filters: Find, Sort, and More. Pipes and filters and, to a lesser extent, redirection and filters, go together naturally.

More

More, as you've seen, pumps command output to the screen one screenful at a time. Normally, one screenful displays 25 lines. If you change the screen mode with the *mode con lines=* command, however, More displays however many lines you specified. When you're viewing long files or directories, consider combining Mode and the More command to reduce the number of times you have to halt the display.

Although the preceding section showed the use of More with the pipe symbol, that's not the only way you can use it. To display a long file, you can also use input redirection, which tells More to use the file as input, as in this example:

```
more < karenina.txt
```

You cannot use More in this form with a command such as Dir, unless you first redirect the output of the command to a file.

Find

Find and Sort are the MS-DOS commands closest to "real" programs. Find is the equivalent of the Find or Search command in your word processor, spreadsheet, or any other application that can comb a document for a specified string of text. As described in Chapter 12, Find can be used on some types of formatted documents, such as those produced by your word processor, but not with particularly happy results because of the formatting codes embedded in the text. When you use Find, you're advised to stick to plain-text, unformatted, ASCII files like those produced by the MS-DOS Editor.

When you use the Find command, you specify a string enclosed in double quotation marks and the names of one or more files (no wildcards) you want to search. When the search is complete, Find displays a line that identifies the file, followed by each line in the file that contains the specified string. As simple and useful as this command format can be, Find also accepts several switches: three that govern the form of its output and one that affects the results of your search. These switches are all described in Chapter 12. To avoid your having to flip back in the book, the command syntax and switches are, briefly, as follows:

find [/v] [/c] [/n] [/i] *"string"* [*filespec1*] [*filespec2*]...[*filespecN*]

- /v displays only lines that don't contain the string you specify. For example, if you want to display all lines in your CONFIG.SYS file that don't contain the string "device=", you would type this:

```
find /v "device=" c:\config.sys
```

- /c displays only a count of the lines containing the string. For example, if you wanted to find the number of commands in CONFIG.SYS containing the string "device=", you would type the following:

```
find /c "device=" c:\config.sys
```

■ /n precedes each line containing the string with its line number. For example, if MS-DOS displays the message *Unrecognized command in CONFIG.SYS* followed by the message *Error in CONFIG.SYS line 15*, you can track down the offending line with a command like the following, which would cover all CONFIG.SYS lines except remarks:

```
find /n "=" c:\config.sys
```

In this case, the output would look something like this (the bad command is produced by a spelling error in line 15):

```
----- C:\CONFIG.SYS
[2]menuitem=ems
[3]menuitem=noems
[6]device=c:\dos\himem.sys
[7]dos=high,umb
[8]lastdrive=z
[9]files=20
[10]buffers=20
[13]include=base
[14]device=c:\dos\emm386.exe ram
[15]deviceehigh=c:\dos\ramdrive.sys 2048 /e
[16]numlock=off
[17]devicehigh=c:\dos\ansi.sys
[20]include=base
[21]device=c:\dos\emm386.exe noems
[22]devicehigh=c:\dos\ansi.sys
[23]numlock=on
```

■ /i tells Find to ignore differences between uppercase and lowercase. Probably the most significant of the Find switches, /i allows you some leeway in specifying the search string. If you don't tell Find to ignore case, it seeks only absolute matches: *dog* if you specify *"dog"*, *Cat* if you specify *"Cat"*, and even *moUSE* if you specify *"moUSE"*. For example, if you are searching for all device and devicehigh lines in CONFIG.SYS but can't remember whether they're uppercase or lowercase, you can type the Find command like this:

```
find /i "device" c:\config.sys
```

Note that the string in the last example excludes the equal sign and merely specifies *device*. Find does not distinguish between whole words and parts of words, so *"device"* covers both *device* and *devicehigh*. Sometimes you have to give a little thought to the string you specify, to ensure that it is inclusive enough to cover all occurrences of the string you want, but exclusive enough to eliminate any similar, but unwanted, strings. For example, suppose you want to use Find to display all lines in a DoubleSpace directory that contain compression ratios. Such a line looks like this:

```
DOSHELP  HLP      5667 03-10-93   6:00a   2.0 to 1.0
```

You might scan the line and assume that the string ".0 to " would do the job because no filename, file size, date, or time would include those characters. In actuality, your search would be incomplete, because not all compression ratios begin with .0 to. If you look at a DoubleSpace DOS directory, you'll see that some ratios are displayed as 2.3 to 1.0, 1.5 to 1.0, 3.2 to 1.0, and so on. What is common to all entries, however, are the characters to 1.0. So, specifying the search string as "to 1.0" would include every line containing a compression ratio, but it would exclude all header lines and lines listing directories. The output would, however, also include a summary line like this:

```
4.6 to 1.0 average compression ratio
```

The line is harmless, but if you wanted to get rid of it as well, you could pipe output from one Find command to another, like this:

```
dir /c | find " to 1.0" | find /v "average compression"
```

Interesting, no?

Finally, if you use Find, also bear in mind that, if you specify more than one word as the search string, as in the preceding example, Find will *not* include any occurrences in which the string is broken by a carriage return at the end of a line. To Find, spaces and carriage returns are as much "real" characters as an A, B, or C, so a string specified as *"hot stuff"* is not the same as an occurrence of the string *hot[carriage return]stuff.*

Sort

Sort is the MS-DOS equivalent of the Sort utility in word processors, spreadsheets, databases, and other applications. You should use Sort, however, only on unformatted ASCII files, and preferably those in which lines are arranged in rows and columns, such as those in a database like the following:

```
snips        37   blue    green   red
snails      254   brown   gray    black
puppy dogs   22   brown   white   spotted
tails        19   bushy   long    short
```

To Sort, each line ends with a carriage return. To avoid confusion as you read the results, avoid files in which words wrap from one line to the next, as they commonly do in letters, books, and other word processed documents. In the same vein, think about how you are going to display a file in which columns of data extend beyond the 80 characters MS-DOS can display on screen. Longer lines, even though they end up sorted correctly, can be difficult to read if you display them with an MS-DOS command, such as Type, because MS-DOS automatically wraps characters beyond 80 columns to a new line. (You won't have trouble viewing such a file, however, with a program such as the MS-DOS Editor, which can scroll to the right to display lines longer than 80 characters.)

When you use Sort on a text file, it sorts the lines of the file alphabetically or numerically, arranging the lines in ascending or descending order, as you request. Characters are sorted in ASCII order (listed in Appendix A). Blank lines appear at the beginning when you sort in ascending order, at the end when you sort in descending order. ASCII characters above 127 are sorted according to the code page (character table) currently in effect. As described in Chapter 12, you can sort on any column you choose, one column being equal to one character or space. For reference, the basic syntax of the Sort command is, briefly, as follows:

sort /r /+n [< source] [> destination]

/r tells Sort to sort in reverse order.

/+n tells Sort to sort on the column you specify as n.

Notice that Sort uses both input and output redirection, getting the lines to sort from a file you specify as source and sending the output to another file you specify as destination. This is the most useful (and safest) syntax to use when sorting a file. You don't, however, have to include both parameters; you can omit source, destination, or both, with the following results:

- If you omit source but include destination, Sort takes its input from the keyboard. You can use this method, if you have a mind to sort lines you type. Sort will keep track of all lines until you press F6 or Ctrl-Z to indicate you are through. At that point, it will sort the lines and send them to the file you specified (which you can then view with the Type command or a text editor).

- If you omit destination but include source, Sort sorts both from and to the file you specify as source. Although Sort can handle files up to 64 K in size, omitting a destination filename is somewhat like giving the command a bowl of alphabet soup and telling it to sort from and to the same bowl. Sort is smart and trustworthy, but why not make it easier on both of you by specifying a separate destination file?

- If you omit both source and destination, Sort acts like an alphabetizing typewriter. As described previously, it soaks up the lines you type until you press F6 or Ctrl-Z. At that time, it sorts and displays the lines for you.

As an alternative, if you want to sort the output of a command rather than the lines of a file, you can use the following syntax:

command ¦ sort /r /+n [> *destination*]

You would use this syntax, for example, in sorting the output of a Dir command or in sorting the lines of a file you display with the Type command. You would also use this syntax in piping the output of a Find command to the Sort command.

Sort used to be really handy in producing a directory listing sorted by name, extension, size, and (to a lesser extent) date or time. You don't need it anymore for that, however, because versions 5 and 6 of MS-DOS can sort a directory listing in just about any way you want. To see how Sort works, however, you can try the following examples. Some tell you what to type; others use your DOS directory, so you can follow along if you want.

Sorting from the keyboard

Suppose you want to alphabetize the following words:

```
panda
fish
elephant
bear
tiger
giraffe
```

First, have Sort display the results on screen:

1. Type the following:

       C:\>sort

2. Type the words in the list, in order, pressing Enter after each. Press F6 when you're done. In a second or two, the alphabetized list appears.

Now try sorting in reverse order and sending the list to a file:

1. Type the following:

       C:\>sort /r > temp.txt

   Type the words again and press F6 when you're done.

2. Now display the destination file. Type the following:

       C:\>type temp.txt

   Impressed? Good.

3. Now delete the file to keep from cluttering up your hard disk:

       C:\>del temp.txt

Sorting columns

To try sorting columns, use your DOS directory. Filenames, of course, begin in column 1, which is the default. Extensions begin in column 10. To sort the directory by extension, use either of the following commands. This command sorts the output of the Dir command directly and displays the results:

```
C:\>dir c:\dos ¦ sort /+10 ¦ more
```

This command sends the output of the Dir command to a file and then sorts the lines of the file. To display the results, use the Type command:

```
C:\>dir c:\dos > dosdir.txt ¦ sort /+10
```

Before you leave this, you might also want to try sorting a directory of your own by date (column 24) or time (column 34). Neither of these sorts will be particularly valuable because of the way the characters are sorted. In the case of dates, *1-01-94* ends up preceding *12-31-93*. If MS-DOS is using a 12-hour clock format for times, you'll find that *6:59p* comes before *8:00a* in the sorted list.

Combining commands

To end this exploration of filter commands, here are two examples, again using your DOS directory, that show how you can combine filter commands to customize output even more. First, use pipes and the following set of commands to display all EXE files in your DOS directory, sorted by file size (the space in front of *exe* in the Find command eliminates AUTOEXEC.BAT from the list).

```
C:\>dir c:\dos ¦ find /i " exe" ¦ sort /+17 ¦ more
```

The next example works only if you have version 6 of MS-DOS and you've used DoubleSpace to compress your hard disk. If you've done this, the command sorts the files in your DOS directory by compression ratio, highest to lowest. As in the earlier compression example, Find is used twice, to eliminate all lines other than the ones that show actual compression ratios. The command is long, but don't worry. Just type the following:

```
C:\>dir c:\dos /c ¦ find " to 1.0" ¦ find /v "average" ¦ sort /+42 ¦ more
```

NOTE: The second Find command here limits the search to "average" rather than "average compression" as shown in the earlier example, because the DOS directory doesn't include any filenames containing "average". The longer string was used earlier to ensure that any file named AVERAGE in any compressed directory would be omitted from the output of the Find command.

The next two chapters take you into the wonderful world of batch files. As you will see, you can use redirection, pipes, and filters in batch files, as well as from the command line.

18

Batch Files and Macros

What You'll Find Here: This chapter is the first of two that deal with finding ways to make your work with MS-DOS easier, faster, and more efficient. For the most part, these chapters deal with batch files, which you can design to carry out any sequence of MS-DOS commands to perform a task you want done. This chapter, however, begins with descriptions of the MS-DOS keyboard template, the Doskey command recorder, and the ways in which you can edit previously used MS-DOS commands. It then goes on to cover simple batch files and Doskey macros. Topics include the use of replaceable parameters, as well as the Echo, Pause, Remark (Rem), and Shift batch commands. The next chapter examines the ways in which you can control the execution of commands in batch files with the help of If, For, Goto, Errorlevel, Call, Shift, and the version 6 Choice command.

*H*ave you ever wondered why computer terminology is so filled with acronyms? Is it because speed, in speech as in program execution, is so important to the technically proficient? Or are these acronyms symptomatic of an arrogance that implies if you can't talk the talk, you might as well limp to the sidelines and not walk the walk? Or could it be that these acronyms are simply tools for clear communication? After all, saying "ansee-dot-sis" to someone who understands what it signifies is a lot easier than describing ANSI.SYS as "you know...that device driver you use when you want enhanced keyboard and screen control according to the guidelines of the American National Standards Institute."

Whatever your belief regarding their origins or meaning, the fact is, acronyms sprout like fungi after rain. Ultimately, the reason they do so is simply because they are useful. While you're probably not in a position to dictate wide use of acronyms like MIPS, ISA, EISA, RAM, ROM, and DOS, in this chapter and the next you get to join the phonetic fray on a personal level by covering the ways in which MS-DOS enables you to create some "acronyms" of your own, the batch files and macros that turn lengthy sets of commands into quick and easy keystrokes. Before you can run, however, you have to walk, and that means knowing about ways to edit your MS-DOS commands.

The keyboard template

The keyboard template is the first and by far the less flexible of your two primary means of editing MS-DOS commands. Along with commands such as Drive Parameters (Drivparm) and Ctty, the keyboard template may well be among the least used of MS-DOS features. The Doskey command recorder is far more useful for most tasks.

The template is a very small area of memory that MS-DOS uses to store one command. This command is usually the last one you carried out by pressing the Enter key. Once in the template, a command can be retrieved, in whole or in part, to be edited or repeated. By way of example, assume you just carried out the following command:

```
C:\>type c:\dos\readme.txt | more
```

To repeat the command, you would press the F3 key and press Enter.

To edit the command, you would use the keys listed in the following table:

Key	Purpose
F1 or Right direction key	Redisplay the command, one character each time you press the F1 key.
F2	Redisplay characters up to, but not including, the character you press after pressing F2.
F3	Redisplay the entire command. Or, if the command has been edited, redisplay what remains of the command in the template. (See the following descriptions for F4 and other keys.)
F4	Delete characters up to, but not including, the character you press after pressing F4.
F5	Copy the command at the system prompt into the template, without carrying out the command. Pressing F5 causes MS-DOS to display an @ symbol and move the cursor to a new line, although without displaying the system prompt. You can use F5 to copy all or part of a command to the template so that you can retrieve and edit it some more, from the beginning (which you probably won't do, but could if you really got carried away with the editing keys). Do not press Enter after pressing F5. Doing so clears the template.
F6	Place a Ctrl-Z (end-of-file) character in the command.
Backspace or Left direction key	Delete one or more characters in the command displayed at the system prompt. These keys do not affect the command in the template.
Del	Delete the character in the template that corresponds to the current cursor position. Using this key, especially in combination with F4, is like catching black cats at the bottom of a lightless well.
Ins	Begin inserting rather than overtyping characters in the template at the position corresponding to the current cursor position. More cats.
Esc	Cancel the current command at the system prompt without changing the template. Otherwise, when you press Esc, MS-DOS displays a backslash and moves the cursor to a new line. If you plan to re-edit the command in the the template, do not press Enter to redisplay the system prompt. Doing so clears the template.

Here are some examples that show the editing keys in action. Each example assumes that the original command, *type c:\dos\readme.txt | more*, is sitting untouched and unedited in the template.

Keystrokes	Result
Press F1 five times.	`C:\>type`
Press F2, followed by the letter R.	`C:\>type c:\dos\`
Press F3.	`C:\>type c:\dos\readme.txt ¦ more`
Press F2, followed by ¦, followed by Del six times.	`C:\>type c:\dos\readme.txt`
Press the following, in order: F2, R, F4, . (period), Ins. Type *appnotes*, press F3.	`C:\>type c:\dos\appnotes.txt ¦ more`
Assuming the original Type command, press the following, in order: F4, Spacebar, Ins. Type *print*, press F3, press Backspace seven times.	`C:\>print c:\dos\readme.txt`
Again assuming the original Type command, press the following, in order: F4, Spacebar, Ins. Type *print*, press F3, F5, F2, ¦, F4, @, F5, F3.	`C:\>print c:\dos\readme.txt`

Doskey

Although it is useful at times, the MS-DOS keyboard template is neither flexible nor particularly intuitive, at least not until using the editing keys becomes automatic to you. But then, it really wasn't meant to be. More useful by far for everyday use of MS-DOS is the Doskey command recorder included with MS-DOS versions 5 and 6.

A small, memory-resident utility that occupies about 4 K of space, Doskey sets aside and manages a buffer in which it stores previously used MS-DOS commands. One of the TSR programs you can load into UMBs with the Loadhigh command, Doskey initially sets aside a 512-byte buffer, enough for about 25 to 30 average-length commands, such as *dir c:\docs*.doc*. If the number of commands you use exceeds the number that can fit into the buffer, Doskey eliminates the oldest command to make way for each incoming new command. If necessary, specify a larger buffer with the /bufsize switch described in Chapter 12.

The full syntax of the Doskey command is given in Chapter 12. The following shows an abbreviated version with key Doskey switches:

doskey /macros /history /insert /overstrike *macroname=commands*

/macros displays the macros currently in memory.

/history displays the commands currently in memory.

/insert and */overstrike* toggle Doskey between inserting and overwriting (the default) existing text. You can use these switches when editing commands, but the Ins key is much easier to use.

macroname=commands lets you define a macro—the Doskey version of a memory-resident batch file.

Keys for display, navigation, and editing

Like MS-DOS with the keyboard template, Doskey responds to a number of function and other keys. The number of keys Doskey responds to, however, is much more extensive. Some of these keys help with command recall, some are used for moving the cursor, others are used for editing, and a few are used for cleanup activities. They are listed and briefly described, by function, in the following tables.

Displaying commands

From the command line, you can type *doskey /history* or *doskey /h* to see a list of the commands currently in memory. For displaying previous commands, you can use the keys in the following table. To execute a displayed command, press Enter.

Key	Function
Up direction key	Redisplays the command that precedes the one currently displayed. (Because Doskey can redisplay any command in memory, this key and the Down direction key let you step through the command history without having to work your way through from the beginning or end to the command you want.)
Down direction key	Redisplays the command that follows the one currently displayed.
Page Up	Redisplays the first command in memory. This is not necessarily the same as the first command you used since loading Doskey. Bear in mind that if the buffer becomes full, Doskey eliminates the oldest command to make room for the newest one.
Page Down	Redisplays the last command in memory.
F7	Displays a numbered list of commands in memory.
F8	Cycles through commands in memory, from newest to oldest.
One or more typed characters followed by F8	Searches for the latest command that begins with the characters you typed before pressing F8. Press F8 repeatedly to cycle back through all matching commands.
F9	Prompts for the number of the command you want to redisplay. If you don't know the number, press F7, and then press F9. When the prompt is displayed, type the number of the command and press Enter. This causes the command to be redisplayed—not re-executed. To carry out the command, press Enter.
F5	Clears the command line and copies it to the template. To redisplay the command, use the editing keys described earlier.
Esc	Clears the command line without copying it to the template.

Moving the cursor

Doskey responds to a number of cursor-movement keys in addition to Backspace (which performs the function you would expect, that of deleting the characters it backs over). The following table lists the Doskey cursor-movement keys. You will no doubt standardize on a few that best fit your typing habits.

Key	Function
Left direction key	Moves the cursor left one character; doesn't delete the character it moves over.
Right direction key	Moves the cursor right one character, again without deleting an existing character.
Ctrl-Left direction key	Moves the cursor left one word.
Ctrl-Right direction key	Moves the cursor right one word.
Home	Moves the cursor to the beginning of the displayed command.
End	Moves the cursor to the end of the displayed command.

Editing keys

Some of the Doskey editing keys correspond closely to those you use when editing a command in the MS-DOS keyboard template. The effect is somewhat different (and disconcerting), however. Remember that with Doskey you are usually working with a displayed command, whereas with MS-DOS you are usually building a command by editing one that otherwise exists only in the template.

The time you're most likely to be confused is when you use the function keys that copy from the command stored in memory. These keys—F1, F2, and F3—work in Doskey as they do under MS-DOS. Because a command is already displayed under Doskey, however, copying from memory to the command line on screen can duplicate existing characters. This duplication sometimes makes it seem as though you are moving the cursor rather than replacing characters with identical copies of themselves. For example, suppose you display the following command and move the cursor to the position shown by the underlined character:

```
C:\>dir c:\dos\*.exe
```

If you were to press the F3 key here, Doskey would copy the characters :\dos\ *.exe and you would end up with the cursor at the end of the command. Because the copied characters duplicate what you already see, however, it seems as though F3 really just moved the cursor to the end of the command. Not so. As you can see if you display a command, backspace to delete characters, and then press F1 or F3, these keys do, indeed, copy characters.

Key	Function
Ins	Toggles between insert and overstrike modes. In insert mode, the cursor is thickened and rectangular. In overstrike mode (the default), the cursor has its normal line shape.
Del	Deletes the character at the cursor position.
When a command is displayed for editing:	
F1	Copies one character corresponding to the current cursor position from the command line stored in memory.
F2, followed by a character key	Copies characters from the current cursor position to the first occurrence of the character you press after pressing F2.
F3	Copies characters from the current cursor position to the end of the command line.
F4, followed by a character key	Deletes characters to the right, from the current cursor position to the first occurrence of the character you press after pressing F4.
F6	Inserts a Ctrl-Z character.
Ctrl-End	Deletes from the cursor position to the end of the line.
Ctrl-Home	Deletes from the cursor position to the beginning of the line.

Cleaning house

When you're working with Doskey, especially if you're using the command history as a temporary warehouse for commands you want to "debug" before saving them as a batch file, you'll sometimes want to clear the buffer. If you create and work with different sets of macros, you might also sometimes want to clear one set out of memory and replace it with another. To do this type of housekeeping, remember the following two key combinations:

Key	Function
Alt-F7	Deletes the command history.
Alt-F10	Clears macro definitions in memory.

Editing a command with Doskey

Doskey is simple to use, so there's not much point in going into detailed descriptions of its personal habits. The preceding lists of keys and key combinations might have seemed a little dizzying, however, so this section includes some examples that should help you see what's going on.

To begin with, you can't do anything with Doskey unless you load it. It's a small program, so unless your upper memory area is packed or you need it for other purposes, Doskey can fit nicely into UMBs with the following command:

```
C:\>lh doskey
```

Once in memory (upper or lower), Doskey sets up its buffer and watches the keyboard, ready for work. Suppose, for example, you later enter the following commands:

```
cls
dir c:\mydocs\*.doc
for %f in (c:\mydocs\*.doc) do find /i "intrepid" %f ¦ more
myword c:\mydocs\fearless.doc
```

To see a list of the commands in the buffer, press F7, and the following appears:

```
1: cls
2: dir c:\mydocs\*.doc
3: for %f in (c:\mydocs\*.doc) do find /i "intrepid" %f ¦ more
4: myword c:\mydocs\fearless.doc
```

To edit the Find command, you press F9, and Doskey displays its prompt for a line number:

```
C:\>Line number:
```

Type the line number (3), press Enter, and this appears:

```
C:\>for %f in (c:\mydocs\*.doc) do find /i "intrepid" %f ¦ more
```

Now for some editing. Suppose your document files are in a state of chaos, and you're forever having to hunt for the one you want. This time, you need to find the file containing your research notes about comb jellies. You know the file is in the JELLY directory. Many people find it much easier to ignore editing keys and simply use Backspace and the keyboard to edit commands. This time, however, you'll use Doskey to edit the command, as follows:

1. Press Home to move the cursor to the beginning of the command line.

2. Press F2, followed by the M key, to copy the command up to, but not including, the pathname after *c:*.

3. Doskey is in overstrike mode by default, and JELLY is shorter than MYDOCS, so type *jelly*. To get rid of the S, press Del.

4. Press F2, followed by I, three times (F2, I, F2, I, F2, I) to copy the characters from the latest cursor position to the beginning of the word *intrepid*.

5. The search string *comb jellies* is longer than *intrepid*, so this time delete the characters between the quotation marks by pressing Del.

6. Press Ins to shift to insert mode, and type *comb jellies*. Press Ins again to shift back to overstrike mode.

7. Finally, because you know there won't be much output displayed, remove the More command at the end. Press Ctrl and then press the Right direction key twice to move the cursor to the pipe symbol. Press Ctrl-End, and you're done. Press Enter to execute your edited command.

This exercise is, admittedly, contrived and too complex for everyday editing chores. Remember the keys, however. You might find yourself reaching for a few of them on a regular basis.

Stringing commands together

At the MS-DOS prompt, you type a command, press Enter, type another command, press Enter, and so on. When you start Doskey, you gain one advantage that takes working at the system prompt part of the way to the capabilities of batch files and macros: the ability to enter more than one command on a single line. Your command line can be up to 128 characters long. To separate one command from another, all you do is press Ctrl-T (which produces a paragraph symbol, ¶, on screen). Here's a simple but useful example that clears the screen before carrying out a Dir command that pauses after each screenful of a long listing:

```
C:\>cls [Ctrl-T] dir /p
```

Creating macros

Command recall and editing represent only half of what Doskey can do. Its ability to generate and carry out macros forms the other, even more useful, half. A macro, as you probably know, is a set of commands you put together and then assign to a keystroke or, in the case of Doskey, a short name that acts as a "trigger" and causes the commands in the macro to be carried out. When you create macros with Doskey, you type them from the keyboard or include them in a batch file in the following form:

doskey *macroname=commands*

The macro name is any name you care to assign, but you should think twice before assigning a name that corresponds to internal MS-DOS commands or to command files ending in COM, EXE, or BAT. Macros remain resident in memory and are carried out before MS-DOS runs its usual check for internal commands, executable files, and batch files. As a result, naming a macro after one of these "reserved" names means that the macro will always be carried out instead of the command or executable file. On the plus side, this feature means you can redefine an MS-DOS command, such as Format, to do what you usually want it to. On the minus side, naming a macro after an executable command or file essentially makes that command or file inaccessible to MS-DOS. If you do assign such a name, intentionally or by mistake, you can delete the macro with the following command:

doskey *macroname=*

The *commands* part of the macro-generating command consists of a set of MS-DOS commands. You can use almost all valid MS-DOS commands, but some restrictions do apply where batch commands are concerned. You can, for example, use Echo to display a message and minimize command echoing, as shown in the SHOWEM macro later in this chapter, but you cannot use Echo off to turn command echoing completely off. Likewise, you can use If and For, but not Goto. For more details, refer to the later section titled "Batch files vs. macros."

When creating a macro, you can do so either directly from the keyboard or with the help of the MS-DOS Editor or another text editor. No matter how you create it, however, each macro must consist of a single line of up to 127 characters. To include multiple commands in a macro, you must separate the commands with the characters $t or $T (lowercase or uppercase doesn't matter). The following macro, for example, includes two commands, Cls to clear the screen, and Chkdsk to run a check on the disk in the current drive:

```
doskey check=cls $t chkdsk
```

To run this macro, you would simply type *check*.

If you're familiar with the Prompt command, the $T combination you've just seen probably reminded you of the dollar-sign special characters that enable you to customize the system prompt in certain ways. The resemblance is real. The $T combination represents one of a number of special character combinations. In Doskey macros, these characters allow you to use redirection and replaceable parameters. The following is the complete list.

Key combination	Meaning
$G	The equivalent of the > redirection symbol. Redirects output to a file or a device.
GG	The equivalent of the >> redirection symbol. Appends output to a file.
$L	The equivalent of the < redirection symbol. Causes a command to get its input from a file or device rather than the keyboard.
$B	The equivalent of the ¦ pipe symbol. Pipes output to another command.
$T	As mentioned, separates commands within a macro.
$$	Allows you to include a $ character in a macro. You would use this, for example, to create a macro to define a new prompt, as in *newprompt=prompt $$d$$_$$p*.
$1 through $9	Represent replaceable parameters—variables typed as part of the command line activating the macro. For example, the macro *subs=dir $1 /s /p* would replace $1 with the name of the WINDOWS directory if you executed the macro by typing *subs windows*.
$*	Represents a special replaceable parameter that substitutes for all command-line parameters you include when executing the macro. For example, the macro *hardcopy=print $** would print all files you specified with the command *hardcopy a.txt b.txt c.txt d.txt*.

NOTE: If you need information on replaceable parameters, see the topic later in this chapter, under batch files, where replaceable parameters are most commonly used.

The following examples show some sample macros, including several that make use of the $ special characters.

Some sample macros

As you've seen, macros are easy to generate, especially if they're simple ones you use to reduce typing for basic but repetitive tasks such as formatting floppies, running the Dir command, and copying files. The following examples show some useful, if not particularly eye-catching, macros. Once you start a macro, by the way, you can't cancel it, as you can with an MS-DOS command or a batch file, by pressing Ctrl-C. Rather, you can't cancel by pressing Ctrl-C once. You must press Ctrl-C for each command in the macro.

This first macro is a simple one that clears the screen and displays the directory of your choice, pausing after each screenful. The macro is named MDIR to keep it from supplanting the Dir command:

```
doskey mdir=cls $t dir $1 /p
```

To run the macro and display your DOS directory, you would type this:

```
C:\>mdir c:\dos
```

If you habitually load ANSI.SYS, you can expand this macro to show more on the screen with this:

```
doskey mdir=mode con lines=43 $t cls $t dir $1 /p
```

Here's a macro that redirects the output of a Dir command to a file named RDIR in the C:\TEMP directory:

```
doskey rdir=dir $1 $g c:\temp\rdir
```

And here's a macro that displays the contents of the C:\TEMP directory, gives you a chance to scan the list, and cleans up the directory if you press Y to confirm deleting all files:

```
doskey cleanup=cls $t dir c:\temp /w /p $t del c:\temp\*.*
```

(Normally, options are difficult to implement in a macro because you can't use the Goto command, and the only way to cancel a macro is to press Ctrl-C for each remaining command. The choice provided by the preceding example, however, takes advantage of the Del command itself, which prompts for confirmation before deleting all the files in a directory.)

As for formatting, the following macro performs a quick format:

```
doskey qformat=cls $t format $1 /q
```

Doskey macros can also help reduce typing with commands, such as Dir and Dblspace, that have a number of switches. The following examples show a set of macros that can help manage disks compressed with the version 6 DoubleSpace command:

Macro	Function
`doskey dcheck=dblspace /chkdsk $1`	Checks the compressed disk in the drive you specify. Add the /f switch to check for fragmentation.
`doskey dcomp=dblspace /compress $1`	Compresses the disk in the drive you specify.
`doskey dcreate=dblspace /create $1`	Creates a compressed drive on the disk you specify.
`doskey dfrag=dblspace /defragment $1`	Defragments the disk in the drive you specify.
`doskey dform=dblspace /format $1`	Formats the compressed disk in the drive you specify.
`doskey dinfo=dblspace /info $1`	Displays information about the disk in the drive you specify.
`doskey dlist=dblspace /list`	Displays compression information about the drives on your system.
`doskey dmount=dblspace /mount $1`	Mounts a compressed floppy disk.
`doskey umount=dblspace /unmount $1`	Unmounts a compressed floppy disk.
`doskey cdir=dir $1 /s /p /c`	Displays a directory, including compression ratios, of the files for the disk or directory (including subdirectories) in the drive you specify.

Here's a more familiar set of macros that can help with directories:

Macro	Function
`doskey pdir=dir $1 /p`	Pauses long directories after each screenful.
`doskey wdir=dir $1 /w /p`	Lists directories in wide format, pausing if necessary.
`doskey adir=dir $1 /a:$2`	Lists files with the attribute specified by $2. For example, *adir private h* would display all hidden files in the PRIVATE directory.
`doskey odir=dir $1 /o:$2`	Sorts the listing in the order specified by $2. For example, *odir c:\ g* would display all files in C:\ with directories listed first.
`doskey sdir=dir $1 /s /p`	Displays all files in the specified directory and all its subdirectories, pausing if necessary.
`doskey bdir=dir $1 /b /p`	Displays only the names and extensions of files in the specified directory.

Earlier in this section on macros, you found that you cannot use Goto within a macro. That restriction would seem to rule out the Shift command for processing more than the nine replaceable parameters MS-DOS allows as part of a command line. You can, however, perform an equivalent of the Shift command from within a macro with the $* special character combination. Here, for example, is a simple batch file that uses Shift to display any number of numbers, characters, or words (separated by spaces) that you type with the name of the batch file:

```
@echo off
:start
if "%1"=="" goto end
for %%f in (%1) do echo %%f
shift
goto :start
:end
```

For example, typing the name of the batch file, followed by the letters of the alphabet, would display each letter on a separate line. To do the same with a macro, you could use the $* replaceable parameter, as follows:

```
doskey showem=echo off $t for %f in ($*) do echo %f $t echo on
```

Here, Echo off minimizes command echoing, but the macro version isn't as clean as the batch file because the Echo off, For, and Echo on commands are still echoed to the screen before they are carried out. The results are otherwise the same, however. The Echo on command at the end of the macro, by the way, is needed to redisplay the system prompt, which is otherwise suppressed by the Echo off command. As you can see from this example, it helps to know your MS-DOS commands and how they behave.

Before we leave these examples, there's one other point about macros that might interest you. Macros, like batch files, can have pretty much any names you want to assign, within the limits mentioned earlier for MS-DOS commands and the names of executable files. You can thus assign an extended character to a macro with the Alt key and numbers on the numeric keypad. For example, on an English-language keyboard, you could assign the following macro to the Greek letter μ by pressing Alt-230 instead of typing a macro name:

```
doskey μ=dir $1 /p
```

You can do the same with a Ctrl-key combination, such as Ctrl-A or Ctrl-J. The key combination will remain in effect until you reboot the system or clear away your macro definitions by pressing Ctrl-F10. If you choose, you can even edit and save a Ctrl-key macro and generate both it and its Ctrl-key "starter" from a batch file, as described in the next section. If you do this, however, be careful about your choice of keys. In particular, don't use any Ctrl-key combinations reserved for other purposes. For example, avoid Ctrl-Z, which MS-DOS interprets as an end-of-file character, and Ctrl-C, which causes MS-DOS to cancel execution of a command.

Reusing macros

Because macros are memory-resident, they go poof when you turn off or restart your computer. Obviously, you don't want to go to the bother of creating a set of macros every time you start your machine. The answer: Save them in a batch file that generates the macros for you. To do this, begin by saving all the macros in memory by redirecting them to a disk file with the Doskey /macros switch and the > redirection symbol, like this:

```
doskey /m > macros.bat
```

Even though you assign the BAT extension to this file, it isn't usable as is. If you start your text editor, you'll see that the file contains the macros themselves, not the Doskey commands that created the macros. To turn the file into one that will re-create the macros for you, you must add the word *doskey* to the beginning of each macro. For example, when you save a macro to a file, it looks like this:

```
wide=dir $1 /w
```

To convert the line to a macro-creating command, you must change the command to this:

```
doskey wide=dir $1 /w
```

In addition, if you use any special characters, such as Ctrl or Esc, enter the character in a way that will ensure that MS-DOS interprets the character correctly. For example, you can enter Ctrl and Esc characters in the MS-DOS Editor by pressing Ctrl-P, followed by the key or key combination you want.

Once you've edited each macro line and cleared away any macros that didn't work or that you don't want, you might also want to add the following command:

```
doskey
```

to the beginning of the file. Doskey doesn't have to be running when you run the batch file because the first macro-generating command in the file will start Doskey whether you want it or not. Including the Doskey command, however, makes your batch file a little more politically correct. When you finish, save the file again. To generate the macros, simply run the batch file by typing its name.

Batch files

Batch files. No other feature of MS-DOS (except maybe Mode or code-page switching) causes such mixed reactions: joy in the hearts of some, fear and loathing in others, and a policy of strict noninvolvement in, probably, the majority of MS-DOS users. Nevertheless, batch files have their place, and now it's their turn in the limelight. If you are or have been one of the "see no evil" group when it comes to batch files, give them a chance. They're fun, if sometimes frustrating to get right.

Batch files vs. macros

The biggest difference between batch files and macros, at least operationally, is that batch files are always disk-based, whereas macros are memory-resident. Batch files can also be longer than the 127-character limit on macros. In most other respects, batch files and macros are remarkably similar—for example, both can make use of redirection and piping. Simple batch files and simple macros can, in fact, be practically interchangeable, as in the following examples.

The batch file:

```
cls
dir %1 /p
```

The macro:

```
doskey pdir=cls $t dir $1 /p
```

Both the batch file and the macro display a screen-by-screen listing of the directory you specify. There are, however, some basic differences between batch files and macros that you should note. For reference, they are all included in the following table. If some don't make sense to you now, they should by the time you finish Chapter 19.

Batch files	Macros
Each command is on a separate line.	Commands are separated by the $T character but are otherwise included in a single line.
@Echo off can be used to suppress display of each command before it is carried out.	@Echo off is not allowed. Commands are echoed to the screen before execution.
Pressing Ctrl-C causes MS-DOS to prompt for confirmation before terminating the entire batch process.	Pressing Ctrl-C cancels only the current command (if you're fast enough). You must press Ctrl-C repeatedly to cancel each command in the macro.
Replaceable parameters are represented by a percent sign followed by a numeral from 0 through 9, as in %1, %2, %3, and so on. The %0 parameter is always replaced by the name of the batch file itself; in other words, you should usually consider %0 out of the range of replaceable parameters.	Replaceable parameters are represented by a dollar sign followed by a numeral from 1 through 9, as in $1, $2, $3, and so on.
Use the Shift and Goto commands to process more than the nine allowable replaceable parameters.	Use the $* special character to represent all information typed after the name of the macro on the command line.

(continued)

Batch files	Macros
Can use all MS-DOS commands, including Call, Choice, Echo, For, Goto, If, Pause, Rem, and Shift.	Can use all MS-DOS commands except Goto. With Goto prohibited, Choice and Shift become unlikely candidates as well because both usually rely on Goto to send execution to a particular set of commands.
Can't run macros, although they can be used to generate macros with the *doskey macroname=commands* command.	Can run batch files, either by name or with the Call command.
Can set and use environment variables, as in the command *set name=boris*, followed by *echo %name%*.	Can set environment variables, but cannot use them in commands.

Batch files as a whole

Batch files are nothing more—well, almost nothing more—than sets of MS-DOS commands strung together to create a procedure you want the operating system to carry out at your command. All batch files have the following three vital characteristics in common:

- They are stored on disk as plain-text (ASCII) files.
- They have filenames.
- They have the extension BAT.

A batch file contains no more than three elements:

- One or more MS-DOS commands.
- Command-line parameters you define.
- Optionally, one or more batch-specific commands that control the way in which the batch procedure is carried out.

A batch file can be simple, like this:

```
win
```

or more complex, like this:

```
@echo off
cls
if not exist %1 goto end
dir %1 | find "file(s)"
echo.
echo Use the number of bytes displayed above
echo to decide whether to compress or copy
echo the files you specified as %1
echo.
```

```
echo Type y to compress, n to copy.
echo.
choice /c:yn Compress files onto drive %2
if errorlevel 2 goto copy
if errorlevel 1 goto compress
:copy
copy %1 %2
goto end
:compress
echo Type y if the disk needs compression first
echo Type n if it doesn't
echo.
choice /c:yn
if errorlevel 2 goto mount
if errorlevel 1 goto double
:double
if not exist %2readthis.txt dblspace /compress %2
goto copy
:mount
dblspace /mount %2
goto copy
:end
```

The first example does nothing more than start Microsoft Windows. The second lets you use the number of bytes of storage needed by a specified set of files to determine whether to use disk compression before copying a group of files to a disk in a floppy drive. The remainder of this chapter covers batch files that are more closely related to the first example than to the second. The next chapter goes on to creating batch files with options you control, as in the second example.

Creating batch files

There are three basic ways to create a batch file. The easiest way, useful for short batch files, is to copy from CON to a file. This is also the most unforgiving of the three methods because you cannot correct errors once you've pressed Enter to end a line. If you're a careful typist, however, copying from CON to a file is great for batch files like the following:

```
@echo off
format %1 /q
```

To end such a file, you would press either F6 or Ctrl-Z to add an end-of-file character to your lines and signal MS-DOS that you have finished typing and want to save the file.

If you're experimenting with commands you want to run from a batch file, Doskey is also a useful tool. Start Doskey and carry out the commands you want, in the order in which you think they should appear in the batch file. If all goes well and the commands do the job you wanted them to do, save them as a file with the command *doskey /history > [filename]*. Note, however, that this approach means you cannot use replaceable parameters and batch commands, such as If and Goto, which can be run only from within a batch file. In addition, redirecting the command history to a file will include the *doskey /history* command. Although Doskey can be useful in testing sequences of commands, don't rely on it as a means of creating anything other than simple batch files. Even then, don't simply save the file and then run it immediately. Edit the file to remove the *doskey* line. While you're at it, examine the commands to see whether replaceable parameters or program-control commands will improve the batch file or make it more flexible.

Slightly more involved, but by far the more adaptable tool to use when you're working out the details of a more elaborate batch file, is a text editor such as the MS-DOS Editor. You can also use your word processor for creating batch files, but if you do, be sure to save the files in unformatted (ASCII or plain text) format. MS-DOS cannot interpret the formatting codes that applications embed in their document files. Trying to run a formatted batch file would not be fun.

Naming batch files

Every batch file has to have a name, and it has to have the BAT extension, even though you don't have to type the extension to get the file to run. Although you can give a batch file any name, you should not give it the same name as

- An internal MS-DOS command, such as Dir.
- A program file with the extension COM or EXE.
- A macro you've loaded into memory.

As explained earlier in this book, MS-DOS searches for commands to execute in a particular, unvarying, order. First it searches itself to determine whether the command is an internal command. Next it searches the command path, one directory at a time. Within each directory, it searches for a file with the extension COM. If it doesn't find a match, it then searches for a file with the extension EXE. If it still is unable to find a match, MS-DOS finally searches for a file with the extension BAT.

If you give a batch file the same name as an internal command, your batch file will never run. Period. MS-DOS will always run the internal command, even if you include the BAT extension in the command line. Giving a batch file the same name as an executable program file is almost as restrictive. Again, your batch file won't run if the external command is in the path ahead of it—or at least it won't run unless you either type the extension as part of your command, like this:

```
C:\>mode.bat
```

or save it in a directory that is not in the command path, and then run the batch file from that directory. Even then, your batch file will still be ignored if it has the same name as an internal command.

As for giving batch files and macros the same names, remember that MS-DOS will run a memory-resident macro before it searches the disk for a batch file of the same name. Until you unload the macro, your batch file won't run.

Building simple batch files

The heart of any batch file lies in the commands you want carried out. Unless you use control commands, such as If and Goto, MS-DOS executes a batch file from beginning to end, one command at a time. A batch file without control commands is thus nothing more than a set of MS-DOS commands that, together, do something that no single MS-DOS command can accomplish on its own. If you've ever found yourself getting sick and tired of typing the same sequence of commands over and over again at the system prompt, what you've really been irritated by is a set of commands that could form the core of a batch file. Here's an example of such a group of commands:

```
cls
dir *.bak /w
del *.bak
cd ..
```

These are the commands you would use to clear unwanted files from one branch of your directory tree—in this example, the automatic backups (BAK files) produced by an application such as a word processor. Starting from the bottom, level by level, you would repeat these commands for each subdirectory. The Dir command is included so that you can be sure you're not deleting anything you might later kick yourself for. It can happen.

Although replaceable parameters and control commands could make this batch file more useful and more fully automated, start at the beginning and build on what you've got. To save these commands as a batch file, you would copy from CON, use Doskey, or start a text editor; type the commands; and save them as a file with the extension BAT.

Giving yourself time to think

As it stands, the commands in this sample batch file work, but the batch file itself could be rather dangerous. It displays a directory, but then it jumps right in and deletes the list of displayed files. Although Undelete could help you out if you made a mistake, it's much easier, and not at all difficult, to build some thinking time into a batch file with the Pause command. Wherever you place the Pause command in a batch file, execution stops and this appears on screen:

```
Press any key to continue . . .
```

On the surface, this message would indicate that all you have to do is press a key, and the next command in the batch file will be carried out. That's true enough, but consider the nature of the batch interpreter itself: It allows you to terminate a batch file whenever you want by pressing Ctrl-C (or Ctrl-Break). Combine this opportunity with the Pause command, and you can control whether the rest of the batch file is even carried out:

```
cls
dir *.bak /w
pause
del *.bak
cd ..
```

Now the batch file will stop after the directory display. To delete the files, you would press any key. If you pressed Ctrl-C instead, however, you would see the following:

```
Terminate batch job (Y/N)?
```

Pressing Y would cancel the batch file; pressing N would carry out the remaining commands in the batch file.

Controlling what is displayed

The Echo command described in Chapter 12 performs either or both of two jobs in a batch file. Placed at the beginning of the file in the form *@echo off*, the command suppresses the display of commands in the batch file until MS-DOS encounters *echo on*. For example, the following batch file, named TEST.BAT:

```
@echo off
echo %1
echo on
echo %2
```

would produce the following output if you typed *test deer antelope*:

```
deer

C:\>echo antelope
antelope
```

The *@echo off* command at the beginning of the file would suppress the batch interpreter's natural inclination to tell you what was coming with the display:

```
C:\>echo deer
```

The *echo on* command, however, turns echoing back on, so you see both the *echo antelope* command and its result, *antelope*.

Echo can be used not only for controlling the display of commands but for displaying messages, cautions, and other remarks. You can also use it to display a blank line by typing the command as *echo.* (echo followed immediately by a period). You can echo to the display even if you turn echo off at the beginning of the file with the *@echo off* command. Combining all these capabilities of Echo, you could dress up the sample batch file as follows:

```
@echo off
cls
dir *.bak /w
echo.
echo.
echo To back out of this operation,
echo press Ctrl-C instead of pressing
echo any key at the the following message.
echo.
pause
del *.bak
cd ..
```

The string of Echo commands in the middle of this example display two blank lines below the directory listing, followed by a message, another blank line, and the message displayed by Pause, like this:

```
(ASSUME THIS IS THE LAST LINE OF THE DIRECTORY DISPLAY)


To back out of this operation,
press Ctrl-C instead of pressing
any key at the following message.

Press any key to continue . . .
```

Now anyone could use the batch file.

When using Echo, don't attempt to display redirection symbols or pipes. The results won't be what you might expect. For example, if you were to use the > redirection symbol to emphasize a message like this:

```
@echo off
echo > this is important
```

nothing would happen on screen, but your Echo command would result in the creation of a file named THIS containing the words *is important*. Not quite what you want.

If you used Echo like this,

```
echo >
```

you would receive the message *File creation error* (because MS-DOS has no "filename" to redirect to). If you tried this,

```
echo |
```

MS-DOS would complain *Syntax error*.

There is, however, one use of Echo and redirection that you might find useful with a laser printer. The following command sends a formfeed character to the printer. You can use this to eject pages without having to take the printer off line and press the formfeed button:

```
echo ^L > prn
```

Unfortunately, you cannot use the MS-DOS Editor to enter the ^L character. To include this command in a batch file, you can copy from CON to a file. If you're creating a long batch file and you want to send formfeeds to the printer, save the Echo command as a one-line batch file and call the file when you need it with the Call command described in the next chapter.

Adding your two cents worth

Unlike Echo, you use the Rem command to include non-displayed comments in a batch file. The syntax of the command, like the other batch commands so far, is simple: Place Rem at the beginning of a line, followed by whatever commentary you want to include. Whenever MS-DOS encounters a line beginning with Rem, it ignores the remainder of the line. You might therefore use Rem to explain the workings of a particularly clever set of commands or, as in the following, to caution people against altering part of a batch file.

```
REM --------------------------------------------
REM DO NOT CHANGE THE COMMANDS IN THIS SECTION
[include your commands here]
REM --------------------------------------------
```

Although too many remarks can serve to clutter a batch file and obscure its logic, you might want to consider starting all or most of your batch files with remarks describing their contents, their purpose, or their time and date of creation, like this:

```
REM This batch file displays a wide directory
REM and then waits for the go-ahead before deleting
REM the displayed files.
@echo off
cls
dir *.bak /w
echo.
echo.
echo To back out of this operation,
echo press Ctrl-C instead of pressing
echo any key at the the following message.
echo.
pause
del *.bak
cd ..
```

An additional use of Rem, common in important batch files such as AUTOEXEC.BAT, is as a means of disabling a command without deleting it from the file, like this:

```
REM Date
REM Time
```

Disabling commands in this way saves them for later reference or reincarnation. This approach is especially useful when you're experimenting with a batch file or when you want to disable an involved command or set of commands that you don't want to have to figure out again.

Replaceable parameters

As useful as Echo, Pause, and Rem are, they don't really do anything to make a batch file suitable for more than one set of circumstances. Replaceable parameters, as you saw earlier for macros and have seen in other places throughout this book, are your ticket to creating open-ended batch files—sets of commands that you can use in more than one situation.

Replaceable parameters in batch files work much like replaceable parameters in macros. In either case, they act as stand-ins for real information—usually directory names, filenames, or drive letters—that you provide as part of the command that sets the batch file (or macro) running. Whereas replaceable parameters in macros are typed as a numeral preceded by a dollar sign ($1, $2, $3, and so on), their equivalents in batch files are entered as any of the numerals from 0 through 9 preceded by a percent sign: %0, %1, %2, and so on.

When you use replaceable parameters in batch files, MS-DOS replaces all occurrences of %1 with the first item of information you type on the command line, all occurrences of %2 with the second item you type, all occurrences of %3 with the third item you type, and so on. Here's a simple example:

```
@echo off
echo %1
echo %2
echo %3
echo %4
echo %5
```

If this batch file were named ECHOTEST.BAT, typing the name of the batch file followed by five words like this:

```
C:\>echotest magicians use hats and rabbits
```

would produce:

```
magicians
use
hats
and
rabbits
```

The replaceable parameter in each Echo command would be replaced by the corresponding word you typed in starting the batch file.

Batch files take a replaceable parameter that macros don't—the %0 combination. When you use %0 in a batch file, it has special meaning to the batch interpreter: It stands for the name of the batch file itself, whereas all the other replaceable parameters, %1 through %9, can stand for any command-line information you enter. If that distinction sounds a little odd, the following example should illustrate the difference. If you changed the preceding batch file to read

```
@echo off
echo %0
echo %1
echo %2
echo %3
echo %4
```

you would still have five replaceable parameters, but typing *echotest magicians use hats and rabbits* would produce the following:

```
echotest
magicians
use
hats
and
```

The %0 parameter would be replaced by the name of the batch file, even if you typed one word for each replaceable parameter in the file.

Hats and rabbits are fun, but replaceable parameters serve on a much more practical level. In the earlier sample batch file, for example, the commands are set up to display and delete BAK files. They're no use if you want to display and delete TXT files, or BMP files, or any other kinds of files. With replaceable parameters, however, you can give this batch file a lot more flexibility, like this:

```
REM This batch file displays a wide directory
REM and then waits for the go-ahead before deleting
REM the displayed files.
@echo off
cls
dir *.%1 /w
echo.
echo.
echo To back out of this operation,
echo press Ctrl-C instead of pressing
echo any key at the the following message.
echo.
pause
del *.%1
cd ..
```

Using the %1 replaceable parameter here means that the batch file will display and, if you choose, delete all files with any extension you specify. If the batch file were named DOIT.BAT, to run the file on TXT files you would type the command as follows:

```
C:\>doit txt
```

Notice, by the way, the positioning of the replaceable parameter, immediately after the *. file specifier. Spacing is important, so be sure the items you type on the command line will appear exactly where they are needed in the command. Here's an example in which one replaceable parameter represents a drive letter, another a different drive or a directory on the current drive:

```
dir %1:
copy %1:*.txt %2
```

So ends coverage of batch-file basics. The next chapter covers ways you can control the execution of commands within a batch file.

19

Controlling Batch Files

What You'll Find Here: The preceding chapter covered the basics of editing commands, using Doskey, and stringing commands together in macros and batch files. In this chapter, you go beyond the basics to, if not the art of programming, at least the logic that supports it all. This is where you'll find the details on batch-control commands you've seen throughout this book: If, For, Goto, and Shift. Here, too, you'll see different ways to run one batch file from another. By the time you reach the end of this chapter, you'll have toured Batchland enough that it will be time to go roaming on your own.

*T*he sample batch file in the preceding chapter—no matter that it grew from a few lines to more than a dozen—doesn't really do a great deal more in its long form than it did in its short one. It ended up being able to accept a replaceable parameter and offering you the chance to read the screen before either deleting files or terminating the process, but the batch file itself still does the same thing: It displays and deletes files. Although usable in its present form, the batch file will change course in this chapter to become something a little more flexible. Currently, for example, the batch file doesn't ask whether you would prefer to copy files instead. Nor does it offer you the chance to format a disk before copying. It could, though, with the help of a few commands that let you build a batch file that responds differently to different conditions. That's what this chapter is about—conditional processing.

If you haven't done this before

Most of this book assumes that you're at least comfortable with using MS-DOS. Many people, however, can become comfortable, even proficient users of MS-DOS commands without ever feeling the need to investigate batch files. Batch files do require you to ascend to a different, and higher, MS-DOS plateau. In describing conditional processing, this chapter should give you the information you need to set up conditions on your own. If you're a relative newcomer to batch files, though, your first attempts won't necessarily end up the way you want. Keep the faith. You're not alone.

Whenever you create a batch file, you are combining commands. When you run the batch file, MS-DOS carries out those commands, one right after the other. Sometimes the order of your commands or the form in which you use them must be adjusted before the batch file does exactly what you want it to do. Here's an example:

```
@echo off
cls
type %1
cls
```

Offhand, this batch file looks logical. It turns echo off, clears the screen, displays a file, and clears the screen again. But there are two obvious errors in it. First, there's nothing to stop the Type command if you decide to display a file that runs to more than one screenful of information. You'd better be quick with the Pause key. Next, the second Cls command, although it might seem to clean up after Type, would actually wipe the screen before you could read it. A better way to accomplish what you want would be this:

```
@echo off
cls
type %1 ¦ more
pause
cls
```

You know that, to make software work correctly, a programmer has to think a lot like a computer "thinks." To control batch files, you have to think a little bit like a programmer thinks. You have to be logical and undeterred by an environment that operates at a faster speed than you normally do and is unfiltered by shades of gray. Judgments are true, or they are not true. There are no degrees of trueness, and certainly no degrees of falseness. You've seen this electronic dedication to truth over and over as you've used MS-DOS commands. If the directory you want is spelled JOUST, MS-DOS will never take you there with a *cd tourney* command. Nor will it even bother with a *cd jousts* command. Like some people, MS-DOS is all or nothing. Get it right, or don't bother.

When you concoct batch files, the need for accuracy and logic increases with each command you add to the file. This is especially true when you use the commands described in this chapter to control the execution of different parts of a batch file. When you use commands such as If and Choice, your batch file must be structured in such a way that the correct commands are carried out not only in one situation, but in at least one other. It's up to you to put the commands in the right order, to have them carried out at the right time, and—most important—to test each alternative to be sure all work as expected.

Because testing and editing can become frustrating, especially when a command in your batch file looks fine but just doesn't work properly, remember that the more complex your batch files become, the more likely it is that they won't work right the first time. When your frustration index begins to rise, remind yourself that you aren't the first, nor will you be the last batch-file maestro to have to examine each command and edit a batch file repeatedly until it all comes right in the end.

Back to the sample batch file

The sample batch file in the preceding chapter looked like this by the time it had collected assorted Echo, Remark (Rem), and Pause commands:

```
REM This batch file displays a wide directory
REM and then waits for the go-ahead before deleting
REM the displayed files.
@echo off
cls
dir *.%1 /w /p
echo.
```

(continued)

```
echo.
echo To back out of this operation,
echo press Ctrl-C instead of pressing
echo any key at the the following message.
echo.
pause
del *.%1
cd ..
```

By the time this chapter ends, the same batch file will have evolved in several ways to illustrate the following:

- How to display a "menu" that lets you choose between copying and deleting the files.
- How to specify more than one filename extension.
- How to use the Type command to display any number of files. (Type does not accept wildcard specifications, so if you use it from the command line, you must specify each file individually.)
- How to run one batch file from another.
- How to run another batch file and return to continue execution with the next line.

There's nothing for it but to do it, so start off with the big one: the If command.

Evaluating conditions in a batch file

You look at the sky and say, "If it's light, it's day; otherwise, it's night." You just set up a condition and, presumably, evaluated it. MS-DOS can evaluate conditions too, although not with the weather, and not unless you set up the conditions in a batch file. The key to it all is the If command, which carries out another command based on whether a condition is true or not true. As described in Chapter 12, the basic syntax of the If command is as follows:

if [not] exist *filename command*

if [not] *string1==string2 command*

if [not] errorlevel *value command*

At first glance, If is a little odd and seemingly complex because you can use it in either of two ways, if and if not, to evaluate any of three conditions:

- Whether a filename exists—that is, whether MS-DOS can find the file specified.
- Whether one string of characters (string1) is the same as another (string2).
- Whether the special value named errorlevel is equal to the value you specify.

Altogether, these various combinations give you six ways of evaluating a condition (non-syntax words are enclosed in brackets to help make the command meaning clearer):

- if exist filename [do this] command
- if not exist filename [do this] command
- if string1==string2 [do this] command
- if not string1==string2 [do this] command
- if errorlevel [equals] value [do this] command
- if not errorlevel [equals] value [do this] command

As you can see, the result of each of these evaluations determines whether an MS-DOS command is carried out. Before you see how If can be used to modify the sample batch file, take a look at these different uses of the command.

If vs. If Not

If and If Not represent mirror images. The easiest way to see how they differ is to put a complementary pair together, as in the following:

```
if exist c:\dos\format.com format a: /q
if not exist c:\dos\format.com echo What did you do with FORMAT.COM?
```

The first statement tests for the FORMAT.COM file and, if it exists, quick formats the disk in drive A. Its companion also tests for FORMAT.COM but, if the file doesn't exist, registers a complaint. In a batch file, you could use the first statement like this:

```
@echo off
if exist c:\dos\format.com format %1 /q
```

Where formatting is involved, of course, you would assume that every MS-DOS computer has FORMAT.COM in its DOS directory. To cover all possibilities, however, you could use the following:

```
@echo off
format %1 /q
if not exist c:\dos\format.com echo What did you do with FORMAT.COM?
```

If, for some reason, MS-DOS could not find FORMAT.COM, this version of the batch file would produce an MS-DOS error message, followed by your own:

```
Bad command or file name
What did you do with FORMAT.COM?
```

Although If and If Not represent opposites, you can sometimes use either to achieve the same desired result. For example,

```
if "%1"=="a" format a: /q
```

ends up doing the same thing as

```
if not "%1"=="b" format a: /q
```

Sometimes, it's all in the way you see the world. If you think about the true/not true side of If, you might find out something interesting about yourself: whether you find it easier to eliminate positives or negatives.

Testing for filenames

The preceding example using FORMAT.COM showed how to use If in checking whether a file exists. You use this approach when you want a command carried out only if a file does (or does not) exist. A far more common use of If in this regard is in checking for files to copy, delete, display, print, and so on. The following batch file contains such a command:

```
@echo off
cls
if exist %1 type %1
```

Here, the batch file substitutes the filename you specify for the replaceable parameter %1 and, if the file exists, displays it on screen. If the file doesn't exist, the batch file ends.

Note here that this If command does not pipe the output of the Type command to the More command. This is intentional. You would normally want to include More to stop scrolling of a long file, but you can't when you use Type as the object of an If command. The output disappears. Although this is jumping ahead a little, a more useful way to use If and Type would be to combine them with the Shift and Goto commands, like this:

```
@echo off
:start
shift
if "%1"=="" goto end
cls
type %1 ¦ more
pause
goto start
:end
echo No more files
```

This version would allow you to specify several files to display because the Shift command would move each, in turn, into the %1 position in the command line. The If command checks for %1. If there is no %1—that is, the string "%1" is the same as "", meaning nothing—the Goto command causes execution to jump to the label :end. Otherwise, the Cls, Type, and More commands display the file.

One final note on this: Although you cannot pipe the output of the Type command to More within an If command, you can redirect output. You can, for example, check for the existence of a set of files and, if they are found, redirect the list to a file with a command like the following:

```
if exist a:%1 dir a:%1 > filelist
```

In this case, the directory on the disk in drive A would be redirected to a file named FILELIST in the current directory of the current drive.

Evaluating strings

The example in the previous section included a common use of If in evaluating strings: *if "%1"=="" goto end*. This command, or one very like it is pretty well inevitable when you use the Shift command because it allows you to control when the batch file ends. Without the If command, the batch file would loop endlessly through the commands between *:start* and *goto start*, displaying error messages until you pressed Ctrl-C to end the unhappy process.

When you check for nothing, be sure to enclose *string1* and *string2* in quotation marks. If you don't, the If command won't have anything to check against. The quotation marks give If something to mull over.

There are other uses for evaluating strings, too. The following example shows one that evaluates a command-line parameter:

```
@echo off
if "%1"=="" goto again
if %1==kate goto kate
if %1==mark goto mark
:again
echo You, forgot to type your name. Try again.
goto end
:kate
cd \kate
:goto end
:mark
cd \mark
:end
```

Here, if the user forgets to type a name, a message is displayed. If the user types *kate*, execution jumps to the label *:kate*, changes the current directory, and goes to the label *:end*. If the user types *mark*, execution jumps to the label *:mark* and changes to the MARK directory. Notice that the batch file first checks for nothing. It does this to avoid *Syntax error* messages that would be produced by the two If commands that follow if the user forgot to type a name and, therefore, those commands had no %1 string to evaluate. Sometimes, small changes make the difference between good and better.

You can use the If command with strings to check for filenames and directories as well. When checking for directories, however, you must take a slightly roundabout approach. The If command can't check for directories directly, so you have to specify a "file"—NUL—that exists in every directory you create. The following example shows a batch file that tests for a directory and, if it exists, changes to the directory and copies the files specified as the %2 parameter:

```
@echo off
if not exist \%1\nul goto nodir
cd \%1
copy %2 \%1
goto end
:nodir
echo The %1 directory does not exist
:end
```

Backslashes are included before %1 to ensure that the parameter is treated as a directory name. Note, however, that this form of the command works only if %1 is typed as a directory name by itself—without a drive or path. If you wanted to allow the user to include a path, the If command would be as follows:

```
if not exist %\nul goto nodir
```

Checking errorlevel

Errorlevel is the name of a special part of memory that some MS-DOS commands use to hold exit codes—numeric values that report on the outcome when these commands are carried out. In version 6 of MS-DOS, errorlevel is the place where the Choice command saves a keystroke received in response to a prompt for input. Although this doesn't sound like such a big deal, it is. Choice plus errorlevel plus If means that you can use keyboard input to control the outcome of a batch file. Prior to version 6, keyboard input could only be processed if you had access to (or created) an assembly language routine or you purchased a utility that included commands that enhanced the native capabilities of the MS-DOS batch interpreter.

Errorlevel doesn't just mean the Choice command, though. In all recent versions of MS-DOS, you could use errorlevel with the If command in a batch file to check on the outcome of a command and, by doing so, control which commands were executed in the batch file. The commands other than Choice that report errorlevel values are: Backup, Check Disk (Chkdsk), Defragmenter (Defrag), Delete Tree (Deltree), Disk Compare (Diskcomp), Diskcopy, Find, Format, Keyboard (Keyb), Microsoft Anti-Virus (Msav), Move, Replace, Restore, Set Version (Setver), and Extended Copy (Xcopy). Format, for example, reports the following:

Exit code	Meaning
0	Success.
3	Terminated by Ctrl-C.
4	Fatal error (any error other than 0, 3, and 5).
5	Response to *Proceed with Format* message was N.

Whether you check errorlevel with a Choice command or one of the more functional commands listed previously, remember one fact when you set up your If command: The If command is true if the errorlevel value found is *equal to or greater than* the value you specify. Because of this, you must put If commands in descending order whenever you use them to check on a series of errorlevel values. To see how this works, start with a look at the Format exit codes. Later, you'll take a look at the more interesting possibilities of the Choice command.

Suppose you were checking the Format errorlevels listed previously. The following If command would be true for errorlevel values 3, 4, and 5:

```
if errorlevel 3 goto stopped
```

If you wanted to display messages simply related to a done/not done outcome of a Format command, you could set up two If commands, like this:

```
if errorlevel 3 goto stopped
if errorlevel 1 goto success
:stopped
echo Format terminated for any of several reasons
goto :end
:success
echo Disk formatted with no problems
:end
```

If, as is likely, you wanted to be more explicit about the matter, your series of If commands would be more like the following, where a successful format is the only one after which files are copied to the newly formatted disk:

```
if errorlevel 5 goto notdone
if errorlevel 4 goto error
if errorlevel 3 goto stopped
if errorlevel 1 goto success
:notdone
echo You pressed N in response to the prompt
goto end
:error
echo Format terminated by a problem
goto end
:stopped
echo You pressed Ctrl-C to stop
goto end
:success
```

(continued)

```
echo Disk formatted with no problems
echo Now copying files
copy %2 %1:
:end
```

Making choices

If you have version 6, the Choice command lets you use keyboard input to determine which part of a batch file is carried out. The syntax of the Choice command
is given in Chapter 12, but to recapitulate briefly, here it is in shortened form:

choice /c[:]*keys* /n [*prompt text*]

/c:keys defines the keys that can be pressed in response to the prompt. The
default is YN.

/n suppresses the prompt, but does display any text you define as *prompt text*.

prompt text specifies any text you want displayed as part of the prompt.
Spaces count, so press the Spacebar at the end of the text message if you want an
extra space between the prompt text and the cursor.

To see Choice at work, the following example uses the skeleton of the sample
batch file developed in the preceding chapter. Some Echo commands and the
Pause command will no longer be needed, so they have been deleted. The result
you see here does not represent a working batch file; it shows the first in a series
of modifications that will produce a more useful file-management tool. In this example, Choice is used with Echo commands to display a "menu" that allows the
user to select between copying and deleting files. The new section is as follows:

```
echo.
echo.
echo You can use this batch file to copy files or to delete them.
echo.
echo.
echo To copy files, press C.
echo To delete files, press D.
echo To quit, press Q.
echo.
choice /c:cdq Copy, Delete, or Quit
if errorlevel 3 goto end
if errorlevel 2 goto delete
if errorlevel 1 goto copy
```

The Choice command defines the acceptable keys as C, D, and Q. Although
Choice can be made case sensitive with the /s switch (described in Chapter 12), it
is omitted here so that the user can type in either uppercase or lowercase. The text
Copy, Delete, or Quit (followed by a space you can't see) produces the following
prompt:

```
Copy, Delete, or Quit [C,D,Q]?
```

When you define keys with the Choice command, the first key you define is assigned errorlevel value 1, the second key has errorlevel value 2, the third key errorlevel value 3, and so on. In this example, for instance, the first key, C, has errorlevel value 1; the second, D, has errorlevel value 2; and the third, Q, has errorlevel value 3.

The three If errorlevel commands following Choice use each errorlevel value to send execution to a different part of the batch file: the copy section, the delete section, or, if the user chooses, to the end to quit.

The following set of commands shows the batch file as it now stands. The remarks are changed slightly, the delete section is modified, and the Change Directory command originally at the end of the file has been altered to change the current directory to the root directory.

```
REM This batch file displays a wide directory
REM and then waits for a choice before copying
REM or deleting the displayed files.
@echo off
cls
echo.
echo.
echo You can use this batch file to copy files or to delete them.
echo.
echo.
echo To copy files, press C.
echo To delete files, press D.
echo To quit, press Q.
echo.
choice /c:cdq Copy, Delete, or Quit
if errorlevel 3 goto end
if errorlevel 2 goto delete
if errorlevel 1 goto copy
*************************************
[new batch commands will be added here]
*************************************
dir %1 /w /p
echo.
echo These files will be deleted.
pause
del %1
cd \
:end
```

Next, it's on to some more batch-control commands. There's more to batch than meets the If.

If you don't have version 6 of MS-DOS

The preceding example and most others based on it in the remainder of this chapter use the Choice command freely. If you don't have version 6 of MS-DOS, these examples won't do anything for you. The following variations on the sample batch file shows two possible ways to get around the lack of Choice. This book focuses primarily on version 6, however, so the remaining examples leave you to work out similar options on your own.

The first workaround relies on three related batch files, the first of which has Echo and Prompt commands masquerade as the Choice command, as follows:

```
REM This batch file waits for a choice before copying
REM or deleting the displayed files.
@echo off
cls
echo.
echo.
echo You can use this batch file to copy files or to delete them.
echo.
echo.
echo To copy files, press C, specify the files to copy,
echo and specify the drive or directory to copy to.
echo.
echo To delete files, press D and specify the files to delete.
echo.
echo When you finish, press Enter.
prompt $_
```

The Echo commands ask the user for input. The altered prompt, which does nothing more than change the system prompt to a linefeed and a flashing cursor, disguises the fact that whatever the user types in response to the Echo commands will, in fact, represent a command that runs one of two additional batch files, C.BAT, which displays a directory and copies the files, or D.BAT, which displays a directory and deletes the files. Both batch files end by restoring the standard MS-DOS prompt.

The following shows sample C.BAT and D.BAT files.
C.BAT looks like this:

```
@echo off
cls
dir %1 /w /p
echo.
pause
copy %1 %2
cd \
prompt $p$g
```

D.BAT looks like this:

```
@echo off
cls
dir %1 /w /p
echo.
echo These files will be deleted.
pause
del %1
cd \
prompt $p$g
```

The second workaround, a faster procedure, relies on more user involvement and replaceable parameters, like this:

```
@echo off
cls
if "%2"=="c" goto copy
if "%2"=="d" goto delete
:copy
cls
dir %1 /w /p
echo.
echo These files will be copied to %3.
pause
copy %1 %3
goto :end
:delete
dir %1 /w /p
echo.
echo These files will be deleted.
pause
del %1
cd \
:end
```

As you can see, this approach requires that the user know what to do. In this case, %2 is a letter specifying whether to copy or delete, and %3 is the letter of the drive to copy to. It works, but if you use batch files a lot and don't have another method of getting keyboard input, version 6 could lighten your load a bit.

Inserting road signs with Goto

In addition to the Choice command in the earlier example, the sample batch file suddenly gained three Goto commands as well. These Goto commands enable the batch interpreter to jump to the portion of the batch file that will soon contain the commands needed to carry out the user's preference for copying or deleting. If you look, you can see that one "cycle" is already complete:

```
if errorlevel 3 goto end
```

This cycle already has a place to go:

```
:end
```

These two commands, in essence, represent the form and function of Goto. For each Goto you include in a batch file, you include a destination known as a *label*. In a sense, Goto labels are older incarnations of the headers you can incorporate in a version 6 CONFIG.SYS file to control which configuration commands are carried out at startup. Both headers and labels must appear on a separate line in the file, but whereas a header always appears within square brackets, as in [normal], a label line is always preceded by a colon, like this:

```
:start
```

Another distinction between headers and labels is that a header can be up to 70 characters long but cannot include spaces. A label, in contrast, can contain spaces but is read only through the eighth character. Thus, even though you can define a label such as *jumbo shrimp*, the batch interpreter will pay attention only to *jumbo sh*.

Although Goto commands and label lines often appear sequentially in a batch file, they don't have to. Whenever the batch interpreter finds a Goto command, it scans the batch file for the label line to which it must go. So, for example, you can set up a repeating cycle of commands with Goto, as in the following:

```
:start
if "%1"=="" goto end
echo %1
shift
goto start
:end
```

Here, for example, the batch file would cycle through the commands between *:start* and *goto start* until the If command in the second line found no more input and sent execution to the label *:end*.

To get back to building the sample batch file, two more labels are needed to give the Choice command somewhere to go. From this point on, the batch file will assume that the current directory is on drive C. The added lines, with the commands they are to carry out, are in italic type. The copy section of the file is set up to copy the specified files to the disk in drive A or drive B:

```
REM This batch file displays a wide directory
REM and then waits for a choice before copying
REM or deleting the displayed files.
@echo off
cls
echo.
echo.
echo You can use this batch file to copy files or to delete them.
```

(continued)

```
echo.
echo.
echo To copy files, press C.
echo To delete files, press D.
echo To quit, press Q.
echo.
choice /c:cdq Copy, Delete, or Quit
if errorlevel 3 goto end
if errorlevel 2 goto delete
if errorlevel 1 goto copy
:copy
cls
dir %1 /w /p
echo.
echo These files will be copied.
echo.
choice /c:abq Press the letter of a drive or Q to quit
if errorlevel 3 goto end
if errorlevel 2 goto b
if errorlevel 1 goto a
:b
copy %1 b:
goto end
:a
copy %1 a:
goto end
:delete
dir %1 /w /p
echo.
echo These files will be deleted.
pause
del %1
cd \
:end
```

Using Goto in AUTOEXEC.BAT

Before you leave the Goto command, you should take a look at one valuable use for it if you have version 6 of MS-DOS and you have set up a multi-configuration CONFIG.SYS file. Version 6 sets an environment variable named CONFIG when you choose one of several configurations at startup, and you can use this variable with a Goto command to send MS-DOS to the section of your AUTOEXEC.BAT file that contains the commands you want to run for the setup you choose. As described in Chapter 17, you refer to an environment variable by placing its name in percent signs, like this:

```
%CONFIG%
```

When you do this, the batch interpreter replaces the name of the variable with its value, much as it substitutes command-line parameters for replaceable parameters in a batch file. To carry out a specific set of commands in AUTOEXEC.BAT that you've tailored to a particular startup option, you use the Goto command. For example, if you start up with the configuration NORMAL, you can carry out the section of your AUTOEXEC.BAT labeled :normal with the following command:

```
goto %config%
```

For an example showing a sample CONFIG.SYS file and a matching AUTOEXEC.BAT file, refer to the section titled, "Linking CONFIG.SYS and AUTOEXEC.BAT" in Chapter 16.

Running one batch file from another

When you build a batch file, you already know that the batch file can contain the name of any legitimate MS-DOS command. Legitimate means the name of any executable command, which includes the names of programs and, if you choose, other batch files. Because of this, you can easily run one batch file from within another. One way, shown earlier, is to disguise the system prompt. There are two other, less devious, ways to do so:

- By transferring execution to another batch file.
- By calling another batch file, running it, and then completing the commands in the original batch file.

Neither approach is difficult, but which you choose can mean the difference between a batch file that does what you want and one that doesn't.

To transfer execution to another batch file, all you have to do is include the name of the batch file you want to carry out. If you do this, however, it's important to remember that *transfer*, in this context, means that you leave the original batch file, never to return. Any remaining commands in the original batch file will not be carried out. The following diagram shows what happens when you transfer execution to another batch file:

```
A.BAT

@echo off
cls
echo Happy
b.bat  ──────────►  B.BAT
echo Birthday
                    @echo off
                    echo Seasons Greetings
```

After clearing the screen and displaying *Happy*, A.BAT transfers execution to B.BAT, which then displays *Seasons Greetings*. Running A.BAT thus produces the following output:

```
Happy
Seasons Greetings
C:\>
```

Because control was transferred to B.BAT, A.BAT never gets the chance to display *Birthday*. In contrast, calling another batch file (with the Call command described in more detail later), causes the commands in the called batch file to be carried out, but then the process returns execution to the caller, so that it can carry out its own remaining commands. Here's how you would call B.BAT instead of transferring to it in the previous example:

```
A.BAT

@echo off
cls
echo Happy
call b.bat    ──────►  B.BAT
►echo Birthday

                       @echo off
                       echo Seasons Greetings ┐
```

Now the output would look like this if you ran A.BAT:

```
Happy
Seasons Greetings
Birthday
```

Dumb, yes. But it should make the point.

As important as knowing the difference between transferring to a batch file and calling one is the fact that you can also run the second batch file directly from the command line whenever you want. Thus, if you create sets of batch files, you have the option of using them separately or including often-used "modules" in other, larger, batch files. The example in this section uses the sample batch file and two new, separate batch files to illustrate the point. One part of the example transfers control to the second batch file. Another uses the Call command. Before we go on to the example itself, here's the basic syntax of Call:

    call [*drive:*][*path*]*filename* [*parameters*]

drive, *path*, and *filename* specify the name and location of the batch file you are calling. The *parameters* parameter represents any command-line parameters, such as drive, directory, or file specification, that the called batch file needs in order to do its job. Although Call is highly useful, don't try to make it too flexible: Don't use either redirection or piping with this command.

Now for the example.

Transferring to a different batch file

As it stands the sample batch file is getting a little long and ambitious. In addition, the copy section of the batch file could easily be used on its own, in other circumstances. Suppose you want to turn that portion into a batch file on its own, yet maintain the ability to use it from within this larger batch file.

```
REM This batch file displays a wide directory
REM and then waits for a choice before copying
REM or deleting the displayed files.
@echo off
cls
echo.
echo.
echo You can use this batch file to copy files or to delete them.
echo.
echo.
echo To copy files, press C.
echo To delete files, press D.
echo To quit, press Q.
echo.
choice /c:cdq Copy, Delete, or Quit
if errorlevel 3 goto end
if errorlevel 2 goto delete
if errorlevel 1 goto copy
:copy
cls
dir %1
echo.
echo These files will be copied.
echo.
choice /c:abq Press the letter of a drive or Q to quit
if errorlevel 3 goto end
if errorlevel 2 goto b
if errorlevel 1 goto a
:b
copy %1 b:
goto end
:a
copy %1 a:
:delete
dir %1 /w /p
echo.
```

(continued)

```
echo These files will be deleted.
pause
del *.%1
cd \
:end
```

The copy section is all in one piece, so all you have to do is edit the file. Save the lines from the Cls command beneath the *:copy* label through the *copy %1 a:* command as a separate batch file with a name such as COPYIT.BAT. Add *@echo off* at the beginning and an *:end* label at the end. The new batch file thus looks like this:

```
@echo off
cls
dir %1 /w /p
echo.
echo These files will be copied.
echo.
choice /c:abq Press the letter of a drive or Q to quit
if errorlevel 3 goto end
if errorlevel 2 goto b
if errorlevel 1 goto a
:b
copy %1 b:
goto end
:a
copy %1 a:
:end
```

To clean up the main batch file and ensure that you can run COPYIT.BAT, you delete the *:copy* label, change the Goto command, and move the delete section up, as shown in the following, in which italics mark the changed Goto command:

```
REM This batch file displays a wide directory
REM and then waits for a choice before copying
REM or deleting the displayed files.
@echo off
cls
echo.
echo.
echo You can use this batch file to copy files or to delete them.
echo.
echo.
echo To copy files, press C.
echo To delete files, press D.
echo To quit, press Q.
echo.
```

(continued)

```
choice /c:cdq Copy, Delete, or Quit
if errorlevel 3 goto end
if errorlevel 2 goto delete
if errorlevel 1 copyit.bat %1
:delete
dir %1 /w /p
echo.
echo These files will be deleted.
pause
del %1
cd \
:end
```

One of the most important changes is the addition of the %1 replaceable parameter to the *if errorlevel 1* command. This addition ensures that the files you specify when using this batch file are passed to the COPYIT.BAT batch file when you transfer control to it. If you didn't include the %1 parameter, COPYIT.BAT would assume that you did not enter a file specification and would default to the current directory of the current drive.

Calling a different batch file

In the preceding example you could, if you wanted, use the Call command instead of transferring to COPYIT.BAT by changing the If command to read

```
if errorlevel 1 call copyit.bat %1
```

There wouldn't be much point in doing this, though, because there's nothing to come home to in the main batch file except the delete section, and you omitted that when you pressed C for Copy. This sample batch file can, however, be modified in a different way to show how Call works. In this version, the batch file lets you format the disk in the drive you want to copy to before copying the files. If you choose to format the disk, the batch file uses Call to run a quick-formatting batch file. The following is the altered version of the main batch file, with changes in italics:

```
REM This batch file displays a wide directory
REM and then waits for a choice before copying
REM or deleting the displayed files.
@echo off
cls
echo.
echo.
echo You can use this batch file to copy files or to delete them.
echo.
echo.
```

(continued)

```
echo To copy files, press C.
echo To delete files, press D.
echo To quit, press Q.
echo.
choice /c:cdq Copy, Delete, or Quit
if errorlevel 3 goto end
if errorlevel 2 goto delete
if errorlevel 1 goto copy
:copy
cls
dir %1
echo.
echo These files will be copied.
echo.
choice /c:yn Does the disk need formatting
if errorlevel 2 goto getdrive
if errorlevel 1 call qformat.bat
:getdrive
choice /c:abq Choose the drive to copy to or press Q to quit
if errorlevel 3 goto end
if errorlevel 2 goto b
if errorlevel 1 goto a
:b
copy %1 b:
goto end
:a
copy %1 a:
goto end
:delete
dir %1 /w /p
echo.
echo These files will be deleted.
pause
del %1
cd \
:end
```

The quick-formatting batch file looks like this. Note that it includes a Choice command to allow a drive to be specified:

```
@echo off
choice /c:ab Press the letter of the drive to format
if errorlevel 2 goto b
if errorlevel 1 goto a
:b
format b: /q
goto end
:a
format a: /q
:end
```

Specifying more than nine parameters

This section of the chapter lessens the emphasis on the sample you've watched grow in the preceding pages. The subject now deals with ways to make a batch file process more than the nine parameters you can include with %1 through %9 or ways to broaden the scope of a batch file to accept more than one drive letter or file specification. The tools you use for these jobs are the For and Shift commands, often in combination.

Repeating commands with For

The For command, as described in Chapter 12, repeats a command for each member of a group of items, called a *set*. Although For is generally used from within a batch file, you can also use it from the command line. The syntax of the command is similar in both cases. When you use For from the command line, you use the following syntax:

for *%variable* in (*set*) do *command* [*parameters*]

From within a batch file, the syntax is this:

for *%%variable* in (*set*) do *command* [*parameters*]

The only difference between the two command forms is the number of percent signs preceding the variable. When For is included in a batch file, the batch interpreter strips off the extra percent sign before processing the variable. Of course, if that's the case, you're probably wondering, why do you need the two percent signs to begin with? The reason becomes apparent when you think about it. Batch files, remember, accept replaceable parameters in the form %1, %2, %3, and so on. To distinguish a variable in the For command from a replaceable variable of the numeric kind, you use two percent signs. To further distinguish a For variable, also avoid using the numerals 0 through 9. Single alphabetic letters work fine.

When MS-DOS carries out a For command, it substitutes, in turn, each item in the set you define for *%variable* and then carries out the command you specify as *command*. You can define a set as any of the following:

- Strings, as in (mike jason christian trevor)
- File specifications, as in (*.txt *.doc)
- Individual drive letters or filenames, as in (a: b: c:) or (file1.txt file2.txt file3.txt)

Although *%variable* appears in the syntax line only before the set you define as (*set*) you can use it elsewhere in the command without bother. For example, this For command uses the *%variable* as the parameter of a Print command:

```
for %f in (c:\batch\*.bat) do print %f
```

If the A.BAT, B.BAT, and C.BAT files are included in the set, MS-DOS changes the command line each time to read as follows:

```
for A.BAT in (c:\batch\*.bat) do print A.BAT
for B.BAT in (c:\batch\*.bat) do print B.BAT
for C.BAT in (c:\batch\*.bat) do print C.BAT
```

Remember when using For, especially in a batch file, that processing goes round and round through the *single* command you specify as the object of For. You cannot, for example, use this command to display a set of files, pausing after each, as follows:

```
for %f in (c:\files\*.txt) do type %f ¦ more
```

The More command is out of bounds and will be ignored. Because processing is so circular with a For command, you should also remember that, if you use For in a batch file, processing will revolve around the For line until the command finishes or you press Ctrl-C. You can't use For to carry out a command on one item in a set, carry out another command line (such as Pause), and then return to carry out the earlier For command on the next member of the set.

To show how For can be used in a batch file, the following example uses part of the sample batch file to either copy files with more than one file specification to the disk in drive A or to delete the files:

```
choice /c:cdq Copy, Delete, or Quit
if errorlevel 3 goto end
if errorlevel 2 goto delete
if errorlevel 1 goto copy
:copy
cls
dir %1
pause
dir %2
pause
dir %3
echo.
echo The files will now be copied.
echo.
for %%f in (%1 %2 %3) do copy %%f a:
:delete
cls
dir %1
pause
dir %2
pause
dir %3
echo.
```

(continued)

```
echo These files will be deleted.
pause
for %%f in (%1 %2 %3) do del %%f
cd \
:end
```

Moving parameters with Shift

The natural companion to replaceable parameters is the Shift command. This command is what you use in a batch file when nine replaceable parameters aren't enough to cover every item you want the batch file to cover or when you want to specify individual items, each of which can be substituted for a %1 replaceable parameter. Unlike For, Shift can be used only from within batch files.

The syntax of the Shift command is not really difficult:

```
shift
```

What happens when you use Shift is intriguing. Whereas MS-DOS substitutes members of a set for the *%variable* you use in a For command, when you use Shift, MS-DOS moves the items you define as a group so that the first item is processed and then eliminated, the second item becomes the first, the third becomes the second, and so on until all items have been moved through the number 1 spot. The following is a simple batch file you could use to display a number of files, one after the other:

```
@echo off
:start
if "%1"=="" goto end
type %1 | more
shift
goto start
:end
```

With such a batch file, you could type the names of as many files as you wanted after the name of the batch file and view each of them in turn.

To wind things up, here's a final look at this chapter's sample batch file—this time a short version that would copy specific files to the disk in drive A or would delete them one by one:

```
choice /c:cdq Copy, Delete, or Quit
if errorlevel 3 goto end
if errorlevel 2 goto delete
if errorlevel 1 goto copy
:copy
cls
echo.
echo The files will now be copied.
```

(continued)

```
:cstart
if "%1"=="" goto end
copy %1 a:
shift
goto cstart
rem this is the delete part of the file
:delete
cls
echo The files will be now be deleted.
pause
:dstart
if "%1"=="" goto end
del %1
shift
goto dstart
:end
```

So ends this look at creating and controlling batch files. Refer to the command descriptions in Chapter 12 for more details and examples of how each batch command can be used. Bon voyage.

20

Beyond MS-DOS

What You'll Find Here: This final chapter of the book takes you a few short steps beyond MS-DOS, into the environment provided by the MS-DOS tool known as QBasic. The chapter is a little bit about programming, but programming is not really its main concern. The following pages will not turn you into a programmer. Nor will they make you even reasonably fluent in the Basic programming language. What this chapter will do, however, is show you that QBasic in many respects is an extension of MS-DOS, and that what you already know about batch files and conditional batch commands carries over into programming fundamentals. The chapter is about becoming comfortable with the idea of exploring QBasic, your first and least expensive resource when you want to push your system a little further and a little harder and MS-DOS alone is not enough.

*I*f you've been using MS-DOS for years, you know that MS-DOS has always been accompanied by some version of the Basic programming language. In the early days, there were cassette Basic, Basic A, and GW Basic. In versions 5 and 6 of MS-DOS, these older programs have been replaced by QBasic.

Languages and their dictionaries

Programming beginners often think that using Basic or another language is a one-two process: Write the instructions, and then tell the computer to carry them out. In a sense that notion is true, but it's not entirely accurate. Like spoken languages such as English, Bantu, Greek, or Hawaiian, a programming language is a set of words—a vocabulary—that you put together according to certain rules that constitute its "grammar," or syntax. If you don't know the vocabulary of a programming language, a program can be difficult to read and understand, but even so, programming languages actually exist to help people, not computers. No matter how exotic they look, languages such as Basic, C, and Pascal allow people to put instructions together in a form that other people can read. Those instructions are not directly executable by computers.

A computer is not by nature multilingual. It understands only one language, the limited vocabulary of binary code—on and off, 1s and 0s in combinations of 8 and multiples of 8. To run a program you've written, you must use a translator that can turn your program instructions into machine-readable, binary code. To do this, you need the help of a language-specific program that uses its own built-in "dictionary" to convert the language instructions into a form the computer can actually carry out. This is where Basic A, GW Basic, and QBasic enter the picture. All of these represent evolutionary steps in a line of programs designed to provide you with the ability to translate and run Basic programs.

QBasic, the newest of these Basic translators, provides you with a complete package for programming in Basic. It includes a "dictionary" of Basic keywords, and it provides a full-screen, menu-driven environment in which you can write, test, debug, and eventually execute the programs you write. QBasic thus provides an excellent tool for learning Basic and for creating small applications of your own.

NOTE: Although QBasic is a programming tool, it is itself an executable program file stored in your DOS directory as QBASIC.EXE. If you want to use and explore QBasic, MS-DOS must be able to find both QBASIC.EXE and the QBasic Help file, QBASIC.HLP. If one or both of these files have been eliminated from your DOS directory to save space, either you'll have to forgo some or all of the pleasure of experimenting with QBasic or you'll have to restore the files by copying them from your original MS-DOS disks with the Expand command.

The QBasic window

When you run QBasic, you work in an on-screen window similar to the one in which you drive the cursor when working with the MS-DOS Editor. This resemblance is more than coincidental—the MS-DOS Editor is actually the text-editing portion of the QBasic program.

You start the MS-DOS Editor by typing the name of the executable file (EDIT.COM) that links you to the text-editing portion of QBASIC.EXE. When you start the Editor, you can either type the startup command alone (*edit*) or include the name of a file you want to work on. When you use QBasic, the same basic options are available to you. You can start QBasic by

■ Typing *qbasic* alone.

■ Typing *qbasic* followed by the name of a program you want to work on. This loads a program but doesn't run it.

■ Typing *qbasic* followed by the /run switch and the name of a program you want to run, like this:

```
C:\>qbasic /run basprog
```

When you include the /run switch, QBasic runs the program before opening its window and displaying the program itself.

No matter how you start, the QBasic window (here cleared of program instructions) looks like this:

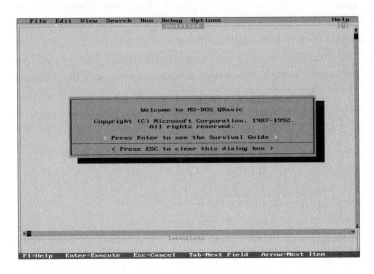

Window panes

In QBasic, as in the Editor, you can open an adjustable Help window at the top of the screen, if you want to display both online Help and the program instructions you are working on. Although the QBasic window looks a lot like the Editor window, it does differ significantly in one respect: The work area is divided into the upper and lower regions, labeled in the following illustration:

The upper area, headed *Untitled* in the preceding illustration, is called the *view window* and is where you enter, edit, and display programs. The small *immediate window* at the bottom is where you can type and run individual instructions to see how they work. This immediate window acts as a "scratchpad" of sorts where you can test instructions without leaving the QBasic editing environment.

Working in the immediate window

Because it accepts and runs single instructions, the immediate window is the best place for getting your QBasic feet wet. If you want to give it a try, follow these steps:

1. Start QBasic by typing *qbasic*. A dialog box appears asking whether you want to see the survival guide.

    □   If you want to cruise online Help, press Enter and take a look at some Help topics. If you have a mouse, you can move from topic to topic either by double-clicking the left button or—faster—by single-clicking the right button. Press Esc when you're through.

    □   If you don't want to bother with help right now, press Esc to clear the dialog box.

2. When QBasic's offer of help is history, move the cursor to the immediate window either by clicking in the window with the mouse or by pressing the F6 key, which moves the cursor from one active window to the next.

Now you can have some fun. First, try a QBasic instruction that has a very familiar counterpart at the system prompt:

1. Type the following (in either uppercase or lowercase, although the convention for QBasic commands in this book is all uppercase):

   ```
   CLS
   ```

   Press Enter to execute the command. As soon as you do, the QBasic view window is replaced by QBasic's *output window*. The output window is cleared by the CLS instruction, and this message appears at the bottom of the screen:

   ```
   Press any key to continue
   ```

2. Press a key, and the QBasic window reappears.

This example serves two purposes: First, it shows that QBasic includes some MS-DOS-like instructions. Second, it gives you a taste of what it's like to run a QBasic "program." Although you don't see any behind-the-scenes work, typing those three letters and pressing Enter causes QBasic to translate your CLS instruction into its binary equivalent, for execution by the microprocessor.

The immediate window is fun, and it's a good place to develop a feel for QBasic. If you want, try the following instructions:

1. The Print statement causes QBasic to "print" data either to a file or, if you omit a filename, to the display. The following instruction prints the result of multiplying (∗) 12 times 12:

   ```
   PRINT 12*12
   ```

   Press a key to return to the QBasic window.

2. You can also use the Print statement to display information on the screen, like this:

   ```
   PRINT "Hello. How are you?"
   ```

   In this case, QBasic displays the words and punctuation you've typed inside the quotation marks, but it doesn't display the quotation marks themselves. The marks here define the object, or *argument*, of the Print statement in two ways. First, as you can see, they identify the beginning and ending characters to display. Second, as you *can't* see, they identify a character, or non-numeric, string. (You have to learn details like this in order to program in QBasic, but no one said it would be easy.)

3. The CHDIR statement causes QBasic to change to the directory you specify within quotation marks. The FILES statement, the QBasic equivalent of the MS-DOS Dir command, lists the files in the current directory. As shown in the following example, you can use these two statements in a QBasic program much as you would use Cd and Dir at the MS-DOS command line or in a batch file or a macro. Even though you're working in the immediate window, you won't see anything happen when you execute the CHDIR statement. C:\DOS will, however, become the current directory, as the FILES statement proves:

```
CHDIR "C:\DOS"
FILES
```

Once again, the quotation marks in the CHDIR statement identify a character string.

Working in the view window

Using the immediate window is a little like using a relatively unsophisticated word processing machine that stores your typing one line at a time and then prints the line onto paper. Using the view window is more like using your word processing application, which lets you wander here and there in a document, making this change and that, until you decide the wording is perfection and you give the order to print.

When you work in the view window, QBasic sits largely in the background, waiting while you enter, edit, arrange, and rearrange the instructions in your program. Quiet as it is, however, QBasic doesn't disconnect entirely from what's happening. Whenever you press Enter to indicate you've finished one line of your program, QBasic translates the line, in the process checking your work for accuracy. If all is well, the line is accepted. If QBasic finds an error, it highlights part of the line, stops translating, and displays a dialog box telling you about the problem and asking you to fix it.

Once you finish writing and editing a program, you run it from the view window by pressing the F5 key or by choosing Start from the Run menu at the top of the screen. QBasic then takes you to its output window and runs the program. To see the difference between using the immediate window and using the view window, you can try typing the following short example in the view window. This example is closely related to the sample statements used earlier, but it adds a SLEEP (for 1 second) instruction to give you time to read the screen. QBasic can be fussy about punctuation and spelling, so to avoid errors, be sure to type the lines exactly as shown here:

```
CLS
CHDIR "C:\"
PRINT "This is what you have in your root directory"
SLEEP 1
FILES
```

When you finish typing, press F5 and something like the following should appear:

```
This is what you have in your root directory
C:\
COMMAND .COM      AUTOEXEC.BAT      WINDOWS   <DIR>...
DOS        <DIR> WINA20 .386      CONFIG  .SYS    ...
```

That's the output of your program.

Making programs interactive

The preceding examples, thrilling as they are, have one thing in common: They act, but they are not acted upon. As you saw in the preceding chapters on batch files and macros, automation gains a great deal of flexibility when it allows for user input and control. QBasic programs benefit from interactivity even more than batch files because the programs you devise with QBasic can fill a variety of needs including, but not limited to, managing files, disks, and directories. QBasic programs can be as simple as small batch files or as complex as "real" games, utilities, and miniature applications. In any of these areas, flexibility is invaluable.

When you start creating QBasic programs, one of the first statements you encounter and use regularly is the INPUT statement. As the name suggests, INPUT gives you a means of reading characters typed at the keyboard or, as you'll see later, from a file. The basic form of an INPUT statement is as follows:

```
INPUT ["PROMPT";] VARIABLE
```

PROMPT represents any string you want to display when requesting input; the semicolon shown in the preceding example, which is optional, adds a question mark to the prompt. VARIABLE is a name you provide that QBasic uses as a substitute for the actual information typed. A variable in QBasic is much like a variable name you assign with the MS-DOS Set command. In QBasic, however, you not only name the variable but indicate what type of information it contains by adding one of several special characters to the end of the name: $ for a character string, for example, and % for an integer.

You can try the INPUT statement easily from the immediate window by following the steps on the next page.

1. First, clear the screen and then have QBasic ask for some input, as follows:

```
CLS
INPUT "What is your name"; NAME$
```

2. Press Enter, and the following appears:

```
What is your name?
```

3. Type your name, and QBasic assigns your typing to the variable NAME$, which, as you can tell from the $ at the end, represents a character string. Is there a way to prove this has happened? Sure. Type this:

```
PRINT NAME$
```

Press Enter, and the output window appears again, this time displaying your name, the string assigned to the variable NAME$.

When you create QBasic programs, you'll seldom want or need to get input from within the immediate window. The following example shows how you might use the Input statement to request information from within a program. (If you don't have an EGA or VGA adapter and a color monitor, omit the SCREEN and COLOR instructions.) Clear the editing window by selecting and deleting the earlier example. Type the following:

```
CLS
INPUT "WHAT IS YOUR NAME"; NAME$
CLS : SCREEN 9 : COLOR 3
PRINT "THANK YOU, "; NAME$
```

Most of these lines should look familiar. The first clears the screen, the second asks for your name, and the fourth displays *thank you*, followed by your name. The third line, however, deserves a little explanation. The SCREEN statement is used to set a particular screen mode, such as 40-column for large characters. When you use this statement, you always follow the SCREEN keyword with a one-digit or two-digit number that specifies the screen mode you want. In this example, screen mode 9 specifies 640-pixel-by-350-pixel graphics, which supports 80 characters across the screen by either 25 lines or 43 lines down. The COLOR statement in the example lets you specify the foreground color, background color, or both. In this case, COLOR is used to set the foreground color to cyan. The colons between the CLS, SCREEN, and COLOR statements are special characters that allow you to enter more than one instruction on a single program line.

Controlling a program

Now you come to the fun part of QBasic, the part where you encounter statements such as IF and FOR, as well as the DO WHILE and DO UNTIL statements you'll wish the MS-DOS batch interpreter supported. When you see these conditional statements in action, you begin to see how your batch-file experience can give you a head start in manipulating QBasic.

As you look through the following examples, you'll see two methods you can use to make your programs easier to understand: indented lines and remarks. Indents aren't necessary, but when you fashion sets of conditional instructions, especially if one condition contains another, *nested*, condition, indented lines can help you visualize the logic of your program and spot errors more quickly. Remarks, like remarks in batch files, are strings of text you include to explain what is going on. QBasic supports a REM command that, like its counterpart in batch files, tells QBasic to ignore a line during processing. As you do in a batch file, you can use REM either to insert a comment or to disable an instruction without removing it from your program. An easier way to add comments to a program, however, is to precede each remark with a single quotation mark (').
You can use the ' symbol either at the beginning of a line or, as shown in some of the later examples, to the right of a QBasic instruction.

Now, on to conditions and how you set them up.

The IF statement

In QBasic, as in a batch file, you use IF as a means of testing whether a condition is true. You set up your program so that it does one thing if the condition is true or does something else if the condition is false. This resemblance between QBasic and the If batch command is relatively strong, but the QBasic IF statement is more flexible than its counterpart in MS-DOS:

if x, then y, else z

if it rains, then turn the sprinklers off, else leave them on

You can't use this sequence of events in a batch file because the IF batch command doesn't recognize *else*. In a batch file, the command form is this:

if x, then do command

if it rains, then turn the sprinklers off

To match the set of conditions in this QBasic IF-THEN-ELSE construction, you would need the following sets of If batch commands:

if x, then do command

if not x, then do command

if it rains, then turn the sprinklers off

if it does not rain, then leave the sprinklers on

In QBasic, the syntax of the IF-THEN-ELSE statement is longer than it is under MS-DOS, but it is also easier to understand. The basic form of IF-THEN-ELSE is as follows:

IF [*condition 1*] THEN

        [do the instructions in block 1]

ELSE

        [do the instructions in block 2]

END IF

The following example shows you such a construction based on a familiar yes/no option:

```
INPUT "Please choose 1 or 2: ", num%
IF NUM% = 1 THEN
     PRINT "You chose 1."
ELSE
     PRINT "You chose 2."
END IF
```

Here, the first line asks the user to choose (type) either a 1 or a 2 and assigns that input to the variable NUM%. When translated, the IF-THEN-ELSE statement that forms the remainder of the example reads as follows: "If the value assigned to the variable NUM% equals 1, then display the words *You chose 1.* Otherwise, display the words *You chose 2.*" END IF, which is necessary at the end of every IF construction, brings the evaluation and its consequences to a close.

Notice, by the way, that the variable NUM in the preceding example is identified by a percent sign, the character you use to tell QBasic that it is dealing with an integer, or whole number.

If all the IF-THEN-ELSE statement in QBasic could do were offer either/or choices, the statement wouldn't be much more flexible than the batch command, but when you introduce an ELSEIF, you can test for more than two conditions, like this:

IF [*condition 1*] THEN

        [do the instructions in block 1]

ELSEIF [*condition 2*] THEN

        [do the instructions in block 2]

ELSE

        [do the instructions in block N]

END IF

Here's an example that shows off IF-THEN-ELSE processing. The three rather gratuitous lines at the beginning are comments:

```
' This example sets the text color to
' red, green, or blue, and prints a sentence
' in the selected color
INPUT "Please type red, green, or blue ", COLOR$
SCREEN 9
IF LCASE$(COLOR$) = "red" THEN
COLOR 4 : PRINT "The foreground color is now ";COLOR$
     ELSEIF LCASE$(COLOR$) = "green" THEN
        COLOR 2 : PRINT "The foreground color is now ";COLOR$
             ELSEIF LCASE$(COLOR$) = "blue" THEN
                COLOR 1 : PRINT "The foreground color is now ";COLOR$
        ELSE PRINT "You didn't type red, green, or blue."
END IF
```

Notice, by the way, there's not a GOTO in sight in the preceding examples, although you use plenty of them in batch files. QBasic supports a GOTO statement, but you're discouraged from using it, for two reasons. One, deciphering a program full of GOTO instructions can make you feel like a bloodhound on the trail of a lost child. Two, QBasic is more flexible by far than the batch interpreter, and you can usually manage to do what you want with IF and DO constructions, as well as with program modules called *subprograms*, or *procedures*. Subprograms, however, are well beyond the scope of this small chapter.

The FOR statement

When you use For at the MS-DOS command line or in a batch file, execution goes round and round horizontally, as MS-DOS processes a command for each item in a set you define:

FOR [*item x*] in [*a set of items*] DO [this MS-DOS command]

The FOR command is thus an economical means of performing the same command repeatedly. When you use QBasic, you have a similar option called a FOR...NEXT loop after the two keywords that define the beginning and end of the loop. The only real difference between the MS-DOS For command and the QBasic FOR...NEXT loop is that, thanks to syntax, processing of the MS-DOS command cycles horizontally from left to right, whereas processing of a QBasic FOR...NEXT loop occurs from top to bottom, like this:

```
FOR i% = 1 to 5
     PRINT i%
NEXT i%
```

As you can see from this example, the FOR statement defines a variable (i%) and the set (the numbers 1 through 5) that are to be assigned, in turn, to i%. Although i% is not explicitly set to 1 to start with, that happens automatically. The PRINT instruction then prints the current value of i%, and the NEXT instruction moves the line along, replacing the current i% with the next value in the set.

When you run a FOR...NEXT loop, processing continues until the last value in the set is reached and then either ends or moves on to the next instruction in the program.

DO...WHILE and DO...UNTIL

The QBasic DO twins offer another way of looping through a set of instructions. In this case, processing continues while (DO...WHILE) or until (DO...UNTIL) a condition you specify is true. Offering a little more variety than FOR...NEXT, the DO statement can be used in either of two forms:

DO WHILE [or UNTIL] this condition

       [carry out this set of instructions]

LOOP

or:

DO

       [carry out this set of instructions]

LOOP WHILE [or UNTIL] this condition

In a sense, these two forms of the DO...LOOP construction are mirror images. One sets the condition to be satisfied at the beginning, the other sets the condition at the end. When you write your own programs, use the DO WHILE or DO UNTIL form if you want the condition evaluated before the instructions are carried out, and use the LOOP WHILE or LOOP UNTIL form if you want the condition evaluated after the instructions have been carried out at least once. The following two examples show both ways of creating a DO loop:

```
i% = 0
DO UNTIL i% = 5
     PRINT i%
     i% = i% + 1
LOOP
```

Here, the value of the variable i% is initially set to 0. The instructions in the DO loop then print the value of i% and increase i% by 1 before the LOOP instruction sends processing back to DO UNTIL, which determines whether the new value of i% is equal to 5. When i% equals 5, the DO UNTIL instruction becomes true, and processing stops (meaning that the only values printed are 0, 1, 2, 3, and 4).

The next example produces the same result, but it places the condition at the end of the loop:

```
i% = 0
DO
        PRINT i%
         i% = i% + 1
LOOP UNTIL i% = 5
```

Putting some of this to work

To finish up this quick look at conditional processing, here's a rather loopy program that combines FOR and DO UNTIL statements to draw circles all over your (EGA or VGA) screen. Comments are included at the beginning of the program and to the right of some instructions. A REM is used in front of the SLEEP statement to disable the line for those who like perpetual-motion displays:

```
' This example draws lots of circles on the screen.
SCREEN 9                                    ' Set screen mode
DO UNTIL INKEY$ <> ""                       ' Do until a key is pressed
FOR i% = 10 TO 150
CIRCLE (300 - i%, i% + 175), i%, i% / 10    ' Draw circles
CIRCLE (300 - i%, 175 - i%), i%, i% / 10    ' of varying sizes
CIRCLE (i% + 300, i% + 175), i%, i% / 10    ' and colors from the
CIRCLE (i% + 300, 175 - i%), i%, i% / 10    ' center to the corners
i% = i% + 1
NEXT i%
CLS
REM SLEEP 1
LOOP
```

This, briefly, is what the instructions do:

- The SCREEN 9 statement sets the screen mode to 640-by-350 graphics, the mode described earlier as suitable for EGA and VGA displays.

- The DO UNTIL statement checks for a condition with the QBasic function called INKEY$, which checks for a character typed on the keyboard. This particular condition becomes true when any key is pressed—that is, INKEY$ is not equal to a null string, "". This null string idea should be familiar from your use of If to check strings in batch files. (Remember the If "string1"=="" command?)

- The FOR statement sets the acceptable values of an integer variable, i%.

- The four CIRCLE statements are variations on a theme that draw circles of different sizes and different colors. The variable i% is used to define the circle centers, their radii, and their color. The following two lines should help you figure out what all those i% variables mean:

      CIRCLE (x coordinate, y coordinate), radius, color

So, for example, in this statement:

```
CIRCLE (300-i%, i% + 175), i%, i%/10
```

300 – i% represents the x coordinate (as a pixel location) for the center of the circle; i% + 175 represents the y coordinate; i% all by itself is the radius, and i%/10 is the color. For color, i% is divided by 10 because screen mode 9 displays any of 15 possible colors. Because i% ranges from 10 to 150, i% divided by 10 gives you each of those colors.

- i% = i% + 1 and NEXT i% are self-explanatory, and you've already met CLS.
- The SLEEP 1 statement, if you remove the REM, causes the computer to pause for 1 second, giving you visual relief from what is otherwise a busy display.
- LOOP, of course, sends QBasic back to the DO UNTIL statement to begin the process over again.

A somewhat more useful program

So far, what you've seen has been cursory in the extreme and seemingly of more entertainment value than utility. QBasic can be trained to more useful tasks, but as you'll find when you develop your own programs, the work involved can produce much larger sets of instructions than you've encountered here. This relationship between length and usability becomes especially apparent when you begin to position output on the screen to make it look better, and it pretty much becomes a fact of life when you test the programs to be sure you've considered every possible way in which you or someone else might try to break them.

The remainder of this section shows how QBasic can be used to read from and write to disk files. The programs work, but do not assume that this material is enough to make you competent in working with files. You'll do little more here than peer through a darkened window. To go further, you'll have to provide some light and some elbow grease of your own. With that in mind, however, here's a short sample program that shows how QBasic can be like MS-DOS at times. Most of these instructions should look familiar:

```
MKDIR "C:\QBTEST"
CHDIR "C:\QBTEST"
INPUT "PLEASE TYPE A SAMPLE FILENAME", FILE$
OPEN FILE$ FOR OUTPUT AS #1
WRITE #1, "THIS TEXT IS IN THE FILE"
CLOSE
OPEN FILE$ FOR INPUT AS #1
INPUT #1, A$
PRINT A$
CLOSE
END
```

First, the program creates a directory named C:\QBTEST with the MKDIR statement and then changes to the new directory. The INPUT statement asks you to provide a filename to use as a sample and assigns the name you type to the variable FILE$. Next, the OPEN statement opens the file (a new one, in this case), prepares it to receive output, and assigns the file the number 1. Now, a WRITE statement "writes" the words *This text is in the file* to the sample file, and the CLOSE statement closes (saves) the file.

Now begins another phase of file management. The next OPEN statement reopens the file assigned to FILE$, but this time it prepares the file to provide input. The INPUT statement that follows then reads from the file and assigns what it reads to the variable A$. The PRINT statement, in due course, takes the characters assigned to A$ and displays them on screen. The CLOSE statement once again closes the file and, finally, the END statement brings the program to an end.

The next sample is based roughly on the same procedures: opening and closing a file, as well as reading from and writing to it. This program, however, uses input to determine whether to read from or write to a "memo" file. If you type in the program, be very careful about spelling, punctuation, and special characters, such as $ and %.

```
CLS
LOCATE 5, 30
PRINT "NOTETAKER"
LOCATE 7, 24
INPUT "READ (R) OR WRITE (W)"; ACTION$
IF UCASE$(ACTION$) = "R" THEN
        OPEN "C:\MEMOS" FOR APPEND AS #1
        CLOSE #1
        OPEN "C:\MEMOS" FOR INPUT AS #1
        CLS
        DO UNTIL EOF(1)
                FOR I% = 1 TO 3
                        INPUT #1, A$
                        PRINT A$
                NEXT I%
                SLEEP 2
                PRINT
        LOOP
ELSE
OPEN "C:\MEMOS" FOR APPEND AS #1
        DO UNTIL UCASE$(NOTE$) = "END"
                CLS
                LOCATE 9
                PRINT "TYPE 80 CHARACTERS OR LESS, AND PRESS ENTER."
                PRINT "TYPE END TO QUIT."
                LOCATE 14
```

(continued)

```
                    PRINT STRING$(80, "-")
                    LOCATE 13
                    INPUT NOTE$
                            IF NOTE$ <> "END" THEN
                                    WRITE #1, DATE$
                                    WRITE #1, TIME$
                                    WRITE #1, NOTE$
                            ELSE CLS : SYSTEM
                            END IF
            LOOP
    END IF
    SYSTEM
```

In this example, the opening lines clear the screen and use the LOCATE statement to position the cursor at line 5, column 30. The PRINT statement displays the word *NOTETAKER*. The next LOCATE and INPUT instructions position the cursor at line 7, column 24, and ask whether you want to read from or write to your memo file.

The main part of the example consists of an IF-ELSE condition:

- If you type *R*, the program first ensures that a file named MEMOS exists in the root directory of drive C. It then opens the file for use and displays your stored memos, along with the date and time each was entered, until it reaches the end of the file (EOF). The UCASE$ function here, by the way, converts your input, if necessary, into uppercase for comparison with the string "R". Using UCASE$, therefore, makes it unnecessary for you to remember whether to type an uppercase R or a lowercase r.

- If, on the other hand, you type *W* (again, uppercase or lowercase doesn't matter), the program opens C:\MEMOS in the mode called APPEND, which adds to existing entries. From that point until you type *end* or *END*, the program displays typing instructions and the message *TYPE END TO QUIT* above a dotted line on which you type a memo of up to 80 characters. For each entry you type, the three WRITE statements in the nested IF send the date, time, and the memo itself to the MEMOS file. When you type *end* to signal that you're through, the program ends and the SYSTEM statement returns you to MS-DOS.

Although the example does not give you an option to quit once you've started, that's not really a problem. To cancel the program, press Ctrl-Break as you do to cancel an MS-DOS command or a batch file. In QBasic, however, pressing Ctrl-Break takes you to the view window, rather than straight to the system prompt. To leave QBasic, you press Alt-F-X (for the File Exit command).

If you saved this example as MEMOS.BAS, you could run the program from the MS-DOS prompt with the command

```
C:\>qbasic /run memos
```

To save time, however, you could also run it from a batch file like this one:

```
@echo off
qbasic /run memos
cls
```

The (MS-DOS) Cls command at the end ensures that you end up with a clear screen, even if you cancel the program by pressing Ctrl-Break. If you try this program, by the way, bear in mind that new entries are appended to existing entries. That means your MEMO file will grow whenever you use it. Clean house now and then by deleting the file.

A final word from your sponsor

If you like what you've seen here and want to know more, you'll find many fine books on programming at your local bookstore. One such, published by Microsoft Press, is *Running MS-DOS QBasic*, by Michael Halvorson and David Rygmyr—two personal acquaintances of mine whose programming know-how will ease your transition from computer user to computer programmer. You'll enjoy their book, and their book will help you enjoy QBasic.

```
CLS
PRINT "THIS IS WHERE WE PART COMPANY."
PRINT "IT'S BEEN FUN, BUT NOW IT'S TIME TO SAY"
PRINT "GOODBYE"
END
```

APPENDIXES

ASCII and IBM Extended Characters

STANDARD ASCII CHARACTERS

Character	Control character	Decimal value	Hexadecimal value
ASCII control characters (displayed as graphics characters by IBM systems)			
NUL		0	00
SOH (start of heading)	^A	1	01
STX (start of text)	^B	2	02
ETX (end of text)	^C	3	03
EOT (end of transmission)	^D	4	04
ENQ (inquiry)	^E	5	05
ACK (acknowledgement)	^F	6	06
BEL (bell)	^G	7	07
BS (backspace)	^H	8	08
HT (horizontal tab)	^I	9	09
LF (linefeed)	^J	10	0A
VT (vertical tab)	^K	11	0B
FF (formfeed)	^L	12	0C
CR (carriage return)	^M	13	0D
SO (shift out)	^N	14	0E
SI (shift in)	^O	15	0F

(continued)

continued

Character	Control character	Decimal value	Hexadecimal value
DLE (data link escape)	^P	16	10
DC1 (device control 1)	^Q	17	11
DC2 (device control 2)	^R	18	12
DC3 (device control 3)	^S	19	13
DC4 (device control 4)	^T	20	14
NAK (negative acknowledgement)	^U	21	15
SYN (synchronous idle)	^V	22	16
ETB (end transmission block)	^W	23	17
CAN (cancel)	^X	24	18
EM (end of medium)	^Y	25	19
SUB (substitute)	^Z	26	1A
ESC (escape)	^[	27	1B
FS (file separator)	^\	28	1C
GS (group separator)	^]	29	1D
RS (record separator)	^^	30	1E
US (unit separator)	^_	31	1F
Printable characters			
(space)		32	20
!		33	21
"		34	22
#		35	23
$		36	24
%		37	25
&		38	26
' (single quotation mark or apostrophe)		39	27
(		40	28
)		41	29
*		42	2A
+		43	2B
, (comma)		44	2C
- (hyphen or minus)		45	2D
. (period)		46	2E
/		47	2F

Character	Control character	Decimal value	Hexadecimal value
Printable characters			
0		48	30
1		49	31
2		50	32
3		51	33
4		52	34
5		53	35
6		54	36
7		55	37
8		56	38
9		57	39
: (colon)		58	3A
; (semicolon)		59	3B
<		60	3C
=		61	3D
>		62	3E
?		63	3F
@		64	40
A		65	41
B		66	42
C		67	43
D		68	44
E		69	45
F		70	46
G		71	47
H		72	48
I		73	49
J		74	4A
K		75	4B
L		76	4C
M		77	4D
N		78	4E
O		79	4F
P		80	50
Q		81	51
R		82	52
S		83	53

(continued)

continued

Character	Control character	Decimal value	Hexadecimal value
T		84	54
U		85	55
V		86	56
W		87	57
X		88	58
Y		89	59
Z		90	5A
[(left square bracket)		91	5B
\		92	5C
] (right square bracket)		93	5D
^ (caret)		94	5E
_ (underscore)		95	5F
´ (accent grave)		96	60
a		97	61
b		98	62
c		99	63
d		100	64
e		101	65
f		102	66
g		103	67
h		104	68
i		105	69
j		106	6A
k		107	6B
l		108	6C
m		109	6D
n		110	6E
o		111	6F
p		112	70
q		113	71
r		114	72
s		115	73
t		116	74
u		117	75
v		118	76
w		119	77
x		120	78

Character	Control character	Decimal value	Hexadecimal value
y		121	79
z		122	7A
{ (opening brace)		123	7B
¦ (pipe)		124	7C
} (closing brace)		125	7D
~ (tilde)		126	7E
△		127	7F

IBM EXTENDED CHARACTERS

ASCII	Dec	Hex	ASCII	Dec	Hex	ASCII	Dec	Hex	ASCII	Dec	Hex
Ç	128	80	á	160	A0	└	192	C0	α	224	E0
ü	129	81	í	161	A1	⊥	193	C1	β	225	E1
é	130	82	ó	162	A2	┬	194	C2	Γ	226	E2
â	131	83	ú	163	A3	├	195	C3	π	227	E3
ä	132	84	ñ	164	A4	─	196	C4	Σ	228	E4
à	133	85	Ñ	165	A5	┼	197	C5	σ	229	E5
å	134	86	ª	166	A6	╞	198	C6	µ	230	E6
ç	135	87	º	167	A7	╟	199	C7	τ	231	E7
ê	136	88	¿	168	A8	╚	200	C8	Φ	232	E8
ë	137	89	⌐	169	A9	╔	201	C9	Θ	233	E9
è	138	8A	¬	170	AA	╩	202	CA	Ω	234	EA
ï	139	8B	½	171	AB	╦	203	CB	δ	235	EB
î	140	8C	¼	172	AC	╠	204	CC	∞	236	EC
ì	141	8D	¡	173	AD	═	205	CD	φ	237	ED
Ä	142	8E	«	174	AE	╬	206	CE	ε	238	EE
Å	143	8F	»	175	AF	╧	207	CF	∩	239	EF
É	144	90	░	176	B0	╨	208	D0	≡	240	F0
æ	145	91	▒	177	B1	╤	209	D1	±	241	F1
Æ	146	92	▓	178	B2	╥	210	D2	≥	242	F2
ô	147	93	│	179	B3	╙	211	D3	≤	243	F3
ö	148	94	┤	180	B4	╘	212	D4	⌠	244	F4
ò	149	95	╡	181	B5	╒	213	D5	⌡	245	F5
û	150	96	╢	182	B6	╓	214	D6	÷	246	F6
ù	151	97	╖	183	B7	╫	215	D7	≈	247	F7
ÿ	152	98	╕	184	B8	╪	216	D8	°	248	F8
ö	153	99	╣	185	B9	┘	217	D9	•	249	F9
Ü	154	9A	║	186	BA	┌	218	DA	·	250	FA
¢	155	9B	╗	187	BB	█	219	DB	√	251	FB
£	156	9C	╝	188	BC	▄	220	DC	η	252	FC
¥	157	9D	╜	189	BD	▌	221	DD	²	253	FD
₧	158	9E	╛	190	BE	▐	222	DE	■	254	FE
ƒ	159	9F	┐	191	BF	▀	223	DF		255	FF

B

ANSI.SYS Escape Sequences and Key Codes

Working as a device driver, ANSI.SYS customizes the screen and keyboard by intercepting, translating, and carrying out special commands known as escape sequences. These escape sequences are strings of characters you cook up and save, either as part of a Prompt command (with the $e parameter) or as the contents of a file you can "run" by displaying it either with the Type command or with an Echo command in a batch file. (A third alternative is to copy the file to the console with the Copy command, but doing this is not as neat or as efficient as using Type or Echo.)

The escape sequences you send to ANSI.SYS are based on a group of standardized codes established by the American National Standards Institute (the source of the ANSI part of the driver name). To "flag" an escape sequence and make it identifiable to ANSI.SYS, you begin by sending an Escape character, followed by a left square bracket. The beginning of an ANSI escape sequence thus always looks like this, where Esc represents the Escape character:

```
Esc[
```

This Esc[part of an ANSI.SYS escape sequence, however, is actually nothing more than your ticket to ANSI country. After the left bracket, you enter the real stuff: a string of characters—alphabetic, numeric, or both—that tell ANSI.SYS what you want to do. After this "definition," you add a single letter that defines the type of control you want. Here, for example, is an ANSI.SYS escape sequence that moves the cursor to the approximate middle of the screen:

```
Esc[12;35f
```

The 12;35 portion of the sequence identifies a particular row and column on the screen (row 12, column 35), and these coordinates are given meaning by the final part of the escape sequence, the single lowercase letter *f* that ANSI.SYS recognizes as a command to position the cursor.

Simple acts, such as positioning the cursor, are just the start, however. You can also string escape sequences together to produce more elaborate results. For example, the following escape sequence clears the screen, positions the cursor at line 12, column 35, displays the string ANSI.SYS in blue letters on a white background, and displays the system prompt in its normal white on black:

```
Esc[2JEsc[12;35fEsc[34;47mANSI.SYSEsc[m
```

And you thought MS-DOS commands were cryptic.

The following sections list and describe the ANSI.SYS escape sequences. To include an Esc character in a batch file as part of a Type or Echo command, use the MS-DOS Editor. Where you want the Esc character to appear, press Ctrl-P, followed by Esc. Bear in mind that all escape sequences begin with the Esc character followed by a left square bracket ([), and that the single-letter ANSI.SYS commands are sensitive to case.

For cursor control

Esc[linesA

Function. Moves the cursor up the number of lines specified by *lines*. This escape sequence is ignored if the cursor is already at the top of the screen.

Example. To position the cursor two lines above the current location:

```
Esc[2A
```

Esc[linesB

Function. Moves the cursor down the number of lines specified by *lines*. This escape sequence is ignored if the cursor is already at the bottom of the screen.

Example. To position the cursor two lines below the current location:

```
Esc[2B
```

Esc[colsC

Function. Moves the cursor right the number of columns (characters) specified by *cols*.

Example. To move the cursor 10 columns to the right of the current position:

```
Esc[10C
```

Esc[colsD

Function. Moves the cursor left the number of columns (characters) specified by *cols*.

Example. To move the cursor 10 columns to the left of the current position:

```
Esc[10D
```

Esc[line;colH

Function. Moves the cursor to the line specified by *line* and the column specified by *col*. The Home position at the upper left corner of the screen is line 0, column 0.

Example. To move the cursor to the Home position:

```
Esc[0;0H
```

Esc[line;colf

Function. Works like the preceding Esc[*line;col*H command.

Example. To move the cursor to the Home position:

```
Esc[0;0f
```

Esc[s

Function. Saves the current cursor position. To move the cursor to this saved position, use the following escape sequence, Esc[u. Note that this escape sequence does not require a user-defined parameter.

Example. To save the current position of the cursor (assume line 10, column 20):

```
Esc[s
```

Esc[u

Function. Restores the cursor to the position saved with the Esc[s sequence. Note that this escape sequence does not require a user-defined parameter.

Example. To restore the cursor to the position saved in the preceding example:

```
Esc[u
```

For screen control

ESC[2J

Function. Clears the screen and moves the cursor to the Home position; the ANSI.SYS equivalent of the Cls command.

Example. To clear the screen and move the cursor to line 0, column 0:

```
Esc[2J
```

Esc[K

Function. Erases the current line, from the cursor position to the end of the line.

Example. To erase the character at the cursor position and all following characters, to the end of the line:

```
Esc[K
```

Esc[=screenmodeh

Function. Sets the screen to the mode specified by *screenmode. screenmode* is any of the following values:

Screen mode	Meaning
0	40 columns by 25 lines, monochrome text
1	40 columns by 25 lines, color text
2	80 columns by 25 lines, monochrome text
3	80 columns by 25 lines, color text
4	320 by 200 screen resolution, four-color graphics
5	320 by 200 screen resolution, monochrome graphics
6	640 by 200 screen resolution, monochrome graphics
7	Enable line wrapping
13	320 by 200 screen resolution, color graphics
14	640 by 200 screen resolution, 16-color graphics
15	640 by 350 screen resolution, monochrome (two-color) graphics
16	640 by 350 screen resolution, 16-color graphics
17	640 by 480 screen resolution, monochrome (two-color) graphics
18	640 by 480 screen resolution, 16-color graphics
19	320 by 200 screen resolution, 256-color graphics

Example. To set the screen to mode 16:

```
Esc[16h
```

Esc[=screenmodel

Function. Resets the screen mode as described previously, except that mode 7 disables line wrapping. The command letter is a lowercase L.

Example. To reset the screen to mode 2 (the typical MS-DOS display):

```
Esc[2l
```

Esc[=graphicsfunction;...graphicsfunctionm

Function. Set screen colors and text attributes as specified by *graphicsfunction*, values for which are listed below. When you use this escape sequence, the settings remain in place until the next time this escape sequence is used. If you forget to reset the screen, colors and attributes can become "sticky." To return the screen to normal, use this escape sequence a second time, but with a setting of 0.

Graphics function	Meaning
Text attributes:	
0	All attributes (see below) off
1	Bold
4	Underscore (monochrome display adapter only)
5	Blink
7	Reverse video
8	Concealed
Foreground colors:	
30	Black
31	Red
32	Green
33	Yellow
34	Blue
35	Magenta
36	Cyan
37	White
Background colors:	
40	Black
41	Red
42	Green
43	Yellow
44	Blue
45	Magenta
46	Cyan
47	White

Example. To use the $e special character and the Prompt command to display the pg prompt in bold yellow on blue, but return to normal for all subsequently typed and displayed text:

```
prompt $e[1;33;44m$p$g$e[0m
```

Esc[keycode;string;...p

Function. Assigns the key or key combination specified by *keycode* to the string specified by *string*. You can use this escape sequence to redefine the character displayed by a key, as shown in the first of the following examples, or to assign a command or set of commands to a key, as shown in the second example. Keycode is entered as one of the values in the table following the examples. Notice that some key codes are combinations of two values separated by a semicolon. Be sure to include this semicolon in addition to the semicolon(s) required by the escape sequence itself.

Example 1. To use the F12 key (key code 0;134) to display the extended character £ (ASCII value 156 in the English-language code page 437):

```
Esc[0;134;156p
```

To reset the key to its original value:

```
Esc[0;134;0;134p
```

Example 2. To "program" the F12 key to display a wide directory listing (/w) of directories (/ad) in the current directory:

```
Esc[0;134;"dir /ad /w";13p
```

The key code 13 at the end of this sequence corresponds to the Enter key and is included to make the command more fully automatic.

ASCII key codes

Key	Code for key alone	Code for Shift-key combination	Code for Ctrl-key combination	Code for Alt-key combination
F1	0;59	0;84	0;94	0;104
F2	0;60	0;85	0;95	0;105
F3	0;61	0;86	0;96	0;106
F4	0;62	0;87	0;97	0;107
F5	0;63	0;88	0;98	0;108
F6	0;64	0;89	0;99	0;109
F7	0;65	0;90	0;100	0;110
F8	0;66	0;91	0;101	0;111

---

* Not available on all keyboards; check your hardware documentation.   *(continued)*

Key	Code for key alone	Code for Shift-key combination	Code for Ctrl-key combination	Code for Alt-key combination
F9	0;67	0;92	0;102	0;112
F10	0;68	0;93	0;103	0;113
F11	0;133	0;135	0;137	0;139
F12	0;134	0;136	0;138	0;140
Home	0;71	55	0;119	—
End	0;79	49	0;117	—
Page Up	0;73	57	0;132	—
Page Down	0;81	51	0;118	—
Up arrow	0;72	56	0;141*	—
Left arrow	0;75	52	0;115	—
Right arrow	0;77	54	0;116	—
Down arrow	0;80	50	0;145*	—
Insert	0;82	48	0;146*	—
Delete	0;83	46	0;147*	—
Print Screen	—	—	0;114	—
Pause/Break	—	—	0;0	—
Backspace	8	8	127	0*
Enter	13	—	10	0;28*
Tab	9	0;15	0;148*	0;165*
Null (Ctrl-2)	0;3	—	—	—
A	97	65	1	0;30
B	98	66	2	0;48
C	99	66	3	0;46
D	100	68	4	0;32
E	101	69	5	0;18
F	102	70	6	0;33
G	103	71	7	0;34
H	104	72	8	0;35
I	105	73	9	0;23
J	106	74	10	0;36
K	107	75	11	0;37
L	108	76	12	0;38
M	109	77	13	0;50
N	110	78	14	0;49
O	111	79	15	0;24
P	112	80	16	0;25

(continued)

Key	Code for key alone	Code for Shift-key combination	Code for Ctrl-key combination	Code for Alt-key combination
Q	113	81	17	0;16
R	114	82	18	0;19
S	115	83	19	0;31
T	116	84	20	0;20
U	117	85	21	0;22
V	118	86	22	0;47
W	119	87	23	0;17
X	120	88	24	0;45
Y	121	89	25	0;21
Z	122	90	26	0;44
1	49	33	—	0;120
2	50	64	0 (NULL)	0;121
3	51	35	—	0;122
4	52	36	—	0;123
5	53	37	—	0;124
6	54	94	30	0;125
7	55	38	—	0;126
8	56	42	—	0;127
9	57	40	—	0;128
0	48	41	—	0;129
-	45	95	31	0;130
=	61	43	—	0;131
[	91	123	27	0;26
]	93	125	29	0;27
\ (backslash)	92	124	28	0;43
; (semi-colon)	59	58	—	0;39
' (single quotation mark)	39	34	—	0;40
, (comma)	44	60	—	0;51
. (period)	46	62	—	0;52
/ (slash)	47	63	—	0;53
` (accent, grave)	96	126	—	0;41*
Enter (keypad)	13	—	10	0;166*
/ (keypad)	47	47	0;142*	0;74*
* (keypad)	42	0;144*	0;78*	—

(continued)

Key	Code for key alone	Code for Shift-key combination	Code for Ctrl-key combination	Code for Alt-key combination
- (keypad)	45	45	0;149*	0;164*
+ (keypad)	43	43	0;150*	0;55*
5 (keypad)	0;76*	53	0;143*	—
101/102-key keyboards:				
Home (gray key)	224;71*	224;71*	224;119*	224;151*
End (gray key)	224;79*	224;79*	224;117*	224;159*
Page Up (gray key)	224;73*	224;73*	224;132*	224;153*
Page Down (gray key)	224;81*	224;81*	224;118*	224;161*
Up arrow (gray key)	224;72*	224;72*	224:141*	224;152*
Left arrow (gray key)	224;75*	224;75*	224;115*	224;155*
Right arrow (gray key)	224;77*	224;77*	224;116*	224;157*
Down arrow (gray key)	224;80*	224;80*	224;145*	224;154*
Insert (gray key)	224;82*	224;82*	224;146*	224;162*
Delete (gray key)	224;83*	224;83*	224;147*	224;163*

C

Code Pages, Countries, and Keyboard Layouts

MS-DOS includes a specialized set of commands you can use to customize your computer to the language, keyboard layout, and conventions (such as time and date format) of a country other than the one for which your system was manufactured. If you want or need to make your computer responsive to more than one language or set of country conventions, the information in the following pages should help you understand the international side of MS-DOS.

NOTE: This appendix explains national language support in terms of what it is, how the commands work together, and the sequence—usually important—in which you use the commands. The commands themselves, including syntax and examples, are described in the reference portion of the book, primarily in Chapter 10, "Devices."

Code pages

Code pages in one form or another lie at the heart of MS-DOS national language support. What are they? They are ASCII tables customized to represent the characters used in different languages, such as English, Portuguese, Canadian French, Norwegian, and Polish. When do you use them? When you want to give MS-DOS the ability to display or reproduce characters in a language not normally supported by your hardware.

MS-DOS recognizes six code pages, each of which is referenced by a number. They are

Code page number	Language
437	English, the MS-DOS default
850	Multilingual, or Latin I, containing the characters used in most European and Latin American countries
852	Slavic, or Latin II, containing the characters used in countries such as Poland, Hungary, the Czech Republic, and Slovakia
860	Portuguese
863	Canadian French
865	Nordic, containing the characters used in countries such as Denmark and Norway

Represented in print, a typical code page looks no different from the ASCII table shown in Appendix A. It is simply a list of characters assigned to the 256 standard and extended ASCII codes. Although the six code pages represent different sets of characters, they really are not as varied as you might think because the first 128 values don't vary. All are assigned to the standard control characters, punctuation marks, numerals, and lowercase and uppercase Roman letters shown in Appendix A.

Where the six code pages do differ, however, is in the upper 128 ASCII values. These are assigned to the various characters unique to different language groups, such as Slavic and Nordic. When a particular code page is active, MS-DOS uses it to determine which character is to be displayed for a particular keypress. For example, in code page 850 (Multilingual), ASCII value 149 stands for the character ò, but in code page 852 (Slavic), the same ASCII value represents the character L. Thus, if code page 850 were active, MS-DOS would display the keypress representing ASCII 149 (entered as Alt-149 on the numeric keypad) as the letter ò; if code page 852 were active, the same keypress would be displayed as L.

In theory, code pages are simple to understand. In practice, they're a little more complex because they come in two varieties, hardware and prepared (software) code pages.

- A hardware code page is built into the computer to provide a "native" language for the keyboard and the display. This code page is used by MS-DOS by default and is the character set responsible for ensuring that the M you press on the keyboard becomes the M displayed by your monitor. If you're uncertain which hardware code page your computer uses, type *chcp* for the Chcp command without any parameters, and MS-DOS will display the number of the active code page.

- A prepared code page is an alternate character set stored on disk as a font file that includes the instructions for matching keypress to character and then displaying the appropriate character shape. MS-DOS versions 5 and 6 provide separate font files for the keyboard and display; version 5 also includes files for IBM Proprinter and Quietwriter printers, which otherwise cannot reproduce alternate character sets. All code-page files have the extension CPI. They are: EGA.CPI (for systems with EGA and VGA displays), and, in version 5, LCD.CPI (for LCD screens) and the 4201.CPI, 4208.CPI, and 5202.CPI files for IBM printers and strict compatibles.

This information about code pages is all the background that you need to understand whether, and when, to use them. Now you can move on to customizing MS-DOS for international needs.

Country conventions

In the United States, most people write, for example, 12/11/93 for the date December 11, 1993, and 8:14 pm for the time. In Brazil, the conventions for the same date and time are 11/12/93 and 20:14. In Poland, the date is usually given as 1993-12-11, although the time format matches the custom in Brazil, 20:14. When MS-DOS displays or asks for the date and time, it uses the conventions of the country your computer is designed to recognize. In addition to the date and time, MS-DOS relies on its country information to determine the currency symbol, alphabetic sort order, and the characters used in filenames and directory names.

To change to the conventions of a different country, you place a Country command in CONFIG.SYS, specifying the code number (shown in the table on the next page) for the country you want and giving the path to the file of information that tells MS-DOS about the country conventions. By default, MS-DOS searches for COUNTRY.SYS and assumes the file is in your root directory. If you use the Country command, the file is probably in your DOS directory, so you'll have to specify the path. You can also specify an alternate country-information file, if you've installed one. As described in Chapter 10, the syntax of the Country command is

country=*code,codepage,filespec*

where *code* is the country code, *codepage* is an optional parameter specifying an alternate code page, and *filespec* is the path to COUNTRY.SYS or a different country file. The table on the next page lists the countries and country codes supported by MS-DOS. To avoid repetition later, this table also includes keyboard codes and the default and alternate code pages you can use for each country.

Country	Country code	Keyboard code	Default code page	Alternate code page
Belgium	032	be	850	437
Brazil	055	br	850	437
Canada (French)	002	cf	863	850
Croatia	038	yu	852	850
Czech Republic	042	cz	852	850
Denmark	045	dk	850	865
Finland	358	su	850	437
France	033	fr	850	437
Germany	049	gr	850	437
Hungary	036	hu	852	850
International English	061	+	437	850
Italy	039	it	850	437
Latin America	003	la	850	437
Netherlands	031	nl	850	437
Norway	047	no	850	865
Poland	048	pl	852	850
Portugal	351	po	850	860
Slovakia	042	sl	852	850
Serbia/ Yugoslavia	038	yu	852	850
Slovenia	038	yu	852	850
Spain	034	sp	850	437
Sweden	046	sv	850	437
Switzerland (French)	041	sf	850	437
Switzerland (German)	041	sg	850	437
United Kingdom	044	uk	437	850
United States	001	us	437	850

If your hardware code page includes all the characters you need for the language of the country you specify, a Country command can be as simple as this:

```
country=039,,c:\dos\country.sys
```

This command sets up MS-DOS to use the date, time, and other country conventions of Italy and gives the path to COUNTRY.SYS. The two commas indicate that a code page was deliberately omitted, as you most likely would do if your hardware code page is 437.

If your hardware code page does not contain the characters you need, you can specify the code page you want, providing

- The code page matches either the default or the alternate code page supported by MS-DOS for that country and its keyboard layout.

- You have prepared the system for national language support as described later.

Keyboard layouts

Keyboard layouts vary from one country to another. Sometimes, as you can see by comparing the United Kingdom and United States layouts, shown here, the differences are minor:

Sometimes the differences are subtle, as you can see by comparing the German layout, shown at the top of the next page, with the United States layout. (Notice the positions of the Y and Z keys.)

And sometimes the differences are striking, as you can see on the Hungarian and Swiss keyboards, shown here:

MS-DOS supports these and other keyboard layouts through the Keyb command, which remaps your keyboard to match the layout used in another country. You can switch to an alternate keyboard layout and even switch between two: Ctrl-Alt-F1 switches to the United States layout; Ctrl-Alt-F2 switches to the alternate layout you chose.

The basic syntax of the Keyb command, described more fully in Chapter 10, is as follows:

keyb *keyboardcode,codepage,filespec*

where *keyboardcode* is the two-letter code of the country whose keyboard layout you want to use; *codepage* is the number of the code page (if different from the active code page) you want to use with the keyboard layout; and *filespec* is the drive, path, and filename of the keyboard definition file that contains the keyboard layout information—by default, KEYBOARD.SYS in your DOS directory.

As with the Country command, if you specify a code page, it must be one of the code pages supported for the keyboard layout you specify, and you must have already prepared the system to use the code page you want.

If you change to a keyboard like the Swiss layout, you'll find that some of the keys contain more than the two characters you can type by pressing the key alone or in combination with the Shift key. On these keyboards, you press the key alone for the lower left character, Shift plus the key for the upper left character, and the following special key combinations for the lower right and upper right characters.

Keyboard	Lower right character (standard keyboard)	Lower right character (enhanced keyboard)	Upper right character (all keyboards)
Canada (French)	Alt-Shift	Alt-Gr	None
Denmark	Alt	Alt-Gr	Alt-Shift
Finland	Alt	Alt-Gr	Alt-Shift
Norway	Alt	Alt-Gr	Alt-Shift
Sweden	Alt	Alt-Gr	Alt-Shift
Others	Alt-Ctrl	Alt-Gr	None

When to use code pages

As already mentioned, you use code pages when your hardware code page does not contain the characters you need for the country or keyboard layout you want. As you can see from the table of countries and code pages earlier in this appendix, many countries use the same code pages. For example, France and Germany both use a default code page of 850 and an alternate code page of 437, so users in either country can switch to the conventions and keyboard layout of the other without specifying a new code page.

If you want to use a character set that is not included in the active code page on your system, however, you turn to code-page switching, which involves preparing the system to use code pages, followed by activating national language support and loading one or more code pages. The procedure is not complicated, but it does involve several MS-DOS commands.

- You must prepare the screen and keyboard for code-page switching with a Device or Devicehigh command in CONFIG.SYS that installs DIS-PLAY.SYS, the device driver that enables code-page switching. Here is a typical such Device command:

    ```
    DEVICE=C:\DOS\DISPLAY.SYS CON=(EGA,437,1)
    ```

    This command identifies the path to DISPLAY.SYS and prepares the console (CON) to display one alternate code page on an EGA or VGA display (EGA covers both) connected to a system on which the hardware code page is 437.

- You must enable national language support with the Nlsfunc command. You can do this from the command line or from AUTOEXEC.BAT with a command like this:

    ```
    nlsfunc
    ```

Or (to save a little memory), you can use an Install command in CONFIG.SYS like this:

```
INSTALL=C:\DOS\NLSFUNC.EXE
```

- You must prepare and load the alternate code page you want (in this case, 850) with a Mode cp prepare command, like this:

    ```
    mode con cp prep=((850)c:\dos\ega.cpi)
    ```

- If you have an IBM printer supported by one of the version 5 CPI files, you also prepare the printer for code-page switching with another Device command in CONFIG.SYS, this one installing PRINTER.SYS, like this:

    ```
    DEVICE=C:\DOS\PRINTER.SYS LPT1=(4201,437,1)
    ```

    This command identifies the path to PRINTER.SYS and the port (LPT1) to which the printer is connected. The items in parentheses specify the 4201.CPI file, the 437 hardware code page native to the printer, and the need for one alternate code page.

- Depending on the language, country, and keyboard you want to specify, you might also need a Country command like the following in CONFIG.SYS:

    ```
    COUNTRY=039,437,C:\DOS\COUNTRY.SYS
    ```

which would tell MS-DOS to use the alternate, rather than default, code page for Italy. And you might need a Keyb command, like this:

```
keyb it,437,c:\dos\keyboard.sys
```

either in AUTOEXEC.BAT or typed at the system prompt.

Pulling it all together, then, to *prepare* for code-page switching—in this case, on a system with an EGA or VGA display and a hardware code page of 437— your CONFIG.SYS file would contain commands like the following:

```
DEVICE=C:\DOS\DISPLAY.SYS CON=(EGA,437,1)
INSTALL C:\DOS\NLSFUNC.EXE
```

and possibly

```
DEVICE=C:\DOS\PRINTER.SYS LPT1=(4201,437,1)
COUNTRY=039,437,C:\DOS\COUNTRY.SYS
```

To *load* an alternate code page and actually enable MS-DOS to switch from one code page to another, you would either type or include in AUTOEXEC.BAT

```
mode con cp prep=((850)c:\dos\ega.cpi)
```

and, perhaps,

```
keyb it,437,c:\dos\keyboard.sys
```

Index

JoAnne Woodcock

Currently a master writer for Microsoft Press, JoAnne Woodcock is author c *Running Microsoft Works 3 for Windows*, the *Concise Guide to MS-DOS 5*, and th *Concise Guide to Microsoft Works for Windows*, coauthor of *Running UNIX* anc *Microsoft Word Style Sheets*, and contributor to the *Microsoft Press Computer Dic tionary*, all published by Microsoft Press.

his book was prepared and submitted to Microsoft Press in
: files were processed and formatted using Microsoft Word

ompositor: Cheryl Whiteside
.er/copy editor: Kathleen Atkins
her: Lisa Iversen
.: Carol L. Luke
ler: Kim Eggleston
or: Lisa Sandburg
Rebecca Geisler
David Lemely
rator: Walker Graphics
iwabata

n by Microsoft Press in Palatino with display type in Palatino
g the Magna composition system. Composed pages were delivered
; electronic prepress files.

Printed on recycled paper stock.

Information
Straight from the Source

Concise Guide to MS-DOS® Batch Files, 3rd ed.
Kris Jamsa

Batch files offer an easy and instantly rewarding way to significantly increase productivity, without programming experience or additional software! Now updated to cover MS-DOS 6—including the new customizable boot tools—this handy reference book provides intermediate to advanced users information on the fundamentals of batch files, new uses for batch files, and even how to debug batch files.

220 pages, softcover   6 x 9 $12.95 ($16.95 Canada)   ISBN 1-55615-549-2

Running Microsoft® FoxPro® for MS-DOS®
Version 2.5
Sal Ricciardi

This comprehensive user's guide is ideal for beginning and intermediate users who want to learn Microsoft FoxPro for MS-DOS inside and out. You'll learn key database concepts, tips, and techniques—many not covered in the manuals. Includes a wealth of easy-to-understand examples, step-by-step tutorials, and helpful screen illustrations. Written by Sal Ricciardi, *PC Magazine* database columnist and member of the ANSI XBase Committee.

550 pages, softcover $29.95 ($39.95 Canada)   ISBN 1-55615-556-5
Available June 1993

Microsoft® Guide to Visual Basic™ for MS-DOS®
Peter G. Aitken

This comprehensive guide teaches Microsoft QuickBasic programmers and users new to programming how to work with this exciting new programming tool. It covers every programming task—from designing the user interface to writing clean, reusable code. Each task is discussed with clarity and supported by clear examples. Most chapters contain programming demonstrations that you can use as tutorials or adapt for inclusion in your own projects.

496 pages, softcover $24.95 ($32.95 Canada)   ISBN 1-55615-478-X

The Authorized Editions on MS-DOS®
from Microsoft Press

Running MS-DOS,® 6th ed.
Van Wolverton

"A book even the PC mavens turn to, it is written by a human being for human beings, in a strange and wonderful tongue: English." **PC Week**

This all-time bestselling guide to MS-DOS for novice to experienced users now covers MS-DOS version 3.3 through version 6.0. It's the sure way to gain a solid grounding in computing fundamentals that will help you better understand and work with other applications. Contains a wealth of easy-to-follow examples, instructions, and exercises.
640 pages, softcover $24.95 ($32.95 Canada)   ISBN 1-55615-542-5

MS-DOS® to the Max
Dan Gookin

This is the ideal book for users who want to use MS-DOS to make their system scream! In his humorous and straightforward style, bestselling author Dan Gookin packs this book with information about getting the most out of your PC using the new MS-DOS 6 utilities. The accompanying disk includes all of the batch files and debug scripts in the book plus two configuration "Wizards" and several bonus tools that will push your system *to the max.*
336 pages, softcover with one 3.5-inch disk
$29.95 ($39.95 Canada)   ISBN 1-55615-548-4

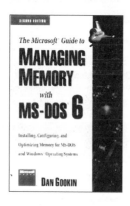

The Microsoft® Guide to Managing Memory with MS-DOS,® 2nd ed.
Dan Gookin

This top-notch guide shows intermediate users how to install, configure, and optimize memory on their MS-DOS or Windows systems. With insight and humor, Gookin provides industrial-strength tips and techniques on the different memory types, describes how memory works, and walks you through the steps necessary to maximize your system with MS-DOS version 6.0.
224 pages, softcover   6 x 9 $14.95 ($19.95 Canada)   ISBN 1-55615-545-X